A TREASURY OF
AMERICAN FOLK HUMOR

A TREASURY OF AMERICAN FOLK HUMOR

*A rare confection of laughter, tall tales,
jests and other gems of merriment
of the American people*

Edited

**with an introduction by
JAMES N. TIDWELL**

BONANZA BOOKS • NEW YORK

PRINTED IN THE UNITED STATES OF AMERICA

This edition published by Bonanza Books,
a division of Crown Publishers, Inc.
a b c d e f g h

ACKNOWLEDGMENTS

The editor and publishers wish to thank the following authors or their representatives, folklore societies, publishers, and publications for their kind permission to use material in this book. Full copyright notices are given on the pages on which the material appears.

American Book Co.; American Folklore Society; *American Mercury;* American Technical Society; *American Speech;* Appleton-Century-Crofts, Inc.; Atlantic Monthly Co.; The Bobbs-Merrill Co.; Albert and Charles Boni; Brandt & Brandt; California Folklore Society; Collier's Magazine; P. F. Collier & Son Co.; Columbia University Press; Conde Nast Publications, Inc.; Thomas Y. Crowell Co.; Curtis Publishing Co.; J. Frank Dobie; Dodd, Mead & Co.; M. A. Donohue Co.; Doubleday & Co.; Duell, Sloan & Pearce, Inc.; Eldridge Entertainment House; Farrar, Straus and Cudahy, Inc.; Greenberg: Publisher; Haldeman-Julius Co.; Hanover House; Harcourt, Brace & Co.; Harper & Bros.; Henry Holt & Co., Inc.; Hoosier Folklore Society; Houghton Mifflin Co.; Macrae Smith Co.; Alfred A. Knopf, Inc.; J. B. Lippincott Co.; Little, Brown & Co.; The Macmillan Co.; G. & C. Merriam Co.; William Morrow & Co.; The New York *Herald-Tribune;* Oxford University Press; G. P. Putnam's Sons; Random House; Rinehart & Co., Inc.; Charles Scribner's Sons; *Southwest Review; Sports Digest;* Stanford University Press; Texas Folklore Society; Transylvania Printing Co.; Tulsa *Daily World; TV Guide;* University of Arizona Press; University of Chicago Press; University of New Mexico Press; University of North Carolina Press; University of Oklahoma Press; Vanguard Press; The Viking Press, Inc.; Archie Walker; Wisconsin Folklore Society.

An exhaustive effort has been made to locate all persons having any rights or interests in material, and to clear reprint permissions. If any required acknowledgments have been omitted or any rights overlooked, it is by accident, and forgiveness is desired.

Author's Note

In choosing material for this collection of American folk humor, two tests were applied to every selection. The first requirement for inclusion was that the selection be funny to an American of 1956. Hence humor of other years was omitted if it dealt with events and conditions which are no longer of concern to us. Most of Petroleum V. Nasby's pieces, for example, deal too much with the Civil War to be funny to modern Americans. The misspelling so much in vogue during the late nineteenth century is no longer amusing, and so most of the radically misspelled humor was excluded. Exceptions were made for pieces such as Josh Billings' essay on the mule—pieces which are funny in spite of the spelling. Some of the best-known pieces of humor were omitted because they were too well known. Mark Twain's "The Jumping Frog of Calaveras County" and the whitewashing-the-fence incident from *Tom Sawyer,* for instance, have been reprinted and reread so often that they no longer have an element of surprise.

The second test for determining whether to include a selection was that it be folk humor. Many definitions of the term "folk humor" could be made, but for the purposes of this volume I have assumed that the term includes humor from any source which has been enjoyed, talked about, and retold by the American people. The stories included may have come from a folklorist's collection of oral material, from a newspaper column, or from the works of a writer of the stature of Twain, Carl Sandburg, or James Thurber. Whatever the source, they were chosen because I felt they represented the American people and their laughter.

Variants of the same story have not ordinarily been included, but when two or more versions were so unlike that they would be funny when read in sequence, an exception was made. When I had the choice of a number of versions of the same story, I selected the one which seemed the most humorous to moderns.

The source of each selection is given in a footnote at the bottom of each page on which the selection begins. If two or more selections begin on the same page, the sources are indicated in order.

My sincerest thanks go to many people who have contributed to the making of this book, but especially the following:

To George Milburn, for his invaluable aid in the research;

To Professor Francis L. Utley, of The Ohio State University, for bibliographical references and friendly encouragement; and to Professor C. Grant Loomis, of the University of California, for valuable suggestions about the material to be included.

JAMES N. TIDWELL.

Contents

Part One: The Flavoring

I. SAVVY

II. SASS

III. RED EYE

Part Two: The Main Course

I. EVERY MAN A CANDIDATE

II. PREACHIN' ALL DAY AND DINNER ON THE GROUND
(The American Slant on Religion)

III. FREE COUNTRY, FREE SPEECH
(Fun with Language)

IV. BET 'EM HIGH AND SLEEP IN THE STREETS
(The Humor in Gambling)

V. A Sucker Is Born Every Minute
(The Lighter Side of Trading and Business)

VI. The Bigger They Are, the Harder They Fall
(Sports Comedy)

VII. Forty Acres and a Government Mule
(Farm and Country Life Topics)

VIII. THE LADDER UP
(Concerning School and Society)

IX. FELONS AND FEVERS
(On the Subjects of Law and Medicine)

X. THE UNHUMAN COMEDY
(About Critters and Varmints)

XI. THERE'S NO PLACE LIKE HOME
(Aspects of Love, Marriage, and Family Life)

XII. ANOTHER DAY, ANOTHER DOLLAR

(Work and Workers' Hero Stories)

Part Three: The Dessert

I. SNIPES AND LEFT-HANDED MONKEY WRENCHES

(Practical Jokes)

II. SPREAD, EAGLE, SPREAD

(Tall Tales)

III. SALMAGUNDI AND SLUMGULLION
(Rhymes and Wordplay)

IV. JOE MILLER RIDES AGAIN
(Anecdotes and Such)

V. A FEW FOR THE ROAD
(Yarns)

Introduction

I

America is a land of laughter, of all-inclusive laughter. The American is ready to laugh at any kind of humor—exaggeration, understatement, puns, nonsense, or what have you—for he has in him the spirit of playfulness in great abundance. In a land where every man is equal before the law, where the vote of the town drunk counts as much as that of the banker or Presbyterian minister, no man feels any reason to restrain laughter. And in the nineteenth century, when a new political system was being developed, a new continent was being won, and new fortunes were being made, Americans were naturally exuberant, and their exuberance continues to affect our attitudes. An exuberant man is a playful man, like a young mountain goat with a new boulder.

American exuberance reveals itself in the comical figures of speech used by our humorists. Any figure of speech is a comparison between two things not totally alike, but the exuberant simile or metaphor stretches the imagination a greater distance—it is fantasy as much as it is comparison. The loser in a fight may look "as if he'd been sorting wildcats"; a slovenly man may look "as if he'd been kicked out of hell for sleeping in the ashes"; or a person or project may be "as disorganized as a bucket of worms." Nimrod Wildfire's wish that he might by "currycomb'd to death by 50,000 tom cats" belongs in this category, as does his statement that "you might as well try to scull a potash kettle up the falls of Niagara with a crowbar for an oar." A figure of speech may also be comical if it is made up of two comparisons and the two are incongruous, as in Mark Twain's "with the calm confidence of a Christian with four aces."

Exuberance is also the cause of exaggeration in American humor. Many people, of course, have come to think of our humor as a formless heap of exaggerations, not realizing that our exaggerations differ from those of other nations in their artistry, not in their quantity. Any humorist knows that a single overstatement is not funny, nor is a string of fifty-two. Here, for example, is a humorless exaggeration: "Before the white man came to America, there lived here a big black bear which weighed a hundred tons." That would not be funny if the weight went up to a million tons or the number of bears were multiplied by the distance in yards to Timbuctoo. What really makes the humor is not the size of an exaggeration but its incongruity, its misfitness in context.

Although a series of parallel exaggerations is not funny, one exaggeration stacked upon another is. One might thus be said to be up the creek with a hole in the boat and no paddle or to know too little to pour water out of a boot with a hole in the toe and instructions on the heel. Or someone after a night out might say that his mouth tasted as if the Russian army had marched through it barefooted.

Humor in exaggeration also comes from the use of concrete detail. The man who said that the road was "sloppy enough to bog down the shadow of a buzzard" gained credence by his detail, for he had apparently recognized that a buzzard's shadow would be larger and hence heavier than that of a sparrow. Numbers, too, give one a feeling of accuracy and concreteness. Note the highly accurate mathematical observation of Ring Lardner:

At high noon the wind was blowing a 2-inch gale backwards and neither scow would move, so the starter postponed it till along came a breath of fresh air, which was a ¼ to 2″. Then away went the two sloops like a snail with paralysis.

Americans seem to enjoy understatement about as much as they do exaggeration. Many of America's well-known humorists are, in fact, more noted for understatement than overstatement—Jack Downing, Josh Billings, and Artemus Ward, to name a few. And the greatest of our humorists, Mark Twain, used a great deal of it, both because its own humorous incongruity was amusing and because it accentuated the exaggeration which he used. Listen to Twain describing his departure from his father's office in terror:

I went away from there. I do not say that I went away in any sort of a hurry, but I simply went—that is sufficient. I went out at the window, and I carried the sash along with me. I did not need the sash, but it was handier to take it than it was to leave it, and so I took it.

Another of Twain's classic understatements occurs in a description of a fire-eating dragon:

He ate men and cattle impartially, and was exceedingly unpopular.

Quite similar to exaggeration or understatement as a source of humor is the incongruity of design, the physical lack of proportion. We are amused by too-muchness or too-littleness, whether in total size or in the size of one part of the anatomy in relation to the others. An over-sized nose like Jimmy Durante's or W. C. Fields' is therefore a physical asset to a stage comedian. The lack of proportion among American comic characters from Simon Suggs to Jiggs would almost make us believe that we have developed a cult of ugliness, for we are amused, not repelled, by the lack of proportion. We don't dislike Durante's nose; we admire it.

The exuberance which leads the American to exaggerate also leads him to enjoy all kinds of incongruities in language. The books on rhetoric and the teachers of English tell him how to write, but he delights in tying tin cans to the rules of good writing. He is told that punning is the lowest form of humor, and so he makes every sort of pun—good, indifferent, puny. He is taught not to use double negatives, but he cantankerously replies, "It don't make no never mind." He is taught to build sentences to climaxes, but he playfully makes them anticlimactic:

> The winds howled like the roaring of Niagara; the thunder rumbled and grumbled and pealed like Vesuvius laboring with an earthquake; the lurid lightnings flashed through the sky like—like—sixty!

> Like Waterloo among battles; Napoleon among warriors; Niagara among falls, and Peck among senators; this magnificent composition stands among Oratorios, Operas, Musical Melodrama and performances of Ethiopian Serenaders, peerless and unrivalled.

The American is taught to say what he means, but he prefers ambiguity: "May all your troubles be little ones." He is told to use the words of standard English—of Webster—but he cuts the lovers of sesquipedalianism down to size with such formations as teetotaciously, exflunctify, segashuate, copasetic, discomboberate, and absquatulate. He uses bad grammar and playfully distorts pronunciation, spelling, and meaning. He may not be proper, but he's having fun.

Another type of incongruity which Americans enjoy is that of the cultural misfit. Our humorists often portray a character of one cultural background thrown among people of a different culture. The transference of a character in time (anachronism) is usually a literary device, as in "Rip Van Winkle" or *The Connecticut Yankee in King Arthur's Court.* But the more frequent transference in American popular humor has been that of place, for the so-called "cracker-box philosophers" are country bumpkins faced with the social and political events of New York and Washington. From the first letters of Jack Downing in 1830 to the death of Will Rogers in 1935 America had an almost unbroken line of these social and political commentators with imaginary hayseed in their hair.

Whether the incongruity is one of time or place, the single outsider is an interloper in the strange social group. In real life he would be considered a misfit, but the better humor comes from letting him be the only completely logical person around. He can view the social and political scene with an eye unclouded by prejudice and can therefore point out the lack of "horse-sense" in what is going on. Whereas most of the humor of these cracker-box commentators is on some topic of the day and disappears when the topic is no longer discussed, the humor of a character shifted in time is less easily dated and can be enjoyed by succeeding generations.

The laughter of Americans at incongruities is large enough also to include nonsense—not pure nonsense, for that, like pure exaggeration, is never funny, but nonsense which leads us to keep trying to make sense out of what doesn't. The last phrase of Artemus Ward's "I was born in Maine of parents" seems at first to be an understatement, but it doesn't really state at all. Another of Ward's remarks also seems to promise sense:

> It would have been ten dollars in Jeff Davis's pocket if he had never been born at all.

Although Americans laugh most at the humor of these different kinds of incongruity, they also enjoy the sharp play of wit. Whereas in humor one describes a funny person or relates a funny happening and is good-humored while doing it, in wit he consciously and derisively makes a joke at someone's expense. Humor pictures; wit punctures. The American is pleased to take his fun either way. Certainly he enjoys the witty derision of George Jean Nathan's opinion that the author of the play *Halfway to Hell* "under-estimated the distance" and of Dorothy Parker's remark that in her new book Margot Asquith "reverts to tripe."

Just as American humor recognizes no limits in technique, so it recognizes no limits in subject. Anything in the land can be laughed about—and probably has been—from sinner to saint and from Maine to mules.

II

There would seem to be little question that America's greatest contribution to the humor of the world has been the humorous story— the rambling, digressive story which is essentially oral in its method. No better analysis of this type of story and the proper method of telling it exists than in "How to Tell a Story," by Mark Twain, and it therefore seems fitting that we reprint Twain's essay and thus let a master of the art tell us how it should be done.

> I do not claim that I can tell a story as it ought to be told. I only claim to know how a story ought to be told, for I have been almost daily in the company of the most expert story-tellers for many years.
>
> There are several kinds of stories, but only one difficult kind— the humorous. I will talk mainly about that one. The humorous story is American, the comic story is English, the witty story is French. The humorous story depends for its effect upon the *manner* of the telling; the comic story and the witty story upon the *matter*.
>
> The humorous story may be spun out to great length, and may wander around as much as it pleases, and arrive nowhere in

From *How to Tell a Story and Other Essays*, by Samuel L. Clemens, pp. 7–15. Copyright, 1897, 1898, 1899, by Harper & Brothers; 1892; by C. L. Webster & Co.; 1898, by The Century Co.; 1898, by The Cosmopolitan; 1899, by Samuel E. Moffett; 1900, by American Publishing Company. Autograph Edition, *The Writings of Mark Twain*, Vol. XXII. Hartford, Conn. The American Publishing Company.

particular; but the comic and witty stories must be brief and end with a point. The humorous story bubbles gently along, the others burst.

The humorous story is strictly a work of art—high and delicate art—and only an artist can tell it; but no art is necessary in telling the comic and the witty story; anybody can do it. The art of telling a humorous story—understand, I mean by word of mouth, not print—was created in America, and has remained at home.

The humorous story is told gravely; the teller does his best to conceal the fact that he even dimly suspects that there is anything funny about it; but the teller of the comic story tells you beforehand that it is one of the funniest things he has ever heard, then tells it with eager delight, and is the first person to laugh when he gets through. And sometimes, if he has had good success, he is so glad and happy that he will repeat the "nub" of it and glance around from face to face, collecting applause, and then repeat it again. It is a pathetic thing to see.

Very often, of course, the rambling and disjointed humorous story finishes with a nub, point, snapper, or whatever you like to call it. Then the listener must be alert, for in many cases the teller will divert attention from that nub by dropping it in a carefully casual and indifferent way, with the pretence that he does not know it is a nub.

Artemus Ward used that trick a good deal; then when the belated audience presently caught the joke he would look up with innocent surprise, as if wondering what they had found to laugh at. Dan Setchell used it before him. Nye and Riley and others use it to-day.

But the teller of the comic story does not slur the nub; he shouts it at you—every time. And when he prints it, in England, France, Germany, and Italy, he italicizes it, puts some whooping exclamation-points after it, and sometimes explains it in a parenthesis. All of which is very depressing, and makes one want to renounce joking and lead a better life.

Let me set down an instance of the comic method, using an anecdote which has been popular all over the world for twelve or fifteen hundred years. The teller tells it in this way:

THE WOUNDED SOLDIER

In the course of a certain battle a soldier whose leg had been shot off appealed to another soldier who was hurrying by to carry him to the rear, informing him at the same time of the loss which he had sustained; whereupon the generous son of Mars, shouldering the unfortunate, proceeded to carry out his desire. The bullets and cannon-balls were flying in all directions, and presently one of the latter took the wounded man's head off—

without, however, his deliverer being aware of it. In no long time he was hailed by an officer, who said:

"Where are you going with that carcass?"

"To the rear, sir—he's lost his leg!"

"His leg, forsooth?" responded the astonished officer; "you mean his head, you booby."

Whereupon the soldier dispossessed himself of his burden, and stood looking down upon it in great perplexity. At length he said:

"It is true, sir, just as you have said." Then after a pause he added, *"But he TOLD me* IT WAS HIS LEG!!!!!"

Here the narrator bursts into explosion after explosion of thunderous horse-laughter, repeating that nub from time to time through his gaspings and shriekings and suffocatings.

It takes only a minute and a half to tell that in its comic-story form; and it isn't worth the telling, after all. Put into the humorous-story form it takes ten minutes, and is about the funniest thing I have ever listened to—as James Whitcomb Riley tells it.

He tells it in the character of a dull-witted old farmer who has just heard it for the first time, thinks it is unspeakably funny, and is trying to repeat it to a neighbor. But he can't remember it; so he gets all mixed up and wanders helplessly round and round, putting in tedious details that don't belong in the tale and only retard it; taking them out conscientiously and putting in others that are just as useless; making minor mistakes now and then and stopping to correct them and explain how he came to make them; remembering things which he forgot to put in in their proper place and going back to put them in there; stopping his narrative a good while in order to try to recall the name of the soldier that was hurt, and finally remembering that the soldier's name was not mentioned, and remarking placidly that the name is of no real importance, anyway—better, of course, if one knew it, but not essential, after all—and so on, and so on, and so on.

The teller is innocent and happy and pleased with himself, and has to stop every little while to hold himself in and keep from laughing outright; and does hold in, but his body quakes in a jelly-like way with interior chuckles; and at the end of the ten minutes the audience have laughed until they are exhausted, and the tears are running down their faces.

The simplicity and innocence and sincerity and unconsciousness of the old farmer are perfectly simulated, and the result is a performance which is thoroughly charming and delicious. This is art—and fine and beautiful, and only a master can compass it; but a machine could tell the other story.

To string incongruities and absurdities together in a wandering and sometimes purposeless way, and seem innocently unaware that they are absurdities, is the basis of the American art, if my position is correct. Another feature is the slurring of the point. A third is the dropping of a studied remark apparently without knowing it, as if one were thinking aloud. The fourth and last is the pause.

Artemus Ward dealt in numbers three and four a good deal. He would begin to tell with great animation something which he seemed to think was wonderful; then lose confidence, and after an apparently absent-minded pause add an incongruous remark in a soliloquizing way; and that was the remark intended to explode the mine—and it did.

For instance, he would say eagerly, excitedly, "I once knew a man in New Zealand who hadn't a tooth in his head"—here his animation would die out; a silent, reflective pause would follow, then he would say dreamily, and as if to himself, "and yet that man could beat a drum better than any man I ever saw."

The pause is an exceedingly important feature in any kind of story, and a frequently recurring feature, too. It is a dainty thing, and delicate, and also uncertain and treacherous; for it must be exactly the right length—no more and no less—or it fails of its purpose and makes trouble. If the pause is too short the impressive point is passed, and the audience have had time to divine that a surprise is intended—and then you can't surprise them, of course.

On the platform I used to tell a Negro ghost story that had a pause in front of the snapper on the end, and that pause was the most important thing in the whole story. If I got it the right length precisely, I could spring the finishing ejaculation with effect enough to make some impressible girl deliver a startled little yelp and jump out of her seat—and that was what I was after. This story was called "The Golden Arm," and was told in this fashion. You can practise with it yourself—and mind you look out for the pause and get it right.

THE GOLDEN ARM

Once 'pon a time dey wuz a monsus mean man, en he live 'way out in de prairie all 'lone by hisself, 'cep'n he had a wife. En bimeby she died, en he tuck en toted her way out dah in de prairie en buried her. Well, she had a golden arm—all solid gold, fum de shoulder down. He wuz pow'ful mean—pow'ful; en dat night he couldn't sleep, caze he want dat golden arm so bad.

When it come midnight he couldn't stan' it no mo'; so he git up, he did, en tuck his lantern en shoved out thoo de storm en dug her up en got de golden arm; en he bent his head down 'gin de win', en plowed en plowed thoo de snow. Den all of a

sudden he stop (make a considerable pause here, and look startled, and take a listening attitude) en say: "My lan', what's dat!"

En he listen—en listen—en de win' say (set your teeth together
and imitate the wailing and wheezing singsong of the wind),
"Bzzz-z—zzz"—en den, way back yonder whah de grave is, he hear
a *voice!*—he hear a voice all mix' up in de win'—can't hardly tell
'em 'part—"Bzzz-zzz—W-h-o—g-o-t—m-y—g-o-l-d-e-n *arm?*—zzz—zzz—
W-h-o g-o-t m-y g-o-l-d-e-n *arm?*" (You must begin to shiver violently now.)

En he begin to shiver en shake, en say, "Oh, my! *Oh,* my lan'!"
en de win' blow de lantern out, en de snow en sleet blow in his
face en mos' choke him, en he start a-plowin' knee-deep towards
home mos' dead, he so sk'yerd—en pooty soon he hear de voice
agin, en (pause) it 'us comin' *after* him! "Bzzz—zzz—zzz—W-h-o—
g-o-t—m-y—g-o-l-d-e-n—*arm?*"

When he git to de pasture he hear it agin—closter now, en
a-comin'!—a-comin' back dah in de dark en de storm—(repeat the
wind and the voice). When he git to de house he rush up-stairs
en jump in de bed and kiver up, head and years, en lay dah
shiverin' en shakin'—en den way out dah he hear it *agin!*—en
a-comin'! En bimeby he hear (pause—awed, listening attitude)—
pat—pat—pat—*hit's a-comin'* up-stairs! Den he hear de latch, en
he know it's in de room!

Den pooty soon he know it's *a-stannin' by de bed!* (Pause.)
Den—he know it's *a-bendin' down over him*—en he cain't skasely
git his breath! Den—den—he seem to feel someth'n *c-o-l-d,* right
down 'most agin his head! (Pause.)

Den de voice say, *right at his year*—"W-h-o—g-o-t—m-y—
g-o-l-d-e-n *arm?* (You must wail it out very plaintively and ac-
cusingly; then you stare steadily and impressively into the face of
the farthest-gone auditor—a girl, preferably—and let that awe-
inspiring pause begin to build itself in the deep hush. When it
has reached exactly the right length, jump suddenly at that girl
and yell, *"You've* got it!"

If you've got the *pause* right, she'll fetch a dear little yelp and
spring right out of her shoes. But you *must* get the pause right;
and you will find it the most troublesome and aggravating and
uncertain thing you ever undertook.)

III

Here then, reader, is enough fun for a series of banquets of American humor, starting with a sample of the flavoring, proceeding to a
main course made up of those things which have been chewed on,
chewed up, or chewed out by our fun-makers, and ending with a
dessert of choice tid-bits.

JAMES N. TIDWELL

PART ONE

The Flavoring

I. SAVVY

Introduction

Running through much of American humor is the flavor of savvy, of know-how. Americans enjoy humor which demonstrates a man's savvy—his ability to exercise horse-sense, to see all sides of a question and judge them fairly, and, most of all, to get along in the world and get along with people while doing it. Savvy, one might say, is a blend of understanding, tact, and ingenuity.

The people have always admired men with the all-round judgment which we call horse-sense. The man with this sort of savvy sees the whole problem, not just a part of it. In showing how short the Mississippi would become if it continued to change its length as it had in the past, Mark Twain was playing a game with the people who have single-track minds, who see only one aspect of a problem. His reasoning seems conclusive to the "scientific" mind, but the fellow with horse-sense knows better.

Jim Baker, the narrator of "The Blue Jay Yarn," showed that he was able to see all sides and make a fair decision when he distinguished the animals which have a limited education and use small words from those which have a large vocabulary and a fluent delivery. In a similar manner the narrator of "Champion Hog-Caller" gave each of the two contestants full praise as the best of his kind, but he was then forced to distinguish two kinds of hog-callers.

A man with savvy recognizes the differences in individuals, and because he does, he knows exactly what kind of appeal will bring the desired response from each. Some readers may damn Madison Tensas as unworthy of a medical degree, but they should also recognize that he had consummate savvy. A duller student would have worked out one technique to use on all the professors, but Tensas, recognizing that even professors are individuals with human differences, devised

1

a different technique for each of them. Bunker Bean, although he had to deal with only one person, had to have a great understanding of Metzeger as an individual in order to make the peculiar appeal which got him a loan. The man with savvy will, as Bunker said, "appeal to the poetry in the man."

Rules for Staying Young

1. Avoid fried meats which angry up the blood.
2. If your stomach disputes you, lie down and pacify it with cool thoughts.
3. Keep the juices flowing by jangling around gently as you move.
4. Go very light on the vices such as carrying on in society. The social ramble ain't restful.
5. Avoid running at all times.
6. Don't look back. Something might be gaining on you.

Champion Hog-Caller

Several years ago I found myself in the pleasant community of Wilson in North Carolina. The town was in an abnormal state of excitement because of a championship hog-calling competition that was to be held in the local ball park. Normally I have small interest in such matters, but I was attracted to the contest for the reason that Olla Ray Boyd was one of the two participants. Mr. Boyd was a candidate for governor of the state. He was reputed to be the best hog-caller in the South and on his calling cards (or hog-calling cards) identified himself as a *hogologist*. He was cheered and saluted and feted wherever he went, and because of the power of his hog-calling voice, his opinions were listened to and respected. It was only natural that such a man, every time election year came round, should run for governor. Somehow he never quite made it, but he went right on building up friendships by calling hogs from one end of the state to the other.

On the afternoon of the contest I made my way to the ball park and found a seat in the crowded stands. A platform had been erected between home plate and the pitcher's mound and the whole park had been decorated with bunting. A brass band played and some girls twirled batons and I sought enlightenment from the people sitting around me. I was told that ole Mist' Boyd had mebby finey met his

From "The Fabulous Satchel Paige," Part 3, by Richard Donovan, in *Collier's* Magazine, June 13, 1953, p. 55.

From *The Rebel Yell, being a Carpetbagger's attempt to establish the truth concerning the screech of the Confederate Soldier plus lesser matters appertaining to the peculiar habits of the South*, by H. Allen Smith, pp. 53–56. Copyright, 1954, by H. Allen Smith. Garden City, New York: Doubleday & Company, Inc. 1954.

match. Someone had dug up a lady by the name of Miz Johnson who was a hog-caller from who-laid-the-chunk.

When Olla Ray Boyd finally climbed to the platform the crowd broke into a wild demonstration. The man sitting next to me was tensed up like a drumhead. He jabbed at me with his elbow and exclaimed, "Yonda's a hwag-calluh! Ah mean hawg-calluh!" Then Mrs. Johnson was introduced and another great cheer arose from the stands. Mrs. Johnson was a lady of middle age, plainly dressed and appearing to be a little nervous.

After some preliminary speeches Olla Ray Boyd stood up and faced the crowd and when the applause faded away he launched into a brief speech, requesting that all present support him for governor. I don't recall just how he stated his qualifications but I seem to remember that he argued that a man with a firm command over hogs would be able to cope with members of the state legislature.

Throughout this little speech there were frequent cries from the audience. "Call 'em hawgs, Mist' Boyd!" And finally he called 'em.

To my everlasting regret I took no notes on Mr. Boyd's opening hog calls. I only remember that they were impressively melodious and that not a sound came from the stands as he stood there bellowing into the breeze. He went on for quite a while, changing tones, skipping from one octave to the next, adding little grace notes here and there, and then the crowd began to yell again. They were chanting "Boah, boah, boah!" The man next to me explained: "They want 'im to do the old boah messin' roun' the ole sow. He allus does it. Mind now."

Mr. Boyd did the old boar messing around the old sow. I have never been present when an old boar was messing around an old sow (otherwise I'd remember it), but apparently Mr. Boyd's take-off of the old boar was perfection itself, for the crowd roared its approval. And then came the cries: "Slop 'em, Mist' Boyd! Slop 'em!" This called for Mr. Boyd's *pièce de résistance*. He impersonated three hogs eating slop. He played all three characters at the same time, filling the air with enormous gruntings and snortings and snufflings and slobberings, and the crowd shrieked its delight. There is no question about it— Olla Ray Boyd is a man of heroic proportions. Completing his performance, he bowed to the stands, then turned and bowed to Mrs. Johnson and resumed his seat.

Now Mrs. Johnson stepped shyly to the front of the platform. She took hold of the rail with both hands, hung her head and began pawing lightly at the wooden floor with one foot. For a few moments I thought that her stage fright was going to prevent her from opening her mouth. Then she seemed to get a grip on herself. She raised her chin and let go.

She was a good fifty yards from me, but I had a feeling that I had been swept up suddenly in the middle of a cyclone. My toes curled up inside my shoes and my eyes seemed to have a strong tendency to cross. What Mrs. Johnson had to say was this:

"Hooooooooooooo-eeeeeeeeeeeee!"

Then a pause. Followed by:

"Hooooooooooooo-eeeeeeeeeeeee!"

Another pause. Followed by:

"Hooooooooooooo-eeeeeeeeeeeee!"

And after that:

"PIG-PIG-PIG-PIG-PIG!"

The people sat as though stunned. They knew. They knew that this was a precious moment, a moment to remember. They had heard a hog-call that was a hog-call.

Mrs. Johnson lowered her head modestly, returned to her chair, and sat down. Olla Ray Boyd got up, walked over and shook hands with her and said something to her. My neighbor interpreted this move: "He ast 'er to do it again. She don't wanna do it again. Airy hawg didn' hear it the first time, he's pure deef."

The judges . . . now went into a huddle and quickly acclaimed Mrs. Johnson as the winner. I felt a little sorry for Olla Ray Boyd and asked my neighbor if this defeat would hurt his political chances.

"Nawp," he said. "Mist' Boyd, he's still the best at what he does. He can do them three hawgs eatin' slop so good you can shet your eyes and you're right smack-dab in th' pigpen. But he's more of a platfawm hog-calluh. He calls hawgs for the benefit of people. That Miz Johnson there, she calls hawgs for the benefit of hawgs. They's a difference."

The Bluejay Story

Animals talk to each other, of course. There can be no question about that; but I suppose there are very few people who can understand them. I never knew but one man who could. I knew he could, however, because he told me so himself. He was a middle-aged, simple-hearted miner who had lived in a lonely corner of California among the woods and mountains, a good many years, and had studied the ways of his only neighbors, the beasts and the birds, until he believed he could actually translate any remark which they made. This was Jim Baker. According to Jim Baker, some animals have only a limited education, and use only very simple words, and scarcely ever a comparison or a flowery figure; whereas, certain other animals have a large vocabulary, a fine command of language and a ready and fluent delivery; consequently these latter talk a great deal; they like

From *A Tramp Abroad*, by Samuel L. Clemens, pp. 12–17. Toronto: Belford & Co. 1880. Also *Collected Works of Mark Twain*, "Author's National Edition" New York: Harper & Brothers. 1899. Vol. I, pp. 24–32. First printed, 1880.

it; they are conscious of their talent, and they enjoy "showing off." Baker said, that after long and careful observation, he had come to the conclusion that the bluejays were the best talkers he had found among the birds and beasts. Said he:—

"There's more *to* a bluejay than any other creature. He has got more moods, and more different kinds of feelings than other creatures; and, mind you, whatever a bluejay feels, he can put into language. And no mere commonplace language, either, but rattling, out-and-out book-talk—and bristling with metaphor, too—just bristling! And for command of language—why *you* never see a bluejay get stuck for a word. No man ever did. They just boil out of him! And another thing: I've noticed a good deal, and there's no bird, or cow, or anything that uses as good grammar as a bluejay. You may say a cat uses good grammar. Well, a cat does—but you let a cat get excited once; you let a cat get to pulling fur with another cat on a shed, nights, and you'll hear grammar that will give you the lockjaw. Ignorant people think it's the *noise* which fighting cats make that is so aggravating, but it ain't so; it's the sickening grammar they use. Now I've heard a jay use bad grammar but very seldom; and when they do, they are ashamed as a human; they shut right down and leave.

"You may call a jay a bird. Well, so he is, in a measure—because he's got feathers on him, and don't belong to no church, perhaps; but otherwise he is just as much a human as you be. And I'll tell you for why. A jay's gifts, and instincts, and feelings, and interests, cover the whole ground. A jay hasn't got any more principle than a Congressman. A jay will lie, a jay will steal, a jay will deceive, a jay will betray; and four times out of five, a jay will go back on his solemnest promise. The sacredness of an obligation is a thing which you can't cram into no bluejay's head. Now, on top of all this, there's another thing: a jay can outswear any gentleman in the mines. You think a cat can swear. Well, a cat can; but you give a bluejay a subject that calls for his reserve powers, and where is your cat? Don't talk to *me*— I know too much about this thing. And there's yet another thing: in the one little particular of scolding—just good, clean, out-and-out scolding—a bluejay can lay over anything, human or divine. Yes, sir, a jay is everything that a man is. A jay can cry, a jay can laugh, a jay can feel shame, a jay can reason and plan and discuss, a jay likes gossip and scandal, a jay has got a sense of humor, a jay knows when he is an ass just as well as you do—maybe better. If a jay ain't human, he better take in his sign, that's all. Now I'm going to tell you a perfectly true fact about some bluejays.

"When I first begun to understand jay language correctly, there was a little incident happened here. Seven years ago, the last man in this region but me moved away. There stands his house,—been empty ever since; a log house, with a plank roof—just one big room, and no more; no ceiling—nothing between the rafters and the floor. Well, one Sunday morning I was sitting out here in front of my cabin, with my cat, taking the sun, and looking at the blue hills, and listening to the leaves rustling so lonely in the trees, and thinking of the home away yonder in the states, that I hadn't heard from in thirteen years, when a bluejay lit on that house, with an acorn in his mouth, and says, 'Hello, I reckon I've struck something.' When he spoke, the acorn dropped out of his mouth and rolled down the roof, of course, but he didn't care; his mind was all on the thing he had struck. It was a knot-hole in the roof. He cocked his head to one side, shut one eye and put the other one to the hole, like a 'possum looking down a jug; then he glanced up with his bright eyes, gave a wink or two with his wings—which signifies gratification, you understand—and says, 'It looks like a hole, it's located like a hole,—blamed if I don't believe it *is* a hole!'

"Then he cocked his head down and took another look; he glances perfectly joyful, this time; winks his wings and his tail both and says, 'O, no, this ain't no fat thing, I reckon! If I ain't in luck!—why it's a perfectly elegant hole!' So he flew down and got that acorn, and fetched it up and dropped it in, and was just tilting his head back, with the heavenliest smile on his face, when all of a sudden he was paralyzed into a listening attitude and that smile faded gradually out of his countenance like breath off'n a razor, and the queerest look of surprise took its place. Then he says, 'Why, I didn't hear it fall!' He cocked his eye at the hole again, and took a long look; raised up and shook his head; stepped around to the other side of the hole and took another look from that side; shook his head again. He studied a while, then he just went into the *details*—walked round and round the hole and spied into it from every point of the compass. No use. Now he took a thinking attitude on the comb of the roof and scratched the back of his head with his right foot a minute, and finally says, 'Well, it's too many for *me* that's certain; must be a mighty long hole; however, I ain't got no time to foot around here, I got to 'tend to business; I reckon it's all right—chance it, anyway.'

"So he flew off and fetched another acorn and dropped it in, and tried to flirt his eye to the hole quick enough to see what become of it, but he was too late. He held his eye there as much as a minute; then he raised up and sighed, and says, 'Confound it, I don't seem to understand this thing, no way; however, I'll tackle her again.' He fetched another acorn, and done his best to see what become of it, but he couldn't. He says, 'Well, *I* never struck no such a hole as this before; I'm of the opinion it's a totally new kind of a hole.' Then he begun to get mad. He held in for a spell, walking up and down the comb of the roof and shaking his head and muttering to himself; but his feelings got the upper hand of him, presently, and he broke loose and cussed himself black in the face. I never see a bird take on so about a little thing. When he got through he walks to the hole and looks in again for half a minute; then he says, 'Well, you're a long hole, and a deep hole, and a mighty singular hole altogether—but I've started in to fill you, and I'm d--d if I *don't* fill you, if it takes a hundred years!'

"And with that, away he went. You never see a bird work so since you was born. He laid into his work . . . and the way he hove acorns into that hole for about two hours and a half was one of the most exciting and astonishing spectacles I ever struck. He never stopped to take a look any more—he just hove 'em in and went for more. Well, at last he could hardly flop his wings, he was so tuckered out. He comes a-drooping down, once more, sweating like an ice-pitcher, drops his acorn in and says, '*Now* I guess I've got the bulge on you by this time!' So he bent down for a look. If you'll believe me, when his head come up again he was just pale with rage. He says, 'I've shoveled acorns enough in there to keep the family thirty years, and if I can see a sign of one of 'em I wish I may land in a museum with a belly full of sawdust in two minutes!'

"He had just strength enough to crawl up to the comb and lean his back agin the chimbly, and then he collected his impressions and begun to free his mind. I see in a second that what I had mistook for profanity in the mines was only just the rudiments, as you may say.

"Another jay was going by, and heard him doing his devotions, and stops to inquire what was up. The sufferer told him the whole circumstance, and says, 'Now yonder's the hole, and if you don't believe me, go and look for yourself.' So this fellow went and looked, and comes back and says, 'How many did you say you put in there?' 'Not any less than two tons,' says the sufferer. The other jay went and looked again. He couldn't seem to make it out, so he raised a yell, and three more jays come. They all examined the hole, they all made the sufferer tell it over again, then they all discussed it, and got off as many leather-headed opinions about it as an average crowd of humans could have done.

"They called in more jays; then more and more till pretty soon this whole region 'peared to have a blue flush about it. There must have been five thousand of them; and such another jawing and disputing and ripping and cussing, you never heard. Every jay in the whole lot put his eye to the hole and delivered a more chuckle-headed opinion about the mystery than the jay that went there before him. They examined the house all over, too. The door was standing half open, and at last one old jay happened to go and light on it and look in. Of course, that knocked the mystery galley-west in a second. There lay the acorns, scattered all over the floor. He flopped his wings and raised a whoop. 'Come here!' he says. 'Come here, everybody; hang'd if this fool hasn't been trying to fill up a house with acorns!' They all came a-swooping down like a blue cloud, and as each fellow lit on the door and took a glance, the whole absurdity of the contract that that first jay had tackled hit him home and he fell over backwards suffocating with laughter, and the next jay took his place and done the same.

"Well, sir, they roosted around here on the housetop and the trees for an hour, and guffawed over that thing like human beings. It ain't any use to tell me a bluejay hasn't got a sense of humor, because I know better. And memory, too. They brought jays here from all over the United States to look down that hole, every summer for three years. Other birds, too. And they could all see the point, except an owl that come from Nova Scotia to visit the Yo Semite, and he took this thing in on his way back. He said he couldn't see anything funny in it. But then he was a good deal disappointed about Yo Semite, too."

Excellent Either Way

That night [John Wesley Hardin] walked into the virtually empty Acme Saloon [in El Paso, Texas,] raised his left foot in familiar posture on the rail, dropped his chin in his left palm, supported by his elbow bent on the bar, and began rolling dice with the tender, Henry Brown, for a quarter a throw. Hardin shook first and tossed the ivories out. "Four sixes to beat," he said, as Brown picked up the dice.

Just then the carefully elusive figure of Old John Selman eased in at the swinging doors behind him and cut loose with his .45. Hardin slid to the floor while Selman still pumped in the lead. Captain Frank Carr, of the police force, was there in a few minutes "after the shooting and he found two guns. Colt forty-ones, but . . . no sign of the mail shirt" Hardin was rumored to wear. And the writer for the *Times*, aware that the hardened Selman was still alive, gave him that partisan portrayal now known as "a good press," saying, "The first shot did the work. It entered the eye and came out at the back of the head."

Justice W. D. Howe was called for the inquest. Jeff [Milton] went down for a last look at Hardin, who, with forty-odd notches on his guns, was now comfortably dead in the middle of the Acme floor. His ready eye saw where the bullet had hit. At a table near by sat Selman, wearing a comical little hat, sweating like an Alabama Negro on election day and receiving the acclaim of the mob. Extending a nervous paw to Jeff, he said, "Shake hands with me, Cap, I've killed the son-of-a-bitch. I shot him right in the eye."

"I don't mix with a murderer," said Milton with contempt. "You shot that feller right in the back of the head. You can't shake hands with me, certain!"

Next day the *Times* revised its original report. Selman was arrested,

From *Jeff Milton, A Good Man with a Gun*, by J. Evetts Haley, pp. 247–248. Copyright, 1948, by the University of Oklahoma Press, Publishing Division of the University. Norman.

but his attorney, Charlie de Pat, got him out on $10,000 bond, while the preliminary hearing was full of ghastly humor resulting from release of the tension.

The police force breathed a sigh of relief, and the *Times* editorialized on the "climate," claiming that the reputation of the town "as a health resort is already firmly established."

But when George H. Higgins, an Episcopal minister transmogrified into a homeopathic surgeon, was put on the stand after examining the corpse, to determine if it was really murder, if Hardin was really shot in the back of the head or in the eye, he sounded the humorous good sense of the whole town.

"If he was shot in the eye," came his conditional answer, "I'd say it was excellent marksmanship. If he was shot in the back of the head, then I'd say it was excellent judgment."

How to Pass an Examination

READER! have you ever taken a shower-bath of a cold winter's morning? or felt a snake crawling over you whilst in bed? or tried to sleep with a deadly fight awaiting you in the morning? or tried to unite the oil of your nature with the agua pura of a chattering damsel, and found no alkali to effect the union—in other words, popped the question and been—refused? or swallowed poison, and no stomach-pump about? or slept with a man with the small-pox? or tried to write, with a couple of gabbling widows in the next room? or run for a political office? or shook hands with the itch? or been without a friend or dollar, thousands of miles from home, and a catch-pole after you for your tavern bill? or had the toothache? or—think of the most uneasy, miserable melancholy, dolesome action, sensation, occurrence, or thought of your life. Read of nothing for two weeks but earthquakes, famines, bankruptcy, murders, suicides, and distress in its blackest form: work on your imagination until you feel yourself labouring under all these combined misfortunes, and perhaps then you may have a slight appreciation of how a young grave rat feels just before he is examined for his degree. Examined, too, by seven old dried-up specimens of humanity, who look as if they had descended for the occasion from some anatomical museum, and who have looked on death, suffering, and annual ranks of medical aspirants, until they have about as much softness of heart as the aforesaid preparations.

The first course of medical lectures the *student* attends, is generally distinguished by his devotion to everything but his studies. At the

From *Odd Leaves from the Life of a Louisiana "Swamp Doctor,"* by Madison Tensas, M.D. (Henry Clay Lewis), pp. 120–131. Republished, 1858, by T. B. Peterson and Brothers, Philadelphia, as a part of *The Swamp Doctor's Adventures in the South-West,* by "Madison Tensas" M.D., and "Solitaire."

commencement of the lectures he purchases a blank-book, for the os-
tensible purpose of taking notes of the lectures; but unwittingly his
fingers, instead of tracing the chirographical characters, are engaged
in caricaturing the professor, who is endeavouring to beat into his
and a few hundred kindred heads, the difference between a dirty
Israelite and the 'nasty moses of an artery. He devotes the midnight
hour to dissecting—pigs-feet, grouse, and devilled bones, or the delicate structure of the epicurean oyster. He strengthens his voice by
making the short hours of the night-clad street alive with the agreeable annunciation, especially to nervous invalids and sick children,
that he "will not go home till morning." He astonishes the professor
of chemistry when lecturing upon electricity, by placing a few pounds
of powder in communication with the machine, and blowing the laboratory to atoms, when the experiments are going on. He forms a
pleasant surprise for his landlady by slipping into the dining-hall
when the meats are on the table, and slyly inserting a dead baby,
stolen from the dissecting-room, under the cover, in place of the ab-
stracted pig, producing a pleasant sensation when discovered, and giving a good appetite to the boarders. He puts quick-lime into the young
ladies' puff-box, and gives them a wash of lunar caustic to allay the
irritation. He and the janitor go halves in raising game-cocks, and the
expenses of a whole winter's lectures are often bet on a *main*. There
is always some medical book that he wishes to purchase, of course
very expensive—and to obtain which he is always writing home for
money to parents or guardian. John Smith suffers, and always appears
in the police reports, when the first course student is put in the watch-
house, and let off by the kind-hearted mayor next morning, on paying
fees and promising to amend. To sum up the whole, the first course,
with few exceptions, conducts himself in such a manner, that but little
injustice is done him when he is classed with free Negroes, rowdies,
and low-flung draymen. But the second course—phew! what a change
comes over the fellow! You would think, to see him, that when he
was born, gravity and soberness had given up the ghost, and their dis-
embodied spirits found a carnal habitation in his cranium.

He now endeavours, by unremitting attention, to retrieve lost time,
and impress the professors favourably in his behalf, for he is now a
candidate for graduation, and he dare not go home without his degree. His care-clad face is now seen on the foremost bench, listening
with a painful absorption, and taking voluminous notes in a book—
not the only thing bound in calf-skin in the room, by long odds—and
always asks, with the utmost deference, long explanations on some
favourite theory of the lecturer, so dazzlingly original, that he did not
perfectly understand it, so bewildered was he by admiration. He smells
of the dissecting-room, and takes occasion, when in the presence of the
professor of anatomy, of jerking out his handkerchief, and with it the
half cut up hand of a subject. He eschews tobacco, whiskey, and

women, joins the physiological temperance society, and collects facts
for a forthcoming work of the professor of practice. He is a strong
vitalist with *"Old Charley,"* and lies-big with the Liebigian follower
of acids and alkalies. He presents the pelvis of the female that obeyed
the Lord's ordinance twenty-six times in ten years, to the professor of
obs—ervations, and has a faculty of making himself generally useful
to the whole faculty. I, to return to particularities, had followed after
the manner of *first coursers,* and would have been a *fac simile* of the
candidate, or second course student, had it not been for my habitual
laziness, and perhaps an overweening confidence in my natural powers
of impudence to push me through. I had had one or two fights the
previous session, in the college, which brought me favourably, of
course, before the notice of the faculty, as a quiet, studious gentleman,
and removed all doubts from my mind of my having a safe and honourable passage. I held a high head, but was confoundedly frightened,
and often wished that I were not an aspirant for the privilege of being a hired assassin, a slayer, without the victim having a chance to
hit back. Many, I say, were my misgivings, as I saw the ides of March,
the time for examination, approach, that my want of medical lore
might knock me higher than the green baize of medicine could cluster
—and yet, never was poor mortal better entitled to write M.D. after
his name than I, miserable devil as I was. But fear would not keep
back the evil day. The bell sounded for class T to go up and be examined, and away we went slowly, as to a summons for pistols and
coffee for two, with feelings resembling those of a gambler who has
staked his whole pile, and found at the *call* that he has been bluffing
up against a *greenhorn* with *"three white aces."*

We were to be examined in separate rooms; our class, consisting of
seven members, by as many professors, fifteen minutes being allotted
to each professor in which to find out the qualifications of the candidate.

I have already indicated the course I intended to pursue in my
examination—impudence and assurance was a new method for a candidate, and might succeed where the old plan would be nearly certain to fail.

Entering boldly, without knocking, the room of one of the professors, who, being a superannuated widower, affected youthfulness very
much, and prided himself very much, like a Durham stock raiser, on
the beauty of his calves, to his dismay I found him arranging a pair
of elaborate false ones, which showed a great disposition to work
around to the front of his spindle-shanks. I had him dead for his vote,
sure. I held the calves, whilst he adapted them to their places, and
smoking a cigar during his fifteen minutes—he congratulated me upon
the progress, he had often remarked, I was making in my studies, and
at the expiration of his time, as he conducted me to the door, assured

me he would vote for me, adding, "by-the-bye, Tensas, you needn't mention anything about the calves."

Well! here's one vote, sure; would I had the other six as safe, thought I. "Physiology, where are you? You are wanted!" said I, as the door enclosed me with the professor of that branch, who, fortunately for me, was what is called a *vitalist*—sticking up for nature, and bitterly denied the Liebigian theory, which refers so many of the living phenomena to chemistry. He and the professor of chemistry were nearly at daggers' points upon the subject, and exceedingly excitable whenever it was mentioned in their presence. I knew my cue.

"Take a seat, Mr. Tensas, you appear wondrous full of vivacity," said the professor, as I entered, singing "A was an artery," &c. "Yes, sir, and I can assure you it is vivacity of the same kind that a beneficent Creator exhaled into the nostrils of the first-created—life in the sense in which every reasonable man—every man with a proper appreciation of the subject—every man of learning and intellect, and physiological acquisition, regards the vital principle—and not that degraded vitality of the Liebigian system, which makes man's assimilating functions a chemical operation, and degrades his mighty nature to the level of the ass"—"hideous doctrine," broke in the old professor. "Mr. Tensas, would that the whole class possessed your discriminative wisdom; then I could descend to the grave with the proud consciousness that man held of his existence the same exalted opinion that I have always tried to teach; then would I see this chemical theory of life exploded. Theory which degrades man lower than the brutes, makes the subtlest operations of his nature a mere chemical effect, and the noble action of the lungs a scape-pipe for extra heat; magnificent—"

And the excited physiologist, carried away by his feelings, burst into one of his wildest harangues, battling for his favourite theory with more vigour than he had ever displayed in the rostrum—and there never had stood his superior for eloquence—until a knock at the door broke in upon his declamatory current and dammed its waters.

"Bless me!" he exclaimed, rubbing his glasses and looking at his watch, "is my time out? Why, I have done all the talking. But go, Mr. Tensas, the views that you advocate attest your qualifications. You may depend upon my vote and influence."

"Two votes safe!" said I, as I regained the lobby, "and now for old 'Roots,' as the professor of Mat. Med. was familiarly called by the class—he's deaf, but thinks no one knows it but himself. I'll talk low, and he won't know whether I am answering correctly or not."

"Take a seat, Mr. Tensas. How are you to-day? I suppose you are ready for being examined? What is calomel?" All this being said *sotto voce*.

"A drug, sir, that may be called the right bower of quackery, and the four aces of medical murder; referred to by Shakespeare when he said, 'Throw physic to the dogs,' and specifically mentioned by him, though a typographical error has somewhat obscured it, evidencing its antiquity and universal administration at his time in the lines:

" 'Be thou as pure as ice, as chaste as snow, thou shalt not escape Calumel.' "

I spoke in a whisper, but moved my lips as if vociferating.

"Right, Mr. Tensas; but you need not holler so as to alarm the college; I am not deaf. What is the usual dose in the South?"

"Half a pound for an infant, and the quadrature of the stomach's circle for a grown Negro!"

"What are its specific effects upon the system?"

"The free use of coffins, spit-boxes, mush-and-milk, and the invention of new oaths with which to curse the doctor!"

"What diseases is it usually given in?"

"In all, and some others, from want of a clean shirt to the death-rattle!"

"Right, sir, right," said the examiner, never doubting, from my aptitude of reply and perfect seriousness, but that they were to the point. "What are emetics?"

"Medicines, that to a man who has dined badly, and wants to conceal it, should never take!"

"What are the most certain?"

"The first cigar, the first quid, or a spoiled oyster!"

"What is their action?"

"That of money won at gambling; going back the way it came, and taking a good deal more than it brought!"

"When should lobelia be given?"

"At elections, where the people are writing a man down an ass, and he wants to be *brought-up* ahead!"

"What dose would you give it in?"

"If the patient was likely to leave a rich widow, I'd certainly give a pound!"

"When would you think an emetic had acted sufficiently?"

"When I was in doubt whether it was the patient's tongue or his stomach that was hanging out of his mouth!"

"What are purgatives?"

"Medicines, whose action bears the same relation to that of emetics, which the possums did to the hollow where the dog was waiting to catch them—they go the other way!"

"Suppose your patient had a diarrhœa, what medicine would you give?"

"A quart of brandy, for it would be sure to make him *tight!*"

"What are the most dangerous preparations of lead?"

"Congressional speeches in Washington, and buckshot in the Southern States!"

"From what does hive syrup derive its name?"

"From the fact of bees living in hives, and there being honey in it!"

"Right, sir! all right! You have answered admirably. I see I must vote for you. You can go, sir!"—and out I went.

"Three votes! Hurrah! Two more, and I'm safe. Now for Old Sawbones. I'm sure of him, though;" for upon surgery I was prepared, and my intimacy with that professor assured me he must be aware of it, and would attribute the errors I might commit to natural trepidation under the circumstances.

He was a man of too much good sense to wheedle or fool with, and notwithstanding my confidence in my good preparation, and his appreciation of it, I anticipated a terrible time with him.

My heart sank as I entered his room. "Be seated, Mr. Tensas. Beautiful weather for this season. Have an apple? Here is an instrument for deligating the subclavian artery, that the maker has done me the honour to call after me. How do you like it? Think I must order a dozen. Do to give to acquaintances," rattled on the kind-hearted professor, trying to reassure me, which he failed to do, for I regarded his pleasantry as somewhat akin to the cat sporting with its victim. "You never shave, Tensas, I believe? Apropos, how old are you?"

I jumped clear out of my seat at the question. The institution required a candidate to be twenty-one, which I was not, by several months.

"It's rather late in the day to inquire that, professor," replied I, "you should have asked that before I paid for your ticket."

"Well, you are old enough to be examined for your degree, I expect, as you'll be rejected, in all probability. How do you make chicken-soup?"

I began to get nettled, thinking he was sporting with me upon my embarrassed condition; but a glance at his face told me he was, or strongly pretending to be, in earnest.

"Professor ——," I said, "I came here, sir, to be examined upon surgery; not to be insulted, sir. What chicken-soup has to do with it, I cannot imagine. If you are disposed to twit me with my early life and humble occupation, I can assure you, sir—"

"Stop! stop! No insult was intended, and though you, with your wisdom of almost twenty-one years, cannot see the connexion between soup and surgery, I can tell you, young man, that the success of the surgeon depends very much upon kitchen medicine. Good soup is easily digested, and strengthens the patient, but bad discomposes, and prevents the reparative action of the system. But this is not answering my question. How do you, sir, make chicken-soup?"

Seeing that if he was not in earnest, it was the best imitation I had seen lately, I vouchsafed to answer the subtle inquiry.

After I had concluded—"Mr. Tensas, you have left out a very important item in the preparation of your soup: you forgot to mention in the first instance whether you would kill the chicken or not."

The glance I shot at him was too much for his gravity. Bursting into a hearty laugh, he said, "Tensas, I knew you were well prepared, but I thought I would teach you that nothing that may be conducive to the recovery of our patient, is too trivial to be remembered by the physician—also to try your temper. You have too much of the latter. The sick-bed is a fine moderator, however. Go, my dear fellow, study hard, and in ten years I will hear from you."

Tears sprung into my eyes as I wrung his hand, and thanked him, on leaving his room.

Four votes safe. One more, and the others may go to Hellespont. Now for chemistry. "How do you do, Mr. Tensas? Be composed, sir. Take a chair. Happy to have the opportunity of gratifying my chemical curiosity at your expense. I expect you candidates think your professors a very inquisitive set of fellows about this time. Ha! ha! Take a chair, sir."

"Professor ——, I am quite well, I am happy to inform you, and desirous of appearing as composed as possible. I also felicitate myself that it is in my power to display to you the fruits, as elaborated in my mind, of those eloquent expositions of chemical science which it has been my good fortune to receive, at such an inadequate remuneration, from your lips. Here is a pamphlet, very denunciatory, I am sorry to announce, of you, that I thought you would like to see. It is by the professor of physiology, and appearing first in a distant city, I thought you might not be aware of its publication; my admiration and friendship for you, together with my anxiety for the promotion of the Liebigian system, led me to procure a copy at an expense which, though considerable in the present dilapidated condition of my finances, never caused the least hesitation in its purchase, when the great good which doubtless would result from your early acquaintance with its pernicious principles was considered."

It took me at least five minutes, in a slow, monotonous, and pompous manner, to deliver this, and only ten were left to the examiner.

"Thank you, Mr. Tensas, thanks for your kind consideration for myself and the system I am proud to advocate, even though it be through detraction and vituperation. I will examine it at my leisure— we have now other business before us. Give me an exposition, Mr. Tensas, of the Atomic or Daltonian theory."

Down below zero went my hitherto buoyant spirits—my scheme had failed—I am gone, thought I, when up my heart bounded again as he interrupted me with, "Ah! how did you say you obtained this atrocious publication? Mr. Tensas, that gentleman, the author, is doing a great and irremediable injury to the cause of truth and scientific controversy. In arguing with a man of philosophical pretensions, it is to be expected that he will combat only those principles which"—and in a tone of grieved and wounded innocence, not giving me an opportunity of giving him the required exposition of the Atomic or Daltonian theory, *which I very much regretted,* the professor concluded the time allotted him for examination, saying, as I bid him adieu, "Mr. Tensas, I shall be happy to see you at my house to-night; you may rest assured of my vote." I stood in the lobby with perfect ease, confident that in having five votes out of the seven—three being required to reject—I was soon to be dubbed Doctor of Medicine. The examinations of the other two professors I got through with very summarily, fainting away before one, and occupying the fifteen minutes to restore me, and before the other, being seized with a violent bleeding at my nose; but in justification of my own honour, I must state that the representations by the rest of the faculty of the splendid examination I had passed before them, influenced their votes, and I obtained all; and, at the appointed time, received my degree, and a square yard of sheepskin, as an attestation of the progress I had made in medicine, giving me a free permit to kill whom I pleased without the fear of the law.

How to Get Elected

The dry-as-dusts solemnly asseverate that humor never did any good. They are cocksure of that. Now, let's see. How did Private John Allen of Mississippi get to Congress? He joked himself in. One "fetching" bit of humor sent him to Washington as a national lawmaker. The first time John ran for the congressional nomination his opponent was the Confederate General Tucker, who had fought gallantly during the Civil War and served with distinction two or three terms in Congress. They met on the stump. General Tucker closed one of his speeches as follows: "Seventeen years ago last night, my fellow citizens, after a hard-fought battle on yonder hill, I bivouacked under yonder clump of trees. Those of you who remember as I do the times that tried men's souls will not, I hope, forget their humble servant when the primaries shall be held."

That was a strong appeal in those days, but John raised the general at his own game in the following amazing manner: "My fellow citizens, what General Tucker says to you about the engagement seventeen years ago on yonder hill is true. What General Tucker says to you about having bivouacked in yon clump of trees on that night is true. It is also true, my fellow citizens, that I was vedette picket and stood guard over him while he slept. Now then, fellow citizens, all of you who were generals and had privates to stand guard over you while you slept, vote for General Tucker; and all of you who were privates and stood guard over the generals while they slept, vote for

From "Wit, Humor, and Anecdote," by Champ Clark, *Library of Southern Literature,* Edwin Anderson Alderman, Joel Chandler Harris, Editors in Chief, Vol. XIV, compiled by C. Alphonso Smith, pp. 6235–6236. Copyright, 1907, 1910, by The Martin and Hoyt Company. Atlanta.

Private John Allen!" The people caught on, took John at his word, and sent him to Congress, where he stayed till the world was filled with his renown.

A Napoleon of Finance

A Napoleon of Finance!

Something, Napoleonic at least for Bunker Bean, had to be done in finance immediately. He had reached the office penniless. He first tried Bulger, who owed him ten dollars. But this was a Waterloo.

"Too bad, old top!" sympathized Bulger. "If you'd only sejested it yesterday. But you know how it is when a man's out; he's got to make a flash; got to keep up his end."

He considered the others in the office. Most of them, he decided, would, like Bulger, have been keeping their ends up. Of course, there was Breede. But Napoleon at his best would never have tried to borrow money of Breede, not even on the day of his coronation. Tully, the chief clerk, was equally impossible. Tully's thick glasses magnified his eyes so that they were terrible to look at. Tully would reach out a nerveless hand and draw forth the quivering heart of his secret. Tully would know right off that a man could have no respectable reason for borrowing five dollars on Thursday.

There remained old Metzeger who worked silently all day over a set of giant ledgers, interminably beautifying their pages with his meticulous figures. True, Bean had once heard Bulger fail interestingly to borrow five dollars of Metzeger until Saturday noon, but a flash of true Napoleonic genius now enabled him to see precisely why Bulger had not succeeded. Metzeger lived for numerals, for columned digits alone. He carried thousands of them in his head and apparently little else. He could tell to the fraction of a cent what Union Pacific had opened at on any day you chose to name. He had a passion for odd amounts. A flat million as a sum interested him far less than one like $107.69¾. He could remember it longer. It was necessary then to appeal to the poetry in the man.

A long time from across his typewriter he studied old Metzeger, tall, angular, his shoulders lovingly rounded above one of the ledgers, a green shade pulled well over his eyes, perhaps to conceal the too-flagrant love-light that shone there for his figures. Napoleon had won most of his battles in his tent.

Bean arose, moved toward the other and spoke in clear, cool tones.

"Mr. Metzeger, I want to borrow five dollars—"

The old man perceptibly stiffened and bent his head lower.

From *Bunker Bean*, by Harry Leon Wilson, pp. 68-71. Doubleday, Page & Company, Garden City, New York. Copyright, 1923. Copyright, 1912, by the Curtis Publishing Company. Copyright 1913, by Doubleday, Page & Company.

"—five dollars and eighty-seven cents until Saturday at ten minutes past twelve."

Metzeger looked up, surveying him keenly from under the green shade.

"*How* much?"

"Five eighty-seven."

There was a curious relenting in the sharpened old face. The man had been struck in a vital spot. With his fine-pointed pen he affectionately wrote the figures on a pad: "$5.87—12:10." They were ideal; they vanquished him. Slowly he counted out money from various pockets, but the sum was $5.90.

"Bring me the change," he said.

Bean brought it from the clerk who kept the stamp-box. Metzeger replaced three pennies in a pocket, and Bean moved off with the sum he had demanded, feeling almost as once he might have felt after Marengo.

Lincoln Tact

President Lincoln was confronted once by two rival hatters, who visited him to present him with hats each had made. After the presentation both hatters stood back expectantly awaiting compliment.

Lincoln looked over the two hats very carefully, and then remarked solemnly: "Gentlemen, they mutually excel each other."

Profiting by Experience

One year my uncle Melik traveled from Fresno to New York. Before he got aboard the train his uncle Garro paid him a visit and told him about the dangers of travel.

When you get on the train, the old man said, choose your seat carefully, sit down, and do not look about.

Yes, sir, my uncle said.

Several moments after the train begins to move, the old man said, two men wearing uniforms will come down the aisle and ask you for your ticket. Ignore them. They will be impostors.

How will I know? my uncle said.

You will know, the old man said. You are no longer a child.

Yes, sir, my uncle said.

Before you have traveled twenty miles an amiable young man will

From *Lincoln Talks, a Biography in Anecdote,* Collected, Collated and Edited by Emanuel Hertz, p. 594. Copyright, 1939, by The Viking Press. New York.

From *My Name Is Aram,* by William Saroyan, pp. 187–191. Copyright 1940 by William Saroyan. New York: Harcourt, Brace & Co.

come to you and offer you a cigarette. Tell him you don't smoke. The cigarette will be doped.

Yes, sir, said my uncle.

On your way to the diner a very beautiful young woman will bump into you intentionally and almost embrace you, the old man said. She will be extremely apologetic and attractive, and your natural impulse will be to cultivate her friendship. Dismiss your natural impulse and go on in and eat. The woman will be an adventuress.

A what? my uncle said.

A whore, the old man shouted. Go on in and eat. Order the best food, and if the diner is crowded, and the beautiful young woman sits across the table from you, do not look into her eyes. If she speaks, pretend to be deaf.

Yes, sir, my uncle said.

Pretend to be deaf, the old man said. That is the only way out of it.

Out of what? my uncle said.

Out of the whole ungodly mess, the old man said. I have traveled. I know what I'm talking about.

Yes, sir, my uncle said.

Let's say no more about it, the old man said.

Yes, sir, my uncle said.

Let's not speak of the matter again, the old man said. It's finished. I have seven children. My life has been a full and righteous one. Let's not give it another thought. I have land, vines, trees, cattle, and money. One cannot have everything—except for a day or two at a time.

Yes, sir, my uncle said.

On your way back to your seat from the diner, the old man said, you will pass through the smoker. There you will find a game of cards in progress. The players will be three middle-aged men with expensive-looking rings on their fingers. They will nod at you pleasantly and one of them will invite you to join the game. Tell them, No speak English.

Yes, sir, my uncle said.

That is all, the old man said.

Thank you very much, my uncle said.

One thing more, the old man said. When you go to bed at night, take your money out of your pocket and put it in your shoe. Put your shoe under your pillow, keep your head on the pillow all night, *and don't sleep.*

Yes, sir, my uncle said.

That is all, the old man said.

The old man went away and the next day my uncle Melik got aboard the train and traveled straight across America to New York. The two men in uniforms were not impostors, the young man with the doped cigarette did not arrive, the beautiful young woman did not sit across the table from my uncle in the diner, and there was no card game in progress in the smoker. My uncle put his money in his shoe and put his shoe under his pillow and put his head on the pillow and didn't sleep all night the first night, but the second night he abandoned the whole ritual.

The second day he *himself* offered another young man a cigarette which the other young man accepted. In the diner my uncle went out of his way to sit at a table with a young lady. He started a poker game in the smoker, and long before the train ever got to New York my uncle knew everybody aboard the train and everybody knew him. Once, while the train was traveling through Ohio, my uncle and the young man who had accepted the cigarette and two young ladies on their way to Vassar formed a quartette and sang *The Wabash Blues.* The journey was a very pleasant one.

When my uncle Melik came back from New York, his old uncle Garro visited him again.

I see you are looking all right, he said. Did you follow my instructions?

Yes, sir, my uncle said.

The old man looked far away in space.

I am pleased that *someone* has profited by my experience, he said.

Steamboat Captain Averse to Racing

Early in the spring of the present year, a magnificent new steamer was launched upon the Ohio river, and shortly afterward made her appearance at the Levee, opposite the flourishing city of Cincinnati. Gilt-edged covers, enveloping the captain's "respects," accompanied with invitations to "see her through," upon her first trip down the river, were forwarded to the editorial corps in that vicinity; the chalked hats were "numerous" on the occasion. It was a grand affair, this *debut* of a floating palace, which has since maintained her repute untarnished as the "crack boat," *par excellence,* upon the Western waters. Your humble servant was among the "invited guests"—and a nice time he had of it!

I found myself on board this beautiful craft in "close communion" with a score of unquestionable "beauties." The company proved to be a heterogeneous conglomeration of character—made up of editors, lawyers, auctioneers, indescribables, and "fancies"—with a sprinkling of "none-such's." There was a stray parson, too, in the crowd—but as his leisure time "between meals" was spent in trading horses, we dispensed with his "grace before meals."

By "The Young 'Un" of Philadelphia (pseudonym for George P. Burnham). First published in New York *Spirit of the Times,* May 16, 1846. From Colonel Thorpe's *Scenes in Arkansaw,* pp. 125–129. Philadelphia: T. B. Peterson and Brothers. 1858.

We left our moorings an hour before sunset, upon a clear cold afternoon, and passed rapidly down stream for a considerable distance, without experiencing any out-of-the-way occurrence. The "sons of temperance," and the parson aforesaid, amused themselves over a smoking whisky toddy—the "boys" were relieving each other of their superfluous dimes and quarters at *euchre,* when a tall gentleman, who was "some," (when he was sober,) stepped suddenly into the cabin, and imparted the information that a well-known "fast boat" had just hove in sight, at the mouth of the Kentucky river. The cards were "dropt" instanter—the punches disappeared—and the "mourners" were soon distributed in knots upon the promenade deck, to watch the progress of events.

Our "bully" boat sped away like a bird, however, and the craft behind gave us early evidence that she should offer no child's play. The "fat was in the fire" at once—a huge column of black smoke curled up in the clear atmosphere—*an extra turn or two* was visible upon our own boat, and away we went! A good deal of excitement existed among the party, as the rival steamer was clearly gaining upon us. A craft like ours, with such a company, and such a captain, mustn't be *beaten.*

As the boat behind us fell in under our stern, and we could "count her passengers," a sort of impression came over us, that, by some mistake, we had got upon the wrong boat! At least, such was the expressed opinion of the parson, as he threatened to "go down *stairs*" and take another drink. Our captain was a noble fellow—he paced the deck quietly, with a constant eye to wind'ard; but he said nothing. A bevy of the mourners stepped up to him, with—

"What speed, cap'n?"

"Fair, gentlemen; I may say *very* fair."

"Smart craft, that, behind," ventured one.

"Very," responded the captain, calmly, as he placed his hand upon a small brass knob at the back of the pilot house. This movement was responded to by the faint jingling of a bell below, followed immediately by a rush of cinders from the smoke-pipes, and an improved action of the paddles.

"Now we move again."

"Some," was the response, and a momentary tremor pervaded the boat as she "slid along" right smartly.

But the craft in our rear moved like our shadow on the calm waters, and as we shot down the river, it seemed as if we had her "in tow," so calmly and uniformly did she follow in our wake. The excitement of the congregation upon deck had by this time become intense, and it was pretty plain that the boats must shortly part company, or "split something!" The rascal behind us took advantage of a turn in the channel, and "helm a-starboard!" was clearly heard from the look-out of our rival, as she "hove off," and suddenly fell alongside us! The parson went below at once, to put his threat into execution, as we came up into the current again, "neck and neck"; and when he returned we were running a twenty-five-knot lick, the steam smack on to 49°!

"She's goin'—goin' go—," muttered an auctioneer to himself.

"A perfect nonsuit," remarked a lawyer.

"Beaten, but not vanquished," added a politician; and away we scudded side by side for half a mile.

"Wouldn't she bear a *leetle* more?" meekly asked the parson.

"She's doing very well," replied the captain. "Don't get excited, gentlemen; my boat is a new one—her reputation and mine is at stake. We mustn't rush her—*racing always injures a boat,* and I am averse to it"; saying which he applied his thumb and finger to the brass knob again—the bell tinkled in the distance—and our rival pilot shortly had an opportunity to examine the architecture of our rudder-post!

I was acquainted with the engineer. I stepped below, (believing we should be beaten at our present speed,) and entering the engine-room—

"Tim," said I, "we'll be licked—give her another turn, eh?"

"I rayther think she moves *some* as it is," said Tim.

"Yes: but the C—— is hard on us—give her a little, my boy—just for—"

"Step in here a moment," remarked Tim; "it's all 'mum,' you know—nothin' to be said, eh? Quiet—, there!—don't she tremble some?"

I noticed, for the first time, that our boat did labour prodigiously!

"But come round *here*," continued Tim: "*look there!—mum's* the word you know."

I stepped out of that engine-room (Tim said afterwards, that I "sprang out at one bound"; but he lied!) in a hurry. *The solder upon the connection-pipe had melted and run down over the seams in a dozen places,* from the excessive heat—a crow-bar was braced athwart the safety-valve, with a "fifty-six" upon one end—and we were shooting down the Ohio, under a head of steam "chock up" to 54 40!!

My "sleeping apartment" was well aft. I entered the state-room—got over upon the *back* side of my berth—and, stuffing the corners of the pillow into my ears, endeavoured to compose myself in sleep. It was out of the question. In attempting to "right myself," I discovered that *my hair stuck out so straight, it was impossible for me to get my head within six inches of the pillow!*

I tossed about till daylight, in momentary expectation of being landed in Kentucky, (or somewhere else!) but we got on finely. We led our rival half an hour into Louisville; and I immediately swore upon my nightcap that I would never accept another invitation, for a pleasure trip, from *a steamboat captain who was averse to racing!*

Science vs. the Mississippi

The Mississippi between Cairo and New Orleans was twelve hundred and fifteen miles long one hundred and seventy-six years ago. It was eleven hundred and eighty after the cut-off of 1722. It was one thousand and forty after the American Bend cut-off. It has lost sixty-seven miles since. Consequently, its length is only nine hundred and seventy-three miles at present.

Now, if I wanted to be one of those ponderous scientific people, and "let on" to prove what had occurred in the remote past by what had occurred in a given time in the recent past, or what will occur in the far future by what has occurred in late years, what an opportunity is here! Geology never had such a chance, nor such exact data to argue from! Nor "development of species," either! Glacial epochs are great things, but they are vague—vague. Please observe:

In the space of one hundred and seventy-six years the Lower Mississippi has shortened itself two hundred and forty-two miles. That is an average of a trifle over one mile and a third per year. Therefore, any calm person, who is not blind or idiotic, can see that in the Old Oölitic Silurian Period, just a million years ago next November, the Lower Mississippi River was upward of one million three hundred thousand miles long, and stuck out over the Gulf of Mexico like a fishing-rod. And by the same token any person can see that seven hundred and forty-two years from now the Lower Mississippi will be only a mile and three-quarters long, and Cairo and New Orleans will have joined their streets together, and be plodding comfortably along under a single mayor and a mutual board of aldermen. There is something fascinating about science. One gets such wholesale returns of conjecture out of such a trifling investment of fact.

An Innocent in Texas

I had heard so much about Texas that I was consumed with curiosity about our great sister republic to the south. Was it true for instance that all Texans are seven feet tall except the football players at Texas Christian and Southern Methodist, who are eight? Was it true that Rhode Island would fit 220 times into Texas, as Texas friends had so often assured me? Was it true that in the early years of the war there were so many Texans in the Royal Canadian Air Force that Canadians

From *Life on the Mississippi*, by Samuel L. Clemens, p. 136. Copyright, 1874 and 1875, by H. O. Houghton and Company; 1883, by Samuel L. Clemens.

From *The Night the Old Nostalgia Burned Down*, by Frank Sullivan, pp. 378–384. Copyright, 1948, by Frank Sullivan. Boston: Little, Brown & Company.

were often tempted to call it the Royal Texan Air Force? Did Oveta Culp Hobby . . .

I wanted to learn the answers. I wanted to see Texas in action. There was only one way to do so. Throwing a few things into my bag I took off for Houston. I travelled light—a spare ten-gallon hat, two pairs of chaps, one for business and one for formal evening wear, a lariat, a few other necessaries, and Rhode Island, which I brought along because, in the interests of accuracy, I was eager to check on that 220 story.

On a typical sparkling Texas morning I debarked at Houston. Two glorious suns were shining, the regular one and the special Texas sun. Above the hum of the city's traffic rose the pleasant susurrus of Texas voices exchanging matutinal howdies in their melodious Confederate drawl.

From the distance came the agreeable gurgle of gushers gushing in the gusheries scattered about the city, with occasionally the triumphant yodel of an oil millionaire who had just discovered a new gusher. Anon, the crack of rifle fire and the sight of a fleeing cattle rustler with a posse at his heels told me plainer than words that Texas could still dispense frontier justice.

"Yippee!" I cried, for I speak Texan fluently, and, drawing two or three six-shooters from my belt, I fired a volley of twenty-one guns in salute to Pecos Bill, John Nance Garner, General Santa Anna, Stephen F. Austin, Maury Maverick and the Alamo.

I made Houston my first port of call because it is the metropolis and chief city of the Texan republic, although I add instantly that Dallas, San Antonio, Galveston, Waco, Wichita Falls, Fort Worth, Austin, Abilene and El Paso are also the chief cities of Texas. Other chief cities may have sprung up since I left. If so, I beg their pardon for not mentioning them.

Houston has a population of 600,000 and, Houstonians informed me, is growing at the rate of 10,000 inhabitants a day, 5,000 of them oil millionaires. Texas grows the largest and most luscious grapefruit in the world and the richest millionaires. Jesse Jones of Houston is the richest Jones in recorded history. At its present rate of growth Houston will outstrip London and New York in a decade. Perhaps sooner, since Texans are twice as big as Londoners or New Yorkers.

My day in Houston was packed with excitement. No sooner was I settled in my suite at one of the city's finer hotels than they struck oil in the cellar and immediately started tearing down the twenty-eight-story hotel to make way for the more profitable gusher. The hospitable Chamber of Commerce quickly found me agreeable quarters in a twenty-nine-story hotel and after washing up I still had time before lunch to measure Rhode Island into Houston. It goes seven times.

I shall not soon forget that lunch. We had steak. Steak is the state flower of Texas. Texas has the finest steaks and the best department stores in the country. I had heard of the Gargantuan meals to which the lusty Texans are accustomed, but after all I come from New York, the home of the late Diamond Jim Brady, who thought nothing of consuming, at one sitting, twelve dozen oysters, eight quarts of orange juice, four adult lobsters, two planked steaks and Lillian Russell, so I set to work with a will and in no time at all was pridefully chasing the last shred of tenderloin around my plate with a piece of bun.

"Yippee!" I remarked. "Here's one dam-yank that can tie on the old feedbag with any varmint in Houston."

Just then a waiter put a steak in front of me twice as big as the steak I had just eaten. The waiter was twice as big as a New York waiter.

"What's that thar, pardner?" says I.

"That thar's yore steak, pardner," says he.

"What was that thar I just et?" says I.

"That thar was jest yore hors d'oeuvre," says he.

"Yippee!" says I, but in a more chastened tone, you may be sure, and that was the last time I bragged of my appetite in Texas.

I tried to tell my hosts how overjoyed I was to be having my first glimpse of their great republic.

"Perhaps no other planet in the universe has contributed as many notable figures to history as Texas," I enthused. "Look at the roster— Martin Dies, Ma Ferguson, Sam Houston, Chester A. Nimitz, Ensign Gay, Abraham Lincoln, George Washington, Queen Victoria, Amon G. Carter, Napoleon Bonaparte, O. Henry, Charlemagne, John the Baptist, the Twelve Apostles . . ."

"Excuse me, pardner," interrupted a Texan, "only nine of the Twelve Apostles was from Texas."

After lunch my hosts asked me if there was anything in particular I wished to see, and I was able to answer them precisely.

"Before I leave Houston I want to see a new gusher come into being," I said.

"Easiest thing in the world. Step this way."

We went to a vacant lot down back of the post office, and the chairman of the Houston Gusher Commission took a folding divining rod from his pocket.

"What kind of oil would you all care to see, pardner?" he asked.

"Some of that black gold I've heard so much about, if you please," said I.

Thereupon the chairman mumbled a few charms, dangled the rod over a cactus plant nearby, and within seconds there was a grumble. There followed a restless groaning and heaving as of oil struggling to reach the surface, the cactus plant hurried off in a kind of panic, and a second later on that very spot a fine geyser of high-octane black gold shot ninety-two feet into the air before us.

"Golly!" I exclaimed, in awesome admiration. "Congratulations. I'll wager this gusher will bring you fellows a pretty penny in royalties."

"Why, she's yours," cried the chairman, jovially.

"Oh, no. Really, I couldn't think . . ."

"Nonsense. It's your luncheon favor. Compliments of the Chamber of Commerce of Houston. We always give gushers to visitors. Why don't you christen her?"

"I christen thee the Pappy O'Daniel," I said to the oil well, and instantly it gulped, gasped and retreated into the bowels of the earth.

"Better try another name," the chairman suggested.

"I christen thee the Davy Crockett," I amended, and this time the gusher gushed joyfully again. I can only add that that gusher has to date brought me $4,390,000 in royalties. As far as I am concerned the accounts of the legendary hospitality of Houston are definitely not exaggerated.

Nor are the accounts of the legendary hospitality of Dallas exaggerated. Dallas, named for Stella Dallas, is 187 light years distant from Houston and is the finest city in Texas. By a stroke of good fortune I visited Dallas just at a time when the traditional rivalry between itself and Fort Worth, the finest city in Texas, had reached one of its periodical boiling points. It seems that the night before I got there a band of marauders from Fort Worth had made a surprise attack on the famous Nieman-Marcus department store in Dallas and with shouts of "Yippee!" and "Southern Methodist is no good, chop 'em up for kindling wood!" had carried off the entire contents of the notion counter, along with several hundred pounds of pecan pralines. Feeling was running high in Dallas and there was talk of reprisals on the Fort Worth Cowboy Lament Works, the great sprawling industrial plant where 20,000 musicians work in three shifts composing the dirges which have made the name of Texas so—what shall I say?—throughout the world.

The rivalry between the various cities of Texas is an interesting phenomenon and, I was told, is the main reason why the founders of the republic felt it wise to place each city at least 800 miles from its nearest neighbor. In telling a Dallasian his community is not as matchless a civic gem as Fort Worth you run an even greater risk than if you told an Irishman from Connemara that County Mayo is the flawless emerald in Erin's diadem.

The Easterner, or tenderfoot, will not comprehend this keen, internecine rivalry. A resident of, let us say, Rochester has no fear of not being made welcome when he visits New York City (one of the larger cities in the state). True, his wallet may be extracted from his pants before he has got three blocks from the Grand Central Terminal, but it is done quietly and with a minimum of discomfort to him. He will be overcharged at hotels and restaurants and will pay one of the better kings' ransoms for theater tickets and on his way home he may be mugged by an acquisitive thug, but it is all in a spirit of detachment, like a surgeon removing a gall bladder. There is absolutely no bias against him simply because he comes from Rochester. In fact, the driver of the taxi which clips him as he crosses Fifth Avenue may himself be a Rochester boy. Truly it is a small world in New York.

Not soon shall I forget my first sight of Fort Worth. I neared the city on foot from the east, meaning east of Fort Worth, at about sunset. My two slaves, Caesar and Pompey, whom I had picked up for a song in one of the large Houston department stores, followed me at a respectful distance, carrying Rhode Island. On the western horizon, enclosing the city in a shimmering, iridescent halo, was a sight of such beauty as to take away my breath—and I had little of it to spare after the day's hike. Reds, golds, crimsons, purples, pinks, mauves, oranges, bananas, a thousand delicate hues intermingled in what cannot but be described as a veritable riot of color. Never, not even over the Hackensack meadows, had I seen so gorgeous a sunset, and for that reason if for none other my disappointment was the keener when I learned that it was not a sunset at all but the great Fort Worth Cowboy Shirt Plant, where they make all those beautiful, vivid shirts that cowboys wear to frighten steers into submission. What I mistook for a sunset was the day's output of the shirt mills, hung out to air. I shall never again see a sunset that will not seem tame.

One of the most agreeable episodes of my trip to Texas was the day I spent on the Regal Ranch, the largest cattle, or any kind of, ranch in the world. Rhode Island fitted into it sixty-seven times. It is so large that although there are 949 billion trillions of blades of grass on it, each blade is three feet from its nearest neighbor. (I am indebted to Professor Harlow Shapley of the Harvard Department of Astronomy for the use of these figures.) The cattle have to be flown in jet planes from one pasturage to another. If they tried to walk they would either die of fatigue or become so tough and muscle-bound that they would be useless for anything except one of those $8 table d'hôte dinners at a swank New York hotel. No matter how large you think the Regal Ranch is, it is twice as large as that. In fact the cowboys from the northern part of the ranch can scarcely understand the dialect spoken by their colleagues from its southern shires.

Last year the Regal exported 5,476,397 head of cattle to Kansas City and 2,397,739 head of cowboy to the Hollywood mart. Of the latter, 726,387 were pure Roy Rogers, 327,835 were Gene Autrys and 14,397 were genuine, antique Gary Coopers. The foreman of one of the counties in the ranch told me they are experimenting on an improved breed of cowboy, who will combine the best features of all cowboys since William S. Hart and will, as one improved feature, have fingernails four times as durable as the present ones, and therefore be better equipped for successful plunking of guitars. Many an otherwise magnificent specimen of cowboy, the foreman told me, has had to be shot because of brittle fingernail, an occupational defect which renders a cowhand useless as a guitar strummer and hence useless. The fingernail snaps off in the middle of "Home on the Range," and lasting shame is the lot of the unfortunate cowboy, through no fault of his own.

With his plunking fingernail thus bolstered, the last defect will be removed from the Texas cowboy, and he will be the most perfect specimen of fine upstanding manhood the world has known. He is eight feet tall, of course. No cowhand under that height can hope to win his lariat. He is not only a paragon of manly beauty but he has a pure mind and worships the ground that women walk on. Womankind, whom he traditionally and respectfully addresses as "Ma'am," takes second place in his affections only to the little dogies whose virtues he has lyricised to the envy of all the rest of the animal kingdom, no species of which has found so eloquent a minstrel to sing its praises. The Texas cowhand is generous to a fault and, unless you are wary, he will give you the shirt off his back. Quick to resent an affront he nevertheless has a heart of gold, and no widow or orphan ever appealed to him for succor in vain.

I shall not name, for I would not dignify him by doing so, a certain viper whom I encountered at a luncheon given for me by the Chamber of Commerce of one of the larger cattle ranches. Chatting casually with this person, who had been introduced to me as a Texan, I said, "You've got a mighty fine state down here, pardner."

"Oh, it's all right," he said, in a tone of diffidence which I did not quite like.

"It's the biggest state in the Union," I said, bridling slightly.

"Size isn't everything," he remarked.

I was now pretty nettled, for in my stay I had come to look upon Texas with great affection.

"Texas has won every war for the United States," I challenged.

"Pooh!" This from a Texan!

"You pooh Texas!" I cried, astounded.

"Yes, and I re-pooh it," said he.

"You deny Texas won the World Wars in addition to the Spanish-American, Civil and Revolutionary wars?"

"I do. Where do you come from?"

"Round Lake, New York."

"I thought so. You foreigners who become enamored of Texas brag worse than our own Chamber of Commerce. Texas is just another state."

I know I acted hastily. I should have turned him over to the Chamber of Commerce. But I couldn't help it. I shot him. No jury convicted me.

A week had passed and my visit to the Lonesome Star State was coming to a close. I do not pretend to have seen all of Texas in my week there. It would take at least another week to do that. But I had completed my research with Rhode Island. It really does go 220 times into Texas. In fact, I had Deaf Smith County left over.

II. SASS

Introduction

Sass is back-talk with backbone. You will not find that definition in the dictionary, nor will you even find an entry for "sass." In fact, even "sassy" will be cross-referenced as a dialectal variant of "saucy." Despite the lexicographers, Americans know what sass is and they enjoy its flavor. It is a tart, witty rejoinder asserting a person's position and his rights. It is amusing both because of its tartness and because of the power which backs it up.

Sometimes sass seems little more than a simple statement which puts all the cards on the table. One way to make it more than a simple statement is to accentuate the strength of position by the terseness of the rejoinder. Such was the reply of the American general in the Battle of the Bulge who, having been requested by the Germans to surrender, replied, "Nuts!" Such, too, is the letter of General Israel Putnam regarding a captured British soldier; the economy of his reply and the decisiveness of his action give sassiness to his plain statements. Terseness reaches its peak when no words at all are used, for actions as well as words may be sassy. There's the classic story, for example, of Babe Ruth's answering the boos of the crowd by pointing with his bat to the centerfield flagpole and then hitting a homer over it. (That's the way I heard it.) Any player can point with a bat, but when he backs his gesture up by hitting the ball over the spot indicated, that's sass.

Another way to make a simple statement sassy is to leave some doubt about the meaning; thus the person sassed is not quite sure whether to be offended or not. Benjamin Franklin's letter to William Strahan is so arranged on the page that it may mean either of two things. In similar vein is Will Rogers' statement, "It was mighty nice of President Hoover to take off time from appointing commissions to open this program."

One of the invasions of privacy which we resent is the nosy question, but it can be diverted with sass. The Squatter in "The Arkansas Traveller" easily avoids answering a whole series of nosy inquiries by misinterpreting the questioner's meaning. Thus when the Traveller asks, ". . . what might your name be?" he replies, "It might be Dick, and it might be Tom; but it lacks right smart uv it." But as a study of American laughter will show, there are countless other situations when sass—not sauce, mind you—is a welcome ingredient.

Straight from the Shoulder

A person of the name of Palmer, who was a lieutenant in the tory new levies, was detected in the camp at Peek's-kiln (Peekskill). Governor Tryon, who commanded the new levies, reclaimed him as a British subject, represented heinous the crime of condemning a man commissioned by his majesty, and threatened vengeance in case he should be executed. General Putnam wrote him the following pithy reply.

"Sir,

"Nathan Palmer, a lieutenant in your King's service, was taken in my camp as a *spy*—he was tried as a *spy*—he was condemned as a *spy*—and you may rest assured, sir, he shall be hanged as a *spy*. I have the honour to be, &c.

ISRAEL PUTNAM.

P.S. Afternoon . . . He is hanged.

Aplomb

It is told of Colonel Ethan Allen of Lisbon, Conn., that once going into the dining room of a New York hotel and no waiter showing him a seat, he walked to the head of the table and took a chair that was turned up there. Then a waiter hurried up and said that the seat was engaged. "To whom?" asked the colonel. "To a gentleman," said the waiter. "He's come," said the colonel, and he ate his dinner undisturbed.

You Are My Friends

An Indian chief of the Creek nation, being once appointed to negotiate a treaty of peace with the people of South Carolina, was desired by the governor and council to speak his mind freely, and not to be afraid, for he was among friends. "I will speak freely; I will not be afraid," said he. "For why should I be afraid among my friends, who never am afraid among my enemies."

From *The American Jest Book, containing a curious variety of Jests, Anecdotes, Bon Mots, Stories* . . . Philadelphia: Printed for M. Carey & W. Spotswood. 1789.

From *American Wit and Humor*, Vol. II, p. 303. Philadelphia: George W. Jacobs & Co. 1900.

From *The American Jest Book, containing a curious variety of Jests, Anecdotes, Bon Mots, Stories* . . . Philadelphia: Printed for M. Carey & W. Spotswood. 1789.

You Are My Enemy

A letter Benjamin Franklin wrote [but did not send] to his British correspondent, William Strahan, July 5, 1775:

You are a member of Parliament, and one of that majority which has doomed my country to destruction.—You have begun to burn our towns and murder our people.—Look upon your hands! They are stained with the blood of your relations!—You and I were long friends:—You are now my enemy,—and

I am
Yours,
BENJAMIN FRANKLIN

War Is Hell

. . . Some time during the latter part of the [Civil] war, or just after it, the society people of the South were in the habit of turning up their noses at "Old Tecumseh" [Gen. W. T. Sherman] as not blue-blooded. In support of their charge it was reported and published in the Southern newspapers that he had once kept a corner grocery. Some of the younger members of the family wrote to the general, inclosing a cutting from a Southern paper to this effect, and asked him to deny it. The old warrior wrote back that he did not think there was any necessity for denial "because, for my part, I think a corner a very good place to keep a grocery."

Hell and Texas

. . . General Sherman . . . is often credited with saying that if he owned both Hell and Texas, he would rent out Texas and live in the other place.

"That's right, every man for his own country," a Texan is said to have retorted.

From *Life & Times of Benjamin Franklin*, by James Parton, p. 88. Vol. II. New York: Mason Brothers, Publishers. 1865.

From *American Wit and Humor*, Vol. II, p. 211. Philadelphia: George W. Jacobs & Co. 1900.

From "A Postscript by the Editor," by J. Frank Dobie, to "Hell in Texas," by George E. Hastings, in *Southwestern Lore*, Publications of the Texas Folk-Lore Society No. IX, edited by J. Frank Dobie, pp. 180, 182. Copyright, 1931, by the Texas Folk-Lore Society. Dallas: Published for the Texas Folk-Lore Society, Austin, Texas, by the Southwest Press.

Grave Question

It is sometimes said, by misguided Yankees, that Southern towns have more than the national average of feeble-minded people wandering their streets. This is not true. Several years ago I was visiting friends in a town in Unoccupied Florida, up near the Georgia border. They were building a new hospital in this town and, though construction had not started, the excavation was almost finished—an immense pit nearly a block long. It happened that a Mr. Dabney, one of the town's leading citizens, was showing me the site. We were standing by the excavation when a boy about twelve years old came along. He was by reputation the town half-wit—that is, he was one of them. He came up alongside of us and stared into the excavation and finally he said, "Mista Dabney, what they gonna do with that big ole hole when they finey git 'er dug?" Mr. Dabney smiled at the boy and then said, "Well, Hoab, I tell you. When they get 'er dug they're gonna take all the sons-of-bitches in this town and pile 'em in there." The boy reflected on this information a bit and then said, "Who they gonna git to cover 'em up?"

A Game Answer

Jim, a coluhed man, was livin' pretty high, puttin' on airs. One day a white man stopped off and started talkin' to de coluhed man. "Jim," he say, "I see dat you been doin' pretty good fo' yo'se'f." "Yessuh," say Jim, "I'se been doin' good. Ev'ything you see is mine." "I guess, Jim, dare's plenty squirrels 'roun' heah." "Yessuh, dare's plenty. I went out yestiddy and kilt a whole mess o' squirrels." "Plenty quail, Jim, I guess." "Yessuh, I went out yestiddy and kilt a big mess." "Jim, you don' know who I is, do you—I'se de gamewarden." "Cap'n, you don' know who I is. Anybody 'roun' heah can tell you dat I'se de biggest liah in dese parts."

From *The Rebel Yell, being a Carpetbagger's Attempt to Establish the Truth Concerning the Screech of the Confederate Soldier plus Lesser Matters Appertaining to the Peculiar Habits of the South,* by H. Allen Smith, pp. 91–92. Copyright, 1954, by H. Allen Smith. Garden City: Doubleday & Company, Inc. 1954.

From "Negro Folktales from Alabama," by Ray B. Browne, in *Southern Folklore Quarterly,* Vol. XVIII (June, 1954), No. 2, p. 131.

I Ain't Lost

A fine city man had a brand-new buggy and a prize-winning pair of trotters that he wished to try out. He drove along the country roads, speeding a little here and walking a little there, studying the good points and admiring the beauty of his new rig. He was so delighted with the prospect that he failed to notice the road. Later on he realized that he was lost, but he hoped by driving on to find his way, or at least to meet someone who could tell him how to get back to the city.

But it was a long lonesome road. For a long time he followed the windings, hoping every hilltop would bring him within sight of some dwelling. When it was almost dark he saw in front of him a cotton patch and a good-sized country boy chopping away in the rows. He reined his tired team near the fence and called out, "Hello, boy."

"Hello yourself," the boy replied, still wielding his hoe.

"Where does this road go to?"

"Hain't never seed it go nowhars. Hit allus stays right whar hit is," said the boy, still digging away.

"How far is it to the next town?"

"Don't know; never measured it," replied the boy.

Thoroughly disgusted, the man said with some heat, "You don't know anything. You are certainly the biggest fool I ever saw."

The boy looked a long time in the man's eyes; then he said with contempt, "I knows I don't know nothing. I knows I'se a fool. But I ain't lost."

Oolah! Oolah!

One time there was a fellow lived just over the line in Oklahoma, and he was running for Congress. There was a lot of Indian farmers out that way, and he got an old chief to round up a lot of them to hear him speak.

"The Government ain't treated you boys right in the past," says he, "but I aim to change all that soon as I get to Washington. After I'm elected, my Indian brothers won't be living in shanties and brush wigwams like they do now. No, siree! Not in my district! I'm going to see that every one of you fellows has got a good house, and fine furniture, and a new cookstove, and a electric ice-box if he wants it."

From "Anecdotes from the Brazos Bottoms," by A. W. Eddins, *Straight Texas*, Publications of the Texas Folk-Lore Society, Number XIII, 1937, edited by J. Frank Dobie and Mody C. Boatright, p. 94. Copyright, 1937, by the Texas Folk-Lore Society. Austin.

From *Who Blowed Up the Church House? and Other Ozark Folk Tales*, by Vance Randolph, pp. 126–127. Copyright, 1952, by Columbia University Press. New York.

The Indians acted like they was might happy to hear this, and they all clapped their hands and hollered "Oolah! Oolah!" The old chief looked kind of surprised, but he did not say nothing.

"And furthermore," says the candidate, "my first act as your Congressman will be to get every Indian voted a good farm, if he ain't got one already. And I'm going to fix it so every one of you boys can have a nice late-model car, instead of some old jalopy. Yes, and we'll build roads fit to drive on, without no mud holes in 'em!"

The Indians was in a fine good humor by this time, laughing and chuckling amongst themselves, and they clapped their hands louder than ever. They was all hollering "Oolah! Oolah!" till you could hear them half a mile off.

"I'm going to bring better livestock into the district, too," says the candidate. "I'll see that good bulls and stallions are available to every Indian stockman, so that our cattle and horses will be second to none in the United States." And with that he set down and all them Indians was so happy they just laughed and slapped each other on the back. They kept a-hollering "Oolah! Oolah!" for five minutes anyhow, while the candidate was a-smiling and shaking hands with everybody that come within reach. He says it is the most enthusiastic audience he ever spoke to, and one of the best meetings of his whole campaign. The old chief he just set there poker-faced and never said a word, but anybody that knows Indians could tell he was just as tickled as the rest of them.

On the way back to town the candidate stopped at a big farm where the ranchman wanted to show him some fine cattle. There was one prize bull that they said was worth ten thousand dollars. "A magnificent animal!" says the candidate, and he started to walk right into the pen, but an Indian ranchhand touched his arm. "You better come around this other gate, Mister," he says. "The boys ain't cleaned up that side yet, and if you walk over there you'll get *oolah* on your shoes."

Straight from the Horse's Mouth

It is said to be a peculiarity of the Yankees that when they are buying a thing they have a habit of depreciating its worth by criticising and finding faults with it in order to cheapen the cost. On one occasion one of this kind wanted to buy a horse from a dealer. A fine-looking animal was led out of the stable for him to examine. He looked him over and saw that apparently there was no defect and no room for complaint.

"Oh," said he, "that horse has a fine head—I won't run him down with so fine a head; it is astonishing how much that head reminds me of

From *Funny Stories* told by Phineas T. Barnum, pp. 161–162. Copyright, 1890, by Phineas T. Barnum. New York and London: George Routledge and Sons, Limited.

a horse my father owned twenty years ago. Well, that is a good shoulder, too; forelegs well-formed. How much they do remind me of a horse my father owned twenty years ago.

Passing along the animal he continued:—

"And those hind quarters are good; and what a beautiful fine tail! It is really wonderful how they remind me of a horse my father owned twenty years ago."

Turning round on the other side of the horse, he said:—

"Fine mane, nice ears, splendid eyes. I declare it is marvellous how much they remind me of a horse my father owned twenty years ago."

And then opening the mouth to look at the teeth, he quietly said, "I guess it's the same horse."

Plain & Fancy Pistol Shooting

SAN DIEGO, Cal., *Sept.* 1, 1854.

I copy the following paragraph from the *Spirit of the Times,* for July 15th:

PISTOL SHOOTING—A CHALLENGE.

Owing to the frequent and urgent solicitations of many of my friends, I am induced to make the following propositions:

1. I will fit a dollar to the end of a twig two inches long, and while a second person will hold the other end in his mouth, so as to bring the coin within an inch and a half of his face, I engage to strike the dollar, three times out of five, at the distance of ten paces, or thirty feet. I will add in explanation, that there are several persons willing and ready to hold the twig or stick described above, when required.

2. I will hit a dollar, tossed in the air, or any other object of the same size, three times out of five *on a wheel and fire.*

3. At the word, I will split three balls out of five, on a knife blade, placed at the distance of thirty feet.

4. I will hit three birds out of five, sprung from the trap, standing thirty feet from the trap when shooting.

5. I will break, at the word, five common clay pipe stems out of seven, at the distance of thirty feet.

6. I engage to prove, by fair trial, that no pistol-shot can be produced who will shoot an apple off a man's head, at the distance of thirty feet, oftener than I can. Moreover I will produce two persons willing and ready to hold the apple on their heads for me, when required to do so.

7. I will wager, lastly, that no person in the United States can be produced who will hit a quarter of a dollar at the distance of thirty feet, oftener than I can, *on a wheel and fire.*

I am willing to bet $5,000 on any of the above propositions, one fourth of that amount forfeit. So soon as any bet will be closed, the money shall be de-

"Pistol Shooting—A Counter Challenge," from *Phoenixiana* . . . , by John Phoenix [George H. Derby], pp. 67–70. New York: D. Appleton & Company. 1856.

posited in the Bank of the State of Missouri, until paid over by the judges, or withdrawn, less forfeit. I will give the best and most satisfactory references that my share will be forthcoming when any of my propositions are taken up. Any one desiring to take up any of my propositions must address me by letter, through the St. Louis Post Office, as the advertisements or notices of newspapers might not meet my eye. Propositions will be received until the first of September next.

EDMUND W. PAUL,
140 Sixth Street, between Franklin Avenue and
Morgan Street, St. Louis, Missouri.

I am unable to see any thing very extraordinary in the above propositions, by Mr. Edmund W. Paul. Any person, acquainted with the merest rudiments of the pistol, could certainly execute any or all of the proposed feats without the slightest difficulty.

"Owing" to my entertaining these opinions, "without solicitation from friends, and unbiassed by unworthy motives," *I* am induced to make the following propositions:—

1. I will suspend *two* dollars by a ring from a second person's nose, so as to bring the coins within three fourths of an inch from his face, and with a double barrelled shotgun, at a distance of thirty feet, will blow dollars, nose and man at least thirty feet further, four times out of five. I will add, in explanation, that, San Diego containing a rather intelligent community, I can find, at present, no one here willing or ready to have his nose blown in this manner; but I have no manner of doubt I could obtain such a person from St. Louis, by Adams & Co.'s Express, in due season.

2. I will hit a dollar, or any thing else that has been tossed in the air (of the same size), on a wheel, *on a pole or axletree, or on the ground,* every time out of five.

3. At the word, I will place five balls on the blade of a penknife, and split them all!

4. I will hit three men out of five, sprung from obscure parentage, and stand within ten feet of a steel-trap (properly set) while shooting!

5. I will break at the word, a whole box of common clay pipes, with a single brick, at a distance of thirty feet.

6. I engage to prove by a fair trial, that no pistol-shot (or other person) can be produced, who will throw more apples at a man's head than I can. Moreover, I can produce in this town more than sixty persons willing and ready to hold an apple on their heads for me, provided they are allowed to eat the apple subsequently.

7. I will wager, lastly, that no person in the United States can be produced, who, with a double barrelled shotgun, while throwing a back-handed summerset, can hit oftener, a dollar and a half, on the perimeter of a *revolving* wheel, *in rapid motion,* than I can.

Any one desiring to take up any of my propositions, will address me through the columns of *The Pioneer Magazine*. Propositions will be received on the first of April next.

JOHN PHŒNIX.

1384 Seventeenth Street, Vallecitos.

"*Se compra oro aqui*, up stairs."

P. S. Satisfactory references given and required. A bet from a steady, industrious person, who will be apt to pay if he loses, will meet with prompt attention.   J. P.

The Law-Abiding Horse Thief

The following cross-examination of a witness in a court in western North Carolina is said to have been an actual occurrence:

District Attorney—Now, Mr. Blinkins, you swear before this court and jury that you know the defendant's reputation in the community in which he lives, and that he is generally reputed an upright, peaceable, law-abiding citizen?

Witness—Yes, sir.

District Attorney—Now, Mr. Blinkins, don't you know that Lafe Huggins has never done anything but loaf around and drink moonshine whisky and fight?

Witness—Yes, sir.

District Attorney—And don't you know that he abuses and beats his wife terribly?

Witness—Yes, sir.

District Attorney—And don't you know that he broke up the Pigeon River camp meeting last winter and whipped the circuit rider?

Witness—Yes, sir.

District Attorney—And don't you know that he kicked his old father down the steps and out of the yard and nearly killed him?

Witness—Yes, sir.

District Attorney—And don't you know that he was convicted in this very court three years ago of maliciously shooting Deacon Smith's hogs?

Witness—Yes, sir.

District Attorney—And don't you know that he was once accused of stealing a horse, and that the owner of the horse and the principal witness for the prosecution were killed just before the trial was to be had?

Witness—Yes, sir.

District Attorney—And don't you know that his neighbors all know these things?

Witness—Yes, sir.

District Attorney—Then how can you sit there and swear that this defendant's reputation is good in the community in which he lives?

From *Waifs of the Press,* collected and edited by Harry L. Work, pp. 198–199. Washington: Walter Neale, Publisher. 1898.

Witness—Why, mister, a man has to do a heap wuss things than that to lose his character in our neighborhood.

The Arkansas Traveler

A lost and bewildered Arkansas Traveler approaches the cabin of a Squatter, about forty years ago, in search of lodgings, and the following dialogue ensues:

DIALOGUE

Traveler.—Halloo, stranger.

Squatter.—Hello yourself.

T.—Can I get to stay all night with you?

S.—No, sir, you can't git to—

T.—Have you any spirits here?

S.—Lots uv 'em; Sal seen one last night by that ar ole hollar gum, and it nearly skeered her to death.

T.—You mistake my meaning; have you any liquor?

S.—Had some yesterday, but ole Bose he got in and lapped all uv it out'n the pot.

T.—You don't understand; I don't mean pot liquor. I'm wet and cold and want some whisky. Have you got any?

S.—Oh, yes—I drunk the last this mornin'.

T.—I'm hungry; havn't had a thing since morning; can't you give me something to eat?

From *The Arkansas Traveler*, B. S. Alford, Photographer, Little Rock, Arkansas. Entered according to Act of Congress, in the Year 1876, by B. S. ALFORD, LITTLE ROCK, ARK., in the Office of the Librarian of Congress, Washington, D. C.

COL. SANDY FAULKNER, the original "Arkansaw Traveler," was born in Georgetown, Scott county, Kentucky, March 3, 1803. He came to Arkansas in 1829, and settled in Chicot county on the Mississippi river, as a cotton planter. In 1839, Col. Faulkner, (with his father, the late Nicholas Faulkner, a Virginian by birth,) took up his residence in Little Rock where he died August 4, 1874, at the age of seventy-one years.

It is well known throughout the Northwest that Col. Faulkner was the original personator of the "Arkansaw Traveler"; it was his pride to be known as such. The story, it is said, was founded on a little incident which occurred in the campaign of 1840, when he made the tour of the state in company with the Hon. A. H. Sevier, Gov. Fulton, Chester Ashley and Gov. Yell. One day in the Boston mountains, the party approached a squatter's for information of the route, and Col. "Sandy" was made spokesman of the company, and it was upon his witty responses the tune and story were founded. On return to Little Rock, a grand banquet was given in the famous "bar room" which used to stand near the Anthony house, and Col. "Sandy" was called upon to play the tune and tell the story. Afterward it grew into popularity. When he subsequently went to New Orleans, the fame of the "Arkansaw Traveler" had gone ahead of him, and at a banquet, amid clinking glasses and brilliant toasts, he was handed a violin by the then governor of Louisiana, and requested to favor them with the favorite Arkansas tune. At the old St. Charles hotel a special room was devoted to his use, bearing in gilt letters over the door, Arkansas Traveler.

S.—Hain't a durned thing in the house. Not a mouffull uv meat, nor a dust uv meal here.

T.—Well, can't you give my horse something?

S.—Got nothin' to feed him on.

T.—How far is it to the next house?

S.—Stranger! I don't know, I've never been thar.

T.—Well, do you know who lives here?

S.—Yes sir!

T.—As I'm so bold, then, what might your name be?

S.—It might be Dick, and it might be Tom; but it lacks right smart uv it.

T.—Sir! will you tell me where this road goes to?

S.—It's never gone any whar since I've lived here; it's always thar when I git up in the mornin'.

T.—Well, how far is it to where it forks?

S.—It don't fork at all; but it splits up like the devil.

T.—As I'm not likely to get to any other house tonight, can't you let me sleep in yours; and I'll tie my horse to a tree, and do without anything to eat or drink?

S.—My house leaks. Thar's only one dry spot in it, and me and Sal sleeps on it. And that thar tree is the ole woman's persimmon; you can't tie to it, 'caze she don't want 'em shuk off. She 'lows to make beer out'n um.

T.—Why don't you finish covering your house and stop the leaks?

S.—It's been rainin' all day.

T.—Well, why don't you do it in dry weather?

S.—It don't leak then.

T.—As there seems to be nothing alive about your place but children, how do you do here anyhow?

S.—Putty well, I thank you, how do you do yourself?

T.—I mean what do you do for a living here?

S.—Keep tavern and sell whisky.

T.—Well, I told you I wanted some whisky.

S.—Stranger, I bought a bar'l more'n a week ago. You see, me and Sal went shars. After we got it here, we only had a bit betweenst us, and Sal she didn't want to use hern fust, nor me mine. You see I had a spiggin in one eend, and she in tother. So she takes a drink out'n my eend, and pays me the bit for it; then I'd take un out'n hern, and give her the bit. Well, we's getting long fust-rate, till Dick, durned skulking skunk, he born a hole on the bottom to suck at, and the next time I went to buy a drink, they wont none thar.

T.—I'm sorry your whisky's all gone; but, my friend, why don't you play the balance of that tune?

S.—It's got no balance to it.

T.—I mean you don't play the whole of it.

S.—Stranger, can you play the fiddul?

T.—Yes, a little, sometimes.

S.—You don't look like a fiddlur, but ef you think you can play any more onto that thar tune, you kin just try it.

(The traveler takes the fiddle and plays the whole of it.)

THE TURN OF THE TUNE.

S.—Stranger, tuck a half a duzen cheers and sot down. Sal, stir your-self round like a six-horse team in a mud hold. Go round in the hollar whar I killed that buck this mornin', cut off some of the best pieces, and fotch it and cook it for me and this gentleman, d'rectly. Raise up the board under the head of the bed, and get the ole black jug I hid from Dick, and gin us some whisky; I know thar's some left yit. Til, drive ole Bose out'n the bread-tray, then climb up in the loft, and git the rag that's got the sugar tied in it. Dick, carry the gentleman's hoss round under the shead, give him some fodder and corn; much as he kin eat.

Til.—Dad, they ain't knives enuff for to sot the table.

S.—Whar's big butch, little butch, ole case, cob-handle, granny's knife, and the one I handled yesterday! That's nuff to sot any gentle-man's table, outer you've lost um. Durn me, stranger, ef you can't stay as long as you please, and I'll give you plenty to eat and drink. Will you have coffey for supper?

T.—Yes, sir.

S.—I'll be hanged if you do, tho', we don't have nothin' that way here, but Grub Hyson,[1] and I reckon it's mighty good with sweetnin'. Play away, stranger, you kin sleep on the dry spot to-night.

T.—(After about two hours' fiddling.) My friend, can't you tell me about the road I'm to travel to-morrow?

S.—To-morrow! Stranger, you won't git out'n these diggins for six weeks. But when it gits so you kin start, you see that big sloo over thar? Well, you have to git crost that, then you take the road up the

---

[1] Sassafras tea.

bank, and in about a mile you'll come to a two-acre-and-a-half corn-patch. The corn's mitly in the weeds, but you needn't mind that: jist ride on. About a mile and a half or two miles from thar, you'll cum to the damdest swamp you ever struck in all your travels; it's boggy enouff to mire a saddle-blanket. Thar's a fust rate road about six feet under thar.

T.—How am I to get at it?

S.—You can't git at it nary time, till the weather stiffens down sum. Well, about a mile beyant, you come to a place whar thar's no roads. You kin take the right hand ef you want to; you'll foller it a mile or so, and you'll find its run out; you'll then have to come back and try the left; when you git about two miles on that, you may know you're wrong, fur they ain't any road thar. You'll then think you're mity lucky ef you kin find the way back to my house, whar you kin cum and play on thata'r tune as long as you please.

The Odds Are Even

One day Bill MacDonald, the famous Texas Ranger captain, racked into our camp on Comanche Creek looking for a bad hombre, but his man wasn't with our outfit. He was a great character, was Bill Mac-Donald. Once when one of the tough towns—Abilene, or one of its hard-boiled neighbors—got boiling with war so bad the sheriff's force threw up their hands, some citizens wired for MacDonald to come a-running. When they met the little hombre at the train they wanted to know where his Rangers was.

"What Rangers?" asks Bill.

"Why, the Rangers to put down the riot."

"Hell, *I'm* here!" grunts Bill. "They ain't only one riot, is they?"

Too Tall

In 1903 the statues of Houston and Austin (by Elisabet Ney) were unveiled with fitting ceremony in the national Capitol, but a brisk exchange between the artist and the curator of the Hall of Fame at Washington immediately ensued. The curator wrote to complain that the two works did not place well. They had no unity, he said: the statue of Austin was a mere scrap, while that of Sam Houston towered six feet two.

By Captain Thomas H. Rynning as told to Al Cohn and Joe Chisholm, p. 44. Copyright, 1931, by Frederick A. Stokes Company.

From *Elisabet Ney*, by Jan Fortune and Jean Burton, p. 270. 1943. Copyright, 1943, by A. A. Knopf, Inc. New York.

"If I am correctly informed," Elisabet wrote back tartly, "God made the two men. I merely reproduced their likenesses. If you are dissatisfied about them, you should take the matter up with God."

Dun In

A banker, newly arrived in Texas and unfamiliar with cattlemen and their problems, refused to accept a borrower's explanation that his cattle were poor and there was no sale for them; and that he would have to wait until fall when his cattle were fat and could be sold. The banker wrote: "Unless I receive a check in full payment by return mail, I will proceed to file suit and take judgment against you."

The old-time cowman turned the letter over and wrote on the back:

Dear Mr. Banker:

If you ain't better prepared to meet your God than I am to meet this obligation, you shore are going to hell.

Yours truly,

Oh! Oh! Pioneers!

. . . At the center of a landscaped circle, from which a tree-bordered avenue leads to the former E. W. Marland home, is the heroic bronze statue of the Pioneer Woman, standing on a broad base of native limestone. In the period of his greatest prosperity as an oilman . . . Marland conceived the idea of this memorial to the pioneer women of the West, provided for its financing, and asked for models from sculptors throughout the country. Bryant Baker's was selected by popular vote, and the statue was dedicated on April 22, 1930.— *Oklahoma: A Guide to the Sooner State,* p. 355.

Will Rogers, a bit weary, but in characteristic good humor, arrived in Ponca City by plane from Los Angeles. . . . His arrival heralded the elaborate festivities attendant upon the unveiling of the "Pioneer Woman" statue, the gift of E. W. Marland, which on the following day, the forty-first anniversary of the opening of the old Oklahoma [Territory] to white settlement, was to become the property of the State. . . .

Rogers was introduced as "Oklahoma's best friend—one who has always defended his state but never apologized for it." Rogers turned to Gov. W. J. Holloway, standing by his side, and said, "I'm here to

From *Texas Tradition,* by Ross Phares, p. 195. Copyright, 1954, by Ross Phares. New York: Henry Holt and Company, Publishers.

From *The Tulsa Daily World,* p. 1, April 23, 1930.

pinch hit for the governor in case he is impeached before the thing is over. The large crowd here came hoping to see an unveiling and an impeachment all at once. Stick around. You may be right."

Someone on the speakers' stand warned him, in the midst of the talk, that he was standing too far from the microphone.

"Oh, I don't care," Rogers answered, waving a hand. "I can talk to the United States any time. I'm here today to talk to home folks.

"Now that the applesauce and baloney is all over," he said, "we'll state a few facts about this affair. The pioneers here sneaked in ahead of the gun. You had to be a crook or you wouldn't be here. If you'd waited until the gun for the run you wouldn't have got any land."

He skipped from that to the census. "Oklahoma takes its census by having a man stand outside the capitol and take the names of the governors as they come out. We've got enough on this fellow (nodding his head toward Governor Holloway) to impeach him, but we haven't found anyone else who'll take the job.

"Pat Hurley is making good as Secretary of War, as long as we have no war. He's trying to start one now. And he'll fight in it if we have one. The Republicans will have one to solve the unemployment problem.

"It was mighty nice of President Hoover to take time off from appointing commissions to open this program. He used to live in Pawhuska and we used to have a clock in Claremore, and he'd come over to see what time it was.

"Coolidge and I usually open these things. We opened a dam the other day. I wanted him to come along, but he couldn't find where it was. Besides, he didn't carry the State and Hoover did, so he spoke to us . . ."

"This statue—I'm all wet about it. I wrote out my notes all about a statue carved in marble and here it's made of pewter or something. Now I've got to rub out this speech and write another.

"But first I want to pay tribute to my wife. It takes a broad-minded woman to let a man fly fifteen hundred miles to take some clothes off a woman.

"The artist has done a wonderful job here. It's the first time I've seen a long skirt in years . . . And she's got on corsets. The kind, remember, that used to come up when you were sitting around at parties—come up so that the girls couldn't see over them.

"I was at a dinner party one time and sat next to a fat woman who was wearing just such a bracer. She kept slidin' over toward me, edgin' me off the bench, and I thought she was tryin' to make room for the fellow on the other side but, you know, I come to find out she wasn't. One of the strings on that corset had busted, and she was just slowly settlin'.''

Two Can Play at That Game

I was on guard duty one night at Fort Armstrong in Hawaii, walking Post No. 2, which extends along the Parade Ground. It was very dark. I couldn't see ten feet in front of me.

All of a sudden I heard footsteps approaching across the Parade Ground. It was the Officer of the Day.

I gave him a snappy challenge and "present arms," since he was a new young looie fresh out of the Academy. He seemed to be impressed. Then he asked me to recite my General and Special Orders for Post No. 2. "Oh," I said to myself, "a wise guy." But I rattled off the orders.

Still he didn't go away.

"Tell me this," he said. "What would you do if you saw a battleship coming at you across the Parade Ground?"

"I would fire a torpedo at it and sink it," I replied.

A gleam came into his eye. "And where would you get the torpedo?" he snapped. He thought he had me.

I came right back, "From the submarine, of course."

"And where," he said, "would you get a submarine out here in the middle of the post?"

"From the same place, sir," I said, "where you got your battleship."

The Superiority of the Superlative

"It's all in this—you haven't got the trick."

"The trick?"

"The trick of conversation. That's not just it. The trick of answering back. Aha, that's better! Scratch out first sentiment. Change signals!"

"There's something in that," said Stover, genuinely amazed.

"You blush."

"What?"

"The word was blush," said Finnegan firmly. "I saw you—Finnegan saw you and grieved. And why? Because you didn't have the trick of answering back."

"Dennis de Brian de Boru Finnegan," said Stover slowly, "I believe you are a whole-hearted little cuss. Also, you're not so far off, either. Now, since this is a serious conversation, this is where I stand: I went through Hades last spring—I deserved it and it's done me good. I've come back to make good. Savez? And that's a serious thing, too. Now

From *Tall Tales They Tell in the Services,* edited by Sgt. Bill Davidson, p. 69. Copyright, 1943, by Thomas Y. Crowell Company. New York.

From *The Varmint, A Lawrenceville Story,* by Owen Johnson, pp. 153–156. Copyright, 1910, by Little, Brown, and Company. Boston.

if you have one particular theory about your art of conversation to elucidate—eluce."

"One theory!" said Finnegan, chirping along as he perceived the danger-point passed. "I'm a theorist, and a real theorist doesn't have one theory; he has dozens. Let me see; let me think, reflect, cogitate, tickle the thinker. Best way is to start at the A, B, C—first principles, all that sort of thing. Supposin', supposin' you come into the room with that hat on—it's a bum hat, by the way—and some one pipes up; 'Get that at the fire sale?' What are you going to answer?"

"Why, I suppose I'd grin," said Stover slowly, "and say: 'How did you guess it?'"

"Wrong," said Finnegan. "You let him take the laugh."

"Well, what?"

"Something in this style: 'Oh, no, I traded it for luck with a squint-eyed, humpbacked biter-off of puppy-dog tails that got it out of Rockefeller's ashcan.' See?"

"No, Dennis, no," said Stover, bewildered. "I see, but there are some things beyond me. Every one isn't a young Shakspere."

"I know," said Finnegan, accepting the tribute without hesitation. "But there's the principle. You go him one better. You make him look like a chump. You show him what you could have said in his place. That shuts him up, makes him feel foolish, spikes the gun, corks the bottle."

"By Jove!"

"It's what I call the Superiority of the Superlative over the Comparative."

"It sounds simple," said Stover pensively.

"When you know the trick."

"You know, Dennis," said Stover, smiling reminiscently, "I used to have the gift of gab once, almost up to you."

"Then let's take a few crouching starts," said Dennis, delighted. "Go ahead."

"Room full of fellows. You enter."

"I enter."

"I speak: 'Dink, I bet Bill here a quarter that you used a tooth-brush.'"

"You lose," said Stover; "I use a whiskbroom."

"Good!" said Dennis professionally, "but a little quicker, on the jump, get on the springboard. Try again. 'Why, Dink, how *do* you get such pink cheeks?'"

"That's a hard one," said Dink.

"Peanuts!"

"Let me think."

"Bad, very bad."

"Well, what would you say?"

"Can't help it, Bill; the girls won't let me alone!"

"Try me again," said Stover, laughing.

"Say, Dink, did your mamma kiss you good-by?"

"Sure, Mike," said Stover instantly; "combed my hair, dusted my hands, and told me not to talk to fresh little kids like you."

"Why, Dick, come to my arms," said Dennis, delighted. "A Number 1. Mark 100 for the term. That's the trick."

"Think I'll do?"

"Sure pop. Of course, there are times when the digestion's jumping fences and you get sort of in the thunder glums. Then just answer, 'Is that the best you can do today?' or 'Why, you're a real funny man; aren't you?' sarcastic and sassy."

"I see."

"But better be original."

"Of course."

"Oh, it's all a knack."

III. RED EYE

Introduction

Red-eye is big-talk. It is often big-talk directed not to another person but to the whole universe—to the sky, the mountains, the rivers, to the Atlantic and Pacific and all intervening points. It is the "whoop" and the "yippee," the rowdy, rough-and-ready element in our fun. It may at times seem to be directed to someone else, but its bigness is meant to go over his insignificant head. "You eternal, yaller-faced, pizen-mouthed, suck-egg son" is really too big to be taken seriously, at least by us ordinary mortals.

Red-eye is often no more than the big-talk of a weakling, for it is a violent statement of power which does not necessarily exist. It is the wildness and violence of the language which Americans enjoy, just as people have enjoyed brags since the time of Beowulf. Nimrod Wildfire's boasts are meaningful only in an emotional sense, but we enjoy the exuberance of his expression: "Why, I'm the yaller flower of the forest. I'm all *brimstone but* the *head,* and that's *aky fortis.*" In contrast to red-eye, sass is mild, ornery, meaningful language backed by a full measure of power. Compare, for instance, the playfully evasive answers of the Squatter to the Arkansas Traveller with the insulting language Crockett uses in answering the landlord: "Travelling to the western country, I presume, mister?" "Presume anything you please, sir. . . ."

Violent action also has the flavor of red-eye. The violence, which is usually intended to scare or intimidate someone, may be an indication that the actor does not have the courage to face the consequences of his deeds. One way to avoid the consequences is to operate in secret as Penrod did with the tar; another way is to run and hide as the fraternity members at Siwash did.

Tennessee Frolic

You may talk of your bar hunts, and your deer hunts, and knottin tigers' tails thru the bungholes of barrels, an cock fitin, and all that, but if a regular bilt frolick in the Nobs of "Old Knox," don't beat 'em all blind for fun, then I'm no judge of fun, that's all! I said *fun,* and I say it agin, from a *kiss* that cracks like a wagin-whip up to a *fite* that rouses up all out-doors—and as to laffin, why they *invented* laffin, and the *last* laff will be hearn at a Nob dance about three in the morning! I'm jest gettin so I can ride arter the motions I made at one at Jo Spraggins's a few days ago.

I'll *try* and tell you who Jo Spraggins is. He's a squire, a school comishoner, overlooker of a mile of Nob road *that leads towards Roody's still-house*—a fiddler, a judge of a hoss, and a hoss himself! He can belt six shillins worth of corn-juice at still-house rates and travel—can out-shute and out-lie any feller from the Smoky Mounting to Noxville, and, if they'll bar one feller in Nox, I'll say to the old Kaintuck Line! (I'm sorter feared of him, for they say that he lied a jackass to death in two hours!)—can make more spinin-wheels, kiss more spinners, thrash more wheat an more men than any one-eyed man I know on. He hates a circuit rider, a Yankee, and a shot gun— loves a woman, old sledge, and sin in eny shape. He lives in a log hous about ten yards squar: it has two rooms, one at the bottom an one at the top of the ladder—has all out ove doors fur a yard, and all the South fur its occupants at times. He gives a frolick onst in three weeks in plowin time, and one every Saturdaynite the balance of the year, and only axes a "fip" [1] for a reel, and two "bits" fur what corn-juice you suck; he throws the galls in, and a bed too in the hay, if you git too hot to locomote. The supper is made up by the fellers; every one fetches sumthin; sum a lick of meal, sum a middlin of bacon, sum a hen, sum a possum, sum a punkin, sum a grab of taters, or a pocket

---

"Dick Harlan's Tennessee Frolic," by "S————L," of Tennessee. From *A Quarter Race in Kentucky and Other Sketches,* edited by William T. Porter, pp. 82–90. Philadelphia: T. B. Peterson and Brothers, 1854. Originally published in Porter's New York *Spirit of the Times,* 1845.

[1] *Fip:* A Spanish silver coin, formerly passing current in the U.S. with a value of about six cents.—*A Dictionary of Americanisms on Historical Principles.* The University of Chicago Press. 1951.

full of peas, or dried apples, an sum only fetches a good appetite and a skin chock full of particular devilry, and if thars been a shutin match for beef the day before, why a *leg* finds its way to Jo's sure, without eny help from the balance of the critter.

* * * * *

The sun had about sot afore I got the things fed an had Barkmill saddled, (you'll larn directly why I call my poney Barkmill,) but an owl couldent have cotch a rat afore I was in site of Jo's with my gall, Jule Sawyers, up behind me. She hugged me mity tite she was *"so feerd of fallin off* that drated poney." She said she didn't mind a fall, but it mought break hir leg an then good bye frolicks—she'd be fit fur nuthin but to nuss brats ollers arterwards. I now hearn the fiddle ting-tong-ding-domb. The yard was full of fellers, and two tall fine-lookin galls was standin in the door, face to face, holdin up the door posts with their backs, laffin, an castin sly looks into the house, an now an then kickin each other with their knees, an then the one kicked wud bow so perlite, and quick at that, and then they'd laff agin an turn red. Jo was a standin in the hous helpin the galls to hold the facins up, an when they'd kick each other he'd wink at the fellers in the yard an grin. Jule, she bounced off just like a bag of wool-rolls, and I hitched my bark-machine up to a saplin that warn't skinned, so he'd git a craw-full of good fresh bark afore mornin. I giv Jule a kiss to sorter molify my natur an put her in heart like, and in we walked. "Hey! hurray!" said the boys; "My gracious!" said the galls, "if here aint Dick and Jule!" Jist like we hadent been *rite thar* only last Saturday nite. "Well, I know we'll have reel now!" "Hurraw!—Go it while you'r young!" "Hurraw for the brimstone kiln—every man praise his country!" "Clar the ring!" *"Misses* Spraggins, drive out these dratted tow-headed brats of your'n—give room!" "Who-oo-whoop! whar's the crock of bald-face, and that gourd of honey? Jim Smith, hand over that spoon, an quit a lickin it like "sank in a bean-pot."

* * * * *

"Whoop! hurraw! Gether your galls for a break down! Give us 'Forked Deer!' " "No, give us 'Natchez-under-the-hill!' " "Oh, Shucks! give us 'Rocky Mounting,' or 'Misses McCloud!' " " 'Misses McCloud' be darned, and 'Rocky Mounting' too! jist give us

"She woudent, and she coudent, and she dident come at all!"

"Thar! that's it! Now make a brake! *Tang!* Thar is a brake—a string's gone!" "Thar'll be a head broke afore long!" "Give him goss [2]—no giv him a horn and every time he stops repeat the dose, and nar another string 'ill brake to nite. Tink-tong! all rite! Now go it!" and if I know what *goin it* is, we *did* go it.

---

[2] Goss: A severe scolding.—*A Dictionary of Americanisms.* A tongue-lashing; also, physical punishment.

About midnite, Misses Spraggins sung out "stop that ar dancin and come and get your supper!" It was sot in the yard on a table made of forks stuck in the ground and plank of the stable loft, with sheets for table cloths. We had danced, kissed, and drank ourselves into a perfect thrashin-machine apetite, and the vittals *hid* themselves in a way quite alarmin to tavern-keepers. Jo sung out "Nives is scase, so give what thar is to the galls an let the balance use thar paws—they was invented afore nives, eney how. Now, Gents, jist walk into the fat of this land. I'm sorter feerd the honey wont last till day break, but the liquor will, *I think*, so you men when you drink your'n, run an kiss the galls fur sweetnin—let them have the honey—it belongs to them, naturaly!"

* * * * *

Well, we danced, and hurrawed without eny thing of *very* perticular interest to happen, till about three o'clock, when the darndest muss was kicked up you ever did see. Jim Smith sot down on the bed along-side of Bet Holden (the steel-trap gall,) and jist fell to huggin of hir bar fashion. She tuck it very kind till she seed Sam Henry a looking on from behind about a dozen galls, *then* she fell to kickin *an* a hollerin, *an* a screetchin like all rath. Sam he come up an told Jim to let Bet go! Jim told him to go to a far off countrie whar they give away brime-stone and throw in the fire to burn it. Sam hit him strate a-tween the eyes, an after a few licks the fitin *started.* Oh hush! It makes my mouth water now to think what a beautiful row we had. One feller from Cady's Cove, nocked a hole in the bottom of a fryin-pan over Dan Turner's head, and left it a hangin round his neck, the handle flyin about like a long que, ane thar it hung till Jabe Thurman cut it off with a cold chissel next day! That was *his share*, fur that nite, sure. Another feller got nocked into a meal-barrel: he was as mealy as an Irish tater and as *hot* as hoss-radish; when he bursted the hoops and cum out he rared a few. Two fellers fit out of the door, down the hill, and into the creek, and thar ended it, in a quiet way, all alone. A perfect mule from Stock Creek hit *me* a wipe with a pair of windin blades [3]: he made kindlin-wood of them, an I lit on him. We had it head-an-tails fur a very long time, all over the house, but the truth must come and shame my kin, he warped me *nice*, so, jist to save his time *I hollered!* The lickin he give me made me sorter oneasy and hostile like; it wakened my wolf wide awake, so I begin to look about for a man I *could* lick and *no mistake!* The little fiddler come a scrougin past, holdin his fiddle up over his head to keep it *in tune*, for the fitin was gettin tolerable brisk. You're the one, thinks I, and I jist grabbed the doughtray and split it plumb open over his head! *He* rotted down, right thar, and I paddled his 'tother end with one of the pieces!—while I was a molifyin my feelings in that way his gall slip'd

---

[3] Winding blades: An antique device for winding yarn after it is spun. Not defined in *A Dictionary of Americanisms.*

up behind me and fetch'd me a rake with the pot-hooks. Jule Sawyer was *thar*, and jist *anexed to her* rite off, and a mity nice fite it was. Jule carried enuf har from hir hed to make a sifter, and striped and checked her face nice, like a partridge-net hung on a white fence. She hollered fur hir fiddler, but oh, shaw! he coudent do hir a bit of good; he was too buisy a rubbin first his broken head and then his blistered extremities, so when I thought Jule had given hir a plenty I pulled hir off and put hir in a good humour by given hir about as many kisses as would cover a barn door.

Well, I thought at last, if I had a drink I'd be *about done*, so I started for the creek; *and* the first thing I saw was more stars with my eyes shut than I ever did with them open. I looked round, and it was the little fiddler's *big brother! I knowed what it meant*, so we locked horns without a word, thar all alone, and I do think we fit an hour. At last some fellers hearn the jolts at the house, and they cum and *dug us out*, for we had fit into a hole whar a big pine stump had burnt out, and thar we was, up to our girths a peggin away, face to face, and *no dodgin!*

Well, it is now sixteen days since that fite, and last nite Jule picked gravels out of my knees as big as squirell shot. Luck rayther run agin me that nite, fur I dident lick eny body but the fiddler, and had three fites—but Jule licked her gall, that's some comfort, and I suppose a feller cant *always* win! Arter my fite in the ground we made friends all round, (except the fiddler—he's hot yet,) and danced and liquored at the tail of every Reel till sun up, when them that was sober enuff went home, and them that was *wounded* staid whar they fell. *I* was in the list of wounded, but could have got away if my bark-mill [4] hadn't *ground* off the saplin and gone home without a parting word; so Dick and Jule had to ride "Shanks' mar," and a rite peart *four-leged* nag she is. She was *weak* in *two* of hir legs, but 'tother two—oh, my stars and possum dogs! they make a man swaller tobacker jist to look at 'em, and feel sorter like a June bug was crawlin up his trowses and the waistband too tite for it to git out. I'm agoin to marry Jule, I swar I am, and *sich* a cross! Think of a locomotive and a cotton gin! Who! whoopee!

Congressman Crockett's Well-Soaked Speech

"Mr. Speaker.

"Who—Who—Whoop—Bow—Wow—Wow—Yough. I say, Mr. Speaker; I've had a speech in soak this six months, and it has swelled me like

---

[4] Bark-mill: a "crib-biter." Some horses have the vicious habit of gnawing wood. Dick's had gnawed down the sapling to which it was hitched.

From *Davy Crockett's Almanac, of Wild Sports in the West, Life in the Backwoods, & Sketches of Texas*, Vol. I, No. 3, 1837, p. 40. Nashville, Tennessee: Published by the heirs of Col. Crockett.

a drowned horse; if I don't deliver it I shall burst and smash the windows. The gentleman from Massachusetts [Mr. Everett] talks of summing up the merits of the question, but I'll sum up my own. In one word I'm a screamer, and have got the roughest racking horse, the prettiest sister, the surest rifle and the ugliest dog in the district. I'm a leetle the savagest crittur you ever *did see*. My father can whip any man in Kentucky, and I can lick my father. I can outspeak any man on this floor, and give him two hours start. I can run faster, dive deeper, stay longer under, and come out drier, than any *chap* this side the big *Swamp*. I can outlook a panther and outstare a flash of lightning, tote a steamboat on my back and play at rough and tumble with a lion, and an occasional kick from a *zebra*. To sum up all in one word *I'm a horse*. Goliah was a pretty hard colt but I could choke him. I can take the rag off—frighten the old folks—astonish the natives—and beat the Dutch all to smash—make nothing of sleeping under a blanket of snow—and don't mind being frozen more than a rotten apple.

"Congress allows *lemonade* to the members and has it charged under the head of stationery—I move also that *whiskey* be allowed under the item of *fuel*. For *bitters* I can suck away at a noggin of aquafortis, sweetened with brimstone, stirred with a lightning rod, and skimmed with a hurricane. I've soaked my head and shoulders in Salt River, so much that I'm always corned. I can walk like an ox, run like a fox, swim like an eel, yell like an Indian, fight like a devil, spout like an earthquake, make love like a mad bull, and swallow a Mexican whole without choking if you butter his head and pin his ears back."

My Name's Nimrod Wildfire

. . . I was riding along the Mississippi one day when I came across a fellow floating down the stream sitting cock'd up in the starn of his boat fast asleep. Well, I hadn't had a fight for as much as ten days—felt as though I must kiver myself up in a salt bin to keep—"so wolfy" about the head and shoulders. So, says I, hullo, stranger, if you don't take keer your boat will run away wi' you. So he looked up at me

From *The Lion of the West*, retitled "The Kentuckian, or A Trip to New York," A Farce in Two Acts, by James Kirke Paulding, revised by John Augustus Stone and William Bayle Bernard, edited and with an introduction by James N. Tidwell, pp. 54–55. Written in 1830 and revised in 1831 and 1833. First dramatic production, April, 1831. First published, December, 1954. Copyright, 1954, by the Board of Trustees of the Leland Stanford Junior University. Stanford, California: Stanford University Press. All dramatic production rights reserved.

For further history and discussion, see Francis Hodge, "Biography of a Lost Play: *Lion of the West*," *The Theatre Annual*, Vol. XII, 1954, pp. 48–61. A report of the speech, "A Fight on the Mississippi," as originally published in the *Daily Louisville Advertiser*, October 17, 1831, is given in *A Treasury of American Folklore* (1944), edited by B. A. Botkin, pp. 13–14, together with the Crockett version and a discussion of Nimrod Wildfire and the backwoods "screamer" tradition (pp. 3–5).

"slantindickular" and I looked down on him "slanchwise." He took out a chaw of tobacco from his mouth and, says he, I don't value you tantamount to that, and then he flopp'd his wings and crowed like a cock. I ris up, shook my mane, crooked my neck, and neighed like a horse. Well, he run his boat foremost ashore. I stopped my wagon and set my triggers. Mister, says he, I'm the best man—if I ain't, I wish I may be tetotaciously exflunctified! I can whip my weight in wild cats and ride strait through a crab apple orchard on a flash of lightning—clear meat axe disposition! And what's more, I once back'd a bull off a bridge. Poh, says I, what do I keer for that? I can tote a steam boat up the Mississippi and over the Alleghany mountains. My father can whip the best man in old Kaintuck and I can whip my father. When I'm good-natured I weigh about a hundred and seventy, but when I'm mad, I weigh a *ton*. With that I fetched him the regular Ingen war-whoop. Out he jumped from his boat and down I tumbled from my wagon—and, I say, we came together like two steam boats going sixty miles an hour. He was a pretty severe colt, but no part of a priming to such a feller as me. I put it to him mighty droll—tickled the varmint till he squealed like a young colt, bellowed "enough" and swore I was a "rip staver." Says I, *ain't* I a horse? Says he, stranger, you're a *beauty*, anyhow, and if you'd stand for Congress I'd vote for you next *lection*. Says I, would you? My name's Nimrod Wildfire. Why, I'm the yaller flower of the forest. I'm all *brimstone but* the *head*, and that's *aky fortis*.

The Wolloping Ways of Mike Hooter

In the Yazoo hills, near the town of Satartia, in the good state of Mississippi, there lived, at no distant date, one Mike Hooter, whose hunting and preaching adventures became famous in all the land. Besides being a great bear-hunter, and hard to beat at preaching, Mike professed to be "considerable" of a fighter, and in a regular knock-down-and-drag-out row, was hard to beat.

In order that the world may not remain in darkness as to his doings in this last behalf, and fearing lest there may be no one who entertains for him that particularly warm regard which animates us towards him, we have thought it incumbent on us in evidence of our attachment for the reverend hero, to jot down an incident that lingers in our memory respecting him—bequeathing it as a rich legacy to remotest time. Entertaining such partiality, we may be pardoned for following Mike in one of his most stirring adventures, related in his peculiar and expressive vernacular.

I'm one of the peaceblest fellers, said Mike, that ever trotted on hind legs, and rather than git into er fuss 'bout nothin', I'd let er chap spit

From *Polly Peablossom's Wedding and Other Tales,* Edited by T. A. Burke, Esq., pp. 146–153. Philadelphia: T. B. Peterson and Brothers. 1851.

on me; but when it comes to rubbin' it in, I always in gen'rally kinder r'ars up an' won't stan' it.

But thar's some fellers up in Yazoo what would rather git into er scrimmage than eat. An' I've seen er few up thar what war so hungry for er fight that they fell away an' got so poor an' thin that they had to lean up agin er saplin' to cuss!

That chap Arch Coony, was er few in that line! He was the durndest, rantankerous hoss-fly that ever clum er tree! I tell you what, ef I hadn't er bin thar I wouldn't er b'leeved it. I seed him one day in Satartia, git up from er jug of whiskey when he hadn't drunk morn'n half of it, and leave t'other half to spile, an' go an' pitch into er privit 'spute 'twene two Injuns, (when he didn't care er durn cent which wolloped t'other,) an' lamin both on um out'n ther mockasins!

Well, you see, Arch was mighty fond of them kinder tricks, an' ef he seed er feller he thought he could lamm without no danger, he wouldn't make no bones, but he'd jest go up to the chap and make faces at him, and harry his feelings er bit, an' ef the feller showed spunky-like, he'd let him alone, an' ax him to take er drink; but ef he sorter tried to sidle out of it, Arch would git as mad as all wrath, an' sw'ar, an' cuss, an' r'ar, an' charge like er ram at er gate-post, and the fust thing you know'd he'd shuck off his coat, an' when the feller warn't 'spectin' nuthin', Arch would fetch him er side-wipe on the head, and knock him into the middle o' next week!

You see I didn't like them sorter doins much, me, myself, I didn't, an' I all'ays ef ever I got er chance at Arch I'd let him down er button-hole er two. He was gettin' too high up in the pictures enny how, an' sez I, one day, in er crowd; sez I, "ef that feller Arch Coony don't mind which side of his bread's buttered, I'll git hold of him one of these days, an' I'll make him see sites!" Well, you see, thar was two or three sheep-stealin' chaps listenin' to what I sed, an' they goes an' tells Arch the fust chance I got, I was gwine to larrup him. Well, that riled him like all fury, an' soon as he hearn it, he begin er cussin' like wrath, and sez he, "dod rot that ole Mike Hooter!—he pertend to be er preacher!— his preachin' ain't nuthin' but loud hollerin' no how!" So you see, them same chaps, they comes an' tells me what Arch had sed, an' I got mad, too, an' we had the durndest rumpus in the neighbourhood you ever hearn!

I didn't see nuthin' of Arch from that time till about er month. Every time I went down to Satartia to buy enything—er barrel of whiskey, or backer, or such like truck, for privit use—I looked for Arch, and Arch he looked for me, but, somehow or 'tother, he never crossed my path. At last, one day I sent him word I believed he was skeer'd of me, and the fust chance I got I'd take the starch out'n him as sure as shooting; and he sent word back to me that was a game two could play at, and when I wanted to try it, he'd see if he couldn't help me.

Well, things went on that way for er long time, and I didn't see nothin' of Arch; so I begin to forgit all about him. At last, one day, when me and two or three other chaps was gwine down to Big Black River, to go bar hunting on t'other side of it, I hearn the darndest clatterwacking and noise in the road behind us, and when I turned round to see what in the name of thunder it was, thar was Arch an' er whole lot of fellers cummin' down the road, er galloping full tilt right up to us, an' er gwine bar huntin' too.

When I seed him, I was so mad I thought I should er burst right wide open! I was hot, I tell you, and sez I to myself, Now Mr. Arch, I've got you, and if you don't keep your eye skin'd, I'll lick you till your hide won't hold shucks.

Toreckly, Arch he cum up along side, and looked me right plum in the face as savage as er meat axe! and, sez he, "Good mornin', ole Preach!—give us your paw!"

I see thar was hell in him as big as er meetin' house, and I 'termined to give him as good as he sent; so I looked at him sorter servagerous like, and, sez I, "Look here, hoss, how can you have the face to talk to me, arter saying what you sed?"

"Why," sez he, "Uncle Mike, didn't you begin it?"

"No," sez I, "an' ef you sez I begun it, I'll larrup you in er inch of your life!"

Sez he, "You eternal ole cuss, ef you want to larrup me, just larrup away as soon as you darn please, and we'll see which 'ell git the wust of it!"

"Now," sez I, "I likes you, Arch, 'cause I all'ays thought you was a fust-rate feller; but ain't you been 'busin' me evry war fur evry thing you could think of?"

"Yes," sez he, "but didn't you say you'd git holt of me one of these days and make me see sites?"

"No," sez I, "I didn't; but this here's what I sed," sez I, "ef that feller Arch Coony *don't mind which side of his bread's buttered*, I'll git holt of him one of these days and make him see sites!"

"Well," sez he, "Uncle Mike, you knows I'm the most peaceablest feller living, and always minds which side of my bread's buttered, and ef that is all you sed 'taint nothin'—so let's take er drink!"

Then he tuck out er tickler of whisky, and arter he'd tuck three er four swallers out'n it, sez he, "Uncle Mike, obleege me by taking er horn!"

"No," sez I, "I won't do no sich er dog on thing, for when I likes a chap I likes him, and when I don't like him, I don't like him; but if you wants to fight, I'm your man."

You oughter seen Arch then! I think he was the most maddest man that ever wobbled on two hind legs! He r'ard an' pitched, and cussed, an' swore, 'tell you'd er thought the day of judgmen' was at hand!

When I see him cuttin up that way, I commence' getting mad, too, an' my knees, they begin to shake, sorter like I had er chill; an'—

Skeer'd—no, sir!—an' I sposed thar was gwine to be the devil to pay!
I give you my word. I ain't bin so wrathy afore but once since, an' that
was t'other day when Mat Cain, the blacksmith, drunk up my last
bottle of "ball-face," an' when I 'tacked him 'bout it, sed he thought it
was milk.

But that ain't neither here nor thar. As I was a sayin', Arch, he
cussed at me, an' I cussed at him, an' the fellers what was along with
me sed I beat him all holler!

Toreckly I begin to get tired of jawin' away so much, an' sez I,
"Arch, what's the use of makin sich er allfired racket 'bout nothin'?
Spose we make it up!"

"Good as wheat," sez he.

"Well," sez I, "give us your paw," sez I, "but," sez I, "thar's one thing
you sed what sorter sticks in my craw yit, an' ef you don't pollogise,
I'll wollop you for it right now!"

"What does yow mean?" sez he.

Sez I, "Didn't you sed one day that my preachin' warn't nuthin' but
loud hollerin'?"

"Yes," sez he, "but didn't you send me word one time that you
b'lieved I was skeered of you, an' the fust chance you got, you'd take
the starch out'n me as sure as er gun?"

Sez I, "Yes, but what does that signify?"

"Well," sez he, "ef you'll take back what you sed, I'll take back what
I sed."

Then I begin to get as mad as all wrath; an' sez I, "You eternal
sheep-stealin', whisky-drinkin', bow-legged, taller-faced son of er—
never mind what—does you want me to tell er lie by chawin up my
own words? Ef that's what's you're arter, jest come on, an' I'll larrup
you tell your mammy won't know you from a pile of sassage meat."

So we kep er ridin' on an' er cussin one another worse than two
Choctaw Injuns, an' toreckly we cum to the ferry-boat whar we had to
cross the river. Soon as we got thar, Arch he hopped down off'n his ole
hoss, an' commenced shuckin' his self fur er fight, an' I jumped down,
too. I see the devil was in him as big as er bull, so I begin grittin' my
teeth, an' lookin' at him as spunky as er Dominicker rooster; an' now,
sez I, "Mister Arch Coony, I sed I'd make you see sites, an' the fust
thing you know, I'll show em to you?" Then I pulled off my ole
Sunday-go-to-meetin' coat, an' slammed it down on er stump, an', sez
I, "Lay thar, ole Methodist, till I learn this coon some sense!"

I soon see thar was gwine to be the bustinest fight that ever was; so
I rolled up my sleeves, an' Arch rolled up his'n, and we was gwine at
it reg'lar.

"Now," sez he, "ole pra'r meet'n, pitch in!"

Well, I jist begin sidelin' up, an' he begin sidelin' up, an' soon as I
got close 'nuff to him, so as I could hit him a jo-darter, sez he, "Hole

on er minit—this ground's too rooty—wait till I clear the sticks away from here, so as I can have a far chance to give it to you good!"

"Don't holler till you're out'n the woods," says I, "p'raps when I'm done with you, you won't say my preachin' ain't nuthin but loud hollerin', I *spec!*"

When he'd done scrapin' off the groun', it looked jest like two bulls had bin thar, pawin' up the dirt—I give you my word it did.

Well, as I sed before, he sidled up and I sidled up, "an' now," sez I, "look out for your bread-basket, ole stud, fur ef I happen to give you er jolt thar, p'raps it'll turn your stomach."

So thar we stood, head and tale up, jest like two chicken cocks in layin' time; an', sez I to him, "Arch, I'm gwine to maul you tell you won't know yerself!"

Soon as we got close 'nuff, an' I see he was erbout to make er lunge at me, sez I, "Hole on, dod drot you! wait till I unbutton my gallowses, an' may-be-so, then I'll show you them sites what we was talkin' 'bout!"

Well, all the fellers was stanin' roun' ready to take sides in the fight, an' toreckly the chap what kep the ferry, he 'gin to get tired of keepin' the ferry-boat waitin', an sez he, "Cuss your pictures, I'm not gwine to keep this here boat waitin' no longer, an' people on t'other side waitin' to get over; so, ef you wants to fight, you come over on t'other side an' fight thar!"

"Good as ole wheat," sez I; "ennything to keep peace away—ef you say so, let's get in the boat and settle it over thar." Well, they all agreed to that without sayin' er word, an' Arch, he got into the ferry-boat, and all the fellers they follered. When the boat was 'bout pushin' off, I jumped into the eend of it, an' was gwine to lead my hoss on too, but the all-fired critter was skeer'd to jump on to it, and sez I to the man what kept the ferry, sez I, "Why in the h–ll don't you wait till I gets this durned four-legged critter into the boat?" He didn't wait to say er word, but kep shovein' the boat out, and toreckly my hoss begin pullin' back with the bridle, an' I er holein on to it, an' the fust thing I know'd I went kerswash into the drink! So you see, in er bout er minit thar was I, on this side of the river, an' thar was Arch on t'other side, an' no chance for me to git at him. I tell you what, I was hot then!—an' what was worser, Arch he holler'd out an' sed he b'lieved I'd skeer'd the hoss an' made him pull back on purpose to git out'n the scrape. When I hearn him say that, I was so mad I farly biled!

Hows'ever, I soon see 'twarn't no use raisin' er racket 'bout what couldn't be helped, so I 'cluded I'd have my satisfaction out'n him enny way, an' I begin shakin' my fist at him, an' er cussin' him. Sez I, "You eternal, yaller-faced, pisen-mouthed, suck-egg son of er—! what is it you ain't mean 'nuff for me to call you?" I tell you what (an' I hope to be forgive for swarin') I cussed him blue!

Well, I was so outdone I didn't wait for the boat to come back, for it was gittin' most night, an' too late for bar huntin' that day—'sides, my wife she would be 'spectin' me at the house, an' might raise per-tickler h–ll if I didn't git thar in time; so I jumped on my ole hoss an' put for home. But the way I cussed and 'bused Arch when I got on that hoss, was er sin!—an' the further I got away from him the louder I hollered! I pledge you my word, you might er hearn me er mile!

To make a long story short, the last word I sed to him, sez I, "Arch, you've 'scaped me this time by er axident, but the next time you cross my path, I'll larrup you worse nor the devil beatin' tan-bark!—I will, by hokey!"

Whew! whistled Mike, drawing a long breath. I tell you what, I come the nearest wollopin' that feller, not to do it, that ever you saw!

At this point Mike donned his coon-skin cap, and giving it a terrific *slam*, that brought it over his eyes, vanished!

Crockett and a Landlord

I mounted my horse and pushed forward on my road to Fulton. When I reached Washington, a village a few miles from the Red river, I rode up to the Black Bear tavern, when the following conversation took place between me and the landlord, which is a pretty fair sample of the curiosity of some folks:—

"Good morning, mister—I don't exactly recollect your name now," said the landlord as I alighted.

"It's of no consequence," said I.

"I'm pretty sure I've seen you somewhere."

"Very likely you may, I've been there frequently."

"I was sure 'twas so; but strange I should forget your name," says he.

"It is indeed somewhat strange that you should forget what you never knew," says I.

"It is unaccountable strange. It's what I'm not often in the habit of, I assure you. I have, for the most part, a remarkably retentive memory. In the power of people that pass along this way, I've scarce ever made, as the doctors say, a *slapsus slinkum* of this kind afore."

"Eh heh!" I shouted, while the critter continued.

"Traveling to the western country, I presume, mister?"

"Presume anything you please, sir," said I; "but don't trouble me with your presumptions."

"O Lord, no, sir—I won't do that, I've no ideer of that—not the least ideer in the world," says he; "I suppose you've been to the westward afore now?"

"Well, suppose I have?"

"Why, on that supposition, I was going to say you must be pretty well—that is to say, you must know something about the place."

From *Life of David Crockett,* the Original Humorist and Irrepressible Backwoods-man . . . , pp. 286–290. Philadelphia: John E. Potter and Company. 1860.

"Eh heh!" I ejaculated, looking sort of mazed full in his face. The tarnal critter still went ahead.

"I take it you're a married man, mister?"

"Take it as you will, that is no affair of mine," says I.

"Well, after all, a married life is the most happiest way of living; don't you think so, mister?"

"Very possible," says I.

"I conclude you have a family of children, sir?"

"I don't know what reason you have to conclude so."

"Oh, no reason in the world, mister, not the least," says he; "but I thought I might just take the liberty to make the presumption, you know; that's all, sir. I take it, mister, you're a man about my age?"

"Eh heh!"

"How old do you call yourself, if I may be so bold?"

"You're bold enough, the devil knows," says I; and as I spoke rather sharp, the varment seemed rather staggered, but he soon recovered himself, and came up to the chalk again.

"No offence I hope—I—I—I—wouldn't be thought uncivil, by any means; I always calculate to treat everybody with civility."

"You have a very strange way of showing it."

"True, as you say, I ginerally take my own way in these ere matters. Do you practise law, mister, or farming, or mechanicals?"

"Perhaps so," says I.

"Ah, I judge so; I was pretty certain it must be the case. Well, it's as good business as any there is followed nowadays."

"Eh heh!" I shouted, and my lower jaw fell in amazement at his perseverance.

"I take it you've money at interest, mister?" continued the varment, without allowing himself time to take breath.

"Would it be of any particular interest to you to find out?" says I.

"Oh, not at all, not the least in the world, sir; I'm not at all inquisitive about other people's matters; I minds my own business—that's my way."

"And a very odd way you have of doing it, too."

"I've been thinking what persuasion you're of—whether you're a Unitarian or Baptist, or whether you belong to the Methodisses."

"Well, what's the conclusion?"

"Why, I have concluded that I'm pretty near right in my conjectures. Well, after all, I'm inclined to think they're the nearest right of any persuasion—though some folks think differently."

"Eh heh!" I shouted again.

"As to pollyticks, I take it, you—that is to say, I suppose you—"

"Very likely."

"Ah, I could have sworn it was so from the moment I saw you. I have a knack at finding out a man's sentiments. I dare say, mister, you're a justice in your own country?"

"And if I may return the compliment, I should say you're a just ass everywhere." By this time I began to get weary of his impertinence, and led my horse to the trough to water, but the darned critter followed me up.

"Why, yes," said he, "I'm in the commission of the peace, to be sure—and an officer in the militia, though, between you and I, I wouldn't wish to boast of it."

My horse having finished drinking, I put one foot in the stirrup, and was preparing to mount. "Any more inquiries to make?" said I.

"Why, no, nothing to speak on," said he. "When do you return, mister?"

"About the time I come back," said I; and leaping into the saddle, galloped off. The pestiferous varment bawled after me, at the top of his voice—

"Well, I shall look for ye, then. I hope you won't fail to call."

Now, who in all natur do you reckon the critter was, who afforded so fine a sample of the impertinent curiosity that some people have to pry into other people's affairs?

I knew him well enough at first sight, though he seemed to have forgotten me. It was no other than Job Snelling, the manufacturer of cayenne pepper out of mahogany sawdust, and upon whom I played the trick with the coon skin. I pursued my journey to Fulton, and laughed heartily to think what a swither I had left poor Job in, at not gratifying his curiosity; for I knew he was one of those fellows who would peep down your throat just to ascertain what you had eaten for dinner.

The Fightin'est Feller in the Holler

Windy Bill Hatfield was the best talker in the entire Holler when he got started, and it wasn't very hard to get him started, either. One day I asked Windy if he had ever known any real honest-to-God bad men in the Ozark country. "Wal now, lemme see," he drawled. "Them James brothers—Jesse slept in our house a many a time—was bad 'nough in some ways, an' th' Younger boys warn't exactly whut you might call sody-squirts, neither. Some o' th' Dalton gang come through hyar oncet in a while, too, an' so did Cherokee Bill an' Henry Starr an' that Doolin feller whut kilt all them folks over t' Southwest City."

But these men, as I pointed out, were merely hard-working bank-robbers, while I wanted to hear about genuine desperadoes, light-hearted gunfighters such as Billy the Kid. Windy had never heard of the Kid, but he got my meaning all right, and immediately bethought himself

"The Saga of Little Ab Yancey," by Vance Randolph. From *Folk-Say IV, The Land Is Ours*, edited by B. A. Botkin, pp. 235–238. Copyright, 1932, by B. A. Botkin. Norman: The University of Oklahoma Press.

of one Abner Yancey, who had terrorized these wilds in the eighties. "Yes sir," he said, "I reckon Leetle Ab was 'bout th' fightin'est feller whut ever showed up in th' Holler. He'd fight a circle-saw, an' turn it hisse'f! He drinked a right smart o' licker, an' played cyards for money, an' run atter th' womenfolks, an' kilt three-four fellers whut crowded him too fur. But me an' him allus got 'long fine—they warn't no rale meanness in him.

"Hit puts me in mind o' whut Lew Merriwether said, th' time they was a-tryin' Ab for killin' a feller over t' Durgenville. Th' prosecutin' attorney was a newcomer, an' he heerd how Lew an' Ab had fit two-three years back, so he got Lew up on th' stand t' testify whut a bad character Ab was. Atter th' jury heerd all 'bout th' fraction th' lawyer he says: 'Now, Mister Merriwether, you think Ab Yancey is a mighty dangerous man, don't ye?' Lew he studied a-while an' then he says: 'Naw, I wouldn't go so fur as t' say that.' Th' 'torney he hollers out: 'Whut? This hyar defendant shot you twicet an' battered your head all up an' run you plumb home an' set your house afire—an' you figger he ain't dangerous?' Lew he jest grinned kinder foolish-like an' says: 'Wal sir, I wouldn't want t' call nobody out'n their name,' says he. Th' pore lawyer was turrible sot back. 'Lord Gawd, Mister Merriwether,' says he, 'whut kind of a man *is* this hyar Yancey, then?' Lew he scratched his head a minute an' then he says: 'Wal Jedge, I reckon Ab is jest a feller whut it won't do t' monkey with, nohow!'

"Ab was a right comical leetle cuss, too—allus a-doin' somethin' t' make folks laugh. I 'member th' time him an' Batty Ross was 'rested for fightin', an' ol' Squire Perkins he fined 'em five dollars apiece. Batty was a turrible big feller, an' he'd ketched Ab drunk an' beat him purty nigh t' death, but Ab he spoke right up in court jest th' same. 'Hell fire, Jedge,' says he, 'hit ain't right t' fine that pore leetle scallywag—ever'body knows he couldn't do no fightin'. Hit was *me* what done th' fightin', Jedge, an' I shore aim t' pay th' hull damage myse'f!'—an' with that he slapped out a ten-spot on th' counter. Batty he jest stood thar plumb flabbergasted, an' even ol' Squire Perkins had t' chuckle a leetle.

"He was purty cagey in his young days, an' had a name for tom-cattin' round atter th' married women. Hit shore did git him into a heap o' trouble, too, but seems like he allus wiggled out'n it some way. One time Ab had snuck in t' visit one o' th' neighbor women—I ain't a-callin' no names, mind ye—an' while he was in thar they heerd somebody open th' gate. Th' heifer she says, 'Oh Gawd, that's my ol' man, shore!' an' Ab he says, 'Wal, whut'd I better do?' She was that skeered she couldn't say nothin', but Ab he run quick an' hid in th' scaldin'-bar'l. Purty soon hyar come a feller in, but it warn't her husband nohow. Hit was Big Jim Applegate, an' he run up t' th' woman an' begin a-huggin' an' a-kissin' an' a-lallygaggin' an' all like that. Ab he jest set thar still as a mouse. He couldn't see nothin', but he shore heerd a plenty. Purty soon th' gate slammed ag'in, an' this time it *was* her ol' man shore 'nough.

Big Jim he put on his hat an' coat mighty quick, an' when th' feller walked in he says, 'Howdy, neighbor! I jest come over t' borry your scaldin'-bar'l—we-uns is aimin' t' butcher t'morrer.' Th' feller didn't like the looks o' things none too good, but he jest says, 'Wal Jim, thar it is, over thar in th' corner.'

"When Big Jim picked th' dang thing up he tuck note it was all-fired heavy, but he figgered this hyar warn't no time t' argufy 'bout th' heft of a scaldin'-bar'l, nohow. So he jest hustled off down th' road with it, an' he never did stop till he was plumb out o' sight. 'My Gawd,' says he, when he finally got whar he could set her down an' rest hisse'f a minute, 'I shore did git out o' that mess mighty slick!' 'Bout that time Leetle Ab he pushed th' led off'n th' bar'l an' crope out. 'You shore did, Jim,' says he, 'an' I didn't do so *turrible* bad myse'f!' "

It seemed to me that this tale was reminiscent of something I had read in Boccaccio, or some other old writer. I intimated as much to Windy Bill, too, but on learning that Boccaccio had lived in Europe several hundred years ago he scouted my theory in no measured terms. "Ab Yancey," he said impressively, "was borned an' raised right up thar on Greasy Creek. He never went nowhar outside th' county, an' he shore didn't have no truck with no furriners. How could this hyar Bo-whut-do-ye-call-him feller of knowed whut Ab done hyar in Poot Holler? Hit's plumb redic'lous, Doc—sometimes I think you ain't jest right in your head!"

No satisfactory reply to this sort of logic occurred to me at the moment, so I dropped the matter of origins rather precipitately, and pressed Bill for more information about Yancey's exploits. Most of them were commonplace enough—Ab's fights and frolics and sprees and adulteries had not differed very much from those of any other mountain bravo. When I asked for the particulars of his death Bill said shortly that he died from drinking too much popskull whisky, but admitted later on that it was no ordinary case of alcoholic poisoning.

"Wal, ye see, Ab got t' drinkin' in th' tavern an' I don't mind tellin' you he drinked jest a leetle more'n he'd orter. Atter while he got t' talkin' kinder wild, a-makin' out like he figgered on killin' somebody afore sun-up. So finally me an' Bob Nowlin jest jumped onto him all of a suddent an' tuck his gun away, an' then we put him t' bed on a pile o' gunnysacks. . . . When he come t' hisse'f next mornin' Ab begun t' holler whar was his gun at? An' then he says how come me all skun up like this, an' my clothes all tore? Frank Pease he was a-tendin' bar that mornin', an' he seen how Ab didn't remember nothin' whut happened last night. So he says, 'Wal Ab, we all drinked a leetle too much, an' you got t' fightin' with a couple o' furriners from th' Injun Terri-tory, an' they jest knocked you plumb senseless,' says he. Frank he didn't mean no harm—he was jest tryin' t' fix it so's Ab wouldn't hold nothin' ag'in me an' Bob Nowlin. So then he give Ab his gun back from under th' counter, an' Ab he jest clicked th' loadin'-gate an' stuck it in his britches same as allus. Hit was one o' these hyar ol' single-action thumb-busters, an' he allus carried it thataway with th' gate stuck out for a hook onto his belt, so's it wouldn't slip down his pants-leg. . . . Ab warn't a-feelin' peart 'nough t' eat no breakfast but he tuck three-four good snorts o' licker an' went a-rampin' off down th' road. An' that's th' last time I ever seen Ab Yancey till they fetched th' corpse back home in th' wagon.

"But th' way I heerd it next mornin', Ab jest walked on down by th' creek, an' purty soon he perked up a leetle—he was a-whistlin' when he passed Ol' Man Joslyn's place, anyhow. He met up with two strangers down by th' ford, an' they howdied him civil as anybody. But Ab he figgered it was maybe these hyar fellers whut got th' best of him last night. 'Whar-bouts do you-uns live at?' he ast 'em, an' when they says they been a-workin' over in th' Nation he out with his six-shooter. 'Wade out in th' creek, Gawd damn ye!' he hollers t' th' biggest 'un. 'Git down on your knees, an' drink water like a cow!' an' th' feller done it. But t'other 'un he jest stood thar, an' when Ab started in a-cussin' *him* he jest pulled out his pistol an' shot Ab right squar' in th' belly! Ab snapped his thumb-buster four times, an' he'd of kilt both of 'em shore, only his gun warn't loaded. Me an' Bob Nowlin had done tuck th' hulls out'n it that night, an' pore Ab was so fuddled he never noticed 'em bein' gone, an' Frank Pease he never thought t' tell him.

"Some o' Ab's kinfolks was mighty high ag'in them fellers from th' Nation, but I never could make out t' blame 'em much myse'f. Whut'd you do, if you was a-walkin' 'long 'tendin' t' your own business, an' some feller tuck t' pullin' out guns an' a-carryin' on like whut Ab done? Ol' Joe Yancey allus helt it ag'in Frank Pease—said he hadn't orter of give Ab no empty gun thataway—an' Ab's woman she 'lowed me an' Bob Nowlin didn't have no business a-takin' th' ca'tridges out like we done. . . . But I allus figgered it was drinkin' bad whisky whut kilt Ab Yancey. Hit stands t' reason, if Ab hadn't of got drunk we wouldn't never of snatched his gun off'n him thataway, or tuck th' hulls out'n it. An' if he'd kept sober he'd of knowed whut happened, an' Frank wouldn't never told him that big windy 'bout fellers from th' Nation, neither. An' more'n that, if his head had been a-workin' he'd of loaded his gun an' kilt both them fellers easy, an' ever'thing would of been all right. . . . We-uns give him a high-tone buryin' as was ever saw in these parts, an' he's got th' biggest grave-rock in th' hull dang country. Hit ain't no more'n right, neither, 'cause Ab was one o' th' best-liked fellers ever lived in th' Holler."

"Change the Name of Arkansas? Hell, No!"

Mr. Speaker, You blue-bellied rascal! I have for the last thirty minutes been trying to get your attention, and each time I have caught your eye, you have wormed, twisted and squirmed like a dog with a flea in his hide, damn you!

Gentlemen, you may tear down the honored pictures from the halls of the United States Senate, desecrate the grave of George Washington, haul down the Stars and Stripes, curse the Goddess of Liberty, and knock down the tomb of U. S. Grant, but your crime would in no wise compare in enormity with what you propose to do when you would change the name of Arkansas! Change the name of Arkansas—hell-fire, no!

Compare the lily of the valley to the gorgeous sunrise; the discordant croak of the bull-frog to the melodious tones of a nightingale; the classic strains of Mozart to the bray of a Mexican mule; the puny arm of a Peruvian prince to the muscles of a Roman gladiator—but never change the name of Arkansas. Hell, no!

II

Here is another version of what is supposed to have been the speech, delivered by Cassius M. Johnson, as printed in a pamphlet at Cleveland, Ohio. Printed by J. H. Philips, Cleveland, Ohio, no date.—F. W. A.

. . . Change the name of Arkansas! Hell, no! stand back and give him room according to his strength. Blood's his natural drink! and the wails of the dying is music to his ears! Cast your eyes on the gentleman, and lay low and hold your breath, for he's 'bout to turn himself loose! He's the bloodiest son of a wild-cat that lives, who would change the name of Arkansas! Hold him down to earth, for he is a child of sin! Don't attempt to look at him with your naked eye, gentlemen; use smoked glass. The man who would change the name of Arkansaw, by gosh, would use the meridians of longitude and the parallels of latitude for a seine,

From *Folklore of Romantic Arkansas*, by Fred W. Allsopp, Volume II, pp. 87–90. Copyright, 1931, by the Grolier Society.

There is a tradition that away back yonder—about the time when the Arkansaw Traveler story came into being—it was proposed to change the name of Arkansas by legislative enactment. Some say the question was actually introduced at a session of the Legislature, and that a member delivered a fiery speech on the subject. "Change the name of Arkansas? Hell, No!" he is supposed to have declared. The writer has been requested many times for a copy of that speech. Investigation fails to reveal any official record of such a deliverance, but it seems certain that there was some discussion of the matter, in or out of the halls of state, and the speech may have been delivered sub rosa at a committee meeting, or, more likely, in a bar-room. It has frequently been referred to at banquets and on other convivial occasions, always being described as a wickedly lurid gem. As often rehearsed by George Williams, a member of the Arkansas Legislature from Pulaski County, some 25 years ago, it went something like this, barring its unprintable profanity and obscenity.—F. W. A.

and drag the Atlantic ocean for whales! He would scratch himself awake with the lightning, and purr himself asleep with the thunder! When he's cold, he would "bile" the Gulf of Mexico and bathe in it! When he's hot, he would fan himself with an equinoctial storm! When he's thirsty, he would reach up and suck a cloud dry like a sponge! When he's hungry, famine follows in his wake! You may put your hand on the sun's face, and make it night on the earth; bite a piece out of the moon, and hurry the seasons; shake yourself and rumble the mountains; but, sir, you will never change the name of Arkansaw!

The man who would change the name of Arkansaw, would massacre isolated communities as a pastime. He would destroy nationalities as a serious business! He would use the boundless vastness of the Great American Desert for his private grave-yard! He would attempt to extract sunshine from cucumbers! Hide the stars in a nail-keg, put the sky to soak in a gourd, hang the Arkansas river on a clothesline; unbuckle the belly-band of Time, and turn the sun and moon out to pasture; but you will never change the name of Arkansaw! The world will again pause and wonder at the audacity of the lop-eared, lantern-jawed, half-breed, half-born, whiskey-soaked hyena who has proposed to change the name of Arkansaw! He's just starting to climb the political banister, and wants to knock the hay-seed out of his hair, pull the splinters out of his feet, and push on and up to the governorship. *But change the name of Arkansaw, hell, no!*

Initiation at Good Old Siwash

Were you ever Hamburgered by a real, live college fraternity? I mean, were you ever initiated into full brotherhood by a Greek-letter society with the aid of a baseball bat, a sausage-making machine, a stick of dynamite and a corn-sheller? What's that? You say you belong to the Up-to-Date Wood-choppers and have taken the josh degree in the Noble Order of Prong-Horned Wapiti? Forget it. Those are n't initiations. They are rest cures. I went into one of those societies which give horse-play initiations for middle-aged daredevils last year and was bored to death because I forgot to bring my knitting. They are stiff enough for fat business men who never do anything more exciting than to fall over the lawn mower in the cellar once a year; but, compared with a genuine, eighteen-donkey-power college frat initiation with a Spanish Inquisition attachment, the little degree teams, made up of grand-fathers, feel like a slap on the wrist delivered by a young lady in frail health.

From *At Good Old Siwash* by George Fitch, pp. 28–49. Copyright, 1910, 1911, by the Curtis Publishing Company, Philadelphia; 1911 by Little, Brown, and Company, Boston.

Mind you, I'm not talking about the baby-ribbon affairs that the college boys use nowadays. It doesn't seem to be the fashion to grease the landscape with freshmen any more. Initiations are getting to be as safe and sane as an ice-cream festival in a village church. When a frat wants to submit a neophyte to a trying ordeal it sends him out on the campus to climb a tree, or makes him go to a dance in evening clothes with a red necktie on. A boy who can roll a peanut half a mile with a toothpick, or can fish all morning in a pail of water in front of the college chapel without getting mad and trying to thrash anyone is considered to be lion-hearted enough to ornament any frat. These are mollycoddle times in all departments.

Eight or ten years ago, when a college fraternity absorbed a freshman, the job was worth talking about. There was no half-way business about it. The freshman could tell at any stage of the game that something was being done to him. They just ate him alive, that was all. Why, at Siwash, where I was lap-welded into the Eta Bita Pies, any fraternity which initiated a candidate and left enough of him to appear in chapel the next morning was the joke of the school. Even the girls' fraternities gave it the laugh. The girls used to do a little quiet initiating themselves, and when they received a sister into membership you could generally follow her mad career over the town by a trail of hairpins, "rats" and little fragments of dressgoods.

Those were the days when the pledgling of a good high-pressure frat wrote to his mother the night before he was taken in and telegraphed her when he found himself alive in the morning. There used to be considerable rivalry between the frats at Siwash in the matter of giving a freshman a good, hospitable time. I remember when the Sigh Whoopsilons hung young Allen from the girder of an overhead railroad crossing, and let the switch engines smoke him up for two hours as they passed underneath, there was a good deal of jealousy among the rest of us who hadn't thought of it. The Alfalfa Delts went them one better by tying roller skates to the shoulders and hips of a big freshman football star and hauling him through the main streets of Jonesville on his back, behind an automobile, and the Chi Yi's covered a candidate with plaster of Paris, with blow-holes for his nose, sculptured him artistically, and left him before the college chapel on a pedestal all night. The Delta Kappa Sonofaguns set fire to their house once by shooting Roman candles at a row of neophytes in the cellar, and we had to turn out at one A.M. one winter morning to help the Delta Flushes dig a freshman out of their chimney. They had been trying to let him down into the fireplace, and when he got stuck they had poked at him with a clothes pole until they had mussed him up considerably. This just shows you what a gay life the young scholar led in the days when every ritual had claws on, and there was no such thing as soothing syrup in the equipment of a college.

Of all the frats at Siwash the Eta Bita Pies, when I was in college,

were preëminent in the art of near-killing freshmen. We used to call
our initiation "A little journey to the pearly gates," and once or twice
it looked for a short time as if the victim had mislaid his return ticket.
Treat yourself to an election riot, a railway collision and a subway explosion, all in one evening, and you will get a rather sketchy idea of
what we aimed at. I don't mean, of course, that we ever killed anyone.
There is no real danger in an initiation, you know, if the initiate does
exactly as he is told and the members don't get careless and something
that was n't expected does n't happen—as did when we tied Tudor
Snyder to the south track while an express went by on the north track,
and then had the time of our young lives getting him off ahead of a
wild freight which we had n't counted on. All we ever aimed at was to
make the initiate so thankful to get through alive that he would love
Eta Bita Pie forever, and I must say we usually succeeded. It is wonderful what a young fellow will endure cheerfully for the sake of passing
it on to someone else the next year. I remember I was pretty mad when
my Eta Bita Pie brethren headed me up in a barrel and rolled me
downhill into a creek without taking the trouble to remove all the
nails. It seemed like wanton carelessness. But long before my nose was
out of splints and my hide would hold water I was perfecting our
famous "Lover's Leap" for the next year's bunch. That was our greatest triumph. There was an abandoned rock quarry north of town with
thirty feet of water in the bottom and a fifty-foot drop to the water.
By means of a long beam and a system of pulleys we could make a
freshman walk the plank and drop off into the water in almost perfect
safety, providing the ropes did n't break. It created a sensation, and the
other frats were mad with jealousy. We took every man we wanted the
next fall before the authorities put a stop to the scheme. That shows
you just how repugnant the idea of being initiated is to the green
young collegian.

Of course, fraternity initiations are supposed to be conducted for
the amusement of the chapter and not of the candidate. But you can't
always entirely tell what will happen, especially if the victim is husky
and unimpressionable. Sometimes he does a little initiating himself.
And that reminds me that I started out to tell a story and not to give
a lecture on the polite art of making veal salad. Did I ever tell you of
the time when we initiated Ole Skjarsen into Eta Bita Pie, and how
the ceremony backfired and very nearly blew us all into the discard?
No? Well, don't get impatient and look in the back of the book. I 'll
tell it now and cut as many corners as I can.

As I have told you before, Ole Skjarsen was a little slow in grasping
the real beauties of football science. It took him some time to uncoil
his mind from the principles of woodchopping and concentrate it on
the full duty of man in a fullback's position. He nearly drove us to a
sanitarium during the process, but when he once took hold, mercy me,
how he did progress from hither to yon over the opposition! He was

the wonder fullback of those times, and at the end of three years there was n't a college anywhere that did n't have Ole's hoofmarks all over its pride. Oh, he was a darling. To see him jumping sideways down a football field with the ball under his arm, landing on someone of the opposition at every jump and romping over the goal line with tacklers hanging to him like streamers would have made you want to vote for him for Governor. Ole was the greatest man who ever came to Siwash. Prexy had always been considered some personage by the outside world, but he was only a bump in the background when Ole was around.

Of course we all loved Ole madly, but for all that he did n't make a frat. He did n't, for the same reason that a rhinoceros does n't get invited to garden parties. He did n't seem to fit the part. Not only his clothes, but also his haircuts were hand-me-down. He regarded a fork as a curiosity. His language was a sort of a head-on collision between Norwegian and English in which very few words had come out undamaged. In social conversation he was out of bounds nine minutes out of ten, and it kept three men busy changing the subject when he was in full swing. He could dodge eleven men and a referee on the football field without trying, but put him in a forty by fifty room with one vase in it, and he could n't dodge it to save his life.

No, he just naturally did n't fit the part, and up to his senior year no fraternity had bid him. This grieved Ole so that he retired from football just before the Kiowa game on which all our young hearts were set, and before he would consent to go back and leave some more of his priceless foot-tracks on the opposition we had to pledge him to three of our proudest fraternities. Talk of wedding a favorite daughter to the greasy villain in the melodrama in order to save the homestead! No crushed father, with a mortgage hanging over him in the third act, could have felt one-half so badly as we Eta Bita Pies did when we had pledged Ole and realized that all the rest of the year we would have to climb over him in our beautiful, beamed-ceiling lounging-room and parade him before the world as a much-loved brother.

But the job had to be done, and all three frats took a melancholy pleasure in arranging the details of the initiation. We decided to make it a three-night demonstration of all that the Siwash frats had learned in the art of imitating dynamite and other disintegrants. The Alfalfa Delts were to get first crack at him. They were to be followed on the second night by the Chi Yi Sighs, who were to make him a brother, dead or alive. On the third night we of Eta Bita Pie were to take the remains and decorate them with our fraternity pin after ceremonies in which being kicked by a mule would only be considered a two-minute recess.

We fellows knew that when it came to initiating Ole we would have to do the real work. The other frats could n't touch it. They might

scratch him up a bit, but they lacked the ingenuity, the enthusiasm—
I might say the poetic temperament—to make a good job of it. We
determined to put on an initiation which would make our past efforts
seem like the effort of an old ladies' home to start a rough-house. It
was a great pleasure, I assure you, to plan that initiation. We revised
our floor work and added some cellar and garret and ceiling and
second-story work to it. We began the program with the celebrated
third degree and worked gradually from that up to the twenty-third
degree, with a few intervals of simple assault and battery for breathing spells. When we had finished doping out the program we shook
hands all around. It was a masterpiece. It would have made Batten-
berg lace out of a steam boiler.

Ole was initiated into the Alfalfa Delts on a Wednesday night. We
heard echoes of it from our front porch. The next morning only three
of the Alfalfa Delts appeared at chapel, while Ole was out at six A.M.,
roaming about the campus with the Alfalfa Delt pin on his necktie.
The next night the Chi Yi Sighs took him on for one hundred and
seventeen rounds in their brand new lodge, which had a sheet-iron
initiation den. The whole thing was a fizzle. When we looked Ole
over the next morning we could n't find so much as a scratch on him.
He was wearing the Chi Yi pin beside the Alfalfa Delt pin, and he
was as happy as a baby with a bottle of ink. There were nine broken
window-lights in the Chi Yi lodge, and we heard in a roundabout way
that they called in the police about three A.M. to help them explain
to Ole that the initiation was over. That's the kind of a trembling
neophyte Ole was. But we just giggled to ourselves. Anybody could
break up a Chi Yi initiation, and the Alfalfa Delts were a set of
narrow-chested snobs with automobile callouses instead of muscles.
We ate a hasty dinner on Friday evening and set all the scenery for
the big scrunch. Then we put on our old clothes and waited for Ole
to walk into our parlor.

He was n't due until nine, but about eight o'clock he came creaking
up the steps and dented the door with his large knuckles in a bashful
way. He looked larger and knobbier than ever and, if anything, more
embarrassed. We led him into the lounging-room in silence, and he
sat down twirling his straw hat. It was October, and he had worn the
thing ever since school opened. Other people who wore straw hats in
October get removed from under them more or less violently; but,
somehow, no one had felt called upon to maltreat Ole. We hated that
hat, however, and decided to begin the evening's work on it.

"Your hat, Mr. Skjarsen," said Bugs Wilbur in majestic tones.

Ole reached the old ruin out. Wilbur took it and tossed it into the
grate. Ole upset four or five of us who could n't get out of the way
and rescued the hat, which was blazing merrily.

"Ent yu gat no sanse?" he roared angrily. "Das ban a gude hat." He
looked at it gloomily. "Et ban spoiled now," he growled, tossing the

remains into a waste-paper basket. "Yu ban purty fallers. Vat for yu do dat?"

The basket was full of papers and things. In about four seconds it was all ablaze. Wilbur tried to go over and choke it off, but Ole pushed him back with one forefinger.

"Yust stay avay," he growled. "Das basket ent costing some more as my hat, I gass."

We stood around and watched the basket burn. We also watched a curtain blaze up and the finish on a nice mahogany desk crack and blister. It was all very humorous. The fire kindly went out of its own accord, and some one tiptoed around and opened the windows in a timid sort of way. It was a very successful initiation so far—only we were the neophytes.

"This won't do," muttered "Allie" Bangs, our president. He got up and went over to Ole. "Mr. Skjarsen," he said severely, "you are here to be initiated into the awful mysteries of Eta Bita Pie. It is not fitting that you should enter her sacred boundaries in an unfettered condition. Submit to the brethren that they may blindfold you and bind you for the ordeals to come." Gee, but we used to use hand-picked language when we were unsheathing our claws!

Ole growled. "Ol rite," he said. "But Aye tal yu ef yu fallers burn das har west lak yu burn ma hat I skoll raise ruffhaus like deekins!"

We tied his hands behind him with several feet of good stout rope and hobbled him about the ankles with a dog chain. Then we blindfolded him and put a pillowslip over his head for good measure. Things began to look brighter. Even a demon fullback has to have one or two limbs working in order to accomplish anything. When all was fast Banks gave Ole a preliminary kick. "Now, brethren," he roared, "bring on the Macedonian guards and give them the neophyte!"

Now I'm not revealing any real initiation secrets, mind you, and maybe what I'm telling you did n't exactly happen. But you can be perfectly sure that something just as bad did happen every time. For an hour we abused that two hundred and twenty pounds of gristle and hide. It was as much fun as roughhousing a two-ton safe. We rolled him downstairs. He broke out sixty dollars' worth of balustrade on the way and he did n't seem to mind it at all. We tried to toss him in a blanket. Ever have a two-hundred-and-twenty-pound man land on you coming down from the ceiling? We got tired of that. We made him play automobile. Ever play automobile? They tie roller skates and an automobile horn on you and push you around into the furniture, just the way a real automobile runs into things. We broke a table, five chairs, a French window, a one-hundred-dollar vase and seven shins. We did n't even interest Ole. When a man has plowed through leather-covered football players for three years his head gets used to hitting things. Also his heels will fly out no matter how careful you are. We took him into the basement and performed our famous trick of boiling the candidate in oil. Of course we wanted to scare him. He accommodated us. He broke away and hopped stiff-legged all over the room. That was n't so bad, but, confound it, he hopped on us most of the time! How would you like to initiate a bronze statue that got scared and hopped on you?

We got desperate. We threw aside the formality of explaining the deep significance of each action and just assaulted Ole with everything in the house. We prodded him with furnace tools and thumped him with cordwood and rolling-pins and barrel-staves and shovels. We walked over him, a dozen at a time. And all the time we were getting it worse than he was. He did n't exactly fight, but whenever his elbows twitched some fellow's face would happen to be in the way, and he could n't move his knee without getting it tangled in some one's ribs. You could hear the thunders of the assault and the shrieks of the wounded for a block.

At the end of an hour we were positively all in. There were n't three of us unwounded. The house was a wreck. Wilbur had a broken nose. "Chick" Struthers' kneecap hurt. "Lima" Bean's ribs were telescoped, and there was n't a good shin in the house. We quit in disgust and sat around looking at Ole. He was sitting around, too. He happened to be sitting on Bangs, who was yelling for help. But we did n't feel like starting any relief expedition.

Ole was some rumpled, and his clothes looked as if they had been fed into a separator. But he was intact, as far as we could see. He was still tied and blindfolded, and I hope to be buried alive in a branch-line town if he was n't getting bored.

"Vat fur yu qvit?" he asked. "It ent fun setting around har."

Then Petey Simmons, who had been taking a minor part in the assault in order to give his wheels full play, rose and beckoned the crowd outside. We left Ole and clustered around him.

"Now, this won't do at all," he said. "Are we going to let Eta Bita Pie be made the laughing-stock of the college? If we can't initiate that human quartz mill by force let's do it by strategy. I've got a plan. You just let me have Ole and one man for an hour and I'll make him so glad to get back to the house that he'll eat out of our hands."

We were dead ready to turn the job over to Petey, though we hated to see him put his head in the lion's mouth, so to speak. I hated it worse than any of the others because he picked me for his assistant. We went in and found Ole dozing in the corner. Petey prodded him. "Get up!" he said.

Ole got up cheerfully. Petey took the dog chain off his legs. Then he threw his sub-cellar voice into gear.

"Skjarsen," he rumbled, "you have passed right well the first test of our noble order. You have faced the hideous dangers which were in reality but shams to prove your faith, and you have borne your sufferings patiently, thus proving your meekness."

I let a couple of grins escape into my sweater-sleeve. Oh, yes, Ole had been meek all right.

"It remains for you to prove your desire," said Petey in curdled tones. "Listen!" He gave the Eta Bita Pie whistle. We had the best whistle in college. It was six notes—a sort of insidious, inviting thing that you could slide across two blocks, past all manner of barbarians, and into a frat brother's ear without disturbing any one at all. Petey gave it several times. "Now, Skjarsen," he said, "you are to follow that whistle. Let no obstacle discourage you. Let no barrier stop you. If you can prove your loyalty by following that whistle through the outside world and back to the altar of Eta Bita Pie we will ask no more of you. Come on!"

We tiptoed out of the cellar and whistled. Ole followed us up the steps. That is, he did on the second attempt. On the first he fell down with melodious thumps. We hugged each other, slipped behind a tree and whistled again.

Ole charged across the yard and into the tree. The line held. I heard him say something in Norwegian that sounded secular. By that time we were across the street. There was a low railing around the parking, and when we whistled again Ole walked right into the railing. The line held again.

Oh, I'll tell you that Petey boy was a wonder at getting up ideas. Think of it! Benjamin Franklin, Thomas Edison, Christopher Columbus, old Bill Archimedes and all the rest of the wise guys had overlooked this simple little discovery of how to make a neophyte initiate himself. It was too good to be true. We held a war dance of pure delight, and we whistled some more. We got behind stone walls, and whistled. We climbed embankments, and whistled. We slid behind blackberry bushes and ash piles and across ditches and over hedge fences, and whistled. We were so happy we could hardly pucker. Think of it! There was Ole Skjarsen, the most uncontrollable force in Nature, following us like a yellow pup with his dinner three days overdue. It was as fascinating as guiding a battleship by wireless.

We slipped across a footbridge over Cedar Creek, and whistled. Ole missed the bridge by nine yards. There isn't much water in Cedar Creek, but what there is is strong. It took Ole fifteen minutes to climb the other bank, owing to a beautiful collection of old barrel-hoops, corsets, crockery and empty tomato cans which decorated the spot. Did you ever see a blindfolded man, with his hands tied behind his back, trying to climb over a city dump? No? Of course not, any more than you have seen a green elephant. But it's a fine sight, I assure you. When Ole got out of the creek we whistled him dexterously into a barnyard and right into the maw of a brindle bull-pup with a capacity of one small man in two bites—we being safe on the other side of the fence, beyond the reach of the chain. Maybe that was mean, but Eta Bita Pie is not to be trifled with when she is aroused. Anyway, the bull got the worst of it. He only got one bite. Ole kicked in the barn door on the first try, and demolished a corn sheller on the second; but on the third he hit the pup squarely abeam and dropped a beautiful goal with him. We went around to see the dog the next day. He looked quite natural. You would almost think he was alive.

It was here that we began to smell trouble. I had my suspicions when we whistled again. There was a pretty substantial fence around that barnyard, but Ole did n't wait to find the gate.

He came through the fence not very far from us. He was conversing under that mangled pillowslip, and we heard fragments sounding like this:

"Purty soon Aye gat yu—yu spindle-shank, vite-face, skagaroot-smokin' dudes! Ugh—ump!"—here he caromed off a tree. "Ven Aye gat das blindfold off, Aye gat yu—yu Baked-Pie galoots!—Ugh! Wow!" —barbed-wire fence. "Vistle sum more, yu vide-trousered polekats. Aye make yu vistle, Aye bet yu, rite avay! Up—pllp—pllp!" That 's the kind of noise a man makes when he walks into a horse-trough at full speed.

"Gee!" said Petey nervously. "I guess we 've given him enough. He's getting sort of peevish. I don't believe in being too cruel. Let's take him back now. You don't suppose he can get his hands loose, do you?"

I did n't know. I wished I did. Of course, when you watch a lion trying to get at you from behind a fairly strong cage you feel perfectly safe, but you feel safer when you are somewhere else, just the same. We got out on the pavement and gave a gentle whistle.

"Aye har yu!" roared Ole, coming through a chicken yard. "Aye har yu, you leetle Baked Pies! Aye gat yu purty soon. Yust vait."

We did n't wait. We put on a little more gasoline and started for the frat house. We did n't have to whistle any more. Ole was right behind us. We could hear him thundering on the pavement and pleading with us in that rich, nutty dialect of his to stop and have our heads pounded on the bricks.

I shudder yet when I think of all the things he promised to do to us. We went down that street like a couple of Roman gladiators pacing a hungry bear, and, by tangling Ole up in the parkings again, managed to get home a few yards ahead.

There was an atmosphere of arnica and dejection in the house when we got there. Ill-health seemed to be rampant. "Did you lose him?" asked Bangs hopefully from behind a big bandage.

"Lose him?" says I with a snort. "Oh, yes, we lost him all right. He loses just like a foxhound. That 's him, falling over the front steps now. You can stay and entertain him; I 'm going upstairs."

Everybody came along. We piled chairs on the stairs and listened while Ole felt his way over the porch. In about a minute he found the door. Then he came right in. I had locked the door, but I had neglected to reënforce it with concrete and boiler iron. Ole wore part of the frame in with him.

"Come on, yu Baked Pies!" he shouted.

"You're in the wrong house," squeaked that little fool, Jimmy Skelton.

"Yu kent fule me!" said Ole, crashing around the loafing-room. "Aye yust can tal das haus by har skagaroot smell. Come on, yu leetle fallers! Aye bet aye inittyate yu some, tu!"

By this time he had found the stairs and was plowing through the furniture. We retired to the third floor. When twenty-seven fellows go up a three-foot stairway at once it necessarily makes some noise. Ole heard us and kept right on coming.

We grabbed a bureau and a bed and barricaded the staircase. There was a ladder to the attic. I was the last man up and my heart was giving my ribs all kinds of massage treatment before I got up. We hauled up the ladder just as Ole kicked the bureau downstairs, and then we watched him charge over our beautiful third-floor dormitory, leaving ruin in his wake.

Maybe he would have been satisfied with breaking the furniture. But, of course, a few of us had to sneeze. Ole hunted those sneezes all over the third floor. He couldn't reach them, but he sat down on the wreck underneath them.

"Aye ent know vere yu fallers ban," he said, "but Aye kin vait. Aye har yu, yu Baked Pies! Aye gat yu yet, by yimminy! Yust come on down ven yu ban ready."

Oh, yes, we were ready—I don't think. It was a perfectly lovely predicament. Here was the Damma Yappa chapter of Eta Bita Pie penned up in a deucedly-cold attic with one lone initiate guarding the trapdoor. Nice story for the college to tell when the police rescued us! Nice end of our reputation as the best neophyte jugglers in the school! Makes me shiver now to think of it.

We sat around in that garret and listened to the clock strike in the library tower across the campus. At eleven o'clock Ole promised to kill the first man who came down. That bait caught no fish. At twelve he begged for the privilege of kicking us out of our own house, one by one. At one o'clock he remarked that, while it was pretty cold, it was much colder in Norway, where he came from, and that, as we would freeze first, we might as well come down.

At two o'clock we were all stiff. At three we were kicking the plaster off of the joists, trying to keep from freezing to death. At four a bunch of Sophomores were all for throwing Petey Simmons down as a sacrifice. Petey talked them out of it. Petey could talk a stone dog into wagging its tail.

We sat in that garret from ten P.M. until the year after the great pyramid wore down to the ground. At least that was the length of time that seemed to pass. It must have been about five o'clock when Petey stopped kicking his feet on the chimney and said:

"Well, fellows, I have an idea. It may work or it may not, but—"

"Shut up, you mental desert!" some one growled. "Another of your fine ideas will wreck this frat."

"As I was saying," continued Petey cheerfully, "it may not succeed, but it will not hurt anyone but me if it does n't. I 'm going to be the Daniel in this den. But first I want the officers of the chapter to come up around the scuttle-hole with me."

Five of us crept over to the hole and looked down. "Aye har yu, yu leetle Baked Pies!" said Ole, waking in an instant. "Yust come on down. Aye ban vaiting long enough to smash yu!"

"Mr. Skjarsen," began Petey in the regular dark-lantern voice that all secret societies use—"Mr. Skjarsen—for as such we must still call you—the final test is over. You have acquitted yourself nobly. You have been faithful to the end. You have stood your vigil unflinchingly. You have followed the call of Eta Bita Pie over every obstacle and through every suffering."

"Aye ban following him leetle furder, if Aye had ladder," said Ole in a bloodthirsty voice. "Ven Aye ban getting at yu, Aye play hal vid yu Baked Pies!"

"And now," said Petey, ignoring the interruption, "the final ceremony is at hand. Do not fear. Your trials are over. In the dark recesses of this secret chamber above you we have discussed your bearing in the trials that have beset you. It has pleased us. You have been found worthy to continue toward the high goal. Ole Skjarsen, we are now ready to receive you into full membership."

"Come rite on!" snorted Ole. "Aye receeve yu into membership all rite. Yust come on down."

"It won't work, Petey," Bangs groaned. Petey kicked his shins as a sign to shut up.

"Ole Skjarsen, son of Skjar Oleson, stand up!" he said, sinking his voice another story.

Ole got up. It was plain to be seen that he was getting interested.

"The president of this powerful order will now administer the oath," said Petey, shoving Bangs forward.

So there, at five A.M., with the whole chapter treed in a garret, and the officers, the leading lights of Siwash, crouching around a scuttle and shivering their teeth loose, we initiated Ole Skjarsen. It was impressive, I can tell you. When it came to the part where the neophyte swears to protect a brother, even if he has to wade in blood up to his necktie, Bangs bore down beautifully and added a lot of extra frills. The last words were spoken. Ole was an Eta Bita Pie. Still, we were n't very sanguine. You might interest a man-eater by initiating him, but would you destroy his appetite? There was no grand rush for the ladder.

As Ole stood waiting, however, Petey swung himself down and landed beside him. He cut the ropes that bound his wrists, jerked off the pillowslip and cut off the blindfold. Then he grabbed Ole's masto-donic paw.

"Shake, brother!" he said.

Nobody breathed for a few seconds. It was darned terrifying, I can tell you. Ole rubbed his eyes with his free hand and looked down at the morsel hanging on to the other.

"Shake, Ole!" insisted Petey. "You went through it better than I did when I got it."

I saw the rudiments of a smile begin to break out on Ole's face. It grew wider. It got to be a grin; then a chasm with a sunrise on either side.

He looked up at us again, then down at Petey. Then he pumped Petey's arm until the latter danced like a cork bobber.

"By ying, Aye du et!" he shouted. "Ve ban gude fallers, ve Baked Pies, if ve did broke my nose."

"What's the matter with Ole?" someone shouted.

"He 's all right!" we yelled. Then we came down out of the garret and made a rush for the furnace.

The Philosophy of Insult

"You ought to see how still that little Georgie Bassett sits," the barber said, reprovingly. "I hear everybody says he's the best boy in town."

"Pfuff! *Phirr!*" There was a touch of intentional contempt in this.

"I haven't heard nobody around the neighbourhood makin' no such remarks," added the barber, "about nobody of the name of Penrod Schofield."

"Well," said Penrod, clearing his mouth after a struggle, "who wants 'em to? Ouch!"

"I hear they call Georgie Bassett the 'little gentleman,' " ventured the barber, provocatively, meeting with instant success.

"They better not call *me* that," returned Penrod truculently. "I'd like to hear anybody try. Just once, that's all! I bet they'd never try it ag— *Ouch!*"

"Why? What'd you do to 'em?"

"It's all right what I'd *do!* I bet they wouldn't want to call me that again long as they lived!"

"What'd you do if it was a little girl? You wouldn't hit her, would you?"

"Well, I'd— Ouch!"

"You wouldn't hit a little girl, would you?" the barber persisted, gathering into his powerful fingers a mop of hair from the top of

From *Penrod*, by Booth Tarkington, pp. 249–282. Copyright, 1914, by Doubleday, Page and Company, Garden City, N. Y.

Penrod's head and pulling that suffering head into an unnatural position. "Doesn't the Bible say it ain't never right to hit the weak sex?"

"Ow! *Say,* look *out!*"

"So you'd go and punch a pore, weak, little girl, would you?" said the barber, reprovingly.

"Well, who said I'd hit her?" demanded the chivalrous Penrod. "I bet I'd *fix* her though, all right. She'd see!"

"You wouldn't call her names, would you?"

"No, I wouldn't! What hurt is it to call anybody names?"

"Well," replied the barber, "that ain't sayin' what you'd do if a young lady ever walked up and called you a little gentleman. *I* want to hear what you'd do to her. I guess I know, though—come to think of it."

"What?" demanded Penrod.

"You'd sick that pore ole dog of yours on her cat, if she had one, I expect," guessed the barber derisively.

"No, I would not!"

"Well, what *would* you do?"

"I'd do enough. Don't worry about that!"

"Well, suppose it was a boy, then: what'd you do if a boy come up to you and says, 'Hello, little gentleman'?"

"He'd be lucky," said Penrod, with a sinister frown, "if he got home alive."

"Suppose it was a boy twice your size?"

"Just let him try," said Penrod ominously. "You just let him try. He'd never see daylight again; that's all!"

"Now what," asked the barber, combing the reeking locks gently, "what would it make you so mad fer, to have somebody call you a little gentleman? It's a kind of compliment, as it were, you might say. What would you want to hit anybody fer *that* fer?"

To the mind of Penrod, this question was without meaning or reasonableness. It was within neither his power nor his desire to analyze the process by which the phrase had become offensive to him, and was now rapidly assuming the proportions of an outrage. He knew only that his gorge rose at the thought of it.

"You just let 'em try it!" he said threateningly, as he slid down from the chair. And as he went out of the door, after further conversation on the same subject, he called back those warning words once more: "Just let 'em try it! Just once—that's all *I* ask 'em to. They'll find out what they *get!*"

The barber chuckled. Then a fly lit on the barber's nose and he slapped at it, and the slap missed the fly but did not miss the nose. The barber was irritated. At this moment his birdlike eye gleamed a gleam as it fell upon customers approaching: the prettiest little girl in the world, leading by the hand her baby brother, Mitchy-Mitch, coming to have Mitchy-Mitch's hair clipped, against the heat.

It was a hot day and idle, with little to feed the mind—and the barber was a mischievous man with an irritated nose. He did his worst.

Meanwhile, the brooding Penrod pursued his homeward way; no great distance, but long enough for several one-sided conflicts with malign insulters made of thin air. "You better *not* call me that!" he muttered. "You just try it, and you'll get what other people got when *they* tried it. You better not ack fresh with *me!* Oh, you *will*, will you?" He delivered a vicious kick full upon the shins of an iron fence-post, which suffered little, though Penrod instantly regretted his indiscretion. "Oof!" he grunted, hopping; and went on after bestowing a look of awful hostility upon the fence-post.

Nearing home, however, his belligerent spirit was diverted to happier interests by the discovery that some workmen had left a caldron of tar in the cross-street, close by his father's stable. He tested it, but found it inedible. Also, as a substitute for professional chewing-gum it was unsatisfactory, being insufficiently boiled down and too thin, though of a pleasant, lukewarm temperature. But it had an excess of one quality—it was sticky. It was the stickiest tar Penrod had ever used for any purposes whatsoever, and nothing upon which he wiped his hands served to rid them of it; neither his polka-dotted shirt waist nor his knickerbockers; neither the fence, nor even Duke, who came unthinkingly wagging out to greet him, and retired wiser.

Nevertheless, tar is tar. Much can be done with it, no matter what its condition; so Penrod lingered by the caldron, though from a neighbouring yard could be heard the voices of comrades, including that of Sam Williams. The caldron was almost full, and the surface of the tar near the rim. Penrod endeavoured to ascertain how many pebbles and brickbats, dropped in, would cause an overflow. Labouring heartily to this end, he had almost accomplished it, when he received the suggestion for an experiment on a much larger scale. Embedded at the corner of a grass-plot across the street was a whitewashed stone, the size of a small watermelon and serving no purpose whatever save the questionable one of decoration. It was easily pried up with a stick; though getting it to the caldron tested the full strength of the ardent labourer. Perspiring, grunting vehemently, his back aching and all muscles strained, he progressed in short stages until the big stone lay at the base of the caldron. He was bending his shoulders for the heave that would lift it over the rim, when a sweet, taunting voice, close behind him, startled him cruelly.

"How do you do, *little gentleman!*"

Penrod squawked, dropped the stone, and shouted. "Shut up, you dern fool!" purely from instinct, even before his about-face made him aware who had so spitefully addressed him.

It was Marjorie Jones. Always dainty, and prettily dressed, she was in speckless and starchy white to-day, and a refreshing picture she made, with the new-shorn and powerfully scented Mitchy-Mitch clinging to her hand. They had stolen up behind the toiler, and now stood laughing together in sweet merriment. Since the passing of Penrod's Rupe Collins period he had experienced some severe qualms at the recollection of his last meeting with Marjorie and his Apache behaviour; in truth, his heart instantly became as wax at sight of her, and he would have offered her fair speech; but, alas! in Marjorie's wonderful eyes there shone a consciousness of new powers for his undoing, and she denied him opportunity.

"Oh, *oh!*" she cried, mocking his pained outcry. "What a way for a *little gentleman* to talk! Little gentleman don't say wicked—"

"Marjorie!" Penrod, enraged and dismayed, felt himself stung beyond all endurance. Insult from her was bitterer to endure than from any other. "Don't you call me that again!"

"Why not, *little gentleman?*"

He stamped his foot. "You better stop!"

Marjorie sent into his furious face her lovely, spiteful laughter.

"Little gentleman, little gentleman, little gentleman!" she said deliberately. "How's the little gentleman, this afternoon? Hello, little gentleman!"

Penrod, quite beside himself, danced eccentrically. "Dry up!" he howled. "Dry up, dry up, dry up, dry *up!*"

Mitchy-Mitch shouted with delight and applied a finger to the side of the caldron—a finger immediately snatched away and wiped upon a handkerchief by his fastidious sister.

" 'Ittle gellamun!" said Mitchy-Mitch.

"You better look out!" Penrod whirled upon this small offender with grim satisfaction. Here was at least something male that could without dishonour be held responsible. "You say that again, and I'll give you the worst—"

"You will *not!*" snapped Marjorie, instantly vitriolic. "He'll say just whatever he wants to, and he'll say it just as *much* as he wants to. Say it again, Mitchy-Mitch!"

" 'Ittle gellamun!" said Mitchy-Mitch promptly.

"Ow-*yah!*" Penrod's tone-production was becoming affected by his mental condition. "You say that again, and I'll—"

"Go on, Mitchy-Mitch," cried Marjorie. "He can't do a thing. He don't *dare!* Say it some more, Mitchy-Mitch—say it a whole lot!"

Mitchy-Mitch, his small, fat face shining with confidence in his immunity, complied.

" 'Ittle gellamun!" he squeaked malevolently. " 'Ittle gellamun! 'Ittle gellamun! 'Ittle gellamun!"

The desperate Penrod bent over the whitewashed rock, lifted it, and then heaved it into the air.

Marjorie screamed.

But it was too late. The big stone descended into the precise midst of the caldron and Penrod got his mighty splash. It was far, far beyond his expectations.

Spontaneously there were grand and awful effects—volcanic spectacles of nightmare and eruption. A black sheet of eccentric shape rose out of the caldron and descended upon the three children, who had no time to evade it.

After it fell, Mitchy-Mitch, who stood nearest the caldron, was the thickest, though there was enough for all. Br'er Rabbit would have fled from any of them.

. . . Penrod descended to dinner. The Rev. Mr. Kinosling had asked for the pleasure of meeting him, and it had been decided that the only course possible was to cover up the scandal for the present, and to offer an undisturbed and smiling family surface to the gaze of the visitor.

Scorched but not bowed, the smouldering Penrod was led forward for the social formulæ simultaneously with the somewhat bleak departure of Robert Williams, who took his guitar with him, this time, and went in forlorn unconsciousness of the powerful forces already set in secret motion to be his allies.

The punishment just undergone had but made the haughty and unyielding soul of Penrod more stalwart in revolt; he was unconquered. Every time the one intolerable insult had been offered him, his resentment had become the hotter, his vengeance the more instant and furious. And, still burning with outrage, but upheld by the conviction of right, he was determined to continue to the last drop of his blood the defense of his honour, whenever it should be assailed, no matter how mighty or august the powers that attacked it. In all ways, he was a very sore boy.

During the brief ceremony of presentation, his usually inscrutable countenance wore an expression interpreted by his father as one of insane obstinacy, while Mrs. Schofield found it an incentive to inward prayer. The fine graciousness of Mr. Kinosling, however, was unimpaired by the glare of virulent suspicion given him by this little brother: Mr. Kinosling mistook it for a natural curiosity concerning one who might possibly become, in time, a member of the family. He patted Penrod upon the head, which was, for many reasons, in no condition to be patted with any pleasure to the patter. Penrod felt himself in the presence of a new enemy.

"How do you do, my little lad," said Mr. Kinosling. "I trust we shall become fast friends."

To the ear of his little lad, it seemed he said, "A trost we shall bick-home fawst frainds." Mr. Kinosling's pronunciation was, in fact, slightly precious; and the little lad, simply mistaking it for some cryptic form of mockery of himself, assumed a manner and expression which argued so ill for the proposed friendship that Mrs. Schofield hastily interposed the suggestion of dinner, and the small procession went in to the dining-room.

"It has been a delicious day," said Mr. Kinosling, presently; "warm but balmy." With a benevolent smile he addressed Penrod, who sat opposite him. "I suppose, little gentleman, you have been indulging in the usual outdoor sports of vacation?"

Penrod laid down his fork and glared, open-mouthed at Mr. Kinosling.

"You'll have another slice of breast of the chicken?" Mr. Schofield inquired, loudly and quickly.

"A lovely day!" exclaimed Margaret, with equal promptitude and emphasis. "Lovely, oh, lovely! Lovely!"

"Beautiful, beautiful, beautiful!" said Mrs. Schofield, and after a glance at Penrod which confirmed her impression that he intended to say something, she continued, "Yes, beautiful, beautiful, beautiful, beautiful, beautiful, beautiful!"

Penrod closed his mouth and sank back in his chair—and his relatives took breath.

Mr. Kinosling looked pleased. This responsive family, with its ready enthusiasm, made the kind of audience he liked. He passed a delicate white hand gracefully over his tall, pale forehead, and smiled indulgently.

"Youth relaxes in summer," he said. "Boyhood is the age of relaxation; one is playful, light, free, unfettered. One runs and leaps and enjoys one's self with one's companions. It is good for the little lads to play with their friends; they jostle, push, and wrestle, and stimulate little, happy struggles with one another in harmless conflict. The young muscles are toughening. It is good. Boyish chivalry develops, enlarges, expands. The young learn quickly, intuitively, spontaneously. They perceive the obligations of *noblesse oblige*. They begin to comprehend the necessity of caste and its requirements. They learn what birth means—ah,—that is, they learn what it means to be well born. They learn courtesy in their games; they learn politeness, consideration for one another in their pastimes, amusements, lighter occupations. I make it my pleasure to join them often, for I sympathize with them in all their wholesome joys as well as in their little bothers and perplexities. I understand them, you see; and let me tell you it is no easy matter to understand the little lads and lassies." He sent to each listener his beaming glance, and, permitting it to come to rest upon Penrod, inquired:

"And what do you say to that, little gentleman?"

Mr. Schofield uttered a stentorian cough. "More? You'd better have some more chicken! More! Do!"

"More chicken!" urged Margaret simultaneously, "Do please! Please! More! Do! More!"

"Beautiful, beautiful," began Mrs. Schofield. "Beautiful, beautiful, beautiful, beautiful—"

It is not known in what light Mr. Kinosling viewed the expression of Penrod's face. Perhaps he mistook it for awe; perhaps he received no impression at all of its extraordinary quality. He was a rather self-engrossed young man, just then engaged in a double occupation, for he not only talked, but supplied from his own consciousness a critical though favourable auditor as well, which of course kept him quite busy. Besides, it is oftener than is suspected the case that extremely peculiar expressions upon the countenances of boys are entirely over-looked, and suggest nothing to the minds of people staring straight at them. Certainly Penrod's expression—which, to the perception of his family, was perfectly horrible—caused not the faintest perturbation in the breast of Mr. Kinosling.

Mr. Kinosling waived the chicken, and continued to talk. "Yes, I think I may claim to understand boys," he said, smiling thoughtfully. "One has been a boy one's self. Ah, it is not all playtime! I hope our young scholar here does not overwork himself at his Latin, at his classics, as I did, so that at the age of eight years I was compelled to wear glasses. He must be careful not to strain the little eyes at his scholar's tasks, not to let the little shoulders grow round over his scholar's desk. Youth is golden; we should keep it golden, bright, glistening. Youth should frolic, should be sprightly; it should play its cricket, its tennis, its hand-ball. It should run and leap; it should laugh, should sing madrigals and glees, carol with the lark, ring out in chanties, folk-songs, ballads, roundelays—"

He talked on. At any instant Mr. Schofield held himself ready to cough vehemently and shout, "More chicken," to drown out Penrod in case the fatal words again fell from those eloquent lips; and Mrs. Schofield and Margaret kept themselves prepared at all times to assist him. So passed a threatening meal, which Mrs. Schofield hurried, by every means with decency, to its conclusion. She felt that somehow they would all be safer out in the dark of the front porch, and led the way thither as soon as possible.

"No cigar, I thank you." Mr. Kinosling, establishing himself in a wicker chair beside Margaret, waved away her father's proffer. "I do not smoke. I have never tasted tobacco in any form." Mrs. Schofield was confirmed in her opinion that this would be an ideal son-in-law. Mr. Schofield was not so sure.

"No," said Mr. Kinosling. "No tobacco for me. No cigar, no pipe, no cigarette, no cheroot. For me, a book—a volume of poems, perhaps. Verses, rhymes, lines metrical and cadenced—those are my dissipation. Tennyson by preference: 'Maud,' or 'Idylls of the King'—poetry of the sound Victorian days; there is none later. Or Longfellow will rest me in a tired hour. Yes; for me, a book, a volume in the hand, held lightly between the fingers."

Mr. Kinosling looked pleasantly at his fingers as he spoke, waving his hand in a curving gesture which brought it into the light of a window faintly illumined from the interior of the house. Then he passed those graceful fingers over his hair, and turned toward Penrod, who was perched upon the railing in a dark corner.

"The evening is touched with a slight coolness," said Mr. Kinosling. "Perhaps I may request the little gentleman—"

"B'gr-r-*ruff!*" coughed Mr. Schofield. "You'd better change your mind about a cigar."

"No, I thank you. I was about to request the lit—"

"*Do* try one," Margaret urged. "I'm sure papa's are nice ones. Do try—"

"No, I thank you. I remarked a slight coolness in the air, and my hat is in the hallway. I was about to request—"

"I'll get it for you," said Penrod suddenly.

"If you will be so good," said Mr. Kinosling. "It is a black bowler hat, little gentleman, and placed upon a table in the hall."

"I know where it is." Penrod entered the door, and a feeling of relief, mutually experienced, carried from one to another of his three relatives their interchanged congratulations that he had recovered his sanity.

" 'The day is done, and the darkness,' " began Mr. Kinosling—and recited that poem entire. He followed it with "The Children's Hour," and after a pause, at the close, to allow his listeners time for a little reflection upon his rendition, he passed his hand again over his head, and called, in the direction of the doorway:

"I believe I will take my hat now, little gentleman."

"Here it is," said Penrod, unexpectedly climbing over the porch railing, in the other direction. His mother and father and Margaret had supposed him to be standing in the hallway out of deference, and because he thought it tactful not to interrupt the recitations. All of them remembered, later, that this supposed thoughtfulness on his part struck them as unnatural.

"Very good, little gentleman!" said Mr. Kinosling, and being somewhat chilled, placed the hat firmly upon his head, pulling it down as far as it would go. It had a pleasant warmth, which he noticed at once. The next instant, he noticed something else, a peculiar sensation of the scalp—a sensation which he was quite unable to define. He lifted his hand to take the hat off, and entered upon a strange experience: his hat seemed to have decided to remain where it was.

"Do you like Tennyson as much as Longfellow, Mr. Kinosling?" inquired Margaret.

"I—ah—I cannot say," he returned absently. "I—ah—each has his own—ugh! flavour and savour, each his—ah—ah—"

Struck by a strangeness in his tone, she peered at him curiously through the dusk. His outlines were indistinct, but she made out that

his arms were uplifted in a singular gesture. He seemed to be wrenching at his head.

"Is—is anything the matter?" she asked anxiously. "Mr. Kinosling,
are you ill?"

"Not at—ugh!—all," he replied, in the same odd tone. "I—ah—I believe—*ugh!*"

He dropped his hands from his hat, and rose. His manner was
slightly agitated. "I fear I may have taken a trifling—ah—cold. I
should—ah—perhaps be—ah—better at home. I will—ah—say good-
night."

At the steps, he instinctively lifted his hand to remove his hat, but
did not do so, and, saying "Good-night," again in a frigid voice, departed with visible stiffness from that house, to return no more.

"Well, of all—!" cried Mrs. Schofield, astounded. "What was the
matter? He just went—like that!" She made a flurried gesture. "In
heaven's name, Margaret, what *did* you say to him?"

"*I!*" exclaimed Margaret indignantly. "Nothing! He just *went!*"

"Why, he didn't even take off his hat when he said good-night!"
said Mrs. Schofield.

Margaret, who had crossed to the doorway, caught the ghost of a
whisper behind her, where stood Penrod.

"You bet he didn't!"

He knew not that he was overheard.

A frightful suspicion flashed through Margaret's mind—a suspicion
that Mr. Kinosling's hat would have to be either boiled off or shaved
off. With growing horror she recalled Penrod's long absence when he
went to bring the hat.

"Penrod," she cried, "let me see your hands!"

She had toiled at those hands herself late that afternoon, nearly
scalding her own, but at last achieving a lily purity.

"Let me see your hands!"

She seized them.

Again they were tarred!

Duel Capacity

"One day this very human and monumental spirit of goodness said,
'My boy don't you know this is no paper for you to be working on.
I've gotten a new position for you this coming Monday on Mr.
O'Malley's very sedate New Orleans daily *Item.* I'm sorry to see you
go but destiny for you beckons to other and larger fields of newspaper
endeavor.'

From *The Honest Rainmaker. The Life and Times of Colonel John R. Stingo*, by
A. J. Liebling, pp. 53–63. Copyright, 1952, 1953, by A. J. Liebling. Garden City,
New York: Doubleday & Company. 1953.

"And, so it was that I reported to the *Item* front boss and was assigned a desk and utensils. No sooner had I gotten well set in my work than two belligerent Editors began shooting at the visiting Chief of Police, the slugs skimming over my head but some of them bouncing merrily off'n a steel pictorial cut extended in front of me for final check up and O.K.

"And that was my beginning in a chosen field of Destiny, the newspaper business, a story of a Lifetime in the pursuit of the Fourth Estate. . . ."

"But what brought you into the line of fire?"

"Mr. O'Malley had abandoned his desk at the usual hour of twelve and betaken himself for prandial relaxation first to the bar of the St. Charles Hotel, where he had a three-bagger of Sazeracs, then to Hymen's bar on Common Street, where he increased his *apéritif* by four silver gin fizzes and after that over to Farbacher's saloon on Royal where he had a schooner or two of Boston Club punch. O'Malley was not of that *sang-pur* elegance which would have got him past the portal of the august Boston Club, the most revered in New Orleans, but he had bribed a fancy girl to wheedle the formula from the Boston Club bartender. It consisted of twelve bottles of champagne, eight bottles of white wine, one and one half bottles raspberry syrup, one half bottle brandy, one half bottle kirschwasser, one quarter bottle Jamaica rum, one quarter bottle Curacao, two pineapples, two dozen oranges, two and one half lbs. sugar, seltzer and ice. This was enough to serve several persons.

"When he had finished his preparations bacchanalic he strolled over to Antoine's, where he had four dozen freshly shucked oysters without any muck on them, a red snapper flambée in absinthe, a salmis of three woodcock and four snipe, a chateaubriand, *bleu,* six bottles of Bass's ale, and a magnum of La Mission Haut Brion of the comet year. After that he smoked a made-to-measure cigar, as long as his arm from the inside of the elbow to the tip of the middle finger, and drank a dipper of Calvados from a cask that had been brought to Louisiana from Normandy with the first cargo of sparkle-eyed Cyprians in 1721. Not more than one quart had been drawn from the cask in any one year since, and it had been carefully replenished each time. Having effectuated the *trou normand,* O'Malley consumed an *omelette au kirsch* and a small baked alaska, followed by a *caffè espresso* for which he sent the maître d'hôtel to a dive operated by the Maffia. 'The hardest thing to get in New Orleans,' he always said, 'is a decent cup of coffee.' He then started to walk back toward the office, which was on Camp Street, with some vague notion of pausing on the way to drape a beautiful octoroon's ivory throat with pearls, and would have arrived at his usual hour, after half-past four, had he not met with an unforeseen vicissitude."

The Colonel paused and looked about him with an expression that

approximated distaste. When he is in such moods his current Gam-
brinian haunts seem to him to lack éclat.

"I'll settle for another beer," he said, and when it had been brought
continued.

"I, a mere kid, had been entranced from the moment of Mr. O'Malley's exit by the notion of seating myself in his swivel chair and cocking
my feet on his desk," he said. "Expecting momentarily his return, for
I had heard that secular newspaper men ate, so to speak, *sur le pouce*,
I refrained for the first four hours and fifteen minutes. Then, deciding
that he might not be back at all, I yielded. I made my way furtively to
his desk, sat down, swung my legs up, and encouraged by the smiles of
the older men, even took the boss's green eyeshade off the blotter and
placed it on my towish potato. I then raised a steel line cut from the
desk and, pretending to inspect it, held it in front of my face, thus
veiling my identity. I did not know it was the habit of Mr. David
Hennessy, the Chief of Police of New Orleans, to arrive at the *Item*
office each afternoon at four thirty-five to shoot at Mr. O'Malley. The
fellows in the composing room set their watches by it and sent the
second edition to press.

"It was a tryst. O'Malley would arrive at four-thirty, hang up his
frock coat, lay out his revolvers on the desk in front of him, and start
to write a leader taking the skin off Hennessy. He would indite daily
a virulent editorial charging the Chief with official dereliction by permitting the poolrooms, policy bazars, brothels and bagnios, the stews
and knocking shops, to run wide open every day including Sunday, a
day of extreme reverence south of the Tennessee River. Mr. O'Malley
was in political control of the city and figured that any madame who
wanted a Sunday turn at bat should apply to him personally. At four
thirty-five the Chief, who had been steaming up on Creole coffee laced
with contraband Cuban rum at McConkey's in Commercial Alley, would
proceed across Camp Street and ascend to the first landing in the *Item*
building. He gave Mr. O'Malley five minutes to get set. With little
knowledge of trigonometry, but with natural copperial intuition, Mr.
Hennessy would select a likely angle of trajectory through the wooden
partition screening the city room and the corner where Mr. O'Malley
sat in pontifical augustity.

"These first shots were a long price to wing Mr. O'Malley but a good
bet to drive him under his desk in search of cover, a position from
which he could not efficiently retaliate. Advancing behind the barrage,
Mr. Hennessy would reach a spot from which he could survey the city
room. But there he would be caught in a cross fire between the sports
editor and the editor of the religious page, and after emptying both
revolvers would be impelled to retreat. It was a lesson in logistics which
I have never forgotten.

"But do not think that Mr. O'Malley had not his troops in elegant
élan and precise readiness for these manoeuvres. At the first muffled

roar and crackling sound of timber rendered, all hands except the enfilading pair, from the city editor to the meekest copy boy,—would secure shotguns conveniently placed for the purpose and rush to the front windows looking out on the street below, knowing full well that the miscreant Hennessy must, perforce, make egress and present briefly a target. After I had survived my first payday I was initiated into the routine. But on this first day of employment I was completely unprepared when a bullet from a Smith and Wesson whammed into the steel plate I held in front of me, knocking it from my hands and me *derrière dessus* behind Mr. O'Malley's desk. I learned afterward that it was the most accurate opening shot Mr. Hennessy had ever fired. 'A perfect carom,' the religious editor said. 'He played it off that new machine, the typewriter. I always said they had no place in a newspaper office.'

"After Mr. Hennessy had retreated, shrinking up close to the front of the *Item* building so as not to give the boys with the fowling pieces a clean shot, all my seniors apologized profusely for not having tipped me off. They hadn't thought I was in any real danger, they explained, and had just wanted to see some of the cockiness taken out of me when the first missile whistled overhead. 'It is ceasing to be fun,' the sports editor said. 'Also, I suspect the Chief of wearing the cover of a wash boiler inside the seat of his pants. The man in the slot had what looked like a clean hit on him day before yesterday and the only result was a loud clang. What worries me, though, is what has happened to the boss? He is either in the clink or some panelworker has stolen his trousers again.' "

The Colonel's wide, generous nose is slightly retroussé, and when he looks up at me his nostrils form a deeply indented M. They have a look of unshakeable sincerity.

"The first surmise was correct," he said. "Mr. O'Malley, returning to the office from his last mysterious port of call, had been hurrying through Commercial Alley, a narrow lane between St. Charles and Camp Streets, in order to arrive at the rendezvous before Mr. Hennessy. Had Hennessy got there first, Mr. O'Malley would have found himself cut off from his base. But in making his way through the alley, the editor, a man of generous girth, came into abrupt collision, like a crack flyer of the Southern Railroad meeting a freight train of the Louisville & Nashville, with the editor of a rival newspaper, the New Orleans *States*, headed in the opposite direction. The two had exchanged acrimonious ink about a suggestion, publicized by Mr. O'Malley, that a bank of which his fellow editor was a director was on the point of failure. Mr. O'Malley had been refused a loan. The bank was the Hibernia National, known in New Orleans of the epoch as the Irish Rock.

"The editor of the *States*, whose name, as I recollect it, was Ewing, invariably carried an umbrella with a sharp ferrule, vouchsafing it served him as a sunshade in the summer. He thrust it immediately at

Mr. O'Malley's left eye, being resigned to an exchange of shots and thinking that by this preliminary he might impair Mr. O'Malley's aim. He missed the eyeball, however, although he put a nice hole in Mr. O'Malley's brow, and forthwith the fusillade began. Of course down there in those days there was so much shooting the general public knew just what to do. The patrolmen on St. Charles and Camp detoured all traffic headed past the ends of the alley, and a number of shopkeepers on Commercial reached out from their doorways and grabbed the right hands of the contestants, an efficacious method of terminating hostilities. Sometimes they made a mistake; one of the duelists was left-handed. The effect of the error could prove lethal. Both Mr. O'Malley and Mr. Ewing, however, were conventionally orientated, and there were no casualties beyond the effusion of gore from Mr. O'Malley's punctured pumpkin.

"The police escorted both men before a magistrate, and from the clutches of these Dogberries O'Malley would soon have talked himself free, had not Ewing, himself a political power, sworn out a warrant against him for impairing the credit of the Hibernia National and causing a run on the Irish Rock. The judge happened to own stock in that institution. O'Malley was therefore immured, soon to be joined by a Mr. Kiernan who published the New Orleans *News*, and who had joined in his campaign of retribution against the Hibernia. A swift messenger informed us at the *Item* office of their predicament."

"What happened to Ewing?" I asked. "He started the fight, didn't he?"

"He was released," the Colonel said. "In those days a mere felonious assault was considered of no moment" . . . .

"A high bail had been set," the Colonel said, "and while the senior members of the staff sought bond for the captives, I was despatched to the St. Charles Parish Prison, where they were incarcerated, in a hired hack with a case of vintage Irroy *brut,* and Mr. O'Malley's English bulldog, Mike, whom he had left tied to the umbrella stand when he went out to lunch. I found the prisoners in good spirits and left them in better after they had emptied the first three bottles, kindly inviting me and the turnkey to have a glass with them. I went out thinking I had landed in the pearl of professions. And so it was, in those days of halcyon, the very cap and zenith of American journalism."

The Colonel appeared to ruminate for a while, and I thought I could visualize the procession of eminent zenithians, like Marse Henry Watterson and the youthful William Randolph Hearst, that must be passing behind his eyelids. But he was thinking of something else.

"I have never ceased to regret, Joe," he said, "that on my first day at the *Item* I was the indirect though innocent cause of Chief Hennessy's death. The bullet that struck the plate in my hand ricocheted through the flimsy ceiling and hit an old-style southern gentleman in the business office in the calf of the leg. His name, as I remember it, was Mr.

Troup Sessams, and he had withheld his fire previously because he considered the shooting downstairs a strictly editorial matter. When the bullet arrived, Mr. Sessams said, 'This is no damn joke.'

"He closed up his roll-top desk, hung his alpaca office coat on a hook, put on his long-tailed frock coat and a hat with a five-inch brim, and withdrew from the lower drawer of the desk a rosewood case containing two long-barreled dueling pistols with which he had eliminated all antebellum rivals for the hand of his wife, at that time heiress to a plantation Faulknerian, but since, like so many of us, non-holding. He loaded the pistols and placed one inside each breast of his frock coat, in the long pockets provided for that purpose by antebellum tailors. He then walked downstairs, limping a little,—the shot had only grazed him,—and followed Hennessy out into the night. It was the end of the Chief. His perforated body was discovered next morning. The year was 1889; the precise date eludes me."

"But wasn't Hennessy the New Orleans police chief who was killed by the Maffia?" I exclaimed, beginning to think I remembered something I had once read.

"That was the common theory, Joe," the Colonel said, "and the citizens of New Orleans acted upon it to the extent of shooting eleven Italians and then hanging them to trees. But those foreigners were desperate characters anyway, and doubtless deserved their fate."

The Sport

Whereas Addison Mizner had many ambitions, Wilson Mizner seemed to have none. Conversation was Wilson's hobby, profession, and neurosis. His fame as a wit has grown steadily since his death, at the age of fifty-seven, in 1933. Although he wrote practically nothing, he is probably quoted more than any other American of this century. His chance remarks have been organized into a literature by his disciples. Like the character in Stendhal who became a noted wit on the strength of six or seven pleasantries inherited from an uncle, scores of men have won recognition as sparkling conversationalists because they have made small private collections of Mizner sayings.

Shortly before he died, a publisher asked him to write the story of his life. "It would be blowing a police whistle," replied Mizner. This was a reasonable excuse. The crime chapters would have occupied a large part of his autobiography. He was fundamentally a confidence man whom circumstances occasionally induced to go straight. But his real reason for refusing to write an autobiography was that he hated to write; he said, "Writing is too damned lonesome." He regarded it as

From *The Legendary Mizners* by Alva Johnston, pp. 64–70. Copyright, 1953, by Evelyn Johnston. Farrar, Straus and Young, N. Y.

an occupation for starvelings. Jim Tully once badgered him into writing a short story, which appeared in the *Liberty* of May 3, 1930. Mizner received a check for $1,000. He was incensed. "It took me eight hours to write it!" he exclaimed.

The short story is rather poor, although it contains a few typical Mizner lines. After a description of the long, tapering fingers of a card-sharp named Bert, Mizner added that Bert "could do more with fifty-two soda crackers than any other ocean grafter could with a new deck." The last paragraph of the story describes a tombstone erected over the grave of the hero, showing him kneeling, with hands clasped in prayer; the last line is "If you pried his hands open, four dice and a pearl neck-lace would fall out." Mizner was a little shamefaced over his literary effort. "I wanted to see something of mine in print except my thumbs," he said.

As a wit, Mizner belonged to two distinct schools—the scientific and the O. Henry. His scientific method consisted of bring a calm spirit of inquiry to bear on boiling emotion. When an excited man rushed up to him exclaiming, "Coolidge is dead," Mizner asked, "How do they know?" The O. Henry school was the school of fantastic exaggeration. During Mizner's formative years, smart conversation consisted mainly of tired hyperboles. A majority of the familiar quotations from Mizner are extravagant figures of speech. He described a thin man as "a trellis for varicose veins." He told a conceited motion-picture producer, "A demitasse cup would fit over your head like a sun bonnet." Regarding a long-nosed Hollywood magnate, he said, "He's the only man who can take a shower and smoke a cigar at the same time" and "I'd like to take him by the feet and plow a furrow with him." Telling of a Klon-dike pal who had frozen to death in the act of tying his shoelaces, he said, "We had to bury him in a drum." A strutting little fellow went through bankruptcy and then strutted more than ever. "Failure has gone to his head," said Mizner. Describing his own flight from a mad-man armed with a revolver, he said, "I got up enough lather to shave Kansas City."

A man with a flourishing head of hair once joined his table at the Brown Derby restaurant in Hollywood, uttered several solemn plati-tudes, and left. "Now I know," said Mizner, "that hair can grow on anything."

A famous stage beauty, who had risen by five marriages to wealth and a title, attempted to bandy insults with him. "You're nothing but a parlayed chambermaid," he said. "You've compromised so many gentlemen that you think you're a lady," he added.

Talking about Tom Sharkey, the great heavyweight prizefighter, who kept a saloon with the old-fashioned swinging doors, Mizner said, "He was so dumb that he crawled under them for two years before he found out that they swung both ways."

He disapproved of San Francisco at the time when Hiram Johnson was sending grafters to jail in large numbers. "They learn to say 'Guilty' here before they can say 'Papa' and 'Mama,' " he said.

He was asked by Lew Lipton, stage and screen writer, if a certain actress wasn't a little "mannish." "Mannish!" he said. "Not at all. I understand it took her all winter to color a meerschaum pipe."

Many of Mizner's lines have passed into the language. Some, like "Life's a tough proposition, and the first hundred years are the hardest," are passing out again after long and hard service. His rules "No opium-smoking in the elevators" and "Carry out your own dead," which he put into effect as manager of the Hotel Rand, in New York, in 1907, have become standard hotel practice. Among his philosophical maxims were "Be nice to people on your way up because you'll meet 'em on your way down," "Treat a whore like a lady and a lady like a whore," and "If you steal from one author, it's plagiarism; if you steal from many, it's research." H. L. Mencken, in his *New Dictionary of Quotations,* attributes to Mizner "I respect faith, but doubt is what gets you an education" and "A good listener is not only popular everywhere, but after a while he gets to know something." Mizner's comment on Hollywood, "It's a trip through a sewer in a glass-bottomed boat," was converted by Mayor Jimmy Walker into "A reformer is a guy who rides through a sewer in a glass-bottomed boat" and has since become a shopworn jewel of stump oratory. Two of Mizner's thirty-year-old lines have recently had revivals in the movies. A magistrate asked him if he was trying to show contempt of court. "No, I'm trying to conceal it," muttered Mizner. A friend argued that a certain Broadway producer "must have a head" to be so successful. "They put better heads on umbrellas," said Mizner.

"I may vomit," the smash line in *The Man Who Came to Dinner,* is a Miznerism. Mizner was seated at his regular table at the Brown Derby in Hollywood, when a young stranger introduced himself as a novelist and said he had a big idea. The trouble with Hollywood, he said, was lack of literary conversation. He asked Mizner to join him in founding a club that would meet an evening or two a week for literary conversation. "Have I offended you?" asked the author, noticing the expression on Mizner's face. "Do you want me to leave?" "No, but you might move over a little," said Mizner, adding the statement that went so big on Broadway.

Among his miscellaneous lines are "You sparkle with larceny," "He'd steal a hot stove and come back for the smoke," "You're a mouse studying to be a rat," "Another pot of coffee, waiter, and bring it under your arm to keep it warm," "I've had better steaks than this for bad behavior," and "If you [a radio chatterer] don't get off the air, I'll stop breathing it."

Mizner usually avoided slang, although he had a few special words of his own, such as "croaker" for "physician," "heart trouble" for "cowardice," and "trap" for a "bank." He disliked puns, although a play on words was worth about $10,000 to him on one occasion. It made a jury laugh and saved him from a verdict for damages. After the Florida real-estate crash, a man had sued him to recover the purchase price of a barren plot, asserting that Mizner had falsely informed him that he could grow nuts on it. "Did you tell the plaintiff that he could grow nuts on the land?" Mizner was asked. "Oh, no," he replied. "I told him he could go nuts on it." He perpetrated a sort of physical pun once when playing poker with a man whose credit was not too good. The man threw his wallet on the table and said, "I raise five hundred dollars." Mizner pulled off a shoe and threw it on the table. "If we're betting leather, I call," he said.

The earliest recorded example of Mizner wit belongs to the scientific school. He was in Nome, Alaska, in 1900. One of Mizner's close pals there was Willus Britt, who later managed Jimmy Britt, Stanley Ketchel, and other fighters. Willus was devoted to a lady known as Nellie, who was as notorious in the Arctic as Chicago May ever was in Chicago. One night, Willus ran out of the Northern Saloon and emptied his revolver at a stranger, who escaped in the darkness. Tradition, which always steals anecdotes from lesser men and pins them on the famous, erroneously states that Tex Rickard did the shooting. The best authorities, however, say it was Britt who fired at the stranger. Everybody wanted to know why he was shooting at the man. "He insulted Nellie!" shouted Britt. The shooting did not excite Mizner. The explanation did. "He *what?*" exclaimed Mizner. "He insulted Nellie," repeated Britt. "For God's sake, *how?*" inquired Mizner.

PART TWO

The Main Course

I. EVERY MAN A CANDIDATE
(Political Stuff)

Introduction

American politics during the first decades of the republic was essentially serious, and the political humor during that period was for the most part urbane and gentlemanly. But the complexion of politics changed radically as population burgeoned and overflowed into the states west of the Alleghenies and Appalachians. The election of Andrew Jackson to the Presidency in 1828 was only one evidence of the great changes that were occurring in political thinking and method. American politics now developed its truly American flavor, for the people since Jackson's time, although serious about politics, have not been serious about their politicians. The political rally became as much a picnic as a time for the serious consideration of campaign issues, and the political speaker was expected to entertain as much as to enlighten. In earlier times offices had sought the men; now men sought the offices, and, if they were to be successful, they had to give the voters what they wanted: jokes, slogans, and brass bands. Candidates "ran" for office, made "stump" speeches, bought liquor for their constituents, kissed babies, and filled the air with promises: free land in the West, forty acres and a government mule, a full dinner pail, a chicken in every pot and two cars in every garage, or thirty dollars every Thursday.

This new attitude encouraged humor in our politics. The continual demand of the voter for political favor is neatly revealed in Alben W. Barkley's story of the explanation one of his constituents gave for voting against him even though Barkley had helped the man a number of times over a period of years. In "On Oratory in Politics" Mr. Dooley indicates that political platforms and speeches are less effective than jobs and handouts in getting elected, for Smith O'Brien Dorgan, the "boy or-ator iv Healey's slough," lost to his opponent, who was "handin' out th' dough that he got fr'm the gas company an' con-ciliatin' th' masses." The spread-eagle oratory so popular during the last century is made amusing by allowing the rhetoric to run away from the idea, as Bill Nye does in his foot-in-mouth imitation of a Fourth of July oration. Nye's speaker keeps the rhetoric rolling, but he doesn't realize the significance of much that he is saying, such as "every inducement held out to accumulate more and more poverty." But votes can be won or lost by humor on the stump, particularly if one of the candidates manages, like Davy Crockett, to ridicule his opponent as superior "in the grinning line," or, like Private John Allen, to turn his opponent's remark into a boomerang.

The fun-maker has also taken delight in the attempts of lobbyists to influence pending legislation. If the lobbyist offers the legislators a hat, the law-maker may refuse the gift, or, like the politician in "The Present Taker," he may feel that a man who won't take a present "is composed of a mixture of fool, liar, and thief," and he may even give the lobbyist a card reading, "This gratuity has not influenced me one damn bit."

The Present-Taker

Another legislative humorist, whose reputation is not sufficiently exploited, represented the county of Pike in that Western State. History has not preserved his name, but his post-office address was Wolf Creek, and, very appropriately, his controversy was with the Rev. Mr. Brown, who resided in Rocky Comfort. The gentleman's remarks are self-explanatory:

"Mr. Speaker, I hope, sir, that you will let me have a few minutes' time in which to place myself square on the record. Mr. Brown has said that I have accepted a new hat from a railroad president, and has hinted, in a way to sting a sensitive man, that I have sold myself.

"I should like to know, Mr. Speaker, if there is anything in our Constitution that prevents a man from accepting a present. I say there is not, and, sir, when our Constitution arises and says that I shan't take everything that is given to me, then will I say, 'Mr. Constitution, attend to your own affairs.'

"Mr. Speaker, I am a present-taker, and as an encouragement to those who contemplate giving me something, let me say that my capacity for taking presents, although well developed, has not been over-taxed. I may also say that the man who won't take a hat, and thereby save himself the expense of buying one, is composed of a mixture of fool, liar, and thief. I'd be afraid to meet such a man away out in the woods. I would feel sure that he would knock me down and rob me. I know of an affair in my county that strongly illustrates the dishonesty of men who are afraid of taking presents:

From *Waifs of the Press.* Collected and Edited by Harry L. Work, pp. 73–74. Washington: Walter Neale, Publisher. 1898.

"A red-bearded fellow named Watson went to work for old man Clark, and made himself so useful that Clark, who well knows how to appreciate merit, went to him one day and said:

" 'Watson, I never had a man that I thought more of than I think of you.'

" 'Much obleeged to you,' replied Watson.

" 'And I have decided,' Clark continued, 'to give you my daughter, Lorena.'

" 'Much obleeged to you,' replied Watson, 'but I ain't acceptin' any presents.'

"Well, Mr. Speaker, that man was so honest that he would not accept the daughter as a present, but the next day he ran away with Clark's wife. Since then I have been extremely suspicious of men who are too high-toned to accept presents, and to keep other fair-minded men from suspecting me, I have determined to refuse nothing."

Keep Scratching My Back

. . . His [Alben W. Barkley's] story of the Ungrateful Constituent . . . has become a classic among politicians. Its moral is: never take your political support for granted.

It is the story of Farmer Jones. It opens with a long chronicle of the political favors done for Farmer Jones over the years, by County Attorney Barkley, Judge Barkley, Congressman Barkley, Senator Barkley. Back in World War I days, Barkley visited Jones in a hospital in France to console him; he interceded with Pershing to get him home sooner after the Armistice; he cut red tape to speed his disability compensation; he helped Jones get loans from the Farm Credit Administration. And so on, down to the mid-1930's, when Barkley got Jones a Disaster Loan to rebuild his farm after the floods washed it away, and an appointment for Mrs. Jones as the local postmistress.

In 1938, when Barkley had a hot fight on his hands with Happy Chandler for renomination to the Senate race in Kentucky, he was thunderstruck to hear that his old protégé, Farmer Jones, was supporting Chandler.

Barkley hastened around to see Jones, who admitted as how he guessed maybe he would vote for Chandler. Barkley, choking down his indignation, recited the long saga of his political labors in Jones' behalf.

"Surely," said Senator Barkley, "you remember all these things I have done for you?"

"Yeah," said Jones sullenly. "But what in hell have you done for me lately?"

From "Washington's Greatest Storyteller," by Beverly Smith, *The Saturday Evening Post,* Vol. 222 (July 2, 1949), No. 1, p. 68. Copyright, 1949, by the Curtis Publishing Company. Philadelphia.

How a Vote Is Decided

On the day that the bill opening the Cherokee Strip was passed by the House, Congressman Heard, of Missouri, who had voted for it, was leaving the Capitol, when he was met by Mrs. Hechmann, the woman who had been so diligently lobbying against the measure.

"What was done with that bill?" asked Mrs. Hechmann.

"It was passed, madam," said Mr. Heard, "by a vote of 142 to 108."

"So," said Mrs. Hechmann, spitefully, "there were 142 railroad thieves, were there?"

"And only 108 cattle thieves, madam, according to the official count," and the polite Congressman made a bow like that of a French courtier, and passed on.

The Greater Crime

A party of six Hinsdale County men started to cross the divide in early winter and were caught in a blizzard . . . Their food was exhausted after a few days and no game was obtainable because of the deep snow.

In this party was a man named Alfred Packer, a tall, wiry fellow with long black hair and an imperial beard. There also was a big, rugged Englishman named Bell and four others named Swan, Miller, Noon and Humphreys.

The next spring Packer hiked into the town of Saguache, about thirty miles south of the Arkansas River. He was fatter than usual and his pockets were filled with money which he began to distribute freely about the Saguache saloons and resorts.

The six men had been reported lost in the Hinsdale County blizzard, so the Saguache marshal questioned Packer. "What became of those men you were with last fall?" he asked . . .

"Oh, those fellows," said Packer, looking at the marshal with drooping eyes. "Four of 'em went south, but that fellow Noon, he died when he was caught in the storm."

"Where'd you get all this money you're spending?"

Packer grinned. "Made it," he said. "I been working."

That answer seemed incredible, so a posse was sent out to visit Packer's old campsite on the plateau . . . and found what was left of the five men's bodies. They had not been eaten by wild animals . . .

Feeling ran high against the broad-browed, saturnine Packer and lynching was narrowly averted. A jury found him guilty of murdering

From *Waifs of the Press*. Collected and Edited by Harry L. Work, p. 72. Washington: Walter Neale, Publisher. 1898.

From *The Arkansas*, by Clyde Brion Davis, pp. 79-81, *The Rivers of America* series. Copyright, 1940, by Clyde Brion Davis. New York: Farrar & Rinehart, Inc.

his five companions and Judge M. P. Gerry sentenced him to hang . . .

Judge Gerry had a poetic streak in his frontiersman's soul and his legendary words in sentencing Packer to death were reported as follows:

"Alfred Packer, . . . you in company with five companions passed through this beautiful mountain valley . . .

"You and your victims had a weary march and, when the shadows of the mountains fell upon your little party and night drew her sable curtain around you, your unsuspecting victims lay down on the ground and were soon lost in the sleep of the weary. And when thus sweetly unconscious of danger from any quarter, and particularly from you, their trusted companion, you cruelly and brutally slew them all.

"I shall pass lightly over the other sickening details of your crime. Enough to say, Alfred Packer, God damn your soul, you have eaten up the Democratic majority in Hinsdale County."

Politics Conquers All

In the campaign of 1900, [Lieutenant Governor Bill] Thorne told the following story in a political speech:

It was just after W. O. Bradley was elected Governor of Kentucky, and the Republicans in my county were holding a big ratification meeting. Brass bands, all kinds of floats and banners, and hundreds of men, women and boys paraded the streets. A young girl claimed that while standing on her front porch, which was almost covered with vines and foliage of different kinds, she was repeatedly hugged and kissed by a young man she hardly knew. A warrant was sworn out for her assailant. He was arrested and it was my duty as Commonwealth's Attorney to prosecute him. John D. Carroll, now Judge of the Kentucky Court of Appeals, had been employed to defend him. I soon finished my examination of the witness and turned her over to Carroll for cross examination.

"What night was this?" thundered Carroll.

"Thursday night," answered the witness.

"Thursday night, you say? What time of night?"

"About eight o'clock."

"That was about the time the parade was passing your house?"

"Yes."

"Did you ever cry out or scream?"

"No, sir, I did not."

"Will you tell this jury," asked Carroll with rising voice, "with the streets thronged with people, and this man hugging and kissing you against your will, as you claim, why you never uttered a single cry for help or assistance?"

From *Stories and Speeches of William O. Bradley,* with Biographical Sketch by M. H. Thatcher, pp. 17–18. Copyright, 1916, by Transylvania Printing Co. Lexington, Kentucky.

"Yes, sir. I will tell the jury, and everybody else, that you'll never ketch me hollerin' at no Republican gatherin'."

What the Governor of Massachusetts Said to the Governor of Maine

Whether they drink or not, most Americans know that the Governor of North Carolina once remarked to the Governor of South Carolina, "It's a long time between drinks." But the circumstances under which that remark was first made are unknown. An early version of the origin occurs in *Puck* on March 5, 1879:

> But we are reminded that once the Governor of North Carolina, after feasting the Governor of South Carolina; and having been told by the Governor of S.C. that the same would be reciprocated, telegraphed: "It's a long time between drinks."

The phrase must have been widely known even in 1879; otherwise *Puck* could not have published the following on June 4:

> *Q.* What did the Governor of Massachusetts say to the Governor of Maine? *Ans.* There's too much drinking between times.

A Wee Bit Wrong

Representative Williams, of Mississippi, commenting on Mr. Dingley's statement as to the conditions of the Government's finances at the opening of the second session of the Fifty-fifth Congress, said the statement reminded him of a story of a man who after presenting an account to another, asked:

"Isn't the account right?"

"Yes; except in two particulars. The figures on the debit side are not right; and figures on the credit side are all wrong."

Hoss Allen's Apology; or, The Candidate's Night in a Mosquito Swamp

"Well, old fellow, you're a *hoss!*" is a western expression, which has grown into a truism as regards Judge Allen, and a finer specimen of a

---

Rewritten from "It's a Long Time Between Drinks," by James N. Tidwell; in *Western Folklore,* XI (1952), 218–219.

From *Waifs of the Press.* Collected and Edited by Harry L. Work, p. 199. Washington. Walter Neale, Publisher. 1898.

From *Streaks of Squatter Life, and Far-West Scenes,* by John S. Robb, pp. 70–83. Copyright, 1843, by Carey & Hart, Philadelphia. Republished, 1858, by T. B. Peterson and Brothers, Philadelphia, as a part of *The Swamp Doctor's Adventures in the South-West,* by "Madison Tensas," M.D., and "Solitaire" (John S. Robb of St. Louis, Mo.).

western judge, to use his constituents' language, "aint no whar," for, besides being a sound jurist, he is a great wag, and the best practical joker within the circuit of six states. Among the wolf-scalp hunters of the western border of Missouri, Judge, or, as they more familiarly style him, *Hoss* Allen is all *powerful* popular, and the "bar" hunters of the southern section equally admire his free and easy manners—they consider him one of the people—none of your stuck-up imported chaps from the dandy states, but a real genuine westerner—in short, a *hoss!* Some of the Judge's admirers prevailed upon him, recently, to stand a canvass for the gubernatorial chair, in which he had Judge Edwards for an antagonist, and many are the rich jokes told of their political encounters. A marked difference characterizes the two men, and more striking opposites in disposition and demeanor would be hard to find, Edwards being slow, dignified, and methodical, while *Hoss* tosses dignity to the winds, and comes right down to a free and easy familiarity with the "boys." Hoss Allen counted strong on the border counties, while his antagonist built his hopes on the centre.

Allen and Edwards had travelled together for a number of days, explaining their separate views upon state government, at each regular place of appointment, and were now nearing the southern part of the state, a section where *Hoss* had filled the judgeship with great unction. Here he resolved to spring a joke upon his antagonist, which would set the south laughing at him, and most effectually insure his defeat among the *bar* hunters. He had been maturing a plan, as they journeyed together, and now having stopped for the night about one day's journey from the town of Benton, one of their places of appointment, and the head quarters of the most influential men of the *bar* section, Hoss proceeded to put his trick in progress of execution. He held a secret conference, at the stable, with the boy who took his horse, and offered him a dollar to take a message that night to Tom Walters, at the forks leading to Benton. The boy agreed, and Hoss penciled a note describing his antagonist, who was unknown in the south of the state, coupled with an earnest request, that he "would keep a look out for Judge Eddards, and by all means be careful not to let him get into that cussed *cedar swamp!*" His express was faithful, and in due time Tom received the missive. In the meantime, the victim, Edwards, in a sweet state of confidence, was unbending his dignity at hearing Hoss relate to their host his amusing yarns about the early settlers. Having talked all the household into a merry mood, he proposed turning in for the night, but first offered his service to unlace the girls' corsets, and in an underbreath asked the old woman to *elope* with him in the morning— Edwards blushed at this, the girls tittered, and the host and his wife said, he was a "raal *hoss!*"—Allen acknowledged he was a leetle inclined that way, and as he had had his *feed*, he now wanted his *straw*.

In the morning Hoss Allen became "dreadful poorly," and it was with great difficulty he could be prevailed upon to get up. All were sympathising with his affliction, and the matron of the house boiled him some hot "sass-tea," which, the old man said, relieved him mightily. Judge Edwards assured Hoss, that it would be necessary for him to lay up for a day or two, and the afflicted candidate signified the same, himself. Before they parted Hoss requested Edwards, as he had the whole field to himself, not to be too *hard* upon him. His antagonist promised to spare him, but chuckled all the while at having a clear field in Allen's most popular district. Shaking the old *Hoss* by the hand, as they were about to separate, he remarked—"we will meet at Benton, I hope, in different trim, Friend Allen." They *did* meet in different *trim*, but Edwards little dreamed the particular kind of trim *he* would appear in. As soon as Judge Edwards was fairly started, it was surprising the rapid change which took place in his antagonist—Hoss' eye lit up, a broad grin spread over his features, and pulling off the handkerchief, which was tied around his head, he twirled it above him like a flag, then stuffed it in his pocket, remarking coolly, at the same time,—"well, that thar swamp, jest at this season, is *awful!*" His express reported himself after his night ride, assured Allen that all was O. K., and received his dollar for delivering the message, upon receiving which intelligence, Allen seated himself quietly and comfortably at his coffee, and imbibed it with a relish that drove the idea of sickness into a hopeless decline.

Judge Edwards rapidly progressed on his way, highly gratified at having his opponent off in this part of the field, and as he, in this happy mood, journeyed onwards he set his brain to work conning a most powerful speech, one that would knock the sand from under Hoss, and leave him in a state of sprawling defeat. He resolved to sweep the south, from that point, like a prairie fire. About noon, or perhaps an hour after, he arrived at Tom Walters' for dinner, and while it was preparing, inquired how far he was from Benton?

"I've an idea," said Tom, "you're well onto nine miles frum thar—jest an easy arternoon ride."

This was highly satisfactory to the Judge, and perceiving that the provender preparing was of a like pleasing character, he spread himself back upon a hickory bottomed chair with a kind of easy dignity, at once comfortable to himself, and edifying to his host.

"Stranger," inquired Tom, "did you *scare* up anythin' like the two candidates, Jedge Eddards and old Hoss Allen, on your way down *yeur?*"

"I did see something of them, my friend," answered the Judge, and then, as if making up his mind to surprise Tom, and give him a striking example of democratic condescension, he inquired, "would you know either of the gentlemen, if they stood before you?"

"Why, as to old Hoss," said Tom, "I don't know anybody else, but this new Jedge I ain't never seed, and ef he is the slicked up finefied sort of a character they pictur' him, I don't *want* to see him—It's my opinion, these squirtish kind a fellars ain't perticular hard baked, and they allers goes in fur *aristocracy* notions."

The Judge had no idea that Tom was smoking him, and he congratulated himself that an opportunity here presented itself, where he could remove a wrong impression personally; so, loftily viewing this southern constituent, he remarked:

"You have heard a calumny, my friend, for *Judge* Edwards now sits before you, and you can see whether his appearance denotes such a person as you describe."

"No!" shouted Tom, with mock surprise, "you ain't comin' a hoax over a fellar?—you raally are the sure enough Jedge?"

"I am really the Judge, my friend," responded his honor, highly elevated with Tom's astonishment.

"Then gin us your paw," shouted Tom, "you're jest the lookin' fellar kin sweep these yeur diggins like a catamount! What in the yearth did you do with old Hoss on the road? I heerd he was a comin' along with you. He ain't gin out, has he?"

The Judge replied, with a smile which expressed disparagement of Hoss Allen's powers of endurance, that he was forced to lie up on the route, from fatigue. Dinner being announced as ready the Judge and Tom seated themselves, and the latter highly expanded his guest's prospects in the district, assuring him that he could lick Hoss "powerful easy, ef he wasn't broken winded." The meal being ended, the Judge demanded his horse, and inquired of his host the direct road to Benton, which Tom thus mapped out:—

"Arter you pass the big walnut, about two miles from yeur, keep *it* a mile on your left, and take the right trail fur about six hundred yards, when you'll cum to the 'saplin acre,' thar you keep to the right agin, and when that trail fotches you up, why right *over from thar* lies Benton."

This was a very clear direction to one who had never before travelled the road, but the Judge, trusting to luck, said, "he thought he would be able to get there without much difficulty," and started off, leaving his late entertainer gazing after him.

"Well, I allow you *will*, Jedge," chuckled Tom,—"You'll git inter that *swamp*, jest as sure as shootin', and you'll hev the biggest and hungryest audience of mosquitors, ever a candidate preached law or larnin' to!" To secure his finding the swamp road, he had stationed his boy *Jim* near the turn off, to make the matter sure.

In the course of a couple of hours along came Hoss Allen, who, as soon as Tom took hold of his bridle, winked his eye at him while he inquired:—

"Did Jedge Eddards come along, Tom?"

"Well, he *did*, Hoss, oncommon extensive in his political feelin's."

"And you didn't let the Jedge stray away from the swamp road?" inquired Hoss.

"Well, I predicate I didn't, fur by this time he's travellin' into the diggins most amazin' innocently," and then the pair enjoyed a regular guffaw!

"He's safe as a skin'd *bar*, then, Tom, and I'll spread his hide afore the Benton boys to-morrow—jest let them into the joke, and I allow, after that, his dandified *a*ristocracy speeches won't have much effect in this section."

"Go it, Jedge," shouted Tom, "ef I ain't thar to hear it, it'll be 'cause the breath'll leave me afore then—gin him goss without sweeten'—rumple his har, but don't spile the varmint!"

After Hoss had stayed his stomach with a cold bite, he bade Tom good-day, and started for Benton, highly tickled with the success of his trick. As he neared the "saplin acre," he met *Jim*, who exhibited a full spread of his ivories, when Hoss inquired which road he had directed the gentleman before him?

"He gone into de swamp road, massa, but what de debil he want dar, 'cept he arter coon skins, dis niggah doesn't hab no idear, whatsomedeber."

Allen passed on, assured that all was right, and as his horse leisurely ambled forward, he broke into singing a verse of a western ditty, which says:—

> "Thar ain't throughout this western nation,
> Another like old Hick*ory*
> He was born jest fur his siteation—
> A bold leader of the free."

As night spread her curtain over this wild district, Hoss neared Benton, and as his nag jogged up the principal street, he broke out into a louder strain, repeating the above verse, on hearing which, the "boys," who were expecting him and Edwards, turned out, and old Hoss was received with a cheer.

"Hello, Jedge!—How are you, Old Hoss?—Give us your paw, Governor!—Here at last, Squire!"—and sundry such expressions of familiar welcome was showered on Allen, by the crowd. "Come in, and git a drink, old fellar," shouted one of the crowd, and forthwith all hands pushed for the hotel bar room, where sweetened corn juice was pushed about with vast liberality—at the *candidate's* expense, of course.

"Whar did you leave the new fellar, Jedge Eddards?" was the general inquiry.

"Why, boys, I stopped to rest on the road, and he slid off to git ahead of me—I heered on him at the forks, and expected he was here. It's my opinion, boys, he's seen a *bar* on the road, and bein' too delicate to make the varmint clar the path, he's taken a long circuit round him!"

This raised a laugh among the crowd, and it was followed up by general inquiries as to what Edwards looked like, but to these Hoss shook his head, remarking, as he raised his hands expressive of how they would be astonished—"jest wait tell you see him yourselves, boys, and then you'll be satisfied."

Let us return to Judge Edwards, who had easily found his way past the "saplin acre," and by the aid of Jim's direction progressed into the swamp road, as easy as if it were his destination. Having travelled, as he thought, about ten miles, he began to look out for Benton, and every now and then uttered an expression of surprise, that they had located the town in such a swampy country—every rod he progressed became more and more obscure, the brush more thick and wild in growth, and the ground more moist and yielding. Night, too, that season for the rendezvous of underbrush and tangle-wood horrors, was fast gathering its forces in the depths of the forest, and beneath the shadows of the thick bushes, shrouding, as with a dark mist, each object on the earth's surface, creeping up the trunks of the old trees, and noiselessly stealing away the light in which they had proudly spread their green foliage, while in lieu of their showy garb he clad them in a temporary mourning. The song of the birds became hushed, while the cry of the startled *wolf* was borne upon the breeze to the ear of the affrighted traveller, interrupted occasionally by the sharp *m-e-o-w!* of the wildcat, making together a vocal concert most unharmonious to the ear of the bewildered candidate. To sum up these horrors a myriad of *mosquitoes*, as musical as hunger and vigorous constitutions could make them, hummed and fi-z-z-zed around him, darting in their stings and darting away from his annoyed blows, with a pertinacity and perseverance only known to the Missouri tribe of insects.

Poor Edwards!—he was fairly in for it—into a swamp at that!—Night was fast making all roads alike obscure, and with amazing rapidity covering our traveller in a mantle of uncertainty. The possibility of his escape that night first became improbable, and then impossible. He hallooed at the highest pitch of his voice, but the wolf was the only live varmint that answered his cry, and a strange fear began to creep over his heart. He remembered well reading accounts of where hungry droves of these animals had eaten the horse from under the saddle, the rider upon it, bones, hide, *har* and all, leaving scarce a vestige of the victims to mark the deed, and his hair grew uneasy on his cranium at the bare thought of such an unpolitical termination to his canvass. At this particular moment a *yell*, as of a thousand devils in his immediate neighbourhood, set his heart knocking against his ribs in a fearful manner. When he partially recovered from the shock he tied his horse to one tree and quickly mounted another—whispering the hope to his heart, at the same time, that a meal on his horse would satisfy the gathering crowd of varmints, who were shouting their death song below him. Having seated himself astride a limb, the mosquitoes had a fair chance at him, and they put the Judge through as active an exercise as ever was inflicted on a recruit—there was this difference, however, between him and a recruit, *they* are generally *raw* at the commencement of a drill, but poor Edwards was most *raw* at the end of his lesson. Every new yell of the swamp pre-emptioners made him climb a limb higher, and each progression upwards appeared to introduce him to a fresh and hungrier company of mosquitoes—the trees in the swamp were like the dwellings in Paris, their *highest* tenants were the most needy. Day at length broke, and our harassed candidate, almost exhausted, clambered from his exalted position. His frightened but unscathed steed uttered a neigh of welcome as he bestrode him, and giving loose to the rein he committed his escape to the animal's sagacity, while he aided his efforts by a devout supplication. Accident favored the horse's footsteps, for striking the trail leading to the road he started off into a trot, and soon broke his rider's spell of terror, by turning into the main avenue leading to Benton. Edwards slowly passed his pimpled hand over his worse pimpled face, sadly remarking:—

"Last night's '*bills*' all passed, for I bear their stinging *signatures* all over my countenance."

When ten o'clock came, on the day following Judge Allen's arrival at Benton, the town swarmed with the southern constituency of Missouri, and as soon as the tavern bell, which had been put in requisition to announce the candidate's readiness, had ceased its clamor, Hoss mounted the balcony of the hotel, and rolling up his sleeves "spread himself" for an unusually brilliant effort.

"Boys!" shouted he, "I want your attention to matters of vital import —of oncommon moment, and replete with a nation's wel*far*." [Here looking down into the crowd at Sam Wilson, who was talking as loud as he could bellow, about an imported heifer he had just bought, Hoss called his attention:] "Sam," said he, "you'd better bring that heifer of your'n up here to address the meetin', and I'll wait till the animal gits through!" This raised a laugh on Sam, and Hoss proceeded. After dilating at some length on the *imported* candidate who was his antagonist, he "*let himself out*," on some of the measures he advocated, and particularly dwelt on the fact that he went in for creating a license law on hunting varmints!

"Would you have the least mite of an idea, boys," said Hoss, "that this creatur' of a faction wants to have every man's rifle stamped with the state arms, and then made pay a license to the state before he can git a bonus for wolf scalps." [At this moment a shrill voice interrupted him again—a girl belonging to the hotel was shouting to a couple of youngsters, who had been despatched to the barn for eggs, to "quit *suckin'* them thar eggs or the candidates would stand a mighty small chance fur thur dinner."] "Jest tell that gall," said Hoss, "to suck my share and stop her screamin'." He again continued: "I want to know what in yearth this Mississippi country's comin' too, when sich fellars finds favor with the people—what do you think of him boys?"

"Why, *cuss his pictur!*" was the general response from the *bar* hunters.

While Hoss was thus arousing public indignation against his antagonist, a stranger entered the crowd, and after listening a moment to the
speaker's imaginary flights he interrupted him by shouting:—

"I deny your assertions, Judge Allen!"

This was a bomb shell, and the crowd cleared a space round the
stranger, in expectation of a fight; but Allen after surveying the stranger, in whom he recognized his antagonist Edwards, coolly inquired
why *he* disputed it?

"What, *me!*" shouted Edwards, "who can better declare your assertions false than the man you are misrepresenting—you know very well
that *I* am that Judge Edwards!"

Hoss Allen turned calmly round to the crowd and said:—"Boys, you
know I never git angry at a man insane or in liquor, and as I don't
know this fellar, and never seed him afore in my life, it's the best proof
that he ain't Jedge Eddards, so you'll oblige me by taking him off the
ground and keeping him from disturbing the meeting."

Expostulation was useless—without any ceremony he was carried into
the hotel, boiling with indignation. There, however, he had to stay, at
a convenient distance to hear that Allen was giving him "*particular
jesse.*"

After the meeting adjourned three cheers were given for Hoss Allen,
and all parties gathered into the bar to take a little *fluid,* and discuss
the speech. Edwards having now been relieved from durance, started
for Hoss;—burning inside with choler and smarting exteriorly from
mosquito-bites,—he looked *bitter.*

"Do you say you don't know me, Judge Allen?" inquired he.

Hoss looked steadily at him, then coolly taking out his spectacles, he
wiped the glasses, adjusted them upon his nose, and surveyed the questioner from head to foot, he then remarked:

"Thar is somethin' about your voice, and the clothes you ware, that
I ought to know—Jedge Eddards wore a coat and kerseys exactly like
your'n, but I'll swar he had a better lookin' face than you carry when
we parted yesterday mornin'. If you are him you're been the wust used
candidate I've seed in an age."

"Yes," responded Edwards, "thanks to that d—n weasel that sent me
into the swamp. I tell you sir that I have passed a night to which the
infernal regions are a scant pattern, and between mosquitoes, wolves,
and wild-cats I should not be surprised if my hair had turned grey."

"I begin to *re*-cognise you, now, Jedge," said Hoss, in a sympathetic
tone, "and no wonder I didn't know you at first sight—your head is
swelled as big as a *pumkin!* I'll do the clean thing, Jedge," said Hoss,
starting for the balcony, I'll apologise afore the boys, publicly, for not
knowin' you."

"No, no!" shouted Edwards, who knew his apology would only place
his night's adventure in a more ridiculous light, "I don't demand any

apology." But he was too late, Hoss had already called the attention of the crowd.

"Boys," said he, "as an honourable man who finds himself in the wrong, I am bound to apologise, publicly, to my friend Jedge Eddards, —the Jedge is a leetle changed in appearance since we wur last together, and I did not *re*-cognise him; I, tharfore, ask his pardon fur orderin' him off the ground."

"I grant it!" shouted Edwards, glad here to wind up the apology, then turning round he added, "come boys, let us drink good friends."

"Wait a minit, boys," said Hoss, "the Jedge and I havin' smoothed that little marter over, I jest want to tell you why I didn't know him at fust sight. You all know that the mosquitoes in cedar swamp are an *oreful* hungry breed, and when they git a passenger they present him with numerous 'relief bills;' well I had gained considerable popularity in that swamp, by presentin' their condition before the legislatur' and askin' for relief for the distressed inhabitants,—the Jedge, to head me down thar, passed all last night on a limb of one of the trees makin' stump speeches to the varmints, and you can see by his countenance that expectin' to be elected he has accepted all their *mosquito bills!*"

One tremendous shout rent the air, followed by bursts of laughter, from which Edwards retreated into the hotel. We have but to add that Hoss carried the *Bar* counties "as easy as rolling off a log!" His antagonist in vain tried to stem the tide of fun,—when he essayed to speak a *m-e-o-w* of a wild-cat or the *hum* of a mosquito imitated by some of his audience would be sure to set the rest *sniggering*, and spoil his effort.

The Voice of the People

I.

Back and forth strode the campaign orator,
back and forth till an Irishman shouted:
"If you're talkin' stop walkin'!
If you're walkin' stop talkin'!"

II.

The classical orator from Massachusetts had pronounced the words "Vox Populi" five times in an Indianapolis speech when one Hoosier Congressman bet another he didn't know what Vox Populi meant. The money was put up and the winner of the bet freely translated Vox Populi to mean "My God, my God, why hast Thou forsaken me?"

From *The People, Yes*, by Carl Sandburg, p. 145. Copyright, 1936, by Harcourt, Brace and Company, Inc. New York.

In the Grinning Line

That Colonel Crockett could avail himself, in electioneering, of the advantages which well applied satire ensures, the following anecdote will sufficiently prove:

In the canvass of the Congressional election of 18–, Mr. ***** was the Colonel's opponent—a gentleman of the most pleasing and conciliating manners—who seldom addressed a person or a company without wearing upon his countenance a peculiarly good humoured smile. The Colonel, to counteract the influence of this winning attribute, thus alluded to it in a stump speech:

"Yes, gentlemen, he may get some votes by *grinning*, for he can *outgrin me*—and you know I ain't slow—and to prove to you that I am not, I will tell you an anecdote. I was concerned myself—and I was fooled a little of the wickedest. You all know I love hunting. Well, I discovered a long time ago that a 'coon couldn't stand my grin. I could bring one tumbling down from the highest tree. I never wasted powder and lead, when I wanted one of the creatures. Well, as I was walking out one night, a few hundred yards from my house, looking carelessly about me, I saw a 'coon planted upon one of the highest limbs of an old tree. The night was very *moony* and clear, and old Ratler was with me; but Ratler won't bark at a 'coon—he's a queer dog in that way. So, I thought I'd bring the lark down in the usual way, *by a grin*. I set myself—and, after grinning at the 'coon a reasonable time, found that he didn't come down. I wondered what was the reason—and I took another steady grin at him. Still he was *there*. It made me a little mad; so I felt round and got an old limb about five feet long, and, planting one end upon the ground, I placed my chin upon the other, and took *a rest*. I then grinned my best for about five minutes; but the cursed 'coon hung on. So, finding I could not bring him down by grinning, I determined to have him—for I thought he must be a droll chap. I went over to the house, got my axe, returned to the tree, saw the 'coon still there, and began to cut away. Down it come, and I ran forward; but d–n the 'coon was there to be seen. I found that what I had taken for one, was a large knot upon the branch of the tree and, upon looking at it closely, I saw that *I had grinned all the bark off, and left the knot perfectly smooth*.

"Now, fellow-citizens," continued the Colonel, "you must be convinced that, in the *grinning line*, I myself am not slow—yet, when I look upon my opponent's countenance, I must admit that he is my superior. You must all admit it. Therefore, be wide awake—look sharp—and do not let him grin you out of your votes."

From *Sketches and Eccentricities of Col. David Crockett, of Western Tennessee.* New York: J. J. Harper. 1833.

"Jist to Git to Holler"

"A constituent of mine from Clearfield County, a newspaper man, spent a few days in Washington during the special session of the Fifty-fifth Congress," said the Hon. W. C. Arnold, of the Twenty-eighth Pennsylvania District. "He occupied a seat in the Visitors' Gallery at each session while here, and one evening he asked me what I thought was Jerry Simpson's idea in, as he expressed it, 'putting in his oar every day when he knew the Speaker would sit on him?'

"I told him that I believed it was a pretty hard matter to fathom any of Jerry's ideas, but that his question reminded me of a story about a newsboy in Pittsburgh, who was interviewed by a benevolent old gentleman as follows:

" 'Where do you get your papers?'

" 'I buys 'em of Jem O'Neil.'

" 'And who is Jem O'Neil?'

" 'He's de big guy in de Dispatch office.'

" 'What do you pay for them?'

" 'Nickel.'

" 'What do you sell them for?'

" 'Nickel.'

" 'You don't make anything at that.'

" 'Nope.'

" 'Then why do you buy them?'

" 'Oh, jist to git to holler.' "

Mr. Dooley on Oratory in Politics

"I mind th' first time Willum J. O'Brien r-run f'r office, th' Raypublicans an' th' Indypindants an' th' Socialists an' th' Prohybitionist (he's dead now, his name was Larkin) nommynated a young man be th' name iv Dorgan that was in th' law business in Halsted Sthreet, near Cologne, to r-run again' him. Smith O'Brien Dorgan was his name, an' he was wan iv th' most iloquint young la-ads that iver made a speakin' thrumpet iv his face. He cud holler like th' impire iv a base-ball game; an', whin he delivered th' sintimints iv his hear-rt, ye'd think he was thryin' to confide thim to a man on top iv a high buildin'. He was prisidint iv th' lithry club at th' church; an' Father Kelly tol' me that, th' day afther he won th' debate on th' pen an' th' soord in favor iv th' pen, they had

From *Waifs of the Press*. Collected and Edited by Harry L. Work, p. 109. Washington: Walter Neale, Publisher. 1898.

From *Mr. Dooley in Peace and in War*, by [Finley Peter Dunne], pp. 218–222. Copyright, 1898, by the *Chicago Journal*; 1898, by Small, Maynard & Company.

to hire a carpenter to mend th' windows, they'd sagged so. They called him th' boy or-rator iv Healey's slough.

"He planned th' campaign himsilf. 'I'll not re-sort,' says he, 'to th' ordin'ry methods,' he says. 'Th' thing to do,' he says, 'is to prisint th' issues iv th' day to th' voters,' he says. 'I'll burn up ivry precin't in th' ward with me iloquince,' he says. An' he bought a long black coat, an' wint out to spread th' light.

"He talked ivrywhere. Th' people jammed Finucane's Hall, an' he tol' thim th' time had come f'r th' masses to r-rise. 'Raymimber,' says he, 'th' idees iv Novimb'r,' he says. 'Raymimber Demosthens an' Cicero an' Oak Park,' he says. 'Raymimber th' thraditions iv ye'er fathers, iv Washin'ton an' Jefferson an' Andhrew Jackson an' John L. Sullivan,' he says. 'Ye shall not, Billy O'Brien,' he says, 'crucify th' voters iv th' Sixth Ward on th' double cross,' he says. He spoke to a meetin' in Deerin' Sthreet in th' same wuruds. He had th' sthreet-car stopped while he coughed up reemarks about th' Constitution until th' bar-rn boss sint down an' threatened to discharge Mike Dwyer that was dhrivin' wan hundherd an' eight in thim days, though thransferred to Wint-worth Avnoo later on. He made speeches to polismin in th' squadroom an' to good la-ads hoistin' mud out iv th' dhraw at th' red bridge. People'd be settin' quite in th' back room playin' forty-fives whin Smith O'Brien Dorgan'd burst in, an' addhress thim on th' issues iv th' day.

"Now all this time Bill O'Brien was campaignin' in his own way. He niver med wan speech. No wan knew whether he was f'r a tariff or again wan, or whether he sthud be Jefferson or was knockin' him, or whether he had th' inthrests iv th' toilin' masses at hear-rt or whether he wint to mass at all, at all. But he got th' superintindint iv th' rollin'-mills with him; an' he put three or four good faml'ies to wurruk in th' gas-house, where he knew th' main guy, an' he made reg'lar calls on th' bar-rn boss iv th' sthreet-ca-ars. He wint to th' picnics, an' hired th' or-chesthry f'r th' dances, an' voted himsilf th' most pop'lar man at th' church fair at an expinse iv at laste five hundherd dollars. No wan that come near him wanted f'r money. He had headquarthers in ivry saloon fr'm wan end iv th' ward to th' other. All th' pa-apers printed his pitcher, an' sthud by him as th' frind iv th' poor.

"Well, people liked to hear Dorgan at first, but afther a few months they got onaisy. He had a way iv breakin' into festive gatherin's that was enough to thry a saint. He delayed wan prize fight two hours, en-couragin' th' voters prisint to stand be their principles, while th' prin-ciples sat shiverin' in their cor-rners until th' polis r-run him out. It got so that men'd bound into alleys whin he come up th' sthreet. People in th' liquor business rayfused to let him come into their places. His fam'ly et in th' coal-shed f'r fear iv his speeches at supper. He wint on talkin', and Willum J. O'Brien wint on handin' out th' dough that he got fr'm th' gas company an' con-ciliatin' th' masses; an', whin iliction day come, th' judges an' clerks waş all f'r O'Brien, an' Dorgan didn't get votes enough to wad a gun. He sat up near all night in his long coat, makin' speeches to himsilf; but tord mornin' he come over to my place where O'Brien sat with his la-ads. 'Well,' says O'Brien, 'how does it suit ye?' he says. 'It's sthrange,' says Dorgan. 'Not sthrange at all,' says Willum J. O'Brien. 'Whin ye've been in politics as long as I have, ye'll know,' he says, 'that th' roly-boly is th' gr-reatest or-rator on earth,' he says. 'Th' American nation in th' Sixth Ward is a fine people,' he says. 'They love th' eagle,' he says, 'on th' back iv a dollar,' he says. 'Well,' says Dorgan, 'I can't undherstand it,' he says. 'I med as manny as three thousan' speeches,' he says. 'Well,' says Willum J. O'Brien, 'that was my majority,' he says. 'Have a dhrink,' he says."

An Oration with Bones in It

. . . After a pleasant and courteous prayer by Rev. Mr. Meeks, in which he laid before the Lord a national policy which he felt certain would make a great hit, our Glee Club sang

Oh, say can you see, etc.

Judge Larraby read the Declaration of Independence in a rich dark red voice, and a self-made man from Hickory township delivered the following impromptu address, the manuscript of which he kindly furnished to the *Record-Statesman:*

"Fellow Citizens: This is the anniversary of the day when freedom towards all and malice towards none first got a foothold in this country. And we are now to celebrate that day. I say that on that day Tireny and uzurpation got a set-back that they will never recover from. We then paved the way for the poor, oppressed foreigner, so that he could come to our shores and take liberties with our form of government. To be a foreigner here in America to-day is one of the sweetest boons. If I could be just what I would like to be, I would be an oppressed foreigner, landing on our shores, free from the taxation and responsibility of government, with no social demands made on me, with nothing in my possession but a hearty Godspeed from both political parties, and a strong yearning for freedom. Oh, why was I not born an alien, that both parties wouldn't dast to reproach; an alien that can come here and find a government already established, with no flies on to it; a government of the people, by the people and for the people? (Firecrackers and applause.)

"On the day that Button Gwinnett put his name to the statement that all men was created more or less equal, the spot on which we now stand was a howling wilderness. Where yonder lemonade-stand now

From "How the Glorious Fourth was Celebrated at Whalen's Grove Last Year," by Bill Nye [Edgar Wilson Nye], from *Bill Nye's Chestnuts, Old and New, Latest Gathering,* pp. 22–29. New York: John W. Lovell Company, n.d. [1896?].

stands and realizes a clean profit of forty-seven dollars and thirty-five cents on an investment of six dollars and fifty cents, the rank thistle nodded in the wynd, and the wild fox dag his hole unscared. If you do not believe this I refer you to the principal of our public school, who is to-day assisting in the band, and who is now in the act of up-ending his alto horn to pour out about a teacupful of liquid melody that he had left over from the last tune.

"And why is this? Why are we to-day a free people, with a surplus in the treasury that nobody can get at? (Loud applause and squeal from a grass-fed horse tied to a tree who is being kicked by a red two-year-old, owned by the Pathmaster of Road District No. 3.)

"Why are our resources so great that they almost equal our liabilities? Why is everything done to make it pleasant for the rich man and every inducement held out for the poor man to accumulate more and more poverty? Why is it that so much is said about the tariff by men who do not support their families? Why is it that when we vote for a president of the United States, we have to take our choice between a statesman-like candidate with great ability and proclivities for grand larceny—why is it that we are given our choice between this kind of a man and what Virgil refers to in his 'Childe Harold' as a chump? (Cheers and cries of 'That's so' from a man who is riveted to the spot by means of a new pitch-plank on which he is sitting and which will not permit him to move out of the sun.)

"One hundred years ago the tastes of our people were simple. Now it takes so much simplicity to keep Congress going that the people don't get a chance at it. A century ago common, home-made rum was the only relaxation known to a plain but abstemious people. Now it takes a man with a mighty good memory to recall the names of some of the things he has drunk when his wife asks him about it on the following morning. I claim to have a good memory of names and things generally, but if you want to get me mixed up and have fun with me, you can do it that way.

"But, fellow-citizens, how can we best preserve the blessing of freedom and fork it over unimpaired to our children? How can we enhance the blood-bought right, which is inherent in every human being, of the people, for the people and by the people, where tyrant foot hath never trod nor bigot forged a chain, for to look back from our country's glorious natal day or forward to a glorious, a happy and a prosperous future with regard to purity of the ballot and free speech. I say for one we cannot do otherwise. (Prolonged applause.)

"I would rather have my right hand cleave to the roof of my mouth than to utter a sentiment that I would regret; but I say that as a people, as a nation or as an inalienable right which no man can gainsay or successfully controvert, not for political purposes, and yet I am often led to inquire whither are we drifting, not only as a people and as a nation, but as a country and as a joint school district, No. 6, where we now stand, and when we are paying a school teacher this summer twenty-two dollars a month to teach the children, little prattling children, during the hot summer weather, how many feet of intestines there are in the human body and what is best to do for it? Last winter we paid thirty-four dollars per month to a man who opened the school with prayer and then made a picture of the digestive organs on the blackboard. And still we wonder that politics is corrupt.

"I tell you that the seeds of vice and wickedness is often sowed at school in the minds of the young by teachers who are paid a large salary to do far different. What do you think of a man who would open a school with prayer and then converse freely about the alimentary canal? Such a man would lead a life of the deepest infamy if he had the least encouragement.

"So I say, fellow-citizens, that we must guard against the influences of the public schools as a nation, for the people, of the people, and by the people. Education is often a blessing in disguise, but we should not pry into things that the finite mind has no business with. How much was Galileo ahead in the long run for going out of his sphere? He was boycotted from morning till night and died poor. Look at Demosthenes. Look at Diogenes. They pried into science, and both of them was poor providers and have since died. Of course their names are frequently used in debating schools, and some claim that this is big pay for what they went through; but I say give me a high-stepping horse, the bright smile of dear ones who are not related to me in any way, the approval of the admiring throng, a large woolly dog that will do as I tell him, a modest little home and unlimited credit at the store, and I do not care how much B. will have to use off from the diameter of a given grindstone, for which he paid an undivided one-fifteenth.

"I know that this is regarded as a queer doctrine by what is called our more Advanced Thinkers, but I say let every man who pants for fame select his own style of pant and go ahead. I bid him a most hearty godspeed and hope he will do well.

"But what makes me mad is for a man to come to me and dictate what I shall pant for. This is called intolerance by people who can afford to use words of that size. Intolerance is a thing that makes me tired. Whether it's religious, political or social intolerance, I dislike it very much. People that think I will enjoy voting for a yaller dog that had been picked out for me, or that I will be tickled to death to indorse the religious dogmas of an effete monicky with my eyes shet, don't know me. I say, let every man rely solely on his own thinker, and damned be he who first cries hold, enough! I am not a profane man, but I quote from a poem in using the above quotation.

"But again. In closing, let me say that we owe it to our common country to be peaceable citizens and pay our taxes without murmuring. The time to get in our fine work is on the valuation, and it is too late to kick after that. Let us cultivate a spirit of lofty patriotism, but believe nothing just to oblige others. I used to be a great believer in anything that was submitted for my approval. That was what kept me back. Now, if a man like Jay Gould says he is not feeling so well as he did, I make him show me his tongue.

"We are here to-day to celebrate the birthday of American freedom, as I understand it, and I am here to say that whatever may be said against our refinement and our pork, our style of freedom is sought for everywhere. It is a freedom that will stand any climate and I hear it very highly spoken of wherever I go.

"I am here to state that, as boy and man, I have been a constant user of American freedom for over fifty years, and I can truly say that I feel no desire to turn back; also that there will be a grand, free-for-all scuffle for a greased pig on the vacant lot south of the church at seven o'clock, after which fireworks will be served to those who desire to remain."

And thus did the Fourth of July pass with all its glories in Whalen's Grove in the year of our independence the 110th.

Political Plagiarism

Soon after Chief Justice Chase assumed the gubernatorial chair in Ohio, he issued his proclamation appointing a Thanksgiving Day. To make sure of being orthodox, the governor composed his proclamation almost entirely of passages from the Bible, which he did not designate as quotations, presuming that every one would recognize them, and admire the fitness of the words as well as his taste of selection. The proclamation meeting the eye of a Democratic editor, he pounced at once upon it, and declared that he had read it before—couldn't say exactly where—but he would take his oath that it was a downright plagiarism from beginning to end. That would have been a pretty fair joke; but the next day the Republican editor came out valiantly in defence of the governor, pronounced the charge libelous, and challenged any man living to produce one single line of the proclamation that had appeared in print before.

Class Will Tell

One day, during a hot political campaign, bets were laid that Gus [the livery-stable keeper] could not, as he said he could, tell a Tillmanite from an Anti-Tillmanite at sight. Presently a well-dressed stranger

From *American Wit and Humor,* Vol. I, p 9. Copyright, 1900, by George W. Jacobs & Co. Philadelphia.

From *I Came Out of the Eighteenth Century,* by John Andrew Rice, pp. 66, 93–97. Copyright, 1942, by Harper & Brothers. New York and London.

came down the street and Gus said, "He's a Anti." When the stranger reached the crowd of loafers and was asked, "Are you for Tillman?" he replied indignantly, "Certainly not," and Gus collected his dollar. Another of the same looks gave the same answer, and Gus collected another dollar. Then a broganed blue-jeaned unwashed customer came along; Gus put him down as a Tillmanite and won again. At last he grew so confident that when another man came in sight, unkempt and unshaven and dressed in a suit that had once been decent but was now spotted and caked with mud, Gus varied his question and said to him, "You're for Tillman, ain't you?" The man gave him a cur-dog look and said, "No, pardner, I ain't. The reason I look this way I bin drunk three days."

II. PREACHIN' ALL DAY AND DINNER ON THE GROUND
(The American Slant on Religion)

Introduction

Americans as a people have been religious, but they have not allowed their religion to dull their sense of humor. One might even say that the depth of their religious conviction is revealed by their readiness to laugh at the comic in religious activities. Because the pompous hypocrite, for example, is not religious as he pretends, devout church members are amused when someone exaggerates such a person's pomposity and sanctimoniousness or reveals the scamp behind the whitewashed facade. The central character of Julia Willhoit's "Cousin Freebody's Last Praying" was such a hypocrite, even though at praying he "couldn't be beat—or stopped, neither."

Ministers themselves have frequently contributed directly to American laughter, for they have often illustrated serious points with humorous anecdotes like the one about the man who saw "G.P.C." in the sky and disagreed with his wife about what it meant. The tired farmer who took his family to a camp meeting or to a Sunday of "preachin' all day and dinner on the ground" went to hear eloquent sermons, yes, but he also went to visit with his neighbors and enjoy a few laughs. If the preacher enlivened his sermon with three or four humorous anecdotes, so much the better.

Some of the religious groups of the last century had no requirement for the ministry except a "call" to preach, and often a man who farmed six days in the week delivered the sermon on the seventh.

Such a man had the advantage of being able to talk the language of the people, but his unschooled interpretations of the Scripture suggested the composing of imitation sermons which began with a text—from the Bible or otherwise—and wandered off into all sorts of comments. Two of the best of such parodies of sermons are "The Harp of a Thousand Strings" and "They Shall Gnaw a File." The educating of the ministry did not, however, eliminate the amusement at such high-flown eloquence from the pulpit as that of George Ade's preacher who "grabbed a rhetorical Roman Candle in each Hand and you couldn't see him for the Sparks." Roark Bradford's "The Projeckin' Son" is also an imitation sermon, but it is amusing principally because of its use of the rhythm of the talking blues.

So much for Sunday. During the week the American felt that God helps them who help themselves and thus could appreciate the reasoning of the preacher who felt that a man shouldn't stop in the middle of a bear fight to pray. This practical attitude of taking care of one's self in this world is tersely stated in the epitaph of Jack King: "Life Ain't in Holding a Good Hand but in Playing a Pore Hand Well."

Sinners First

When Mr. Moody was on a journey, in the western part of Massachusetts, he called on a brother in the ministry on Saturday, to spend the Sabbath with him. He offered to preach, but his friend objected on account of his congregation having got into a habit of going out before the meeting was closed. "If that is all, I must and will stop and preach for you," was Moody's reply. When Mr. Moody had opened the meeting and named his text, he looked around on the assembly and said:—"My hearers, I am going to speak to two sorts of folks to-day—saints and sinners! Sinners! I am going to give you your portion first, and would have you give good attention." When he had preached to them as long as he thought best, he paused and said, "There, sinners, I have done with you now; you may take your hats and go out of the meeting-house as soon as you please." But all tarried and heard him through.

The Brakeman at Church

One bright winter morning, the twenty-ninth day of December, Anno Domini 1879, I was journeying from Lebanon, Indiana, where I had

From *Flashes and Sparks of Wit and Humor by Our American Humorists . . .*, p. 33. New York: M. J. Ivers & Co., 1880.

"The Brakeman at Church," Chapter XV from *Chimes from a Jester's Bells . . .*, by Robert J. Burdette, pp. 197–205. Indianapolis and Kansas City: The Bowen-Merrill Company, 1897. [First printed in the Burlington (Iowa) *Hawkeye*, 1879.]

["Its popularity was immediate, and after its publication . . . as a pamphlet, . . . was distributed by tens of thousands. It was copied by every newspaper of more than the slightest importance . . ."—Clara B. Burdette, *Robert J. Burdette, His Message*, p 127. Pasadena and Philadelphia, 1922.]

sojourned Sunday, to Indianapolis. I did not see the famous cedars, and I supposed they had been used up for lead-pencils, and moth-proof chests, and relics, and souvenirs; for Lebanon is right in the heart of the holy land. That part of Indiana was settled by Second Adventists, and they have sprinkled goodly names all over their heritage. As the train clattered along, stopping at every station to trade off some people who were tired of traveling for some other people who were tired of staying at home, I got out my writing-pad, pointed a pencil, and wondered what manner of breakfast I would be able to serve for the ever hungry "Hawkeye" next morning.

I was beginning to think I would have to disguise some "left-overs" under a new name, as the thrifty house-keeper knows how to do, when my colleague, my faithful yoke-fellow, who has many a time found for me a spring of water in the desert place—the Brakeman, came down the aisle of the car. He glanced at the tablet and pencil as I would look at his lantern, put my right hand into a cordial compress that abode with my fingers for ten minutes after he went away, and seating himself easily on the arm of the seat, put the semaphore all right for me by saying:

"Say, I went to church yesterday."

"Good boy," I said, "and what church did you attend?"

"Guess," was his reply.

"Some Union Mission chapel?" I ventured.

"N-no," he said, "I don't care to run on these branch roads very much. I don't get a chance to go to church every Sunday, and when I can go, I like to run on the main line, where your trip is regular, and you make schedule time, and don't have to wait on connections. I don't care to run on a branch. Good enough, I reckon, but I don't like it."

"Episcopal?" I guessed.

"Limited express!" he said, "all parlor cars, vestibuled, and two dollars extra for a seat; fast time, and only stop at the big stations. Elegant line, but too rich for a brakeman. All the trainmen in uniform; conductor's punch and lanterns silver-plated; train-boys fenced up by themselves and not allowed to offer anything but music. Passengers talk back at the conductor. Trips scheduled through the whole year, so when you get aboard you know just where you're going and how long it will take you. Most systematic road in the country and has a mighty nice class of travel. Never hear of a receiver appointed on that line. But I didn't ride in the parlor car yesterday."

"Universalist?" I suggested.

"Broad gauge," the Brakeman chuckled; "does too much complimentary business to be prosperous. Everybody travels on a pass. Conductor doesn't get a cash fare once in fifty miles. Stops at all way-stations and won't run into anything but a union depot. No smoking-car allowed on the train because the company doesn't own enough brimstone to head a match. Train orders are rather vague, though; and I've noticed the trainmen don't get along very well with the passengers. No, I didn't go on the broad gauge, though I have some good friends on that road who are the best people in the world. Been running on it all their lives."

"Presbyterian?" I hinted.

"Narrow gauge, eh?" said the Brakeman; "pretty track; straight as a rule; tunnel right through the heart of a mountain rather than go around it; spirit level grade; strict rules, too; passengers have to show their tickets before they get on the train; cars a little bit narrow for sleepers; have to sit one in a seat and no room in the aisle to dance. No stop-over tickets allowed; passenger must go straight through to the station he's ticketed for, or stay off the car. When the car's full, gates are shut; cars built at the shops to hold just so many, and no more allowed on. That road is run right up to the rules and you don't often hear of an accident on it. Had a head-on collision at Schenectady union station and run over a weak bridge at Cincinnati, not many years ago, but nobody hurt, and no passengers lost. Great road."

"May be you rode with the Agnostics?" I tried.

The Brakeman shook his head emphatically.

"Scrub road," he said, "dirt road-bed and no ballast; no time-card, and no train dispatcher. All trains run wild and every engineer makes his own time, just as he pleases. A sort of 'smoke-if-you-want-to' road. Too many side tracks; every switch wide open all the time, switchman sound asleep and the target-lamp dead out. Get on where you please and get off when you want. Don't have to show your tickets, and the conductor has no authority to collect fare. No, sir; I was offered a pass, but I don't like the line. I don't care to travel over a road that has no terminus.

"Do you know, I asked a division superintendent where his road run to, and he said he hoped to die if he knew. I asked him if the general superintendent could tell me, and he said he didn't believe they had a general superintendent, and if they had, he didn't know any more about the road than the passengers did. I asked him who he reported to, and he said, 'Nobody.' I asked a conductor who he got his orders from, and he said he didn't take no orders from any living man or dead ghost. And when I asked the engineer who gave him orders, he said he'd just like to see any man on this planet try to give him orders, black-and-white or verbal; he said he'd run that train to suit himself or he'd run it into the ditch. Now, you see, I'm not much of a theologian, but I'm a good deal of a railroad man, and I don't want to run on a road that has no schedule, makes no time, has no connections, starts anywhere and runs nowhere, and has neither signal man, train dispatcher or superintendent. Might be all right, but I've railroaded too long to understand it."

"Did you try the Methodist?"

"Now you're shoutin'!" he cried with enthusiasm; "that's the hummer! Fast time and crowds of passengers! Engines carry a power of steam, and don't you forget it. Steam-gauge shows a hundred and enough all the time. Lively train crews, too. When the conductor shouts 'All a-b-o-a-r-d!' you can hear him to the next hallelujah station. Every train lamp shines like a head-light. Stop-over privileges on all tickets; passenger can drop off the train any time he pleases, do the station a couple of days and hop on to the next revival train that comes thundering along with an evangelist at the throttle. Good, whole-souled, companionable conductors; ain't a road on earth that makes the passengers feel more at home. No passes issued on any account; everybody pays full traffic rate for his own ticket. Safe road, too; well equipped; Wesleyanhouse air brakes on every train. It's a road I'm fond of, but I didn't begin this week's run with it."

I began to feel that I was running ashore; I tried one more lead:

"May be you went with the Baptists?"

"Ah, ha!" he shouted, "now you're on the Shore line! River Road, eh? Beautiful curves, lines of grace at every bend and sweep of the river; all steel rail and rock ballast; single track, and not a siding from the round-house to the terminus. Takes a heap of water to run it, though; double tanks at every station, and there isn't an engine in the shops that can run a mile or pull a pound with less than two gauges. Runs through a lovely country—river on one side and the hills on the other; and it's a steady climb, up grade all the way until the run ends where the river begins, at the fountain head. Yes, sir I'll take the River Road every time for a safe trip, sure connections, good time, and no dust blowing in when you open a window. And yesterday morning, when the conductor came around taking up fares with a little basket punch, I didn't ask him to pass me; I paid my fare like a little Jonah— twenty-five cents for a ninety-minute run, with a concert by the passengers thrown in. I tell you what it is, Pilgrim, never mind your baggage, you just secure your passage on the River Road if you want to go to—"

But just here the long whistle announced a station, and the Brakeman hurried to the door, shouting—

"Zions-VILLE! ZIONS-ville! All out for Zionsville! This train makes no stops between here and Indianapolis!"

Cousin Freebody's Last Praying

When it come to praying, Cousin Freebody Tillman just couldn't be beat—or stopped, neither, till he'd prayed his self out. When he got up to pray, everybody at Pilgrim Beauty Church House knowed they was

By Julia Willhoit. From *God Bless the Devil! Liars' Bench Tales* by James R. Aswell, Julia Willhoit, Jennette Edwards, E. E. Miller, and Lena E. Lipscomb, of the Tennessee Writers' Project, pp. 25–32. Copyright, 1940, by the University of North Carolina Press. Chapel Hill.

in for a spell of squirming, because Cousin Freebody cried aloud and spared none.

He had a special kind of slow solemn way to get down on his knees. He'd turn his round red face up towards the rafters and give a sweet smile in the Lord's direction. Then he'd pull at his white chinbrush two or three times and sail in. "Oh Looord, oh Looord," he'd say, each time a mite louder. "Oh Looord, this is Freebody Tillman asking you to send the Holy Spirit down upon them whiskey-making Barfieldses! Oh Looord, drive out the demons from the heart of pore Della Creasy, for she's been galavanting around and got herself in a fix.

"Oh Looord," he'd beller, "who is beknowing to all things, clean with them holy hands of yores the vile hands of them that charges two prices for brought-on goods that they got half price at the county seat. You know who I mean." And he'd open one eye and look at Storekeeper Boshears.

That's why they all called him Cousin Freebody, when he wasn't nobody's cousin at all. Cousin-like, he knowed everybody's business and was just dying to tell it around. Yes, when he got warmed up praying, Cousin Freebody would run right through the community, naming names and telling what they'd done against the teaching of the Book since last meeting night.

Cousin Freebody left his own self to the tag end. "Oh Looord," he says, "bless thy humble servant that calls yore attention to these here sinners. Send yore holy lamb to bless his mission of righteousness, oh Looord, *Amen!*" Then he'd get off his knees, looking mighty satisfied and proud of his self.

Some said it wasn't right the way Cousin Freebody taken on his self to tell the Lord all such things in public. But some claimed it was a genuwine service to the community. Both sides argued back and forth and Cousin Freebody kept right on pointing the sinners out every chance he got to pray.

Old Hub Peegrum lived joining farms to Cousin Freebody and knowed him might near as well as anybody, or maybe better. "You know," he says, "it's a queer thing to me that them Freebody Tillmanses will eat possum, come any season, and any fool knowing possum ain't good only from frost till Easter. Why, I've seen the meat on the platter, and it don't have that greasy look that possum meat does. It's sort of pink and all lean like—well, it just *couldn't* be sheep meat, because Cousin Freebody don't raise sheep. But I will say it's the sheepiest-looking possum meat ever I seen!"

You could take it or leave it. Old Hub Peegrum hadn't put his self on no limb, but it did set folks to thinking. They got to thinking about the way the farmers had been missing lambs and couldn't figger what was going with them.

Far and near the folks begun talking about Cousin Freebody's sheepylooking possum meat. Some of them says to him, "What kind of possum is that you folks eat, Cousin Freebody?"

"Regular old simmon tree possum, brother," says Cousin Freebody. "Eats good, too. I've eat so much possum, reckon you might say I'm half a possum my own self."

It didn't take the wind out of *his* sails none at all. If anything, he prayed louder and spilled other people's sins out in public harder than ever. His "Oh Looords" got to be so long that some said he counted up to ten in his mind before he'd turn one aloose.

One reason Cousin Freebody got away with all he did was the way he could pray up a rain. Just let it come a drouth and there'd be a special prayer service for rain. By the time Cousin Freebody had got through his prayer, wasn't no need of nobody else trying. Wasn't nothing else left to promise the Lord if he sent rain. So the meeting would break up and the crowd go home. Most usually by that time the sun would be gone behind a cloud. All the womenfolks would go home and get the rain barrels and tubs out, for they knowed that rain was sure coming.

Some that read their almanacs said they noticed Cousin Freebody seemed to pick out the days to pray for rain when the signs were right for it. Some said so to his face.

But Cousin Freebody just laughed. "Well, anyhow," says he, "it *did* rain, didn't it? Almanac or no almanac, you don't see it raining after anybody else prays, do you?"

He had them *there*.

Cousin Freebody not only prayed, but he was likewise visited by visions.

"Didn't a white dog come sneaking out from under Malinda's bed one night and didn't I try to kick it out the door, because Malinda wouldn't have no such truck as a dog in the house, let alone under a body's bed, and didn't my foot go clean through that hant, and didn't it just sort of fade away without going out the door nor nothing? And, of course, it wasn't no time till Malinda taken with pneumonia fever and died.

"That was a warning for certain," Cousin Freebody would say. "And furthermore than that, I see visions the times I pray for sinners. Yes, the Lord sends me signs, and the sinners most always get converted."

The way Cousin Freebody got warnings and had his prayers answered gave lots of people the all-overs and brought heaps of them to the mourners' bench. But there was one time when Cousin Freebody's vision wasn't just what he bargained for.

The regular Wednesday night prayer meeting was being held over at the Edwardses away across the ridge, and Cousin Freebody and Old Hub Peegrum went over together. On the way, Cousin Freebody said it would be weathering before long, because he had heard a hoot owl hooting that day.

"It's not a sign of weathering," says Hub Peegrum, "to hear a hoot owl, but just them whiskey-making Barfieldses signaling somebody's coming towards their still. Some day," he says, "you'll find out all them signs you go by don't hold water, Cousin Freebody."

Now that didn't set well with Cousin Freebody—Old Hub's belittling his signs and visions. So he just puffed and blowed, mad as a hornet, all the rest of the way to the meeting.

The womenfolks were there in the parlor and each one had their Bible and songbook and fan. The menfolks were chewing tobacco and smoking out in the yard till Cousin Freebody come in. Then they followed him inside to begin the meeting.

"Cousin Freebody must have a powerful good speaking or something on his mind tonight," everybody says. "He never stopped to swap gossip with the men outside like always. Just come right on in."

"Pears to me," somebody says, "he looks sort of unusually pious too, or else something's troubling his mind a plenty. Maybe another one of them visions he talks about."

The song services ended with them all joining in on "When I Shall See Him Face to Face," and Cousin Freebody got ready to pray. Down on both knees, face lifted to high heaven, hands folded.

"Oh, Looord! Oh Lord Almighty God! You who are beknowing to our every need. Oh Looord, send a vision to these sinful people. Something as a token, Lord, to thy faithful servant for telling you all these things these folks been doing all these years. Oh, Loooord, one of our deacons don't believe in warnings from thy holy hand. Lord, just a little vision to them as needs it most is all I'm asking."

Somebody giggled from over next to the wall where the young bucks was setting with their girls. Cousin Freebody cocked one eye open to see how Old Hub's face was looking. Everybody was bound to know the prayer for a vision was aimed at Hub, the doubting deacon.

And that was the downfall of Cousin Freebody, opening that one eye. If he hadn't done it, likely nothing would have happened. But he did.

He sprung up with both eyes wild and he threw his arms out in front of him like he was trying to push away the devil his self.

"Almighty God, remove this evil vision from me!" he howled. "I'll pay Tom Edwards and Hub Peegrum for every last lamb of theirs I et and told it was possum. Almighty God, this ain't the little lamb I et today, you done made a mistake, Lord, it was a young ewe I et today. Oh God Almighty, stop the pitiful bleating of that poor little stolen lamb of Hub's I et last week! Oh, Loooooord—!"

And there it was, out before God and everybody else what he'd been doing.

Everybody was laughing so hard, and Cousin Freebody howling so loud that Tom Edwards' house near shaken down.

"It ain't no vision, Cousin Freebody!" Tom kept yelling at him. "It's a little pet lamb of Nancy's. A lamb that's been raised up in the house and taken a notion to stroll in. It ain't no vision, Cousin Freebody."

Well, when Cousin Freebody seen what he'd done to his self, he lost his religion. He waved his arms and raved, "You ornery razor-backed, throat-cutting, whiskey-drinking bastards can have all the meetings you want to from now on, but I won't be there to help you. Anybody that would make a poor old man think he was getting such a bushwhacking from the Holy Spirit is worthless as frog spit!"

He stomped towards the door, but stopped long enough to say, "And as for you, Tom Edwards, anybody that'd stoop to raising sheep in the house ain't fitten for even a sheep thief to associate with."

And Cousin Freebody never went to another meeting and never prayed again.

The Harp of a Thousand Strings

. . . "Thar may be some here to-day, my brethering, as don't know what persuasion I am uv. Well, I may say to you, my brethering, that I am a Hard-Shell Baptist. Thar's some folks as don't like the Hard-Shell Baptists, but I'd rather hev a hard shell as no shell at all. You see me here to-day, my brethering, dressed up in fine close; you mout think I was proud, but I am not proud, my brethering; and although I've been a preacher uv the gospel for twenty years, and although I'm capting uv that flat-boat that lies at your landing, I'm not proud, my brethering.

"I'm not gwine ter tell you *edzackly* whar my tex may be found: suffice it tu say, it's in the leds of the Bible, and you'll find it somewhar 'tween the fust chapter of the book of Generation, and the last chapter of the book of Revolutions, and ef you'll go and sarch the Scripturs, you'll not only find *my* tex thar, but a great many other *texes* as will do you good to read; and my tex, when you shill find it, you shill find it to read thus:

" 'And he played on a harp uv a thousand strings—sperits of just men made perfeck.'

"My tex, brethren, leads me to speak uv sperits. Now thar's a great many kind of sperits in the world—in the fust place, thar's the sperits as som folks call ghosts; then thar's the sperits uv turpen*time;* and then thar's the sperits as some folks call liquor, and I've got as good artikel uv them kind uv sperits on my flat-boat as ever was fotched down the Mississippi River; but thar's a great many other kind of sperits, for the tex says: 'He played on a harp uv a *thou*-sand strings— sperits of just men made perfeck.'

From *The Harp of a Thousand Strings;* or, *Laughter for a Lifetime,* "Konceived, Compiled, and Komically Konkokted by Spavery [S. P. Avery?], pp. [9]–11. New York: Dick & Fitzgerald, Publishers. 1858.

"But I'll tell you the kind of sperits as is ment in the tex: it's *fire*. That is the kind of sperits as is ment in the tex, my brethering. Now thar's a great many kinds of fire in the world. In the fust place, thar's the common sort uv fire you light a segar or pipe with, and then thar's camfire, fire before you're ready to fall back, and many other kinds uv fire, for the tex ses: 'He played on a harp uv a *thou*-sand strings— sperits uv just men made perfeck.'

"But I'll tell you the kind of fire as is ment in the tex, my brethering —it's *hell-fire!* an' that's the kind of fire as a great many of you'll come to, ef you don't do better nor what you have bin doin'—for 'He played on a harp uv a *thou*-sand strings—sperits of just men made perfeck.'

"Now, the different sorts uv fire in the world may be likened unto the different persuasions in the world. In the first place, we have the 'Piscapalions, and they are a high salin' and a highfalutin' set, and they may be likened unto a turkey-buzzard, that flies up into the air, and he goes up and up till he looks no bigger than your finger-nail, and the fust thing you know, he comes down and down, and is a fillin' himself on the karkiss of a dead hoss by the side uv the road— and 'He played on a harp uv a *thou*-sand strings—sperits of just men made perfeck.'

"And then, thar's the Methodis, and they may be likened unto the squirrel, runnin' up into a tree, for the Methodis believes in gwine on from one degree uv grace to another, and finally on to perfecshun; and the squirrel goes up and up, and he jumps from lim' to lim', and branch to branch, and the fust thing you know, he falls, and down he comes kerflummux; and that's like the Methodis, for they is allers fallin' from Grace, ah! And 'He played on a harp of a *thou*-sand strings —sperits of just men made perfeck.'

"And then, my brethering, thar's the Baptist, ah! and they hev bin likened unto a possum on a 'simmon tree, and the thunders may roll, and then the earth may quake, but that possum clings there still, ah! And you may shake one foot loose, and the other's thar; and you may shake all feet loose, and he laps his tail around the lim', and he clings fur ever—for 'He played on a harp of a *thou*-sand strings—sperits of just men make perfeck.' "

> "If you want to make old Satan run,
>   Play on the golden harp!
> Just shoot him with the gospel gun,
>   Play on the golden harp!
> Play on the golden harp! play on the golden harp!"

They Shall Gnaw a File

My Beloved Brethering: I am a unlarnt Hard-Shell Baptist preacher, of whom you've no doubt hearn afore, and I now appear here to expound the scripters and pint out the narrow way which leads from a vain world to the streets of Jaroosalem; and my tex which I shall choose for the occasion is in the leds of the Bible, somewhar between the Second Chronik-ills and the last chapter of Timothytitus; and when you find it, you'll find it in these words: "And they shall gnaw a file, and flee unto the mountains of Hepsidam, whar the lion roareth and the wang-doodle mourneth for his first-born."

Now, my brethering, as I have before told you, I am an oneddicated man, and I know nothing about grammar talk and collidge highfalutin, but I am a plane unlarnt preacher of the Gospil, what's been foreordaned and called to prepare a pervarse generashun for the day of wrath—ah! "For they shall gnaw a file, and flee unto the mountains of Hepsidam, whar the lion roareth and the wang-doodle mourneth for his first-born"—ah!

My beloved brethering, the tex says they shall gnaw a file. It does not say they *may*, but shall. Now, there is more than one kind of file. There's the hand-saw file, the rat-tail file, the single file, the double file, and profile; but the kind spoken of here isn't one of them kind nayther, bekaws it's a figger of speech, and means going it alone and getting ukered; "for they shall gnaw a file, and flee unto the mountains of Hepsidam, whar the lion roareth and the wang-doodle mourneth for his first-born"—ah!

And now there be some here with fine close on thar backs, brass rings on thar fingers, and lard on thar har, what goes it while they're yung; and thar be others here what, as long as thar constitooshins and forty-cent whiskey last, goes it blind. Thar be sisters here what, when they gets sixteen years old, cut thar tiller-ropes and goes it with a rush. But I say, my dear brethering, take care you don't find, when Gabriel blows his last trump, your hand's played out, and you've got ukered—ah! "For they shall gnaw a file, and flee unto the mountains of Hepsidam, whar the lion roareth and the wang-doodle mourneth for his first-born."

Now, my brethering, "they shall flee unto the mountains of Hepsidam"; but thar's more dams than Hepsidam. Thar's Rotter-dam, Had-dam, Amster-dam, and "Don't-care-a-dam"—the last of which, my brethering, is the worst of all, and reminds me of a sirkumstans I onst knowed in the state of Illenoy. There was a man what built him a mill on the north fork of Ager Crick, and it was a good mill and ground a

By William P. Brannan. From *Tall Tales of the Southwest*, An Anthology of Southern and Southwestern Humor, 1830–1860, edited by Franklin J. Meine, pp. 253–255. Copyright, 1930, by Alfred A. Knopf, Inc.

sight of grain; but the man what built it was a miserable sinner, and never give anything to the church; and, my dear brethering, one night there came a dreadful storm of wind and rain, and the mountains of the great deep was broke up, and the waters rushed down and swept that man's milldam to kingdom cum, and when he woke up he found that he wasn't worth a dam—ah! "For they shall gnaw a file, and flee unto the mountains of Hepsidam, whar the lion roareth and the wang-doodle mourneth for his first-born"—ah!

I hope I don't hear any body larfin; do I?

Now, "whar the lion roareth and the wang-doodle mourneth for his first-born"—ah! This part of my tex, my beseaching brethering, is not to be taken as it says. It don't mean the howling wilderness, whar John the Hard-Shell Baptist fed on locusts and wild asses, but it means, my brethering, the city of New Y'Orleans, the mother of harlots and hard lots, whar corn is wuth six bits a bushel one day and nary a red the nex; whar suckers are as thick as black bugs in spiled bacon ham, and gamblers, thieves, and pickpockets goes skiting about the streets like weasels in a barn-yard; whar honest men are scarcer than hen's teeth; and whar a strange woman once took in your beluved teacher, and bamboozled him out of two hundred and twenty-seven dollars in the twinkling of a sheep's-tail; but she *can't* do it again! Hallelujah—ah! "For they shall gnaw a file, and flee unto the mountains of Hepsidam, whar the lion roareth and the wang-doodle mourneth for his first-born"—ah!

My brethering, I am the captain of that flat-boat you see tied up thar, and have got aboard of her flour, bacon, taters, and as good Monongahela whiskey as ever was drunk, and am mighty apt to get a big price for them all; but what, my dear brethering, would it all be wuth if I hadn't got religion? Thar's nothing like religion, my brethering: it's better nor silver or gold gimcracks; and you can no more get to heaven without it than a jay-bird can fly without a tail—ah! Thank the Lord! I'm an oneddicated man, my brethering; but I've sarched the Scripters from Dan to Beersheba, and found Zion right side up, and hard-shell religion the best kind of religion—ah! 'Tis not like the Methodists, what specks to get to heaven by hollerin' hell-fire; nor like the Univarsalists, that get on the broad gage and goes the hull hog—ah!; nor like the Yewnited Brethering, that takes each other by the slack of thar breeches and hists themselves in; nor like the Katherliks, that buys threw tickets from their priests; but it may be likened unto a man what has to cross the river—ah!—and the ferry-boat was gone; so he tucked up his breeches and waded acrost—ah! "For they shall gnaw a file, and flee unto the mountains of Hepsidam, whar the lion roareth and the wang-doodle mourneth for his first-born!"

Pass the hat, Brother Flint, and let every Hard-Shell Baptist shell out.

Correction, Please

Commodore William F. Davidson of the old White Collar Line of Mississippi River steamboats was a very pious man. It was his custom to assemble the members of his crew on deck on Sunday mornings and to there hold a prayer meeting. On such occasions he always offered the prayer himself. One of these prayers he once concluded, according to a river tale, with the following words:

"And, Oh Lord, bless the poor. Give to every poor family a Barrel of Pork—a Barrel of Flour—a Barrel of Sugar—a Barrel of Salt—a Barrel of Pepper." Then, hesitating for a moment, he added: "Oh, h——l no—that's too much Pepper!"

The Fable of the Preacher Who
Flew His Kite. . . .

A certain Preacher became wise to the Fact that he was not making a Hit with his Congregation. The Parishioners did not seem inclined to seek him out after Services and tell him he was a Pansy. He suspected that they were Rapping him on the Quiet.

The Preacher knew there must be something wrong with his Talk. He had been trying to Expound in a clear and straightforward Manner, omitting Foreign Quotations, setting up for illustration of his Points such Historical Characters as were familiar to his Hearers, putting the stubby Old English words ahead of the Latin, and rather flying low along the Intellectual Plane of the Aggregation that chipped in to pay his Salary.

But the Pew-Holders were not tickled. They could Understand everything he said, and they began to think he was Common.

So he studied the Situation and decided that if he wanted to Win them and make everybody believe he was a Nobby and Boss Minister he would have to hand out a little Guff. He fixed it up Good and Plenty.

On the following Sunday Morning he got up in the Lookout and read a Text that didn't mean anything, read from either Direction, and then he sized up his Flock with a Dreamy Eye and said: "We cannot more adequately voice the Poetry and Mysticism of our Text than in those familiar Lines of the great Icelandic Poet, Ikon Navrojk:

From *Old Man River*, Upper Mississippi River Steamboating Days Stories, Tales of the Old Time Steamboats and Steamboatmen [by Charles E. Brown], p. 5. Madison, Wisconsin: Charles E. Brown, Wisconsin Folklore Society. 1940.

From *Fables in Slang*, by George Ade, pp 63–74. Illustrated by Clyde J. Newman. Copyright, 1899, by Herbert S. Stone & Co. New York.

"To hold is not to have—
Under the seared Firmament,
Where Chaos sweeps, and Vast Futurity
Sneers at these puny Aspirations—
There is the full Reprisal."

When the Preacher concluded this extract from the Well-Known Icelandic Poet he paused and looked downward, breathing heavily through
his Nose, like Camille in the Third Act.

A Stout Woman in the Front Row put on her Eye-Glasses and leaned
forward so as not to miss Anything. A Venerable Harness Dealer over
at the Right nodded his Head solemnly. He seemed to recognize the
Quotation. Members of the Congregation glanced at one another as if
to say: "This is certainly Hot Stuff!"

The Preacher wiped his Brow and said he had no Doubt that every
one within the Sound of his Voice remembered what Quarolius had
said, following the same Line of Thought. It was Quarolius who disputed the Contention of the great Persian Theologian Ramtazuk, that
the Soul in its reaching out after the Unknowable was guided by the
Spiritual Genesis of Motive rather than by mere Impulse of Mentality.
The Preacher didn't know what all This meant, and he didn't care, but
you can rest easy that the Pew-Holders were On in a minute. He talked
it off in just the Way that Cyrano talks when he gets Roxane so Dizzy
that she nearly falls off the Piazza.

The Parishioners bit their Lower Lips and hungered for more First-
Class Language. They had paid their Money for Tall Talk and were
prepared to solve any and all Styles of Delivery. They held on to the
Cushions and seemed to be having a Nice Time.

The Preacher quoted copiously from the Great Poet Amebius. He
recited 18 lines of Greek and then said: "How true this is!" And not a
Parishioner batted an Eye.

It was Amebius whose Immortal Lines he recited in order to prove
the Extreme Error of the Position assumed in the Controversy by the
Famous Italian, Polenta.

He had them Going, and there wasn't a Thing to it. When he would
get tired of faking Philosophy he would quote from a Celebrated Poet
of Ecuador or Tasmania or some other Seaport Town. Compared with
this Verse, all of which was of the same School as the Icelandic Masterpiece, the most obscure and clouded Passage in Robert Browning was
like a Plate-Glass Front in a State Street Candy Store just after the
Colored Boy gets through using the Chamois.

After that he became Eloquent, and began to get rid of long Boston
Words that hadn't been used before that Season. He grabbed a rhetorical
Roman Candle in each Hand and you couldn't see him for the Sparks.

After which he sunk his Voice to a Whisper and talked about the
Birds and the Flowers. Then, although there was no Cue for him to

Weep, he shed a few real Tears. And there wasn't a dry Glove in the Church.

After he sat down he could tell by the Scared Look of the People in Front that he had made a Ten-Strike.

Did they give him the Joyous Palm that Day? Sure!

The Stout Lady could not control her Feelings when she told how much the Sermon had helped her. The venerable Harness Dealer said he wished to indorse the Able and Scholarly Criticism of Polenta.

In fact, every one said the Sermon was Superfine and Dandy. The only thing that worried the Congregation was the Fear that if it wished to retain such a Whale it might have to Boost his Salary.

In the Meantime the Preacher waited for some one to come and ask about Polenta, Amebius, Ramtazuk, Quarolius and the great Icelandic Poet, Navrojk. But no one had the Face to step up and confess his Ignorance of these Celebrities. The Pew-Holders didn't even admit among themselves that the Preacher had rung in some New Ones. They stood Pat, and merely said it was an Elegant Sermon.

Perceiving that they would stand for Anything, the Preacher knew what to do after that.

MORAL: *Give the People what they think they want.*

Little David and Ole Goliar

Well, de Hebrews whupped de Philistines and de Philistines whupped de Hebrews. But neither side wouldn't stay whupped. So finally de Lawd sort of got tired stayin' round to he'p out de Hebrews all de time, so he app'inted a man name King Saul to be king er de Hebrews.

"King Saul," say de Lawd, "you take and lead my people while I go on back and 'tend to my angels a little."

Ole King Saul was a purty good king when hit come to fightin', but when hit come to jest plain ev'yday kingin', ole Saul wa'n't so much. But as long as he whupped de Philistines de people hung wid him, and sort of put up wid him for de rest er de time. So Saul started to think he was purty good all de way round.

"What a king needs," say ole King Saul, "is a heap er music round de camp." So he sont out and got a little boy name Little David to come and play on his harp round de camp.

Little David was one er deseyar boys which could do mighty nigh anything and could do hit good. But when hit come right down to hit, he could make up songs and sing 'em better'n he could do anything else. He always was makin' up a song and playin' hit on his harp and singin'. Even while he was out herdin' his daddy's sheep he'd take and put his harp in his pocket and set out on de hillside and sing:

From *Ol' Man Adam an' His Chillun*, by Roark Bradford, pp. 212–219. Copyright, 1928, by Harper and Brothers. New York.

> "Ef I could I sholy would,
> I wanter stand on de rocks whar Moses stood.
> Little David, play on yo' harp, hallelu! hallelu!
> Little David, play on yo' harp, hallelu!"

So while he was singin' a big bear come and stole a sheep and he had to git up and run de bear down to git de sheep back. Den he went on back and sung some mo':

> "Old Joshua was de son of Nun,
> And he never quit fightin' to de fightin' was done.
> Little David, play on yo' harp, hallelu! hallelu!
> Little David, play on yo' harp, hallelu!"

So 'bout dat time yar come a line and stole another sheep, so Little David had to git up and run him down.

"Dis ain't gittin' nowheres," he say. "I'm gittin' sick and tired er runnin' deseyar thievin' varmints down ev'y time they steals a sheep. I bet I'm gonter fix me somethin' which'll do my runnin' for me." So he tuck and cut de tongue outer his shoe and got two strings and make him a sling-shot. So he set down and started singin' again:

> "Old Joshua stood on de top er de hill,
> And he looked at de sun and de sun stood still.
> Little David, play on yo' harp, hallelu! hallelu!
> Little David, play on yo' harp, hallelu!"

So 'bout dat time a wolf come up and steal hisse'f a sheep. But David didn't git up and run after him. He jest got a rock and put hit in de sling-shot and slung hit round his head about twice, and ker-blip! de wolf thought de lightnin' had done struck him!

So when ole King Saul sont for Little David, Little David not only tuck 'long his harp, but he tuck 'long his sling-shot, too. So one day he was settin' out in front of ole King Saul's tent, playin' and singin' away, to all at once hit started to git dark and de yearth started to tremble and de ground started to shake.

"What dat, ole King Saul?" say Little David.

"Dat's ole Goliar," say old King Saul.

"Who he?" say David.

"De he-coon er de Philistines," say King Saul.

"What do he want?" say David.

"Trouble," say ole King Saul.

"Well, you de king, ain't you?" say Little David. "Can't you ease his worries 'long dat line?"

"Who, me?" say Saul. "I'm a married man. Cou'se I ain't skeered of him, but still and at de same time I got a wife and a family dependin' on me for s'port. So I don't see no reason how come I should git out and git hurted by no gi'nt."

"He's a gi'nt?" say Little David.

"Twenty foot tall," say King Saul.

"What else is he?" say David.

"Jest wait to he gits out in de clearin' and starts makin' his say-so," say King Saul.

So 'bout dat time ole Goliar stepped out in de clearin' and commenced makin' his say-so.

"I'm a cross betwixt a wild cat and de yaller ianders," he say. "I'm sired by Trouble and dammed by Sudden Death. I drinks nothin' but stump water and a rattlesnake bit me and died. I breathes out forked lightnin' and I spits out thunder. When I laughs de skies pop open, and when I groans hit rolls up like a ball er yarn. I kills my friends and I makes hamburgers outer my enemies. Tornadoes and harrycanes follow me round like pet dogs, and lines and tigers is my playmates. I'm bad. I'm mean. I'm vicious, and jest natchally can't he'p it. When I gits sick hit takes nothin' less'n a Hebrew man's meat to cyore me. And I feel a buck auger comin' on. So look out! I'm reekin' wid meanness and I'm huntin' trouble."

"Sounds hard, don't he?" say Little David.

"Sounds?" say ole King Saul. "Son, dat big scound'el is hard!"

"Is you skeered of him?" say Little David.

"Naw, I ain't skeered of him," say ole King Saul, " 'cause I got sense enough to keep out'n his way."

"I ain't skeered of him," say Little David.

"You kin run purty fast, kin you?" say Saul.

"Naw, I ain't de runnin' kind," say Little David. "I'm jest goin' up yonder and whup dat scound'el befo' supper time."

"You gonter which?" say ole King Saul.

"I'm gonter whup him," say Little David, "or else he gonter whup me."

"Well," say ole King Saul, "be keerful and don't meet up wid de ole Fool Killer on yo' way over, 'cause efn de Fool Killer meet up wid you, he gonter beat ole Goliar to you."

Little David didn't said a word. He jest tuck his harp in one hand and his sling-shot in de yuther, and he went off singin':

> "When I gits to heaven I'm gonter be like Job.
> I'm gonter wawk all around in my long, white robe.
> Little David, play on yo' harp, hallelu! hallelu!
> Little David, play on yo' harp, hallelu!"

So when ole Goliar seed Little David he say, "What you doin' over yar on my side, little ole Hebrew boy?"

"I thought I yared somebody say you was lookin' for trouble," say Little David.

"Don't play wid me, little boy," say Goliar. "I'm in a bad humor and I ain't kilt me no Hebrew since yistiddy. Trot 'long back home befo' I gits mad and spatters you up ag'in' de side er de yearth."

"You don't want to fight wid me?" say Little David. "I yared 'bout deseyar boys wid de big say-so, and f'm what I yars, hit's all say-so and no do-so."

Well, dat made old Goliar good and hot, so he arch up his back and squnch down his shoulders and start stiff-laiggin' round and roarin' and bellowin'. "I'm comin', so jest watch out for me," he say. "I'm dealin' death and destruction right yar and now." And he dance stiff-laigged round Little David, jest groanin' and gruntin' like hit's hurtin' him powerful bad to hold hisse'f back to he gits done wid his dancin' and tawkin'.

"I'm comin', 'cause I can't hold myse'f back no longer," say ole Goliar and he started twarg Little David.

So Little David jest drap a rock into his sling-shot and slung hit round his head, and ker-blop! he tuck ole Goliar right between de eyes and ole Goliar never knowed what hit him.

So 'bout dat time de Lawd stepped out f'm behind a bush and say: "Well, dat settles hit, Little David. You gonter be king over my people."

"Aw, Lawd," say Little David, "ole King Saul is de king."

"You mean he was de king," say de Lawd. "I been holdin' on to him 'cause he makes out like he kin fight. But you not on'y kin sing, but you kin outfight him, too, and ev'ybody knows ole King Saul can't sing. So hit's jest like I say, son. You de king, and no argyment wid me 'bout hit."

"Well, thanky, Lawd," say Little David. So he picks up his harp and wawked on back to camp, singin':

> "Little David was a shepherd's boy,
> And he killed ole Goliar and he hollered wid joy.
> Little David, play on yo' harp, hallelu! hallelu!
> Little David, play on yo' harp, hallelu!"

A Bird in the Hand

Uncle Bob Jordan was the out-prayingest Christian on the Green plantation. He had long been known for his prayers, but now he was praying more than he had ever prayed. He was seventy-two years old and, as he could no longer work much, his master had promised him his freedom for twenty dollars. So Uncle Bob would go down into the woods near the big house every night about seven o'clock and get down on his knees and pray, asking God to please send him twenty dollars for his freedom.

He had been praying for about a month, when the master passed near the tree where Uncle Bob was praying one night and overheard

From "Juneteenth," by J. Mason Brewer, in *Tone the Bell Easy*, Publications of the Texas Folk-Lore Society, Number X, 1932, edited by J. Frank Dobie, pp. 28–29. Copyright, 1932, by the Texas Folk-Lore Society. Austin, Texas.

the prayer. The master decided that the next night he would have some fun out of Uncle Bob. So just before dark he went down to the prayer tree and climbed up in it.

At dark Uncle Bob came under the tree, got down on his knees, and started praying as usual, "Oh, Lawd, sen' me twenty dollers to buy my freedom. Oh, Lawd, sen' me twenty dollers to buy my freedom."

"All right, Uncle Bob," came the master's voice from overhead, "look down at the foot of the tree and you will find a ten-dollar bill."

Sure enough, Uncle Bob looked and found a ten-dollar bill.

"Come back tomorrow night," said the voice, "and you will find a five-dollar bill."

"Sho, sho, Lawd," said Uncle Bob, taking the ten-dollar bill and sticking it in his pocket. "Thank you, thank you."

The next night the master beat Uncle Bob to the tree again and hid in its branches. At dark Uncle Bob came and prayed his accustomed prayer: "Oh Lawd, please sen' me ten mo' dollers to buy my freedom."

"Uncle Bob," responded the voice from overhead, "look at the foot of the tree and you will find another five-dollar bill. Take the ten-dollar bill I gave you last night, and the five-dollar bill I gave you tonight, and bring them back tomorrow night. Put them underneath the tree so that I can get them, and the next night I will bring you a twenty-dollar bill."

"No, sah, no sah, dat's aw right, Lawd," answered Uncle Bob. "I sho thanks you for de fifteen, but I'll git de udder five some place else."

Don't Send a Boy

There is a story told of an old colored woman, who had been walking on the streets in Charleston when the great earthquake came, many years ago.

Desperately and in terror she started to run. The rocking, quaking earth, trembling beneath her feet, made running an impossibility. She fell to her knees, and as a rescuing party reached her, she was praying with all the intensity of her race.

"Oh mah Gawd an mah Father, ain' Yuh see how dis ground do trimble same like Jedgement Day? Come down hyuh, Lawd, an help po people in dere trial and tribbilation, but, oh do, Mass Gawd, be sho an come Yoself an doan sen Yo Son, because dis ain' no time fu chillun!"

From *Cryin' in de Wilderness*, Sermons and Adventures of Reb'ren Nichodemus Ezra Malachi Lee of Maxfield on Santee, by Alfred Holmes von Kolnitz, pp. 30, 44–45. (n.d.) Charleston, South Carolina: Walker Evans and Cogswell Company.

Alabama Parables

I

Man had twin sons, Johnny and Willie, who he loved very much. Johnny died and de father grieved very much over his great loss. He got to goin' out to de grabeyard and grievin' over de grabe. Now, Willie he got tired of his father's grievin', an' thinkin' maybe to he'p him, one night he t'rew a sheet ober his head an' fol'd him to de grabeyard. De father was bendin' over de grabe prayin': "Oh, Lord, please send Johnny back to earth so I can see him jes' one mo' time." Willie, behin' de tom'stone, at dis point said, "O.K. Pa, here I is." De father riz up an' looked hine him at de ghos'. He started backin' off from de ghos', holin' up his han' and sayin', "Now, Johnny, go on back, and lemme lone." But de ghos' kep' on comin' and sayin', "Naw, I wanta go home witcha." Den de father say, "Dat's wa's wrong witcha, Johnny, you always was hard headed. Dat's wha' got you *in* dis mess."

II

Heah's a little story about Sunday school catechism class.—Teacher had been tellin' her pupils all about how God had made ev'ything and ev'ybody. Den she ast one little boy who made him. "Papa," he answered. "No," de teacher said. "I jes' tole you dat God made ev'ybody. Now remember dat." So de nex' Sunday while the first little boy had gone to de spring, de teacher ast 'nother little boy who made him. "Papa," he answered. "No," de teacher answered. "Di'nt you hear me last Sunday say dat God made you?" "Yes, but dat boy dat God made is down at de spring. Papa made me."

III

One day de preacher was goin' to his 'pointment. He had to cross a creek on a log. When he right in de middle o' de log a bear step up on de end o' de log. De preacher scared, so he turn round to go off de other end, but he saw dat a bear had step up on dat en' too. De bears start walkin' towards de preacher. He start prayin': "Lord, I has jes' one request to make o' you. Help me if you can, but don' help dose bears." Den he div' in de water and de bears watch him swim away an' crawl out o' de water downstream.

De preacher went on to church and tole his 'perience. When he finish

From "Negro Folktales from Alabama," by Ray B. Browne, in *Southern Folklore Quarterly*, Vol. XVIII (June, 1954), No. 2, pp. 129–133.

. . . [These] stories are representative of this Negro-preacher-parable-anecdote *genre*. They are not, however, restricted to this parable-anecdote type, for they are Negro folktales in the fullest sense of the word. They just happen to have been told me by a Negro preacher who has used them in his sermons as long as he has been preaching. R.B.B.

one o' de sisters tole him dat he should a prayed. "Prayer, Sister," said de preacher, "is all right at *prayer*-meetin' but it ain't worth a damn at *bear*-meetin'.".

IV

One time dere was a man what was a farmer. One year he had a real good crop. But dis man was kinda lazy, and when it come time to gather de crop he tole ole lady dat he could not he'p gather de crop cause he felt de Lord was callin' him to go preach. He tole her to look up in de sky, and he pointed out de letters G P C, which he say meant, "Go Preach Christ" and he had to go.

But de ole lady she was too much for him. "Dose letters don' mean, Go Preach Christ," she said. "Dey mean, 'Go Pick Cotton'."

V

Two preachers was arguin' 'bout which was de merits ob de Baptist and Methodist 'nominations. De Baptist was makin' some good points. He say: "You can take a piece o' cloth" (le's say domeskic); "you can take a piece of domeskic and you can roll it roun' an' get it dirty, and bur' it in water an' wash it an' it come forth an' will glitter all beauti-ful an' white." "Yes," say de Methodist preacher, "but you got to sprin-kle it 'fore you i'on it, else it won' i'on worth a damn."

VI

Long time ago we got up some money to send a missionary to Africa. You know dat ober dare dey eat people, 'specially if deyre fat, and do other things 'gainst Scripture; so we got up de money to send dis mis-sionary. He had been ober dere 'bout a year and was doin' pretty good about Christianity. Fact, he was doin' so good dat de Empire [Emperor] got worried. So one day de missionary saw an ad in de paper dat any-body dat had anything to do with Christianity was goin' to get kilt. Well de preacher got holt o' de law and read it good. Den one day de Empire's police came and got de preacher and was goin' to kill him. But he say, "Hole on, I'se not guilty o' breakin' dis law." "Why," dey ast, "ain't you been goin' 'round preachin' dis here Christianity?" "No," he say, "I'se been preachin' Baptistism." "Ain't you a Christian?" dey ast, "No, I'se a *Baptist*," he say. And dey let him off.

Celebrating a Funeral

"These yere obsequies which I'm about mentionin'," observed the Old Cattleman, "is the first real funeral Wolfville has."

The old fellow had lighted a cob pipe and tilted his chair back in a fashion which proclaimed a plan to be comfortable. He had begun to

From *Wolfville* by Alfred Henry Lewis, pp. 1–8. A. L. Burt Company, Publishers, New York. Copyright, 1897, by Frederick A. Stokes Company.

tolerate—even encourage—my society, although it was clear that as a tenderfoot he regarded me with a species of gentle disdain.

I had provoked the subject of funeral ceremonies by a recurrence to the affair of the Yellowhouse Man, and a query as to what would have been the programme of the public-spirited hamlet of Wolfville if that invalid had died instead of yielding to the nursing of Jack Moore and that tariff on draw-poker which the genius of Old Man Enright decreed.

It came in easy illustration, as answer to my question, for the Old Cattleman to recall the funeral of a former leading spirit of Southwestern society. The name of this worthy was Jack King; and with a brief exposition of his more salient traits, my grizzled *raconteur* led down to his burial with the remark before quoted.

"Of course," continued the Old Cattleman, "of course while thar's some like this Yallerhouse gent who survives; thar's others of the boys who is downed one time an' another, an' goes shoutin' home to heaven by various trails. But ontil the event I now recalls, the remainders has been freighted east or west every time, an' the camp gets left. It's hard luck, but at last it comes toward us; an' thar we be one day with a corpse all our'n, an' no partnership with nobody nor nothin'.

"'It's the chance of our life,' says Doc Peets, 'an' we plays it. That's nothin' too rich for our blood, an' these obsequies is goin' to be spread-eagle, you bet! We'll show Red Dog an' sim'lar villages they ain't sign-camps compared with Wolfville.'

"So we begins to draw in our belts an' get a big ready. Jack King, as I says before, is corpse, eemergin' outen a game of poker as sech. Which prior tharto, Jack's been peevish, an' pesterin' an' pervadin' 'round for several days. The camp stands a heap o' trouble with him an' tries to smooth it along by givin' him his whiskey an' his way about as he wants 'em, hopin' for a change. But man is only human, an' when Jack starts in one night to make a flush beat a tray full for seven hundred dollars, he asks too much.

"Thar ain't no ondertakers, so we rounds up the outfit, an' knowin' he'd take a pride in it, an' do the slam-up thing, we puts in Doc Peets to deal the game unanimous.

"'Gents,' he says, as we-alls turn into the Red Light to be refreshed, 'in assoomin' the present pressure I feels the compliments paid me in the seelection. I shall act for the credit of the camp, an' I needs your he'p. I desires that these rites be a howlin' vict'ry. I don't want people comin' 'round next week allowin' thar ain't been no funeral, an' I don't reckon much that they will. We've got the corpse, an' if we gets bucked off now it's our fault.'

"So he app'ints Old Monte an' Dan Boggs to go for a box for Jack, an' details a couple of niggers from the corral to dig a tomb.

"'An' mind you-alls,' says Peets, 'I wants that hole at least a mile from camp. In order to make a funeral a success, you needs distance. That's where deceased gets action. It gives the procession a chance to spread an' show up. You can't make no funeral imposin' except you're plumb liberal on distances.'

"It all goes smooth right off the reel. We gets a box an' grave ready, an' Peets sticks up a notice on the stage-station door, settin' the excitement for third-drink time next day. Prompt at the drop of the hat the camp lets go all holds an' turns loose in a body to put Jack through right. He's laid out in splendid shape in the New York Store, with nothin' to complain of if he's asked to make the kick himse'f. He has a new silk necktie, blue shirt an' pearl buttons, trousers, an' boots. Some one—Benson Annie, I reckons—has pasted some co't plaster over the hole on his cheek-bone where the bullet gets in, an' all 'round Jack looks better than I ever sees him.

" 'Let the congregation remove its hats,' says Peets, a-settin' down on a box up at Jack's head, 'an' as many as can will please get somethin' to camp on. Now, my friends,' he continues, 'thar ain't no need of my puttin' on any frills or gettin' in any scroll work. The objects of this convention is plain an' straight. Mister King, here present, is dead. Deceased is a very headstrong person, an' persists yesterday in entertainin' views touchin' a club flush, queen at the head, which results in life everlastin'. Now, gents, this is a racket full of solemnity. We wants nothin' but good words. Don't mind about the trooth; which the same ain't in play at a funeral, nohow. We all knows Jack; we knows his record. Our information is ample that a-way; how he steals a hoss at Tucson; how he robs a gent last fall at Tombstone; how he downs a party at Cruces; how that scar on his neck he gets from Wells-Fargo's people when he stands up the stage over on the Lordsburg trail. But we lays it all aside to-day. We don't copper nary bet. Yesterday mornin', accompanied by the report of a Colt's forty-five, Mister King, who lies yere so cool an' easy, leaves us to enter in behind the great white shinin' gates of pearl an' gold, which swings inwards to glory eternal. It's a great set back at this time thar ain't no sky-pilot in the camp. This deeficiency in sky-pilots is a hoss onto us, but we does our best. At a time like this I hears that singin' is a good, safe break, an' I tharfore calls on that little girl from Flagstaff to give us "The Dyin' Ranger." '

"So the little Flagstaff girl cl'ars her valves with a drink, an' gives us the song; an' when the entire congregation draws kyards on the last verse it does everybody good.

> " 'Far away from his dear old Texas,
>   We laid him down to rest;
>   With his saddle for a pillow,
>   And his gun across his breast.'

"Then Peets gets out the Scriptures. 'I'm goin' to read a chapter outen these yere Testaments,' he says. 'I ain't makin' no claim for it, except it's part of the game an' accordin' to Hoyle. If thar's a preacher yere he'd do it, but bein' thar's no sech brand on this range I makes it as a forced play myse'f.'

"So he reads us a chapter about the sepulcher, an' Mary Magdalene, an' the resurrection; an' everybody takes it in profound as prairie-dogs, for that's the lead to make, an' we knows it.

"Then Peets allows he'd like to hear from any gent onder the head of 'good of the order.'

" 'Mister Ondertaker an' Chairman,' says Jim Hamilton, 'I yields to an inward impulse to say that this yere play weighs on me plumb heavy. As keeper of the dance-hall I sees a heap of the corpse an' knows him well. Mister King is my friend, an' while his moods is variable an' on-certain; an' it's cl'arly worth while to wear your gun while he's hoverin' near, I loves him. He has his weaknesses, as do we all. A disp'sition to make new rooles as he plays along for sech games of chance as enjoys his notice is perhaps his greatest failin'. His givin' way to this habit is primar'ly the cause of his bein' garnered in. I hopes he'll get along thar, an' offers a side bet, even money, up to five hundred dollars, he will. He may alter his system an' stand way up with the angels an' seraphs, an' if words from me could fix it, I'd shorely stack 'em in. I would say further that after consultin' with Billy Burns, who keeps the Red Light, we has, in honor of the dead an' to mark the occasion of his cashin' in, agreed upon a business departure of interest to all. This departure Mister Burns will state. I mournfully gives way to him for said purpose.'

" 'Mister Peets, an' ladies an' gents,' says Burns, 'like Mister Hamilton, who I'm proud to meet yere as gent, citizen, an' friend, I knows deceased. He's a good man, an' a dead-game sport from 'way back. A protracted wrastle with the remorseless drinks of the frontier had begun to tell on him, an' for a year or so he's been liable to have spells. Referrin' to the remarks of Mister Hamilton, I states that by agreement between us an' in honor to departed, the quotations on whiskey in this yere camp, from now on, will be two drinks for two bits, instead of one as previous. We don't want to onsettle trade, an' we don't believe this will. We makes it as a ray of light in the darkness an' gloom of the hour.'

"After this yere utterance, which is well received, we forms the procession. Doc Peets, with two buglers from the Fort, takes the lead, with Jack an' his box in one of the stage coaches comin' next. Enright, Tutt, Boggs, Short Creek Dave, Texas Thompson, an' me, bein' the six pall-bearers, is on hosses next in line; an' Jack Moore commandin' of the rest of the outfit, lines out permiscus.

" 'This is a great day for Wolfville,' says Peets, as he rides up an' down the line. 'Thar ain't no camp this side of St. Looey could turn this trick. Which I only wishes Jack could see it himse'f. It's more calculated to bring this outfit into fav'rable notice than a lynchin'.'

"At the grave we turns in an' gives three cheers for King, an' three for Doc Peets; an' last we gives three more an' a tiger for the camp. The buglers cuts loose everythin' they knows, from the 'water-call' to the 'retreat,' an' while the niggers is a-shovelin' in the sand we bangs away with our six-shooters for general results delightful. You can gamble thar ain't been no funeral like it before or since.

"At the last Peets hauls outen the stage we uses for Jack, a headboard. When it's set up it looks like if Jack ain't satisfied, he's shorely hard to suit. On it in big letters is:

JaCK KInG

LIfE AiN'T

in

HOLDING A GOOD HAND

BUT

In PLAYING A PORE HAnd

weLL.

" 'You sees, we has to work in a little sentiment,' says Doc Peets.

"Then we details the niggers to stand watch-an'-watch every night till further orders. No; we ain't afraid Jack'll get out none, but the coyotes is shore due to come an' dig for him, so the niggers has to stand gyard. We don't allow to find spec'mens of Jack spread 'round loose after all the trouble we takes."

III. FREE COUNTRY, FREE SPEECH
(Fun with Language)

Introduction

Serious writers generally feel it necessary to know and obey the rules of composition and rhetoric, but much of American humor comes from disobeying the rules and stretching language as far as it will go—if not a little farther. The fun of violating rules is obvious in series which are not parallel: "We rescued him with difficulty and a long rope" or "John liked history, algebra, and blondes." Irvin S. Cobb did this sort of thing when he said that the doctor "took my temperature and fifteen dollars." There is humor, too, in such misuse of words as Dizzy Dean's "they's a lotta nerve-wrackin out there on the field." Instead of disobeying the rules of composition, one may, of course, imitate John Phoenix and make up some new ones.

The humorist may also amuse us by using language which is inappropriate, either because it is too slangy or because it is too hoity-toity. H. L. Mencken's version of the Gettysburg Address illustrates the fun of dignified ideas expressed in such American slang as "to put the skids under it"; in contrast, the version "rephrased by a professor" gives us such delightful gobbledygook as this, "We cannot assign—we cannot integrate—we cannot implement this area." But the language of the American folk can be a medium for literary expression as well as for humor, as the selections from Carl Sandburg, Damon Runyon, George Ade, and Ring Lardner show.

The American Language and Dizzy Dean

Much of the stuff that has been written about [Dizzy Dean] since his assignment to the Yankees has missed the mark. Even as astute a writer as Joe Williams insists that Dizzy says "slud" for "slid." Never. What he says is "slood," making it rhyme with wood. . . .

Sometimes a batter "walks disgustilly" to the dugout after fanning. Sometimes he "stands confidentially" at the plate. And the players come off the "bainch" to "take their respectable positions."

A ball is "farred over to second" and a third strike sometimes "retarrs the side." When a pitcher fields a bunt Diz says: "He bounced on it like a cat on a mouse." A hard-hit ground ball that gets away from an infielder is usually described as having "karmed off his glove."

Dizzy speaks of "sprang training" and "peench hitters" and the relief hurler "throwin' down his plimminary pitches." He summarizes, "No hits, no runs, and no airs." Errors are always airs. He describes conferences "in the middle of the diament." He says time has been called while a base runner "is lacening up his shoes." He becomes the baseball expert when he remarks, "They's gonna be a little fancy stragedy pulled now." The adverb "far" is always "for" in the Dean lexicon. "Lopat's got five strike-outs in the ball game so for," he says. Or, "As you seen on your screen, that's the first air of the ball game so for." He describes a hard-laboring pitcher as having "pussperation clean thew his uniform." And in announcing a pamphlet which the public may get by writing in, he says, "You can have the new Yankee sketch book if you woosh."

During a close shot of a batter, Dizzy advises: "Look careful now and you can see the heesive tape on his neck." Once when Joe DiMaggio

From *Three Men On Third*, by Ira L. Smith and H. Allen Smith, pp. 10–14. New York: Doubleday and Company. 1951.

made a magnificent catch deep in center—running with his back toward the plate and reaching high above his head to snag a fly ball, Dizzy yelled: "Holy cow! He caught it with his back in front of the pitcher's box!"

In a pre-season exhibition game at the stadium Dizzy uttered the following remarkable sentence: "That loads the Brooklyn Dodgers fulla bases." Speaking once of a player coming up to bat, he said, "He resembles Crosetti like he used to look." And on the occasion of a spirited rhubarb, he remarked: "They better watch out. That umparr used to be an ex-fighter." He is usually contrite when he makes a mistake in calling a play. "I *bag* your pardon!" he says.

"This is what you call a real slugger's fest," he explained one day. And for the benefit of the amateur scorekeepers: "You gotta give the pitcher a sist on that." Discussing Ted Williams admiringly, he said: "Look at that stance on him! Brother, they's rhythm in that stance!" And of the Red Sox catcher: "Most all ballplayers got nicknames and Birdie Tebbett's is Birdie because he's always a-hollerin' like a little ole kinairy bird." Recalling the career of Dolph Camilli he said: "There was one of the gracefulest first basemens I ever seen." And during a tight situation in a close game, he remarked, "Brother, they's a lotta nerve-wrackin' out there on that field right now." Dizzy's comment on the lazily relaxed manner of Joe Gordon was: "Look at 'im. There's a fella you look at 'im you say, there's a fella dreads to do *anything*."

Sometimes Dizzy tries to be helpful to his audience, explaining things about baseball itself or about his own manner of speech. He spoke once of the futility of quarreling with an umpire, saying, "You might as well try to argy with a stump." After a moment's reflection, he continued: "Some of you New York folks might not know what a stump is. Well, I'll tell ya. A stump is a wood thing . . . well, it's somethin' a tree has been cut down off of."

One day when a visiting manager was making his way to the mound for the purpose of yanking his pitcher, Dizzy filled in with information out of his own vast experience.

"You folks," he said, "prob'ly wonder what's goin on out there— what they're sayin' to one another. Well, I had some experience pitchin' and I can tell you what's goin' on. In the first place, that pitcher he's hot as a farrcracker. And he prob'ly don't like the idee of bein' took out. So when the manager comes walkin' nonchalantly out to the mound, the pitcher he says, 'Aw, fer cryin' out loud!' So the manager he says 'Now take it easy, son. You cain't win *ever*' day.' So the pitcher he says, 'Aw fer cryin 'out loud! If I coulda got that one guy out, that bum, they never woulda got nowheres offa me.' Then the manager he says, 'Now take it easy son. You go on and take a sharr and git some rest and maybe you can beat 'em tuhmarr.' So the pitcher's purty burned up, and he says, 'Aw, fer cryin' out loud!' But he's gotta go, so he goes. That's approxi-mate-aly what goes on out there at the mound, folks." . . .

A New System of English Grammar

I have often thought that the adjectives of the English language were not sufficiently definite for the purposes of description. They have but three degrees of comparison—a very insufficient number, certainly, when we consider that they are to be applied to a thousand objects, which, though of the same general class or quality, differ from each other by a thousand different shades or degrees of the same peculiarity. Thus, though there are three hundred and sixty-five days in a year, all of which must from the nature of things, differ from each other in the matter of climate,—we have but half a dozen expressions to convey to one another our ideas of this inequality. We say— "It is a fine day;" "It is a *very* fine day;" "It is the *finest* day we have seen;" or, "It is an unpleasant day;" "A *very* unpleasant day;" "The *most* unpleasant day we ever saw." But it is plain, that none of these expressions give an *exact* idea of the nature of the day; and the two superlative expressions are generally untrue. I once heard a gentleman remark, on a rainy, snowy, windy and (in the ordinary English language) indescribable day, that it was "most preposterous weather." He came nearer to giving a correct idea of it, than he could have done by any ordinary mode of expression; but his description was not sufficiently definite.

Again:—we say of a lady—"She is beautiful;" "She is *very* beautiful," or "She is *perfectly* beautiful;"—descriptions, which, to one who never saw her, are no descriptions at all for among thousands of women he has seen, probably no two are equally beautiful; and as to a *perfectly* beautiful woman, he knows that no such being was ever created—unless by G. P. R. James, for one of the two horsemen to fall in love with, and marry at the end of the second volume.

If I meet Smith in the street, and ask him—as I am pretty sure to do—"How he does?" he infallibly replies—"*Tolerable,* thank you"— which gives me no *exact* idea of Smith's health—for he has made the same reply to me on a hundred different occasions—on every one of which there *must* have been some slight shade of difference in his physical economy, and of course a corresponding change in his feelings.

To a man of a mathematical turn of mind—to a student and lover of the exact sciences these inaccuracies of expression—this inability to understand *exactly* how things are, must be a constant source of annoyance; and to one who, like myself, unites this turn of mind to an ardent love of truth, for its own sake—the reflection that the English

From *Phoenixiana; Or, Sketches and Burlesques,* by John Phoenix (George H. Derby), pp. 32–41. New York: D. Appleton and Co., 1856.

language does not enable us to speak the truth with exactness, is peculiarly painful. For this reason I have, with some trouble, made myself thoroughly acquainted with every ancient and modern language, in the hope that I might find some one of them that would enable me to express precisely my ideas; but the same insufficiency of adjectives exist in all except that of the Flathead Indians of Puget Sound, which consists of but forty-six words, mostly nouns; but to the constant use of which exists the objection, that nobody but that tribe can understand it. And as their literary and scientific advancement is not such as to make a residence among them, for a man of my disposition, desirable, I have abandoned the use of their language, in the belief that for me it is *hyas. cultus.,* or as the Spaniard hath it, *no me vale nada.*

Despairing, therefore, of making new discoveries in foreign languages, I have set myself seriously to work to reform our own; and have, I think, made an important discovery, which, when developed into a system and universally adopted, will give a precision of expression, and a consequent clearness of idea, that will leave little to be desired, and will, I modestly hope, immortalize my humble name as the promulgator of the truth and the benefactor of the human race.

* * * * *

This system—shall I say this great system—is exceedingly simple, and easily explained in a few words. In the first place, *"figures won't lie."* Let us then represent by the number 100, the maximum, the *ne plus ultra* of every human quality—grace, beauty, courage, strength, wisdom, learning—every thing. Let *perfection,* I say, be represented by 100, and an absolute minimum of all qualities by the number 1. Then by applying the numbers between, to the adjectives used in conversation, we shall be able to arrive at a very close approximation to the idea we wish to convey; in other words, we shall be enabled to speak the truth. Glorious, soul-inspiring idea! For instance, the most ordinary question asked of you is, "How do you do?" To this, instead of replying, "Pretty well," "Very well," "Quite well," or the like absurdities—after running through your mind that *perfection* of health is 100, no health at all, 1—you say, with a graceful bow, "Thank you, I'm 52 to day;" or, feeling poorly, "I'm 13, I'm obliged to you," or "I'm 68," or "75," or "87½," as the case may be! Do you see how very close in this way you may approximate to the truth; and how clearly your questioner will understand what he so anxiously wishes to arrive at—your *exact* state of health?

Let this system be adopted into our elements of grammar, our conversation, our literature, and we become at once an exact, precise, mathematical, truth-telling people. It will apply to every thing but politics; there, truth being of no account, the system is useless. But in literature, how admirable! Take an example:

As a 19 young and 76 beautiful lady was 52 gaily tripping down the sidewalk of our 84 frequented street, she accidently come in contact— 100 (this shows that she came in close contact) with a 73 fat, but 87 good-humored looking gentleman, who was 93 (i.e. intently) gazing into the window of a toy-shop. Gracefully 56 extricating herself, she received the excuses of the 96 embarrassed Falstaff with a 68 bland smile, and continued on her way. But hardly—7—had she reached the corner of the block, ere she was overtaken by a 24 young man, 32 poorly dressed, but of an 85 expression of countenance; 91 hastily touching her 54 beautifully rounded arm, he said, to her 67 surprise—

"Madam, at the window of the toy-shop yonder, you dropped this bracelet, which I had the 71 good fortune to observe, and now have the 94 happiness to hand to you." (Of course the expression "94 happiness" is merely the young man's polite hyperbole.)

Blushing with 76 modesty, the lovely (76, as before, of course), lady took the bracelet—which was a 24 magnificent diamond clasp—(24 *magnificent,* playfully sarcastic; it was probably *not* one of Tucker's) from the young man's hand, and 84 hesitatingly drew from her beautifully 38 embroidered reticule a 67 port-monnaie. The young man noticed the action, and 73 proudly drawing back, added—

"Do not thank me; the pleasure of gazing for an instant at those 100 eyes (perhaps too exaggerated a compliment), has already more than compensated me for any trouble that I might have had."

She thanked him, however, and with a 67 deep blush and a 48 pensive air, turned from him, and pursued with a 33 slow step her promenade.

Of course you see that this is but the commencement of a pretty little tale, which I might throw off, if I had a mind to, showing in two volumes, or forty-eight chapters of thrilling interest, how the young man sought the girl's acquaintance, how the interest first excited, deepened into love, how they suffered much from the opposition of parents (her parents of course), and how, after much trouble, annoyance, and many perilous adventures, they were finally married—their happiness, of course, being represented by 100. But I trust that I have said enough to recommend my system to the good and truthful of the literary world; and besides, just at present I have something of more immediate importance to attend to.

*   *   *   *   *

P. S. I regret to add that having just read this article to Mrs. Phoenix, and asked her opinion thereon, she replied, that "if a first-rate magazine article were represented by 100, she should judge this to be about 13; or if the quintessence of stupidity were 100, she should take this to be in the neighborhood of 96." This, as a criticism, is perhaps a little discouraging, but as an exemplification of the merits of my system it is exceedingly flattering. How could she, I should like to know, in ordinary language, have given so *exact* and truthful an idea—how expressed so forcibly her opinion (which, of course, differs from mine) on the subject?

As Dr. Samuel Johnson learnedly remarked to James Boswell, Laird of Auchinleck, on a certain occasion—

"Sir, the proof of the pudding is in the eating thereof."

The Exactness of the Inexact

Many of you have no doubt heard a person say that he didn't know someone else from Adam's off ox, but you may not have stopped to consider the peculiar aptness of this folk expression. Of Adam's two oxen, the near ox is better known that the off ox for two reasons: first, he is nearer the driver, and, second, the sight of him is unobstructed. We can say, then, that the off ox is less known than the near ox, who in turn is less known than Adam, who is not known at all. This expression illustrates one method of making the inexact exact: The unknown or inexact is divided exactly into the parts which it must logically possess.

The common folk have long known and used this method. Their expressions often particularize the unparticularable, both to lend the drama of the concrete to what would otherwise be abstract and to gain credence by adding minute detail. One might indicate height by saying a thing is knee-high to a half-grown jack-rabbit, length by saying it is as long as a short piece of rope, or depth, by saying it is hip-deep to a tall Indian. These divisions within the inexact could be made even more exact by the use of numbers, a system of exactness which we shall discuss later. Hence a thing could be said to be three inches less than hip-deep to a tall Indian.

Those of us who say that a person is ugly enough to stop an eight-day clock use this principle of exactness, although we may never have stopped to verbalize it. Just as there are obvious differences in clocks, so there are obvious differences in ugliness, and, if it takes x-ugliness to stop a twenty-four-hour clock, it must take $8x$-ugliness to stop the eight-day kind. This is assuming, of course, that the progression is arithmetic, not geometric.

One of the sayings reported in the *Publications of the American Dialect Society* is that a girl was so buck-toothed that she could eat a pumpkin to the hollow through a crack in a board fence. We must of necessity admire the truthfulness, the courage, and the discrimination of the speaker, for he has obviously divided buck-toothedness carefully into at least three categories—that by which one can eat only the inner rind, that by which one can eat to the hollow, and that by

"Adam's Off Ox. A Study in the Exactness of the Inexact," by James N. Tidwell. *The Journal of American Folklore*, Vol. 66 (Oct.-Dec., 1953), No. 262, pp. 291–294.

which one can eat the whole pumpkin. Is it conceivable that a man who is so precise in his statements could be lying?

Many more folk sayings illustrate a similar exactness in handling the inexact. *Cold enough to freeze the tail off a brass monkey,* for instance, shows the speaker's knowledge of the freezing point of such things as glass, porcelain, and iron as compared to that of brass, and his knowledge of the difference in the freezing levels of the various parts of the anatomy. *A smile crossed his face like a wave over a slop-bucket* indicates a knowledge of the differences in wave motion over areas of varying size and through liquids of different viscosity. *As slow as molasses in January* implicitly divides the slowness of molasses into twelve degrees corresponding to the twelve months of the year. *As small as the little end of nothing* assumes that, just as there is a horn of plenty, there is a horn of un-plenty, and this is at the little end of the horn. *As ugly as home-made sin* recognizes that store-bought sin is less ugly than the home-made variety. *As poor as Job's turkey,* like *as unknown as Adam's off ox,* makes a comparison, not with the central unknown thing, but with a lesser-known thing connected with it. *As much as Carter had oats,* although structurally comparable to *as poor as Job's turkey,* does not illustrate the same type of particularization, for Job's complete and general poverty is legendary and hence everything he owned must have been poor, but Carter's reputation rests solely on the fact that he grew so many oats that he didn't have land enough to stack them on.

Many examples of particularizing within the area of the inexact occur in our popular literature. A. B. Longstreet's statement that Ransy Sniffle was in height "five feet nothing; and his average weight in blackberry season, ninety-five" indicates that Ransy's weight varied during the year and that the author's love of exactness made him give the weight at a specific season of the year. By saying that "one might as well attempt to twist a streak of lightning into a true lover's knot as to stop him," Davy Crockett was indirectly pointing out how much harder it is to tie a streak of lightning into a true lover's knot than it is to tie one into an overhand, a slip, or even a square knot. And there is T. B. Thorpe's remark that "the fire of his eyes would have singed a cat's hair." The discrimination exercised here is evident to those who have ever rubbed cat's hair in the dark and thus know of its unsingeability.

Another technique of making the inexact more exact is that of using numbers. Exact figures help to confound the realist who might doubt one's veracity, for ours is an age which respects numbers, true or otherwise. No one that I know of has ever calculated the value of one whoop in hell, although many of us speak of things as not being worth two whoops in hell. Now unless the whoop has a negative value in the nether regions, a thing worth only one whoop is even more valueless than that which is worth two whoops. Time, similarly, may be expressed numerically in shakes of a lamb's tail (usually two), and fastidiousness may be exactly defined by the number of bites (two, three, or four) a person makes of a cherry. Speaking loosely, we may say that a thing is as hot as hell, but the specific temperature can be better communicated by saying that it is as hot as the seven brass hinges of hell, for hinges are hotter than the surrounding area and the number seven reveals a close mathematical observation. And so the second method of making the inexact exact is to number the innumerable with extreme accuracy.

Because any approximation must of necessity include a certain amount of inexactness, it follows that one should never approximate. If there are no exact numbers available, one should make them up—there are forty-'leven ways of doing it. A bad number is always better than a good approximation. Paul Bunyan's blue ox Babe, for example, was forty-two axe-handles and a plug of Star tobacco between the eyes—that's exactness for you! Using this method, a man might be as hungry as a she-wolf sucking *nine* to a side, but bet one of his friends a *hundred* acres of red hogs and win the bet *nine* ways from Sunday. More important, of course, would be for him to have a clear deed to a *ten*-acre lot in heaven.

A folk language form related to this particularizing of the unparticularable is the so-called redundancy. Grammarians have called redundant whatever seemed to them to be repetitious or irrelevant, but in a number of instances their decisions may be questioned. If we respect usage as the arbiter of language, we will admit that *widow woman, widow,* and *woman* mean *three* things, as do *dog, hound,* and *hound dog.* A good example of the particularizing use of the redundant occurred in one of the late Huey Long's campaigns for office. Long was opposed by a successful young dentist, who seemed to be leading in public favor until Huey vanquished him with the remark, "I'm going to beat that there *tooth dentist!*" The grammarians may have winced, but the unredundant redundancy certainly must have hurt the professional reputation of Long's opponent, making him in the mind of many voters nothing more than a tooth puller, a tooth mechanic.

Just as redundancy occurs because something is added which seems unnecessary, so many folk exaggerations are formed by adding one exaggeration to another, a method which Professor Archer Taylor has aptly termed whimsical enlargement. You might say that the exaggerator believes in such slogans as "Don't be half safe," "Why use one when two wipe dry," and "If your first does not exceed, try again." Users of this method seem to assume that two exaggerations are more nearly true than one. Instead of being as cross as a bear, or as cross as a bear with two cubs, or as cross as a bear with a sore tail, the speaker may compound the three and say he is as cross as a bear with two cubs and a sore tail. Or, instead of saying something is as fast as lightning, he may add the known fact that grease speeds up machinery and say it as fast as greased lightning. Or, instead of simply raising hell, he may make the job more difficult by saying he intends to jack up the four corners of hell and put chocks under them. Instead of saying simply that he will fight until hell freezes over, he may add some whimsy and say he'll fight until hell freezes over and then write on the ice, "Come on, you bastards!"

Many folk sayings illustrate this kind of expansion: to have a crow to pick with someone and a poke to put the feathers in; to feel like a three-cent piece with a hole in it; to be low down enough to walk under a snake's belly (or a trundle bed) with a top hat on; as little chance as a blind calf in a cane brake, as a snowball in hell on an August afternoon, or as a celluloid cat chasing an asbestos dog in hell; as hot as a sheep in a pepper patch, or as a fox in a forest fire; as gloomy as a graveyard on a wet Sunday; as happy as a dead pig in the sunshine; as quiet as a one-legged man on a tin roof; as busy as a one-armed paper-hanger with the hives; as fine as frog hair split in the middle; as funny as a barrel of monkeys, as crooked as a barrel of eels; and as quiet as an eel swimming in oil.

A variation of this method is to add, not elements of further and greater exaggeration, but elements of much less exaggeration. By giving the exaggerative parts in a descending order of importance, one seems to be returning whimsically to reality and hence truth. One may thus say that he loves a girl a bushel and a peck and a hug around the neck, or, less arguably in the descending order of importance, that he loves her a bushel and a peck and some in a gourd. Or one might say that he could whip all hell and half of Georgia. Using this principle, Simon Suggs spoke of blood flowing "like all the world! Yes, like all the world . . . and the Tallapussey river!" This principle, too, was used by one author in speaking of Paul Bunyan as "eating the frozen bears like blackberries, and spitting out their fuzzy fur like peach skins."

Instead of adding exaggeration to the already exaggerated in either an ascending or descending order, one can simply add a little truth— or at least apparent truth—to the original exaggeration. An assertion that has nine parts falsehood and one part truth is almost as likely to be believed as one in which the proportions are reversed. It may be best, then, to qualify an exaggeration as Sut Lovingood did one of his: "[He] can make more spinnin' wheels, kiss more spinners, thrash more wheat and more men than any *one-eyed* man I know on." At another time Sut made this brag: "He . . . can out shute and out lie any feller from the Smoky Mountings to Noxville, and, if they'll bar one feller in Nox, I'll say to the old Kaintuck line!"

A speaker could, of course, stop just inside the bounds of truth, and thus not exaggerate at all, as Davy Crockett did when he spoke of fourteen dogs that were so poor "that when they would bark they would *almost* have to lean up against a tree and take a rest." But the more common practice seems to be to reduce the size of the lie, not to eliminate it entirely. Note the realistic qualifications in "I could stretch a mile if I wouldn't have to walk back," "So hungry I could eat a sow and seven pigs and run a boar hog a mile," and "The room was too small to cuss a cat in without getting hairs in your teeth." Herman Melville did this sort of thing when he converted "Take everything but the galley stove" into "Everything was filled with sperm, except the captain's pantaloons pockets."

The exuberant exaggerator might say that he could ride a streak of greased lightning indefinitely, but the man with a respect for truth like Nimrod Wildfire will admit that he can ride it only a short distance—such as across a crab-apple orchard. The former might say that someone couldn't hit the side of a barn, but the truthful man, recognizing the added difficulty of hitting a moving target, would say that the fellow couldn't hit the side of a barn if the door were swinging. Davy Crockett didn't claim that he could swallow Santa Anna *au naturel* without gagging, but that he could swallow him if you'd skewer his ears back and grease his head a little.

Whatever the method used by the folk in forming proverbial expressions about the inexact—whether by particularizing the unparticularable, numbering the innumerable, measuring the immeasurable, or enlarging upon the already enlarged—there is in them the drama and the freshness of the concrete and unusual.

Behold the Proverbs of a People

I[1]

A code arrives; language; lingo; slang;
behold the proverbs of a people, a nation:
Give 'em the works. Fix it, there's always
a way. Be hard boiled. The good die young.

Be a square shooter. Be good; if you can't
be good be careful. When they put you in
that six foot bungalow, that wooden kimono,
you're through and that's that.

Sell' em, sell 'em. Make 'em like it. What
if we gyp 'em? It'll be good for 'em. Get their
names on the dotted line and give 'em the haha.

The higher they go the farther they drop.
The fewer the sooner. Tell 'em. Tell 'em.
Make 'em listen. They got to listen when

[1] From *Good Morning, America*, by Carl Sandburg, pp. 15–18. Copyright, 1928, by Carl Sandburg. New York: Harcourt, Brace & Company.

they know who you are. Don't let 'em know
what you got on your hip. Hit 'em where
they ain't. It's good for whatever ails
you and if nothing ails you it's good for
that. Where was you raised—in a barn?

They're a lot of muckers, tin horns; show
those slobs where they get off at. Tell 'em
you're going to open a keg of nails. Beat 'em
to a fare-thee-well. Hand 'em the razz-berries.
Clean 'em and then give 'em car-fare home.
Maybe all you'll get from 'em you can put in
your ear, anyhow.

They got a fat nerve to try to tie a can
on you. Send 'em to the cleaners. Put the
kibosh on 'em so they'll never come back.
You don't seem to know four out of five
have pyorrhea in Peoria.

Your head ain't screwed on wrong, I trust.
Use your noodle, your nut, your think tank,
your skypiece. God meant for you to use it.
If they offer to let you in on the ground
floor take the elevator.

Ef you wants to see how much folks is goin' to miss you, jest stick yo'
finger in de pond den pull it out an' look at de hole.

Put up a sign: Don't worry; it won't last;
nothing does. Put up a sign: In God we
trust, all others pay cash. Put up a sign:
Be brief, we have our living to make. Put
up a sign: Keep off the grass.

Aye, behold the proverbs of a people:
The big word is Service.
Service—first, last and always.
Business is business.
What you don't know won't hurt you.
Courtesy pays.
Fair enough.
The voice with a smile.
Say it with flowers.
Let one hand wash the other.
The customer is always right.

Who's your boy friend?
Who's your girl friend?
O very well.
God reigns and the government at Washington lives.
Let it go at that.
There are lies, damn lies and statistics.
Figures don't lie but liars can figure.
There's more truth than poetry in that.
You don't know the half of it, dearie.
It's the roving bee that gathers the honey.[1]
A big man is a big man whether he's a president or a prizefighter.[2]
Name your poison.
Take a little interest.
Look the part.
It pays to look well.
Be yourself.
Speak softly and carry a big stick.[3]
War is hell.
Honesty is the best policy.
It's all in the way you look at it.
Get the money—honestly if you can.
It's hell to be poor.
Well, money isn't everything.
Well, life is what you make it.
Speed and curves—what more do you want?
I'd rather fly than eat.[4]
There must be pioneers and some of them get killed.[5]
The grass is longer in the backyard.[6]
Give me enough Swedes and snuff and I'll build a railroad to hell.[7]
How much did he leave? All of it.[8]
Can you unscramble eggs? [9]
Early to bed and early to rise and you never meet any prominent
    people.[10]

---

[1] On hearing from his father "A rolling stone gathers no moss," John L. Sullivan won one of his important early fights and telegraphed this reply.—C.S.

[2] John L. Sullivan's greeting spoken to President Theodore Roosevelt in the White House.—C.S.

[3] A Spanish proverb first Americanized by Theodore Roosevelt.—C.S.

[4] & 5 Charles A. Lindbergh.—C.S.

[6] Based on a Republican campaign story in 1892 alleging that a man on all fours eating grass on the White House lawn told President Grover Cleveland, "I'm hungry" and was advised, "The grass is longer in the backyard."—C.S.

[7] A saying that took rise from James J. (Jim) Hill.—C.S.

[8] A folk tale in Chicago chronicles two ditch diggers on the morning after Marshall Field I died, leaving an estate of $150,000,000, as having this dialogue.—C.S.

[9] J. Pierpont Morgan's query as to court decrees dissolving an inevitable industrial combination.—C.S.

[10] George Ade.—C.S.

Let's go. Watch our smoke. Excuse our dust.
Keep your shirt on.

II

*　　*　　*　　*　　*

aw nuts aw go peddle yer papers[1]
where did ja cop dat monkeyface
　　jeez ja see dat skirt
　　did ja glom dat moll
who was tellin you we wuz brudders
how come ya get on dis side deh street
go home and tell yer mudder she wants yuh
chase yer shadder aroun deh corner
yuh come to me wid a lot uh arkymalarky
　　a bing in de bean fer you yeah
how come ya get on dis side deh street
go home and get yer umbreller washed
　　den get yer face lifted
dis corner is mine—see dis corner is mine
　　gwan ja tink ya gonna get dis f'm me fer nuttin
　　　nobody gets nuttin fer nuttin
　　　gwan monkeyface peddle yer papers
ya can't kiss yerself in here　dis is all fixed

*　　*　　*　　*　　*

The rich own the land and the poor own the water.[2]
The rich get richer and the poor get children.
The rich have baby napkins, and the poor have diapers.
The big houses have small families and the small
　　houses big families.
Why did Death take the poor man's cow and the rich
　　man's child?

The mazuma, the jack, the shekels, the kale,[3]
　　The velvet, the you-know-what,
　　The what-it-takes, a roll, a wad,
　　Bring it home, boy.
　　Bring home the bacon.
　　Start on a shoestring if you have to.
　　Then get your first million.
The second million is always easier than the first.
And if you get more of them round iron men than you can use

---

[1] From *The People, Yes,* by Carl Sandburg. Copyright, 1936, by Harcourt, Brace
& Co. This and succeeding lines are from pp. 130–131.
[2] *Ibid.,* p. 164.
[3] *Ibid.,* pp. 165–166.

you can always throw them at the birds: it's been done.

Now take some men, everything they touch turns into money: they know how the land lays: they can smell where the dollars grow.

Money withers if you don't know how to nurse it along: money flies away if you don't know where to put it.

The first question is, Where do we raise the money, where is the cash coming from?

A little horse sense helps: an idea and horse sense take you far: if you got a scheme ask yourself, Will it work?

And let me put one bug in your ear: inside information helps: how many fortunes came from a tip, from being on the ground first, from hearing a piece of news, from fast riding, early buying, quick selling, or plain dumb luck?

Yes, get Lady Luck with you and you're made: some fortunes were tumbled into and the tumblers at first said, Who would have believed it? and later, I knew just how to do it.

Yes, Lady Luck counts: before you're born pick the right papa and mama and the news-reel boys will be on the premises early for a shot of you with your big toe in your mouth.

The cauliflower is a cabbage with a college education.[1]

All she needs for housekeeping is a can opener.

They'll fly high if you give them wings.

Put all your eggs in one basket and watch that basket.

Everybody talks about the weather and nobody does anything about it.

The auk flies backward so as to see where it's been.

Handle with care women and glass.

Women and linen look best by candlelight.

One hair of a woman draws more than a team of horses.

Blessed are they who expect nothing for they shall not be disappointed.

You can send a boy to college but you can't make him think.

The time to sell is when you have a customer.

Sell the buffalo hide after you have killed the buffalo.

The more you fill a barrel the more it weighs unless you fill it with holes.

A pound of iron or a pound of feathers weighs the same.

Those in fear they may cast pearls before swine are often lacking the pearls.

May you live to eat the hen that scratches over your grave.

He seems to think he's the frog's tonsils but he looks to me like a plugged nickel.

If you don't like the coat bring back the vest and I'll give you a pair of pants.

---

[1] *Ibid.*, pp. 62–63.

The coat and the pants do the work but the vest gets the gravy.

"You are singing an invitation to summer," said the teacher, "you are
not defying it to come."

* * * * *

Why repeat? I heard you the first time.[1]

You can lead a horse to water, if you've
got the horse.

The rooster and the horse agreed not to
step on each other's feet.

The caterpillar is a worm in a raccoon coat
going for a college education.

The cockroach is always wrong when it
argues with the chicken.

If I hadn't done it Monday somebody else
would have done it Tuesday.

Money is like manure—good only when
spread around.

You're such a first-class liar I'll take a
chance with you.

A short horse is soon curried.

A still pig drinks the swill.

Small potatoes and few in a hill.

A fat man on a bony horse: "I feed myself
—others feed the horse."

No peace on earth with the women, no life
anywhere without them.

Some men dress quick, others take as much
time as a woman.

"You're a liar." "Surely not if you say so."

He tried to walk on both sides of the street
at once.

He tried to tear the middle of the street in
two.

"When is a man intoxicated?" "When he
tries to kiss the bartender good-night."

"He says he'll kick me the next time we
meet. What'll I do?" "Sit down."

He's as handy as that bird they call the
elephant.

Now that's settled and out of the way what
are you going to do next?

"From here on," said the driver at an
imaginary line near the foothills of the
Ozarks, "the hills don't get any higher
but the hollers get deeper and deeper."

---

[1] *Ibid.*, pp. 83–84.

So slick he was his feet slipped out from
    under him.

The ground flew up and hit him in the face.

Trade it for a dog, drown the dog, and
    you'll be rid of both of them.

There'll be many a dry eye at his funeral.

"Which way to the post-office, boy?" "I
    don't know." "You don't know much,
    do you?" "No, but I ain't lost."

* * * * *

You can't come back to a home unless it was a[1]
    home you went away from.

Between hay and grass neither one nor the other.

Can't you be useful as well as ornamental?

Why don't you go roll a peanut around the corner?
    When did they let you out?

The mules went to ask horns and came back without ears.

When you get hold of a good thing freeze onto it.
    Nothing to do and all day to do it in.

So dumb he spent his last dollar buying a pocketbook to put it in.
    A little more sandpaper and this will be smooth.

Write on one side of the paper and both sides of the subject.

Swear to it on a stack of Bibles and they wouldn't believe you.
    Be not a baker if your head be of butter.

Yesterday? It's a nickel thrown on a Salvation Army drum.

How could I let go when it was all I could do to hold on?

Thousands drink themselves to death before ones dies of thirst.
    He didn't have much till he married a hunk of tin.
    There's always a nut on every family tree.
    The mosquitoes organized and drove me out of bed.

We'll fight till hell freezes over and then write on the ice, "Come on,
    you bastards."

The yes-man spent his vacation yelling, "No, no! I tell you No!"

A man having nothing to feed his cow sang to her of the fresh green
    grass to come; this is the tune the old cow died on.

The man feeding a hatful of doughnuts to a horse explained to the
    curious, "I want to see how many he'll eat before he asks for a cup
    of coffee."

"I fired the man," said the new section boss, "not because I had any-
    thing agin him but because I had the authority."

"Don't I argue? Don't I sputify?" the backwoods preacher inquired of
    the complaining committee whose chairman responded, "Yes, you
    do argue and you do sputify but you don't tell wherein!"

---

[1] *Ibid.*, 111–113.

The late riser is asked, "Are you up for all day?"

Shut the door—do you want to heat all outdoors?

He won't go to a wedding unless he's the bride nor a funeral unless he's the corpse.

"May you have the sevenyear itch," was answered, "I hope your wife eats crackers in bed."

He was always a hell of a big fellow in Washington when he was in Rhode Island and a hell of a big fellow in Rhode Island when he was in Washington.

You say you are going to Warsaw (or Boston) because you want me to think you are going to Lemberg (or Buffalo) but I know you are going to Warsaw (or Boston.)

He got on a horse and rode off in all directions at once.

Did they let you out or did you let yourself out?

"Why!" said a Republican Governor of Illinois, "Why the Democrats can't run the government! It's all us Republicans can do."

This will last a thousand years and after that to the end of the world.

When a member died the newspaper men of the Whitechapel Club of Chicago gave the toast:

"Hurrah for the next who goes!"

In Vermont a shut-mouthed husband finally broke forth to his wife, "When I think of how much you have meant to me all these years, it is almost more than I can do sometimes to keep from telling you so."

*   *   *   *   *

"A long, tall man won't always make a good fireman," said the Santa[1] Fe engineer to a couple of other rails deadheading back. "Out of a dozen wants to be firemen you can pick 'em. Take one of these weakly fellers he'll do his best but he's all gone time you get nine miles. Take a short, stout feller, low down so he can get at his coal, and he'll beat one of those tall fellers has to stoop. But if a tall feller's got long arms he can do wonders. I knowed one engineer used to say he had a fireman he never saw him throw a shovel of coal on the fire—his arms was so long he just reached and laid the coal on!"

He can turn around on a dime.

He has an automobile thirst and a wheelbarrow income.

I don't know where I'm going but I'm on my way.

I'll knock you so high in the air you'll starve coming down.

A bonanza is a hole in the ground owned by a champion liar.

All you get from him you can put in your eye.

He tried to get a bird in the hand and two in the bush but what he got was a horse of another color.

---

[1] *Ibid.*, pp. 59–60.

If the government tried to pay me for what I don't know there wouldn't
be enough money in all the mints to pay me.

You can't tell him anything because he thinks he knows more now
than he gets paid for.

It's a slow burg—I spent a couple of weeks there one day.

He bit off more than he could chew.

Don't take a mouthful bigger than your mouth.

Let's take it apart to see how it ticks.

If we had a little ham we could have some ham and eggs if we had
some eggs.

He always takes off his hat when he mentions his own name.

What's the matter with him? The big I, always the big I.

"Why didn't you zigzag your car and miss him?" "He was zigzagging
himself and outguessed me."

"Are you guilty or not guilty?" "What else have you?"

"Are you guilty or not guilty?" "I stands mute."

> "I never borrowed your umbrella," said a [1]
>   borrower, "and if I did I brought it back."
> He was quiet as a wooden-legged man on a tin roof
>   and busy as a one-armed paper hanger with the
>   hives.
> When a couple of fried eggs were offered the new
>   hired man he said, "I don't dirty my plate for
>   less than six."

> Ugly? Sleep stays away from him till he covers his [2]
>   face.
> Poor? He can't raise money enough to buy lumber
>   for a backhouse.
> Big Feet? Buying shoes he don't ask for a number,
>   he says, "Lemme see the biggest you got."

The name of a stub line under the Lone Star banner is The Houston [3]
Eastern and Western Texas railroad.

On the passenger and freight cars is the monogram, the initials
H. E. W. T.

And nearly everybody in the territory traversed and the adjacent right
of way calls it "Hell Either Way you Take It."

The Never Did and Couldn't railway is the N. D. & C., Newburgh,
Duchess and Connecticut.

The Delay Linger and Wait is the D. L. & W., the Delaware, Lacka-
wanna and Western.

---

[1] *Ibid.,* p. 64.
[2] *Ibid.,* p. 119.
[3] *Ibid.,* p. 149.

Come Boys and Quit Railroading ran the slogan of the 1888 engineer's
strike on the C. B. & Q. RR., the Chicago Burlington & Quincy
Rail Road.

No matter how thick or how thin you slice it it's still baloney.[1]

I would if I could and I could if I would but if I couldn't how could
I, could you?

I never made a mistake in grammar but once in my life and as soon as
I done it I seen it.

He was a good shoveler but I don't know as I would say he was a
fancy shoveler.

"You're always talking about liberty, do you want liberty?" "I don't
know as I do and I don't know *as* I do."

"The train is running easier now." "Yes, we're off the track now."

The chorus goes, "They take him by the hand, and they lead him to
the land, and the farmer is the man who feeds them all."

"I hear a burglar in the house." "Wait, if he finds anything worth
stealing we'll take it away from him."

"Did you say the sky is the limit?" "Yes, we won't go any higher than
the sky."

"That dwarf ain't worth ten cents to see—he's five feet high if he's a
foot." "Exactly, my good sir, he's the tallest dwarf in the world."

> The big fish eat the little fish,[2]
> the little fish eat shrimps
> and the shrimps eat mud.
> You don't know enough to come in when it rains.
> You don't know beans when the bag is open.
> You don't know enough to pound sand in a rat hole.
> All I know is what I hear.
> All I know is what I read in the papers.
> All I know you can put in a thimble.
> All I know I keep forgetting. . . .

The Old Doll's House

Now it seems that one cold winter night, a party of residents of
Brooklyn comes across the Manhattan Bridge in an automobile wishing to pay a call on a guy by the name of Lance McGowan, who is
well known to one and all along Broadway as a coming guy in the
business world.

---

[1] *Ibid.*, p. 160.
[2] *Ibid.*, p. 234.

From *Damon Runyan's Blue Plate Special*, pp. 199–216. New York: Frederick A.
Stokes Company, 1934. Copyright, 1934, by Damon Runyon.

In fact, it is generally conceded that, barring accident, Lance will someday be one of the biggest guys in this country as an importer, and especially as an importer of such merchandise as fine liquors, because he is very bright, and has many good connections throughout the United States and Canada.

Furthermore, Lance McGowan is a nice-looking young guy and he has plenty of ticker, although some citizens say he does not show very sound business judgment in trying to move in on Angie the Ox over in Brooklyn, as Angie the Ox is an importer himself, besides enjoying a splendid trade in other lines, including artichokes and extortion.

Of course Lance McGowan is not interested in artichokes at all, and very little in extortion, but he does not see any reason why he shall not place his imports in a thriving territory such as Brooklyn, especially as his line of merchandise is much superior to anything handled by Angie the Ox.

Anyway, Angie is one of the residents of Brooklyn in the party that wishes to call on Lance McGowan, and besides Angie the party includes a guy by the name of Mockie Max, who is a very prominent character in Brooklyn, and another guy by the name of The Louse Kid, who is not so prominent, but who is considered a very promising young guy in many respects, although personally I think The Louse has a very weak face.

He is supposed to be a wonderful hand with a burlap bag when anybody wishes to put somebody in such a bag, which is considered a great practical joke in Brooklyn, and in fact The Louse Kid has a burlap bag with him on the night in question, and they are figuring on putting Lance McGowan in the bag when they call on him, just for a laugh. Personally, I consider this a very crude form of humor, but then Angie the Ox and the other members of his party are very crude characters, anyway.

Well, it seems they have Lance McGowan pretty well cased, and they know that of an evening along toward ten o'clock he nearly always strolls through West Fifty-fourth Street on his way to a certain spot on Park Avenue that is called the Humming Bird Club, which has a very high-toned clientele, and the reason Lance goes there is because he has a piece of the joint, and furthermore he loves to show off his shape in a tuxedo to the swell dolls.

So these residents of Brooklyn drive in their automobile along this route, and as they roll past Lance McGowan, Angie the Ox and Mockie Max let fly at Lance with a couple of sawed-offs, while The Louse Kid holds the burlap bag, figuring for all I know that Lance will be startled by the sawed-offs and will hop into the bag like a rabbit.

But Lance is by no means a sucker, and when the first blast of the slugs from the sawed-offs breezes past him without hitting him, what does he do but hop over a brick wall alongside him and drop into a yard on the other side. So Angie the Ox, and Mockie Max and The Louse Kid get out of their automobile and run up close to the wall themselves because they commence figuring that if Lance McGowan starts popping at them from behind this wall, they will be taking plenty the worst of it, for of course they cannot figure Lance to be strolling about without being rodded up somewhat.

But Lance is by no means rodded up, because a rod is apt to create a bump in his shape when he has his tuxedo on, so the story really begins with Lance McGowan behind the brick wall, practically defenseless, and the reason I know this story is because Lance McGowan tells most of it to me, as Lance knows that I know his real name is Lancelot, and he feels under great obligation to me because I never mention the matter publicly.

Now, the brick wall Lance hops over is a wall around a pretty fair-sized yard, and the yard belongs to an old two-story stone house, and this house is well known to one and all in this man's town as a house of great mystery, and it is pointed out as such by the drivers of sight-seeing buses.

This house belongs to an old doll by the name of Miss Abigail Ardsley, and anybody who ever reads the newspapers will tell you that Miss Abigail Ardsley has so many potatoes that it is really painful to think of, especially to people who have no potatoes whatever. In fact, Miss Abigail Ardsley has practically all the potatoes in the world, except maybe a few left over for general circulation.

These potatoes are left to her by her papa, old Waldo Ardsley, who accumulates same in the early days of this town by buying corner real estate very cheap before people realize this real estate will be quite valuable later on for fruit-juice stands and cigar stores.

It seems that Waldo is a most eccentric old bloke, and is very strict with his daughter, and will never let her marry, or even as much as look as if she wishes to marry, until finally she is so old she does not care a cuss about marrying, or anything else, and becomes very eccentric herself.

In fact, Miss Abigail Ardsley becomes so eccentric that she cuts herself off from everybody, and especially from a lot of relatives who are wishing to live off of her, and any time anybody cuts themselves off from such characters they are considered very eccentric, indeed, especially by the relatives. She lives in the big house all alone, except for a couple of old servants, and it is very seldom that anybody sees her around and about, and many strange stories are told of her.

Well, no sooner is he in the yard than Lance McGowan begins looking for a way to get out, and one way he does not wish to get out is over the wall again, because he figures Angie the Ox and his sawed-offs are bound to be waiting for him in Fifty-fourth Street. So Lance looks around to see if there is some way out of the yard in another direction, but it seems there is no such way, and pretty soon he sees the snozzle of a sawed-off come poking over the wall, with the ugly kisser of Angie the Ox behind it, looking for him, and there is Lance McGowan all cornered up in the yard, and not feeling so good, at that.

Then Lance happens to try a door on one side of the house, and the door opens at once and Lance McGowan hastens in to find himself in the living-room of the house. It is a very large living-room with very nice furniture standing around and about, and oil paintings on the walls, and a big old grandfather's clock as high as the ceiling, and statuary here and there. In fact, it is such a nice, comfortable-looking room that Lance McGowan is greatly surprised, as he is expecting to find a regular mystery-house room such as you see in the movies, with cobwebs here and there, and everything all rotted up, and maybe Boris Karloff wandering about making strange noises.

But the only person in this room seems to be a little old doll all dressed in soft white, who is sitting in a low rocking-chair by an open fireplace in which a bright fire is going, doing some tatting.

Well, naturally Lance McGowan is somewhat startled by this scene, and he is figuring that the best thing he can do is to guzzle the old doll before she can commence yelling for the gendarmes, when she looks up at him and gives him a soft smile, and speaks to him in a soft voice, as follows:

"Good evening," the old doll says.

Well, Lance cannot think of any reply to make to this at once, as it is certainly not a good evening for him, and he stands there looking at the old doll, somewhat dazed, when she smiles again and tells him to sit down.

So the next thing Lance knows, he is sitting there in a chair in front of the fireplace chewing the fat with the old doll as pleasant as you please, and of course the old doll is nobody but Miss Abigail Ardsley. Furthermore, she does not seem at all alarmed, or even much surprised, at seeing Lance in her home, but then Lance is never such a looking guy as is apt to scare old dolls, or young dolls either, especially when he is all slicked up.

Of course Lance knows who Miss Abigail Ardsley is, because he often reads stories in the newspapers about her the same as everybody else, and he always figures such a character must be slightly daffy to cut herself off from everybody when she has all the potatoes in the world, and there is so much fun going on, but he is very courteous to her, because after all he is a guest in her home.

"You are young," the old doll says to Lance McGowan, looking him in the kisser. "It is many years since a young man comes through yonder door. Ah, yes," she says, "so many years."

And with this she lets out a big sigh, and look so very sad that Lance McGowan's heart is touched.

"Forty-five years now," the old doll says in a low voice, as if she is talking to herself. "So young, so handsome, and so good."

And although Lance is in no mood to listen to reminiscences at this time, the next thing he knows he is hearing a very pathetic love story, because it seems that Miss Abigail Ardsley is once all hotted up over a younger guy who is nothing but a clerk in her papa's office.

It seems from what Lance McGowan gathers that there is nothing wrong with the young guy that a million bobs will not cure, but Miss Abigail Ardsley's papa is a mean old waffle, and he will never listen to her having any truck with a poor guy, so they dast not let him know how much they love each other.

But it seems that Miss Abigail Ardsley's ever-loving young guy has plenty of moxie, and every night he comes to see her after her papa goes to the hay, and she lets him in through the same side-door Lance McGowan comes through, and they sit by the fire and hold hands, and talk in low tones, and plan what they will do when the young guy makes a scratch.

Then one night it seems Miss Abigail Ardsley's papa has the stomach ache, or some such, and cannot sleep a wink, so he comes wandering downstairs looking for the Jamaica ginger, and catches Miss Abigail Ardsley and her ever-loving guy in a clutch that will win the title for any wrestler that can ever learn it.

Well, this scene is so repulsive to Miss Abigail Ardsley's papa that he is practically speechless for a minute, and then he orders the young guy out of his life in every respect, and tells him never to darken his door again, especially the side-door.

But it seems that by this time a great storm is raging outside, and Miss Abigail Ardsley begs and pleads with her papa to let the young guy at least remain until the storm subsides, but between being all sored up at the clutching scene he witnesses, and his stomach ache, Mr. Ardsley is very hard-hearted, indeed, and he makes the young guy take the wind.

The next morning the poor young guy is found at the side-door frozen as stiff as a board, because it seems that the storm that is raging is the blizzard of 1888, which is a very famous event in the history of New York, although up to this time Lance McGowan never hears of it before, and does not believe it until he looks the matter up afterwards. It seems from what Miss Abigail Ardsley says that as near as anyone can make out, the young guy must return to the door seeking shelter after wandering about in the storm a while, but of course by this time her papa has the door all bolted up, and nobody hears the young guy.

"And," Miss Abigail Ardsley says to Lance McGowan, after giving him all these details, "I never speak to my papa again as long as he lives, and no other man ever comes in or out of yonder door, or any other door of this house, until your appearance tonight, although," she says, "this side-door is never locked in case such a young man comes seeking shelter."

Then she looks at Lance McGowan in such a way that he wonders if Miss Abigail Ardsley hears the sawed-offs going when Angie the Ox and Mockie Max are tossing slugs at him, but he is too polite to ask.

Well, all these old-time memories seem to make Miss Abigail Ardsley feel very tough, and by and by she starts to weep, and if there is one thing Lance McGowan cannot stand it is a doll weeping, even if she is nothing but an old doll. So he starts in to cheer Miss Abigail Ardsley up, and he pats her on the arm, and says to her like this:

"Why," Lance says, "I am greatly surprised to hear your statement about the doors around here being so little used. Why, Sweetheart," Lance says, "if I know there is a doll as good-looking as you in the neighborhood, and a door unlocked, I will be busting in myself every night. Come, come, come," Lance says, "let us talk things over and maybe have a few laughs, because I may have to stick around here a while. Listen, Sweetheart," he says, "do you happen to have a drink in the joint?"

Well, at this Miss Abigail Ardsley dries her eyes, and smiles again, and then she pulls a sort of rope near her, and in comes a guy who seems about ninety years old, and who seems greatly surprised to see Lance there. In fact, he is so surprised that he is practically tottering when he leaves the room after hearing Miss Abigail Ardsley tell him to bring some wine and sandwiches.

And the wine he brings is such wine that Lance McGowan has half a mind to send some of the lads around afterwards to see if there is any more of it in the joint, especially when he thinks of the un-locked side-door, because he can sell this kind of wine by the carat.

Well, Lance sits there with Miss Abigail Ardsley sipping wine and eating sandwiches, and all the time he is telling her stories of one kind and another, some of which he cleans up a little when he figures they may be a little too snappy for her, and by and by he has her laughing quite heartily indeed.

Finally he figures there is no chance of Angie and his sawed-offs being outside waiting for him, so he says he guesses he will be going, and Miss Abigail Ardsley personally sees him to the door, and this time it is the front door, and as Lance is leaving he thinks of something he once sees a guy do on the stage, and he takes Miss Abigail Ardsley's hand and raises it to his lips and gives it a large kiss all of which is very surprising to Miss Abigail Ardsley, but more so to Lance McGowan when he gets to thinking about it afterwards.

Just as he figures, there is no one in sight when he gets out in the street, so he goes on over to the Humming Bird Club, where he learns that many citizens are greatly disturbed by his absence, and are won-dering if he is in The Louse Kid's burlap bag, for by this time it is pretty well known that Angie the Ox and his fellow citizens of Brooklyn are around and about.

In fact, somebody tells Lance that Angie is at the moment over in Good Time Charley's little speak in West Forty-ninth Street, buying drinks for one and all, and telling how he makes Lance McGowan hop a brick wall, which of course sounds most disparaging of Lance.

Well, while Angie is still buying these drinks, and still speaking of making Lance a brick-wall hopper, all of a sudden the door of Good Time Charley's speak opens and in comes a guy with a Betsy in his hand and this guy throws four slugs into Angie the Ox before anybody can say hello.

Furthermore, the guy throws one slug into Mockie Max, and one slug into The Louse Kid, who are still with Angie the Ox, so the next thing anybody knows there is Angie as dead as a door-nail, and there is Mockie Max even deader than Angie, and there is The Louse making a terrible fuss over a slug in his leg, and nobody can remember what the guy who plugs them looks like, except a couple of stool pigeons who state that the guy looks very much like Lance McGowan.

So what happens but early the next morning Johnny Brannigan, the plain-clothes copper, puts the arm on Lance McGowan for plugging Angie the Ox, and Mockie Max and The Louse Kid, and there is great rejoicing in copper circles generally because at this time the newspapers are weighing in the sacks on the coppers quite some, claiming there is too much lawlessness going on around and about and asking why somebody is not arrested for something.

So the collar of Lance McGowan is water on the wheel of one and all because Lance is so prominent, and anybody will tell you that it looks as if it is a sure thing that Lance will be very severely punished, and maybe sent to the electric chair, although he hires Judge Goldstein, who is one of the surest-footed lawyers in this town, to defend him. But even Judge Goldstein admits that Lance is in a tough spot, especially as the newspapers are demanding justice, and printing long stories about Lance, and pictures of him, and calling him some very uncouth names.

Finally Lance himself commences to worry about his predicament, although up to this time a little thing like being charged with murder in the first degree never bothers Lance very much. And in fact he will not be bothering very much about this particular charge if he does not find the D. A. very fussy about letting him out on bail. In fact, it is nearly two week before he lets Lance out on bail, and all this time Lance is in the sneezer, which is a most mortifying situation to a guy as sensitive as Lance.

Well, by the time Lance's trial comes up, you can get 3 to 1 anywhere that he will be convicted, and the price goes up to 5 when the prosecution gets through with its case, and proves by the stool pigeons that at exactly twelve o'clock on the night of January 5th,

Lance McGowan steps into Good Time Charley's little speak and plugs Angie the Ox, Mockie Max and The Louse Kid.

Furthermore, several other witnesses who claim they know Lance McGowan by sight testify that they see Lance in the neighborhood of Good Time Charley's around twelve o'clock, so by the time it comes Judge Goldstein's turn to put on the defense, many citizens are saying that if he can do no more than beat the chair for Lance he will be doing a wonderful job.

Well, it is late in the afternoon when Judge Goldstein gets up and looks all around the courtroom, and without making any opening statement to the jury for the defense, as these mouthpieces usually do, he says like this:

"Call Miss Abigail Ardsley," he says.

At first nobody quite realizes just who Judge Goldstein is calling for, although the name sounds familiar to one and all present who read the newspapers, when in comes a little old doll in a black silk dress that almost reaches the floor, and a black bonnet that makes a sort of a frame for her white hair and face.

Afterwards I read in one of the newspapers that she looks like she steps down out of an old-fashioned ivory miniature and that she is practically beautiful, but of course Miss Abigail Ardsley has so many potatoes that no newspaper dast to say that she looks like an old chromo.

Anyway, she comes into the courtroom surrounded by so many old guys you will think it must be recess at the Old Men's Home, except they are all dressed up in claw-hammer coat tails, and high collars, and afterwards it turns out that they are the biggest lawyers in this town, and they all represent Miss Abigail Ardsley one way or another, and they are present to see that her interests are protected, especially from each other.

Nobody ever see so much bowing and scraping before in a courtroom. In fact, even the judge bows, and although I am only a spectator I find myself bowing too, because the way I look at it, anybody with as many potatoes as Miss Abigail Ardsley is entitled to a general bowing. When she takes the witness-stand, her lawyers grab chairs and move up as close to her as possible, and in the street outside there is practically a riot as word goes around that Miss Abigail Ardsley is in the court, and citizens come running from every which way, hoping to get a peek at the richest old doll in the world.

Well, when all hands finally get settled down a little, Judge Goldstein speaks to Miss Abigail Ardsley as follows:

"Miss Ardsley," he says, "I am going to ask you just two or three questions. Kindly look at this defendant," Judge Goldstein says, pointing at Lance McGowan, and giving Lance the office to stand up. "Do you recognize him?"

Well, the little old doll takes a gander at Lance, and nods her head yes, and Lance gives her a large smile, and Judge Goldstein says:

"Is he a caller in your home on the night of January fifth?" Judge Goldstein asks.

"He is," Miss Abigail Ardsley says.

"Is there a clock in the living-room in which you receive this defendant?" Judge Goldstein says.

"There is," Miss Abigail Ardsley says. "A large clock," she says. "A grandfather's clock."

"Do you happen to notice," Judge Goldstein says, "and do you now recall the hour indicated by this clock when the defendant leaves your home?"

"Yes," Miss Abigail Ardsley says, "I do happen to notice. It is just twelve o'clock by my clock," she says. "Exactly twelve o'clock," she says.

Well, this statement creates a large sensation in the courtroom, because if it is twelve o'clock when Lance McGowan leaves Miss Abigail Ardsley's house in West Fifty-fourth Street, anybody can see that there is no way he can be in Good Time Charley's little speak over five blocks away at the same minute unless he is a magician, and the judge begins peeking over his specs at the coppers in the court-room very severe, and the cops begin scowling at the stool pigeons, and I am willing to lay plenty of 6 to 5 that the stools will wish they are never born before they hear the last of this matter from the gendarmes.

Furthermore, the guys from the D. A.'s office who are handling the prosecution are looking much embarrassed, and the jurors are muttering to each other, and right away Judge Goldstein says he moves that the case against his client be dismissed, and the judge says he is in favor of the motion, and he also says he thinks it is high time the gendarmes in this town learn to be a little careful who they are arrest-ing for murder, and the guys from the D. A.'s office do not seem to be able to think of anything whatever to say.

So there is Lance as free as anybody, and as he starts to leave the courtroom he stops by Miss Abigail Ardsley, who is still sitting in the witness-chair surrounded by her mouthpieces, and he shakes her hand and thanks her, and while I do not hear it myself, somebody tells me afterwards that Miss Abigail Ardsley says to Lance in a low voice, like this:

"I will be expecting you again some night, young man," she says.

"Some night, Sweetheart," Lance says, "at twelve o'clock."

And then he goes on about his business, and Miss Abigail Ardsley goes on about hers, and everybody says it is certainly a wonderful thing that a doll as rich as Miss Abigail Ardsley comes forward in the interests of justice to save a guy like Lance McGowan from a wrong rap.

But of course it is just as well for Lance that Miss Abigail Ardsley

does not explain to the court that when she recovers from the shock
of the finding of her ever-loving young guy frozen to death, she stops
all the clocks in her house at the hour she sees him last, so for forty-
five years it is always twelve o'clock in her house.

A Letter to Al

Paso Robles, California, March 2.

Old Pal Al: Well Al we been in this little berg now a couple of days
and its bright and warm all the time just like June. Seems funny to
have it so warm this early in March but I guess this California climate
is all they said about it and then some.

It would take me a week to tell you about our trip out here. We
came on a Special Train De Lukes and it was some train. Every place
we stopped there was crowds down to the station to sees us go through
and all the people looked me over like I was a actor or something. I
guess my hight and shoulders attracted their attention. Well Al we
finally got to Oakland which is across part of the ocean from Frisco.
We will be back there later on for practice games.

We stayed in Oakland a few hours and then took a train for here.
I have road one night at a time but this was four straight nights. You
know Al I am not built right for a sleeping car birth.

The hotel here is a great big place and got good eats. We got in at
breakfast time and I made a B line for the dining room. Kid Gleason
who is a kind of asst. manager to Callahan come in and sat down with
me. He says Leave something for the rest of the boys because they will
be just as hungry as you. He says Ain't you afraid you will cut your
throat with that knife. He says There ain't no extra charge for using
the forks. He says You shouldn't ought to eat so much because you're
overweight now. I says You may think I am fat, but it's all solid bone
and muscle. He says Yes I suppose it's all solid bone from the neck
up. I guess he thought I would get sore but I will let them kid me
now because they will take off their hats to me when they see me work.

Manager Callahan called us all to his room after breakfast and give
us a lecture. He says there would be no work for us the first day but
that we must all take a long walk over the hills. He also says we must
not take the training trip as a joke. Then the colored trainer give
us our suits and I went to my room and tried mine on. I ain't a bad
looking guy in the White Sox uniform Al. I will have my picture
taken and send you boys some.

My roommate is Allen a left hander from the Coast League. He
don't look nothing like a pitcher but you can't never tell about them

From *You Know Me Al, A Busher's Letters*, by Ring W. Lardner, pp. 15–18.
New York: George H. Doran Company. Copyright, 1916, by George H. Doran Company; Copyright, 1914, by the Curtis Publishing Company.

dam left handers. Well I didn't go on the long walk because I was tired out. Walsh stayed at the hotel too and when he seen me he says Why didn't you go with the bunch? I says I was too tired. He says Well when Callahan comes back you better keep out of sight or tell him you are sick. I says I don't care nothing for Callahan. He says No but Callahan is crazy about you. He says You better obey orders and you will git along better. I guess Walsh thinks I am some rube.

When the bunch come back Callahan never said a word to me but Gleason come up and says Where was you? I told him I was too tired to go walking. He says Well I will borrow a wheel-barrow some place and push you round. He says Do you sit down when you pitch? I let him kid me because he has not saw my stuff yet.

Next morning half the bunch mostly veterans went to the ball park which isn't no better than the one we got at home. Most of them was veterans as I say but I was in the bunch. That makes things look pretty good for me don't it Al? We tossed the ball round and hit fungos and run round and then Callahan asks Scott and Russell and I to warm up easy and pitch a few to the batters. It was warm and I felt pretty good so I warmed up pretty good. Scott pitched to them first and kept laying them right over with nothing on them. I don't believe a man gets any batting practice that way. So I went in and after I lobbed a few over I cut loose my fast one. Lord was to bat and he ducked out of the way and then throwed his bat to the bench. Callahan says What's the matter Harry? Lord says I forgot to pay up my life insurance. He says I ain't ready for Walter Johnson's July stuff.

Well Al I will make them think I am Walter Johnson before I get through with them. But Callahan come out to me and says What are you trying to do kill somebody? He says Save your smoke because you're going to need it later on. He says Go easy with the boys at first or I won't have no batters. But he was laughing and I guess he was pleased to see the stuff I had.

There is a dance in the hotel to-night and I am up in my room writing this in my underwear while I get my suit pressed. I got it all mussed up coming out here. I don't know what shoes to wear. I asked Gleason and he says Wear your baseball shoes and if any of the girls gets fresh with you spike them. I guess he was kidding me.

Write and tell me all the news about home.

Yours truly,   JACK.

The Words are the Words of English

. . . After Buck Fanshaw's inquest, a meeting of the shorthaired
brotherhood was held, for nothing can be done on the Pacific coast
without a public meeting and an expression of sentiment. Regretful
resolutions were passed and various committees appointed; among
others, a committee of one was deputed to call on the minister, a
fragile, gentle, spiritual new fledgling from an Eastern theological
seminary, and as yet unacquainted with the ways of the mines. The
committeeman, "Scotty" Briggs, made his visit; and in after days it was
worth something to hear the minister tell about it. Scotty was a stalwart rough, whose customary suit, when on weighty official business,
like committee work, was a fire helmet, flaming red flannel shirt,
patent leather belt with spanner and revolver attached, coat hung
over arm, and pants stuffed into boot tops. He formed something of a
contrast to the pale theological student. . . . Being admitted to the
presence he sat down before the clergyman, placed his firehat on an
unfinished manuscript sermon under the minister's nose, took from it
a red silk handkerchief, wiped his brow and heaved a sigh of dismal
impressiveness, explanatory of his business. He choked, and even shed
tears; but with an effort he mastered his voice and said in lugubrious
tones:

"Are you the duck that runs the gospel-mill next door?"

"Am I the—pardon me, I believe I do not understand?"

With another sigh and a half-sob, Scotty rejoined:

"Why, you see, we are in a bit of trouble, and the boys thought
maybe you would give us a lift, if we'd tackle you—that is, if I've got
the rights of it and you are the head clerk of the doxology-works
next door."

"I am the shepherd in charge of the flock whose fold is next door."

"The which?"

"The spiritual adviser of the little company of believers whose
sanctuary adjoins these premises."

Scotty scratched his head, reflected a moment, and then said:

"You ruther hold over me, pard. I reckon I can't call that hand.
Ante and pass the buck."

"How? I beg your pardon. What did I understand you to say?"

"Well, you've ruther got the bulge on me. Or maybe we've both
got the bulge, somehow. You don't smoke me and I don't smoke you.
You see, one of the boys has passed in his checks, and we want to give

From *Roughing It*, by Samuel L. Clemens, Ch. VI. Entered according to Act of
Congress, in the year 1872, by The American Publishing Company in the office of
the Librarian of Congress, at Washington; copyright, 1899, by The American Publishing Company; 1899, by Samuel L. Clemens.

him a good sendoff, and so the thing I'm on now is to roust out somebody to jerk a little chin-music for us and waltz him through handsome."

"My friend, I seem to grow more and more bewildered. Your observations are wholly incomprehensible to me. Cannot you simplify
them in some way? At first I thought perhaps I understood you, but I
grope now. Would it not expedite matters if you restricted yourself
to categorical statements of fact unencumbered with obstructing accumulations of metaphor and allegory?"

Another pause, and more reflection. Then, said Scotty:

"I'll have to pass, I judge."

"How?"

"You've raised me out, pard."

"I still fail to catch your meaning."

"Why, that last lead of yourn is too many for me—that's the idea.
I can't neither trump nor follow suit."

The clergyman sank back in his chair perplexed. Scotty leaned
his head on his hand and gave himself up to thought. Presently his
face came up, sorrowful but confident.

"I've got it now, so's you can savvy," he said. "What we want is a
gospel-sharp. See?"

"A what?"

"Gospel-sharp. Parson."

"Oh! Why did you not say so before? I am a clergyman—a parson."

"Now you talk! You see my blind, and straddle it like a man. Put
it there!"—extending a brawny paw, which closed over the minister's
small hand and gave it a shake indicative of fraternal sympathy and
fervent gratification.

"Now we're all right, pard. Let's start fresh. Don't you mind my
snuffling a little—becuz we're in a power of trouble. You see, one of
the boys has gone up the flume—"

"Gone where?"

"Up the flume—throwed up the sponge, you understand."

"Thrown up the sponge?"

"Yes—kicked the bucket—"

"Ah—has departed to that mysterious country from whose bourne
no traveler returns."

"Return! I reckon not. Why, pard, he's *dead!*"

"Yes, I understand."

"Oh, you do? Well, I thought maybe you might be getting tangled
some more. Yes, you see he's dead again—"

"*Again!* Why, has he ever been dead before?"

"Dead before? No! Do you reckon a man has got as many lives as a
cat? But you bet you he's awful dead now, poor old boy, and I wish
I'd never seen this day. I don't want no better friend than Buck
Fanshaw. I knowed him by the back; and when I know a man and

like him, I freeze to him—you hear *me*. Take him all round, pard, there never was a bullier man in the mines. No man ever knowed Buck Fanshaw to go back on a friend. But it's all up, you know, it's all up. It ain't no use. They've scooped him."

"Scooped him?"

"Yes—death has. Well, well, well, we've got to give him up. Yes, indeed. It's a kind of a hard world, after all, *ain't* it? But pard, he was a rustler! You ought to seen him get started once. He was a bully boy with a glass eye! Just spit in his face and give him room according to his strength, and it was just beautiful to see him peel and go in. He was the worst son of a thief that ever drawed breath. Pard, he was *on* it! He was on it bigger than an Injun!"

"On it? On what?"

"On the shoot. On the shoulder. On the fight, you understand. *He* didn't give a continental for *any*body. *Beg* your pardon, friend, for coming so near saying a cussword—but you see I'm on an awful strain, in this palaver, on account of having to cramp down and draw everything so mild. But we've got to give him up. There ain't any getting around that, I don't reckon. Now if we can get you to help plant him—"

"Preach the funeral discourse? Assist at the obsequies?"

"Obs'quies is good. Yes. That's it—that's our little game. We are going to get the thing up regardless, you know. He was always nifty himself, and so you bet you his funeral ain't going to be no slouch—solid silver door-plate on his coffin, six plumes on the hearse, and a nigger on the box in a biled shirt and a plug hat—how's that for high? And we'll take care of *you*, pard. We'll fix you all right. There'll be a kerridge for you; and whatever you want, you just 'scape out and we'll 'tend to it. We've got a shebang fixed up for you to stand behind, in No. 1's house, and don't you be afraid. Just go in and toot your horn, if you don't sell a clam. Put Buck through as bully as you can, pard, for anybody that knowed him will tell you that he was one of the whitest men that was ever in the mines. You can't draw it too strong. He never could stand it to see things going wrong. He's done more to make this town quiet and peaceable than any man in it. I've seen him lick four Greasers in eleven minutes, myself. If a thing wanted regulating, *he* warn't a man to go browsing around after somebody, to do it, but he would prance in and regulate it himself. He warn't a Catholic. Scasely. He was down on 'em. His word was, 'No Irish need apply!' But it didn't make no difference about that when it came down to what a man's rights was—and so, when some roughs jumped the Catholic boneyard and started in to stake out town-lots in it he *went* for 'em! And he *cleaned* 'em, too! I was there, pard, and I see it myself."

"That was very well indeed—at least the impulse was—whether the act was strictly defensible or not. Had deceased any religious con-

victions? That is to say, did he feel a dependence upon, or acknowl-
edge allegiance, to a higher power?"

More reflection.

"I reckon you've stumped me again, pard. Could you say it over
once more, and say it slow?"

"Well, to simplify it somewhat, was he, or rather had he ever been
connected with any organization sequestered from secular concerns
and devoted to self-sacrifice in the interests of morality?"

"All down but nine—set 'em up on the other alley, pard."

"What did I understand you to say?"

"Why, you're most too many for me, you know. When you get in
with your left, I hunt grass every time. Every time you draw, you fill;
but I don't seem to have any luck. Let's have a new deal."

"How? Begin again?"

"That's it."

"Very well. Was he a good man, and—"

"There—I see that; don't put up another chip till I look at my
hand. A good man, says you? Pard, it ain't no name for it. He was
the best man that ever—pard, you would have doted on that man.
He could lam any galoot of his inches in America. It was him that
put down the riot last election before it got a start; and everybody
said he was the only man that could have done it. He waltzed in with
a spanner in one hand and a trumpet in the other, and sent fourteen
men home on a shutter in less than three minutes. He had that riot
all broke up and prevented nice before anybody ever got a chance to
strike a blow. He was always for peace, and he would *have* peace—he
could not stand disturbances. Pard, he was a great loss to this town.
It would please the boys if you could chip in something like that and
do him justice. Here once when the Micks got to throwing stones
through the Methodis' Sunday-school windows, Buck Fanshaw, all of
his own notion, shut up his saloon and took a couple of six-shooters
and mounted guard over the Sunday-school. Says he, 'No Irish need
apply!' And they didn't. He was the bulliest man in the mountains,
pard! He could run faster, jump higher, hit harder, and hold more
tanglefoot whisky without spilling it than any man in seventeen
counties. Put that in, pard—it'll please the boys more than anything
you could say. And you can say, pard, that he never shook his mother."

"Never shook his mother?"

"That's it—any of the boys will tell you so."

"Well, but why *should* he shake her?"

"That's what *I* say—but some people does."

"Not people of any repute?"

"Well, some that averages pretty so-so."

"In my opinion the man that would offer personal violence to his
own mother, ought to—"

"Cheese it, pard; you've banked your ball clean outside the string.

What I was drivin' at, was, that he never *throwed off* on his mother—don't you see? No indeedy. He give her a house to live in, and town lots, and plenty of money; and he looked after her and took care of her all the time; and when she was down with the smallpox I'm d—d if he didn't set up nights and nuss her himself! *Beg* your pardon for saying it, but it hopped out too quick for yours truly. You've treated me like a gentleman, pard, and I ain't the man to hurt your feelings intentional. I think you're white. I think you're a square man, pard. I like you, and I'll lick any man that don't. I'll lick him till he can't tell himself from a last year's corpse! Put it *there!*" [Another fraternal hand shake—and exit.] . . .

Malaprop Courting

"Tom," said a girl to her sweetheart, " you have been paying your distresses to me long enough. It is time you made known your contentions, so as not to keep me in expense any longer."

Does This *W?*

It is interesting to trace the evolution of words and expressions. Cultured people say "how do you do?" Those who are less precise say "howdy do?" In the backwoods of Tennessee they say "howdy?" The noble red man of the west says "how?" While the cat on the fence says "ow?"

Double Talk

"Our paper is two days late this week," writes a Nebraska editor, "owing to an accident to our press. When we started to run the press Wednesday night, as usual, one of the guy ropes gave way, allowing the forward glider fluke to fall and break as it struck the flunker flopper. This, of course, as any one who knows anything about a press will readily understand, left the gang-plank with only the flip flap to support it, which also dropped and broke off the wooper-chock. This loosened the fluking from between the ranrod and the flibber-snatcher, which also caused trouble. The report that the delay was caused by the over-indulgence in stimulants by ourselves, is a tissue of falsehoods,

From *Gus Williams' World of Humor*. New York: De Witt, Publishers. 1880.

From *American Wit and Humor*, Vol. II, p. 48. Philadelphia: George W. Jacobs & Co. 1900.

From *American Wit and Humor*, Vol. II, p. 197. Philadelphia: George W. Jacobs & Co. 1900.

the peeled appearance of our right eye being caused by our going into the hatchway of the press in our anxiety to start it, and pulling the coupling pin after the slap-bang was broken, which caused the dingus to rise up and welt us in the optic. We expect a brand-new glider fluke on this afternoon's train.

Noun into Verb

"Yesterday," said the college boy home on vacation, "we autoed to the country club, golfed till dark, bridged a while, and autoed home."

"Yesterday," said the father, "I muled to the cornfield and gee-hawed till sundown, then I suppered till dark, piped till nine, bedsteaded till five, breakfasted and went muling again."

Ladle Rat Rotten Hut

Wants pawn term, dare worsted ladle gull hoe lift wetter murder inner ladle cordage honor itch offer lodge dock florist. Disc ladle gull orphan worry ladle cluck wetter putty ladle rat hut, end fur disc raisin pimple caulder ladle rat rotten hut. Wan moaning rat rotten hut's murder colder inset: "Ladle rat rotten hut, heresy ladle basking winsome burden barter and shirker cockles. Tick disc ladle basking tudor cordage offer groin murder hoe lifts honor udder site offer florist. Shaker lake, dun stopper laundry wrote, end yonder nor sorghum stenches dun stopper torque wet strainers."

"Hoe-cake, murder," resplendent ladle rat rotten hut, end tickle ladle basking an stuttered oft. Honor wrote tudor cordage offer groin murder, ladle rat rotten hut mitten anomalous woof.

"Wail, wail, wail," set disc wicket woof, "evanescent ladle rat rotten hut! Wares or putty ladle gull goring wizard ladle basking?"

"Armor goring tumor groin murder's" reprisal ladle gull. "Grammars seeking bet. Armor ticking arson burden barter end shirker cockles."

"O hoe! Heifer blessing woke," setter wicket woof, butter taught tomb shelf, "Oil tickle shirt court tudor cordage offer groin murder. Oil ketchup wetter letter, an den—O bore!"

Soda wicket woof tucker shirt court, end whinney retched a cordage

From *The People, Yes,* by Carl Sandburg, p. 154. Copyright, 1936, by Harcourt, Brace and Company, Inc. New York.

From *Word Study,* Vol. XXVIII (May, 1953), Number 5, p. 4.
A subsequent issue of *Word Study,* [Vol. XXIX (Oct., 1953), Number 1] identifies the author as Prof. Howard Chace, Department of Romance Languages, Miami University, Oxford, Ohio. Professor Chace's hobby is reducing folk tales to what he calls "Anguish Languish."

offer groin murder, picket inner widow an sore debtor port oil worm-
ing worse lion inner bet. Inner flesh disc abdominal woof lipped
honor betting adder rope. Zany pool dawn a groin murder's nut cup
an gnat gun, any curdle dope inner bet.

Inner ladle wile ladle rat rotten hut a raft attar cordage an ranker
dough ball. "Comb ink, sweat hard," setter wicket woof, disgracing is
verse. Ladle rat rotten hut entity bet rum end stud buyer groin
murder's bet. "Oh grammar," crater ladle gull, "Wart bag icer gut!
A nervous sausage bag ice!" "Buttered lucky chew whiff, doling,"
whiskered disc ratchet woof, wetter wicket small. "Oh grammar, water
bag noise! A nervous sore suture anomalous prognosis!" "Buttered
small your whiff," inserter woof, ants mouse worse wadding. "Oh
grammar, water bag mousey gut! A nervous sore suture bag mouse!"

Daze worry on forger nut gull's lest warts. Oil offer sodden throne
offer carvers an sprinkling otter bet, disc curl an bloat Thursday woof
ceased pore ladle rat rotten hut an garbled erupt.

Mural: Yonder nor sorghum stenches shut ladle gulls stopper torque
wet strainers.

Bills of Fare

Some tact should be observed in arranging a *menu*. They are generally written in French; this one therefore is prepared in United States:

Oysters or eggs on the half shell.

Bean Soup.

Shad.   Sauce from the cook.

Sliced cucumbers and Jamaica Ginger.

Colt steaks.   Sheepshead sauce.

Roast beef, plenty of gravy.

Tired eggs, turned over.

Hens, stuffed with soldier buttons.

Tame cheese.

Ice cream garnished with green peas.

Apples and Peanuts.

Sage Tea.

Here's another in French:

MENU.

Huitres, 6 per quartre.

Potage au taisez vous.

Saumon aux no bones.

Ris de veaux.   Sauce, new mown hay.

Ris de Daible.   Sauce nixey.

From *The Berkshire News Comic Cook Book and Dyspeptics Guide to the Grave*,
by Fred H. Curtiss, pp. 14–15. Copyright, 1890, by Douglas Bros., Publishers. Great
Barrington, Massachusetts.

Fillet de bœuf red hot.

Punch *a la* John L.

Bicasses; pommes de terre au peeled.

Salad; marseillaise dressing.

Asperges; *a la* skim milk.

Ramequins au Lambrequins.

Fruit; fi cent a grab.

Glace de creme *a la* Hunter's Point.

Dessert (of Sahara)

The following bill-of-fare is particularly intended for large hotels:

SOUP.

Inthe.   Ox Yoke.   Whalebone.   Cold.

FISH.

Red herring.   Blue herring.   Hamilton Fish.

COLD DISHES.

Cracked ice.   Cold ice.   Cold shoulder.   Thawed ice.

ROAST.

Goat, with drawn butter.   Umpires with batter.

Buffalo, robe sauce.

GAME.

Poker.   Tennis.   Croquet.   Old Sledge.   Old Maid.

Keno.   Pitch.   Pool.   High Low Jack.

ENTREES.

Singed Cat.   Friccassed Frog's Ears.   Liver Pads

and Bacon.   Shakespeare and Bacon.

VEGETABLES.

Dead Beets.   Green Corn.   Soft Corn.   Lettuce alone.

Hay.   Sweet Potatoes.   Sour Potatoes.

Darn Body Oat Meal Stream

Darn body oat meal stream,
    Wear a first mate shoe,
Ouija eyesore blue
    Dresden gingham, too.
It was there anew
    Thatch a loft me too.
You were sixteen,
    Marvel itch Queen,
Darn body oat meal stream!

From *Sillynyms* by Dave Morrah, p. 16. Copyright 1956, by Rinehart and Company. New York.

The Declaration of Independence in American

When things get so balled up that the people of a country have got to cut loose from some other country, and go it on their own hook, without asking no permission from nobody, excepting maybe God Almighty, then they ought to let everybody know why they done it, so that everybody can see they are on the level, and not trying to put nothing over on nobody.

All we got to say on this proposition is this: first, me and you is as good as anybody else, and maybe a damn sight better; second, nobody ain't got no right to take away none of our rights; third, every man has got a right to live, to come and go as he pleases, and to have a good time whichever way he likes, so long as he don't interfere with nobody else. That any government that don't give a man them rights ain't worth a damn; also, people ought to choose the kind of government they want themselves, and nobody else ought to have no say in the matter. That whenever any government don't do this, then the people have got a right to can it and put in one that will take care of their interests. Of course, that don't mean having a revolution every day like them South American coons and yellow-bellies and Bolsheviki, or every time some job-holder goes to work and does something he ain't got no business to do. It is better to stand a little graft, etc., than to have revolutions all the time, like them coons and Bolsheviki, and any man that wasn't a anarchist or one of them I.W.W.'s would say the same. But when things get so bad that a man ain't hardly got no rights at all no more, but you might almost call him a slave, then everybody ought to get together and throw the grafters out, and put in new ones who won't carry on so high and steal so much, and then watch them. . . .

Lincoln's Gettysburg Address in American

Eighty-seven years ago them old-timers that you heard about in school signed the Declaration of Independence, and put the kibosh on the English king, George III. From that day to this, this has been a free country. An American citizen don't have to take offen his hat to nobody, excepting maybe God. He is the equal to anybody on this earth, high or low. If anybody steps on his toes, then they have got

From *The American Language*, An Inquiry into the Development of English in the United States, by H. L. Mencken, pp. 398–402. Third Edition. Copyright, 1923, by Alfred A. Knopf, New York. First printed, as "Essay in American," in the Baltimore *Evening Sun*, Nov. 7, 1921.

Ibid., pp. 402–403.

a fight on their hands, and it ain't over until the other fellow is licked.

Well, now we have got a war on our hands, and them crooks from the South are trying to do to us what they done to the poor coons. The question is whether this free country is going on or whether they are going to put the skids under it. On this very spot where we stand our boys went over the top, and the enemy took to the woods. A great many of them give their lives in that battle. Everyone was a hero. Nobody hung back when the bullets began to fly. Well, we will take care of those who got out of it alive, or maybe with only a leg cut off. No American business man will ever turn a hero away. There will be jobs for all, and plenty of them. But all we can do for the dead is to put up a monument to them, and see that their graves are kept green.

Well, a monument sure ain't much. The fact is, them heroes don't need no monument. Nobody will ever forget them. Schoolchildren will be studying about them long after all us here is gone. Nobody will ever ask what I said in my speech here, or what you said here, but everybody will want to know what our boys done here. The best thing we can do is to not forget what the battle was about that they fought in, and make up our minds to keep this a free country. Suppose we didn't do it? Then what sense would it of been for them heroes to go over the top? Who could look into the eyes of their little children and say "Your papa died for democracy, but now it has gone blooey"? No. This is the freest country in the whole world and it is up to us to keep it free. Let each and everyone here today lift up their right hand and take an oath that they will never support no government withouten it is elected by the people, always remembers who elected it, and never does nothing withouten it is sure the people want it.

The Gettysburg Address for Professors

ED. NOTE: An M.I.T. professor pokes fun at some of his colleagues who *hide* their important messages in language only intelligible to other professors. He says he rewrote this address "so that professors can understand it."

Eight and seven-tenths decades ago the pioneer workers in this continental area implemented a new group based on an ideology of free boundaries and initial conditions of equality. We are now actively engaged in an over-all evaluation of conflicting factors in order to determine whether or not the life expectancy of this group or of any group operating under the stated conditions is significant.

We are met in an area of maximum activity among the conflicting

From *Tech Training*, published by the American Technical Society, as reprinted in *Word Study*, Vol. XXVII (April, 1952). No. 4, pp. 4–5. Springfield, Massachusetts: G. & C. Merriam Company.

factors. The purpose of the meeting is to assign permanent positions to the units which have been annihilated in the process of attaining a steady state. This procedure represents standard practice at the administrative level.

From a more comprehensive viewpoint we cannot assign—we cannot integrate—we cannot implement this area.

The courageous units, in being annihilated, who were active in this area have integrated it to the point where the application of simple arithmetical operations to include our efforts would produce only negligible effects.

The reaction of the general public to this colloquium will be non-essential and transitory but the reaction to the impingement of the combat group is invariant. It is for this group in being rather to be integrated with the incomplete activities for which the combat groups who were active in this area have so comprehensively effected the initial implementation.

It is preferable for this group to be integrated with the incompleted implementation—that from the standards set by these respected deceased units we take accelerated intensive effort—that we here resolve at a high ethical level that the deceased shall not have been annihilated without furthering the project—that this group under divine leadership shall implement a new source of unhampered activity—and that political supervision composed of the integrated units, for the integrated units, and by the integrated units shall not perish from the superficial area of this planet.

Lincoln's Language

I

PRESIDENT LINCOLN'S POPULAR LANGUAGE

The criticism was often made, as to President Lincoln's public papers, that they lacked dignity of style and language. Mr. Carpenter, in his recollections of Mr. Lincoln, tells the following anecdote in illustration of this fact:—

It will be remembered that an extra session of Congress was called in July following Mr. Lincoln's inauguration. In the message then sent in, speaking of secession, and the measures taken by the Southern leaders to bring it about, there occurs the following remark: "With rebellion thus sugar-coated, they have been drugging the public mind of their section for more than thirty years, until at length they have brought many good men to a willingness to take up arms against the

From the Springfield *Republican*, July 8, 1865. Reprinted in *Word Study*, Vol. XXVII (April, 1952), No. 4, p. 4. Springfield, Massachusetts: G. & C. Merriam Company.

government," etc. Mr. Defrees, the government printer, told me that, when the message was being printed, he was a good deal disturbed by the use of the term "sugar-coated," and finally went to the President about it. Their relations to each other being of the most intimate character, he told Mr. Lincoln frankly that he ought to remember that a message to Congress was a different affair from a speech at a mass meeting in Illinois—that the message became a part of history, and should be written accordingly.

"What is the matter now?" inquired the President.

"Why," said Mr. Defrees, "you have used an undignified expression in the message"; and then, reading the paragraph aloud, he added, "I would alter the structure of that, if I were you."

"Defrees," replied Mr. Lincoln, "that word expresses precisely my idea, and I am not going to change it. The time will never come in this country when the people won't know exactly what 'sugar-coated' means."

II

. . . [Lincoln] rarely used a Latin word. He felt that the average juryman could not follow high-flown language in his native tongue, and he preferred to talk with him, man to man. A colleague who relied on different methods, once quoted a legal maxim and turned to him asking, "Isn't that so, Mr. Lincoln?"

"If that is Latin, you had better call another witness," he answered. . . .

IV. BET 'EM HIGH AND SLEEP IN THE STREETS

(The Humor in Gambling)

Introduction

From dolls to dotage man seems to love to take small chances for big profits. In boyhood he learns to draw straws and play even-or-odd, hull-gull, or keeps. Later he puts away childish things, replacing them with grown-up games involving dice, cards, horses, bank nights, lotteries, bingo, keno, roulette wheels, and the like. And his bets, like his interests, become man-sized.

From *Personal Traits of Abraham Lincoln*, by Helen Nicolay, p. 87. Copyright, 1912, by The Century Company. New York.

There have been those who have tried to make betting an even-steven proposition and thus a matter of pure chance. The mathematical odds for every possible combination in cards and dice can be calculated, and the racing handicapper hopes to make all the horses finish in a dead heat, but such things don't bother the sucker, who will draw to an inside straight and bet on a sure thing in a horse race. "After all," he says, "Columbus took a chance."

The humorist is interested not in the mathematical but the human element in gambling, in the personality of the players, in the sharpers who make sure that Lady Luck does not rule, and in the suckers who are always sure they can spot the shell with the pea under it, see when cards are marked or stacked, and tell by their feel whether dice are loaded. The people laugh at a banker's willingness to back good odds in "Any Bank Will Lend On It," at Canada Bill's willingness to take any odds, at the uneven odds in "Little Looloo" and "The Heathen Chinee," and at the judge in "Science vs. Luck," who gathers sufficient evidence to rule that seven-up is "a game not of chance but of science." We understand but are amused by the anxiety of the horse player who uses almost every means to bring his horse home in front or the dice player who chants, "Baby needs a new pair of shoes."

A Very Pious Story

At the Derby, Walt Haight, a well-fed horse author from Washington, told it this way.

There's this horse player and he can't win a bet. He's got patches in his pants from the way even odds-on favorites run up the alley when he's backing them and the slump goes on until he's utterly desperate. He's ready to listen to any advice when a friend tells him: "No wonder you don't have any luck, you don't live right. Nobody could do any good the way you live. Why, you don't even go to church. Why don't you get yourself straightened out and try to be a decent citizen and just see then if things don't get a lot better for you?"

Now, the guy has never exactly liked to bother heaven with his troubles. Isn't even sure whether they have horseracing up there and would understand his difficulties. But he's reached a state where steps simply have to be taken. So, the next day being Sunday, he does go to church and sits attentively through the whole service and joins in the hymn-singing and says "Amen" at the proper times and puts his buck on the collection plate.

All that night he lies awake waiting for a sign that things are going to get better; nothing happens. Next day he gets up and goes to the track, but this time he doesn't buy a racing form or scratch sheet or

From *Out of the Red*, by Red [Walter W.] Smith, pp. 159–162. Copyright, 1950, by Walter W. Smith. New York: Alfred A. Knopf.

Jack Green's card or anything. Just gets his program and sits in the stands studying the field for the first race and waiting for a sign. None comes, so he passes up the race. He waits for the second race and concentrates on the names of the horses for that one, and again there's no inspiration. So again he doesn't bet. Then, when he's looking them over for the third, something seems to tell him to bet on a horse named Number 4.

"Lord, I'll do it," he says, and he goes down and puts the last fifty dollars he'll ever be able to borrow on Number 4 to win. Then he goes back to his seat and waits until the horses come onto the track.

Number 4 is a little fractious in the parade, and the guy says, "Lord, please quiet him down. Don't let him get himself hurt." The horse settles down immediately and walks calmly into the starting gate.

"Thank you, Lord," says the guy. "Now please get him off clean. He don't have to break on top, but get him away safe without getting slammed or anything, please." The gate comes open and Number 4 is off well, close up in fifth place and saving ground going to the first turn. There he begins to move up a trifle on the rail and for an instant it looks as though he might be in close quarters.

"Let him through, Lord," the guy says. "Please make them horses open up a little for him." The horse ahead moves out just enough to let Number 4 through safely.

"Thank you, Lord," says the guy, "but let's not have no more trouble like that. Have the boy take him outside." Sure enough, as they go down the backstretch the jockey steers Number 4 outside, where he's lying fourth.

They're going to the far turn when the guy gets agitated. "Don't let that boy use up the horse," he says. "Don't let the kid get panicky, Lord. Tell him to rate the horse a while." The rider reaches down and takes a couple of wraps on the horse and keeps him running kind, just cooking on the outside around the turn.

Wheeling into the stretch, Number 4 is still lying fourth. "Now, Lord," the guy says. "Now we move. Tell that kid to go to the stick." The boy outs with his bat and, as Ted Atkinson says, he really "scouges" the horse. Number 4 lays his ears back and gets to running.

He's up to third. He closes the gap ahead and now he's lapped on the second horse and now he's at his throat latch and now he's past him. He's moving on the leader and everything behind him is good and cooked. He closes ground stride-by-stride with the boy working on him for all he's worth and the kid up front putting his horse to a drive.

"Please, Lord," the guy says. "Let him get out in front. Give me one call on the top end, anyway."

Number 4 keeps coming. At the eighth pole he's got the leader collared. He's past him. He's got the lead by two lengths.

"Thank you, Lord," the guy says, "I'll take him from here. Come on, you son of a bitch!"

Science *vs.* Luck

At that time, in Kentucky (said the Hon. Mr. K——), the law was very strict against what is termed "games of chance." About a dozen of the boys were detected playing "seven up" or "old sledge" for money, and the grand jury found a true bill against them. Jim Sturgis was retained to defend them when the case came up, of course. The more he studied over the matter, and looked into the evidence, the plainer it was that he must lose a case at last—there was no getting around that painful fact. Those boys had certainly been betting money on a game of chance. Even public sympathy was roused in behalf of Sturgis. People said it was a pity to see him mar his successful career with a big prominent case like this, which must go against him.

But after several restless nights an inspired idea flashed upon Sturgis, and he sprang out of bed delighted. He thought he saw his way through. The next day he whispered around a little among his clients and a few friends, and then when the case came up in court he acknowledged the seven-up and the betting, and, as his sole defense, had the astounding effrontery to put in the plea that old sledge was not a game of chance! There was the broadest sort of a smile all over the faces of that sophisticated audience. The judge smiled with the rest. But Sturgis maintained a countenance whose earnestness was even severe. The opposite counsel tried to ridicule him out of his position, and did not succeed. The judge jested in a ponderous judicial way about the thing, but did not move him. The matter was becoming grave. The judge lost a little of his patience, and said the joke had gone far enough. Jim Sturgis said he knew of no joke in the matter—his clients could not be punished for indulging in what some people chose to consider a game of chance until it was *proven* that it was a game of chance. Judge and counsel said that would be an easy matter, and forthwith called Deacons Job, Peters, Burke, and Johnson, and Dominies Wirt and Miggles, to testify; and they unanimously and with strong feeling put down the legal quibble of Sturgis by pronouncing that old sledge *was* a game of chance.

"What do you call it *now?*" said the judge.

"I call it a game of science!" retorted Sturgis; "and I'll prove it, too!"

They saw his little game.

He brought in a cloud of witnesses, and produced an overwhelming mass of testimony, to show that old sledge was not a game of chance but a game of science.

Instead of being the simplest case in the world, it had somehow

From *Sketches New and Old*, by Samuel L. Clemens, pp. 184–187. Copyright, 1875, by Samuel L. Clemens; 1899 and 1903, by Samuel L. Clemens; 1917, by Clara Gabrilowitsch. New York: P. F. Collier & Son Company. n.d.

turned out to be an excessively knotty one. The judge scratched his head over it awhile, and said there was no way of coming to a determination, because just as many men could be brought into court who would testify on one side as could be found to testify on the other. But he said he was willing to do the fair thing by all parties, and would act upon any suggestion Mr. Sturgis would make for the solution of the difficulty.

Mr. Sturgis was on his feet in a second.

"Impanel a jury of six of each, Luck *versus* Science. Give them candles and a couple of decks of cards. Send them into the jury-room, and just abide by the result!"

There was no disputing the fairness of the proposition. The four deacons and the two dominies were sworn in as the "chance" jurymen, and six inveterate old seven-up professors were chosen to represent the "science" side of the issue. They retired to the jury-room.

In about two hours Deacon Peters sent into court to borrow three dollars from a friend. [Sensation.] In about two hours more Dominie Miggles sent into court to borrow a "stake" from a friend. [Sensation.] During the next three or four hours the other dominie and the other deacons sent into court for small loans. And still the packed audience waited, for it was a prodigious occasion in Bull's Corners, and one in which every father of a family was necessarily interested.

The rest of the story can be told briefly. About daylight the jury came in, and Deacon Job, the foreman, read the following

We, the jury in the case of the Commonwealth of Kentucky *vs.* John Wheeler *et al.,* have carefully considered the points of the case, and tested the merits of the several theories advanced, and do hereby unanimously decide that the game commonly known as old sledge or seven-up is eminently a game of science and not of chance. In demonstration whereof it is hereby and herein stated, iterated, reiterated, set forth, and made manifest that, during the entire night, the "chance" men never won a game or turned a jack, although both feats were common and frequent to the opposition; and furthermore, in support of this our verdict, we call attention to the significant fact that the "chance" men are all busted, and the "science" men have got the money. It is the deliberate opinion of this jury, that the "chance" theory concerning seven-up is a pernicious doctrine, and calculated to inflict untold suffering and pecuniary loss upon any community that takes stock in it.

"That is the way that seven-up came to be set apart and particularized in the statute-books of Kentucky as being a game not of chance but of science, and therefore not punishable under the law," said Mr. K——. "That verdict is of record, and holds good to this day."

Dat's Gamblin'

At the regular meeting of the Thompson Street Poker Club, on Saturday evening, owing to the fact that both his eyes had that morning accidentally collided with the knuckles of the Rev. MR. THANKFUL SMITH, after a slight financial misunderstanding, and that for two hours he had lost every jackpot he had opened, Mr. TOOTER WILLIAMS presented somewhat the aspect of gloom. Mr. GUS JOHNSON was one dollar and forty-nine cents ahead, having had an unusually steady two-pair streak; Mr. RUBE JACKSON had sixty-nine cents' worth of velvet before him; Professor BRICK was a few coppers and a postage stamp on the right side; and Mr. WILLIAMS, who was banking, was the only loser. It being his deal, three kings wandered into his hand, and might have proved effectual but for the sad fact that everybody noticed the expression of his eye and fled. A jack-pot was then in order, and after it had climbed to aces the players braced up and knew that the event of the evening had come. At that moment the door opened and the Rev. Mr. SMITH, accompanied by a slight odor of hiccoughs, entered, took his seat behind Mr. JACKSON's chair, and glared a renewal of the morning's hostilities at Mr. WILLIAMS. That gentleman haughtily refused to notice it, however, but opened the pot with a burst of chips which scared Mr. JOHNSON half to death. Professor BRICK came in.

"Rise dat," said the Rev. Mr. SMITH to Mr. JACKSON. Then he whispered audibly: "Dem tree nines'll win dat pot, sho."

Mr. JACKSON elevated the bet as directed. Mr. WILLIAMS was delighted, for he had three jacks. He returned the raise.

"Rise him agin," commanded the Rev. Mr. SMITH, and then whispered as before: "Doan leggo dem nines."

Back came Mr. WILLIAMS, and then the Rev. Mr. SMITH counseled Mr. JACKSON to "jess call," and "and see what dem nines'll ketch in the draw."

Mr. JACKSON wanted two cards, and caught a pair of trays. Mr. WILLIAMS held up a king and drew one card, which, after elaborately combing his hand, he discovered to be another king. The battle was then resumed.

"I'll back dem nines for all I'se wuff," said Mr. SMITH, slipping his wallet into Mr. JACKSON's hand. And so they went at each other until even Mr. WILLIAMS' new collar button was up, and he was forced to call.

"What yo' got, man?"

From *The Thompson Street Poker Club* [by Henry Guy Carleton], pp. 24–26. Illustrated [by E. W. Kemble]. Copyright, 1884, by Mitchell and Miller; 1888, by White and Allen, New York. These sketches appeared originally in *Life*.

"Whad yo' got yo'se'f?" retorted Mr. JACKSON.

"I'se got er jack-full—*dat's* what *I* got," said Mr. WILLIAMS.

"Shome down," said Mr. SMITH, imperturbably.

Mr. WILLIAMS proudly skinned out three jacks and a pair of kings, and inquired rather superciliously, was "dat good?"

"We'se loaded fer bar over yar," retorted Mr. SMITH, evasively.

"Whad?" asked Mr. WILLIAMS, astonished; for, as dealer, he was certain he had not given Mr. WILLIAMS a fourth nine.

"We'se jess—jess loaded fer bar."

"Whad's dat?" reiterated Mr. WILLIAMS, turning as pale as he could. "Shope dem nines!"

Mr. SMITH's only reply was to spread Mr. JACKSON's hand out. It consisted mainly of queens, with a flavor of trays to give it strength. He then gathered in the pot and, with Mr. JACKSON, quitted the room. Mr. WILLIAMS sat in deep thought. After a little he said: "I like de game for fun—jess, jess to pass away de time. But *dat*"—here Mr. WILLIAMS waved his hand towards the débris of the recent encounter, with the air of one inculcating a lofty moral—"dat's gamblin'!"

Little Looloo

Luck favored the stranger from the start, and he won steadily. Finally, he drew four aces, and after the stakes had been run up to a comfortable figure, he manganimously refused to bet further.

"This is downright robbery," he exclaimed, "and I don't want to end the game here by bankrupting you. So here goes." He threw down four aces and reached for the money.

"Hold on!" cried his antagonist. "I'll take care of the dust, if you please."

"But I held four aces—see?"

"Well, what of it. I've got a looloo."

The stranger was dazed, "A looloo?" he repeated. "What is a looloo, anyway?"

"Three clubs and two diamonds," coolly replied the miner, raking in the stakes. "I guess you ain't accustomed to our Poker rules out here. See there?"

He jerked his thumb toward a pasteboard sign which ornamented the wall of the saloon. It read:

A LOOLOO
BEATS FOUR ACES

From *Poker Stories*, as Told by Statesmen, Soldiers, Lawyers, Commercial Travelers, Bankers, Actors, Editors, Millionaires, Members of the Ananias Club, and the Talent, Embracing the Most Remarkable Games, 1894–95, collected and edited by John F. B. Lillard, New York, 1896. Cited in *Sucker's Progress*, An Informal History of Gambling in America from the Colonies to Canfield, by Herbert Asbury, pp. 30–31. Copyright, 1938, by Dodd, Mead and Company, Inc. New York.

The game proceeded, but it was plainly evident that the unsophisticated tiger hunter had something on his mind. Within five minutes he suddenly braced up, his face was wreathed in smiles, and he began betting once more with his former vigor and recklessness. . . .

The stranger threw down his cards with an exultant whoop. "It's my time to howl just about now!" he cried, as he reached for the money. "There's a looloo for you—three clubs and two diamonds."

"Tut! Tut!" exclaimed the miner. "Really this is too bad. You evidently don't understand our rules at all. You certainly don't mean to tell me that you play Poker in such a fast-and-loose, slipshod way down East, do you? Why, look at that rule over there."

He pointed directly over the head of the busy bartender. The bit of pasteboard bore this legend:

THE LOOLOO CAN BE PLAYED
BUT ONCE IN A NIGHT.

Any Bank Will Lend On It

One morning the janitor of a Denver bank opened the door and was surprised to observe three rather tired-looking citizens seated on the steps, the center one of whom held a sealed envelope carefully in sight of his companions.

"Want to make a deposit, gentlemen?" asked the cashier, who shortly arrived. "Step inside."

"No, I want to negotiate a loan," said the man with the envelope, "and there ain't a minute to lose. I want $5,000 quicker than hell can scorch a feather."

"What collaterals have you—Government?" inquired the bank official.

"Government nothin'. I've got something that beats four per cents all hollow. You see I've been sitting in a poker game across the street, and there's over $4,000 in the pot. There are three or four pretty strong hands out, and as I've every cent in the center the boys have given me thirty minutes to raise a stake on my hand. It's in this envelope. Just look at it, but don't give it away to these gentlemen. They're in the game, and came along to see I don't monkey with the cards."

"But, my dear sir," said the cashier, who had quietly opened the envelope and found it to contain four kings and an ace. "This is certainly irregular—we don't lend money on cards."

"But you ain't going to see me raised out on a hand like that?"

From *Poker Stories*, collected and edited by John F. B. Lillard (New York, 1896), pp. 88–90. Cited in *Sucker's Progress*, An Informal History of Gambling in America from the Colonies to Canfield, by Herbert Asbury, pp. 28–29. Copyright, 1938, by Dodd, Mead and Company, Inc. New York.

whispered the pokerist. "These fellows think I'm bluffing and I can just clean out the whole gang. I've got 'em right in the door."

"Can't help it, sir. Never heard of such a thing," said the cashier, and the disappointed applicant and friends drifted sadly out. On the corner they met the bank's president, who was himself just from a quiet little all-night game. They explained the case again, and the next moment the superior officer darted into the bank, seized a bag of twenties and followed the trio. In about ten minutes he returned with the bag and an extra handful of twenties, which he flung on the counter.

"Here, credit five hundred to interest account," he said to the cashier. "Why, I thought you had more business snap. Ever play poker?"

"No, sir."

"Ah, thought not—thought not. If you did you'd know what good collateral was. Remember that in future four kings and an ace are always good in this institution for our entire assets, sir—our entire assets."

Gamblers Must Gamble

It was Canada Bill who originated the story which has become the classic gambling anecdote. He and one of his partners were marooned for the night in a little Louisiana river town a few years before the Civil War, and after diligent search Canada Bill found a faro game and began to play. His partner urged him to stop.

"The game's crooked!" he declared.

"I know it," replied Bill, "but it's the only one in town!"

Faded by Fate

One day, the master at arms aboard our ship stumbled on a crap game in the crew's quarters. He broke up the game, and took the offenders to the Captain's Mast to be judged and sentenced. Gambling aboard ship is against Navy regulations.

One by one the offenders pleaded guilty and received thirty-day restrictions.

The last man to appear before the skipper was a little colored mess attendant. "How do you plead?" asked the captain.

From *The French Quarter*, An Informal History of the New Orleans Underworld, by Herbert Asbury, p. 209. Copyright, 1936, by Alfred A. Knopf, Inc. New York and London.

From *Tall Tales They Tell in the Services*, Edited by Sgt. Bill Davidson. P. 10. Copyright, 1943, by Thomas Y. Crowell Company, 1943. New York.

"Not guilty," said the mess attendant.

"But didn't you find this man with the rest of the crap shooters?" said the captain to the master at arms.

"Yes, sir," said the master at arms.

"Did you actually see him rolling the dice?"

"No, sir. But he had a few bills in his hand. And just as I broke up the game, he picked up all the money on the deck."

Grimly the captain turned back to the little mess attendant. "Do you know that if you're lying, you can be brought up on charges of falsehood as well as gambling?"

"Ah know, sir," said the mess attendant, "but Ah ain't lyin'. You see, sir, it was like this. Ah owed some money and no one could change my twenty dollah bill, so Ah took it to the game, knowin' Ah could get some change theah. The fella that changed it fo' me had just won a handful of money and was kinda nervous. So when he handed me my change, he dropped some of it on the deck. The other fella, who was just then rollin' the dice, rolled a four. And before Ah could pick up my change, it was faded."

Sassy Susie

A horse room-operator had a big player he wanted to keep. The player was always wagering folding money of large denominations, but he was the bookies' biggest chump because none of his selections ever won.

However, the bookie was worried because the sucker was cooling off on horse racing. So he went to the man he had calling the races over the speaker in his horse room and told him, I want you to give this guy some sort of encouragement. Even if his horse is an absolute last give him a call somewhere up close once in a while. Just so he thinks that he is getting a run for his money and keeps playing the horses. Just kid him along. Do you understand, just kid him along?"

When the next race went to the post Mr. Big Bettor had a bundle of coarse notes riding on an extreme outsider named Sassy Susie. Word was passed to the man on the speaker who Mr. Big Bettor was wagering on and he began to call the race as follows.

"They're off! Sassy Susie breaks well and takes the rail. Sassy Susie is full of run and moving on the leaders. Sassy Susie goes to the front. At the half Sassy Susie leads by two. In the stretch Sassy Susie is bidding them all good evening . . ."

The bookie was beside himself with glee as he mentally pocketed the big bet the player had made with him. Mr. Big Bettor was also very happy. During the call he was jumping up and down, yelling at

From *Best Sports Stories of 1945*, edited by Irving T. Marsh and Edward Ehre, pp. 150–151. Copyright, 1946, by E. P. Dutton and Co., Inc. New York.

the top of his lungs each time the announcer paused, and carrying on generally.

The man at the speaker was perspiring freely as he brought his broadcast to a close, saying:

"The winner . . . SASSY SUSIE! . . . And Boss . . . I ain't been kiddin'!"

Win, Place and Show

. . . Two old turfmen were engaged in the usual swap session. The first had just finished telling about a mare he had started in a mile race on a half-mile oval. "She was so much the best," he said, "that she finished the race before the others got around the first lap."

"Hmmmmmmph," snorted the second. "I was racing out in the bush one time and I had a real good mare. She was ready to foal, and I knowed it, but I was hard up for coffee money and I had to race her. The race ran twice around the oval and after the first time around she stopped and foaled twins—a colt and a filly. The colt came first and he got right up and run and won the race. Meanwhile, the filly arrives and to make matters worse she takes off and would have finished second if her mother hadn't nipped her at the wire."

"Why do you say 'to make matters worse'?" warily queried the first horseman. "You took down three ends of the purse, didn't you?"

"Oh, that?" answered the second horseman, climbing to his feet and setting himself to go. "You see I took a chance and named the mare and the filly as an entry, so when the colt won I was disqualified and liked to get ruled off for running a ringer."

A Bet on a Badger

This particularly old story was last told, in its present shape, by Will Visscher, in a Chicago paper. The writer trusts the shade of the departed Nye will not lay it up against him, but will hold Visscher responsible:

Only a few weeks before his death Nye wrote me from his home at Asheville, N. C., saying: "I have on my farm here a very promising field of rye that looks as if it would run 15 to 20 gallons to the acre. Come down."

Years ago, when Nye was running an afternoon newspaper in Laramie, Wyo., I went over from Cheyenne one day to pay him a visit. He

From *Best Sports Stories of 1945*, edited by Irving T. Marsh and Edward Ehre, p. 151. Copyright, 1946, by E. P. Dutton and Co., Inc. New York.

From *Waifs of the Press*. Collected and Edited by Harry L. Work, pp. 96–98. Washington: Walter Neale, Publisher. 1898.

was hard at work in his office, which was upstairs over a livery stable, a fact that caused him to live in mortal dread of hay fever.

As soon as I went in he said: "Sit down there and write something to help me get the paper out, and we will get off quicker and have some fun with the boys."

"What shall I write about?"

"Oh, 'bout a column."

So I wrote about a column, headed it "About a Column," and commented on columns. In a little while we were out and Nye led the way to a place where a man kept all sorts of sporting arrangements. He had a cockpit for fighting roosters in, and a ring for boxers to practice on each other, billiard tables, tenpin alleys and other accommodations. While we were there a man came in with a live eagle that he proposed to pit against the proprietor's best bird. The old sport took him up at once, and the Roman-nosed bird of freedom was thrown in with a healthy-looking chicken that would have fought a buzz saw. The rooster made a dab at the eagle, and that "fierce gray bird with a bending beak" and an unwarranted reputation for gameness, ignominiously, ingloriously, and incontinently fled and hid under a chair, where he looked out in a piteous sort of way and as good as said: "Take him off; I want to go home."

Among the other things this man of sport had was a badger that he was prepared to back for large sums on the statement that no dog of anybody's could take the beast out of a barrel that lay lengthwise on the floor, with one head knocked out and in which the badger was ensconced. I had wondered why it was that Nye had been coaxing an "onary" looking cur to follow us, and now the problem was about to be solved. Nye made a bet that he had a dog that would take the badger out of the barrel. The money was "put up" and Nye caught that dog by the "nape of the neck and seat of his breeches," so to speak, and threw him into the barrel, tail foremost. The badger nabbed the dog by one ham and the dog went right away from there like a blue streak, taking the badger with him. The last that was ever seen of that dog, or badger either, both were going toward the North Platte River, the dog making the best time he ever had made, and the badger hanging straight out behind, a close second. Nye won.

Judging the Thimble Game

In the early days of the West, when justice was dispensed after a free-and-easy fashion in log-cabin courthouses, a case was on trial in

From *The Lance, Cross and Canoe; The Flatboat, Rifle and Plough in the Valley of the Mississippi, The Backwoods Hunter and Settler, The Flatboatman, The Saddle-Bags Parson, The Stump Orator and Lawyer, as the Pioneers of Its Civilization, Its Great Leaders, Wit and Humor, Remarkable Extent and Wealth of Re-*

which the plaintiff sought to avoid payment of a gambling debt on the ground that the money had been won by "thimblerigging." His counsel, who was an expert in the game, was giving an illustration of its operation to his Honor and the jury. "Then, may it please the court, the defendant, placing the cups on his knee, *thus,* began shifting them *so,* offering to bet that my client could not tell under which cup was the 'little joker'—meaning, thereby, may it please the court, this ball —with the intention of defrauding my client of the sum thus wagered. For instance, when I raise the cup *so,* your Honor supposes that you see the ball."

"*Suppose* I see!" interrupted the judge, who had closely watched the performance, and was sure that he had detected the ball as one of the cups was accidentally raised. "Why, any fool can see where it is, and bet on it and be sure to win. There ain't no defraudin' *thar.*"

"Perhaps your Honor would like to go a *V* on it," insinuated the counsel.

"Go a *V!* Yes, and double it too, and here's the rhino. It's under the middle cup."

"I'll go a *V* on that," said the foreman of the jury.

"And I, and I," joined in the jury, one after another, until each one had invested his pile.

"Up!" said his Honor.

"Up" it was, but the "little joker" had mysteriously disappeared. Judge and jury were enlightened, and found no difficulty in bringing in a verdict in favor of the plaintiff on the ground that "it was the biggest kind o' defraudin'." His Honor adjourned the court, and "stood for drinks all round" in consideration of being "let off" from his wager.

A Louse Race

It was one day in the rainy winter of '54 and '55, and too wet to work in the mines, so the boys begun to wander in early down at the Long Tom. By noon all the tables was full and the gambling got more exciting as the day wore on. Some of the boys set right there at the tables from morning through all the day and on into the evening, without stopping except to take on a drink or to make room for more.

source, Its Past Achievements and Glorious Future, by W. H. Milburn, pp. 577–578. Entered . . . 1892, by William Henry Milburn. New York and St. Louis: N. D. Thompson Publishing Company.

From *Ghost Town,* Wherein Is Told Much That Is Wonderful, Laughable, and Tragic, and Some That Is Hard to Believe, about Life during the Gold Rush and Later in the Town of Columbia on California's Mother Lode, as Remembered by the Oldest Inhabitants and Here for the First Time Set Down by G. Ezra Dane in collaboration with Beatrice J. Dane, pp. 13–18. Copyright, 1941, by G. Ezra Dane. New York: Alfred A. Knopf.

If you once get the gambling fever, you know, in a place like that, the longer you keep at it, the higher the fever gets. That fever's catching and it'll spread through a crowd like any other fever. So monte, faro, seven-up, and the different brands of poker got too slow for some, and they begun laying bets on any chance that offered. At some of the tables they was betting on the turn of a card, and they was one crowd having a spitting tournament at the stove. Then they was some fellows betting which of two flies on the wall would move first, and others at the door laying bets whether or not the next man to come in would be Irish. But the greatest bet in betting history was laid that night by young Ad Pence. An inspiration it was, no less.

"Boys," says Ad, pounding on the bar to get the attention of the crowd, "boys," says he, "luck's been agin me so far, but I've got five hundred here that says I've a louse that can beat, in a fair race, any louse that ever cut his teeth on any miner's hide."

He'd caught a good lively one and held him up for all the boys to see.

"I say this louse is the champeen," says Ad, "for I've been chasing him around my carcass for a week and I've only just caught up with him. Five hundred backs him against all comers."

Well, at that all the games stopped short, and everybody crowded up to the bar where Ad was showing off this champeen louse. But none of the boys would admit that he kept this kind of stock and it begun to look as though nobody was going to take the bet. Then a stranger, a big Irishman with a red beard, come elbowing his way through the crowd and up to the bar where Ad was standing.

"Will ye let me have a look at that louse?" he says.

So Ad held it out and the stranger squinted at it from one side and then from the other. "A dainty crayther indade he is," says he, "but I think he's no racer. His belly's too low and his legs are too short by a long ways. Now wait just a bit and I'll have something to show ye."

So the stranger puts his hand inside his shirt, and scrabbled around in there for a minute, and when he pulled it out again, between his thumb and finger he held a struggling louse.

"Me boy," he says, "your five hundred is as good as gone. But before I take it from ye, I want ye to have a good look at *this* louse. Ye'll never see the likes of him again. Ye say yours is the champeen, but ye've only had him a wake, and he has not so much as a name. I say he's but a mongrel! Now *this* one is the greatest racing louse in all the world, and he has the most distinguished pedigray that ever a louse did boast. And I don't want to be taking your money under any false pretenses, so I'm going to tell ye his history, and when ye've heard it, if ye want to withdraw, I'll freely let ye do so.

"Just before me old grandfather died, back in Ireland, he called me to his bedside and he said to me: 'Grandson,' says he, 'I'm a pore man. I've no money to lave ye, nor any property. But there's wan threasure I have, Grandson,' says the old man, 'Katie, the finest little seam squirrel in all of Ireland, and a direct discindent of one that fed on Saint Patrick.

" 'Take her, Grandson,' says he, 'kape good care of her and fade her well, and she'll surely bring ye luck.'

"Now, me boy, this louse ye see here is Larry, Katie's great-great-great-grandson, and the blood of Saint Patrick himself runs in his veins, so he's bound to bring me luck. And to show the faith I have in him and in Holy Saint Patrick, bejayziz, I'll lay a thousand to that five hundred ye bet on yer mongrel louse! Now, do ye still want to make that bet?"

"I do," says Ad. "Your louse may be good, but I know what mine can do from long chasing of him, and my bet on him still stands."

So Ad and the stranger placed their stakes with Doc Johns, and side betting begun in the crowd.

"There can be no race without a racetrack," says the stranger, and he calls to the bar-tender: "Bring us a plate," he says. "Now, boys, the middle's the start, the edge is the goal, and the first little pants rabbit over the rim is the winner."

So the bar-tender brought the plate, and the stranger felt of it. "No louse," says he, "would ever set a good pace on this cold plate. Let's hate it up a bit, and then you'll see them kick up their heels and run."

So they heated the plate piping hot over the stove and set it on a table where all could see. And when Doc Johns counted off: "One, two, three, go!" each man dropped his louse in the middle of the plate, and they were off, a-scrambling and a-jumping because it was so hot, you know. The boys was cheering and yelling and standing on chairs to see, and laying bets right and left.

Well, neck and neck it was at the start acrost the bottom of the plate, but Ad's louse pulled ahead a bit and he was the first to reach the rise of the rim. Then came the last hard pull for the edge. He started up the rise, but when he got about half-way up he lost his footing on the slippery rim and slid down again. So he backed up and he took another run for it, and got up a little further, but again he slid back. He was a game one, that louse was. He tried it again and again, but he couldn't quite make it. No, sir, it was on that last hard pull up the rim of the plate that the blood of Saint Patrick began to tell, for Larry, the stranger's lucky louse, he started up slow and careful, and he kept on a-pulling and a-scrambling and up and up he went and *over* the edge to victory and into his master's hand. A hero he was, for sure!

The fellows jumped down from the tables then and Jack White, he says: "Three cheers for Larry and the blood of Saint Patrick!" So the boys roared out the three cheers. And they *was* cheers too, for them young fellows didn't have no colds, nor consumption neither.

Well, then Doc Johns paid over the fifteen hundred dollars to the stranger, and Ad went up to shake his hand. "Stranger," he says, "it

was a fair race, and the best louse won. The money's yours and I
don't begrudge it to you. But I've one request to make of you, stranger,
and if you'll grant it, I'll be forever grateful."

"And what may that be?" says the stranger.

"Just let me borrow Larry till tomorrow," says Ad.

"But what for?" says the stranger. "Why might ye be wanting to
borry me pet?"

"Why, man!" says Ad, "I want to improve my breed!"

Epitaph to a Gambler

> Played five aces,
> Now playing a harp.

The Heathen Chinee

> Which I wish to remark,—
>   And my language is plain,—
> That for ways that are dark
>   And for tricks that are vain,
> The heathen Chinee is peculiar.
>   Which the same I would rise to explain.
>
> Ah Sin was his name
>   And I shall not deny
> In regard to the same
>   What that name might imply,
> But his smile it was pensive and childlike,
>   As I frequent remarked to Bill Nye.
>
> It was August the third
>   And quite soft the skies:
> Which it might be inferred
>   That Ah Sin was likewise;
> Yet he played that day upon William
>   And me in a way I despise.
>
> Which we had a small game,
>   And Ah Sin took a hand:

From *Texas Tradition*, by Ross Phares, p. 212. Copyright, 1954, by Ross Phares.
New York: Henry Holt and Company.

"Plain Language from Truthful James," from *Poems*, by Bret Harte, pp. 79–83.
Entered . . . 1870, by Bret Harte. Boston: James R. Osgood and Company, 1875.

It was Euchre. The same
   He did not understand:
But he smiled as he sat by the table,
   With the smile that was childlike and bland.

Yet the cards they were stocked
   In a way that I grieve,
And my feelings were shocked
   At the state of Nye's sleeve:
Which was stuffed full of aces and bowers,
   And the same with intent to deceive.

But the hands that were played
   By that heathen Chinee,
And the points that he made,
   Were quite frightful to see,—
Till at last he put down a right bower,
   Which the same Nye had dealt unto me.

Then I looked up at Nye,
   And he gazed upon me;
And he rose with a sigh,
   And said, "Can this be?
We are ruined by Chinese cheap labor,"—
   And he went for that heathen Chinee.

In the scene that ensued
   I did not take a hand,
But the floor it was strewed
   Like leaves on the strand
With the cards that Ah Sin had been hiding,
   In the game "he did not understand."

In his sleeves, which were long,
   He had twenty-four packs,—
Which was coming it strong,
   Yet I state but the facts;
And we found on his nails, which were taper,
   What is frequent in tapers,—that's wax.

Which is why I remark,
   And my language is plain,
That for ways that are dark,
   And for tricks that are vain,
The heathen Chinee is peculiar,—
   Which the same I am free to maintain.

Ladies Wild

In the exclusive set (No diphtheria cases allowed) in which I travel, I am known as a heel in the matter of parlor games. I will drink with them, wrassle with them, and, now and again, leer at the ladies, but when they bring out the bundles of pencils and the pads of paper and start putting down all the things they can think of beginning with "W," or enumerating each other's bad qualities on a scale of 100 (no hard feeling results, mind you—just lifelong enmity), I tiptoe noisily out of the room, and say:

"The hell with you."

For this reason, I am not usually included in any little games that may be planned in advance. If they foresee an evening of "Consequences" coming over them, they whisper:

"Get Benchley out of the house. Get him a horse to ride, or some beads to string—anything to get him out of the way."

For, I forgot to tell you, not only am I a non-participant in parlor games, but I am a militant non-participant. I heckle from the sidelines. I throw stones and spit at the players. Hence the nickname: "Sweet Old Bob," or sometimes just the initials.

One night last Summer I detected, from the general stir among the ladies and the more effete gents, that I was being eased out of the house. This meant that the gaming was about to begin. But instead of the usual clatter of pencils among the croupiers, I saw someone sneaking in with a tray of poker chips. They almost had me out the door when I discovered what was up.

"Well, so long, Bob," they said. "Good bowling to you."

"What's this?" I came back into the room. "Are these poker chips?"

"Sure, they're poker chips. It's all right to play poker, isn't it? The reform administration's gone out."

I assumed a hurt air. In fact, I didn't have to assume it. I was hurt.

"I don't suppose I'm good enough to play poker with you," I said. "All I'm good enough for is to furnish the liquor and the dancing girls."

"Why, we thought you didn't like games. You always acted like such a goddamned heel whenever a game is suggested."

"My dear people," I said, trying to be calm. "There are games and games. 'Twenty Questions' is one game, if you will, but poker— why, poker is a man's game. It's my dish. I'm an old newspaperman, you know. Poker is the breath of life to a newspaperman." (As a matter of fact, I never played poker once when I was on a newspaper,

From *After 1903—What?* by Robert Benchley, pp. 1-7. New York: Harper & Brothers, 1938. Copyright, 1938, by Robert C. Benchley.

and was never allowed to do more than kibitz at the Thanatopsis
games of Broun, Adams, Kaufman, and that bunch, but poker is still
my favorite game in a small way, or at least it *was*.)

Then there was a great scrambling to get me a chair and sell me
chips.

"Old Bob's going to play!" was the cry. "Old Bob likes poker!"
People came in from the next room to see what the commotion was,
and one woman said that if I was going to play she had a headache.

(I had ruined a game of "Who Am I?" for her once by blowing
out a fuse from the coat closet.)

As for me, I acted the part to the hilt. I took off my coat, unbut-
toned my vest so that just the watch chain connected it, lighted my
pipe, and kept my hat on the back of my head.

"This is the real poker costume," I said. "The way we used to play
it down on the old Trib. There ought to be a City News ticker over
in the corner to make it seem like home."

"I'm afraid he's going to be too good for us," said one of the more
timid ladies. "We play for very small stakes, you know."

"The money doesn't matter," I laughed. "It's the game. And anyway," I added modestly, "I haven't played for a long time. You'll
probably take me good." (I wish now that I had made book on that
prediction.)

It was to be Dealer's Choice, which should have given me a tip-off
right there, with three women at the table, one the dealer.

"This," she announced, looking up into space, as if for inspiration,
"is going to be 'Hayfever.'"

"I beg your pardon," I said, leaning forward.

"'Hayfever,'" explained one of the men. "The girls like it. One
card up, two down, the last two up. One eyed jacks, sevens, and nines
wild. High-low."

"I thought this was going to be poker," I said.

"From then on you play it just like regular poker," said the dealer.

From then on! My God! Just like regular poker!

Having established myself as a regular poker fan, I didn't want to
break down and cry at the very start, so I played the hand through.
I say I "played" it. I sat looking at my cards, peeking now and then
just to throw a bluff that I knew what I was doing. One eyed jacks,
sevens and nines wild, I kept saying to myself, and puffing very hard
at my pipe.

After a minute of owlish deliberation, I folded.

The next hand was to be "Whistle Up Your Windpipe," another
one which the girls had introduced into the group and which the men,
weak-kneed sissies that they were, had allowed to become regulation.

This was seven card stud, first and last cards up, deuces, treys, and
red-haired queens wild, high-low-and-medium. I figured out that I had
a very nice straight, bet it as I would have bet a straight in the old

days, and was beaten for eleven dollars and sixty cents by a Royal Straight Flush.

Amid general laughter, I was told that an ordinary straight in these games is worth no more than a pair of sixes in regular poker. A Royal Straight Flush usually wins. Well, it usually won in the old days, too.

By the time the deal came to me, my pipe had gone out and I had taken my hat off. Between clenched teeth, I announced:

"And this, my frands, is going to be something you may not have heard of. This is going to be old-fashioned draw poker, with nothing wild."

The women had to have it explained to them, and remarked that they didn't see much fun in that. However, the hand was played. Nobody had anything (in comparison to what they had been having in the boom days), and nobody bet. The hand was over in a minute and a half, amid terriffic silence.

That was the chief horror of this epidemic of "Whistle Up Your Windpipe," "Beezy-Weezy," and "Mice Afloat." It made old-fashioned stud seem tame, even to me.

Every time it came to me, I elected the old game, just out of spite, but nobody's heart was in it. I became the spoil-sport of the party again, and once or twice I caught them trying to slip the deal past me, as if by mistake.

Even a round of jackpots netted nothing in the way of excitement, and even when I won one on a full house, there was no savor to the victory, as I had to explain to the women what a full house was.

They thought I was making up my own rules. Nothing as small as a full house had ever been seen in that game.

The Big Newspaper Man was taken for exactly sixty-one dollars and eight cents when the game broke up at four A.M. Two of the women were the big winners. They had finally gotten it down to a game where everything was wild but the black nines, and everyone was trying for "low."

From now on, I not only walk out on "Twenty Questions" and "Who am I?" but, when there are ladies present (God *bless* them!) I walk out on poker.

And a fine state of affairs it is when an old newspaperman has to walk out of poker!

V. A SUCKER IS BORN EVERY MINUTE
(The Lighter Side of Trading and Business)

Introduction

Buying, selling, and trading are necessary in a free enterprise system such as ours, but it may be that we have made too much of getting the better of the other fellow in a trade, of making more profit than our neighbor, of accumulating more cattle, chattels, and cash. At least English travelers in this country during the nineteenth century almost invariably commented upon the materialism of the Americans. But they were not alone in their estimate of our love for the material, for many of our own writers were saying the same thing. It was Washington Irving who coined "Almighty Dollar" and Q. K. Philander Doesticks (Mortimer Thompson), another American, who wrote:

> But the god he wildly worshipped,
> Traded off his heart and soul for,
> (As of old did Doctor Faustus,
> Swapping jackknives with the Devil),
> Was the king of dimes and quarters,
> Was the god of Pluri-bus-tah.
> And the prayers which he, on Sunday,
> Offered to the King of Heaven,
> From his lips fell strange and coldly.
> But the week-day prayer he uttered,
> From his heart came hot and earnest,
> And the language runs this wise:
> 'Potent, and ALMIGHTY DOLLAR!'

It is, of course, the social historian who should tell us just how much Americans have loved the material, but our humorists have seen at least enough materialism in our society to get many laughs from it. Their laughter has come from both sides of the mouth, but principally it has come from the materialistic side. Davy Crockett's use of the same coonskin to buy rum over and over again was trickery, but his constituents seemed to consider it a mark of ingenuity. And Simon Suggs' dictum might serve as a golden rule for the materialists: "It is good for a man to be shifty in a new country."

Materialists or not, Americans enjoy stories of sharp bartering practices, of trades for fast hounds or for horses which are balky, spavined, sore-backed, and false-tailed. And they like stories of super-salesmanship and of grandiose schemes for making money by selling ingenious sleep prolongers or raising whales on a cattle ranch.

An Old-Time Pitchman Spiel

The itinerant fellows who frequent our village, during the sessions of the Courts, and on all other occasions of popular assembling—vending their small wares, a la the Razor-Strop man—are sometimes very amusing. We noticed one of 'em, last week, crying his *erasive soap* to as simple a crowd as we have observed in some time. He was a sharp-eyed fellow, with a sanctified look, black whiskers, and a still blacker and enormous straw hat.

"Gentlemen," he said, or rather sang—"gentlemen, I offer you a splendid article, a superb article, an incomparable article—magical, radical, tragical article!" [Here he displayed a cake of his soap.] "Magical, radical, tragical, *erasive* soap! Yes, in its effects upon its inventor most tragical! Shall I tell you how? It was invented by a celebrated French chemist, after twenty years of toil, labour and privation. In just fifteen minutes, two seconds and a half after the discovery, he fell into the arms of death, and his name became immortal! You can draw your own conclusions, gentlemen!

"Magical, radical, tragical, e-ra-sive soap! Dime a cake! Hand me the money!—served me right—there's the soap! Yes, there's a man has got a cake of the incomparable, inappreciable, infallible, invaluable, magical, radical, tragical, e-ra-sive soap!

"Gentleman, you'd open your eyes, if I were to tell you half the wonders performed by this in-com-pa-rable article.—It cleans oil-spots, removes stains, hides dirt, brightens good colours and obliterates ugly ones!—such is the virtue of the all-healing, never-failing, spot-removing, beauty-restoring, health-giving, magical, radical, tragical, e-ra-sive Soap!" The vender wiped his brow, heaved a sigh, and recommenced, standing at ease against a piazza-post.

"Why, gentlemen, when I first became acquainted with this in-extollable gift of divine Providence to erring man, I had an obstruction of the vocal organs, an impediment of speech, that bid fair to destroy the hopes of the fond parents who intended me for the bar or the pulpit. I was *tongue-tied*—but I came across this precious compound—swallowed just half an ounce, and ever since, to the satisfaction of my parents, myself, and an assembled world, I have been volubly, rapidly, and successfully, interminably, unremittingly, most eloquently, sounding the praises of the incomparable, infallible, inimitable, inappreciable, never-failing, all-healing, spot-removing, beauty-restoring, magical, radical, tragical, erasive soap!

"Ah, gentlemen, a world without it would be naught! It takes the

---

"The Erasive Soap Man," from *The Widow Rugby's Husband . . . and Other Tales of Alabama*, by Johnson J. Hooper, pp. 109–111. Philadelphia: T. B. Peterson & Brothers. 1851.

stains from your breeches, the spots from your coat, removes the dirt, and diffuses a general cheerfulness over the character of the whole outer man! True, gentlemen, I've worn the forefinger of my right-hand to the first joint, in illustrating the efficacy of this ineffable compound; but I hold that the forefinger of one man—yea, or the forefinger of TEN MEN—are as nothing when compared with the peace and welfare of society and the world!

"Oh, magical Soap! oh, radical Soap! oh, tragical Soap! What wonders thou dost perform! The frightened locomotive leaves its track (*as it were*) on thy approach! The telegraphic wires tremble and are dumb in thy presence!

"Why, gentlemen, it clears the complexion of a Negro, and makes a curly-headed man's hair straight! It removes the stains from the breeches and the spots from your coats—in like manner, it purifies the conscience and brightens the character! If you're a little dishonest or dirty, try it! If your reputation or clothing is a little smutted, I'll warrant it! For ladies whose slips—I mean these little brown, yellow, white, blue, and many-coloured *slippers*—have become soiled, it is the only cure, panacea, medicamentum, vademecum, in all globular creation. Then come up, tumble up, run up, and jump up, like Hung'ry patriots, and buy my incomparable, infallible, ineffable, inappreciable, coat-preserving, beauty-restoring, dirt-removing, speech-improving, character-polishing, virtue-imparting, compound, ERASIVE Soap!"

Here Hard-Cheek's oratory was interrupted by a shower of dimes from boys, men, and hobble-de-hoys, and the "show" was considered "closed."

David Harum's Horse Trade

Mrs. Bixbee went on with her needlework, with an occasional side glance at her brother, who was immersed in the gospel of his politics. Twice or thrice she opened her lips as if to address him, but apparently some restraining thought interposed. Finally, the impulse to utter her mind culminated. "Dave," she said, "d' you know what Deakin Perkins is sayin' about ye?"

David opened his paper so as to hide his face, and the corners of his mouth twitched as he asked in return, "Wa'al, what's the deakin sayin' now?"

"He's sayin'," she replied, in a voice mixed of indignation and apprehension, "thet you sold him a balky horse, an' he's goin' to hev the law on ye." David's shoulders shook behind the sheltering page, and his mouth expanded in a grin.

"Wa'al," he replied after a moment, lowering the paper and look-

From *David Harum, A Story of American Life*, by Edward Noyes Westcott, pp. 4–21. Copyright, 1898, by D. Appleton and Company. New York.

ing gravely at his companion over his glasses, "next to the deakin's religious experience, them of lawin' an' horse-tradin' air his strongest p'ints, an' he works the hull on 'em to once sometimes."

The evasiveness of this generality was not lost on Mrs. Bixbee, and she pressed the point with, "Did ye? an' will he?"

"Yes, an' no, an' mebbe, an' mebbe not," was the categorical reply.

"Wa'al," she answered with a snap, "mebbe you call that an answer. I s'pose if you don't want to let on you won't, but I do believe you've ben playin' some trick on the deakin, an' won't own up. I do wish," she added, "that if you hed to git rid of a balky horse onto somebody you'd hev picked out somebody else."

"When you got a balker to dispose of," said David gravely, "you can't alwus pick an' choose. Fust come, fust served." Then he went on more seriously: "Now I'll tell ye. Quite a while ago—in fact, not long after I come to enjoy the priv'lidge of the deakin's acquaintance—we hed a deal. I wasn't jest on my guard, knowin' him to be a deakin an' all that, an' he lied to me so splendid that I was took in, clean over my head. He done me so brown I was burnt in places, an' you c'd smell smoke 'round me fer some time."

"Was it a horse?" asked Mrs. Bixbee gratuitously.

"Wa'al," David replied, "mebbe it *had* ben some time, but at that partic'lar time the only thing to determine that fact was that it wa'n't nothin' else."

"Wa'al, I declare!" exclaimed Mrs. Bixbee, wondering not more at the deacon's turpitude than at the lapse in David's acuteness, of which she had an immense opinion, but commenting only on the former. "I'm 'mazed at the deakin."

"Yes'm," said David with a grin, "I'm quite a liar myself when it comes right down to the hoss bus'nis, but the deakin c'n give me both bowers ev'ry hand. He done it so slick that I had to laugh when I come to think it over—an' I had witnesses to the hull confab, too, that he didn't know of, an' I c'd 've showed him up in great shape if I'd had a mind to."

"Why didn't ye?" said Aunt Polly, whose feelings about the deacon were undergoing a revulsion.

"Wa'al, to tell ye the truth, I was so completely skunked that I hadn't a word to say. I got rid o' the thing fer what it was wuth fer hide an' taller, an' stid of squealin' 'round the way you say he's doin', like a stuck pig, I kep' my tongue between my teeth an' laid to git even some time."

"You ort to 've hed the law on him," declared Mrs. Bixbee, now fully converted. "The old scamp!"

"Wa'al," was the reply, "I gen'all prefer to settle out of court, an' in this partic'lar case, while I might 'a' ben willin' t' admit that I hed ben did up, I didn't feel much like swearin' to it. I reckoned the time 'd come when mebbe I'd git the laugh on the deakin, an' it did, an' we're putty well settled now in full."

"You mean this last pufformance?" asked Mrs. Bixbee. "I wish you'd quit beatin' about the bush, an' tell me the hull story."

"Wa'al, it's like this, then, if you *will* hev it. I was over to Whiteboro a while ago on a little matter of wordly bus'nis, an' I seen a couple of fellers halter-exercisin' a hoss in the tavern yard, I stood 'round a spell watchin' 'em, an' when he come to a standstill I went an' looked him over, an' I liked his looks fust rate.

"'Fer sale?' I says.

"'Wa'al,' says the chap that was leadin' him, 'I never see the hoss that wa'n't if the price was right.'

"'Your'n?' I says.

"'Mine an' his'n," he says, noddin' his head at the other feller.

"'What ye askin' fer him?' I says.

"'One-fifty,' he says.

"I looked him all over agin putty careful, an' once or twice I kind o' shook my head 's if I didn't quite like what I seen, an' when I got through I sort o' half turned away without sayin' anythin', 's if I'd seen enough.

"'The' ain't a scratch ner a pimple on him,' says the feller, kind o' resentin' my looks. 'He's sound an' kind, an' 'll stand without hitchin', an' a lady c'n drive him 's well 's a man.'

"'I ain't got anythin' agin him,' I says, 'an' prob'ly that's all true, ev-ry word on't; but one-fifty's a considerable price fer a hoss these days. I hain't no pressin' use fer another hoss, an', in fact,' I says, 'I've got one or two fer sale myself.'

"'He's wuth two hundred jest as he stands,' the feller says. 'He hain't had no trainin', an' he c'n drawn two men in a road-wagin better'n fifty.'

"Wa'al, the more I looked at him the better I liked him, but I only says, 'Jes' so, jes so, he may be wuth it to *me,* an' I hain't got that much money with me if he was,' I says. The other feller hadn't said nothin' up to that time, an' he broke in now. 'I s'pose you'd take him fer a gift, wouldn't ye?' he says, kind o' sneerin'.

"'Wa'al, yes,' I says, 'I dunno but I would if you'd throw in a pound of tea an' a halter.'

"He kind o' laughed an' says, 'Wa'al, this ain't no gift enterprise, an' I guess we ain't goin' to trade, but I'd like to know,' he says, 'jest as a matter of curios'ty, what you'd say he *was* wuth to ye?'

"'Wa'al,' I says, 'I come over this mornin' to see a feller that owed me a trifle o' money. Exceptin' of some loose change, what he paid me 's all I got with me,' I says, takin' out my wallet. 'That wad's got a hundred an' twenty-five into it, an' if you'd sooner have your hoss an' halter than the wad,' I says, 'why, I'll bid ye good-day.'

"'You're offerin' one-twenty-five fer the hoss an' halter?' he says.

" 'That's what I'm doin',' I says.

" 'You've made a trade,' he says, puttin' out his hand fer the money an' handin' the halter over to me."

"An' didn't ye suspicion nuthin' when he took ye up like that?" asked Mrs. Bixbee.

"I did smell woolen some," said David, "but I had the *hoss* an' they had the *money,* an', as fur 's I c'd see, the critter was all right. How-somever, I says to 'em: 'This here's all right, fur 's it's gone, but you've talked putty strong 'bout this hoss. I don't know who you fellers be, but I c'n find out,' I says. Then the fust feller that done the talkin' 'bout the hoss put in an' says, 'The' hain't ben one word said to you about this hoss that wa'n't gospel truth, not one word.' An' when I come to think on't afterward," said David with a half laugh, "it mebbe wa'n't *gospel* truth, but it was good enough *jury* truth. I guess this ain't over 'n' above interestin' to ye, is it?" he asked after a pause, looking doubtfully at his sister.

"Yes, 'tis," she asserted. "I'm lookin' forrered to where the deakin comes in, but you jest tell it your own way."

"I'll git there all in good time," said David, "but some of the point of the story'll be lost if I don't tell ye what come fust."

"I allow to stan' it 's long 's you can," she said encouragingly, "seein' what work I had gettin' ye started. Did ye find out anythin' 'bout them fellers?"

"I ast the barn man if he knowed who they was, an' he said he never seen 'em till the yestiddy before, an' didn't know 'em f'm Adam. They come along with a couple of hosses, one drivin' an' t'other leadin— the one I bought. I ast him if they knowed who I was, an' he said one on 'em ast him, an' he told him. The feller said to him, seein' me drive up: 'That's a putty likely-lookin' hoss. Who's drivin' him?' An' he says to the feller: 'That's Dave Harum, f'm over to Homeville. He's a great feller fer hosses,' he says."

"Dave," said Mrs. Bixbee, "them chaps jest laid fer ye, didn't they?"

"I reckon they did," he admitted; "an' they was as slick a pair as was ever drawed to," which expression was lost upon his sister. David rubbed the fringe of yellowish-gray hair which encircled his bald pate for a moment.

"Wa'al," he resumed, "after the talk with the barn man, I smelt woolen stronger'n ever, but I didn't say nothin', an' had the mare hitched an' started back. Old Jinny drives with one hand, an' I c'd watch the new one all right, an' as we come along I begun to think I wa'n't stuck after all. I never see a hoss travel evener an' nicer, an' when we come to a good level place I sent the old mare along the best she knew, an' the new one never broke his gait, an' kep' right up 'ithout 'par'ntly half tryin'; an' Jinny don't take most folks' dust neither. I swan! 'fore I got home I reckoned I'd jest as good as made seventy-five anyway."

"Then the' wa'n't nothin' the matter with him, after all," commented Mrs. Bixbee in rather a disappointed tone.

"The meanest thing top of the earth was the matter with him," declared David, "but I didn't find it out till the next afternoon, an' then I found it out good. I hitched him to the open buggy an' went 'round by the East road, 'cause that ain't so much travelled. He went along all right till we got a mile or so out of the village, an' then I slowed him down to a walk. Wa'al, sir, scat my ——! He hadn't walked more'n a rod 'fore he come to a dead stan'still. I clucked an' gitapp'd, an' finely took the gad to him a little; but he only jest kind o' humped up a little, an' stood like he'd took root."

"Wa'al, now!" exclaimed Mrs. Bixbee.

"Yes'm," said David; "I was stuck in ev'ry sense of the word."

"What d'ye do?"

"Wa'al, I tried all the tricks I knowed—an' I could lead him—but when I was in the buggy he wouldn't stir till he got good an' ready; 'n' then he'd start of his own accord an' go on a spell, an'——"

"Did he keep it up?" Mrs. Bixbee interrupted.

"Wa'al, I s'd say he did. I finely got home with the critter, but I thought one time I'd either hev to lead him or spend the night on the East road. He balked five sep'rate times, varyin' in length, an' it was dark when we struck the barn."

"I should hev thought you'd a wanted to kill him," said Mrs. Bixbee; "an' the fellers that sold him to ye, too."

"The' *was* times," David replied, with a nod of his head, "when if he'd a fell down dead I wouldn't hev figgered on puttin' a band on my hat, but it don't never pay to git mad with a hoss; an' as fur 's the feller I bought him of, when I remembered how he told me he'd stand without hitchin', I swan! I had to laugh. I did, fer a fact. 'Stand without hitchin'!' He, he, he!"

"I guess you wouldn't think it was so awful funny if you hadn't gone an' stuck that horse onto Deakin Perkins—an' I don't see how you done it."

"Mebbe that *is* part of the joke," David allowed, "an' I'll tell ye th' rest on't. Th' next day I hitched the new one to th' dem'crat wagin an' put in a lot of straps an' rope, an' started off fer the East road agin. He went fust rate till we come to about the place where we had the fust trouble, an', sure enough, he balked agin. I leaned over an' hit him a smart cut on the off shoulder, but he only humped a little, an' never lifted a foot. I hit him another lick, with the self-same result. Then I got down an' I strapped that animal so't he couldn't move nothin' but his head an' tail, an' got back into the buggy. Wa'al, bomby, it may 'a' ben ten minutes, or it may 'a' ben more or less—it's slow work settin' still behind a balkin' hoss—he was ready to go on his own account, but he couldn't budge. He kind o' looked around, much as to say, 'What on earth's the matter?' an' then he tried another move, an' then another, but no go. Then I got down an' took the hopples off an' then climbed back into the buggy, an' says 'Cluck' to him, an' off he stepped as chipper as could be, an' we went joggin' along all right mebbe two mile, an' when I slowed up, up he come agin. I gin him another clip in the same place on the shouder, an' I got down an' tied him up agin, an' the same thing happened as before, on'y it didn't take him quite so long to make up his mind about startin', an' we went some further without a hitch. But I had to go through the puf-formance the third time before he got it into his head that if he didn't go when *I* wanted he couldn't go when *he* wanted, an' that didn't suit him; an' when he felt the whip on his shoulder it meant bus'nis."

"Was that the end of his balkin'?" asked Mrs. Bixbee.

"I had to give him one more go-round," said David, "an' after that I didn't have no more trouble with him. He showed symptoms at times, but a touch of the whip on the shoulder alwus fetched him. I alwus carried them straps, though, till the last two or three times."

"Wa'al, what's the deakin kickin' about, then?" asked Aunt Polly. "You're jest sayin' you broke him of balkin'."

"Wa'al," said David slowly, "some hosses will balk with some folks an' not with others. You can't most alwus gen'ally tell."

"Didn't the deakin have a chance to try him?"

"He had all the chance he ast fer," replied David. "Fact is, he done most of the sellin', as well 's the buyin', himself."

"How's that?"

"Wa'al," said David, "it come about like this: After I'd got the hoss where I c'd handle him I begun to think I'd had some int'restin' an' valu'ble experience, an' it wa'n't scurcely fair to keep it all to myself. I didn't want no patent on't, an' I was willin' to let some other feller git a piece. So one mornin', week before last—let's see, week ago Tuesday it was, an' a mighty nice mornin' it was, too—one o' them days that kind o' lib'ral up your mind—I allowed to hitch an' drive up past the deakin's an' back, an' mebbe git somethin' to strengthen my faith, et cetery, in case I run acrost him. Wa'al, 's I come along I seen the deakin putterin' 'round, an' I waved my hand to him an' went by a-kitin'. I went up the road a ways an' killed a little time, an' when I come back there was the deakin, as I expected. He was leanin' over the fence, an' as I jogged up he hailed me, an' I pulled up.

" 'Mornin', Mr. Harum,' he says.

" 'Mornin', deakin,' I says. 'How are ye? an' how's Mis' Perkins these days?'

" 'I'm fair,' he says; 'fair to middlin', but Mis' Perkins is ailin' some—*as usyul*,' he says."

"They do say," put in Mrs. Bixbee, "thet Mis' Perkins don't hev much of a time herself."

"Guess she hez all the time the' is," answered David. "Wa'al," he went on, "we passed the time o' day, an' talked a spell about the weather an' all that, an' finely I straightened up the lines as if I was goin' on, an' then I says: 'Oh, by the way,' I says, 'I jest thought on't. I heard Dominie White was lookin' fer a hoss that 'd suit him.' 'I hain't heard,' he says; but I see in a minute he had—an' it really was a fact—an' I says: 'I've got a roan colt risin' five, that I took on a debt a spell ago, that I'll sell reasonable, that's as likely an' nice ev-ry way a young hoss as ever I owned. I don't need him,' I says, 'an' didn't want to take him, but it was that or nothin' at the time an' glad to git it, an' I'll sell him a barg'in. Now what I want to say to you, deakin, is this: That hoss 'd suit the dominie to a tee in my opinion, but the dominie won't come to me. Now if *you* was to say to him— bein' in his church an' all thet,' I says, 'that you c'd get him the right kind of a hoss, he'd believe you, an' you an' me'd be doin' a little stroke of bus'nis, an' a favor to the dominie into the bargain. The dominie's well off,' I says, 'an' c'n afford to drive a good hoss.' "

"What did the deakin say?" asked Aunt Polly as David stopped for breath.

"I didn't expect him to jump down my throat," he answered; "but I seen him prick up his ears, an' all the time I was talkin' I noticed him lookin' my hoss over, head an' foot. 'Now I 'member,' he says, 'hearin' sunthin' 'bout Mr. White's lookin' fer a hoss, though when you fust spoke on't it had slipped my mind. Of course,' he says, 'the' ain't any real reason why Mr. White shouldn't deal with you direct, an' yit mebbe I *could* do more with him 'n you could. But,' he says, 'I wa'n't cal'latin' to go t' the village this mornin', an' I sent my hired man off with my drivin' hoss. Mebbe I'll drop 'round in a day or two,' he says, 'an' look at the roan.'

" 'You mightn't ketch me,' I says, 'an' I want to show him myself; an' more'n that,' I says, 'Dug Robinson's after the dominie. I'll tell ye,' I says, 'you jest git in 'ith me an' go down an' look at him, an' I'll send ye back or drive ye back, an' if you've got anythin' special on hand you needn't be gone three quarters of an hour,' I says."

"He come, did he?" inquired Mrs. Bixbee.

"He done *so*," said David sententiously. "Jest as I knowed he would, after he'd hem'd an' haw'd about so much, an' he rode a mile an' a half livelier 'n he done in a good while, I reckon. He had to pull that old broadbrim of his'n down to his ears, an' don't you fergit it. He, he, he, he! The road was jest *full* o' hosses. Wa'al, we drove into the yard, an' I told the hired man to unhitch the bay hoss an' fetch out the roan, an' while he was bein' unhitched the deakin stood 'round an' never took his eyes off'n him, an' I knowed I wouldn't sell the deakin no roan hoss *that* day, even if I wanted to. But when he come out I begun to crack him up, an' I talked hoss fer all I was wuth. The deakin looked him over in a don't-care kind of a way, an' didn't 'parently give much heed to what I was sayin'. Finely I says, 'Wa'al, what do you think of him?' 'Wa'al,' he says, ' he seems to be a likely enough critter, but I don't believe he'd suit Mr. White—'fraid not,' he says. 'What you askin' fer him?' he says. 'One-fifty,' I says, 'an' he's a cheap hoss at the money'; but," added the speaker with a laugh, "I knowed I might 's well of said a thousan'. The deakin wa'n't buyin' no roan colts that mornin'."

"What did he say?" asked Mrs. Bixbee.

"'Wa'al,' he says, 'wa'al, I guess you ought to git that much fer him, but I'm 'fraid he ain't what Mr. White wants.' An' then, 'That's quite a hoss we come down with,' he says. 'Had him long?' 'Jest long 'nough to git 'quainted with him,' I says. 'Don't you want the roan fer your own use?' I says. 'Mebbe we c'd shade the price a little.' 'No,' he says, 'I guess not. I don't need another hoss jest now.' An' then, after a minute he says: 'Say, mebbe the bay hoss we drove 'd come nearer the mark fer White, if he's all right. Jest as soon I'd look at him?' he says. 'Wa'al, I hain't no objections, but I guess he's more of a hoss than the dominie 'd care for, but I'll go an' fetch him out, I says. So I brought him out, an' the deakin looked him all over. I see it was a case of love at fust sight, as the storybooks says. 'Looks all right,' he says. 'I'll tell ye,' I says, 'what the feller I bought him of told me.' 'What's that?' says the deakin. 'He said to me,' I says, '"that hoss hain't got a scratch ner a pimple on him. He's sound an' kind, an' 'll stand without hitchin', an' a lady c'd drive him as well 's a man."'

"'That's what he said to me,' I says, 'an' it's every word on't true. You've seen whether or not he c'n travel,' I says, 'an', so fur's I've seen, he ain't 'fraid of nothin'.' 'D'ye want to sell him?' the deakin says. 'Wa'al,' I says, 'I ain't offerin' him fer sale. You'll go a good ways,' I says, ''fore you'll strike such another; but, of course, he ain't the only hoss in the world, an' I never had anythin' in the hoss line I wouldn't sell at *some* price.' 'Wa'al,' he says, 'what d' ye ask fer him?' 'Wa'al,' I says, 'if my own brother was to ask me that question I'd say to him two hundred dollars, cash down, an' I wouldn't hold the offer open an hour,' I says."

"My!" ejaculated Aunt Polly. "Did he take you up?"

"'That's more'n I give fer a hoss 'n a good while,' he says, shakin' his head, 'an' more'n I c'n afford, I'm 'fraid.' 'All right,' I says; 'I c'n afford to keep him'; but I knew I had the deakin same as the wood-chuck had Skip. 'Hitch up the roan,' I says to Mike; 'the deakin wants to be took up to his house.' 'Is that your last word?' he says. 'That's what it is,' I says. 'Two hundred, cash down.'"

"Didn't ye dast to trust the deakin?" asked Mrs. Bixbee.

"Polly," said David, "the's a number of holes in a ten-foot ladder." Mrs. Bixbee seemed to understand this rather ambiguous rejoinder.

"He must 'a' squirmed some," she remarked. David laughed.

"The deakin ain't much used to payin' the other feller's price," he said, "an' it was like pullin' teeth; but he wanted that hoss more'n a

cow wants a calf, an' after a little more squimmidgin' he hauled out
his wallet an' forked over. Mike come out with the roan, an' off the
deakin went, leadin' the bay hoss."

"I don't see," said Mrs. Bixbee, looking up at her brother, "thet
after all the' was anythin' you said to the deakin thet he could ketch
holt on."

"The' wa'n't nothin'," he replied. "The only thing he c'n complain
about's what I *didn't* say to him."

"Hain't he said anthin' to ye?" Mrs. Bixbee inquired.

"He, he, he, he! He hain't but once, an' the' wa'n't but little of it
then."

"How?"

"Wa'al, the day but one after the deakin sold himself Mr. Stickin'-
Plaster I had an arrant three four mile or so up past his place, an'
when I was comin' back, along 'bout four or half past, it come on to
rain like all possessed. I had my old umbrel'—though it didn't hender
me f'm gettin' more or less wet—an' I sent the old mare along fer all
she knew. As I come along to within a mile f'm the deakin's house I
seen somebody in the road, an' when I come up closter I see it was
the deakin himself, in trouble, an' I kind o' slowed up to see what
was goin' on. There he was, settin' all humped up with his ole broadbrim hat slopin' down his back, a-sheddin' water like a roof. Then I
seen him lean over an' larrup the hoss with the ends of the lines fer
all he was wuth. It appeared he hadn't no whip, an' it wouldn't done
him no good if he'd had. Wa'al, sir, rain or no rain, I jest pulled up
to watch him. He'd larrup a spell, an' then he'd set back; an' then he'd
lean over an' try it agin, harder'n ever. Scat my——! I thought I'd die
a-laughin'. I couldn't hardly cluck to the mare when I got ready to
move on. I drove alongside an' pulled up. 'Hullo, deakin,' I says,
'what's the matter?' He looked up at me, an' I won't say he was the
maddest man I ever see, but he was long ways the maddest-*lookin'*
man, an' he shook his fist at me jest like one o' the unregen'rit.
'Consarn ye, Dave Harum!' he says, 'I'll hev the law on ye fer this.'
'What fer?' I says. 'I didn't make it come on to rain, did I?' I says.
'You know mighty well what fer,' he says. 'You sold me this *damned
beast,*' he says, 'an' he's balked with me *nine* times this afternoon, an'
I'll fix ye for 't,' he says. 'Wa'al, deakin,' I says, 'I'm 'fraid the squire's
office 'll be shut up 'fore you *git* there, but I'll take any word you'd
like to send. You know I told ye,' I says, 'that he'd stand 'ithout
hitchin'. ' An' at that he only jest kind o' choked an' sputtered. He
was so mad he couldn't say nothin', an' on I drove, an' when I got
about forty rod or so I looked back, an' there was the deakin a-comin'
along the road with as much of his shoulders as he could git under
his hat an' *leadin'* his new hoss. He, he, he, he! Oh, my stars an'
garters! Say, Polly, it paid me fer bein' born into this vale o' tears.
It did, I declare for't!" Aunt Polly wiped her eyes on her apron.

"But, Dave," she said, "did the deakin really say—*that word?*"

"Wa'al," he replied, "if 'twa'n't that it was the puttiest imitation on't that ever I heard."

"David," she continued, "don't you think it putty mean to badger the deakin so't he swore, an' then laugh 'bout it? An' I s'pose you've told the story all over."

"Mis' Bixbee," said David emphatically, "if I'd paid good money to see a funny show I'd be a blamed fool if I didn't laugh, wouldn't I? That specticle of the deakin cost me consid'able, but it was more'n wuth it. But," he added, "I guess, the way the thing stands now, I ain't so much out on the hull."

Mrs. Bixbee looked at him inquiringly.

"Of course, you know Dick Larrabee?" he asked.

She nodded.

"Wa'al, three four days after the shower, an' the story 'd got aroun' some—as *you* say, the deakin *is* consid'able of a talker—I got holt of Dick—I've done him some favors an' he natur'ly expects more—an' I says to him: 'Dick,' I says, 'I hear 't Deakin Perkins has got a hoss that don't jest suit him—hain't got knee-action enough at times,' I says, 'an' mebbe he'll sell him reasonable.' 'I've heerd somethin' about it,' said Dick, laughin'. 'One of them kind o' horses 't you don't like to git ketched out in the rain with,' he says. 'Jes' so,' I says. 'Now,' I says, 'I've got a notion 't I'd like to own that hoss at a price, an' that mebee *I* c'd git him home even if it did rain. Here's a hundred an' ten,' I says, 'an' I want you to see how fur it'll go to buyin' him. If you git me the hoss you needn't bring none on't back. Want to try?' I says. 'All right,' he says, an' took the money. 'But,' he says, 'won't the deakin suspicion that it comes from you?' 'Wa'al,' I says, 'my portrit ain't on none o' the bills, an' I reckon *you* won't tell him so, out an' out,' an' off he went. Yistidy he come in, an' I says, 'Wa'al, done anythin'?' 'The hoss is in your barn,' he says. 'Good fer you!' I says. 'Did you make anythin'?' 'I'm satisfied,' he says. 'I made a ten-dollar note.' An' that's the net results on't," concluded David, "that I've got the hoss, an' he's cost me jest thirty-five dollars."

How Jack Downing Saved His Eye-Teeth

. . . Well, I kept jogging along on the farm after the same old sort, year after year, so long, and there didn't nothing happen to me, that sometimes I almost begun to give it up, and think sure enough it was all nothing but a dream. Still I kept having spells that I felt terrible uneasy, and was tempted forty times to pack up and go and

From *The Life and Writings of Major Jack Downing* [Seba Smith] of Downing-ville, away down east in the State of Maine, written by himself, pp. 29–33. Boston: Lilly, Watt, Colman, & Holden. 1834.

seek my fortune. I might tell a good deal more about my life, and my uncles and ants and cousins, and the rest of the neighbors: but I begin to feel a most tired of writing my life, and believe I shall have to serve it pretty much as I planted my watermillion seeds. And that was this. When I was about six or seven years old, our folks give me a pint of watermillion seeds and told me to go out into the field and plant 'em for myself, and I might have all I could raise. So off I goes tickled enough. And I went to work and punched little holes down in the ground and put in one seed to time along in a row, three or four inches apart, till I got about half the seeds planted. It was rather a warm afternoon and I begun to feel a little tired, so I took and dug a hole and poured the rest of the seeds all in together, and covered 'em up, and went into the house. Well, mother asked me if I'd planted my seeds; yes mam, says I. What, all of 'em, says she? Yes mam, says I. But you've been very spry, says she, how did you get them done so quick? O, says I, easy enough; I planted 'em in a *hill and a row.* And, when they begun to come up, they found 'em in a hill and a row sure enough. So I believe I shall have to pour the rest of my life into a hill, and let it go.

To come then right to the pint—I don't mean the pint of watermillion seeds, but the pint in my life which seemed to be the turning pint—In the fall of the year 1829, I took it into my head I'd go to Portland. I had heard a good deal about Portland, what a fine place it was, and how the folks got rich there proper fast; and that fall there was a couple of new papers come up to Downingville from there, called the Portland Courier and Family Reader; and they told a good many queer kind of things about Portland, and one thing another; and all at once it popped into my head, and I up and told father; and says I, I'm going to Portland whether or no; and I'll see what this world is made of yet. Father stared a little at first, and said he was afraid I should get lost; but when he see I was bent upon it, he give it up; and he stepped to his chist and opened the till, and took out a dollar and give to me, and says he, Jack, this is all I can do for you; but go, and lead an honest life, and I believe I shall hear good of you yet. He turned and walked across the room, but I could see the tears start into his eyes, and mother sot down and had a hearty crying spell. This made me feel rather bad for a minute or two, and I almost had a mind to give it up; and then again father's dream came into my mind, and I mustered up courage, and declared I'd go. So I tackled up the old horse and packed in a load of ax handles and a few notions, and mother fried me some dough-nuts and put 'em into a box along with some cheese and sassages, and ropped me up another shirt, for I told her I didn't know how long I should be gone; and after I got all rigged out, I went round and bid all the neighbors good bye, and jumped in and drove off for Portland.

Ant Sally had been married two or three years before and moved to Portland, and I inquired round till I found out where she lived, and went there and put the old horse up and eat some supper and went to bed. And the next morning I got up and straightened right off to see the Editor of the Portland Courier, for I knew by what I had seen in his paper that he was jest the man to tell me which way to steer. And when I come to see him I knew I was right; for soon as I told him my name and what I wanted, he took me by the hand as kind as if he had been a brother; and says he, Mr. Downing, I'll do any thing I can to assist you. You have come to a good town; Portland is a healthy thriving place, and any man with a proper degree of enterprise may do well here. But says he, Mr. Downing, and he looked mighty kind of knowing, says he, if you want to make out to your mind, you must do as the steamboats do. Well, says I, how do they do? for I didn't know what a steam boat was, any more than the man in the moon. Why, says he, they *go ahead*. And you must drive about among the folks here jest as though you were at home on the farm among the cattle. Dont be afraid of any of 'em, but figure away, and I dare say you will get into good business in a very little while. But says he, there's one thing you must be careful of, and that is not to get into the hands of them are folks that trades up round Huckler's Row; for there's some sharpers up there, if they get hold of you, would twist your eye teeth out in five minutes. Well after he had gin me all the good advice he could I went back to Ant Sally's again and got some breakfast, and then I walked all over the town to see what chance I could find to sell my ax handles and things, and to get into business.

After I had walked about three or four hours I come along towards the upper end of the town where I found there were stores and shops of all sorts and sizes. And I met a feller, and says I, what place is this? Why this says he, is Huckler's Row. What, says I, are these the stores where the traders in Huckler's Row keep? And says he, yes. Well then, thinks I to myself, I have a pesky good mind to go in and have a try with one of these chaps, and see if they can twist my eye teeth out. If they can get the best end of a bargain out of me, they can do what there aint a man in Downingville can do, and I should jest like to know what sort of stuff these ere Portland chaps are made of. So in I goes into the best looking store among 'em. And I see some biscuit lying on the shelf, and says I, Mister, how much do you ax apiece for them are biscuit? A cent apiece, says he. Well, says I, I shant give you that, but if you've a mind to, I'll give you two cents for three of 'em, for I begin to feel a little as though I should like to take a bite. Well, says he, I wouldn't sell 'em to any body else so, but seeing it's you I dont care if you take 'em. I knew he lied, for he never see me before in his life. Well he handed down the biscuits and I took 'em, and walked round the store awhile to see what else he had to sell. At last, says I, Mister, have you got any good new cider? Says he, yes, as good as ever you see. Well, says I, what do you ax a glass for it?

Two cents, says he. Well, says I, seems to me I feel more dry than I do hungry now. Aint you a mind to take these ere biscuit again and give me a glass of cider? And says he I dont care if I do; so he took and laid 'em on the shelf again, and poured out a glass of cider. I took the cider and drinkt it down, and to tell the truth it was capital good cider. Then, says I, I guess it's time for me to be a going, and I stept along towards the door. But, says he, stop Mister. I believe you have'nt paid me for the cider. Not paid you for the cider, says I, what do you mean by that? Didn't the biscuit that I give you jest come to the cider? Oh, ah, right, says he. So I started to go again; and says he, but stop, Mister, you didn't pay me for the biscuit. What, says I, do you mean to impose upon me? do you think I am going to pay you for the biscuit and let you keep 'em tu? Aint they there now on your shelf, what more do you want? I guess sir, you dont whittle me in that way. So I turned about and marched off, and left the feller staring and thinking and scratching his head, as though he was struck with a dunderment. Howsomever, I didn't want to cheat him, only jest to show 'em it want so easy a matter to pull my eye teeth out, so I called in next day and paid him his two cents. Well, I staid at Ant Sally's a week or two, and I went about town every day to see what chance I could find to trade off my ax handles, or hire out, or find some way or other to begin to seek my fortune. . . .

How to Buy a Dog

A good many times people have asked me how I came to own the fastest hound dog in the State of Maine, and why he was known to be the fastest, and I want to tell it just the way it happened so you'll all know the facts. I came from Wytopitlock, where I was living at the time, down to Mattawamkeag on the Bangor & Aroostook Railroad one day to buy myself a hound dog. Up to Wytopitlock we was having a run on long-legged rabbits then, and I didn't want none of these short-legged dogs that can run all day and not move any. I wanted one with rangy pins that could get close enough to a Wytopitlock rabbit so he'd exert himself and know he was chased. The short-legged dogs we'd been using was no good at all, and I says to myself, "The Hell with that!"

So I set out on purpose to find me a dog that was high-posted, limber and lickety, clever and able, and why I came down to Mattawamkeag I don't right know, but I'm quite a cuss on dogs and have a sense of smelling them out once I know what I want. So here I was in Mattawamkeag and not knowing a soul there, but I wandered

From *The Fastest Hound Dog in the State of Maine,* by John Gould, pp. 17–33. Copyright, 1953, by John Gould and F. Wenderroth Saunders. New York: William Morrow and Company.

around thinking if they had a likely dog in those parts I'd soon find out, and if they warn't, I'd soon know that, too, and no harm done.

Well, I circulated some, and had made up my mind it was a day thrown away, and I started back to the depot, meaning to pick up a copy of the Bangor Daily *News* to read on the train going home, and to get there quicker I cut across and came up onto the back end of a barn, and when I did I had this premonition of Dog, and I says to myself that I'd been led to this barn by some power unknown.

So I said to myself, "Dog!" And just as I did they commenced to bark, and I'd say offhand without exaggeration that the barn had fifty dogs in it, at least fifty, and just then a little door opened and a fellow stuck his head out and wanted to know what I was up to.

I said I was just cutting across to the Bangor & Aroostook depot, and moved up closer while I was saying it, and when I got close enough to holler above the dogs I said, "What you got in there?"

"In where?" he says.

"In that barn," I says.

"In what barn?" he says.

I could see we warn't getting any place that way, and where I didn't have much time for the train I says, "Sounds like dogs."

"It might be," he says.

I says, "I'm looking for a dog if I find the one I want."

"Mine ain't for sale," he says.

So I says all right, but where I had a few minutes to train time, did he mind if I looked at them, and he said he didn't see no harm in that, so we went in. Well, sir, I never see such a bevy of dogs. He had every kind of dog that the mind of God had ever devised, and some nobody had thought up yet, and on top of that he had crossed them up somewhat, but they were all fat and nice and all glad to see me. I patted some of them and made of them, and kept looking for one that might match up with a Wytopitlock rabbit, but I didn't see any that took my fancy, and I got to thinking I'd better be getting on down to the depot.

But something made me dilly-dally, no doubt it was Providence, and all to once over in the far corner I heard a new bark, some dog that hadn't been saying anything was starting in, and for some reason I liked the sound of it. So I says, "What's that?"

"What's what?" he says.

"That barking," I says.

"Dog, I guess," he says.

So I went over, and he had a piece of chicken wire strung kitty-cornered, and where it was back from the window I couldn't rightly see, but I run my hand in, and I got the friendliest lapping I ever had from a dog, and I knew right off that I'd come onto the very dog I was after and no doubt about it. I could tell from the way he lapped that he had a kind heart and a knowing eye, and his bark was the bark of a hound, and where I held my hand he come up about belt high or so. I made up my mind to have him first and look him over afterward. I was that sure. So I took my hand out and says, "That might be the very dog I want!"

"He ain't for sale," the fellow says.

I says, "I take it he's a hound."

"Sort of," he says. "But he ain't for sale."

I says, "Probably ain't much of a dog, then."

"Oh, yes," he says. "He's a good dog, but I'm sentimental over him, and don't plan to let him go."

So looking at my watch I says, "Time's running on and I got a train to catch, so I got to be getting along." I says, "If this dog was for sale, which you say he ain't, and you was to take a liking to me, knowing I could give him a good home," I says, "what price would you put on him?"

"He ain't for sale," he says.

"I know that," I says. "And I'm not interested in him, but if I was to be interested in him, and you was to offer him for sale, what kind of value would you set on him?"

"I don't know," he says. "I ain't thought of selling him, and ain't put my mind to it."

So I says, "That's true, and I appreciate your feelings, but what I'm talking is purely supposing-if, and I give you my word I ain't got the slightest hankering for that dog at all, and if you was to offer him to me as an outright present, I doubt if you could make me take him," I says. "So what I mean is by way of passing the time until the train comes, and I'd like to have your opinion as to what a dog like that is worth, so I'd know what to offer if I ever run up against one like him that takes my eye."

"Well," he says. "Putting it that way I got to tell you that he's really a valuable dog."

I says, "That's an opinion, and I respect your right to hold it, but I was hoping you'd express it in terms of money"—and I slapped my wallet—"so I'd know just how valuable you think he is."

"Well," he says. "He's worth a good deal."

I says, "How much is a good deal?"

So he says, "Well, he ain't for sale, as I told you, and I don't want to make no remarks that would mislead you, but if he was for sale, which he ain't, and I was to put a price on him, which I refuse to do, I'd say he was no good to me at all unless he'd fetch—well, let's say about . . . Oh, I'd say about a dollar and a quarter."

"Well," I says. "I admire your honesty and I thank you for your opinion, but I can see that your sentimental attachment to him has given you some erroneous ideas, but if he was for sale, which I understand he ain't, and if I was to be interested in buying him, which I ain't, I don't believe I could possibly bring myself to make an offer for him of anything above seventy-five cents," I says.

So the fellow says, "Sold!"

False Tail

One time there was a fellow up in Missouri owned a big fine-looking saddle mare, except she didn't have no tail, as it had got cut off some way. But there was a wigmaker in Kansas City that fixed a false tail so good you couldn't tell the difference, and it was fastened onto the stub with eelskin and rubber.

The trader that owned the mare got a fine saddle and bridle with silver on it, and rode around to all the fairs. He would sell the mare for a good price, but he never sold the saddle and bridle. Soon as he got the money in his pocket, he always took off the saddle and bridle, and then he would pull the mare's tail off. She just had a little stub about six inches long, and it was shaved smooth and dyed yellow. It sure did look funny, so all the people would laugh, and the fellow that bought the mare begun to holler for his money back. But the horse trader says the tail does not belong to the mare, because it come off another animal. He says he bought the tail separate in Kansas City, and he has got a bill of sale to prove it. False tails is just like a woman's bustle, and if any gentleman wants an artificial tail, they can go to Kansas City and see the wigmaker, says he.

So then he would go set in the livery stable, and pretty soon the fellow that bought the mare would come around talking turkey. Then the horse trader would say, "I always try to do the right thing, and not work no hardship on the customers. So I will take the mare back, if you will give me twenty dollars for my trouble." That's the way it went all over the country, and sometimes he would sell the mare three or four times in one day. The horse trader was a-living the life of Riley, and putting money in the bank besides.

One day he rode into a little town in Arkansas, and right away an old man bought the mare for two hundred dollars. When the horse trader pulled the mare's tail off, the old man didn't bat an eye, and just laughed like the rest of the boys. The horse trader hung around the livery stable all day, but the old man never showed up. The horse trader stayed at the hotel that night, and the next day he borrowed a pony and rode out to the old man's place. He says he don't feel right about the sale, so he will take the mare and give the old man his money back, and no hard feelings.

The old man just laughed, and says he hasn't got no complaint, as a bargain is a bargain. He says he likes the mare fine, and he is going

From *Who Blowed Up the Church House? and Other Ozark Folk Tales,* by Vance Randolph, pp. 175–177. Copyright, 1952, by Columbia University Press. New York.

to braid a new tail out of corn shucks, and paint it blue to match his wife's eyes. The horse trader figured the old man must be out of his head. But he had to get the snide mare back somehow, so he offered to pay the two hundred dollars and give the old man ten dollars besides. The old man just laughed louder than ever, and he says the mare is worth four hundred dollars easy, and she ain't for sale anyway. So the horse trader comes back to town. He sets around the hotel mighty glum, and all the home boys was laughing about it.

Next morning he went out to see the old man again, and says he will give two hundred and twenty-five dollars for the snide mare. The old man says, "Don't talk foolish, because me and my wife has got attached to the mare now, and she is just like one of the family." And then he says he knowed that tail was a fake all the time, because he used to swap horses with the Indians when he was a young fellow.

The horse trader thought about it awhile, and then he says, "Listen, that snide's all I've got to live on, and feed a big family. Do you want to take the bread out of my little children's mouth?" The old man says, "No, I wouldn't do nothing like that. Give me three hundred dollars and you can have your mare back." The horse trader started to write a check, but the old man wouldn't take no check, so they went to the bank, and the horse trader give him three hundred dollars in cash. All the loafers was a-laughing about it, and the banker laughed louder than anybody. So then the horse trader put the mare's tail where it belonged, and he rode out of town. He never did come back, neither.

Lots of people up North think the folks that live down in Arkansas are all damn fools. But it ain't so, particular when it comes to swapping horses and things like that.

Ma Pettengill and the Boys at the Ranch

I. RAISING WHALES IN THE WEST

I told you about whales, didn't I? Whales started it—whales for table use. It come in the Sunday paper—with the picture of a handsome whale and the picture of a French cook kissing his fingers over the way he has cooked some of it; and the picture of a pleased young couple eating whale in a swell restaurant; and the picture of a fair young bride in her kitchenette cutting up three cents' worth of whale meat into a chafing dish and saying how glad she was to have something tasty and cheap for dearie's lunch; and the picture of a poor labouring man being told by someone down in Washington, D. C.,

From *Ma Pettengill*, by Harry Leon Wilson, pp. 12–37. Copyright, 1919, by Doubleday, Page & Company. New York: Grosset & Dunlap.

that's making a dollar a year, that a nickel's worth of prime whale meat has more actual nourishment than a dollar's worth of porter-house steak; and so on, till you'd think the world's food troubles was going to be settled in jig time; all people had to do was to go out and get a good eating whale and salt down the side meat and smoke the shoulders and grind up some sausage and be fixed for the winter, with plenty to send a mess round to the neighbours now and then.

And knocking beef, you understand, till you'd think no one but criminals and idiots would ever touch a real steak again, on account of its being so poor in food values, like this Washington scientist says that gets a dollar a year salary and earns every cent of it. It made me mad, the slanderous things they said about beef; but I read the piece over pretty carefuly and I really couldn't see where the whale was going to put me out of business, at least for a couple years yet. It looked like I'd have time, anyway, to make a clean-up before you'd be able to go into any butcher shop and get a rib roast of young whale for six cents, with a bushel or two of scraps thrown in for the dog.

Then this Sunday paper goes out to the bunk house and the boys find the whale piece and get excited about it. Looks like if it's true that most of 'em will be driving ice wagons or something for a living. They want me to send down for a mess of whale meat so they can see if it tastes like regular food. They don't hardly believe these pictures where people dressed up like they had money are going into spasms of delight about it. Still, they don't know—poor credulous dubs! They think things you see in a Sunday paper might be true now and then, even if it is most always a pack of lies thought up by dissipated newspaper men.

I tell 'em they can send for a whole whale if they want to pay for it, but none of my money goes that way so long as stall-fed beef retains its present flavour; and furthermore I expect to be doing busi-ness right here for years after the whale fad has died out—doing the best I can with about ten silly cowhands taking the rest cure at my expense the minute I step off the place. I said there was no doubt they should all be added to the ranks of the unemployed that very minute—but due to other well-known causes than the wiping out of the cattle industry by cold whale hash in jelly, which happened to be the dish this French chef was going crazy over.

They chewed over that pointed information for a while, then they got to making each other bets of a thousand dollars about what whale meat would taste like; whether whale liver and bacon could be told from natural liver and bacon, and whether whale steak would prob-ably taste like catfish or mebbe more like mud turtle. Sandy Sawtelle, who always knows everything by divine right, like you might say, he says in superior tones that it won't taste like either one but has a flavour all its own, which even he can't describe, though it will be something like the meat of the wild sea cow, which roams the ocean in vast herds off the coast of Florida.

Then they consider the question of a whale round-up in an expert manner. It don't look none too good, going out on rodeo in water about three miles too deep for wading, though the idea of lass'ing a whale calf and branding it does hold a certain fascination. Sandy says it would be the only livestock business on earth where you don't always have to be fearing a dry season; and Buck Devine says that's so, and likewise the range is practically unlimited, as any one can see from a good map, and wouldn't it be fine riding herd in a steam yacht with a high-class bartender handy, instead of on a so-and-so cayuse that was liable any minute to trade ends and pour you out of the saddle on to your lame shoulder.

They'd got to kidding about it by this time, when who should ride up but old Safety First Timmins. They spring the food whale on Safety with much flourish. They show him the pictures and quote prices on the hoof—which are low, but look what even a runt of a yearling whale that was calved late in the fall would weigh on the scales!—and no worry about fences or free range or winter feeding or water holes; nothing to do but ride round on your private steamboat with a good orchestra, and a chance to be dissolute and count your money. And look what a snap the pioneers will have with all the mavericks; probably not a single whale in the ocean yet branded! And does Timmins want to throw in with us? If he does mebbe they can fix up a deal with me because I want a good business man at the head of the new outfit.

But Safety says right off quick that it's all a pack of nonsense. He says it's the mad dream of a visionary or feeble-minded person. He don't deny there would be money in whales if they could be handled, but you couldn't handle anything that had the whole ocean to swim in that covers three quarters of the earth's surface, as he has often read. And how would you get a branding iron on a whale, and what good would it do you? He'd beat it out for Europe. He said they was foolish to think whales would stay in a herd, and he guessed I'd been talking just to hear myself talk, or more likely I'd been kidding 'em to get a good laugh.

Sandy says: "Well, I wasn't going to tell you at first, but I guess it'll be safe with you, you being a good friend of the Arrowhead, only don't let it go no farther; but the fact is the boss is negotiating for the whale privilege in Great Salt Lake. Yes, sir, she's bribing the Utah legislature this very minute to let the bill go through! And I guess that don't look much like kidding. As soon as the governor has signed the bill she'll put in a couple of good three-year-old bull whales and a nice little herd of heifers and have the world's meat supply at her finger ends in less than five years—just killing off the yearling steers."

Safety looks a bit startled at this, and Sandy goes on to say that though whale meat is now but a fad of the idle rich it's bound to be the meat of rich and poor alike in future. He'd bet a thousand dollars to a dime that by the time the next war come along, the first thing they'd do would be to establish a whaleless day. He said whale meat was just that good.

Safety chewed his gum quite a time on this—he says if a man chews gum he won't ruin himself in pocket for tobacco—and he read the whale article over carefully and looked at the pictures again, but he still said it didn't sound to him like a legitimate business enterprise. He said for one thing there'd be trouble shipping the original herd up to Salt Lake. Sandy said it was true; there would be the initial expense of loading on to flat cars, and a couple of tunnels would have to be widened so the bulls wouldn't be rasped going through, but that I have already taken this up with the railroad company.

Safety says that may all be true, but, mark his word, the minute my herd gets into inland waters it will develop some kind of disease like anthrax or blackleg, and the whole bunch will die on me. Sandy says it will be a simple matter to vaccinate, because the animals will be as affectionate as kittens by that time through having been kindly handled, which is all a whale needs. He says they really got a very social nature and are loyal unto death. Once a whale is your friend, he says, it's for life, rain or shine, just so long as you treat him square. Even do a whale a favour just once and he'll remember your face, make no difference if it's fifty years; though being the same, it is true, in his hatreds, because a whale never forgives an injury. A sailor he happens to know once give a whale he had made friends with a chew of tobacco just for a joke and the animal got into an awful rage and tried to tear the ship down to get at him, and then he followed the ship all over the world waiting for this sailor to fall off or get wrecked or something, till finally the hunted man got so nervous he quit the sea and is now running a newsstand in Seattle, if Safety don't believe it. It just goes to show that a whale, as long as you're square with him, is superior in mind and morals to a steer, which ain't got sense enough to know friend from foe.

Safety still shakes his head. He says "safe and sane" has been his motto thoughout a long and busy life and this here proposition don't sound like neither one to him. The boys tell him he's missing a good thing by not throwing in with us. They say I'm giving 'em each a big block of stock, paid up and non-assessable, and they don't want him to come round later when they're rolling in wealth and ask why they didn't give him a chance too.

"I can just hear you talk," said Sandy. "You'll be saying: "I knew that whole fool bunch when not one ever had a dollar he could call his own the day after he was paid off, and now look at 'em—throwing their hundreds of thousands right and left; houses with pianos in every room; new boots every week; silver-mounted saddles at a thousand each; choice wines, liquors, and cigars, private taxicabs; and Alexander J. Sawtelle, the wealthy banker, being elected to Congress by an overwhelming majority!' That's the way you'll be talking," said Sandy, "with regret eating into your vitals like some horrible acid that is fatal to man and beast."

Safety says he thinks they're all plumb crazy, and a fool and his money is soon parted—this being a saying he must have learned at the age of three and has never forgotten a word of—and he comes up to the house to see me. Mebbe he wanted to find out if I had really lost my mind, but he said nothing about whales. Just set round and talked the usual hard luck. Been in the stock business thirty years and never had a good year yet. Nothing left of his cattle but the running gear; and his land so poor you couldn't even raise a row on it unless you went there mad; and why he keeps on struggling in the bitter clutch of misfortune he don't know. But I always know why he keeps on struggling. Money! Nothing but money. So when he got through mourning over his ruined fortunes, and feebly said something about taking some mules off my hands at a fair price, I shut him off firmly. Whenever that old crook talks about taking anything off your hands he's plotting as near highway robbery as they'll let him stay out of jail for. He was sad when I refused two hundred and fifty dollars a span for my best mules.

He went off shaking his head like he hadn't expected such inhumanity from an old friend and neighbour to one who through hard luck was now down and out.

II. The Elephant Ranch

Well, I hear no more about whales; but a circus is coming to Red Gap and old Pete, the Indian, says he must go down to it, his mind being inflamed by some incredible posters pasted over the blacksmith shop at Kulanche. He says he's a very old man and can't be with us long, and when he does take the one-way trail he wants to be able to tell his friends on the other side all about the strange animals that they never had a chance to see. The old pagan was so excited about it I let him go. And he was still more excited when he got back two days later. Yes, sir; he'd found a way to fortune.

He said I'd sure think he was a liar with a crooked tongue and a false heart, but they had an animal at that circus as big as our biggest covered mess wagon and it would weigh as much as the six biggest steers I ever shipped. It has a nose about five feet long—he was sure I wouldn't believe this part—that it fed itself with, and it carried so much meat that just one ham would keep a family like Pete's going all winter. He said of course I would think he was a liar, but I could write down to Red Gap to a lawyer, and the lawyer would get plenty of people to swear to it right in the courthouse. And so now I must hurry up and stock the place with these animals and have more meat than anybody in the world and get rich pretty quick. Forty times he stretched his arms to show me how big one of these hams would be, and he said the best part was that this animal hardly ate anything at all but a little popcorn and a few peanuts. Hadn't he watched it for hours? And if I didn't hurry others would get the idea and run prices up.

I guess Pete's commercial mind must of been engaged by hearing the boys talk about whales. He hadn't held with the whale proposition, not for a minute, after he learned they live in the ocean. He once had a good look at the ocean and he promptly said "Too much water!" But here was a land animal packing nearly as much meat as a whale, eating almost nothing, and as tame as a puppy. "I think, 'Injun how you smart!' " he says when he got through telling me all this in a very secret and important way.

I told him he was very smart indeed and ought to have a job with the Government at a dollar a year telling people to quit beef meat for the elephant. I said I was much obliged for the tip and if I ever got to going good in elephants I'd see he had a critter of his own to butcher every fall. So Pete went out with all his excitement and told the boys how I was going to stock the ranch with these new animals which was better than whales because you wouldn't have to get your feet wet. The boys made much of it right off.

In no time at all they had all the white-faces sold off and vast herds of pure-bred elephants roaming over the ranch with the Arrowhead brand on 'em. Down on the flat lands they had waving fields of popcorn and up above here they had a thousand acres of ripening peanuts; and Sandy Sawtelle, the king of the humourists, he hit on another idea that would bring in fifty thousand dollars a year just on the side. He said if a crowd come along to a ranch and bought the rancher's own hay for the sake of feeding it to his own steers they would be thought weak-minded. Not so with elephants. He said people would come from far and near and bring their little ones to buy our own peanuts and popcorn to feed our own elephants. All we needed to do was put the stuff up in sacks at a nickel a throw. He said of course the novelty might die out in time, but if he could only get the peanut-and-popcorn concession for the first three years that would be all he'd want for his simple needs of living in a swell marble house in Spokane, with a private saloon and hired help to bring him his breakfast in bed and put on another record and minister to his lightest whim. Buck Devine said he'd be able to throw his own good money right and left if he could get the ivory privilege, which is made from the horns of the elephant and is used for many useful purposes; and one of the other boys says they'll develop a good milk strain and get a dairy herd, because the milk of this noble animal ought to be fine for prize fighters and piano movers.

In about ten minutes they was doing quite a business for old Pete's benefit, and Pete very earnest about it. He says I've promised him a young animal to butcher every fall, and they tell him there ain't no meat so good as a prime young popcorn-fed elephant, and he'll certainly live high. And just then up rides old Safety First again. So they get silent and mysterious all at once and warn Pete, so Safety will hear it, not to say a word to any one. Pete looks secretive and hostile at the visitor and goes back to his woodpile. Safety naturally says what fool thing have they got into their head now, and he supposes it's some more of that whale nonsense.

The boys clam up. They say this is nothing like whales, but a dry-land proposition too important to talk about; that I've sworn everyone to secrecy, but he'll see soon enough what it is when the big money begins to roll in. They don't mind telling him it's an African proposition of new and nourishing food, a regular godsend to the human race, but they got to keep quiet until I get my options bought up so I'll have the cream of the business.

Safety sniffs in a baffled manner and tries to worm out a hint, but they say it's a thing would go like wildfire once it got known, being so much tastier than whale meat and easier to handle, and eating almost nothing.

"Whales was pretty good," says Sandy; "but since the boss got a line on this other animal she's disposed of her whale interests for seventy-three thousand dollars."

Buck Devine says I showed him the check, that come in yesterday's mail, and let him hold it a minute so he could say he once held seventy-three thousand dollars in his hand just like that. And the money was to be put into this new business, with the boys being let in on the ground floor, like they had been with the whales. Sandy says that in probably a year from now, or eighteen months at the most, he won't be a thing but a dissipated millionaire. Nothing but that!

Safety is peculiar in his mind. If you told him you found a million gold dollars up in the top of that jack pine he wouldn't believe it, yet still and all he'd get a real thrill out of it. He certainly does cherish money. The very notion of it is romantic to him. And he must of been thrilled now. He hung round, listening keenly while the boys squandered their vast wealth in various reprehensible ways, trying to get some idea about the new animal. Finally he sniffed some more, and they was all crazy as loons, and went off. But where does he go but over to old Pete at the woodpile and keeps him from his work for ten minutes trying to get the new animal's name out of Pete. But he can't trap the redman into any admissions. All he can find out is that Pete is serious and excited.

Then he come up to ask me once more if he couldn't take some mules off my hands. He found out quick and short that he couldn't. Still he hung round, talking nonsense as far as I could make out, because I hadn't yet been let in on the new elephant proposition. He says he hears I'm taking up a new line of stock, the same not being whales nor anything that swims, and if it's more than I can swing by myself, why, he's a good neighbour of long standing, and able in a pinch, mebbe, to scrape up a few thousand dollars, or even more if it's a sure cinch, and how about it, and from one old friend to another just what is this new line?

Being busy I acted short. I said I was sticking to cattle in spite of the infamous gossip against 'em, and all reports to the contrary was mere society chatter. Still he acted like I was trying to fool him. He went out saying if I changed my mind any time I was to let him know, and he'd be over again soon to talk mules at least, if nothing else, and anything he could do for me any time, just say the word, and try some of this gum, and so forth. I was right puzzled by these here refined civilities of his until Pete comes in and tells me how the boys have stocked the old ranch with elephants and how Safety has tried to get him to tell the secret. I tell Pete he's done right to keep still, and then I go down to the bunk house and hear the whole thing.

By this time they're shipping thousands of steer elephants at top prices; they catch 'em up off soft feed and fatten' em on popcorn and peanuts, and every Thanksgiving they send a nice fat calf to the White House, for no one looks at turkey any more. Sandy is now telling what a snap it will be to ride herd on elephants.

"You pick out a big one," he says, "and you build a little cupalo up on top of him and climb up into it by means of a ladder, and set there in this little furnished room with a good book, and smoke and pass the time away while your good old saddle elephant does the work. All you got to do is lean out of the front window now and then jab him in the forehead with an ice pick, whichever way you want him to turn."

I said trust a cow-puncher to think up some way where he'd have to do as little work with his hands as he does with his head. But I admitted they seemed to have landed on old Timmins for once, because he had tried to get Pete to betray the secret and then come wheedling round to me about it. I said I could talk more intelligently next time, and he would sure come again because he had lavished two sticks of gum on me, which was an incredible performance and could not have been done except for an evil purpose.

"Now say," says Sandy, "that does look like we got him believing. I was going to kid him along about once more, then spring elephants on him, and we'd all have a good laugh at the old wolf. But it looks to me like a chance for better than a laugh; it looks to me like we might commit a real crime against him."

"He never carries anything on him," I says, "if you're meaning something plain, like highway robbery."

Sandy says he don't mean that; he means real Wall Street stuff, such as one gentleman can pull on another and still keep loose; crooked, he says, but not rough. I ask what is the idea, and Sandy says get him more and more feverish about the vast returns from this secret enterprise. Then we'll cut out a bunch of culls—thin stuff and runts and cripples—and make him give about four times what they're worth on a promise to let him into the new deal; tell him we must be rid of this stuff to make room for the new animals, and naturally we'll favour our friends.

"There, now!" says Sandy. "I should be in Wall Street this minute, being able to think up a coop as pernicious as that: and I would of been there, too, only I hate city life."

"For once in the world's history," I says, "there may be a grain of sense in your words. Only no cows in the deal. Even to defraud the old crook I wouldn't let him have hide nor hair of a beef, not since he worked on my feelings in the matter of them bull calves two years ago. Mules, yes. But the cow is too worthy a beast to be mixed up in anything sinful I put over on that profiteer. Now I'll tell you what," I says, very businesslike: "you boys tole him along till he gets hectic enough to take that bunch of mule runts down in the south field, and anything you get over fifty dollars a head I'll split with you."

Sandy hollers at this. He says this bunch ain't mules but rabbits, and that I wouldn't refuse forty a head for 'em this minute. He says even a man expecting to be let in on a sure-thing elephant ranch would know something wicked was meant if asked to give even as much as fifty dollars for these insects. I tell him all very true; but this is just the margin for his lasting financial genius which he displays so little reticence about that it'll get into the papers and make him a marked man from coast to coast if he ain't careful. He says oh, all right, if I want to take it that way, and he'll see what he can do. Mebbe he can get fifty-five a head, which would not only give the boys a good laugh but provide a little torch money.

I left 'em plotting against a man that had never been touched by any plot whatever. I resolved to remain kind of aloof from their nefarious doings. It didn't seem quite dignified for one of my standing to be mixed up in a deal so crooked—at least no more than necessary to get my share of the pickings.

Sure enough, the very next day here come the depraved old outcast marauding round again at lunch time and et with the boys in the kitchen. He found 'em full of suppressed excitement and secret speech and careless talk about large sums of money. It must of been like sweetest music to his ears. One says how much would it be safe to count on cutting up the first year—how much in round numbers; and another would say that in round numbers, what with the expense of getting started and figuring everything down to the last cent, it wouldn't be safe to count on more than a hundred thousand dollars; but, of course, for the second year, now, why it would be nearer two hundred thousand in round numbers, even figuring everything fine and making big allowance for shrinkage. After that they handed money back and forth in round numbers till they got sick of the sound of it.

They said Safety set and listened in a trance, only waking up now and then to see if he couldn't goad someone into revealing the name of this new animal. But they always foiled him. Sandy Sawtelle drew an affecting picture of himself being cut off by high living at the age of ninety, leaving six or eight million dollars in round numbers and having his kin folks squabble over his will till the lawyers got most of it. They said Safety hardly et a morsel and had an evil glitter in his eyes.

III. Profit in Mules

After lunch he went out to the wood-pile where old Pete was working and offered him two bits in money to tell him the secret, and when old Pete scorned him he raised it to four bits. I guess the idea of any one refusing money merely for a little talk had never seemed possible to him. He must of thought there was sure something in it. I was away that day, but when I got back and heard about his hellish attempt to bribe old Pete I told the boys they sure had the chance of a lifetime. I said if there was a mite of financial prowess in the bunch they would start the price on them runt mules at one hundred dollars flat, because it was certain that Safety had struck the skids.

Next day it looked better than ever. Safety not only appeared in the afternoon but he brought me a quart jar of honey from his own bees. Any one not having looked up his criminal record would little understand what this meant. I pretended to be too busy to be startled at the gift, which broke thirty years of complete inactivity in that line. I looked worried and important with a litter of papers on my desk and seemed to have no time to waste on callers. He mentioned mules once or twice with no effect whatever, then says he hears I'm going into a new line that seems like it might have a few dollars in it, and he hopes I won't lose my all, because so many things nowadays look good till they're tried. I was crafty. I said I might be going into a new line, then again it might be nothing but idle talk and he better not believe everything he hears. . . .

He took up the jar of honey and fondled it, with his face looking like he was laying a loved one to rest, and said he wouldn't mind going into something new himself if he could be sure it was sound, because the stock business at present was a dog's life. . . . And as a matter of fact now, as between old friends and neighbours, if I had something that looked good, why not keep it all together just with us here in the valley, he, though a poor man, being able to scrape up a few thousand dollars in round numbers for any enterprise that was a cinch.

And the old hound being worth a good half million dollars at that instant! But I kept control of my face and looked still more worried and important and said I might have to take in a good man, and then again I might not. I couldn't tell till I got some odd lots of stock cleaned up. Then I looked at some more documents and, like I was talking unconsciously to myself, I muttered, though distinctly: "Now that there bunch of runt mules—they'll have to go; but, of course, not for any mere song."

Then I studied some more documents in a masterful manner and forgot my caller entirely till at last he pussyfooted out, having caught sight of Sandy down by the corral.

Pretty soon Sandy reports to me. He says Safety is hurt at my cold manner to an old friend and neighbour that's always running in with a jar of honey or some knickknack; and he had mentioned the runt mules, saying he might be induced to consider 'em though I probably won't let 'em go for any mere song, contemptible as they are. Sandy says he's right; that it's got to be a whole opera with words and music for them mules. He says I got a reason for acting firm about the price, the reason being that this new line I'm going to embark in is such a sure thing that I want only friends to come in, and I got to be convinced first that their heart is in the right place.

Safety says his heart is always getting the best of his head in stock deals, but just how foolish will I expect an old and tried friend to seem about these scrub mules that nobody in his right mind would touch at any price.

Sandy yawns like he was weary of it all and says a hundred dollars flat. He said Safety just stood still and looked at him forever without batting an eye, till he got rattled and said that mebbe ninety-five might be considered. That's a trick with this old robber when a party's got something to sell him. They tell their price and he just keeps still and looks at 'em—not indignant nor astonished, not even interested, but merely fishlike. Most people can't stand it long, it's that uncanny. They get fussed and nervous, and weaken before he's said a single word.

But it was certain now that the mystery was getting to Safety, because otherwise he'd have laughed his head off at the mention of a hundred dollars for these mules. Three months before he'd heard me himself offer 'em for forty a head. You see, when I bought bands of mules from time to time I'd made the seller throw in the little ones to go free with the trade. I now had twenty-five or so, but it had begun to get to me that mebbe those sellers hadn't been so easy as I thought at the time. They was knotty-headed little runts that I'd never bothered to handle.

Last spring I had the boys chink up the cracks in the corral and put each one of the cunning little mites into the chute and roach it so as to put a bow in its neck; then I put the bunch on good green feed where they would fatten and shed off; but it was wasted effort. They looked so much like field mice I was afraid that cats would make a mistake. After they got fat the biggest one looked as if he'd weigh close up to seven hundred and fifty. It was when they had begun to buy mules too; that is to say, mules! But no such luck as a new West Pointer coming to inspect these; nothing but wise old cavalry captains that when they put an eye on the bunch would grin friendly at me and hesitate only long enough to put some water in the radiator. I bet there never was a bunch of three-year-old mules that stood so much condemning.

After offering 'em for forty a head one time to a party and having him answer very simply by asking how the road was on beyond and which turn did he take, I quit bothering. After that when buyers come along I told the truth and said I didn't have any mules. I had to keep my real ones, and it wasn't worth while showing those submules. And this was the bunch Sandy had told S. F. Timmins he could take away for a hundred a head—or even ninety-five. And Safety hadn't laughed!

And would you have wondered when he sifts in a couple days later and makes me a cold offer of sixty dollars a head for this choice live-stock? Yes, sir! He says "Live and let live" is his motto, and he wants to prove that I have wronged him in the past if I ever had the faintest suspicion that he wasn't the ideal party to have in on a deal that was going to net everyone concerned a handsome fortune. He says the fact is money goes through his fingers like water if you come right down to it; and sixty or even sixty-five if I want to push him to extremes, because he's the last man on God's green earth to let five dollars split up old neighbours that ought to be hand and glove in any new deal that come up.

It like to of keeled me over, but I recovered and become busier than ever and got out my bank book and begun to figure over that. I said Sandy Sawtelle had the handling of this particular bunch of my assets and I couldn't be bothered by it.

So he mooches down to the barn till Sandy come in with Buck Devine. They was chattering about three hundred thousand dollars in round numbers when they got near enough for him to overhear their private conversation. They wondered why they had wasted so much of their lives in the cattle business, but now them old hard-working days was over, or soon would be, with nothing to do but travel round in Pullman palace cars and see America first, and go to movies, and so forth. Safety wished to haggle some about the mules, but Sandy says he's already stated the price in clear, ringing tones, and he has no time to waste, being that I must send him down that night to get an order on the wire for two carloads of the Little Giant peanut. Safety just blinked at this, not even asking why the peanuts; and the boys left him cold.

When I told 'em about the offer to me of sixty or a possible sixty-five, they at once done a medicine dance.

"This here will be the richest coop ever pulled off west of Cheyenne," says Buck; and Sandy says he guesses anybody not blind can now see that well-known street in New York he ought to have his office on. He says he hopes Safety don't fall too easy, because he wants more chance to work it up.

But Sandy is doomed to disappointment. Safety holds off only two days more. Two days he loafs round at mealtimes, listening to their rich converse and saying he'd like to know who's a better friend of this outfit than he's been for twenty years. The boys tell him if he's such a good friend to go ahead and prove it with a little barter that would be sure to touch my heart. And the first day Safety offers seventy-five a head for these here jack rabbits, which they calmly ignore and go on talking about Liberty Bonds being a good safe investment; and the second day he just cries like a child that he'll pay eighty-five and trust to their honour that he's to have in on this new sure-thing deal.

That seemed enough, so they all shook hands with the spendthrift and slapped him on the back in good fellowship, and said they knew all the time he had a heart of gold and they feel free to say now that once the money has passed he won't be let to go off the place till he has heard all about the new enterprise and let in on the ground floor, and they hope he won't ever forget this moment when the money begins to roll in fit to smother him in round numbers. So Safety says he knows they're a good square set of boys, as clean as a hound's tooth, and he'll be over to-morrow to take over the stock and hear the interesting details.

The boys set up late that night figuring their share of the burglary. There was twenty-five of these ground squirrels. I was to get my fifty a head, at least ten of which was illegitimate. Then for the thirty-five, which was the real robbery, I was to take half, and eight of the boys the other half. I begun to wonder that night just what could be done to us under the criminal law. It looked like three years in some good jail wouldn't be a bit too harsh.

Next day bright and early here comes frugal Safety, gangling along behind his whiskers and bringing one of his ill-fed hirelings to help drive the stuff back. Safety is rubbing his hands and acting very sprightly, with an air of false good fellowship. It almost seems like he was afraid they had thought better of the trade and might try to crawl out. He wants it over quick. They all go down and help him drive his purchase out of the lower field, where they been hiding in the tall grass, and in no time at all have the bunch headed down the lane on to the county road, with Safety's man keeping well up to protect 'em from the coyotes.

Next there's kind of a solemn moment when the check it being made out. Safety performs that serious operation down at the bunk house. Making out any check is always the great adventure with him. He writes it with his heart's blood, and not being the greatest scholar in the world he has to count the letters in his name after it's written—he knows there ought to be nine together—and then he has to wipe the ink off his hands and sigh dismally and say if this thing keeps up he'll be spending his old age at the poor farm, and so forth. It all went according to schedule, except that he seemed strangely eager and under a severe nervous strain.

Me? I'd been sort of hanging round on the edge of events while the dastardly deed was being committed, not seeming to be responsible in any way. My Lord! I still wanted to be able to face the bereaved man as an honest woman and tell him it was only some nonsense of the boys for which I could not be held under the law, no matter how good a lawyer he'd get. When they come trooping out of the bunk house I was pretending to consult Abner, the blacksmith, about some mower parts. And right off I was struck by the fact that Safety seemed to be his old self again; his air of false gayety and nervous strain had left him and he was cold and silent and deadly, like the poisonous cobra of India.

But now they was going to spring the new secret enterprise on him, so I moved off toward the house a bit, not wanting to be too near when his screams begun. It did seem kind of shameful, taking advantage of the old miser's grasping habits; still, I remembered a few neat things he'd done to me and I didn't slink too far into the background. Safety was standing by his horse with the boys all gathered close round him, and I heard Sandy say "Elephants—nothing but elephants—that's the new idea!"

Then they all begun to talk at once, jabbering about the peanuts and popcorn that crowds of people will come to buy from us to feed back to our stock, and how there's more meat in an elephant than in six steers, and about how the punchers will be riding round in these little cupalos up on top of their big saddle elephants; and they kept getting swifter and more excited in their talk, till at last they just naturally exploded when they made sure Safety got the idea and would know he'd been made a fool of. They had a grand time; threw their hats in the air and danced round their victim and punched each other, and their yells and hearty laughter could of been heard for miles up and down the creek. Two or three had guns they let off to add to the gleeful noise. Oh, it was deuces wild for about three minutes. They nearly died laughing.

Then the whole thing kind of died a strange and painful death. Safety wasn't taking on one bit like a man that's been stung. He stood there cold and malignant and listened to the noise and didn't bat an eye till he just naturally quelled the disorder. It got as still as a church, and then Safety talked a little in a calm voice.

"Elephants?" says he, kind of amused. "Why, elephants ain't no good stock proposition because it takes 'em so long to mature. Elephants is often a hundred and twenty years old. You'd have to feed one at least forty years to get him fit to ship. I really am surprised at you boys, going into a proposition like that without looking up the details. It certainly ain't anything for my money. Why, you couldn't even veal an elephant till he was about fifteen years old, which would need at least six thousand dollars' worth of peanuts; and what kind of a stock business is that, I'd like to know. And even if they could rustle their own feed, what kind of a business is it where you could only ship once in a life-time? You boys make me tired, going hell-bent into an enterprise where you'd all be dead and forgotten before the first turnover of your stock."

He now looked at 'em in a sad, rebuking manner. It was like an icy blast from Greenland the way he took it.

Two or three tried to start the big laugh again, but their yips was feeble and died quickly out. They just stood there foolish. Even Sandy Sawtelle couldn't think of anything bright to say.

Safety now climbs on his horse, strangely cheerful, and says: "Well, I'll have to be getting along with them new mules of mine." Then he kind of giggled at the crowd and says: "I certainly got the laugh on this outfit, starting a business where this here old Methusalem hisself could hardly get it going good before death cut him off!"

And away he rides, chuckling like it was an awful joke on us. Not a single scream of agony about what had been done to him with them stunted mules.

Of course that was all I needed to know. One deadly chill of fear took me from head to foot. I knew perfectly well our trench was mined and the fuse lighted. Up comes this chucklehead of a Sawtelle, and for once in his life he's puzzled.

"Well," he says, "you got to give old S. F. credit for one thing. Did you see the way he tried to switch the laugh over on to us, and me with his trusty check right here in my hand? I never would have thought it, but he is certainly one awful good game loser!"

"Game loser nothing!" I says. "He's just a game winner. Any time you see that old boy acting game he's won. And he's won now, no matter how much the known facts look against it. I don't know how, but he's won."

They all begin to tell me I must be mistaken, because look at the price we got for stuff we hadn't been able to sell at any price before. I says I am looking at that, but I'm also obliged to look at Safety after he's paid that price, and the laws of Nature certainly ain't been suspended all at once. I offer to bet 'em what they've made on the deal that Safety has run true to form. "Mark my words," I says, "this is one sad day for the Arrowhead! I don't know how or why, but we'll soon find out; and if you don't believe me, now's the time to double your money."

But they hung off on that. They got too much respect for my judgment. And they admitted that Safety's way of standing the gaff had been downright uncanny. So there was nothing to do but pay over their share of this tainted money and wait for the blow, eight hundred and seventy-five dollars being the amount I split with 'em for their masterly headwork in the depredation.

That very day in the mail comes a letter that has been delayed because this here Government of ours pinches a penny even worse than old Timmins does. Yes, sir; this letter had been mailed at Seattle with a two-cent stamp the day after the Government had boosted the price to three cents. And what does the Government do? Does it say: "Oh, send it along! Why pinch pennies?" Not at all. It takes a printed card and a printed envelope and the time of a clerk and an R.F.D. mail carrier to send me word that I must forward one cent if I want this letter—spends at least two cents to get one cent. Well, it takes two days for that notice to reach me; and of course I let it lie round a couple of days, thinking it's probably an advertisement; and then two days for my one-cent stamp to go back to this parsimonious postmaster; and two days for the letter to get here; making about eight days, during which things had happened that I should of known about. Yes, sir; it's a great Government that will worry over one cent and then meet one of these smooth profiteers and loosen up on a million dollars like a cowhand with three months' pay hitting a wet town. Of course it was all over when I read this letter.

I rolled another cigarette for the injured woman, it being no time for words.

"It just goes to show," she observed after the first relishing draft, "that we should be honest, even with defectives like old Timmins. This man in Seattle that keeps track of prices for me writes that the top of the mule market has blown sky-high; that if I got anything looking at all like a mule not to let it go off the place for less than two hundred dollars, because mule buyers is sure desperate. Safety must of got the same tip, only you can bet his correspondent put the full three cents on the letter. Safety would never have trusted a strange postmaster with the excess. Anyway he sold that bunch of rabbits a week later for one hundred and seventy-five a head, thus adding twenty-two hundred and fifty dollars of my money to his tainted fortune. You can imagine the pins and needles he'd been on for a week, scared I'd get the tip and knowing if he even mentioned them runts at any price whatever that I'd be wise at once. That joke of the boys must of seemed heaven-sent to him.

"You ought to heard the lecture I read them fool punchers on common honesty and how the biter is always bit. I scared 'em good;

there hasn't been an elephant on the place since that day. They're a chastened lot, all right. I was chastened myself. I admit it. I don't hardly believe I'll ever attempt anything crooked on old Safety again —and yet, I don't know."

The lady viciously expelled the last smoke from her cigarette and again took up the knitting.

"I don't really know but if there was some wanton duplicity come up that I could handle myself and not have to leave to that pack of amateur thieves out in the bunk house, and it was dead sure and I didn't risk doing more than two years' penal servitude—yes, I really don't know. Even now mebbe all ain't over between us."

The Fable of the Inveterate Joker Who Remained in Montana

The Subject of this Fable started out in Life as a Town Cut-Up. He had a keen Appreciation of Fun, and was always playing Jokes. If he wanted a few Gum-Drops he would go into the Candy Store and get them, and then ask the Man if he was willing to take Stamps. If the Man said he was, then the Boy would stamp a couple of times, which meant that the Laugh was on the Man. It was considered a Great Sell in Those Parts.

Or else he would go out into a Grocery with another tricky Tad and get some Article of Value, and they would pretend to Quarrel as to which should Pay for it. One would ask the Proprietor if he cared who paid for it, and if he said he did not, they would up and tell him to Pay for it Himself. This one was so Cute that they had a little Piece in the Paper about it.

Or they would go and Purchase a Watermelon to be paid for as soon as a Bet was decided, and afterward it would Develop that the Bet was whether the Saw-Mill would fall to the East or the West, in case the Wind blew it over.

It was Common Talk that the Boy was Sharp as a Tack and Keen as a Brier and a Natural-Born Humorist.

Once he sold a Calf to the Butcher, several Hours after the Calf had been struck by Lightning. As for ordering Goods and having them charged to his Father, that was one of the Slickest Things he ever did.

About the time the Joker was old enough to leave Home, he traveled out through the Country selling Bulgarian Oats to the Farmers. When the Contract for the Seed Oats got around to the Bank, it proved to be an iron-clad and double-riveted Promissory Note. The Farmer always tried to get out of Paying it, but when the Case came to Trial

From *More Fables,* by George Ade, pp. 121–127. Illustrated by Clyde J. Newman. Copyright, 1900, by Herbert S. Stone & Co. New York. Toronto: George J. McLeod.

and the Jurors heard how the Agent palavered the Hay-Seed they had to Snicker right out in Court. They always gave Judgment for the Practical Joker, who would take them out and buy Cigars for them, and they would hit him on the Back and tell him he was a Case.

One Day the Joker had an Inspiration, and he had to tell it to [his] Friend, who also was something of a Wag.

They bought a Cat-Tail Swamp remote from Civilization and divided it into Building Lots. The Marsh was Advertised as a Manufacturing Suburb, and they had side-splitting Circulars showing the Opera House, the Drill Factory, Public Library, and the Congregational Church. Lots were sold on the Instalment Plan to Widows, Cash-Boys, and Shirt-Factory Girls who wanted to get Rich in from fifteen to twenty Minutes.

The Joker had a Lump of Bills in every Pocket. If asked how he made his Roll, he would start to Tell, and then he would Choke Up, he was so full of Laugh. He certainly had a Sunny Disposition.

Finally he went to the State of Montana. He believed he could have a Season of Merriment by depositing some Valuable Ore in a Deserted Mine, and then selling the Mine to Eastern Speculators. While he was Salting the Mine, pausing once in a while to Control his Mirth, a few Natives came along, and were Interested. They were a slow and uncouth Lot, with an atrophied Sense of Humor, and the Prank did not Appeal to them. They asked the Joker to Explain, and before he could make it Clear to them or consult his Attorney they had him Suspended from a Derrick. He did not Hang straight enough to suit, so they brought a Keg of Nails and tied [it] to his Feet, and then stood off and Shot at the Buttons on the Back of his Coat.

MORAL: *Don't Carry a Joke too far, and never Carry it into Montana.*

De Ducks

When the crops were garnered, would come the settlement between the owner and tenant. The value of the products was ascertained, and fifty percent of the whole was credited to the landowner and fifty percent to the tenant. Then from the tenant's half was deducted the amount charged against him for supplies. This system, practiced with honesty as between the conscientious land owner and the ignorant tenant, worked in an equitable and satisfactory manner, but, as might have been expected, the time came when the land fell into the hands of some who had no scruples about dealing with the poor, and out of this condition grew a long chain of abuses. The "advance merchant" came upon the scene, removing from the shoulders of the land owner

From *The Book of Birmingham*, by John R. Hornady, pp. 206–211. Copyright, 1921, by Dodd, Mead and Company, Inc. New York.

the burden of providing the tenant with the things needful for producing the crop and maintaining his family between seasons.

Many of these merchants played a useful and constructive part in keeping the agriculture of the South moving, but as always under such circumstances, the man looking for a big profit, and having no compunctions as to how it was obtained, found this a lucrative field. The schemes to which he would resort in robbing the farmer of the fruit of his toil is the theme of many a story, and they illustrate a genius for wrongdoing, as well as a surprising indifference to the Golden Rule. One of the common practices of this element is said to have been to start a "charge column" with the year, then add the purchases from time to time, thus:

Bought:	Sept. 1, 1868
1 sack of meal	$2.40
1 pr. shoes	3.00
10 lbs. coffee	1.50

When the time of settlement came, the year went into the total charged against the farmer, along with such other extraordinary charges as might have suggested themselves during the twelve months, and he was a lucky individual who had anything left after the settlement.

The impression made upon the mind of the farmer-tenant by practices of this kind was well illustrated on one occasion when a wealthy citizen from the North came into Alabama with a view to buying a large plantation which had been offered for sale. The deal was considered so important that the real estate man handling the matter called upon the Agricultural Department of the State for the assistance of an expert in explaining the nature of the soil and the wide variety of products to which it was adapted. The visitor was much impressed and was about to close the deal when he fell into conversation with an aged tenant, and then it looked for a few minutes as though the real estate man might lose a fat commission and the State a new citizen.

While the parties to the transaction were seated upon the broad veranda of the old mansion which adorned this plantation, the prospective buyer observed an aged tenant seated by an overflowing artesian well that bubbled up near the house, and he strolled over to the farmer, whereupon the following conversation was overheard by the real estate dealer and the agent from the Agricultural Department:

"How long have you lived here?" asked the prospective buyer.

"All my life, Boss; I was borned on this here place befo' de wah, an' when de slaves was freed I stayed on here," was the reply of the farmer.

"Then you know this plantation very well?"

"I does dat; I knows every foot of it, an' I knows it am de best place in dis whole country. I knows mo' cawn an' cotton is hauled off'n dis place every year dan off'n nair uther place hereabout."

At this the prospective buyer smiled his appreciation, and the real estate man whispered "that ought to cinch matters," but the conversation at the well was not over, for the gentleman continued:

"Then I ought to make a lot of money off of this plantation, eh?"

"No, sah, Boss, you can't make no money. If you does it'll be the fust time anybody ever done it since de wah."

The jaw of the Northerner sagged and he gasped:

"If it's such fine land and produces such splendid crops, why is it money cannot be made here?"

"Well, Boss, to tell you de truf, de ducks eats it all up; yes sah, de ducks takes it all!"

"The ducks eat it up! What on earth do you mean by that?"

"Yes, sir, de ducks eats it up, just like I's tellin' you. We tenants raises heaps of cotton an' heaps of cawn, an' den we takes it to town to de sto'. Den de white folks dey figgers an' figgers, an' dey ducks dis and dey ducks dat, and 'fo de Lawd, by time dey's done, de ducks is et up ever' thing we's raised!"

*   *   *   *   *

Today the old-time advance merchant largely is a creature of the past, education and diversification having proved his undoing. Many farmers are able to finance their own operations, and those who cannot have the help of the banker or the legitimate merchant. So "de ducks" are not so destructive of farm values as they were in olden times.

The Complete Sleep Prolonger

". . . This thing is simple," said [The Tennessee Shad], stretching out on his bed and pulling a string at one side. "Opens hot-air register. No applause necessary. But this is a little, comforting idea of my own. Protection from sudden change of temperature without bodily exposure." Extending his hand he pulled the other rope, which, running through the pulley over his head, brought the counterpane quickly over him. "How's that? No sitting up, reaching down, fumbling about in zero weather."

"That's good as far as it goes," said Dennis, whose natural state was not one of reverence; "but how about the window? Some one has to get up and shut the window."

"Simple as eggs," said the Shad, yawning disdainfully. "A string and a pulley do the trick, see? Down comes the window. All worked at the same exchange. Well, Dink, you may lead the cheer."

Now, Stover suddenly remembered a device he had been told of,

From *The Varmint*, A Lawrenceville Story of Owen Johnson, pp. 175–200. Copyright, 1910, by Little, Brown, and Company, Boston.

and, remembering it, to give it the appearance of improvisation he pretended to deliberate.

"Well," said the Tennessee Shad, surprised, "my humble little inventions don't seem to impress you."

"Naw."

"They don't, eh! Why not?"

"Oh, it's the right principle," said Stover, assuming a deliberate look; "but crude, very crude, backwoods, primitive, and all that sort of thing."

The Tennessee Shad, amazed, looked at Finnegan, who spoke: "Crude, Dink?"

"Why, yes. All depends on whether the Shad wakes up or not. And then, why hand labor?"

"I suppose you have something more recherché to offer," said the Tennessee Shad cuttingly, having recovered.

"Why, yes, I might," said Stover coolly. "A real inventor would run the whole thing by machinery. Who's got an alarm clock?"

Dennis, mystified, returned running with his.

Stover, securing it with strings, fastened it firmly on the table, which he moved near the scene of operations. He then lowered the upper half of the window, assuring himself that a slight impetus would start it. To the sash he attached a stout string which he ran through a pulley fixed to the top of the window frame; to the string he fastened a weight which he carefully balanced on the edge of a chair; to the weight, thus fastened, he attached another string which he led to the clock and made fast to the stem that wound the alarm. Then he straightened up, cast a glance over the Shad's handiwork and went to the register.

"When the window shuts it should open the register, of course—first principles," he said crushingly. He disconnected the string from the bed and arranged it on the window. Having wound the clock he addressed his audience:

"It's a simple little thing," he said with a wave of his hand. "I happened to remember that the key of an alarm clock turns as the alarm works. That's all there is to it. Set the alarm when you want to wake up—see—like this. Alarm goes off, winds up spring, throws weight off balance, weight falls, shuts the window, opens the register and you stay under the covers. Practical demonstration now proceeding."

The mechanism worked exactly as he had predicted. The Tennessee Shad and the Wild Irishman, transfixed with awe, watched with dropped mouths the operation. Finnegan, the first to recover, salaamed in true Oriental fashion.

"Mr. Edison," he said in a whisper, "don't take advantage of two innocent babes in the wood. Did you honestly just work this out?"

"Oh, no, of course not," said Dink loftily. "My father told me,—it cost him a fortune; he gave years of his life to perfecting it!"

"And this to me!" said the exponent of the superlative reproachfully.

The Tennessee Shad rose and offered his hand with a gesture worthy of Washington.

"Sir to you. I am your humble servant. Wonderful! Marvelous! Smashing! Terrific! Sublime!"

"Do it again," said Dennis de Brian de Boru.

The alarm being wound and set, the operation was repeated with the same success, while Dennis danced about excitedly and the Tennessee Shad contemplated it with dreamy absorption.

"Jemima!" said Dennis. "And it works for any time?"

"Any time," said Dink, with one hand gracefully resting on his hip.

"Cracky!" exclaimed Dennis, prancing excitedly toward the door. "I'll get the whole House up."

"Dennis!"

Finnegan stopped, surprised at the note of authority in the Tennessee Shad's voice.

"Dennis de Brian de Boru Finnegan; back and sit down."

"What's wrong?"

"You would call in the whole House, would you?"

"Why not?" said Dink, thirsting for the applause of the multitude.

"Dink, oh, Dink!" said the Shad, in profound sorrow. "You would throw away a secret worth millions, would you?"

Dink looked at Dennis, who returned the look, and then with a simultaneous motion they sat down.

"This invention has millions in it, millions," said the Tennessee Shad, promoter. "It is simple, but revolutionary. Every room in the school must be equipped with it."

"Then there's all the apartment houses," said Dennis eagerly.

"That will come later," said the Tennessee Shad.

"We'll patent it," said Stover, seeing clouds of gold.

"Certainly," said the promoter. "We will patent the principle."

"Let's form a company."

The three rose and solemnly joined hands.

"What shall we call it?"

"The Third Triumvirate?" said Dennis.

"Good!" said the Tennessee Shad.

"What shall we charge?" said Dink.

"We must make a dollar profit on each," said the Tennessee Shad. "That means—four hundred fellows in the school—allowing for roommates; we should clear two hundred and ten dollars at the lowest. That means seventy dollars apiece profit."

"Let's begin," said Dennis.

"I'm unalterably opposed," said Dink, "to allowing Doc Macnooder in the firm."

"Me, too," said Dennis.

"Doc is strong on detail," said the Tennessee Shad doubtfully.

"I'm unalterably opposed," said Dink, "to allowing Doc Macnooder to swallow this firm."

"Me, too," said Dennis.

"Doc has great business experience," said the Tennessee Shad; "wonderful, practical mind."

"I'm unalterably—" said Dink and stopped, as the rest was superfluous.

"Me, too," said Dennis.

"Some one's got to work for us in the other Houses."

"Make him our foreign representative," said Stover.

"And give him a commission?"

"Sure—ten per cent."

"No more," said Dennis. "Even that cuts down our profits."

"All right," said the Tennessee Shad. "As you say, so be it. But still I think Doc Macnooder's business sagacity—"

At this moment Doc Macnooder walked into the room. The three future millionaires responded to his greeting with dignity, keeping in mind that distance which should separate a board of directors from a mere traveling man.

"Hello," said Macnooder glibly. "All shipshape and ready for action. Tea served here and chafing-dish ready for the midnight rabbit. Ha, ha, Dink, still got the souvenir toilet set, I see."

"Still, but not long," said Dink. "But that story comes later. Sit down, Doc, and pay attention."

"Why so much chestiness?" said Doc, puzzled. "I haven't sold anything to any of you, have I?"

"Doc," said Stover, "we have formed a company and we want to talk business."

"What company?"

"The Third Triumvirate Manufacturing Company," said Dennis.

"What does it manufacture?"

"This," said Stover, indicating the appliance. "A combined window closer and alarm clock that also opens the register."

"Let's see it," said Macnooder, all excitement.

The demonstration took place. Macnooder the enthusiast was conquered, but Macnooder the financier remained cold and controlled. He sat down, watched by three pairs of eyes, took from his pocket a pair of spectacles, placed them on his nose and said indifferently:

"Well?"

"What do you think of it?"

"It's a beaut!"

"I say, Doc," said Finnegan, "now, won't every fellow in the school be crying for one, won't be happy till he gets it, and all that sort of thing?"

"Every fellow in the school will have one," said Macnooder carefully, making a distinction which was perceived only by the Tennessee Shad.

"Now, Doc," said Dink, still glowing with his triumph over the Tennessee Shad, "let's talk business."

Macnooder took off the glasses and minutely polished them with his handkerchief.

"You've formed a company, eh?"

"The Third Triumvirate—the three of us."

"Well, where do I come in?"

"You're to be our foreign representative."

"Commission ten per cent," added Finnegan carefully.

The Tennessee Shad said nothing, waiting expectantly. Macnooder rose whistling through his teeth and stood gazing down at the alarm clock.

"Foreign representative, commission ten per cent," he said softly.

"We thought we'd give you first whack at it," said Stover in a careless, business-like way.

"So. What's your idea of developing it?"

"Why, we thought of installing it for a dollar."

"With the clock?"

"Oh, no! The clock extra."

"Charging a dollar for string and pulley?"

"And the invention."

"Humph!"

"Well, Doc, is it a go?" said Dink, observing him fall into a revery.

"No, I guess I'm not much interested in this," said Macnooder, taking up his hat. "There's no money in it."

"Why, Doc," said Finnegan, aghast, "you said yourself every fellow would have to have it."

"Would have it," said Macnooder in correction. "The invention's all right, but it's not salable."

"Why not?"

"Nothing to sell. First fellow who sees it can do it himself."

Finnegan looked at Stover, who suddenly felt his pockets lighten.

"Doc is very strong on detail," said the Tennessee Shad softly, in a reminiscent way.

"You might sell it to one fellow," said Macnooder, "without telling him. But soon as you set it up every one will copy it."

"Great business head," continued the Tennessee Shad.

"It's a good idea," said Macnooder condescendingly. "You might get a vote of thanks, but that's all you would get. Do you see the rub?"

"I see," said Dink.

"Me, too," said Dennis.

"And a wonderful practical mind," concluded the Tennessee Shad dreamily.

"Well, let's be public benefactors then," said Dennis in a melancholy tone.

"And such a beautiful idea," said Dink mournfully.

"I move the Third Triumvirate disband," said the Tennessee Shad; and there was no objection.

"Now," said Doc Macnooder briskly, sitting down, "I'll put my own proposition to you amateurs. There's only one way to make the thing go, and I've got the way. I take all responsibility and all risks. All I ask is control of the stock—fifty-one per cent."

Ten minutes later the Third Triumvirate Manufacturing Company was reformed on the following basis:

PRESIDENT..Doc Macnooder, 51 shares.
ADVISORY BOARD.......................................The Third Triumvirate.
TREASURER..Doc Macnooder.

PAID-UP CAPITAL

Macnooder $5.10
The Tennessee Shad 1.70
Dink Stover 1.70
Dennis de B. de B. Finnegan 1.50

"Now," said Macnooder, when the articles were safely signed and the capital paid up, "here's the way we work it. We've got to do two things: first, conceal the way it's done until we sell it; and second, keep those who buy from letting on."

"That's hard," said the Tennessee Shad.

"But necessary. I'm thinking out a plan."

"Of course the first part is a cinch," said Dennis. "A few extras, etcetera, etceteray. It's putting the ribbons in the lingerie, that's all."

"Exactly."

"You don't think it's selling goods under false pretenses?"

"Naw," said Macnooder. "Same principle as the patent medicine—the only wheel that goes round there is a nice, fat temperance measure of alcohol, isn't it? We'll have the first public demonstration to-morrow afternoon. I'll distribute a few more pearls to-night. Ta, ta."

The three sat quietly, listening to the fall of his departing steps.

"If we'd asked him in the first place," said the Tennessee Shad, gazing out the window, "we'd only given up twenty-five per cent—great business head, Doc; great mind for detail."

Macnooder, that night, formed the Eureka Purchasing Company, incorporated himself, and secured, at jigger rates, every second-hand alarm clock on which he could lay his hands—but more of that hereafter.

At five o'clock the next afternoon the combined Kennedy House packed itself into the Tennessee Shad's room, where Doc Macnooder rose and addressed them:

"Gentlemen of the Kennedy: I will only detain you an hour or so; I have only a few thousand words to offer. We are gathered here on an auspicious occasion, a moment of history—the moment *is* historical. Your esteemed Housemate, Mr. Dink Stover, has completed, after years of endeavor, an invention that is destined to be a household word from the northernmost wilds of the Davis House to the sun-kissed fragrance of the Green, from the Ethiopian banks of the fur-bearing canal to the Western Tins of Hot-dog Land! . . . Gentlemen, in a few moments I shall have the pleasure of placing before you an opportunity to become shareholders in one of the most epoch-making inventions the world has ever known."

"What's it called?" said a voice.

"It's called," said Macnooder slowly, secure now of the attention of his audience, "it's called The Complete Sleep Prolonger. The title itself is a promise and a hope. I will claim nothing for this wonderful little invention. It not only combats the cold, but it encourages the heat; it prolongs not only the sleep, but the existence; it will increase the stature, make fat men thin, thin men impressive, clear the complexion, lighten the eye and make the hair long and curly."

"Let's have it," cried several voices.

"Gentlemen," said Macnooder, seeing that no further delay was possible, "our first demonstration will be entitled The Old Way."

Dennis de Brian de Boru Finnegan, in pajamas, appeared from a closet, went to the window, opened it, shut the register, yawned, went to his bed and drew the covers over his head. The faint sounds of a mandolin were heard from the expert hands of the Tennessee Shad.

"Scene," said Macnooder, fitting his accents to low music as is the custom of vaudeville—"scene represents the young Lawrenceville boy, exhausted by the preparation of the next day's lessons, seeking to rest his too conscientious brain. The night passes, the wind rises. It grows cold. Hark the rising bell. He hears it not. What now? He rises in his bed, the room is bitter cold. He bounds to the window over the frozen ground. He springs to the register and back to his bed. He looks at his watch. Heavens! Not a moment to lose. The room is bitter cold, but he must up and dress!"

Finnegan, completing the pantomime, returned with thunders of applause.

"Gentlemen," cried Macnooder, "is this picture a true one?"

And the roar came back:

"You bet!"

"Our next instructive little demonstration is entitled The Scientific Way or The Sleep Prolonger Watches Over Him. Observe now the modest movements of the Dink, the Kennedy House Edison."

Dink, thus introduced, connected the hot-air register to the window sash, the window sash to the weight—specially covered with tin foil—and brought forth the table on which was the now completed Sleep Prolonger. Only the face of the clock appeared, the rest was buried under an arrangement of cardboard boxes and perfectly useless spools, that turned with the rope that took a thrice devious way to the alarm key. In front, two Kennedy House flags were prominently displayed.

"Is everything ready, Mr. Stover?" said Macnooder, while the crowd craned forth, amazed at the intricacy of the machine.

"Ready, Mr. President."

"Second demonstration," said Macnooder.

Finnegan again entered, fixed the register, lowered the window and, going to the clock, set the alarm.

"He sets the alarm for half-past seven," said Macnooder in cadence. "One half-hour gained. The night passes. The wind rises. It grows cold. Hark the rising bell. He hears it not; he doesn't have to. The Sleep Prolonger is there."

The alarm shot off with a suddenness that brought responsive jumps from the audience, the weight fell, and to the amazement of all, the window closed and the register opened.

"Watch him now, watch him," cried Macnooder, hushing the tumult of applause. "Observe the comfort and the satisfaction in his look. He has not stirred, not a limb of his body has been exposed, and yet the room grows warm. His eye is on the clock; he will rise in time, and he will rise in comfort!

"Gentlemen, this great opportunity is now before you. This marvel of human ingenuity, this baffling example of mechanical intricacy is now within your reach. It can do anything. It is yours. It is yours at prices that would make a miner turn from picking up gold nuggets. It is yours for one dollar and twenty-five cents—twenty-five cents is our profit, gentlemen, and you get one profit-sharing bonus. And, furthermore, each of the first fifteen purchasers who will pay the sum of one-fifty will receive not one, but three eight-per-cent, accumulative, preferred bonuses."

"Bonus for what?" said an excited voice.

"Twenty-five per cent of the net profits," cried Macnooder, thumping the table, "will be set aside for pro-rata distribution. The device itself remains for three days a secret, until the completion of the patents. Orders from the model set up and installed in twenty-four hours now acceptable, cash down. No crowding there, first fifteen get three bonuses—one at a time; keep back there—no crowding, no pushing—no pushing, boys. Here, stop! Owing to the extraordinary demand, have I the advisory board's consent to give every purchaser present who pays one-fifty three bonuses? I have? Let her go! Mr. Finnegan, take down the names. Cash, right over here!"

"I don't like this idea of bonuses," said Finnegan, when the rooms had returned to their quiet again.

"Twenty-five per cent, Doc!" said the Tennessee Shad reproachfully.

"Why, you chump," said Macnooder proudly, "that's what's called the profit-sharing system. It keeps 'em quiet, and it also keeps 'em from going out and giving the game away. Mark my words."

"But twenty-five per cent," said the Tennessee Shad, shaking his head.

"Of the profits—net profits," said Macnooder. "There's a way to get around that. I'll show you later."

"We must get to work and round up some alarm clocks," said Stover.

"I've already thought of that," said Doc, as he took his leave. "Don't worry about that. Now I'll canvas the Dickinson."

"A slight feeling of uneasiness," said the Tennessee Shad solemnly, when Macnooder had departed—"a slight feeling of uneasiness is stealing over me, as the poet says."

"Let's have a look at the articles of incorporation," said Stover, who sat down with Dennis to study them.

"We're the advisory board," said Dennis stoutly.

"He's got fifty-one per cent of the stock, though," said Dink.

"But we've got forty-nine!"

The Tennessee Shad, who had not risen from his chair as it involved extraordinary exertion, was heard repeating in a lonely sort of way to himself:

"A slight feeling of uneasiness."

By the next nightfall every room in the Kennedy was equipped with a Complete Sleep Prolonger. Their reception was exactly as Macnooder had foreseen. At first a roar went up as soon as the simplicity of the device was unearthed, but the thought of the precious bonuses soon quelled the revolt.

Besides, there was no doubt of the great humanizing effects of the invention, and the demand that it would awaken throughout the whole school.

But an obstacle arose to even the deep-laid plans of Macnooder himself. As the Third Triumvirate Manufacturing Company had bought its stock from the Eureka Purchasing Company—which had cornered the alarm-clock market—it followed that the alarm clocks were distinctly second rate.

The consequence was that, though all were set for half-past seven, the first gun went off at about quarter-past two in the morning, bringing Mr. Bundy, the assistant house master, to the middle of the floor in one terrified bound, and starting a giggle that ran the darkened house like an epidemic.

At half-past three another explosion took place, aggravated this time by the fact that, the window pulleys being worn, the sash flew up with enough force to shatter most of the glass.

At four o'clock, when three more went off in friendly conjunction, The Roman met Mr. Bundy in the hall in light marching costume, and made a few very forcible remarks on the duties of subordinates— the same being accentuated by the wailing complaint of the youngest Roman which resounded through the house.

From then on the musketry continued intermittently until half-past seven, when such a salvo went off that the walls of the house seemed jarred apart.

The Third Triumvirate went down to breakfast with small appetite. . . .

At noon, by virtue of an extraordinary order from headquarters, all alarm clocks were confiscated and ordered to be surrendered.

"It's all the Old Roman," said Stover doggedly. "He knew it was my invention. He's got it in for me, I tell you."

"Anyhow," said Finnegan, "since Doc planted a few Prolongers in the Dickinson and the Woodhull we ought to be able to stack up a few nice, round plunks."

The Tennessee Shad looked very thoughtful.

At this moment the Gutter Pup and P. Lentz, representing the profit-sharing stockholders, called to know when the surplus was to be divided.

"Macnooder is now at work on the books," said Dink. "We expect him over at any time."

But when at eight o'clock that evening no word had been received from the president, the Third Triumvirate held a meeting and sent the Tennessee Shad over to the Dickinson, with orders to return only with the bullion, for which purpose he was equipped with a small, black satchel.

Just before lights the Tennessee Shad's dragging step was heard returning.

"I don't like the sound," said Dink, listening.

"He always shuffles his feet," said Dennis, clinging to hope.

The door opened and the Tennessee Shad, carrying the black satchel, solemnly entered. Dink flung himself on the bag, wrenched it open and let it drop, exclaiming:

"Nothing!"

"Nothing?" said Dennis, rising.

"Nothing," said the Tennessee Shad, sitting down.

"But the profits?"

"The profits," said the Tennessee Shad, pointing sarcastically to the bag, "are in there."

"Do you mean to say—" began Dink and stopped.

"I mean to say that the Third Triumvirate Manufacturing Company is insolvent, bankrupt, busted, up the spout."

"But then, who's got the coin?"

"Doc Macnooder," said the Tennessee Shad, "and it's all legal."

"Legal?"

"All legal. It's this way. Our profits depended upon the price we paid for alarm clocks. See? Well, when Doc Macnooder, as president of the Third Triumvirate Manufacturing Company looked around for clocks, he found that Doc Macnooder, as president of the Eureka Purchasing Company, had cornered the market and could dictate the price."

"So that?" said Stover indignantly.

"So that each clock was charged up to us at a rate ranging from one dollar and forty cents to one dollar and fifty."

"By what right?" said Dennis.

"It's what is called a subsidiary company," said the Tennessee Shad. "It's quite popular nowadays."

"But where's the stock we subscribed?" said Dennis, thinking of his one dollar and fifty cents. "We get that back?"

"No."

"What!" said the two in unison.

"It's this way. Owing to executive interference, the Third Triumvirate Manufacturing Company is liable to the Eureka Purchasing Company for ten alarm clocks, which it has ordered and can't use."

"But then, out of the whole, blooming mess," said Dennis, quite overcome, "where do I stand?"

The Tennessee Shad unfolded a paper and read:

"You owe the Eureka, as your share of the assessment, two dollars and forty cents."

"Owe!" said Finnegan with a scream.

"Just let him come," said Dink, doubling up his fists. "Let him come and assess us!"

The three sat in long silence. Finally the Tennessee Shad spoke:

"I am afraid Doc was sore because we tried to freeze him out at first. It was a mistake."

No one noticed this.

"Great Willie Keeler!" said Dennis suddenly. "If this thing had been a success we'd have been ruined!"

"But what right," said Dink, unwilling to give up the fight, "had he to pay the Eureka such prices. Who authorized him?"

"A vote of fifty-one per cent of the stock," said the Tennessee Shad.

"But he never said anything to us—the forty-nine per cent. Has the minority no rights?"

"The minority," said the Tennessee Shad, speaking beyond his horizon, "the minority has only one inalienable right, the right to indorse."

"I'll get even with him," said Dink, after a blank period.

"I suppose," said Dennis de Brian de Boru Finnegan, "that's what's called Finance."

And the Tennessee Shad nodded assent:

"Higher Finance, Dennis."

Packsaddle Jack and the Eye-Glass Englishmen

Then old Packsaddle Jack got to telling about Senator Dorsey, of Star Route fame, selling a little herd of cattle he had in northern New Mexico. He said the Senator had got hold of some eye-glass Englishmen, and, representing to them that he had a large herd of cattle, finally made a sale at $25 a head all around. The Englishmen however, insisted on counting the herd and wouldn't take the Senator's books for them. Dorsey agreed to this; he then went to his foreman, Jack Hill.

"Jack," he said, "I want you to find me a small mountain around which a herd of cattle can be circled several times in one day. This mountain must have a kind of natural stand where men can get a good count on cattle stringing by but where they can't possibly get a view of what is going on outside. Sabe?"

Jack selected a little round mountain with a canyon on one side of it. Here on the bank of the canyon he stationed the Englishmen and their bookkeepers and Senator Dorsey. The Senator had only about 1,000 cattle, and these Jack and the cowboys separated into two bunches out in the hills. Keeping the two herds about a mile apart, they now drove the first herd into the canyon. . . . It was hardly out of sight before the second bunch came stringing along. Meantime cowboys galloped the first herd around back of the mountain and had them coming down the canyon past the Englishmen again for a second count. And they were hardly out of sight before the second division was around the mountain and coming along to be tallied again. Thus the good work went on all morning, the Senator and the Englishmen having only a few minutes to snatch a bite and tap fresh bottles.

At noon Dorsey's foreman told the English party that his men were yet holding an enormous herd back in the hills from which they were cutting off these small bunches of 500 and bringing them along to be tallied. But about three o'clock in the afternoon the cattle began to

---

From *A Vaquero of the Brush Country*, by J. Frank Dobie, pp. 165–166. Copyright, 1929, by the Southwest Press. Dallas.

The average old time range man would not have known a "folk-tale," by name, from Adam's off ox; just the same the open range was "lousy" with folk-tales, and one of them was about the way a cowman sold cattle to a greenhorn and in delivering them had the buyer count the same animals over and over. This tale has been told many times in connection with many cowmen and many greenhorns—generally some unnamed Englishman; but perhaps the best of all versions of the yarn fastens the trick on Senator Dorsey. It is to be found in a small, rollicky, and long out-of-print book called *Cowboy Life on a Sidetrack*, by Frank Benton. It seems appropriate here to quote the story as Frank Benton, a thoroughgoing waddie, spun it.—J.F.D.

get thirsty and footsore. Every critter had already traveled thirty miles that day, and lots of them began to drop out and lie down. In one of the herds was an old yellow steer. He was bobtailed, lophorned, and had a game leg. When for the fifteenth time he limped by the crowd that was counting, milord screwed his eyeglass a little tighter on his eye and says:

"There is more bloody, blarsted, lophorned, bobtailed, yellow crippled brutes than anything else, it seems."

Milord's dogrobber speaks up and says, "But, me lord, there's no hanimal like 'im hin the other 'erd."

The Senator overheard this interesting conversation, and, taking the foreman aside, told him when they got that herd on the other side of the mountain again to cut out the old yellow reprobate and not let him come by again. So Jack cut him out and ran him off a ways. But old yellow had got trained to going around that mountain, and the herd wasn't any more than tallied again till here come old Buck, as the cowboys called him, limping down the canyon, the Englishmen staring at him with open mouths and Senator Dorsey looking at old Jack Hill in a reproachful, grieved kind of way. The cowboys ran old Buck off still farther next time, but half an hour afterwards he appeared over a little rise and slowly limped by again.

The Senator now announced that there was only one herd more to count and signalled to Jack to ride around and stop the cowboys. . . . But as the party broke up and started for the ranch, old Buck came by again, looking like he was in a trance. That night the cowboys said the Senator was groaning in his sleep in a frightful way, and when one of them woke him up and asked if he was sick, he told them, while big drops of cold sweat dropped off his face, that he'd had a terrible nightmare. He said that he thought he was yoked up with a yellow, bobtailed, lophorned, lame steer and was being dragged by the animal through a canyon and around a mountain, day after day, in a hot, broiling sun, while crowds of witless Englishmen and jibbering cowboys were looking on. He insisted on saddling up and going back through the moonlight to the mountain to see if old Buck was still there. A cowboy went with him and after they had got to the canyon and waited a while they heard something coming. Sure enough, directly in the bright moonlight they saw old Buck painfully limping along, stopping now and then to rest.

A week later a cowboy reported finding old Buck dead on his well-worn trail. No one ever rides that way on moonlight nights now, for the cowboys have a tradition that during each full moon old Buck's ghost still limps down the canyon.

The Go-Getter Coroner

" 'The fact of it is,' said old Dr. Potts, the Los Angeles Coroner, the other day, as he strolled through the morgue with Judge Van Snyder, 'the fact of it is, that these San Francisco coroners don't really understand how to work up their business for all its worth, and make it boom as it were.'

" 'What do you mean?' said the Judge, somewhat horrified.

" 'Why, they don't know how to really run a corpse for all the coin that is in it. They don't handle 'em scientifically, so to speak. Now we do that sort of thing better down our way.'

" 'Do, eh?'

" 'Yes. For instance, there was a Chinaman killed by smoking opium a few months ago, out in the suburbs of our town, and of course I was around there and had sworn in a jury before the cadaver got cold, and what with summoning witnesses, taking testimony, &c., before night I had a bill against the county for $96.50.'

" 'More than the Chinaman was worth, I should think,' said the Judge.

" 'But wait. I opened the grave in the county burial-ground the same night, rushed the corpse down to the laboratory and had it embalmed, and all ready for emergencies. Well, about three nights after that they had a free fight out at the Digger Indian encampment, and so I had the Celestial pigtail cut short, a few feathers twisted in it, and hid him in a bush out that way. Of course it was discovered pretty soon, and reported; and as the jury couldn't agree as to the particular tribe of Indians the deceased belonged to, I impaneled another one—nearly double the fees, don't you see?—and gave the papers a rousing good item. It's a way-up plan to keep in with the reporters, by the way.'

" 'How much did that make?'

" 'Well, I was about $240 ahead on the speculation then, so I waited until a lot of Dago emigrants passed through the town, and the next day one of 'em was found dropped dead on the road of heart-disease—don't you see. Same old corpse, with a big felt hat and rawhide boots, and his pocket full of macaroni. I think I squeezed about $175 more out of the taxpayers that time. Well, I kinder let up for about a week after that, and then had the remains doubled up in a packing-box and found among the unclaimed freight down at the railroad station. The papers wrote it up as a "Mysterious Murder Case," and we had a ten days' examination. Lemme see, I think it was $445.50 the whole thing

From *Camps in the Rockies,* Being a Narrative of Life on the Frontier, and Sport in the Rocky Mountains, with an Account of the Cattle Ranches of the West, by William A. Baillie-Grohman, pp. 370–373. Copyright, 1882, by William A. Baillie-Grohman. New York: Charles Scribner's Sons.

panned out before we were through that time. What do you think of that?'

" 'Why, it's the most extraordinary—'

" 'Why, that's nothing, my dear sir, nothing. I haven't got half through with that Chinaman yet. When I left home I just kinder wedged him in among the top branches of a tree in the woods just out of town, dressed in a suit of complete black with an old telescope in his coat-tail pocket, and a pair of big green spectacles on his nose. Catch the idea, don't you?'

" 'Can't say I do.'

" 'Why, that's the aeronaut dodge, don't you see? Unknown scientific party, fallen out of a balloon. My own design entirely. Splendid, isn't it? The corpse is a little worn by this time, I know; but what are you going to do with such an infernally unhealthy climate as Los Angeles? I expect to send the old lady and the girls to Paris on those remains yet, if I have to wire 'em together to do it. No, my dear sir, depend upon it what those metropolitan coroners lack is push, enterprise, sir, and ingenuity.'

"And the doctor reluctantly stopped poking a defunct stock speculator with his cane, and permitted the Judge to take him out for a drink."

Bidder Beware!

The great attention getter of the day is the Saturday Sale. Missourians dearly love to match wits in any kind of trade, and this Saturday Sale is an outlet for anyone's trade emotion, if you know what I mean. The sale is held in an alley between two buildings, where large counters are permanently placed for things that can be carried. . . . No household item is too small, or too trivial, to be brought to the sales alley. There's always a box of broken china and a stack of old magazines, carefully tied. Old dresses, long-since out of style, funny stocking caps, men's long underwear, circular dining tables, broken rockers, Morris chairs, stoves, and baking pans, all showing marks of long usage, are mixed, higgledy-piggledy on those long counters. Around ten o'clock, a leather-lunged auctioneer . . . begins the auction. . . .

Some day, I hope, I shall find what I've always been seeking at these Saturday sales. A large iron kettle, and I mean *big!* The kind in which Grandma used to make soap.

Only once has such a kettle shown up at the Saturday sale. There it was, flanked by a broken plow and an antique sewing machine. I presumed the overalled man lounging nearby was the owner.

From *Take to the Hills*. A Chronicle of the Ozarks, by Marguerite Lyon, pp. 75–81. Copyright, 1941, by the Bobbs-Merrill Company. Indianapolis and New York.

I asked what he wanted for the iron kettle.

He wa'nt the owner, he said, but he would find him and ask the price. I waited until he returned.

"He wants two dollars f'r the pot, ma'am."

Then he whispered guardedly: "Better thump it, ma'am."

Thump an iron pot. I had never heard of such a thing. One thumps watermelons. Why should a pot be thumped?

Lowering his head, he explained confidentially: "Sometimes these here pots freeze and bust, but you cain't see no crack. You jis' thump 'em!"

I thumped.

"Hear that!" he exclaimed triumphantly. "I'm a-tellin' you, hit's cracked. Like as not, it'd bust wide open first time you put it on the f'ar!"

Of course I didn't want a cracked pot. I was so disappointed I didn't even stay for the auction.

An hour later, my shopping finished at Roy Charles' grocery, meat, dry goods, and handmade furniture emporium, I was carrying my packages across the street to the car, when my way was blocked for a moment. It was one of the Ozark station wagons, drawn by a flea-bitten white mule. I looked up at the driver, who grinned widely and flourished a sassafras buggy whip. He was my friend of the sales alley, the man who had taught me to thump. I waved back. But I didn't grin.

In the back end of the homeward-bound wagon, snugly bedded in straw, along with four tow-headed youngsters, was the big, black iron kettle.

VI. THE BIGGER THEY ARE, THE HARDER THEY FALL

(Sports Comedy)

Introduction

Americans love sports, but they like just as much to talk about them. They tell stories about a bull winning a race against horses, a thirty-five-inch midget or a talking horse getting into a big-league baseball game, and snakes and minnows which help the fishermen. Sometimes their fiction sounds like truth, and sometimes their truth sounds like fiction—the Brooklyn Dodgers did once have three men on third.

They make up humorous explanations for not catching a fish or not shooting a deer. They tell yarns of the best marksmen, the best coon

dogs, the fattest bears. They like success stories about the men who won
bets on horse races or took home the beef in a shooting match, but they
also enjoy stories of dramatic failures such as mighty Casey's time at bat.

Sham Hays and His Racing Bull

Some forty years ago the managers of the race course near Brownsville
on the Monongahela, published a notice of a race, one mile heats, on
a particular day, for a purse of $100, fee for anything with four legs,
and hair on. A man in the neighborhood, named Hays, had a bull that
he was in the habit of riding to the mill with his bag of corn, and he
determined to enter him for the race. He said nothing about it to any
one; but he rode him around the track a number of times on several
bright nights, and the bull had the lay of the ground pretty well, and
would keep the right course. He rode him with spurs, which the bull
considered particularly disagreeable; so much so that he always bellowed when they were applied to his sides. On the morning of the race,
Hays came upon the ground 'on horseback' on his bull. Instead of a
saddle he had a dried oxhide, the head part of which, with the horns
still on, he had placed on the rump. He carried a short tin horn in his
hand. He rode up to the judges' stand and offered to enter his bull for
the race, but the owners of the horses objected. Hays appealed to the
terms of the notice, insisted that his bull had 'four legs and hair on,'
and that therefore he had a right to enter him. After a good deal of
'cussin' and discussin',' the judges declared themselves compelled to
decide that the bull had the right to run, and he entered accordingly.
When the time for starting arrived the bull and the horses took their
places. The horseracers were out of humor at being bothered with the
bull and at the burlesque which they supposed was intended, but
thought that would be over as soon as the horses started.

The signal was given, and they did start. Hays gave a blast with his
horn, and sank his spurs into the bull's sides, which bounded with a
terrible bellow, at no trifling speed, the dried oxhide flapped up and
down, rattling at every jump, making a combination of noises that had
never been heard on a race course before. The horses all flew off the
track, every one seemed to be seized with a sudden determination to
take the shortest cut to get out of the Redstone country, and not one
of them could be brought back in time to save their distance. The purse
was given to Hays under a great deal of hard swearing on the part of
the owners of the horses. A general row ensued, but the fun of the thing
put the crowd all on the side of the bull. The horsemen contended that
they were swindled out of the purse, and that if it had not been for

"Sham Hays and His Race Bull," in *Frontier Times*, Vol. 17 (December, 1939)
No. 3, pp. 128–129. Bandera, Texas. Originally published in *The Western Stock
Journal*, Pleasanton, Texas, December 2, 1873.

Hays' horn and oxhide, which he ought not to have been permitted to bring on the ground the thing would not have turned out as it did. Upon this Hays told them that his bull beat any of their horses anyhow, and if they would put up $100 against the purse he had won, he would take off his oxhide and leave his tin horn and run a fair race with them. His offer was accepted and his money staked. They again took their places at the starting post and the signal was given. Hays gave the bull another touch with his spurs, and the bull gave another tremendous bellow. The horses remembered the horrible sound, and thought all the rest was coming as before. Away they went again, in spite of all the exertions of their riders, while Hays galloped his bull around the track again, and won the money. From that time they nicknamed him Sham Hays. He afterward removed to Ohio, but his nickname stuck to him as long as he lived.

You Could Look It Up

It all begun when we dropped down to C'lumbus, Ohio, from Pittsburgh to play a exhibition game on our way out to St. Louis. It was gettin' on into September, and though we'd been leadin' the league by six, seven games most of the season, we was now in first place by a margin you could 'a' got it into the eye of a thimble, bein' only a half a game ahead of St. Louis. Our slump had given the boys the leapin' jumps, and they was like a bunch a old ladies at a lawn fete with a thunderstorm comin' up, runnin' around snarlin' at each other, eatin' bad and sleepin' worse, and battin' for a team average of maybe .186. Half the time nobody'd speak to nobody else, without it was to bawl 'em out.

Squawks Magrew was managin' the boys at the time, and he was darn near crazy. They called him "Squawks" 'cause when things was goin' bad he lost his voice, or perty near lost it, and squealed at you like a little girl you stepped on her doll or somethin'. He yelled at everybody and wouldn't listen to nobody, without maybe it was me. I'd been trainin' the boys for ten year, and he'd take more lip from me than from anybody else. He knowed I was smarter'n him, anyways, like you're goin' to hear.

This was thirty, thirty-one year ago; you could look it up, 'cause it was the same year C'lumbus decided to call itself the Arch City, on account of a lot of iron arches with electric-light bulbs into 'em which stretched acrost High Street. Thomas Albert Edison sent 'em a telegram, and they was speeches and maybe even President Taft opened the celebration by pushin' a button. It was a great week for the Buckeye capital, which was why they got us out there for this exhibition game.

From *My World and Welcome to It*, by James Thurber, pp. 85–110. Copyright, 1942, by Harcourt, Brace & Company.

Well, we just lose a double-header to Pittsburgh, 11 to 5 and 7 to 3, so we snarled all the way to C'lumbus, where we put up at the Chittaden Hotel, still snarlin'. Everybody was tetchy, and when Billy Klinger took a sock at Whitey Cott at breakfast, Whitey throwed marmalade all over his face.

"Blind each other, whatta I care?" says Magrew. "You can't see nothin' anyways."

C'lumbus win the exhibition game, 3 to 2, whilst Magrew set in the dugout, mutterin' and cursin' like a fourteen-year-old Scotty. He bad-mouthed everybody on the ball club and he bad-mouthed everybody offa the ball club, includin' the Wright brothers, who, he claimed, had yet to build a airship big enough for any of our boys to hit it with a ball bat.

"I wisht I was dead," he says to me. "I wisht I was in heaven with the angels."

I told him to pull hisself together, 'cause he was drivin' the boys crazy, the way he was goin' on, sulkin' and bad-mouthin' and whinin'. I was older'n he was and smarter'n he was, and he knowed it. I was ten times smarter'n he was about this Pearl du Monville, first time I ever laid eyes on the little guy, which was one of the saddest days of my life.

Now, most people name of Pearl is girls; but this Pearl du Monville was a man, if you could call a fella a man who was only thirty-four, thirty-five inches high. Pearl du Monville was a midget. He was part French and part Hungarian, and maybe even part Bulgarian or somethin'. I can see him now, a sneer on his little pushed-in pan, swingin' a bamboo cane and smokin' a big cigar. He had a gray suit with a big black check into it, and he had a gray felt hat with one of them rainbow-colored hatbands onto it, like the young fellas wore in them days. He talked like he was talkin' into a tin can, but he didn't have no foreign accent. He might a been fifteen or he might a been a hundred, you couldn't tell. Pearl du Monville.

After the game with C'lumbus, Magrew headed straight for the Chittaden bar—the train for St. Louis wasn't goin' for three, four hours —and there he set, drinkin' rye and talkin' to this bartender.

"How I pity me, brother," Magrew was tellin' this bartender. "How I pity me." That was alwuz his favorite tune. So he was settin' there, tellin' this bartender how heartbreakin' it was to be manager of a bunch a blindfolded circus clowns, when up pops this Pearl du Monville outa nowheres.

It give Magrew the leapin' jumps. He thought at first maybe the D.T.'s had come back on him; he claimed he'd had 'em once, and little guys had popped up all around him, wearin' red, white and blue hats.

"Go on, now!" Magrew yells. "Get away from me!"

But the midget clumb up on a chair acrost the table from Magrew and says, "I seen that game today, Junior, and you ain't got no ball club. What you got there, Junior," he says, "is a side show."

"Whatta ya mean, 'Junior'?" says Magrew, touchin' the little guy to satisfy hisself he was real.

"Don't pay him no attention, mister," says the bartender. "Pearl calls everybody 'Junior' 'cause it alwuz turns out he's a year older'n anybody else."

"Yeh?" says Magrew. "How old is he?"

"How old are you, Junior?" says the midget.

"Who, me? I'm fifty-three," says Magrew.

"Well, I'm fifty-four," says the midget.

Magrew grins and asts him what he'll have, and that was the beginnin' of their beautiful friendship, if you don't care what you say.

Pearl du Monville stood up on his chair and waved his cane around and pretended like he was ballyhooin' for a circus. "Right this way, folks!" he yells. "Come on in and see the greatest collection of freaks in the world! See the armless pitchers, see the eyeless batters, see the infielders with five thumbs!" and on and on like that, feedin' Magrew gall and handin' him a laugh at the same time, you might say.

You could hear him and Pearl du Monville hootin' and hollerin' and singin' way up to the fourth floor of the Chittaden, where the boys was packin' up. When it come time to go to the station, you can imagine how disgusted we was when we crowded into the doorway of that bar and seen them two singin' and goin' on.

"Well, well, well," says Magrew, lookin' up and spottin' us. "Look who's here. . . . Clowns, this is Pearl du Monville, a monseer of the old, old school. . . . Don't shake hands with 'em, Pearl, 'cause their fingers is made of chalk and would bust right off in your paws," he says, and he starts guffawin' and Pearl starts titterin' and we stand there givin' 'em the iron eye, it bein' the lowest ebb a ball-club manager'd got hisself down to since the national pastime was started.

Then the midget begun givin' us the ballyhoo. "Come on in!" he says, wavin' his cane. "See the legless base runners, see the outfielders with the butter fingers, see the southpaw with the arm of a little chee-ild!"

Then him and Magrew begun to hoop and holler and nudge each other till you'd of thought this little guy was the funniest guy than even Charlie Chaplin. The fellas filed outa the bar without a word and went on up to the Union Depot, leavin' me to handle Magrew and his new-found crony.

Well, I got 'em outa there finely. I had to take the little guy along, 'cause Magrew had a holt onto him like a vise and I couldn't pry him loose.

"He's comin' along as masket," says Magrew, holdin' the midget in the crouch of his arm like a football. And come along he did, hollerin' and protestin' and beatin' at Magrew with his little fists.

"Cut it out, will ya, Junior?" the little guy kept whinin'. "Come on, leave a man loose, will ya, Junior?"

But Junior kept a holt onto him and begun yellin', "See the guys with the glass arm, see the guys with the cast-iron brains, see the fielders with the feet on their wrists!"

So it goes, right through the whole Union Depot, with people starin' and catcallin', and he don't put the midget down till he gets him through the gates.

"How'm I goin' to go along without no toothbrush?" the midget asts. "What'm I goin' to do without no other suit?" he says.

"Doc here," says Magrew, meanin' me—"doc here will look after you like you was his own son, won't you, doc?"

I give him the iron eye, and he finely got on the train and prob'ly went to sleep with his clothes on.

This left me alone with the midget. "Lookit," I says to him. "Why don't you go on home now? Come mornin', Magrew'll forget all about you. He'll prob'ly think you was somethin' he seen in a nightmare maybe. And he ain't goin' to laugh so easy in the mornin', neither," I says. "So why don't you go on home?"

"Nix," he says to me. "Skiddoo," he says, "twenty-three for you," and he tosses his cane up into the vestibule of the coach and clam'ers on up after it like a cat. So that's the way Pearl du Monville come to go to St. Louis with the ball club.

I seen 'em first at breakfast the next day, settin' opposite each other; the midget playin' "Turkey in the Straw" on a harmonium and Magrew starin' at his eggs and bacon like they was a uncooked bird with its feathers still on.

"Remember where you found this?" I says, jerkin' my thumb at the midget. "Or maybe you think they come with breakfast on these trains," I says, bein' a good hand at turnin' a sharp remark in them days.

The midget puts down the harmonium and turns on me. "Sneeze," he says; "your brains is dusty." Then he snaps a couple drops of water at me from a tumbler. "Drown," he says, tryin' to make his voice deep.

Now, both them cracks is Civil War cracks, but you'd of thought they was brand new and the funniest than any crack Magrew'd ever heard in his whole life. He started hoopin' and hollerin', and the midget started hoopin' and hollerin', so I walked on away and set down with Bugs Courtney and Hank Metters, payin' no attention to this weak-minded Damon and Phidias acrost the aisle.

Well, sir, the first game with St. Louis was rained out, and there we was facin' a double-header next day. Like maybe I told you, we lose the last three double-headers we play, makin' maybe twenty-five errors in the six games, which is all right for the intimates of a school for the blind, but is disgraceful for the world's champions. It was too wet to go to the zoo, and Magrew wouldn't let us go to the movies, 'cause they flickered so bad in them days. So we just set around, stewin' and frettin'.

One of the newspaper boys come over to take a pitture of Billy

Klinger and Whitey Cott shakin' hands—this reporter'd heard about the fight—and whilst they was standin' there, toe to toe, shakin' hands, Billy give a back lunge and a jerk, and throwed Whitey over his shoulder into a corner of the room, like a sack a salt. Whitney come back at him with a chair, and Bethlehem broke loose in that there room. The camera was tromped to pieces like a berry basket. When we finely got 'em pulled apart, I heard a laugh, and there was Magrew and the midget standin' in the door and givin' us the iron eye.

"Wrasslers," says Magrew, cold-like, "that's what I got for a ball club, Mr. Du Monville, wrasslers—and not very good wrasslers at that, you ast me."

"A man can't be good at everythin'," says Pearl, "but he oughta be good at somethin'."

This sets Magrew guffawin' again, and away they go, the midget taggin' along by his side like a hound dog and handin' him a fast line of so-called comic cracks.

When we went out to face that battlin' St. Louis club in a double-header the next afternoon, the boys was jumpy as tin toys with keys in their back. We lose the first game, 7 to 2, and are trailin', 4 to 0, when the second game ain't but ten minutes old. Magrew set there like a stone statue, speakin' to nobody. Then, in their half a the fourth, somebody singled to center and knocked in two more runs for St. Louis.

That made Magrew squawk. "I wisht one thing," he says. "I wisht I was manager of a old ladies' sewin' circus 'stead of a ball club."

"You are, Junior, you are," says a familyer and disagreeable voice.

It was that Pearl du Monville again, poppin' up outa nowheres, swingin' his bamboo cane and smokin' a cigar that's three sizes too big for his face. By this time we'd finely got the other side out, and Hank Metters slithered a bat acrost the ground, and the midget had to jump to keep both his ankles from bein' broke.

I thought Magrew'd bust a blood vessel. "You hurt Pearl and I'll break your neck!" he yelled.

Hank muttered somethin' and went on up to the plate and struck out.

We managed to get a couple runs acrost in our half a the sixth, but they come back with three more in their half a the seventh, and this was too much for Magrew.

"Come on, Pearl," he says. "We're gettin' outa here."

"Where you think you're goin'?" I ast him.

"To the lawyer's again," he says cryptly.

"I didn't know you'd been to the lawyer's once, yet," I says.

"Which that goes to show how much you don't know," he says.

With that, they was gone, and I didn't see 'em the rest of the day, nor know what they was up to, which was a God's blessin'. We lose the nightcap, 9 to 3, and that puts us into second place plenty, and as low in our mind as a ball club can get.

The next day was a horible day, like anybody that lived through it can tell you. Practice was just over and the St. Louis club was takin' the field, when I hears this strange sound from the stands. It sounds like the nervous whickerin' a horse gives when he smells somethin' funny on the wind. It was the fans ketchin' sight of Pearl du Monville, like you have prob'ly guessed. The midget had popped up onto the field all dressed up in a minacher club uniform, sox, cap, little letters sewed onto his chest, and all. He was swingin' a kid's bat and the only thing kept him from lookin' like a real ballplayer seen through the wrong end of a microscope was this cigar he was smokin'.

Bugs Courtney reached over and jerked it outa his mouth and throwed it away. "You're wearin' that suit on the playin' field," he says to him, severe as a judge. "You go insultin' it and I'll take you out to the zoo and feed you to the bears."

Pearl just blowed some smoke at him which he still has in his mouth.

Whilst Whitey was foulin' off four or five prior to strikin' out, I went on over to Magrew. "If I was as comic as you," I says, "I'd laugh myself to death," I says. "Is that any way to treat the uniform, makin' a mockery out of it?"

"It might surprise you to know I ain't makin' no mockery outa the uniform," says Magrew. "Pearl du Monville here has been made a bone-of-fida member of this so-called ball club. I fixed it up with the front office by long-distance phone."

"Yeh?" I says. "I can just hear Mr. Dillworth or Bart Jenkins agreein' to hire a midget for the ball club. I can just hear 'em." Mr. Dillworth was the owner of the club and Bart Jenkins was the secretary, and they never stood for no monkey business. "May I be so bold as to inquire," I says, "just what you told 'em?"

"I told 'em," he says, "I wanted to sign up a guy they ain't no pitcher in the league can strike him out."

"Uh-huh," I says, "and did you tell 'em what size of a man he is?"

"Never mind about that," he says. "I got papers on me, made out legal and proper, constitutin' one Pearl du Monville a bone-of-fida member of this former ball club. Maybe that'll shame them big babies into gettin' in there and swingin', knowin' I can replace any one of 'em with a midget, if I have a mind to. A St. Louis lawyer I seen twice tells me it's all legal and proper."

"A St. Louis lawyer would," I says, "seein' nothin' could make him happier than havin' you makin' a mockery outa this one-time baseball outfit," I says.

Well, sir, it'll all be there in the papers of thirty, thirty-one year ago, and you could look it up. The game went along without no scorin' for seven innings, and since they ain't nothin' much to watch but guys poppin' up or strikin' out, the fans pay most of their attention to the goin's-on of Pearl du Monville. He's out there in front a the dugout, turnin' hand-springs, balancin' his bat on his chin, walkin' a imaginary line, and so on. The fans clapped and laughed at him, and he ate it up.

So it went up to the last a the eighth, nothin' to nothin', not more'n seven, eight hits all told, and no errors on neither side. Our pitcher gets the first two men out easy in the eighth. Then up come a fella name of Porter or Billings, or some such name, and he lammed one up against the tobacco sign for three bases. The next guy up slapped the first ball out into left for a base hit, and in come the fella from third for the only run of the ball game so far. The crowd yelled, the look a death come onto Magrew's face again, and even the midget quit his tom-foolin'. Their next man fouled out back a third, and we come up for our last bats like a bunch a schoolgirls steppin' into a pool of cold water. I was lower in my mind than I'd been since the day in Nineteen-four when Chesbro throwed the wild pitch in the ninth inning with a man on third and lost the pennant for the Highlanders. I knowed something just as bad was goin' to happen, which shows I'm a clairvoyun, or was then.

When Gordy Mills hit out to second, I just closed my eyes. I opened 'em up again to see Dutch Muller standin' on second, dustin' off his pants, him havin' got his first hit in maybe twenty times to the plate. Next up was Harry Loesing, battin' for our pitcher, and he got a base on balls, walkin' on a fourth one you could a combed your hair with.

Then up come Whitey Cott, our lead-off man. He crotches down in what was prob'ly the most fearsome stanch in organized ball, but all he can do is pop out to short. That brung up Billy Klinger, with two down and a man on first and second. Billy took a cut at one you could a knocked a plug hat offa this here Carnera with it, but then he gets sense enough to wait 'em out, and finely he walks, too, fillin' the bases.

Yes, sir, there you are; the tyin' run on third and the winnin' run on second, first a the ninth, two men down, and Hank Metters comin' to the bat. Hank was built like a Pope-Hartford and he couldn't run no faster'n President Taft, but he had five home runs to his credit for the season, and that wasn't bad in them days. Hank was still hittin' better'n anybody else on the ball club, and it was mighty heartenin', seein' him stridin' up towards the plate. But he never got there.

"Wait a minute!" yells Magrew, jumpin' to his feet. "I'm sendin' in a pinch hitter!" he yells.

You could a heard a bomb drop. When a ball-club manager says he's sendin' in a pinch hitter for the best batter on the club, you know and I know and everybody knows he's lost his holt.

"They're goin' to be sendin' the funny wagon for you, if you don't watch out," I says, grabbin' a holt of his arm.

But he pulled away and run out towards the plate, yellin', "Du Monville battin' for Metters!"

All the fellas begun squawlin' at once, except Hank, and he just stood there starin' at Magrew like he'd gone crazy and was claimin' to be Ty Cobb's grandma or somethin'. Their pitcher stood out there with his hands on his hips and a disagreeable look on his face, and the plate umpire told Magrew to go on and get a batter up. Magrew told him again Du Monville was battin' for Metters, and the St. Louis manager finely got the idea. It brung him outa his dugout, howlin' and bawlin' like he'd lost a female dog and her seven pups.

Magrew pushed the midget towards the plate and he says to him, he says, "Just stand up there and hold that bat on your shoulder. They ain't a man in the world can throw three strikes in there 'fore he throws four balls!" he says.

"I get it, Junior!" says the midget. "He'll walk me and force in the tyin' run!" And he starts on up to the plate as cocky as if he was Willie Keeler.

I don't need to tell you Bethlehem broke loose on that there ball field. The fans got onto their hind legs, yellin' and whistlin', and everybody on the field begun wavin' their arms and hollerin' and shovin'. The plate umpire stalked over to Magrew like a traffic cop, waggin' his jaw and pointin' his finger, and the St. Louis manager kept yellin' like his house was on fire. When Pearl got up to the plate and stood there, the pitcher slammed his glove down onto the ground and started stompin' on it, and they ain't nobody can blame him. He's just walked two normal-sized human bein's, and now here's a guy up to the plate they ain't more'n twenty inches between his knees and his shoulders.

The plate umpire called in the field umpire, and they talked a while, like a couple doctors seein' the bucolic plague or somethin' for the first time. Then the plate umpire come over to Magrew with his arms folded acrost his chest, and he told him to go on and get a batter up, or he'd forfeit the game to St. Louis. He pulled out his watch, but somebody batted it outa his hand in the scufflin', and I thought there'd be a free-for-all, with everybody yellin' and shovin' except Pearl du Monville, who stood up at the plate with his little bat on his shoulder, not movin' a muscle.

Then Magrew played his ace. I seen him pull some papers outa his pocket and show 'em to the plate umpire. The umpire begun lookin' at 'em like they was bills for somethin' he not only never bought it, he never even heard of it. The other umpire studied 'em like they was a death warren, and all this time the St. Louis manager and the fans and the players is yellin' and hollerin'.

Well, sir, they fought about him bein' a midget, and they fought about him usin' a kid's bat, and they fought about where'd he been all season. They was eight or nine rule books brung out and everybody was thumbin' through em, tryin' to find out what it says about midgets, but it don't say nothin' about midgets, 'cause this was somethin' never'd come up in the history of the game before, and nobody'd ever dreamed about it, even when they has nightmares. Maybe you can't send no midgets in to bat nowadays, 'cause the old game's changed a lot, mostly for the worst, but you could then, it turned out.

The plate umpire finely decided the contrack papers was all legal and proper, like Magrew said, so he waved the St. Louis players back to their places and he pointed his finger at their manager and told him to quit hollerin' and get on back in the dugout. The manager says the game is percedin' under protest, and the umpire bawls, "Play ball!" over 'n above the yellin' and booin', him havin' a voice like a hog-caller.

The St. Louis pitcher picked up his glove and beat at it with his fist six or eight times, and then got set on the mound and studied the situation. The fans realized he was really goin' to pitch to the midget, and they went crazy, hoopin' and hollerin' louder'n ever, and throwin' pop bottles and hats and cushions down onto the field. It took five, ten minutes to get the fans quieted down again, whilst our fellas that was on base set down on the bags and waited. And Pearl du Monville kept standin' up there with the bat on his shoulder, like he'd been told to.

So the pitcher starts studyin' the setup again, and you got to admit it was the strangest setup in a ball game since the players cut off their beards and begun wearin' gloves. I wisht I could call the pitcher's name —it wasn't old Barney Pelty nor Nig Jack Powell nor Harry Howell. He was a big right-hander, but I can't call his name. You could look it up. Even in a crotchin' position, the ketcher towers over the midget like the Washington Monument.

The plate umpire tries standin' on his tiptoes, then he tries crotchin' down, and he finely gets hisself into a stanch nobody'd ever seen on a ball field before, kinda squattin' down on his hanches.

Well, the pitcher is sore as a old buggy horse in fly time. He slams in the first pitch, hard and wild, and maybe two foot higher'n the midget's head.

"Ball one!" hollers the umpire over 'n' above the racket, 'cause everybody is yellin' worsten ever.

The ketcher goes on out towards the mound and talks to the pitcher and hands him the ball. This time the big right-hander tried a undershoot, and it comes in a little closer, maybe no higher'n a foot, foot and a half above Pearl's head. It would a been a strike with a human bein' in there, but the umpire's got to call it, and he does.

"Ball two!" he bellers.

The ketcher walks on out to the mound again, and the whole infield comes over and gives advice to the pitcher about what they'd do in a case like this, with two balls and no strikes on a batter that oughta be in a bottle of alcohol 'stead of up there at the plate in a big-league game between the teams that is fightin' for first place.

For the third pitch, the pitcher stands there flatfooted and tosses up the ball like he's playin' ketch with a little girl.

Pearl stands there motionless as a hitchin' post, and the ball comes in big and slow and high—high for Pearl, that is, it bein' about on a level with his eyes, or a little higher'n a grown man's knees.

They ain't nothin' else for the umpire to do, so he calls, "Ball three!"

Everybody is onto their feet, hoopin' and hollerin', as the pitcher sets to throw ball four. The St. Louis manager is makin' signs and faces like he was a contorturer, and the infield is givin' the pitcher some more advice about what to do this time. Our boys who was on base stick right onto the bag, runnin' no risk of bein' nipped for the last out.

Well, the pitcher decides to give him a toss again, seein' he come closer with that than with a fast ball. They ain't nobody ever seen a slower ball throwed. It come in big as a balloon and slower'n any ball ever throwed before in the major leagues. It come right in over the plate in front of Pearl's chest, lookin' prob'ly big as a full moon to Pearl. They ain't never been a minute like the minute that followed since the United States was founded by the Pilgrim grandfathers.

Pearl du Monville took a cut at that ball, and he hit it! Magrew give a groan like a poleaxed steer as the ball rolls out in front a the plate into fair territory.

"Fair ball!" yells the umpire, and the midget starts runnin' for first, still carryin' that little bat, and makin' maybe ninety foot an hour. Bethlehem breaks loose on that ball field and in them stands. They ain't never been nothin' like it since creation was begun.

The ball's rollin' slow, on down towards third, goin' maybe eight, ten foot. The infield comes in fast and our boys break from their bases like hares in a brush fire. Everybody is standin' up, yellin' and hollerin', and Magrew is tearin' his hair outa his head, and the midget is scamperin' for first with all the speed of one of them little dashhounds carryin' a satchel in his mouth.

The ketcher gets to the ball first, but he boots it on out past the pitcher's box, the pitcher fallin' on his face tryin' to stop it, the shortstop sprawlin' after it full length and zaggin' it on over towards the second baseman, whilst Muller is scorin' with the tyin' run and Loesing is roundin' third with the winnin' run. Ty Cobb could a made a three-bagger outa that bunt, with everybody fallin' over theirself tryin' to pick the ball up. But Pearl is still maybe fifteen, twenty feet from the bag, toddlin' like a baby and yeepin' like a trapped rabbit, when the second baseman finely gets a holt of that ball and slams it over to first. The first baseman ketches it and stomps on the bag, the base umpire waves Pearl out, and there goes your old ball game, the craziest ball game ever played in the history of the organized world.

Their players start runnin' in, and then I see Magrew. He starts after Pearl, runnin' faster'n any man ever run before. Pearl sees him comin' and runs behind the base umpire's legs and gets a holt onto 'em. Magrew comes up, pantin' and roarin', and him and the midget plays ring-around-a-rosy with the umpire, who keeps shovin' at Magrew with one hand and tryin' to slap the midget loose from his legs with the other.

Finely Magrew ketches the midget, who is still yeepin' like a stuck sheep. He gets holt of that little guy by both his ankles and starts whirlin' him round and round his head like Magrew was a hammer thrower and Pearl was the hammer. Nobody can stop him without gettin' their head knocked off, so everybody just stands there and yells. Then Magrew lets the midget fly. He flies on out towards second, high and fast, like a human home run, headed for the soap sign in center field.

Their shortstop tries to get to him, but he can't make it, and I knowed the little fella was goin' to bust to pieces like a dollar watch on a asphalt street when he hit the ground. But it so happens their center fielder is just crossin' second, and he starts runnin' back, tryin' to get under the midget, who had took to spiralin' like a football 'stead of turnin' head over foot, which give him more speed and more distance.

I know you never seen a midget ketched, and you prob'ly never even seen one throwed. To ketch a midget that's been throwed by a heavy-muscled man and is flyin' through the air, you got to run under him and pull your hands and arms back and down when you ketch him, to break the compact of his body, or you'll bust him in two like a matchstick. I seen Bill Lange and Willie Keeler and Tris Speaker make some wonderful ketches in my day, but I never seen nothin' like that center fielder. He goes back and back and still further back and he pulls that midget down outa the air like he was liftin' a sleepin' baby from a cradle. They wasn't a bruise onto him, only his face was the color of cat's meat and he ain't got no air in his chest. In his excitement, the base umpire, who was runnin' back with the center fielder when he ketched Pearl, yells, "Out!" and that give hysterics to the Bethlehem which was ragin' like Niagry on that ball field.

Everybody was hoopin' and hollerin' and yellin' and runnin', with the fans swarmin' onto the field, and the cops tryin' to keep order, and some guys laughin' and some of the women fans cryin', and six or eight of us holdin' onto Magrew to keep him from gettin' at that midget and finishin' him off. Some of the fans picks up the St. Louis pitcher and the center fielder, and starts carryin' 'em around on their shoulders, and they was the craziest goin's-on knowed to the history of organized ball on this side of the 'Lantic Ocean.

I seen Pearl du Monville strugglin' in the arms of a lady fan with a ample bosom, who was laughin' and cryin' at the same time, and him beatin' at her with his little fists and bawlin' and yellin'. He clawed his way loose finely and disappeared in the forest of legs which made that ball field look like it was Coney Island on a hot summer's day.

That was the last I ever seen of Pearl du Monville. I never seen hide nor hair of him from that day to this, and neither did nobody else. He just vanished into the thin of the air, as the fella says. He was ketched for the final out of the ball game and that was the end of him, just like it was the end of the ball game, you might say, and also the end of our losin' streak, like I'm goin' to tell you.

That night we piled onto a train for Chicago, but we wasn't snarlin' and snappin' any more. No, sir, the ice was finely broke and a new spirit come into that ball club. The old zip come back with the disappearance of Pearl du Monville out back a second base. We got to laughin' and talkin' and kiddin' together, and 'fore long Magrew was laughin' with us. He got a human look onto his pan again, and he quit whinin' and complainin' and wishtin' he was in heaven with the angels.

Well, sir, we wiped up that Chicago series, winnin' all four games, and makin' seventeen hits in one of 'em. Funny thing was, St. Louis was so shook up by that last game with us, they never did hit their stride again. Their center fielder took to misjudgin' everything that come his way, and the rest a the fellas followed suit, the way a club'll do when one guy blows up.

'Fore we left Chicago, I and some of the fellas went out and bought a pair of them little baby shoes, which we had 'em golded over and give 'em to Magrew for a souvenir, and he took it all in good spirit. Whitey Cott and Billy Klinger made up and was fast friends again, and we hit our home lot like a ton of dynamite and they was nothin' could stop us from then on.

I don't recollect things as clear as I did thirty, forty year ago. I can't read no fine print no more, and the only person I got to check with on the golden days of the national pastime, as the fella says, is my friend, old Milt Kline, over in Springfield, and his mind ain't as strong as it once was.

He gets Rube Waddell mixed up with Rube Marquard, for one thing, and anybody does that oughta be put away where he won't bother nobody. So I can't tell you the exact margin we win the pennant by. Maybe it was two and a half games, or maybe it was three and a half. But it'll all be there in the newspapers and record books of thirty, thirty-one year ago and, like I was sayin', you could look it up.

A Fine Stream for Trout

"Paddy, my boy," said a gentleman to an Irishman, whom he observed fishing away at a favorite pool, "that must be a fine stream for trout." "Faith and sure it must be that same, for I have been standing here this three hours, and not one of 'em will stir out of it."

From *Gus Williams' World of Humor*. New York: De Witt, Publishers, 1880.

Who's on First?

Lou Costello Has Been Asking
Bud Abbott for the Last 17 Years

Practically everyone's chuckled at Abbott & Costello's "Who's on First?" routine, one they've performed more than 10,000 times during the past 17 years. Given the same material, can you get the same laughs? By publishing, for perhaps the first time, part of the famed skit, *TV Guide* now offers you a chance to find out.

ABBOTT—You know, strange as it may seem, they give ballplayers nowadays very peculiar names . . . Now, on the St. Louis team Who's on first, What's on second, I Don't Know is on third—

COSTELLO—That's what I want to find out. I want you to tell me the names of the fellows on the St. Louis team.

ABBOTT—I'm telling you. Who's on first, What's on second, I Don't Know is on third—

COSTELLO—You know the fellows' names?

ABBOTT—Yes.

COSTELLO—Well, then, who's playin' first?

A.—Yes.

C.—I mean the fellow's name on first base.

A.—Who.

C.—The fellow playin' first base.

A.—Who.

C.—The guy on first base.

A.—Who is on first.

C.—Well, what are you askin' me for?

A.—I'm not asking you—I'm telling you. Who is on first.

C.—I'm asking you—who's on first?

A.—That's the man's name!

C.—That's who's name?

A.—Yes.

C.—Well, go ahead tell me!

A.—Who.

C.—Have you got a first baseman on first?

A.—Certainly.

C.—Then who's playing first?

A.—Absolutely.

C.—Well, all I'm trying to find out is what's the guy's name on first base.

A.—Oh, no, no. What is on second base.

C.—I'm not asking you who's on second.

A.—Who's on first.

c.—That's what I'm trying to find out.

a.—Now, take it easy.

c.—What's the guy's name on first base?

a.—What's the guy's name on second base.

c.—I'm not askin' ya who's on second.

a.—Who's on first.

c.—I don't know.

a.—He's on third.

c.—If I mentioned the third baseman's name, who did I say is playing third?

a.—No, Who's playing first.

c.—Stay offa first, will ya?

a.—Well, what do you want me to do?

c.—Now, what's the guy's name on first base?

a.—What's on second.

c.—I'm not asking ya who's on second.

a.—Who's on first.

c.—I don't know.

a.—He's on third.

c.—There I go back to third again.

a.—Please. Now what is it you want to know?

c.—What is the fellow's name on third base?

a.—What is the fellow's name on second base.

c.—I'm not askin' ya who's on second.

a.—Who's on first.

c.—I don't know. (Makes noises) You got an outfield?

a.—Oh, sure.

c.—The left fielder's name?

a.—Why.

c.—I just thought I'd ask.

a.—Well, I just thought I'd tell you.

c.—Then tell me who's playing left field.

a.—Who's playing first.

c.—Stay out of the infield. I want to know what's the fellow's name in left field.

a.—What is on second.

c.—I'm not asking you who's on second.

a.—Now take it easy, take it easy.

c.—And the left fielder's name?

a.—Why.

c.—Because.

a.—Oh, he's center field.

c.—Wait a minute. You got a pitcher?

a.—Wouldn't this be a fine team without a pitcher?

c.—Tell me the pitcher's name.

a.—Tomorrow.

c.—You don't want to tell me today?

a.—I'm telling you, man.

c.—Then go ahead.

a.—Tomorrow.

c.—What time tomorrow are you gonna tell me who's pitching?

a.—Now listen. Who is not pitching. Who is on—

c.—I'll break your arm if you say who's on first.

a.—Then why come up here and ask?

c.—I want to know what's the pitcher's name.

a.—What's on second.

c.—Ya gotta catcher?

a.—Yes.

c.—The catcher's name?

a.—Today.

c.—Today. And Tomorrow's pitching.

a.—Yes.

c.—I'm a good catcher too, you know.

a.—I know that.

c.—I would like to catch. Tomorrow's pitching and I'm catching.

a.—Yes.

c.—Tomorrow throws the ball and the guy up bunts the ball.

a.—Yes.

c.—Now when he bunts the ball—me being a good catcher—I want to throw the guy out at first base, so I pick up the ball and throw it to who?

a.—Now, that's the first thing you've said right.

c.—I DON'T EVEN KNOW WHAT I'M TALKING ABOUT.

a.—Well, that's all you have to do.

c.—Is to throw it to first base.

a.—Yes.

c.—Now who's got it?

a.—Naturally.

c.—Who has it?

a.—Naturally.

c.—O.K.

a.—Now you've got it.

c.—I pick up the ball and I throw it to Naturally.

a.—No you don't. You throw the ball to first base.

c.—Then who gets it?

a.—Naturally.

c.—I throw the ball to Naturally.

a.—You don't. You throw it to Who.

c.—Naturally.

a.—Well, naturally. Say it that way.

c.—I said I'd throw the ball to Naturally.

a.—You don't. You throw it to Who.

c.—Naturally.

a.—Yes.

c.—So I throw the ball to first base and Naturally gets it.

a.—No. You throw the ball to first base—

c.—Then who gets it?

a.—Naturally.

c.—That's what I'm saying.

a.—You're not saying that.

c.—I throw the ball to first base.

a.—Then Who gets it.

c.—He better get it.

a.—That's it. All right now, don't get excited. Take it easy.

c.—Now I throw the ball to first base, whoever it is grabs the ball, so the guy runs to second.

a.—Uh-huh.

c.—Who picks up the ball and throws it to what. What throws it to I don't know. I don't know throws it back to tomorrow—a triple play.

a.—Yeah. It could be.

c.—Another guy gets up and it's a long fly ball to center. Why? I don't know. And I don't care.

a.—What was that?

c.—I said, I don't care.

a.—Oh, that's our shortstop.

c.—(Makes noises—steps close to Abbott and they glare at each other)

Three Men on Third

The day that Brooklyn accumulated three runners on third was August 15, 1926, when the Dodgers were engaging the Braves at Ebbets Field. In case you don't remember it, here are the details:

Brooklyn came to bat in the seventh. Johnny Butler singled. DeBerry hit a two-bagger scoring Butler. Dazzy Vance singled and DeBerry went to third. Fewster was hit by the pitcher, filling the bases. Jacobson popped out. Babe Herman now took his place at the plate. The stage was all set for the drama. Herman belted a line drive to right field and DeBerry vacated third base and crossed the plate. Vance, who had been on second, thought Herman's drive was going to be caught, and held up until he was certain the outfielder had missed it; then Dazzy started for home. He rounded third, ran halfway to the plate, decided he wouldn't be able to beat the throw-in, reversed himself and started back to third. Meanwhile Fewster was tearing around the base paths from first, arriving at the third sack about the time Vance returned to it. They stood and looked at each other in astonishment for a few moments and

From *Three Men On Third*, by Ira L. Smith & H. Allen Smith, pp. 16–17. Copyright, 1951, by Doubleday and Company. New York.

then switched their attention to an even more astonishing sight. Babe Herman figured he had a double, possibly a triple, and he preferred a triple of course, and was bent on trying to stretch it. He had his head down and was running for all he was worth, with no suspicion in his mind that a traffic jam had already developed at third. He didn't raise his head until he was a few feet from third and then when he looked up, there stood Vance and Fewster, and the Boston third baseman was just taking the throw. This third baseman, Taylor, was understandably excited. He received the throw and started tagging people. He tagged every human being within reach, including the third base umpire. Herman, however, had got himself out of range and was heading back for second. Taylor fired the ball down to the shortstop and Herman was tagged out before he could reach the bag.

That episode became a sort of baseball classic, possibly because the unpredictable Babe Herman was involved in the making of it. Bennett Cerf has told the story of the time a few years later, when Quentin Reynolds was sitting in the last row of seats in the grandstand at Ebbets Field during the early innings of an important game. Chancing to look into the street outside the park, Reynolds saw a late-comer, a Brooklyn fan who was running along the pavement, puffing heavily as he headed for the entrance.

"Better hurry up!" Reynolds yelled down to the man. "You're missing something big. The Dodgers have three men on base."

"Yehr?" cried the fan. "Which base?"

The Helpful Snake

One day, when my basic training was over, there wasn't much to do around camp, so I decided to sneak away and go fishing.

I went to a little stream near by, and settled back with a pint of whiskey and a can of worms. My luck wasn't so good, though. Every once in a while there was a pull on my line, but each time the bait was taken, so that the can of worms became empty long before the bottle did. I began to look around for more worms.

I looked and I looked and I couldn't find a single one. Finally I turned over a rotten board. There sat a big, old snake. In the snake's mouth was a juicy worm.

"How," I said to myself, "am I going to get the worm away from this snake without getting him sore?" After a while I got an idea. I reached into my pocket and took out the pint of whiskey. I carefully tilted the bottle and poured a few drops into the snake's half-open mouth. The snake looked at me gratefully, and with a happy wriggle, dropped the worm neatly into my hand.

I went back to my fishing, and a few minutes later had landed a whopper.

I didn't have to look for bait for the rest of the afternoon.

Every five minutes the snake was back at the bottle—with a worm in his mouth.

The Helpful Minnow

On a warm day Bob was fishing for perch in the middle of Round Lake. His luck had been so bad that he had to rely for his sole amusement on the quart of liquid refreshment that was part of every fishing trip. By the time half of it was gone he had become rather unsteady, and it was fortunate that half of the remaining pint was spilled into the minnow bucket.

Bob baited his hook with a fresh minnow several minutes later and dropped it listlessly over the side. The line started a wild dash out and around the boat, and a few seconds later he felt the tug of a speckled two-pounder, which he immediately pulled in. The fish had not swallowed the hook in the attempt to get the minnow, however. The pleasantly alcoholized minnow had bitten the big perch in the back of the neck and pulled him in with the assistance of the line.

In half an hour, with the assistance of several refreshing rests in the minnow bucket, the bait had dragged in the day's limit.

Little Jonah

Whenever the rains came, truth fled. One day a man showed up with three fine bass which, he said, he had taken on bay crabs cast from the dock at the Quarry.

"I had a better one," he said, "but a funny thing happened. I got these three and another fellow took two and they were the only fish caught from the dock this morning. My only other bite was that real big one. He swallowed the bait and I thought I had him solid.

"I didn't know it at the time, of course, but he had a big minnow inside of him. When he took the hook down, it caught in the head of this minnow. I was bringing him in slowly, taking it easy because he was a brute.

"All of a sudden he gave a lunge and the minnow came out of his belly and I brought the minnow in. The bass was gone."

From *The Yazoo River*, by Frank E. Smith, p. 235. Copyright, 1954, by Frank E. Smith. *The Rivers of America*, edited by Carl Carmer. New York & Toronto: Rinehart & Company, Inc.

By Red Smith. New York *Herald Tribune*, August 1, 1956.

The Fish that Caught Itself

Then there's the tale of the record muskellunge of Butternut Lake, which is up north in the Flambeau country. He weighed, the story goes, more than seventy pounds, but nobody ever saw him alive.

He was found dead with a beer can stuck in his throat. It was a bright and shiny beer can, colored like a new plug in a sporting goods showcase.

Obviously, the muskie had hit the floating can and strangled. The story doesn't say what brand of beer.

Casey at the Bat

The outlook wasn't brilliant for the Mudville nine that day;
The score stood four to two, with but one inning more to play;
And so when Cooney died at first and Burrough did the same,
A sickly fear came o'er the patrons of the game.

A few got up to go, but on the other hand the rest
Stayed with the hope that springs eternal in the human breast.
They thought if only Casey could get a whack at that,
They'd put up even money now with Casey at the bat.

But Flynn preceded Casey and so did Jimmy Blake;
The former was a hoodoo, the latter was a fake;
But Flynn let drive a single, to the wonderment of all,
And Blake, the much despiséd, tore the cover off the ball.

And when the dust had risen and they saw what had occurred;
There was Blake safe on second and Flynn hugging third;
Then from the maddened thousands there went up such a yell,
It beat against the hillsides, it echoed in the dell;
It thundered on the mountain top, it recoiled upon the flat,
For Casey, mighty Casey, was advancing to the bat.

There was ease in Casey's manner as he stepped into his place,
There was pride in Casey's bearing and a smile on Casey's face;
And when, responding to the cheers, he lightly doffed his hat,
No stranger in the crowd could doubt 'twas Casey at the bat.

By Red Smith. New York *Herald Tribune*, August 1, 1956.

By Ernest Lawrence Thayer. Reprinted in *Casey at the Bat, and Other Humorous Favorites*, edited by George Milburn. Little Blue Book No. 1025. Girard, Kansas: Haldeman-Julius Company, 1926. First printed in the San Francisco *Examiner*, June 3, 1888.

Ten thousand eyes were on him as he rubbed his hands with dirt,
Five thousand tongues applauded as he wiped them on his shirt.
Then while the writhing pitcher ground the ball into his hip,
Defiance gleamed in Casey's eye, a sneer curled Casey's lip.

And now the leather-covered sphere came hurtling through the air,
And Casey stood a-watching it in haughty grandeur there.
Close by the sturdy batsman the ball unheeded sped—
"That ain't my style," said Casey. "Strike one!" the umpire said.

From the benches, black with people, there went up a muffled roar,
Like the beating of storm waves on a stern and distant shore.
"Kill him! Kill the umpire!" shouted someone in the stand,
And it's likely they'd have killed him had not Casey raised his hand.

With a smile of Christian charity great Casey's visage shone;
He stilled the rising tumult; he bade the game go on.
He signaled to the pitcher, and once more the spheroid flew;
But Casey still ignored it, and the umpire said "Strike two!"

"Fraud!" cried the maddened thousands, and an echo answered "Fraud!"
But one scornful look from Casey and the audience was awed.
They saw his face grow stern and cold, they saw his muscles strain,
And they knew that Casey wouldn't let that ball go by again.

The sneer is gone from Casey's lip, his teeth are clinched in hate,
He pounds with cruel violence his bat upon the plate;
And now the pitcher holds the ball, and now he lets it go,
And now the air is shattered by the force of Casey's blow.

Oh somewhere in this favored land the sun is shining bright,
The band is playing somewhere, and somewhere hearts are light,
And somewhere men are laughing, and somewhere children shout,
But there is no joy in Mudville—mighty Casey has struck out!

The Untruthful Horse

A drunk was staggering home one morning when he passed a parked
milk wagon and stopped to pat the bag of old bones standing between
the shafts.

"Hello," said the horse, much to the surprise of Mr. Alcoholic
Anonymous. "I hope you don't mind me addressing you so familiarly,
sir, but it gets terribly lonely for me, prowling these streets all night
with nobody to talk to except my driver, who doesn't even listen to me.

From *Best Sports Stories of 1945*, edited by Irving T. Marsh and Edward Ehre,
p. 147. Copyright, 1946, by E. P. Dutton and Co., Inc. New York.

"You'd never guess it to look at me, now, sir," he went on, "but I was once a famous race horse. Just eleven years ago, and it seems like yesterday, I won the Kentucky Derby. They put a wreath of roses around my neck and I was the toast of the country.

"But that's the way it goes. I've had my moment of glory and now I am a drudge. My only comfort is my memories."

The drunk was flabbergasted almost to the point of sobriety. When the driver returned he offered to buy the horse. He shoved $100 into the man's hand, and started to take possession.

"This is the most wonderful horse I ever saw," he remarked in awe. "He is so intelligent I can scarcely believe my ears."

The driver yawned and said: "Yeah? He's probably been giving you that old bunk about winning the Kentucky Derby. He tells everybody that."

Run, Run, Run!

It seems that because of the manpower shortage, Leo Durocher, manager of the Brooklyn Dodgers, was forced to buy a horse to play the outfield for his team. He was a little dubious about his equine purchase, but the situation was desperate and a bookmaker friend of his touted him on the horse by telling of the equine's prowess at bat.

When the horse reported, Leo gave him the lead-off spot in the batting order. However, he reported so late that the manager didn't have time to try him out, but was forced to place him right in the lineup, cold.

After looking over a couple of pitches in a professional manner, the horse connected solidly. He stood there calmly watching his hit bounce off the fence until Durocher, who was coaching at third, screamed at him, "RUN! RUN! DAMN IT, RUN!"

"Don't be silly," whinnied the horse scornfully as he lurched back to the bench. "If I could run I'd be out to Belmont Park."

A Tight Race Considerin'

"You see, Doc, I'd heered so much from mam 'bout her dad's Shumach and his rider Swage, and the mile a minute, and the Croton water what was gin him, and how she bleved that if it warn't for bettin', and the cussin' and fightin', running race-hosses warn't the sin folks said it war; and if they war anything to make her 'gret gettin' religion and

From *Best Sports Stories of 1945*, edited by Irving T. Marsh and Edward Ehre, pp. 147–148. Copyright, 1946, by E. P. Dutton and Co., Inc. New York.

From "A Tight Race Considerin'" in *Odd Leaves from the Life of a Louisiana "Swamp Doctor*," by Madison Tensas, M.D. (Henry Clay Lewis), pp. 47–53. Republished, 1858, by T. B. Peterson and Brothers, Philadelphia, as a part of *The Swamp Doctor's Adventures in the South-West*, by "Madison Tensas," M.D., and "Solitaire."

jinin' the church, it war cos she couldn't 'tend races, and have a race-colt of her own to comfort her 'clinin' years, sich as her daddy had afore her, till she got me; so I couldn't rest for wantin' to see a hoss-race, and go shares, p'raps, in the colt she war wishin' for. And then I'd think what sort of a hoss I'd want him to be—a quarter nag, a mile critter, or a hoss wot could run (fur all mam says it can't be did) a whole four mile at a stretch. Sometimes I think I'd rather own a quarter nag, for the suspense wouldn't long be hung, and then we could run up the road to old Nick Bamer's cow-pen, and Sally is almost allers out thar in the cool of the evenin'; and in course we wouldn't be so cruel as to run the poor critter in the heat of the day. But then agin, I'd think I'd rather have a miler,—for the 'citement would be greater, and we could run down the road to old Wither's orchard, an' his gal Miry is frightfully fond of sunnin' herself thar, when she 'spects me 'long, and she'd hear of the race, certain; but then thar war the four miler for my thinkin', and I'd knew'd in such case the 'citement would be greatest of all, and you know, too, from dad's stable to the grocery is jist four miles, an' in case of any 'spute, all hands would be willin' to run over, even if it had to be tried a dozen times. So I never could 'cide on which sort of a colt to wish for. It was fust one, then t'others, till I was nearly 'stracted, and when mam, makin' me religious, told me one night to say grace, I jes shut my eyes, looked pious, and yelled out, 'D—n it, go!' and in 'bout five minutes arter, came near kickin' dad's stumak off, under the table, thinkin' I war spurrin' my critter in a tight place. So I found the best way was to get the hoss fust, and then 'termine whether it should be Sally Bamers, and the cow-pen; Miry Withers, and the peach orchard; or Spillman's grocery, with the bald face.

"You've seed my black colt, that one that dad's father gin me in his will when he died, and I 'spect the reason he wrote that will war, that he might have wun then, for it's more then he had when he was alive, for granma war a monstrus overbearin' woman. The colt would cum up in my mind, every time I'd think whar I was to git a hoss. 'Git out!' said I at fust—*he* never could run, and 'sides if he could, mam rides him now, an' he's too old for anything, 'cept totin' her and bein' called mine; for you see, though he war named Colt, yet for the old lady to call him old, would bin like the bar 'fecting contempt for the rabbit, on account of the shortness of his tail.

"Well, thought I, it does look sorter unpromisin', but its Colt or none; so I 'termined to put him in trainin' the fust chance. Last Saturday, who should cum ridin' up but the new cirkut preacher, a long-legged, weakly, sickly, never-contented-onless-the-best-on-the-planta-tion-war-cooked-fur-him sort of a man; but I didn't look at him twice, his hoss was the critter that took my eye; for the minute I looked at him, I knew him to be the same hoss as Sam Spooner used to win all his splurg-in' dimes with, the folks said, and wot he used to ride past our house so fine on. The hoss war a heap the wuss for age and change of masters;

for preachers, though they're mity 'ticular 'bout thar own comfort, seldom tends to thar hosses, for one is privit property and 'tother generally borried. I seed from the way the preacher rid, that he didn't know the animal he war straddlin'; but I did, and I 'termined I wouldn't lose sich a chance of trainin' Colt by the side of a hoss wot had run real races. So that night, arter prayers and the folks was abed, I and Old Bill tuck the hosses and carried them down to the pastur'. It was a forty-aker lot, and consequently jist a quarter across—for I thought it best to promote Colt, by degrees, to a four-miler. When we got thar, the preacher's hoss showed he war willin'; but Colt, dang him! commenced nibblin' a fodder-stack over the fence. I nearly cried for vexment, but an idea struck me; I hitched the critter, and told Bill to get on Colt and stick tight wen I giv' the word. Bill got reddy, and unbeknownst to him I pulled up a bunch of nettles, and, as I clapped them under Colt's tail, yelled, 'Go!' Down shut his graceful like a steel-trap, and away he shot so quick an' fast that he jumpt clean out from under Bill, and got nearly to the end of the quarter 'fore t' po' cus toch the ground: he lit on his head, and in course warn't hurt—so we cotched Colt, an' I mounted him.

"The next time I said 'go' he showed that age hadn't spiled his legs or memory. Bill an' me 'greed we could run him now, so Bill mounted Preacher and we got ready. Thar war a narrer part of the track 'tween two oaks, but as it war near the end of the quarter, I 'spected to pass Preacher 'fore we got thar, so I warn't afraid of barkin' my shins.

"We tuck a fair start, and off we went like a peeled ingun, an' I soon 'scovered that it warn't such an easy matter to pass Preacher, though Colt dun delightful; we got nigh the trees, and Preacher warn't past yet, an' I 'gan to get skeered, for it warn't more than wide enuf for a horse and a half; so I hollered to Bill to hold up, but the imperdent fool turned his ugly pictur, and said, 'he'd be cussed if he warn't goin' to play his han' out.' I gin him to understand he'd better fix for a foot-race when we stopt, and tried to hold up Colt, but he wouldn't stop. We reached the oaks, Colt tried to pass Preacher, Preacher tried to pass Colt, and cowollop, crosh, cochunk! we all cum down like 'simmons arter frost. Colt got up and won the race; Preacher tried hard to rise, but one hind leg had got threw the stirrup, an' tother in the head stall, an' he had to lay still, doubled up like a long scarecrow in a short bed. I lit on my feet, but Old Bill war gone entire. I looked up in the fork of one of the oaks, and thar he war sittin', lookin' very composed on surroundin' nature. I couldn't git him down till I promised not to hurt him for disobeyin' orders, when he slid down. We'd 'nuff racin' for that night, so we put up the hosses and went to bed.

"Next morning the folks got ready for church, when it was diskivered that the hosses had got out. I an' Bill started off to look for them; we found them cleer off in the field, tryin' to git in the pastur' to run the last night's race over, old Blaze, the reverlushunary mule, bein' along to act as judge.

"By the time we got to the house it war nigh on to meetin' hour; and dad had started to the preachin', to tell the folks to sing on, as preacher and mam would be 'long bimeby. As the passun war in a hurry, and had been complainin' that his creetur war dull, I 'suaded him to put on uncle Jim's spurs what he fotch from Mexico. I saddled the passun's hoss, takin' 'ticular pains to let the saddle-blanket come down low in the flank. By the time these fixins war threw, mam war 'head nigh on to a quarter. 'We must ride on, passun,' I said, 'or the folks 'll think we is lost.' So I whipt up the mule I rid, the passun chirrupt and chuct to make his crittur gallop, but the animal didn't mind him a pic. I 'gan to snicker, an' the passun 'gan to git vext; sudden he thought of his spurs, so he ris up, an' drove them *vim* in his hoss's flanx, till they went through his saddle-blanket, and like to bored his nag to the holler. By gosh! but it war a quickener—the hoss kickt till the passun had to hug him round the neck to keep from pitchin' him over his head. He next jumpt up 'bout as high as a rail fence, passun holdin' on and tryin' to git his spurs—but they war lockt—his breeches split plum across with the strain, and the piece of wearin' truck wot's next the skin made a monstrous putty flag as the old hoss, like drunkards to a barbacue, streakt it up the road.

"Mam war ridin' slowly along, thinkin' how sorry she was, cos Chary Dolin, who always led her off, had sich a bad cold, an' wouldn't be able to 'sist her singin' to-day. She war practisin' the hymns, and had got as far as whar it says, 'I have a race to run,' when the passun huv in sight, an' in 'bout the dodgin' of a diedapper, she found thar war truth in the words, for the colt, hearin' the hoss cumin' up behind, began to show symptoms of runnin'; but when he heard the passun holler 'wo! wo!' to his hoss, he thought it war me shoutin' 'go!' and sure 'nuff off they started jis as the passun got up even; so it war a fair race. Whoop! git out, but it war egsitin'—the dust flew, and the rail-fence appeered strate as a rifle. Thar war the passun, his legs fast to the critter's flanx, arms lockt round his neck, face as pale as a rabbit's belly, and the white flag streemin' far behind—and thar war Mam, fust on one side, then on t'other, her new caliker swelled up round her like a bear with the dropsy, the old lady so much surprized she cuddent ride steddy, an' tryin' to stop her colt, but he war too well trained to stop while he heard 'go!' Mam got 'sited at last, and her eyes 'gan to glimmer like she seen her daddy's ghost axin' 'if he ever trained up a child or a race-hoss to be 'fraid of a small brush on a Sunday,' she commenced ridin' beautiful; she braced herself up in the saddle, and began to make calkerlations how she war to win the race, for it war nose and nose, and she saw the passun spurrin' his critter every jump. She tuk off her shoe, and the way a number ten go-to-meetin' brogan commenced givin' a hoss particular Moses, were a caution to hoss-flesh—but still it kept nose and nose. She found she war carryin' too much weight for Colt, so she 'gan to throw off plunder, till nuthin' was left but her saddle and close, and the spurs kept tellin' still. The old woman commenced strippin' to lighten, till it wouldn't bin the clean thing for her to have taken off one dud more; an' then when she found it war no use while the spurs lasted, she got cantankerous. 'Passun,' says she, 'I'll be cust if it's fair or gentlemanly for you, a preacher of the gospel, to take advantage of an old woman this way, usin' spurs when you know *she* can't wear 'em—'taint Christian-like nuther,' and she burst into cryin'. 'Wo! Miss Hibbs! Wo! Stop! Madam! Wo! Your son'—he attempted to say, when the old woman tuck him on the back of the head, and fillin' his mouth with right smart of a saddle-horn, and stoppin' the talk, as far as his share went for the present.

"By this time they'd got nigh on to the meetin'-house, and the folks were harkin' away on 'Old Hundred,' and wonderin' what could have become of the passun and mam Hibbs. One sister in a long beard axt another brethren in church, if she'd heered anything 'bout that New York preacher runnin' way with a woman old enough to be his muther. The brethrens gin a long sigh an' groaned 'it ain't possible! marciful heavens! you don't 'spicion?' wen the sound of the hosses comin', roused them up like a touch of the agur, an' broke off their sarpent-talk. Dad run out to see what was to pay, but when he seed the hosses so close together, the passun spurrin', and mam ridin' like close war skase whar she cum, he knew her fix in a second, and 'tarmined to help her; so clinchin' a saplin', he hid 'hind a stump 'bout ten steps off, and held on for the hosses. On they went in beautiful style, the passun's spurs tellin' terrible, and mam's shoe operatin' 'no small pile of punkins,'—passun stretched out the length of two hosses, while mam sot as stiff and strate as a bull yearling in his fust fight, hittin' her nag, fust on one side, next on t'other, and the third for the passun, who had chawed the horn till little of the saddle, and less of his teeth war left, and his voice sounded as holler as a jackass-nicker in an old saw-mill.

"The hosses war nose and nose, jam up together so close that mam's last kiverin' and passun's flag had got lockt, an' 'tween bleached domestic and striped linsey made a beautiful banner for the pious racers.

"On they went like a small arthquake, an' it seemed like it war goin' to be a draun race; but dad, when they got to him, let down with all his might on Colt, scarin' him so bad that he jumpt clean ahead of passun, beatin' him by a neck, buttin' his own head agin the meetin'-house, an' pitchin' mam, like a lam for the sacryfise, plum through the winder 'mongst the mourners, leavin' her only garment flutterin' on a nail in the sash. The men shot their eyes and scrambled outen the house, an' the women gin mam so much of their close that they like to put themselves in the same fix.

"The passun quit the circuit, and I haven't been home yet."

The Way Old Tige Barked

There was once a backwoodsman who boasted that his hound Tige was the best hunting dog in seven counties. He said that he never went hunting that Tige did not tree a varmint and that by the way he barked old Tige always told him what the varmint was.

A newcomer to the settlement, who thought that the old-timer must be stretching the blanket a bit, offered to bet that old Tige could not tell one varmint from another. So to settle the wager the men went hunting the next night. They turned Tige loose in the creek bottom and told him to sic.

"There ain't no use in walking around a lot," said the backwoodsman. "Old Tige will let us know when he finds something."

They had not been sitting long when old Tige was heard.

"Jest wait," said the settler. "He ain't treed yet."

They sat for a few minutes longer, then old Tige sounded a new note.

"He's treed now," said the backwoodsman.

"What's he got?" asked the newcomer.

"I reckon that must be a bobcat."

When they reached the tree and held up their torch, sure enough there was a bobcat. They shot it and put Tige on the trail again.

After a while Tige bayed.

"He's treed," said the old-timer.

"What's he got this time?"

"I reckon that must be a possum."

They came to the tree, and sure enough there was the possum.

Again they sat while Tige ranged and again Tige bayed.

"What's Tige got this time?"

"I reckon that must be a coon."

Again the prediction proved correct.

The newcomer was ready to pay the wager, but the night was young and old-timer was eager for more hunting. So Tige was put on the trail and presently he bayed again.

Then suddenly his bark changed to a long howl that seemed to shake the trees and hills.

"What's Tige got now?" asked the newcomer.

"Tige ain't got nothing," replied the backwoodsman, jumping to his feet. "Something's got Tige."

From *Folk Laughter on the American Frontier*, by Mody C. Boatright, pp. 100–101. New York: The Macmillan Company, 1949.

The Double Wabble

Shooting-matches are probably nearly coeval with the colonization of Georgia. They are still common throughout the Southern States, though they are not as common as they were twenty-five or thirty years ago. Chance led me to one about a year ago. I was travelling in one of the northeastern counties, when I overtook a swarthy, bright-eyed, smerky little fellow, riding a small pony and bearing on his shoulder a long, heavy rifle, which, judging from its looks, I should say had done service in Morgan's corps.

"Good-morning, sir!" said I, reining up my horse as I came beside him.

"How goes it, stranger?" said he, with a tone of independence and self-confidence that awakened my curiosity to know a little of his character.

"Going driving?" inquired I.

"Not exactly," replied he, surveying my horse with a quizzical smile. "I haven't been a-driving *by myself* for a year or two; and my nose has got so bad lately I can't carry a cold trail *without hounds to help me.*"

Alone, and without hounds as he was, the question was rather a silly one; but it answered the purpose for which it was put, which was only to draw him into conversation, and I proceeded to make as decent a retreat as I could.

"I didn't know," said I, "but that you were going to meet the huntsmen, or going to your stand."

"Ah, sure enough," rejoined he, "that *mout* be a bee, as the old woman said when she killed a wasp. It seems to me I ought to know you."

"Well, if you *ought,* why *don't* you?"

"What *mout* your name be?"

"It *might* be anything," said I, with borrowed wit, for I knew my man, and knew what kind of conversation would please him most.

"Well, what *is* it, then?"

"It *is* Hall," said I; "but you know it might as well have been anything else."

"Pretty digging!" said he. "I find you're not the fool I took you to be; so here's to a better acquaintance with you!"

"With all my heart," returned I; "but you must be as clever as I've been, and give me your name."

"To be sure I will, my old coon; take it—take it, and welcome. Anything else about me you'd like to have?"

"No," said I, "there's nothing else about you worth having."

"Oh yes, there is, stranger! Do you see this?" holding up his ponderous rifle with an ease that astonished me. "If you will go with me to the shooting-match, and see me knock out the *bull's-eye* with her a few

From *Georgia Scenes* . . . , by a Native Georgian [Augustus Baldwin Longstreet], pp. 274–297. New York: Harper & Brothers, 1840.

times, you'll agree the old *Soap-stick's* worth something when Billy Curlew puts his shoulder to her."

This short sentence was replete with information to me. It taught me that my companion was *Billy Curlew;* that he was going to a *shooting-match;* that he called his rifle the *Soap-stick,* and that he was very confident of winning beef with her; or, which is nearly but not quite the same thing, *driving the cross with her.*

"Well," said I, "if the shooting-match is not too far out of my way, I'll go to it with pleasure."

"Unless your way lies through the woods from here," said Billy, "it'll not be much out of your way; for it's only a mile ahead of us, and there is no other road for you to take till you get there; and as that thing you're riding in a'n't well suited to fast travelling among brushy knobs, I reckon you won't lose much by going by. I reckon you hardly ever was at a shooting-match, stranger, from the cut of your coat?"

"Oh yes," returned I, "many a time. I won beef at one when I was hardly old enough to hold a shot-gun offhand."

"*Children* don't go to shooting-matches about here," said he, with a smile of incredulity. "I never heard of but one that did, and he was a little *swinge* cat. He was born a-shooting, and killed squirrels before he was weaned."

"Nor did *I* ever hear of but one," replied I, "and that one was myself."

"And where did you win beef so young, stranger?"

"At Berry Adams's."

"Why, stop, stranger, let me look at you good! Is your name *Lyman Hall?*"

"The very same," said I.

"Well, dang my buttons, if you a'n't the very boy my daddy used to tell me about. I was too young to recollect you myself; but I've heard daddy talk about you many a time. I believe mammy's got a neck-handkerchief now that daddy won on your shooting at Collen Reid's store when you were hardly knee-high. Come along, Lyman, and I'll go my death upon you at the shooting-match, with the old Soap-stick at your shoulder!"

"Ah, Billy," said I, "the old Soap-stick will do much better at your own shoulder. It was my mother's notion that sent me to the shooting-match at Berry Adams's; and, to tell the honest truth, it was altogether a chance shot that made me win beef; but that wasn't generally known, and 'most everybody believed that I was carried there on account of my skill in shooting; and my fame was spread far and wide, I well remember. I remember too, perfectly well, your father's bet on me at the store. *He* was at the shooting-match, and nothing could make him believe but that I was a great shot with a rifle as well as a shot-gun. Bet he would on me, in spite of all I could say, though I assured him that I had never shot a rifle in my life. It so happened, too, that there were but two bullets, or, rather, a bullet and a half; and so confident was your father in my skill that he made me shoot the half-bullet; and, strange to tell, by another chance shot I'd like to have drove the cross and won his bet."

"Now I know you're the very chap, for I heard daddy tell that very thing about the half-bullet. Don't say anything about it, Lyman, and darn my old shoes if I don't tare the lint off the boys with you at the shooting-match! They'll never 'spect such a looking man as you are of knowing anything about a rifle. I'll risk your *chance* shots."

I soon discovered that the father had eaten sour grapes, and the son's teeth were on edge; for Billy was just as incorrigibly obstinate in his belief of my dexterity with a rifle as his father had been before him.

We soon reached the place appointed for the shooting-match. It went by the name of Sims's Cross Roads, because here two roads intersected each other; and because, from the time that the first had been laid out, Archibald Sims had resided there. Archibald had been a justice of the peace in his day (and where is the man of his age in Georgia who has not?); consequently, he was called *Squire* Sims. It is the custom in this State, when a man has once acquired a title, civil or military, to force it upon him as long as he lives; hence the countless number of titled personages who are introduced in these sketches.

We stopped at the squire's door. Billy hastily dismounted, gave me the shake of the hand which he had been reluctantly reserving for a mile back, and, leading me up to the squire, thus introduced me: "Uncle Archy, this is Lyman Hall; and for all you see him in these fine clothes, he's a *swinge* cat; a darn sight cleverer fellow than he looks to be. Wait till you see him lift the old Soap-stick and draw a bead upon the bull's-eye. You *gwine* to see fun here to-day. Don't say nothing about it."

"Well, Mr Swinge-cat," said the squire, "here's to a better acquaintance with you," offering me his hand.

"How goes it, Uncle Archy?" said I, taking his hand warmly (for I am always free and easy with those who are so with me; and in this course I rarely fail to please). "How's the old woman?"

"Egad," said the squire, chuckling, "there you're too hard for me; for she died two-and-twenty years ago, and I haven't heard a word from her since."

"What! and you never married again?"

"Never, as God's my judge!" (A solemn asseveration, truly, upon so light a subject.)

"Well, that's not my fault."

"No, nor it's not mine *ni*ther," said the squire.

Here we were interrupted by the cry of another Ransy Sniffle: "Hello, here! All you as wish to put in for the shoot'n'-match, come on here! for the putt'n' in's *riddy* to begin."

About sixty persons, including mere spectators, had collected, the most of whom were more or less obedient to the call of Mealy Whitecotton—for that was the name of the self-constituted commander-in-chief. Some hastened and some loitered, as they desired to be first or last on the list; for they shoot in the order in which their names are entered.

The beef was not present, nor is it ever upon such occasions; but several of the company had seen it, who all concurred in the opinion that it was a good beef, and well worth the price that was set upon it —eleven dollars. A general inquiry ran round, in order to form some opinion as to the number of shots that would be taken; for, of course, the price of a shot is cheapened in proportion to the increase of that number. It was soon ascertained that not more than twenty persons would take chances; but these twenty agreed to take the number of shots at twenty-five cents each.

The competitors now began to give in their names; some for one, some for two, three, and a few for as many as four shots.

Billy Curlew hung back to the last; and when the list was offered him, five shots remained undisposed of.

"How many shots left?" inquired Billy.

"Five," was the reply.

"Well, I take 'em all. Put down four shots to me, and one to Lyman Hall, paid for by William Curlew."

I was thunderstruck; not at his proposition to pay for my shot, because I knew that Billy meant it as a token of friendship, and he would have been hurt if I had refused to let him do me this favor; but at the unexpected announcement of my name as a competitor for beef, at least one hundred miles from the place of my residence. I was prepared for a challenge from Billy to some of his neighbors for a *private* match upon me; but not for this.

I therefore protested against his putting in for me, and urged every reason to dissuade him from it that I could, without wounding his feelings.

"Put it down!" said Billy, with the authority of an emperor, and with a look that spoke volumes intelligible to every by-stander. "Reckon I don't know what I'm about?" Then wheeling off, and muttering in an under, self-confident tone, "Dang old Roper," continued he, "if he don't knock that cross to the north corner of creation and back again before a cat can lick her foot!"

Had I been king of the cat tribe they could not have regarded me with more curious attention than did the whole company from this moment. Every inch of me was examined with the nicest scrutiny; and some plainly expressed by their looks that they never would have taken me for such a bite. I saw no alternative but to throw myself upon a third chance shot; for though, by the rules of the sport, I would have been allowed to shoot by proxy, by all the rules of good-breeding I was bound to shoot in person. It would have been unpardonable to disappoint the expectations which had been raised on me. Unfortunately, too, for me, the match differed in one respect from those which I had been in the habit of attending in my younger days. In olden time the contest was carried on chiefly with *shot-guns,* a generic term which, in those days, embraced three descriptions of fire-arms—*Indian-traders* (a long, cheap, but sometimes excellent kind of gun that Mother Britain used to send hither for traffic with the Indians), *the large musket,* and the *shot-gun;* properly so-called rifles were, however, always permitted to compete with them, under equitable restrictions. These were, that they should be fired offhand, while the shot-guns were allowed a rest, the distance being equal; or that the distance should be one hundred yards for a rifle to sixty for the shot-gun, the mode of firing being equal.

But this was a match of rifles exclusively; and these are by far the most common at this time.

Most of the competitors fire at the same target, which is usually a board from nine inches to a foot wide, charred on one side as black as it can be made by fire, without impairing materially the uniformity of its surface; on the darkened side of which is *pegged* a square piece of white paper, which is larger or smaller according to the distance at which it is to be placed from the marksmen. This is almost invariably sixty yards, and for it the paper is reduced to about two and a half inches square. Out of the centre of it is cut a rhombus of about the width of an inch, measured diagonally; this is the *bull's-eye* or *diamond,* as the marksmen choose to call it; in the centre of this is the cross. But every man is permitted to fix his target to his own taste; and, accordingly, some remove one-fourth of the paper, cutting from the centre of the square to the two lower corners, so as to leave a large angle opening from the centre downward, while others reduce the angle more or less; but it is rarely the case that all are not satisfied with one of these figures.

The beef is divided into five prizes, or, as they are commonly termed, five *quarters*—the hide and tallow counting as one. For several years after the Revolutionary War a sixth was added—the *lead* which was shot in the match. This was the prize of the sixth best shot; and it used to be carefully extracted from the board or tree in which it was lodged, and afterwards remoulded. But this grew out of the exigency of the times, and has, I believe, been long since abandoned everywhere.

The three master shots and rivals were Moses Firmby, Larkin Spivey, and Billy Curlew; to whom was added, upon this occasion, by common consent and with awful forebodings your humble servant.

The target was fixed at an elevation of about three feet from the ground; and the judges (Captain Turner and Squire Porter) took their stands by it, joined by about half the spectators.

The first name on the catalogue was Mealy Whitecotton. Mealy stepped out, rifle in hand, and toed the mark. His rifle was about three inches longer than himself, and near enough his own thickness to make the remark of Darby Chislom, as he stepped out, tolerably appropriate: "Here comes the corn-stock and the sucker!" said Darby.

"Kiss my foot!" said Mealy. "The way I'll creep into that bull's-eye's a fact."

"You'd better creep into your hind sight," said Darby. Mealy raised and fired.

"A pretty good shot, Mealy!" said one.

"Yes, a blamed good shot!" said a second.

"Well done, Meal!" said a third.

I was rejoiced when one of the company inquired, "Where is it?" for I could hardly believe they were founding these remarks upon the evidence of their senses.

"Just on the right-hand side of the bull's-eye," was the reply.

I looked with all the power of my eyes, but was unable to discover the least change in the surface of the paper. Their report, however, was true; so much keener is the vision of a practised than an unpractised eye.

The next in order was Hiram Baugh. Hiram was like some race-horses which I have seen; he was too good not to contend for every prize, and too good for nothing ever to win one.

"Gentlemen," said he, as he came to the mark, "I don't say that I'll win beef, but if my piece don't blow I'll eat the paper, or be mighty apt to do it, if you'll b'lieve my racket. My powder are not good powder, gentlemen; I bought it *thum* [from] Zeb Daggett, and gin him three-quarters of a dollar a pound for it; but it are not what I call good powder, gentlemen; but if old Buck-killer burns it clear, the boy you call Hiram Baugh eats paper, or comes mighty near it."

"Well, blaze away," said Mealy, "and be d—d to you, and Zeb Daggett, and your powder, and Buck-killer, and your powder-horn and shot-pouch to boot! How long you gwine stand thar talking 'fore you shoot?"

"Never mind," said Hiram, "I can talk a little and shoot a little too; but that's nothin'. Here goes!"

Hiram assumed the figure of a note of interrogation, took a long sight, and fired.

"I've eat paper," said he, at the crack of the gun, without looking, or seeming to look, towards the target. "Buck-killer made a clear racket. Where am I, gentlemen?"

"You're just between Mealy and the diamond," was the reply.

"I said I'd eat paper, and I've done it; haven't I, gentlemen?"

"And s'pose you have!" said Mealy; "what do that 'mount to? You'll not win beef, and never did."

"Be that as it mout be, I've beat Meal 'Cotton mighty easy; and the boy you call Hiram Baugh are able to do it."

"And what do that 'mount to? Who the devil a'n't able to beat Meal

'Cotton? I don't make no pretence of bein' nothin' great, nohow; but you always makes out as if you were gwine to keep 'em makin' crosses for you constant, and then do nothin' but *'eat paper'* at last; and that's a long way from *eatin' beef,* 'cordin' to Meal 'Cotton's notions, as you call him."

Simon Stow was now called on.

"Oh, Lord!" exclaimed two or three; "now we have it. It'll take him as long to shoot as it would take Squire Dobbins to run round a *track* o'land."

"Good-bye, boys," said Bob Martin.

"Where are you going, Bob?"

"Going to gather in my crop; I'll be back agin, though, by the time Sime Stow shoots."

Simon was used to all this, and therefore it did not disconcert him in the least. He went off and brought his own target, and set it up with his own hand.

He then wiped out his rifle; rubbed the pan with his hat; drew a piece of tow through the touchhole with his wiper; filled his charger with great care; poured the powder into the rifle with equal caution; shoved in with his finger the two or three vagrant grains that lodged round the mouth of his piece; took out a handful of bullets, looked them all over carefully, selected one without flaw or wrinkle; drew out his patching, found the most even part of it; sprung open the grease-box in the breech of his rifle; took up just so much grease, distributed it with great equality over the chosen part of his patching; laid it over the muzzle of his rifle, grease side down; placed his ball upon it, pressed it a little; then took it up and turned the neck a little more perpendicularly downward, placed his knife-handle on it, just buried it in the mouth of the rifle; cut off the redundant patching just above the bullet, looked at it, and shook his head, in token that he had cut off too much or too little—no one knew which—sent down the ball; measured the contents of his gun with his first and second fingers on the protruding part of the ramrod; shook his head again, to signify there was too much or too little powder; primed carefully; placed an arched piece of tin over the hind sight to shade it; took his place; got a friend to hold his hat over the fore sight to shade it; took a very long sight, fired, and didn't even eat the paper.

"My piece was badly *loadned,*" said Simon, when he learned the place of his ball.

"Oh, you didn't take time," said Mealy. "No man can shoot that's in such a hurry as you is. I'd hardly got to sleep 'fore I heard the crack o' the gun."

The next was Moses Firmby. He was a tall, slim man, of rather sallow complexion; and it is a singular fact that though probably no part of the world is more healthy than the mountainous parts of

Georgia, the mountaineers have not generally robust frames or fine complexions; they are, however, almost inexhaustible by toil.

Moses kept us not long in suspense. His rifle was already charged, and he fixed it upon the target with a steadiness of nerve and aim that was astonishing to me and alarming to all the rest. A few seconds, and the report of his rifle broke the deathlike silence which prevailed."

"No great harm done yet," said Spivey, manifestly relieved from anxiety by an event which seemed to me better calculated to produce despair. Firmby's ball had cut out the lower angle of the diamond, directly on a right line with the cross.

Three or four followed him without bettering his shot; all of whom, however, with one exception, "eat the paper."

It now came to Spivey's turn. There was nothing remarkable in his person or manner. He took his place, lowered his rifle slowly from a perpendicular until it came on a line with the mark, held it there like a vise for a moment, and fired.

"Pretty *sevigrous,* but nothing killing yet," said Billy Curlew, as he learned the place of Spivey's ball.

Spivey's ball had just broken the upper angle of the diamond, beating Firmby about half its width.

A few more shots, in which there was nothing remarkable, brought us to Billy Curlew. Billy stepped out with much confidence, and brought the Soap-stick to an order, while he deliberately rolled up his shirt-sleeves. Had I judged of Billy's chance of success from the looks of his gun, I should have said it was hopeless. The stock of Soap-stick seemed to have been made with a case-knife, and had it been, the tool would have been but a poor apology for its clumsy appearance. An auger-hole in the breech served for a grease-box; a cotton string assisted a single screw in holding on the lock; and the thimbles were made, one of brass, one of iron, and one of tin.

"Where's Lark Spivey's bullet?" called out Billy to the judges, as he finished rolling up his sleeves.

"About three-quarters of an inch from the cross," was the reply.

"Well, clear the way! the Soap-stick's coming, and she'll be along in there among 'em presently."

Billy now planted himself astraddle, like an inverted V; shot forward his left hip, drew his body back to an angle of about forty-five degrees with the plane of the horizon, brought his cheek down close to the breech of old Soap-stick, and fixed her upon the mark with untrembling hand. His sight was long, and the swelling muscles of his left arm led me to believe that he was lessening his chance of success with every half-second that he kept it burdened with his ponderous rifle; but it neither flagged nor wavered until Soap-stick made her report.

"Where am I?" said Billy, as the smoke rose from before his eye.

"You've jist touched the cross on the lower side," was the reply of one of the judges.

"I was afraid I was drawing my bead a *leetle* too fine," said Billy. "Now, Lyman, you see what the Soap-stick can do. Take her, and show the boys how you used to do when you was a baby."

I begged to reserve my shot to the last; pleading, rather sophistically, that it was, in point of fact, one of Billy's shots. My plea was rather indulged than sustained, and the marksmen who had taken more than one shot commenced the second round. This round was a manifest improvement upon the first. The cross was driven three times —once by Spivey, once by Firmby, and once by no less a personage than Mealy Whitecotton, whom chance seemed to favor for this time, merely that he might retaliate upon Hiram Baugh; and the bull's-eye was disfigured out of all shape.

The third and fourth rounds were shot. Billy discharged his last shot, which left the rights of parties thus: Billy Curlew first and fourth choice, Spivey second, Firmby third, and Whitecotton fifth. Some of my readers may perhaps be curious to learn how a distinction comes to be made between several, all of whom drive the cross. The distinction is perfectly natural and equitable. Threads are stretched from the uneffaced parts of the once intersecting lines, by means of which the original position of the cross is precisely ascertained. Each bullet-hole being nicely pegged up as it is made, it is easy to ascertain its circumference. To this I believe they usually, if not invariably, measure, where none of the balls touch the cross; but if the cross be driven, they measure from it to the centre of the bullet-hole. To make a draw-shot, therefore, between two who drive the cross, it is necessary that the centre of both balls should pass directly through the cross—a thing that very rarely happens.

The Bite alone remained to shoot. Billy wiped out his rifle carefully, loaded her to the top of his skill, and handed her to me. "Now," said he, "Lyman, draw a fine bead, but not too fine; for Soap-stick bears up her ball well. Take care, and don't touch the trigger until you've got your bead, for she's spring-trigger'd, and goes mighty easy; but you hold her to the place you want her, and if she don't go there, dang old Roper."

I took hold of Soap-stick, and lapsed immediately into the most hopeless despair. I am sure I never handled as heavy a gun in all my life. "Why, Billy," said I, "you little mortal, you! what do you use such a gun as this for?"

"Look at the bulls-eye yonder!" said he.

"True," said I, "but *I* can't shoot her; it is impossible."

"Go 'long, you old coon!" said Billy; "I see what you're at," intimating that all this was merely to make the coming shot the more remarkable. "Daddy's little boy don't shoot anything but the old Soap-stick here to-day, I know."

The judges, I knew, were becoming impatient, and, withal, my situation was growing more embarrassing every second; so I e'en resolved to try the Soap-stick without further parley.

I stepped out, and the most intense interest was excited all around me, and it flashed like electricity around the target, as I judged from the anxious gaze of all in that direction.

Policy dictated that I should fire with a falling rifle, and I adopted this mode, determining to fire as soon as the sights came on a line with the diamond, *bead* or no *bead*. Accordingly, I commenced lowering old Soap-stick; but, in spite of all my muscular powers, she was strictly obedient to the laws of gravitation, and came down with a uniformly accelerated velocity. Before I could arrest her downward flight she had not only passed the target, but was making rapid encroachments on my own toes.

"Why, he's the weakest man in the arms I ever seed," said one, in a half-whisper.

"It's only his fun," said Billy; "I know him."

"It may be fun," said the other, "but it looks mightily like yearnest to a man up a tree."

I now, of course, determined to reverse the mode of firing, and put forth all my physical energies to raise Soap-stick to the mark. The effort silenced Billy, and gave tongue to all his companions. I had just strength enough to master Soap-stick's obstinate proclivity, and, consequently, my nerves began to exhibit palpable signs of distress with her first imperceptible movement upward. A trembling commenced in my arms, increased, and extended rapidly to my body and lower extremities; so that, by the time that I had brought Soap-stick up to the mark I was shaking from head to foot, exactly like a man under the continued action of a strong galvanic battery. In the meantime my friends gave vent to their feelings freely.

"I swear poin'-blank," said one, "that man can't shoot."

"He used to shoot well," said another; "but can't now, nor never could."

"You better *git* away from 'bout that mark!" bawled a third, "for I'll be dod darned if Broadcloth don't give some of you the dry gripes if you stand too close thare."

"The stranger's got the *peedoddles*," [1] said a fourth, with humorous gravity.

"If he had bullets enough in his gun he'd shoot a ring round the bull's-eye big as a spinning-wheel," said a fifth.

As soon as I found that Soap-stick was high enough (for I made

---

[1] This word was entirely new to me; but like most, if not all, words in use among the common people, it is doubtless a legitimate English word, or, rather, a compound of two words, the last a little corrupted, and was very aptly applied in this instance. It is a compound of *"pee,"* to peep with one eye, and *"daddle,"* to totter or wabble.

no further use of the sights than to ascertain this fact), I pulled trigger, and off she went. I have always found that the most creditable way of relieving myself of derision was to heighten it myself as much as possible. It is a good plan in all circles, but by far the best which can be adopted among the plain, rough farmers of the country. Accordingly, I brought old Soap-stick to an order with an air of triumph, tipped Billy a wink, and observed, "Now Billy, 's your time to make your fortune. Bet 'em two to one that I've knocked out the cross."

"No, I'll be dod blamed if I do," said Billy; "but I'll bet you two to one you ha'n't hit the plank."

"Ah, Billy," said I, "I was joking about *betting,* for I never bet; nor would I have you to bet: indeed, I do not feel exactly right in shooting for beef, for it is a species of gaming at last; but I'll say this much, if that cross isn't knocked out I'll never shoot for beef again as long as I live."

"By dod," said Mealy Whitecotton, "you'll lose no great things at that!"

"Well," said I, "I reckon I know a little about wabbling. Is it possible, Billy, a man who shoots as well as you do never practised shooting with the double wabble? It's the greatest take in in the world when you learn to drive the cross with it. Another sort for getting bets upon, to the drop-sight, with a single wabble! And the Soap-stick's the very yarn for it."

"Tell you what, stranger," said one, "you're too hard for us all here. We never *hearn* o' that sort o' shoot'n' in these parts."

"Well," returned I, "you've seen it now, and I'm the boy that can do it."

The judges were now approaching with the target, and a singular combination of circumstances had kept all my party in utter ignorance of the result of my shot. Those about the target had been prepared by Billy Curlew for a great shot from me; their expectations had received assurance from the courtesy which had been extended to me; and nothing had happened to disappoint them but the single caution to them against the "dry gripes," which was as likely to have been given in irony as in earnest; for my agonies under the weight of the Soap-stick were either imperceptible to them at the distance of sixty yards, or, being visible, were taken as the flourishes of an expert who wished to "astonish the natives." The other party did not think the direction of my ball worth the trouble of a question; or if they did, my airs and harangue had put the thought to flight before it was delivered. Consequently, they were all transfixed with astonishment when the judges presented the target to them and gravely observed, "It's only second best, after all the fuss."

"Second best!" exclaimed I, with uncontrollable transports.

The whole of my party rushed to the target to have the evidence of their senses before they would believe the report; but most marvellous

fortune decreed that it should be true. Their incredulity and astonishment were most fortunate for me; for they blinded my hearers to
the real feelings with which the exclamation was uttered, and allowed
me sufficient time to prepare myself for making the best use of what I
had said before with a very different object.

"Second best!" reiterated I, with an air of despondency, as the company turned from the target to me. "Second best only? Here, Billy,
my son, take the old Soap-stick; she's a good piece, but I'm getting
too old and dim-sighted to shoot a rifle, especially with the drop-sight
and double wabbles."

"Why, good Lord a'mighty!" said Billy, with a look that baffles all
description, "a'n't you *driv* the cross?"

"Oh, driv the cross!" rejoined I, carelessly. "What's that? Just look
where my ball is! I do believe in my soul its centre is a full quarter
of an inch from the cross. I wanted to lay the centre of the bullet
upon the cross, just as if you'd put it there with your fingers."

Several received this palaver with a contemptuous but very appropriate curl of the nose; and Mealy Whitecotton offered to bet a half-
pint "that I couldn't do the like again with no sort of wabbles, he
didn't care what." But I had already fortified myself on this quarter
by my morality. A decided majority, however, were clearly of opinion
that I was serious; and they regarded me as one of the wonders of the
world. Billy increased the majority by now coming out fully with my
history, as he had received it from his father; to which I listened with
quite as much astonishment as any other one of his hearers. He begged
me to go home with him for the night, or, as he expressed it, "to go
home with him and swap lies that night, and it shouldn't cost me a
cent"; the true reading of which is, that if I would go home with him,
and give him the pleasure of an evening's chat about old times, his
house should be as free to me as my own. But I could not accept his
hospitality without retracing five or six miles of the road which I had
already passed, and therefore I declined it.

"Well, if you won't go, what must I tell the old woman for you? for
she'll be mighty glad to hear from the boy that won the silk handkerchief for her, and I expect she'll lick me for not bringing you home
with me."

"Tell her," said I, "that I send her a quarter of beef, which I won, as
I did the handkerchief, by nothing in the world but mere good luck."

"Hold your jaw, Lyman!" said Billy; "I a'n't a gwine to tell the old
woman any such lies; for she's a *real* reg'lar built Meth'dist."

As I turned to depart—"Stop a minute, stranger!" said one; then,
lowering his voice to a confidential but distinctly audible tone, "What
you offering for?" continued he. I assured him I was not a candidate
for anything; that I had accidentally fallen in with Billy Curlew, who
begged me to come with him to the shooting-match, and, as it lay
right on my road, I had stopped. "Oh," said he, with a conciliatory

nod, "if you're up for anything, you needn't be mealy-mouthed about it 'fore us boys; for we'll all go in for you here up to the handle."

"Yes," said Billy, "dang old Roper if we don't go our death for you, no matter who offers! If ever you come out for anything, Lyman, jist let the boys of Upper Hogthief know it, and they'll go for you to the hilt, against creation, tit or no tit, that's the *tatur.*"

I thanked them kindly, but repeated my assurances. The reader will not suppose that the district took its name from the character of the inhabitants. In almost every county in the State there is some spot or district which bears a contemptuous appellation, usually derived from local rivalships, or from a single accidental circumstance.

Charity Pays Off

A nun was sitting at a window in her convent one day . . . when she was handed a letter from home. Upon opening it a ten-dollar bill dropped out. She was most pleased at receiving the gift from her home folks, but as she read the letter her attention was distracted by the actions of a shabbily dressed stranger who was leaning against a post in front of the convent.

She couldn't get him off her mind and, thinking that he might be in financial difficulties, she took the ten-dollar bill and wrapped it in a piece of paper, on which she had written, 'Don't despair, Sister Eulalia,' and threw it out of the window to him. He picked it up, read it, looked at her with a puzzled expression, tipped his hat and went off down the street.

The next day she was in her cell saying her beads when she was told that some man was at her door who insisted on seeing her. She went down and found the shabbily dressed stranger waiting for her. Without saying a word he handed her a roll of bills. When she asked what they were for he replied, 'That's the sixty bucks you have coming. Don't Despair paid 5-to-1.'

The Fat Bears of Arkansaw

"The season for bear hunting, stranger," said the man of Arkansaw, "is generally all the year round, and the hunts take place about as reg-

From *Best Sports Stories of 1945,* edited by Irving T. Marsh and Edward Ehre, p. 149. Copyright, 1946, by E. P. Dutton and Company, Inc. New York.

From "The Big Bear of Arkansas" by T[homas] B[angs Thorpe], in *The Hive of "the Bee Hunter,"* pp. 79–80. New York: D. Appleton & Company. 1854. Originally published in *The Spirit of the Times,* Vol. XI, pp. 43–44 (March 27, 1841); reprinted in *The Big Bear of Arkansas and Other Sketches, Illustrative of Characters and Incidents in the South and South-west,* edited by William T. Porter, pp. 13–31. Philadelphia: Carey & Hart, 1845.

ular. I read in history that varmints have their fat season, and their lean season. That is not the case in Arkansaw, feeding as they do upon the *spontenacious* productions of the sile, they have one continued fat season the year round; though in winter things in this way is rather more greasy than in summer, I must admit. For that reason bear with us run in warm weather, but in winter they only waddle.

"Fat, fat! it's an enemy to speed; it tames every thing that has plenty of it. I have seen wild turkeys, from its influence, as gentle as chickens. Run a bear in this fat condition, and the way it improves the critter for eating is amazing; it sort of mixes the ile up with the meat, until you can't tell t'other from which. I've done this often.

"I recollect one perty morning in particular, of putting an old he fellow on the stretch, and considering the weight he carried, he run well. But the dogs soon tired him down, and when I came up with him wasn't he in a beautiful sweat—I might say fever; and then to see his tongue sticking out of his mouth a feet, and his sides sinking and opening like a bellows, and his cheeks so fat that he couldn't look cross. In this fix I blazed at him, and pitch me naked into a briar patch, if the steam didn't come out of the bullet-hole ten foot in a straight line. The fellow, I reckon, was made on the high-pressure system, and the lead sort of bust his biler."

"That column of steam was rather curious, or else the bear must have been very *warm*," observed the foreigner with a laugh.

"Stranger, as you observe, that bear was WARM, and the blowing off of the steam show'd it, and also how hard the varmint had been run. I have no doubt if he had kept on two miles farther his insides would have been stewed; and I expect to meet with a varmint yet of extra bottom, that will run himself into a skinfull of bear's grease: it is possible; much onlikelier things have happened."

How to Shoot Quail

An English sportsman came to West Texas to shoot blue quail. He induced a cowboy to go along with him as a guide. On a mountainside they located a large covey. The birds began running for the valley below, as they are prone to do, keeping just out of range.

The cowboy leveled his gun and began running after them.

The Englishman was astonished. "My dear fellow," he said, "surely you are not going to shoot the birds running, are you?"

"No," said the cowboy. "I'm not going to shoot 'em running. But if they ever stop I'll give 'em hell."

From *Folk Laughter on the American Frontier,* by Mody C. Boatright, pp. 102–3. New York: The Macmillan Company. 1949.

He Wouldn't Waste His Powder

A southern Colonel went deer hunting and took with him a Negro man who had served the family faithfully and loyally for many years. The Colonel thought Mose would be pleased to have an opportunity to kill a deer.

So on the first day of their hunt, having located a deer run, the white man gave Mose a rifle and told him to remain very still behind a bush. He would circle around and try to drive a buck by him.

The Colonel then made a wide semicircular approach to a clump of trees at the head of a ravine, where he threw some rocks into the brush and frightened out a large buck. The deer, running at terrific speed, leaping boulders and brush, took the path the hunter had anticipated, and passed within a few yards of Mose, who, because of a severe attack of buck ague, was unable to draw a bead.

The Colonel returned somewhat nettled.

"Mose," he said, "I drove that buck right by you. Why didn't you shoot?"

Mose stammered a moment and said: "I'll tell you, Colonel. It was like this. I didn't see no use wastin' no powder and lead on dat buck. The way he was a-comin' I jest thought I'd leave him alone and he'd kill hisself."

VII. FORTY ACRES AND A GOVERNMENT MULE
(Farm and Country Life Topics)

Introduction

Machinery has changed not only the methods of farming but the farmer himself. The modern farmer often drives the same model car, wears the same suits, and watches the same television programs as his city neighbor. But farmers of a generation or more ago were much more isolated and hence much more unlike city men. Having milked the same cows and slopped the same pigs night and morning for months, having repaired the same fences year after year, and having looked at the same end of the same pair of mules for days on end, the old-time

---

From *Folk Laughter on the American Frontier*, by Mody C. Boatright, p. 104. New York: The Macmillan Company, 1949.

farmer was accustomed to monotony and silence. To such a man conversations in anything other than monosyllables were garrulous. His silence may have been accentuated by the strangeness of the city environment, but even in the country he was a man of few words. He needed practice, of course, for mules are notoriously poor conversationalists.

Usually, however, the old-time farmer, although out of place in the city and in many ways a laughable figure, was laughed with rather than laughed at. He was the man with horse-sense, with a down-to-earth judgment which made him a symbol of the good citizen. Whether part fact or pure fiction—whether a Jack Downing, a Davy Crockett, a Nimrod Wildfire, or a Will Rogers,—he was the man who was never stampeded by some new-fangled idea, who always reduced the problem to simple terms.

But life in the country also had, and still has, its pleasures. There are baseball games, dances, barbecues, school programs, corn shuckings, and other social events. And to many farmers the most enjoyable hours are those spent with their fellows in the country store or on the steps of the county courthouse, swapping stories and exaggerations about poor land and dry years, rich land and big crops.

Nobottom Swamp

Wildfire. The soil—oh, the soil's so rich you may travel under it.

Mrs. Wollope. Travel under ground, sir? . . .

Wildfire. Yes, Madam, particularly after the spring rains. Look you here now, tother day, I was a horseback paddling away pretty comfortably through Nobottom swamp, when suddenly—I wish I may be curry-comb'd to death by 50,000 tom cats, if I didn't see a white hat getting along in mighty considerable style all alone by itself on the top of the mud—so up I rid, and being a bit jubus, I lifted it with the butt end of my whip when a feller sung out from under it, Hallo, stranger, who told you to knock my hat off? Why, says I, what sort of sample of a white man are you? What's come of the rest of you? Oh, says he, I'm not far off—only in the next county. I'm doing beautifully —got one of the best horses under me that ever burrowed—claws like a mole—no stop in him—but there's a waggon and horses right under me in a mighty bad fix, I reckon, for I heard the driver say a spell ago one of the team was getting a leetel tired.

Mrs. Wollope. What a geological novelty.

Wildfire. So, says I, you must be a pretty considerable feller on your own, but you had better keep you mouth shut or you'll get your teeth

From *The Lion of the West*, retitled *The Kentuckian, or A Trip to New York, A Farce in Two Acts*, by James Kirke Paulding, revised by John Augustus Stone and William Bayle Bernard, edited by James N. Tidwell, pp. 35–36. Copyright, 1954, by the Board of Trustees of the Leland Stanford Junior University. Stanford, California: Stanford University Press.

sunburnt. So, says I, good bye, stranger. I wish you a pleasant ride, but I prognosticate afore you get through the next sandbank you'll burst you biler.

Dry Rain

An El Pasoan, an Amarillan, and a Beaumontian met at the State Fair, the story goes.

"How do you like living in El Paso, John?" said Beaumont. "I understand it gets mighty hot out there."

"Yeah," replied the El Pasoan. "The thermometer goes to 110 in the shade and there isn't much shade. We have our thermometers made with rubber bulbs so's they won't blow off the top. It sure does get hot; but then it's a *dry* heat, and we don't mind it."

"Bill, I've heard Amarillo gets pretty cold in the winter," persisted Beaumont.

"Well," admitted the Amarillan, "there's nothing between us and the North Pole but some barb-wire fences with the gates open. So what would you expect but cold when one of them Dakota blizzards gets going good? It gets so cold sometimes that a poor cow will freeze standing up and not fall down till the thaw. But you see our cold is a *dry sort* of cold, and we enjoy it."

"By the way, I understand you have quite a lot of rain at Beaumont," said El Paso. "We don't have to put up with more'n ten or fifteen inches a year out our way. More sunshine days than Yuma!"

Beaumont did not hesitate. "Sure we have rain—fifty—sixty inches a year. Furnishes fine muskrat range and irrigates our rice. Plenty of rain at Beaumont, yes sirree. But it's a kind of ·*dry rain,* and it doesn't bother us a-tall!"

Rotating Soils

It was reported that dust had been found in the vault at the bank, that a banana crate used as a wastepaper basket by the local editor was full and running over with dust. One man claimed that gravel had come through his windowpane and wakened him during the night. Another, finding his car stalled by the grit in the engine, opened the door and shot ground squirrels overhead which were tunneling upward for air! A local paper reported finding gold nuggets in

From *East Texas,* Its History and Its Makers, by Dabney White and T. C. Richardson, Vol. I, pp. 46–47. Copyright, 1940, by Lewis Historical Publishing Company. New York.

From *Short Grass Country,* by Stanley Vestal, pp. 205–206, 208. *American Folkways,* edited by Erskine Caldwell. Copyright, 1941, by Stanley Vestal. New York: Duell, Sloan & Pearce.

the street which had been blown from the mines in New Mexico. The county farm agent advised his clients that it would be unnecessary to rotate crops in the future, since the wind was rotating soils. One of the natives proposed a test for wind velocity: "Fasten one end of a logchain to the top of a fence-post. If the wind does not blow the chain straight out from the post, the breeze is moderate. You have a calm day."

Allergy in its various forms became so common that, it was said, even the snakes had learned to sneeze; in the night you could tell when a duster was coming by the sneezing of the rattlesnakes on the prairie. Everyone jestingly referred to a dust storm as an "Oklahoma rain." A man caught some huge bullfrogs, so he said, and put them in his watertank to multiply; but, he said, the poor things all drowned immediately. It hadn't rained for so long that they had never had a chance to learn to swim.

A housewife claimed that she scoured her pans by holding them up to a keyhole. The sand coming through in a stream polished them better than she could by the usual method. One old lady, on hearing a man compare the climate to that of hell, put her chin up and declared that if the good Lord sent *her* to hell, he'd have to give her a constitution to stand it.

They laughed about the Black Snow which covered their fields. One farmer said he was going to leave Texas and move to Kansas to pay taxes—"There's where my farm is now."

Another said he could not keep up with his farm, which had taken a trip north. "But next week she'll be back," he said. "I can plow then."

One leather-faced dry farmer said, "I hope it'll rain before the kids grow up. They ain't never seen none." . . .

Those who left the Plains generally did so unwillingly, and, in the midst of their disaster, with a joke on their lips: "Well, the wind blew the dirt away. But we haven't lost everything. We still got the mortgage!"

That Soil Was Too Rich

Early in the forenoon Dr. Binninger, Tom Fenton, Jim Hart, the retired miner, and Fraser, the Canadian, came up and began inspecting the crops.

"Oh, this is very well; very well, indeed, for Jersey," said Dr. Binninger, at last, as they sat on the fence by the cornfield, after their labors, smoking; "but nothing to what I have seen. In Gastley County, Missouri, I once saw the corn growing to such an unprecedented height, and the stalks so exceptionally vigorous, that nearly every

From *The Book of Lies*, by John Langdon Heaton, pp. 143–146. Copyright, 1896, by John Langdon Heaton. New York: The Morse Company.

farmer stacked up, for winter firewood, great heaps of cornstalks, cut up into cord-wood length by power saws run by the threshing engines. One man, Barney Gregory, took advantage of the season to win a fortune by preparing cornstalks for use as telegraph poles. . . ."

"What is one man's meat is another man's poison," said Fenton. "Fine growing weather, similar to that which made Gregory's fortune in Missouri, has come near ruining those of the Western Nebraska farmers who raised pumpkins. Just as, by all ordinary rules, the crop should have been ready to house, a mysterious rot began to destroy the great green globes glowing to yellow in the sun. An examination by the chemists of the State Agricultural College, showed that the trouble was due to the too rapid growth of the vines, which dragged the pumpkins about after them, all over the fields, until the pumpkins' lower cuticle, being worn out by the abrasion, they succumbed easily to rot in the bruised portion. Should another such year come, the farmers will avoid a like catastrophe by providing each pumpkin with a straw-lined nest, or a little truck with casters.

"A good illustration of nature's bounty happened some time ago in Doniphan County, Kansas," continued Fenton. "A seven-year-old daughter of James Steele was sent, in the middle of the forenoon, to carry a jug of switchel to the men, who were at work near the middle of one of those vast Kansas cornfields. The corn was about up to little Annie's shoulders as she started, but as she went along it rose and rose before her eyes, shooting out of the soil under the magic influence of the sun and the abundant moisture. Almost crazed with fear, she hastened on, but before she could reach the men, the stalks were waving above her head. The men were threatened in a like manner, but by mounting a little fellow on a big man's shoulders, to act as a lookout, they managed to get out, when they promptly borrowed a dog, to follow little Annie's trail. It was not until late in the afternoon that they reached her, where she lay, having cried herself to sleep, with the tear-stains streaking her plump cheeks."

"The soil of some of the Southern California counties is so rich as to become an actual detriment to the farmer," observed Eckels. "In San Bernardino County, a farmer, named Jones, has been forced entirely to abandon the culture of corn, because the stalks, under the influence of the genial sun, mild air, and mellow soil, shoot up into the air so fast that they draw their roots after them; when, of course, the plant dies as a rule. Cases have been known, however, where cornstalks thus uprooted, and lifted into the air, have survived for some time upon the climate alone."

"Why," said Dr. Binninger, "we used to have the same trouble in Kentucky, but it was solved long ago by burying a heavy stone under each cornstalk, and wiring the stalk down to it. I have known the price of stone to treble in one season in consequence of the purely agricultural demand."

Dat Land Wasn't So Rich

"Yeah," said Sack Daddy, "you sho is tellin' de truth 'bout dat big old mosquito, 'cause my old man bought dat same piece of land and raised a crop of pumpkins on it and lemme tell y'all right now—mosquito dust is de finest fertilizer in de world. Dat land was so rich and we raised pumpkins so big dat we et five miles up in one of 'em and five miles down and ten miles acrost one and we ain't never found out how far it went. But my old man was buildin' a scaffold inside so we could cut de pumpkin meat without so much trouble, when he dropped his hammer. He tole me, he says, 'Son, Ah done dropped my hammer. Go git it for me.' Well, Ah went down in de pumpkin and begin to hunt dat hammer. Ah was foolin' 'round in there all day when I met a man and he ast me what Ah was lookin' for. Ah tole him my ole man had done dropped his hammer and sent me to find it for him. De man tole me Ah might as well give it up for a lost cause, he had been lookin' for a double mule-team and a wagon that had got lost in there for three weeks and he hadn't found no trace of 'em yet. So Ah stepped on a pin, de pin bent and dat's de way de story went."

"Dat was rich land but my ole man had some rich land too," put in Will House. "My old man planted cucumbers and he went along droppin' de seeds and befo' he could git out de way he'd have ripe cucumbers in his pockets. What is the richest land you ever seen?"

"Well," replied Joe Wiley, "my ole man had some land dat was so rich dat our mule died and we buried him down in our bottom-land and de next mornin' he had done sprouted li'l jackasses."

"Aw, dat land wasn't so rich," objected Ulmer. "My old man had some land and it was so rich dat he drove a stob [1] in de ground at de end of a corn-row for a landmark and next morning there was ten ears of corn on de corn stalk and four ears growin' on de stob."

"Dat lan' y'all talkin' 'bout might do, if you give it plenty commercial-nal [2] but my old man wouldn't farm no po' land like dat," said Joe Wiley. "Now one year we was kinda late puttin' in our crops. Everybody else had corn a foot high when papa said, 'Well, chillun, Ah reckon we better plant some corn.' So I was droppin' and my brother was hillin' up behind me. We had done planted 'bout a dozen rows when Ah looked back and seen de corn comin' up. Ah didn't want it to grow too fast 'cause it would make all fodder and no roastin' ears so Ah hollered to my brother to sit down on some of it

From *Mules and Men*, by Zora Neale Hurston, pp. 135–136. Copyright, 1935, by Zora Neale Hurston. Philadelphia and London: J. B. Lippincott Company.

[1] Stake.—Z.N.H.
[2] Commercial fertilizer.—Z.N.H.

to stunt de growth. So he did, and de next day he dropped me back a note—says: 'passed thru Heben yesterday at twelve o'clock sellin' roastin' ears to de angels.' "

Small Potatoes

In the Snake River Valley lives an old-timer who is known as Old Jim. Old Jim comes to town now and then and boasts of the fertility of his land, but complains that he is unable to market the stuff. He grew pumpkins, but they were so large he could not get them on to a wagon, and then ventured into potatoes. When, two years ago, a CCC camp was established nearby, Old Jim was approached by a man who wanted to buy a hundred pounds of spuds. "Only a hundred pounds?" he asked, scratching his pate. "No, I can't do it. I wouldn't cut a spud in two for no one."

Weather or Not

When he had got all his calcerlations figgered down to his satisfaction he says, "I've got it this pop shore."

"Well, what is it?" says I.

"High thermometer, low barometer, and a warm wave for the Gulf States durin' the next forty-eight hours."

"And for Texas too?" says I.

"Yes, for Texas too," says he. "And I hope it will be hot enough to scorch hell out of it from the Sabine to the Rio Grande." (And from that you may know the medicin was workin' splendid.)

"Now," says he, "I reckon I kin made a satisfactory report to the Bureau at Washington."

And he tuck his cheer to a table and begun scribblin' as hard as he could. I sot patiently waitin' to hear what he had to say to the Bureau for more'n an hour, but still he kept on writin'. At last when I was tired of waitin' for him to git through, I hearn a door go slam! and then the shutters went bang! and the house shivered from top to

From *Idaho Lore*, prepared by the Federal Writers' Project of the Work Projects Administration, Vardis Fisher, State Director, American Guide Series, p. 139. Copyright, 1939, by George H. Curtis, Secretary of State for the State of Idaho. Caldwell, Idaho: The Caxton Printers, Ltd.

From "Old Prob's Visit to Texas," by John C. Duval, a story with a forenote by J. Frank Dobie, *Southwest Review*, Vol. XXIV, No. 3 (April, 1939), pp. 295–297. Copyright, 1939, by the *Southwest Review*. Dallas.

The story of Old "Prob"—short for Probability—seems to have had a particular fascination for Duval (1816–1897). He wrote it at least twice in divergent ways. The version here given is from the manuscript possessed by Mrs. John Maddox of Austin. J.F.D.

bottom. I stepped to the door and looked out, though I knowed well enough what was the matter.

"What's the row now?" says Old Prob,[1] layin' down his pen and lookin' oneasy-like toward me. For by this time, you see, he was gettin' mity suspicious of Texas weather.

"Oh, it's nothin'," says I, "but a reg'lar ole blue norther comin' butt-end foremost."

Ole Prob jumped up from his cheer like a stingin' lizard had popped his behind.

"Git my horse right off," says he, screwin' his azermuth past the last notch and wrenchin' the left limb clean off. "Git my horse at once," says he, "and I'll quit this confounded Texas of yourn as soon as I kin git on top of him. And if the Bureau at Washington," says he, "don't knock Texas out 'n my beat, I'll resign," says he, "as shore as shootin'."

I tried my best to get him to hold on till the norther had blowed out, tellin' him it was impossible to travel agin' it, but he wouldn't listen to me. (You see, the medicin was just gittin' down to its work.)

"I don't care a durn," says he, "if it's rainin' cats and dogs and hailin' millstones—git my horse quick," says he, "for I won't stay in sich a country another minit."

Findin' I had give Old Prob ruther an overdost of the medicin, and that he was bent on goin', I went to the stable, saddled up old Whitey and hitched him under the lee of the house out'n the wind. Then I helped Ole Prob tie all his contraptions to his saddle (except the left limb of his azermuth, which was layin' on the floor where he had throwed it in his tantrum).

When he had mounted ole Whitey and was ready to start, I says to him, "Well," says I, "if you will go, there's one little favor I would like to ask of you afore you leave."

"What's that?' says he.

"Well," says I, "off-hand like, what sort of weather are we goin' to have for the next forty-eight hours?"

Ole Prob laughed—he couldn't help it.

"Well," says he, lookin' up at the sky and then around at the mottes of timber scattered over the perera, "off-hand like, my perdiction is high thermometer, low barometer, and warm and pleasant in the Gulf States for the next forty-eight hours."

"And for Texas?" says I.

"No," says he, "for Texas it will be as hot as Hades, er cold as flugens, as wet as a drowned rat, er as dry as a dried apple, jest whichever it damn pleases."

And saying this, he sot his spurs inter ole Whitey's flanks, and the

---

[1] "Old Prob"—that is, Old Probabilities. "Weather columns in nineteenth century American newspapers often bore the heading: "Old Probabilities Says—" J.C.D.

last thing I seed of Ole Prob, he was weathern' a pint of post oak timber in the direction of Washington with his coat-tails stickin' out straight behind and his long nose splittin' as cold a norther as ever blowed over the pereras of Texas.

A Legend of Country Baseball

After I left the Giants in '24, crops down here wasn't so good, so for a couple of summers I got together a nine called the Gray Travelers, and we went around playing the country and town teams with us always as the visiting club. They was good money in it—if you win. Mostly we played winner-take-all, with a side bet I seen run as high as nine-ten hunnert dollars. Crops was bad, but they was lots of money loose in them days and people had real pride and dug deep for their local nines.

All through this country—not only here in Arkansas, but in Missouri, Kansas and Oklahomy—they was sending up some great young ball players. Fellers like Bill Dickey, Arky Vaughan, the Waner boys, Glenn Wright, the Deans, Schoolboy Rowe. Purt near every town and pea patch had three-four young fellers so good they made the rest of their club look real solid.

Traveling, batting agin home town empires, playing on diamonds that was mostly on the sides of mountings, we had a lot of strikes on us. The crowds was no pleasure. They wasn't above flashing mirrors in your eyes or flinging them giant firecrackers under your feet or running you lickety-split out of town if you done a little hard sliding into their favor-ites.

So my nine had to be a whole lot better. The first year we win about seven out of every ten games, and when I totted up the season's figgers, we done jist a little better than even. Then the second year I got ol' Heinie Aunfeldt who use to catch for the Cubs, Cornbread Jones who had been up too, three real good young infielders, and a big farmer from Pea Ridge who was good enough finally to go up to Brooklyn. Day, this Pea Ridge feller was named. You recollect him. I heerd he always gave a hog call in Ebbets Field when he was slated to pitch and scared them Dodger fans most to death. My legs was too fur gone to play the outfield, so I took over third base.

They's things you do in the big leagues, natcher'ly, that's way past town ball, and up there they expect you to do things a certain way. That's why they's called the big leagues, I reckon. But after being up twelve years, I had to re-learn myself some ol' town ball tricks with my Travelers. I had to learn Pea Ridge to pull his cap right down over the bridge of his nose so the home-town rooters can't blind him

From *The Spitter*. A Legend of Country Baseball, by Paul Fisher, pp. 6–29. Copyright, 1950, by Paul Fisher. Privately Printed.

with mirrors. I had to learn my outfielders how to run down the side of the mountings spraddle-legged to take low liners. Me and ole Heine and the first baseman got to learn ourselves how to climb like mounting goats up on the hoods of the autos parked all along the field to catch them foul balls. In fact, by '26, I done away with spiked shoes. We played in tennis slippers. You could climb up on Fords and Dorts and Chevvies purty good in spikes, but for Marmons and Hupmobiles and Franklins in them days, tennis slippers was best.

Anyways, by the time July rolled around in my second year with the Travelers, we was going real good. We was up through Missouri and over through Kansas and we got clear down into Oklahomy before we lost a game. We was way ahead financially. We win twenty-three before we lost that game in Oklahomy. Pea Ridge Day had pitched most every other day, so we took two weeks off, and decided for me to work up a schedule in Arkansas where things was a-booming.

When I got back home here, all the people in the hills was talking about a nine over at Simmons Run, not too fur from the Oklahomy line. They was putting a railroad through there, and some oil had been sighted, so they was a kinda boom on. Folks said this Simmons Run nine was made up entirely of local fellers except for pitchers. They brung in pitchers from outside, most of the time one of three left-handed Indians which had made life so mizzible for us Travelers in '25. They was three Indians in three separate hearses, two black and one pearl gray. . . .

You never *heerd* of them three left-handed Indians?

No, they wasn't dead Indians. I shore wished many a time that they was. They owned them hearses personally. They was three things them three Indians liked to do that I knowed of. They liked to drive them hearses. They liked to carry their whole famblies and most of their tribe everywhere in the hearses with 'em. And they shore liked to pitch. I expect the thing they liked to do most was sit back in the hearse with a little mounting water, because when they pitched agin you, they made return trips to the closed end of the hearse. They would go back in them hearses in the third, fifth, sixth, seventh, eighth and ninth innings, and a thing I allus noticed was that all three, after the sixth inning, pitched with one eye closed, sump'n a man only does when he's shooting a fararm or drinking stimulates.

The folks said this Simmons Run nine had got both Little Rock and Fort Smith's perfessional teams to come up fur games and beat 'em both. I was told that the Indian in the gray hearse, Willie Wild-flower his name was, the one who allus wore the miller's cap and the striped overhalls when he pitched, had shut both of 'em out. I knowed these Indians had oil wells over by Miami, Oklahomy, so I got in my car and went over there.

They was home all right. I seen a million Indian wimmern and young uns out in the backyards of the three big stone houses the three left-handed Indians had built, but I was real formal and went to the door of the middle house. It had a pure big silver knocker and I purt near tore that door off, knocking. Nobody answered. Finally I went around to the back, and down in a grove, maybe fifty yards away, there was the three hearses and the three Indian wrongarms. They had put up tents in the grove of trees. They wasn't living in them big stone houses at all. They had jist built them houses fur show.

They knowed me all right. We talked about how good they was the year before and they says they was even better this year. Then I done a thing that wasn't real ethical. I says I heerd the big distilleries up at Peory, Illinois, was hiring left-handed pitchers, paying regular money and a bonus of gov'ment spirits for every win. I says it was a real fast league, but having seen the three of 'em pitch, I figgered they could win. Jist by chance I had a road map and if they wanted I'd be glad to pencil out the best route. I never seen three more excited Indians. They didn't give a dang about salaries, but that bonus shore whetted 'em. Even before I walked back up to my car, they was slinging their wimmern and kids in the hearses, the hulabaloo was deaf'-ning, and I knowed they was off, fur three weeks or a month, any-ways.

So I clumb in my auto and drove lickety-split over to Simmons Run. The town barber was running the Simmons Run nine—funny how often in country ball you find a barber who thinks he's a Connie Mack, John McGraw, and Colonel Ruppert all rolled into one. Be-fore we talked two minutes, I seen he thought they was going to really clean our plow. So I ast him about the very next Sunday and he says they'd have to cancel out on the Watts, Oklahomy, club, but if they did, they would have to have a tolable big side bet. I says we might scrape up five hunnert, but, no, he figgers that was purty small. Twelve hunnert dollars, he says, and winner take all the gate. He near choked on that figger, so I knowed it was the biggest bet in the history of Simmons Run.

"I reckon you'll pitch the Indians?" I says to him.

"I reckon we will," he says, real chipper. "And to win, we'll rotate 'em, three innings a-piece, if we think it need be. But it won't. You fellers never beat 'em onct last year."

"They're mighty good," I says. "But it's worth a try. You figger to have much of a gate with this little notice?"

"We shore do," he says. "This is the Sunday we plan to unveil our nine in the new sateen uniforms we bought 'em fur beating Fort Smith and Little Rock. Folks have heerd so much about the nine and now about these sateen uniforms that they's coming all the way from Siloam Springs and Gravette and Fayetteville, jist to see us."

"Well," I says, "we'll be in Sunday morning, and I'll meet you here with the twelve hunnert. We know a good base empire—"

"Don't you worry about empires," he says. "Home club furnishes the empires. We allus use one on the bases, too; we wasn't born yestidday."

I lost there, but still and all, I feels purty keen. I never knowed a lefthander to leave a forrarding address, and I was purty certain left-handed Indians was no exception. But keen as I feels then, I feels keener Sunday morning as young Pea Ridge Day and me was driving toward Simmons Run. Thirty miles away, even early in the morning, the road was lined with buckboards and buggies and even ol' hayricks, with people hanging on from every which side. And I never seen so many autos out in Arkansas in my life. The traffic was all one-way to Simmons Run.

It's peculiar thing about this here hill country. You can stand up on a mounting and look fur miles and maybe you won't see more'n three-four houses. Country seems real empty. But have a fox hunt or a square dance or a fight or a ball game where the home nine is going to play some perfessionals like Cornbread and ole Heinie and I used to be, and the folks just seem to spring from the hills and the hollers. They come pouring out of every cranny, packing their young uns and their wimmern folks and follered by their hounds. Every auto and every buggy has a market basket filled plumb up with cold-fried chicken and smoked ham and 'tater salad and picca-lilli, and they's stone jugs full of spring-cold buttermilk or sweet cider, and all the folks is grinning and real neighbor-like, willing to feed you till you bust. They's quick to fight, but down deep, these here folks is as good a friends as you'll find.

I drapped young Pea Ridge at the railroad commissary where our nine was dressing and picked up five hunnert dollars from both ole Heinie and Cornbread to fill out the bet. Then I went to the barber shop. Simmons Run is only two roads intersecting, you might say, but I was about tuckered out fighting my way through the crowd. They was firecrackers going off right and left and hounds baying and dozens of young uns already lost and howling fur their folks. The barber had pervailed on Judge Damon to hold the stakes. We counted out the money and when I seen we wasn't being short-changed none, I says to the barber,

"You starting Dryshell or Willie Wildflower?"

"Here at Simmons Run," he says, swelling up and looking real smart-alecky, "we make it a practice never to reveal our plans. Aint that right, judge?"

The judge looked sour at such high-falutin' manners, but he didn't say nothing.

"Fact is," says the barber, "we may start John Bearpaw."

"Well," I says, "I didn't see their hearses. Most usually them Indians get right in the middle of all the firecracker shooting."

"Don't let it worry you none at all," this here barber says, and he winks knowing like at Judge Damon. "Whoever we pitch will purely dazzle you fellers. And we'll dazzle you some more when you see our brand new uniforms. Slickest in three states."

Going back to the commissary to get in my own monkey suit, I seen quite a few fellers I knowed personal and ast if they had seen the three Indians or even the three hearses. Nobody had. I reckon I was like every feller that's laid out a slick plan. I feared I'd missed some place. But purty soon I got to listening to our shortstop, Tommy Ringle, who says he's seen this Simmons Run nine a couple of times and played agin 'em onct. He was briefing Pea Ridge on how to pitch to 'em.

Tommy says they can hit but he figgers Pea Ridge is too fast for 'em —they won't get around quick enough theirselves to pull the ball fur distance. They's one exception, Tommy says—the catcher.

"He's bigger'n a horse and jist as strong," Tommy says. "His name's Ory. He's got the stutters, but it shore don't hurt his hitting none. I aint never seen a man who could hit a ball so fur. He hits 'em off his ears and off his shoe tops. You'll jist have to figger him out yourselves."

"Them kind," says ole Heinie, who's lacing up his tennis slippers, "sometimes can't hit a change-up. We'll tippy up a couple to him, Pea Ridge, and see how he likes the slow stuff."

We was the first nine on the diamond. Ball fields down here is a lot more uniform than in the big leagues, if that surprises you. They's no place with enough level ground fur a complete field, so they mostly set on the side of the mounting with home plate at the foot and the infield sloping upwards. I never seen a diamond in all these hills with home plate at the top of the mounting. Onct I figgered out why. These boys hit fur distance in these here hills, and if they was swinging down hill, it would take a mint to keep 'em in baseballs. They's another advantage. The autos and buggies and wagons can park along the foul lines, and being as one is parked a little higher than the other, right on out to the top of the mounting, it makes seeing easier fur all concerned.

I never seen a crowd in Arkansas like they had there that day at Simmons Run. The furthest auto on the left field line looked like a speck. A stand had been built back of home plate to seat eight-nine hunnert, but they musta been a full thousand packed on the seats. The Simmons Run nine was charging admission fur everything except hounds and suckling young, fifty cents each fur the grownups and a quarter fur the walking young. The gate come to eighteen hunnert and ten dollars. So I figger a good five thousand had paid to get in.

We was warming up along the third base line when I seen everybody craning their necks looking into the crowd back of first. My heart shore sunk then. Usually that's where the three lefthanded Indians pulled up in their hearses and slid open the back doors fur a million Indians to fly out, most of 'em carrying greenbacks in big wads to buy sarsparilly and popcorn and hot dogs. But it turned out diff'runt. Thirty-forty

Simmons Run folks was clearing a path through the crowd. Purty soon they had a big hole. A covered wagon was backed up to the hole, and all at once someone inside the wagon slung up the canvas and out jumped the Simmons Run nine, one after the other, and come running out into the middle of the field.

I never heerd sich a roar, not even at the Polo Grounds when the Babe hit one agin us in the '21 series. The noise jist growed and growed. Man, they was never a sight or sound like it in the history of baseball. They had stole a leaf from them big football colleges like Illinois U. and Michigan U. and Pennsylvania U. One by one they'd drap out of the covered wagon and run all alone over to the pitcher's mound where they squatted in a perfect line.

It was stupendjous. The folks was standing up shouting, the hounds was baying and the young uns, scared by all the hulabaloo, was screaming. Firecrackers was going off every which way, and every horn in every auto was sounding. It wasn't that they was jist the undefeated Simmons Run nine. It wasn't that they was jist local boys who wasn't afeerd to cross bats with any club, amateur or perfessional. Mostly it was them new uniforms the barber had bragged up.

They was sateen, jist as he said, and while I never seen sateen ball suits before, that didn't stun me near so much as the color. They was purely black. When the sun struck that black sateen, it purt near blinded you. I seen ball suits with lots of red and lots of green and lots of yaller, and onct when I was with Telsy on my way up to the big leagues, we had powder blue road uniforms till the fans near hooted us out of the league. But fur a real eye-catching ball suit, them black sateen outfits the Simmons Run nine had beat anything I ever hope to lay eyes on.

They was country boys so they couldn't hold on to the pose in the center of the field long. As they begun to go back to the first base line, I seen one more player crawling out of that covered wagon. He was in a gray road suit, well made, too, and when he turned around, he made two quick tugs at his cap brim and then quick wets his right finger tips with his tongue. Fur me, that was as much as if he had wrote his name. I knowed him before he follered up by tugging twice at his belt.

Yes, sir, you're right, it was ol' Tug Monahan. And onct he had got onto the field, he done jist like he allus did at Forbes Field in Pittsburgh—he begin lookin all 'round, counting the house.

In country and town ball, you're expected to do a little social visiting before a game so I went right over. Ol' Tug looked at me as if it had only been yestidday since I seen him, but least ways he shook hands.

"I thought you was still with the Pirates?" I says.

"I got waived out the same year you did," he says. "And you should know it."

"Where'd these fellers find you?" I says.

"You know and they know I live in K.C.," he says, "and that's where you can always find me."

"I reckon, Tug," I says, "that it's no fun pitching without your spitter—" but I didn't get in a word more.

"They outlawed the spitter only in organized ball," he says. "This is a hell of a long ways from organized ball."

"These are jist kids, Tug," I says, "and they might walk right into that spitter."

"Some kids, Muley," Tug says. "Ole Heinie must have grandsons up there, and Cornbread Jones and you both broke in before I did."

Right about then I had a feeling I was standing in the shade. I was, too. The big Simmons Run catcher, Ory he was called, has moseyed up and he was standing on the sunny side of me. He was six foot six-seven inches and built to fit. I never seen a uniform fit a man so snug. But the thing I seen about his uniform that struck me as strange was his sweat shirt. Most wrist bands on sweat shirts don't have a long bunch of ridges running from half-way up to the elbow, but his did. Then it come to me that was no sweat shirt he had on—that was the top part of long underwear sich as they was selling down in these hills fur several years. And when I looked down at his legs, I seen the legs of his long drawers had been folded under his baseball stockings. Glancing here and there, I noticed all the Simmons Run nine was wearing long underwear, and I reckoned the answer was that never having had sweat shirts, and seeing pitchers of full baseball outfits, they had reasoned that even in the big leagues, the players wore long underwear right through the heat of the summer.

I must have missed some of the talk between Ory and Tug, because when I come to, Tug was saying,

"Speak up, man, I won't bite you."

"I-I-I-I fou-fou-fou-fought we sh-sh-should t-t-talk over the s-s-s-s-signals," Ory says. You see, he stuttered some.

"Signals?" Tug says. "What signals?"

"He means your signs," I says. "This here is your catcher, Tug."

Ory laid a hand on my shoulder and I purt near was pushed through the ground.

"I-I-I'll d-do my own t-t-t-talking," he says to me. "I-I-I'm b-big enough to s--sp-speak my own m-m-mind."

"You shore are," I says and I wandered over by the water keg at the end of the Simmons Run bench. I aint planning to listen in, but you couldn't help yourself, what with that high squeaky voice of Ory and that deep cellar voice of ol' Tug.

Well, it was a long conversation without much said for several minutes. I heerd Tug say he'd sign for pitchouts, and then I missed a few lines and purty soon both their voices rose up stronger than ever.

"You mean," Tug says real loud, "that you won't catch a spitter?"

"N-n-n-no, sir-e-ee," Ory screams, and hurls his little two-bit kid's catching glove on the ground. "A s-s-s-spitter t-t-takes off every wh-wh-which way. A-a-and th-there's g-g-g-germs on sp-s-spit."

"What?" Tug hollers.

"G-g-g-germs," screams Ory. "S-s-s-spit is un-un-un-s-s-unsanitary."

"Gaddlemighty," Tug hollers. "You afraid of a little old germ? Don't you know my spitter is my best pitch?"

"C-c-can't help it," Ory says. "D-d-don't th-th-th-throw that g-g-g-gol-danged spitter."

"Listen, you big ape," Tug screams, "you know who's hitting agin us? Take a look. Muley hit in the five spot for McGraw for years. Cornbread Jones was as good a hitter as I ever hope to see in the big leagues. Ol' Aunfeldt won more games in the clutch for the Cubs than any hitter they had. You think I came 250 miles to have my ears pinned back?"

"I-I-I w-w-won't catch n-n-n-no sp-spitters," Ory says coldly.

Well, finally it ended up in a compromise, you might say. Tug would throw his spitter only if he got in a bad hole and only if Ory gave him the sign. They used the oldest set of signs in baseball, as it worked out. One finger was for Tug's fast ball, two for his hook, the fist for his change-up, and they decided that if Ory put down three fingers, that was for the spitter. I slaunched off about then, and went back to my bench.

Tug begin warming up, and he looked as loose and easy as he ever looked up there. But he aint what took my eye. This Ory was a ball player if I ever seen one. He drapped in a natural crouch on the first warmup toss, and you could see every muscle in his body as he set there on his toes. Fact is, so tight was his black sateen suit and his long drawers that I could count the four buttons on the trap door of the underdrawers—the buttons that hold up the flap. If you could forget the clo'es and the little toy mitt he wore, you'da swore he was the purtiest catcher you ever seen in all your born days.

And one thing I knowed. Watching him, I knowed simple as their signs was, we wasn't going to steal them signs. He was one of them natcheral catchers that hide their signing hand from everyone except the pitcher and even the pitcher's got to look sharp to see how many fingers are down for the called pitch.

Well, in a ways it was a dull game the first seven innings. But purty. Ol' Tug Monahan was pulling the ball up to his mouth purty near every pitch, faking saliver on it, but he never throwed a spitter onct. He was pitchin me and Cornbread low, half-speed hooks, and he kept his stuff high and tight on ole Heinie, so none of us was getting any wood on the ball. His control was perfect and he was sneaky fast. Pea Ridge was slinging his high hard one till it jist whistled. Except to this big Ory. First time Ory came up Pea Ridge slang two fast balls way wide, then jist ante-ed a soft one up, and Ory like to broke his back sending a little toy fly down to me near the third sack. He did it again

in the fifth and we went into the last of the eighth without either them
or us getting a man as fur as second, much less scoring.

The sun was bearing down, and when Ory come up with one out and
nobody on in the eighth, he was something to see. His black britches
was so soaked with sweat that they seem glued to him and every time
he took a practice swipe with his war club, the sweat jist flew all round
him. Pea Ridge throwed him a couple way wide, and then, like young
pitchers jist natcherally seem to do, he let one go right down the alley
but Ory jist stood there and watched her sail by for a strike.

Heinie came out from behind the plate and he was sore.

"You young fool," he shouts to Pea Ridge, "pitch like I tell you to.
No more of that."

So Pea Ridge wastes another, and I reckon he was smarter'n ol'
Heinie. He ra'red back and slang another right in the gut.

Ory swang and before I could even duck, the ball shot past my ear,
climbing fast. I turned and seen Cornbread beginning to spin to go
back on his ol' legs, but it was no use. That ball was still lifting when
it went over the mounting top. In all my born days, I never seen a ball
hit so fast or so fur. And as I turned back, I knowed without a piece of
stupendjous luck we're gone gooses.

Ory was half way between first and second when the real roar went
up from all that mob of hill folks. He was one of them big fellers that
run with all their arms and legs spraddled and their head down. All
he knowed was that he had hit one on the nose, the crowd was yelling
their lungs loose, and so he was putting on all his horses to run till
someone tole him to stop.

Right then I figgered out two of the things in a thinking way that
won that ball game.

I knowed if we could get Ory out of there, Simmons Run prolly didn't
have no one to hold Tug Monahan and maybe we could push a run or
two across. I knowed, too, that outside Ory, none of them is going to
hit Pea Ridge, if we play a week of Sundays. Sitting here now—jist as
I did seven-eight years ago when that womern baseball writer came to
write up my greatest day in baseball—I can recollect jist as clear how
my mind was churning and I was reaching for a solution to win by.

One thing I gave up immejiately as Ory rounded second. I knowed
I couldn't give him the hip as he swang around third. He'd a knocked
me stem-winding, and all of us woulda got rid out of Simmons Run on
a rail to boot. So to keep away from that devil idey, I begun backing
toward home plate, acting as if I was going to take a relay throw and
whip it home.

Ory swang round third and he was still going hell-bent with his head
down. So I eased over toward the line and when he was about twenty-
five feet from the plate and the panjemonium was so stupendjous I
couldn't hardly think, I drawed in all the air I could and hollered as
I never hollered before,

"SLIDE, ORY, SLIDE!"

He heerd me. He slud. He musta weighed 270-280 pounds and he was no Ty Cobb or Max Cary fur sliding grace. He flang hisse'f up in the air and came down square on his hine-end, with his feet up off the ground. A reg'lar explosion of dust blew in the air. He slud fifteen-twenty feet before he hit the plate and he slud right on for another ten feet. Before I got choked up on the dust, I smelled the burnt sateen he had skidded off from the friction, you might say, of all that meat hitting on that sun-baked ground.

I never expect to hear a crowd like that agin. They purely blowed that huge cloud of dust away, they made so much racket. You couldn't have made a-body hear you if you'da clumb right in their ear. It was that deaf'ning. And Ory was up to the occasion. He clumb to his feet after sitting there about two minutes. First he bowed to the thousand folks crammed into the stands back of home. Then he decided to dust hisse'f off with his cap and that took a couple of minutes. Presently he marched over to home plate and bows to all the folks stretched out along third base to the mounting top. After he figgered they should be satisfied, he executes a right-about face, and makes a big long bow to the folks stretched out along the right field line.

When he made the turn-about, I seen his backside fur the first time. I knowed then why people not only was cheering but was laughing fit to kill and nudging at each other's ribs and p'inting. Ory's whole hine-end was out. When he slud, he not only burned up the seat of them black sateen britches, but he created so much heat he burned the flap off his long drawers. One of the buttons was hanging by a thread, and the light brown piece of cloth—a kinda reinforcement they had on them models of underdrawers—was all that was left of the whole flap. An it was ready to break loose and fall down between his legs like a ribbon with the first strain he put on it.

You ever notice what happens when a man gits in a fix like Ory was in? Not only down here in this country—everywhere. Like the saying—not even their best friends will tell him. Ory figgered, I reckon, that the p'inting and the mixed laughing and cheering was for his homer. They was no breeze stirring to give him a idey of his raw state, and before he was done bowing, one of their men had made the last out and his own nine, pleased to be winning and maybe jist a little bit willing for Ory to look as much fool as hero, had tooken to the field.

Ory quit bowing long enough to put on his two-bit mask and his two-bit glove and get behind the plate. They was still so much noise you couldn't hear nothing. I was trying to far up our nine on the bench, but they couldn't hear me and most of 'em, anyways, was craning around, trying to get a glance at Ory's backside to see if the button still held up that brown ribbon.

With two out, Ringle worked Tug fur a free pass—the only one he given us that day. Ol' Cornbread laid into the first pitched and lined a hard single into left field. He hit a hook, I seen, which hung and I knowed Tug was tiring. Ol' Heinie come up and he didn't waste a second. He cracked one a mile a minute down the third base line. Their third sacker knocked it down deep behind third, but it was a hit and the bases was full and I was up.

I allus had a superstition about crossing to the plate in front of the catcher, specially with men on. I wasn't thinking about Ory's bare hiney but when I went around him, I seen that there last button had bit the dust and the brown reinforcement ribbon was flapping around between his legs with his action. Om'nous as things was for Simmons Run and noisy as the crowd was, people was making half the noise, jist enjoying Ory's delicate condition. Only he never knowed it.

The first pitch Tug throwed me was around my ankles and the Simmons Run empire called it a strike. Tug faked a spitter and come in with a curve ball that was way wide. He faked twice more and they was too wide even for the Simmons Run empire to call anything but balls. Then Tug put one in there, and run the count to three and two.

You recollect how Tug allus rested his left hand on his left knee and leaned way forrard to get his signs? Well, I was watching him like a hawk and I seen his whole face light up sudden-like. He scrooched forrard to take still another look and a kinda grin comes over his face and then he r'ars back in his holding stance and puts the ball up to his mouth. He done this maybe twenty-five—thirty times through the game, faking his spitter. But this time I suspicioned from his grin and his action that it was the real spitter coming, a pitch that allus troubled me up there and I knowed would trouble me here.

I got cocked, and the second he came around, I knowed it was a spitter. All told I got maybe a fifth of a second to figger what to do. This pitch is coming right down the middle fast as a bullet, titty-high, right where I like 'em. But when it was no more than twenty feet out of Tug's hand, you could feel it getting ready to sail. I knowed when the saliver on it took a real hold, it would jump at least two feet and would be so fur outside that I'd draw me a free pass and force in the tying run.

Same time, churning through my head, was the fact Ory didn't like them there spitters. If I swang wild and lit fur first, chances was Ory would miss the ball complete, and we'd be free to take all the bases we could on a passed third strike. Maybe we'd score two-three runs and win.

All this passed through my brain in the blink of the eye. I made the most desperate swing a man ever made and knowed the minute the ball jumped by me I done the right thing. Ory was still squatting. He jist let that spitter sail by.

Everybody, natcherally, was running with the count full and two out. As I rounded first I seen Ringle and Cornbread high-tailing it in, and right behind 'em ole Heinie was chuffing. My legs was killing me time I got to second, so I slowed up to look. Ory was standing straight up, his face purple behind the little toy mask and his Adam's apple jumping up and down. The whole Simmons Run nine was standing jist friz in their tracks. The ball was way back by the back stop, so I lit out for third, and it wasn't till I was heading into home that their first sacker woken up and started for the ball. So I scored and that made four runs for us on my strikeout.

Ory was standing about three feet in front of home plate when I crossed. Sudden-like he took off his toy mask and slang it on the ground and then he slang his toy mitt on the ground and jumped up and down on it. Then real puppusful he started marching out toward ol' Tug. Tug kin take care of hisse'f agin most people, but with this big baboon Ory I figgered I better go out to give him a hand.

When Ory gets about ten feet from Tug, he stops and screams.

"I-I-I-I f-f-f-f-f-fought I t-t-t-tole you to n-n-never to th-th-throw that sp-sp-spitter!"

"Gaddlemighty, boy!" Tug says. "You give me the spitter sign, didn't you? You showed me three fingers, didn't you?"

"S-s-s-sign?" Ory shouts. "Three f-f-f-fingers? I-I-I-I g-g-give you the s-s-s-sign for a curve b-b-ball. Two f-f-f-fingers. L-l-l-like this."

He scrooched down and wagged two fingers. But hanging right down beside his middle finger so it looked like a third finger was the brown reinforcement piece of his long drawers. Tug and me studied it for maybe a minute before the whole thing lighted up for us and then we fell down right there on the pitcher's mound and laughed till we near died.

I tole the story of that game to this here women baseball writer, jist about word for word as I tole you. I tole her how it all ended up regulation. They had their last bats and Pea Ridge fanned the side and it ended 4-1, our favor. Shore, I got no hits and didn't do nothing mechanical to rave about. But fur pure puppusful thinking that was my greatest day in baseball. . . .

The Spelling Bee

. . . What a dress party is to Fifth Avenue, a spelling-school is to Hoopole County. It is an occasion which is metaphorically inscribed with this legend, "Choose your partners." Spelling is only a blind in Hoopole County, as is dancing on Fifth Avenue. But as there are some in society who love dancing for its own sake, so in Flat Creek district there were those who loved spelling for its own sake, and who, smelling the battle from afar, had come to try their skill in this tournament, hoping to freshen the laurels they had won in their school-days.

From *The Hoosier School-Master*, A Novel, by Edward Eggleston, pp. 42–47. New York: Orange Judd and Company, 1871.

"I 'low," said Mr. Means, speaking as the principal school trustee, "I 'low our friend the Square is jest the man to boss this ere consarn to-night. Ef nobody objects, I'll appint him. Come, Square, don't be bashful. Walk up to the trough, fodder or no fodder, as the man said to his donkey."

There was a general giggle at this, and many of the young swains took occasion to nudge the girls alongside them, ostensibly for the purpose of making them see the joke, but really for the pure pleasure of nudging. The Greeks figured Cupid as naked, probably because he wears so many disguises that they could not select a costume for him.

The Squire came to the front. Ralph made an inventory of the agglomeration which bore the name of Squire Hawkins, as follows:

1. A swallow-tail coat of indefinite age, worn only on state occasions when its owner was called to figure in his public capacity. Either the Squire had grown too large or the coat too small.

2. A pair of black gloves, the most phenomenal, abnormal, and unexpected apparition conceivable in Flat Creek district, where the preachers wore no coats in the summer, and where a black glove was never seen except on the hands of the Squire.

3. A wig of that dirty, waxy color so common to wigs. This one showed a continual inclination to slip off the owner's smooth, bald pate, and the Squire had frequently to adjust it. As his hair had been red, the wig did not accord with his face, and the hair ungrayed was sadly discordant with a face shriveled by age.

4. A semicircular row of whiskers hedging the edge of the jaw and chin. These were dyed a frightful dead black, such as no natural hair or beard ever had. At the roots there was a quarter of an inch of white, giving the whiskers the appearance of having been stuck on.

5. A pair of spectacles "with tortoise-shell rim." Wont to slip off.

6. A glass eye, purchased of a peddler, and differing in color from its natural mate, perpetually getting out of focus by turning in or out.

7. A set of false teeth, badly fitted, and given to bobbing up and down.

8. The Squire proper, to whom these patches were loosely attached.

It is an old story that a boy wrote home to his father begging him to come West, because "mighty mean men got in office out here." But Ralph concluded that some Yankees had taught school in Hoopole County who would not have held a high place in the educational institutions of Massachusetts. Hawkins had some New England idioms, but they were well overlaid by a Western pronunciation.

"Ladies and gentlemen," he began, shoving up his spectacles, and sucking his lips over his white teeth to keep them in place, "ladies and gentlemen, young men and maidens, raley I'm obleeged to Mr. Means fer this honor," and the Squire took both hands and turned the top of his head round several inches. Then he adjusted his spectacles. Whether he was obliged to Mr. Means for the honor of being compared to a donkey, was not clear. "I feel in the inmost compartments of my animal spirits a most happifying sense of the success and futility of all my endeavors to sarve the people of Flat Crick deestrick, and the people of Tomkins township, in my weak way and manner." This burst of eloquence was delivered with a constrained air and an apparent sense of a danger that he, Squire Hawkins, might fall to pieces in his weak way and manner, and of the success and futility (especially the latter) of all attempts at reconstruction. For by this time the ghastly pupil of the left eye, which was black, was looking away round to the left, while the little blue one on the right twinkled cheerfuly toward the front. The front teeth would drop down so that the Squire's mouth was kept nearly closed, and his words whistled through.

"I feel as if I could be grandiloquent on this interesting occasion," twisting his scalp round, "but raley I must forego any such exertions. It is spelling you want. Spelling is the corner-stone, the grand, underlying subterfuge of a good eddication. I put the spellin'-book prepared by the great Daniel Webster alongside the Bible. I do, raley. I think I may put it ahead of the Bible. For if it wurnt fer spellin'-books and sich occasions as these, where would the Bible be? I should like to know. The man who got up, who compounded this little work of inextricable valoo was a benufactor to the whole human race or any other." Here the spectacles fell off. The Squire replaced them in some confusion, gave the top of his head another twist, and felt of his glass eye, while poor Shocky stared in wonder, and Betsey Short rolled from side to side at the point of death from the effort to suppress her giggle. Mrs. Means and the other old ladies looked the applause they could not speak.

"I appint Larkin Lanham and Jeems Buchanan fer captings," said the Squire. And the two young men thus named took a stick and tossed it from hand to hand to decide which should have the "first chice." One tossed the stick to the other, who held it fast just where he happened to catch it. Then the first placed his hand above the second, and so the hands were alternately changed to the top. The one who held the stick last without room for the other to take hold had gained the lot. This was tried three times. As Larkin held the stick twice out of three times, he had the choice. He hesitated a moment. Everybody looked toward tall Jim Phillips. But Larkin was fond of a venture on unknown seas, and so he said, "I take the master," while a buzz of surprise ran round the room, and the captain of the other side, as if afraid his opponent would withdraw the choice, retorted quickly, and with a little smack of exultation and defiance in his voice: "And *I* take Jeems Phillips."

And soon all present, except a few of the old folks, found themselves ranged in opposing hosts, the poor spellers lagging in, with what grace they could, at the foot of the two divisions. The Squire opened his spelling-book and began to give out the words to the two captains, who stood up and spelled against each other. . . .

The Question Bee

When I was eighteen years of age, my good father gave me an interest in his business, and I settled down to a mercantile life. It was an old-fashioned store—general stock, as we called it; a little of everything that the humble, primitive people of the country wanted. I learned more of human nature there than I ever learned anywhere, and I learned civility. We sold goods on a year's time, and then lapped over a part of the debt if the customer could not pay it all. Sometimes a feller run away, and my father balanced his account with a G. T. T., "gone to Texas," and that was the end of it. I used to think there was a power of rascals roosting in those Texas woods, and I reckon there was, for everybody run there from our county when they got into trouble and wanted to dodge the sheriff or the jail. We sold goods at a hundred per cent. generally, and could afford to lose a few debts. All the little things like lace, and thimbles, and combs, and jew's-harps, and so forth, we sold for three or four times what they cost us. I used to sell fiddles for six dollars that cost me a dollar and a half. Lawyers used to take half of a man's land for defending the title. Old Doctor Banks used to charge $500 for cutting a rock out of a man. Dr. Wildman charged a whole slave for curing him of the small-pox. Nobody but a few rich folks could ride in a carriage or wear boots, and store clothes, and linen bosoms, and palpitating lace, and cook on a stove, and have glass windows, and a piano, and book music. Most of our people were just tolerably well off—just comfortable; and my father used to say he made all his money out of them, that he never made anything out of rich folks. They wouldn't pay a fair profit, and they wanted too much indulgence. There was a clever old man lived over there whose name was Simmons —A. Q. Simmons—and once a month he brought into our store for us to sell on commission a few dozen or so packages of yellow powder done up in brown paper and tied up with old strings. He said it was made of white ash root and may apple, and would cure chills—the "fever and ager," as it was called. He dried the roots and ground them up in a coffee mill. We sold the first medicine he ever put up, and by and by it got to be popular, for it was a good medicine, and the old man extended his circuit and peddled 'round in his little wagon. He never advertised any. After he died some Macon men took it up without any credentials, and then Zellin got it, and now Simmons' liver medicine is known all over the wide world; but whether it is the same or not, nobody knows. The old man never called it liver medicine. I don't think he knew that folks had livers. But most everybody have got livers now, and most of 'em are sick or diseased, and we are finding out that we

"Old Times," from *Bill Arp's Scrap Book*, by Bill Arp [Charles H. Smith], pp. 197–199. Atlanta: Jas. P. Harrison & Co., Publishers. 1884.

have all got a pair of kidneys. I have heard of 'em, but knew nothing hardly until this man Warner began to sound such an alarm bell all over the country. He has mighty nigh scared half the people into a belief that they have got Bright's disease. These patent medicine fellers are mighty smart, but they haven't got any of my small change yet. I don't believe that any druggist ought to be allowed to sell any patent medicine that has not been inspected, and analyzed, and indorsed by the State Medical Board.

When I got to be twenty-one years old I suddenly took a notion that measuring off tape and calico, and weighing out copperas and nails and the like, was a business most too limited for my ambition, and so I studied a little passel of law and began to attend the Justices' courts around in the county. Tom Alexander was doing the same thing, and the first case we had was down at Ben Smith's district, where a feller had sued another feller for thirty dollars' worth of slander. I dident know that a slander case couldent be tried in a Justice's court, and Tom dident know it, nor the old 'Squire, nor the jury, and so we rolled up our sleeves and pitched into the case like killing snakes. We beat the atmosphere and clawed around and used language immensely for an hour or two, and then submitted the case to the jury, and they retired and soon came back with a verdict: "We, the jury, find for the plaintiff three dollars unless the defendant will take back what he said." Well, I was for the defendant, and so I took my client out in the bushes and advised him to take it back, and he did it, and then the question came up as to who should pay the cost. We argued that luminously for awhile, and the jury retired and came back with a verdict: "We, the jury, find that the lawyers shall pay the cost." Tom and I stood square to the rack and paid it. We took our clients' notes for five dollars apiece (which we never did collect) and came home proud of our laurels.

Not long after this I married me a wife and went regularly into the family business and have succeeded beyond my most sanguine expectations. A numerous progeny have grown up around us, and children's children are never so happy as when they get to grandpa's. For twenty-five years we lived in town and I practiced law and made a good living, but as the years rolled on the more I longed to revive the pleasures of my youth, and so a few years ago I bought me a farm—a farm with creeks and branches and springs and meadows and mountains close by; and I can sit in my piazza and look off upon a beautiful prospect, and see the sun go down behind the western hills.

By invitation I made a speech not long ago at a farmers' barbecue in a naboring county, and I spread myself in encouraging our people to keep up with the progress of the age, and I pictured the innocence and honesty and independence of a farmer's life in multitudinous language. I was cheered and congratulated of course when I got through, but an old grizzly feller with brass-bound spectacles came up and says he to me, "My friend, you talk mighty well; you talk like a lawyer; but I would like to know if you can tell what kind of a calf makes the best milch cow." "A heifer calf," said I, and the crowd just yelled. I got the grin on the old man, and so says I, "Now, let me ask you a question, and you may ask me another, and the man who can't answer his own question must treat to cigars." "All right," said he, "now go ahead."

Said I: "How does a ground squirrel dig his hole without leaving any dirt round the top?"

He studied awhile and gave it up, and called on me to answer. "Why," said I, "he begins at the bottom."

"Well, but how does he get to the bottom?" said the old man, as though he had me.

"I don't know," said I; "I never did know; and as it is your question, you must answer or pay."

The crowd yelled again, and the old man surrendered and bought the cigars.

Well, there are a heap of things just that way about farming; we take too much for granted. The ground squirrel does leave dirt around the top. . . .

The Pioneer Pessimist

It was during the period when pioneers had partially recovered from their early consternation at the idea of such a thing as a steam railroad, at first looked upon as an invention of the devil himself. They had become somewhat reconciled to the idea of such nerve-wracking speed as ten miles an hour, which they had declared to be greater than a gracious Providence ever intended that man should travel on wheels, and the thought of a railroad was slowly becoming an accepted fact. Indeed, at some time in the future, when the good Lord so willed it, a railroad might pass through their own community.

There was one individual in central Illinois, however, who was somewhat inclined to discount things about him, particularly the supposed attractions of his own immediate locality. In his estimation it was no Arcady, and he was, indeed, inclined to adopt a pessimistic attitude toward everything concerning it.

Time came when Dame Rumor began to assert that a railroad would be forthcoming in that community in the immediate future, and the tidings were hurriedly carried to the pessimistic one by his 12-year-old son.

"A railroad in this God-forsaken place? Why, they won't even survey the line," he declared.

A few months intervened, when the son again approached his father. "Say, Dad, they're surveyin' the line."

From the Manuscripts of the Federal Writer's Project of the Works Progress Administration for the State of Illinois. Library of Congress Folklore Collection.

"O well," retorted the disgusted father, "they may survey, but they'll never build a grade."

After a further lapse of time the boy approached his father with the latest report.

"Say, Dad," he said, "they're a-building a grade."

"Buildin' a grade, eh?" with great scorn. "Well, that's all the good it'll ever do 'em. They'll never lay a tie."

It was not long after this that the boy came running, announcing breathlessly, "Say, Dad, they're a-laying the ties."

This was a poser, but there was no sign of surrender in the parent's manner as he confidently asserted, "Well, they may lay some ties, but they'll never string a rail."

And then, when the ever-watchful offspring had brought the news that they were stringing the rails, the prompt reply was, "They may string some rails, but they'll never run a train through."

It was not very long after this that the boy came running to him, one day, with the most stirring news of all, "Say, Dad, they're runnin' a train through."

The calm, unwavering reply of the confident father was—"Well, it may go through, *but it'll never come back.*"

Profits of Sin

A Missouri farmer recently learned that the grand jury was about to indict him for working on Sunday. He didn't try to evade the charge, but on the contrary had his four sons summoned as witnesses against him. He was fined one dollar and costs, a total of five dollars. But as the mileage and witness fees of his sons amounted to $10.40, the family cleared $5.40 on the transaction.

How to Secure Land

Out in Wyoming there are settled quite a number of Swedes, who, as a rule, make good citizens. That they readily grasp conditions as they find them is evidenced by the following anecdote, which is told by Representative John E. Osborne, of that State:

A Swede stepped into a Rawlins attorney's office one day and asked: "Is hare ben a lawyer's place?"

"Yes; I'm a lawyer."

"Well, Maister Lawyer, I tank I shall have a paper made."

From *American Wit and Humor,* Vol. II, p. 77. Philadelphia: George W. Jacobs & Co. 1900.

From *Waifs of the Press.* Collected and Edited by Harry L. Work, p. 121. Washington: Walter Neale, Publisher. 1898.

"What kind of a paper do you want?"

"Well, I tank I shall have a mortgage. You see, I buy me a piece of land from Nels Petersen, and I want a mortgage on it."

"Oh, no. You don't want a mortgage; what you want is a deed."

"No, Maister; I tank I want a mortgage. You see, I buy me two pieces of land before, and I got deed for dem, and 'nother faller come along with mortgage and take the land; so I tank I better get mortgage this time."

If You Can't Wash Dishes, Don't Eat

Cooks were paid from fifteen to twenty-five dollars a month more than riders. Long before the wagon crew was gathered for the spring work, the wagon boss had his cook hired, frequently paying him wages for a month or two before he was needed, just to hold him.

The cook was monarch of all he surveyed. Everybody paid him homage, and the wise "stray man" with the outfit or casual drifter dropping in for a meal or two always grabbed one of the flour-sack towels and helped him get his dirty dishes out of the way. Nor has this situation changed with the passing years. Four or five years ago, at the headquarters ranch of a big cow outfit in the Black Hills of South Dakota, the kitchen was decorated with large plainly read signs, such as:

IF YOU CAN'T WASH DISHES, DON'T EAT.

WE USE WOOD IN THE COOKSTOVE CUT 16 INCHES
LONG, BUT *No Longer.*

A BUSY COOK LOVES A FULL WOOD BOX.

A FULL WATER BUCKET MAKES A HAPPY COOK.

STRAY MEN ARE NOT EXEMPT FROM HELPING WASH
DISHES, BRINGING WOOD OR WATER.

THE WELL IS JUST 110 STEPS FROM THE KITCHEN,
MOSTLY DOWNHILL BOTH WAYS.

The Pride of Texas

The older woman remembers well the flour-sack days of Texas, and she doesn't have to be so old, either. The sheets, the pillowcases, the tablecloths, the dishtowels, the children's underwear, the doilies and antimacassars and center-table covers, the jelly-strainers, milk-strainers, pudding bags, and overnight cases! Miles of Mexican drawn work

From *Cattle*, by William MacLeod Raine and Will C. Barnes, pp. 297-298. Copyright, 1930, by William MacLeod Raine and Will C. Barnes. Garden City, New York: Doubleday, Doran & Company, Inc.

From *The Golden Hoof*, The Story of the Southwest, by Winifred Kupper, pp. 174–175. Copyright, 1945, by Alfred A. Knopf, Inc. New York.

went into the flour-sack cloth, miles of hemstitching and tiny tucks, millions of fine, painstaking stitches. The flour sack played a major role in the Texas woman's household economy and art of living.

"I married John," a little lady, now a sprightly seventy-five, often tells, "and I came to Texas to take what might befall. I had been brought up in Philadelphia and been trained for a musical career, so I'd hardly washed a dish or mended a stocking before I came to Texas. But it was all such fun! After two years in our camp my trousseau clothes began to wear out. My dresses were of good, strong material, and I had mended them here and there where the brush had torn them, so that they did very nicely. But my underwear had got quite beyond mending. So one day I asked John about it. 'John,' I said, 'do you think you could get me a few yards of white material at the store the next time you go to town?' 'Honey,' he said, 'I wish I could, but we've barely enough for some things I need for the sheep, and I don't want to ask Schreiner for another dollar till I've paid something back. Could you possibly wait till the wool is sold this fall?' I give you my word that I hadn't heard of flour-sack underwear at the time. I had seen very little of women in those two years. So I thought my idea was quite original. I took two flour sacks and fashioned a pair of drawers. Such work as went into them! I always did like pretty underwear; so I stitched ruffles and tucks, very fine tucks, and then added feather-stitching. I was very, very proud of them, and I could hardly wait to see John. He came in at last, and as soon as I could I danced out in front of him. 'How do you like my handiwork?' I asked him, and I lifted my skirts and twirled around. He burst out laughing, and he laughed until he had to hold his sides. I was surprised and even a little hurt. I'd spent *hours* on those drawers. But still he laughed. And finally, when he could talk, I found out why. You see, nobody had ever told me how to bleach out the lettering that was on every sack. I had tried boiling, but it had only turned the red letters to a delicate pink. 'Oh, well,' I had told myself, 'the letters will all be lost in the folds.' But they hadn't been; and on the side of me, in back, was plainly printed in large pink letters 'THE PRIDE' and on the other side 'OF TEXAS.' "

Young Melvin

After his pappy passed on Young Melvin decided he wanted to travel. He'd always lived back at the forks of the creek and he hadn't ever at no time been farther from there than the crossroads.

So Young Melvin put out the fire and hid the ax and skillet and

By James R. Aswell. From *God Bless the Devil! Liars' Bench Tales*, by James R. Aswell, Julia Willhoit, Jennette Edwards, E. E. Miller, and Lena E. Lipscomb, of the Tennessee Writers' Project, pp. 3–10. Copyright, 1940, by the University of North Carolina Press. Chapel Hill.

called up his hound named Bulger and he was on his way. He went over the hill and a good piece further and he come to the crossroads. He went straight to Old Man Bill Blowdy's house there. He knocked on the oor.

Old Man Bill Blowdy come to the door and stuck his nose out the crack. "Who's there?" says he, not daring to come out for fear it was somebody he'd beat in some deal.

"It's me," says Young Melvin. "Just me and my hound dog Bulger."

Old Man Bill Blowdy opened the door then and gave Young Melvin a sly look. "Come in and rest and eat a bite," he says, faint-like.

He was a great big fat red man that was always grinning and easy talking, like butter wouldn't melt in his mouth. And he was just about the slickest, double-dealingest old cooter in the country or anywhere else at all. Nobody could beat him in a deal—never had, anyway—or when it come to a law-suit. Always lawing somebody, Old Man Bill Blowdy was.

"Why don't you come in, Young Melvin?" he says.

"Because I'm on my way, Mister Old Man Bill Blowdy. I'm a-going to town for sure. It's forty miles and across two counties but I aim to see that town. That's why I come to see you."

Old Man Bill Blowdy started shutting the door. "Now, now, Young Melvin," he says. "I'm hard up for money right now. I couldn't loan my sweet mother, now in heaven praise be, so much as a penny."

"I don't want no money," says Young Melvin. "I ain't the borrowing kind."

So Old Man Bill Blowdy poked his head out again. "What can I do for you then?"

"Well, it's like this. You're my twenty-third cousin, my only kin in this world. I got a favor for you to do for me."

Old Man Bill Blowdy started sliding that door shut. "No, no favors. I make it a rule to do no favors and don't expect none from nobody."

"It's a favor I'm aiming to pay for," says Young Melvin.

"Oh," says Old Man Bill Blowdy, opening the door once more, "that's different now. Come right in, Young Melvin."

"No, sir, no need to come in, for I'd just be coming out again. What I want you to do is keep my fox hound Bulger while I'm off on my travels. I'll pay his keep, I'll pay what's right when I come back to get him."

Old Man Bill Blowdy grinned all over his face. He thought he saw a way to make himself something extry or get him a fox hound of his own. Everybody knew Young Melvin was simple. Honest as the day's long but simple.

"Why yes," says Old Man Bill Blowdy. "Why yes, I'll keep Bulger for you, Young Melvin, and glad to."

So Young Melvin gave his hound dog over and bid Old Man Bill Blowdy farewell. "I'll be back next week or month or sometime. I don't know how long it'll be, for it's forty miles and across two counties to town."

Well, one day the week or month or anyhow sometime after that, here come Young Melvin down the pikeroad to the crossroads, limping and dusty and easy in mind. He went straight to Old Man Bill Blowdy's house and knocked his knuckles on the door.

Old Man Bill Blowdy stuck his nose out the crack and says, "Who's there?"

"It's me, it's Young Melvin."

"How are you, Young Melvin?"

"Fair to piddling. I walked to town and saw all the sights and then walked back here again. Forty miles and across two counties. Don't never want to roam no more. I'm satisfied now."

Old Man Bill Blowdy started shutting the door. "Glad to hear it, Young Melvin. Next time you come down to the crossroads, drop in and say hello. Any time, just any time, Young Melvin."

"Hold there! Wait a minute!" says Young Melvin.

"I'm busy," says the old man.

But Young Melvin got his foot in the door. "How about Bulger, Old Man Bill Blowdy? How about him?"

Old Man Bill Blowdy kept trying to shut the door and Young Melvin kept shoving his foot in.

"See here!" says Young Melvin. "I mean my fox hound."

"Oh him? Why, I declare to my soul I'd almost forgot that hound dog, Young Melvin. I sure almost had."

"Where is he at?" says Young Melvin, still trying to keep the old man from closing the door.

"I'll tell you," says Old Man Bill Blowdy, still trying to shut it, "I feel mighty bad about it, Young Melvin, but your Bulger is no more."

"How come? What do you mean?"

"Why, he's perished and gone, Young Melvin. The first night after you left I sort of locked him up in that little busted-down house over in the Old Ground. Well sir, Young Melvin, those last renters of mine that lived there was powerful dirty folks. They left the place just lousy with chinch bugs. Them bugs was mortal hungry by this time. So they just eat that Bulger of yours alive. Eat all but the poor thing's bones by morning—and the bones was pretty well gnawed.

"It was my fault in one way. I ought to known better than put your dog in there, Young Melvin. But I done it. So I won't charge you a penny for his keep the night I had him. I aim to do the fair thing."

Well, Old Man Bill Blowdy stuck his sly eye to the crack of the door to see how Young Melvin was taking it. He knew the boy was simple. He figured he had him. Because Old Man Bill Blowdy had Bulger hid out and he aimed to swap him for something to a man he knew in the next county.

So Young Melvin stood there looking like the good Lord had shaken him off His Christian limb. Tears come in his eyes and he sleeved his nose. "That dog was folks to me," he says. "Them chinch bugs don't know what they done to me."

He pulled his foot out of the door and he backed down the steps. He started towards home.

Old Man Bill Blowdy eased out on the porch to watch him go.

About that time Young Melvin turned around. "Mister Old Man Bill Blowdy," he says, "my place is way over the hill and a good piece further. I'm beat out and tired. Wonder if you'd loan me your mule to ride on? I'll bring it back tomorrow."

The old man knew Young Melvin was honest as the livelong day. Besides, he was so tickled with how he'd got him a good hound to swap and it not costing anything that he just called across the way to the crossroads store and got a witness to the loan and let Young Melvin take the mule. It was a fine mule, too, with the three hind ribs showing, the best sort of sign in a mule—shows he's a hard worker.

Next morning Young Melvin never showed up and Old Man Bill Blowdy got worried. He got worrieder still in the middle of the day when no sign of Young Melvin did he see.

But along about afternoon he saw Young Melvin come walking over the hill and down towards the crossroads. He run out on his porch and yelled, "Hey, Young Melvin, where's my mule?"

Young Melvin kept walking. He just shook his head. "I feel mighty bad about that mule, Mister Old Man Bill Blowdy," he called. "I sure do."

"Hey! Wait there!"

But Young Melvin went on, heading for the store at the crossroads.

So Old Man Bill Blowdy was so mad he didn't wait to get his shoes. He just jumped off the porch and run across to Square Rogers, that good old man's house up the road a ways.

"Square," he says, "I want you to handle Young Melvin. He stole my mule."

The Square waked up his deputy and the deputy went down and brought in Young Melvin. Everybody at the crossroads come tagging along behind.

Square said, "Son, they tell me you stole a mule."

"No sir, Square Rogers, I never done it," says Young Melvin.

Old Man Bill Blowdy stomped his bare feet and shook his fists. "He's a bald-faced liar!"

"Curb yourself down, Old Man Bill Blowdy," says the Square, "and let the boy tell his side. Go ahead, Young Melvin."

So Young Melvin told his side, told how he borrowed the mule and started for home. "Well," he says, "you know I live over the hill and a good piece further. I rode that mule to the top of the hill. I was mind-ing my own business and not giving nobody any trouble. Then all on a sudden I see a turkey buzzard dropping down out of the sky. Here it come, dropping fast and crowing like a game rooster.

"First thing I knew that old buzzard just grabbed Old Man Bill Blowdy's mule by the tail and started heaving and the mule's hind legs lifted off the ground and I went flying over his head and hit a rock head-on. I failed in my senses a minute. When I could see straight I saw that buzzard sailing away with the mule, most a mile high and getting littler all the time.

"And that's how it happened. I sure am sorry, but there ain't much you can do with a thing like that, Square."

"Hold on there!" says Square Rogers, that good old man. "I've seen many a turkey buzzard in my time, Young Melvin, but never a one that could crow."

"Well," says Young Melvin, "it surprised me some too. But in a county where chinch bugs can eat up a full-grown fox hound in one night, why I just reckon a turkey buzzard has a right to crow and fly off with a mule if he wants to."

So it all come out and Square Rogers, that good old man, made Old Man Bill Blowdy fork up Bulger and then Young Melvin gave back the mule.

Old Man Bill Blowdy was mocked down to nothing. He just grieved and pined away and it wasn't no more than ten years before he taken sick and wasted away and died.

Putting Up a Stove Pipe

Putting up a stove is not so difficult in itself. It is the pipe that raises four-fifths of the mischief and all the dust. You may take down a stove with all the care in the world, and yet that pipe won't come together again as it was before. You find this out when you are standing on a chair with your arms full of pipe and your mouth full of soot. Your wife is standing on the floor in a position that enables her to see you, the pipe, and the chair, and here she gives utterance to those remarks that are calculated to hasten a man into the extremes of insanity. Her dress is pinned over her waist, and her hands rest on her hips. She has got one of your hats on her head, and your linen coat on her back, and a pair of rubbers on her feet. There is about five cents' worth of pot black on her nose, and a lot of flour on her chin, and altogether she is a spectacle that would inspire a dead man with distrust. And while you are up there trying to circumvent the awful contrariness of the pipe, and telling that you know some fool has been mixing it, she stands safely on the floor and bombards you

From *Life in Danbury* . . . , by James M. Bailey, "The Danbury News Man" . . . , pp. 150–155. Boston: Shepard and Gill, 1873.

with such domestic mottoes as—"What's the use of swearing so?" "You know no one has touched that pipe." "You ain't got any more patience than a child." "Do be careful of that chair." And then she goes off and reappears with an armful more of pipe, and before you are aware of it she has got that pipe so horribly mixed up that it does seem no two pieces are alike.

You join the ends and work them to and fro, and to and fro again, and then you take them apart and look at them. Then you spread one out and jam the other together, and mount them once more. But it is no go. You begin to think the pieces are inspired with life, and ache to kick them through the window. But *she* doesn't lose her patience. She goes around with that awful exasperating rigging on, with a length of pipe under each arm and a long-handled broom in her hand, and says she don't see how it is some people never have any trouble putting up a stove. Then you miss the hammer. You don't see it anywhere. You stare into the pipe along the mantel, and down the stove, and off to the floor. Your wife watches you, and is finally thoughtful enough to inquire what you are looking after; and on learning, pulls the article from her pocket. Then you feel as if you could go out doors and swear a hole twelve feet square through a block of brick buildings, but she merely observes, "Why on earth don't you speak when you want anything, and not stare around like a dummy."

When that part of the pipe which goes through the wall is up, she keeps it up with the broom, while you are making the connection, and stares at it with an intensity that is entirely uncalled for. All the while your position is becoming more and more interesting. The pipe don't go together, of course. The soot shakes down into your eyes and mouth, the sweat rolls down your face and tickles your chin as it drops off, and it seems as if your arms were slowly but surely drawing out of their sockets.

Here your wife comes to the rescue by inquiring if you are going to be all day doing nothing, and if you think *her* arms are made of cast iron; and then the broom slips off the pipe, and in her endeavor to recover her hold she jabs you under the chin with the handle, and the pipe comes down on your head with its load of fried soot, and then the chair tilts forward enough to discharge your feet, and you come down on the wrong end of that chair with a force that would bankrupt a pile driver. You don't touch that stove again. You leave your wife examining the chair and bemoaning its injuries, and go into the kitchen and wash your skinned and bleeding hands with yellow soap. Then you go down street after a man to do the business, and your wife goes over to the neighbor's with her chair, and tells them about its injuries, and drains the neighborhood dry with its sympathy long before you get home.

Uses of a Wheelbarrow

If you have occasion to use a wheelbarrow, leave it, when you are through with it, in front of the house with the handles toward the door. A wheelbarrow is the most complicated thing to fall over on the face of the earth. A man will fall over one when he would never think of falling over anything else. He never knows when he has got through falling over it, either; for it will tangle his legs and his arms, turn over with him and rear up in front of him, and just as he pauses in his profanity to congratulate himself, it takes a new turn, and scoops more skin off of him, and he commences to evolute anew, and bump himself on fresh places. A man never ceases to fall over a wheelbarrow until it turns completely on its back, or brings up against something it cannot upset. It is the most inoffensive-looking object there is, but it is more dangerous than a locomotive, and no man is secure with one unless he has a tight hold of its handles, and is sitting down on something. A wheelbarrow has its uses, without doubt, but in its leisure moments it is the great blighting curse on true dignity.

How Much Stone for a Fireplace?

I got a span of mules from the ranch, borrowed a wagon from my neighbor, and took Virgil off duty to haul rock. He and I went over the ridges hand-picking every stone that went into the house. When we had a great pile for the masons, I asked the contractor to tell me when we had enough. He looked at the pile, spat, and then said: "Ever fool with stone much?"

He knew very well I hadn't, but he waited for an answer.

"No."

"Well, I tell you; haul 'er up here til ya got enough, then haul 'bout five, six loads more."

"The Intricacies of a Wheelbarrow," from *Life in Danbury* . . . , by James N. Bailey, "The Danbury News Man" . . . , pp. 140–141. Boston, Shepard and Gill, 1873.

From *Talking to the Moon*, by John Joseph Mathews, p. 8. Copyright, 1945, by The University of Chicago Press, Chicago.

VIII. THE LADDER UP

(Concerning School and Society)

Introduction

Down through the years a little boy trudging slowly toward a little red schoolhouse has been for most of us a nostalgic symbol of school days. The boy was trudging slowly because he was of divided mind about continuing to school. The teacher was there to make him be quiet and try in every way to get him to learn, but his playmates were also there. Was it worth sitting still most of the day to get an hour of play during recesses? Could he risk breaking the routine by throwing a few spitballs during recitation hours, or would it be more fun to get two or three of his friends to play hooky and go fishing?

The teacher represented authority, and authority always galls. Because of the boy's resentment of the teacher's discipline, he was always trying to outwit her in some way. Often he tried practical jokes: stopping up the flue of the stove, cutting her paddle so that it would break when she applied it with vigor, or putting tacks in her chair or a snake in her desk drawer. But regularly he tried to disrupt schoolroom monotony by making faces at one of his classmates when the teacher's back was turned, by talking under his breath to his friend across the aisle, by tripping someone walking by him, by continually asking permission to leave the room, by throwing spitballs or little darts made of a dress pin, some paper, and a match, or by putting a pin through the toe of his shoe and gently skewering someone beneath the desk—all these and more he tried. Like Doc Macnooder, he may even have tried smoking on the school grounds.

On the other side of the desk sat another human being, although the students might sometimes doubt her humanity. She really needed to be superhuman in order to maintain discipline against 30-to-1 odds and a schoolground code which placed the tattle-tale at the bottom of the ladder. Since she could not get information from other students, she had to catch the culprits herself. And catching them made necessary ears like the antennae of a grasshopper to determine the direction of a whistle, eyes in the back of her head to see the face-maker and spit-baller, and perfect composure when a mouse jumped out of her desk drawer. If she hadn't been born with these attributes, she had to develop them. If the teacher were a man instead of a woman, he was always felt to be a little peculiar, for despite his knowledge of algebra and Latin, he wasn't much good at practical men's activities such as selling hardware, plowing corn, or shooting craps. And he was absent-minded.

Everyone has heard, of course, of the time he telephoned the police to find his car. They did—he had left it in front of the post office with the motor running. Richard M. Dorson's "The Folklore of Colleges" shows, however, that this man's absent-mindedness is no more than that of other professors.

School, though, is the hard way. It is easier to pretend that you have an education and an appreciation of the arts than to secure one by training. But when you pretend, you are likely to become the butt of a fun-maker's jokes. John Phoenix showed the pretentiousness of many small-town reports of musical performances in his review of "The Plains," *par* Jabez Tarbox, which "stands out among Oratorios, Operas, Musical Melodramas and performances of Ethiopian Serenaders, peerless and unrivalled." His needless use of foreign language fragments adds another element of fun, for it causes us to laugh at the person who uses that method to show that he has been to school. Mark Twain and Will Rogers had their fun by pretending to be completely uninformed about the arts. With a perfectly straight face Twain could say, ". . . yesterday when I learned that Michael Angelo was dead." And equally straight-faced was Will Rogers when he argued that ". . . when you get down and write of Cabbages, Potatoes, and Tomatoes, you just about hit on a Universal subject."

Guying the Guides

. . . In this connection I wish to say one word about Michael Angelo Buonarotti. I used to worship the mighty genius of Michael Angelo—that man who was great in poetry, painting, sculpture, architecture—great in everything he undertook. But I do not want Michael Angelo for breakfast—for luncheon—for dinner—for tea—for supper—for between meals. I like a change, occasionally. In Genoa, he designed everything; in Milan he or his pupils designed everything; he designed the Lake of Como; in Padua, Verona, Venice, Bologna, who did we ever hear of, from guides, but Michael Angelo? In Florence, he painted everything, designed everything, nearly, and what he did not design he used to sit on a favorite stone and look at, and they showed us the stone. In Pisa he designed everything but the old shot-tower, and they would have attributed that to him if it had not been so awfully out of the perpendicular. He designed the piers of Leghorn and the custom-house regulations of Civita Vecchia. But, here—here it is frightful. He designed St. Peter's; he designed the Pope; he designed the Pantheon, the uniform of the Pope's soldiers, the Tiber, the Vatican, the Coliseum, the Capitol, the Tarpeian Rock, the Bar-

From *The Innocents Abroad*, by Samuel L. Clemens, pp. 223–229. Copyright, 1869, 1897, and 1899, by The American Publishing Company; 1911, by Clara Gabrilowitsch; 1927, by The Macmillan Company.

berini Palace, St. John Lateran, the Campagna, the Appian Way, the Seven Hills, the Baths of Caracalla, the Claudian Aqueduct, the Cloaca Maxima—the eternal bore designed the Eternal City, and unless all men and books do lie, he painted everything in it! Dan said the other day to the guide, "Enough, enough, enough! Say no more! Lump the whole thing! say that the Creator made Italy from designs by Michael Angelo!"

I never felt so fervently thankful, so soothed, so tranquil, so filled with a blessed peace, as I did yesterday when I learned that Michael Angelo was dead.

But we have taken it out of this guide. He has marched us through miles of pictures and sculpture in the vast corridors of the Vatican; and through miles of pictures and sculpture in twenty other palaces! He has shown us the great picture in the Sistine Chapel, and frescoes enough to fresco the heavens—pretty much all done by Michael Angelo. So with him we have played that game which has vanquished so many guides for us—imbecility and idiotic questions. These creatures never suspect—they have no idea of a sarcasm.

He shows us a figure and says: "Statoo brunzo." (Bronze statue.)

We look at it indifferently and the doctor asks: "By Michael Angelo?"

"No—not know who."

Then he shows us the ancient Roman Forum. The doctor asks: "Michael Angelo?"

A stare from the guide. "No—a thousan' year before he is born."

Then an Egyptian obelisk. Again: "Michael Angelo?"

"Oh, *mon dieu,* genteelmen! Zis is *two* thousan' year before he is born!"

He grows so tired of that unceasing question sometimes, that he dreads to show us anything at all. The wretch has tried all the ways he can think of to make us comprehend that Michael Angelo is only responsible for the creation of a *part* of the world, but somehow he has not succeeded yet. Relief for overtasked eyes and brain from study and sightseeing is necessary, or we shall become idiotic sure enough. Therefore this guide must continue to suffer. If he does not enjoy it, so much the worse for him. We do.

In this place I may as well jot down a chapter concerning those necessary nuisances, European guides. Many a man has wished in his heart he could do without his guide; but knowing he could not, has wished he could get some amusement out of him as a remuneration for the affliction of his society. We accomplished this latter matter, and if our experience can be made useful to others they are welcome to it.

Guides know about enough English to tangle everything up so that a man can make neither head nor tail of it. They know their story by heart—the history of every statue, painting, cathedral, or other

wonder they show you. They know it and tell it as a parrot would—
and if you interrupt, and throw them off the track, they have to go
back and begin over again. All their lives long, they are employed
in showing strange things to foreigners and listening to their bursts
of admiration. It is human nature to take delight in exciting admiration. It is what prompts children to say "smart" things, and do absurd
ones, and in other ways "show off" when company is present. It is
what makes gossips turn out in rain and storm to go and be the first
to tell a startling bit of news. Think, then, what a passion it becomes
with a guide, whose privilege it is, every day, to show to strangers
wonders that throw them into perfect ecstasies of admiration! He
gets so that he could not by any possibility live in a soberer atmosphere. After we discovered this, we *never* went into ecstasies any
more—we never admired anything—we never showed any but impas-
sible faces and stupid indifference in the presence of the sublimest
wonders a guide had to display. We had found their weak point. We
have made good use of it ever since. We have made some of those people savage, at times, but we have never lost our own serenity.

The doctor asks the questions, generally, because he can keep his
countenance, and look more like an inspired idiot, and throw more
imbecility into the tone of his voice than any man that lives. It
comes natural to him.

The guides in Genoa are delighted to secure an American party,
because Americans so much wonder, and deal so much in sentiment
and emotion before any relic of Columbus. Our guide there fidgeted
about as if he had swallowed a spring mattress. He was full of animation—full of impatience. He said:

"Come wis me, genteelmen!—come! I show you ze letter-writing by
Christopher Colombo!—write it himself!—write it wis his own hand—
come!"

He took us to the municipal palace. After much impressive fumbling of keys and opening of locks, the stained and aged document
was spread before us. The guide's eyes sparkled. He danced about us
and tapped the parchment with his finger:

"What I tell you, genteelmen! Is it not so? See! handwriting Christopher Colombo!—write it himself!"

We looked indifferent—unconcerned. The doctor examined the document very deliberately, during a painful pause. Then he said, without any show of interest:

"Ah—Ferguson—what—what did you say was the name of the party
who wrote this?"

"Christopher Colombo! ze great Christopher Colombo!"

Another deliberate examination.

"Ah—did he write it himself, or—or how?"

"He write it himself!—Christopher Colombo! he's own handwriting,
write by himself!"

Then the doctor laid the document down and said:

"Why, I have seen boys in America only fourteen years old that could write better than that."

"But zis is ze great Christo—"

"I don't care who it is! It's the worst writing I ever saw. Now you mustn't think you can impose on us because we are strangers. We are not fools, by a good deal. If you have got any specimens of penmanship of real merit, trot them out!—and if you haven't, drive on!"

We drove on. The guide was considerably shaken up, but he made one more venture. He had something which he thought would overcome us. He said:

"Ah, genteelmen, you come wis me! I show you beautiful, oh, magnificent bust Christopher Colombo!—splendid, grand, magnificent!"

He brought us before the beautiful bust—for it *was* beautiful—and sprang back and struck an attitude:

"Ah, look, genteelmen!—beautiful, grand,—bust Christopher Colombo!—beautiful bust, beautiful pedestal!"

The doctor put up his eyeglass—procured for such occasions:

"Ah—what did you say this gentleman's name was?"

"Christopher Colombo!—ze great Christopher Colombo!"

"Christopher Colombo—the great Christopher Colombo. Well, what did *he* do?"

"Discover America!—discover America, oh, ze devil!"

"Discover America. No—that statement will hardly wash. We are just from America ourselves. We heard nothing about it. Christopher Colombo—pleasant name—is—is he dead?"

"Oh, *corpo di Baccho!*—three hundred year!"

"What did he die of?"

"I do not know!—I cannot tell."

"Smallpox, think?"

"I do not know, genteelmen!—I do not know *what* he die of!"

"Measles, likely?"

"Maybe—maybe—I do *not* know—I think he die of somethings."

"Parents living?"

"Im-posseeble!"

"Ah—which is the bust and which is the pedestal?"

"Santa Maria!—*zis* ze bust!—*zis* ze pedestal!"

"Ah, I see, I see—happy combination—very happy combination, indeed. Is—is this the first time this gentleman was ever on a bust?"

That joke was lost on the foreigner—guides cannot master the subtleties of the American joke.

We have made it interesting for this Roman guide. Yesterday we spent three or four hours in the Vatican again, that wonderful world of curiosities. We came very near expressing interest, sometimes—even admiration—it was very hard to keep from it. We succeeded though. Nobody else ever did, in the Vatican museums. The guide was bewildered—nonplussed. He walked his legs off, nearly, hunting up extraordinary things, and exhausted all his ingenuity on us, but it was a failure; we never showed any interest in anything. He had reserved what he considered to be his greatest wonder till the last—a royal Egyptian mummy, the best-preserved in the world, perhaps. He took us there. He felt so sure, this time, that some of his old enthusiasm came back to him:

"See, genteelmen!—Mummy! Mummy!"

The eyeglass came up as calmly, as deliberately as ever.

"Ah,—Ferguson—what did I understand you to say the gentleman's name was?"

"Name?—he got no name!—Mummy!—'Gyptian mummy!"

"Yes, yes. Born here?"

"No! *'Gyptian* mummy!"

"Ah, just so. Frenchman, I presume?"

"No!—*not* Frenchman, not Roman!—born in Egypta!"

"Born in Egypta. Never heard of Egypta before. Foreign locality, likely. Mummy—mummy. How calm he is—how self-possessed. Is, ah—is he dead?"

"Oh, *sacré bleu,* been dead three thousan' year!"

The doctor turned on him savagely:

"Here, now, what do you mean by such conduct as this! Playing us for Chinamen because we are strangers and trying to learn! Trying to impose your vile second-hand carcasses on *us!*—thunder and lightning, I've a notion to—to—if you've got a nice *fresh* corpse, fetch him out!—or, by George, we'll brain you!"

We make it exceedingly interesting for this Frenchman. However, he has paid us back, partly, without knowing it. He came to the hotel this morning to ask if we were up, and he endeavored as well as he could to describe us, so that the landlord would know which persons he meant. He finished with the casual remark that we were lunatics. The observation was so innocent and so honest that it amounted to a very good thing for a guide to say.

There is one remark (already mentioned) which never yet has failed to disgust these guides. We use it always, when we can think of nothing else to say. After they have exhausted their enthusiasm pointing out to us and praising the beauties of some ancient bronze image or broken-legged statue, we look at it stupidly and in silence for five, ten, fifteen minutes—as long as we can hold out, in fact—and then ask:

"Is—is he dead?"

That conquers the serenest of them. It is not what they are looking for—especially a new guide. Our Roman Ferguson is the most patient, unsuspecting, long-suffering subject we have had yet. We shall be sorry to part with him. We have enjoyed his society very much. We trust he has enjoyed ours, but we are harassed with doubts. . . .

Musical Review Extraordinary

SAN DIEGO, July 10th, 1854.

As your valuable work is not supposed to be so entirely identified with San Franciscan interests, as to be careless what takes place in other portions of this great *kedntry*, and as it is received and read in San Diego with great interest (I have loaned my copy to over four different literary gentlemen, most of whom have read some of it), I have thought it not improbable that a few critical notices of the musical performances and the drama of this place might be acceptable to you, and interest your readers. I have been, moreover, encouraged to this task by the perusal of your interesting musical and theatrical critiques on San Francisco performers and performances; as I feel convinced that, if you devote so much space to them, you will not allow any little feeling of rivalry between the two great cities to prevent your noticing ours, which, without the slightest feeling of prejudice, I must consider as infinitely superior. I propose this month to call your attention to the two great events in our theatrical and musical world—the appearance of the talented MISS PELICAN, and the production of Tarbox's celebrated "Ode Symphonie" of "The Plains."

The critiques on the former are from the columns of *The Vallecetos Sentinel,* to which they were originally contributed by me, appearing on the respective dates of June 1st and June 31st.

From The Vallecetos Sentinel, *June 1st.*

MISS PELICAN.—Never during our dramatic experience, has a more exciting event occurred than the sudden bursting upon our theatrical firmament, full, blazing, unparalleled, of the bright, resplendent and particular star, whose honored name shines refulgent at the head of this article. Coming among us unheralded, almost unknown, without claptrap, in a wagon drawn by oxen across the plains, with no agent to get up a counterfeit enthusiasm in her favor, she appeared before us for the first time at the San Diego Lyceum, last evening, in the trying and difficult character of Ingomar, or the Tame Savage. We are at a loss to describe our sensations, our admiration, at her magnificent, her superhuman efforts. We do not hesitate to say that she is by far the superior of any living actress; and, as we believe hers to be the perfection of acting, we cannot be wrong in the belief that no one hereafter will ever be found to approach her. Her conception of the character of Ingomar was perfection itself; her playful and ingenuous manner, her light girlish laughter, in the scene with Sir Peter, showed an appreciation of the savage character, which nothing but the most arduous study, the most elaborate training could produce; while her awful change to the stern, unyielding, uncompromising father in the tragic scene of Duncan's murder, was indeed nature itself. Miss Pelican is about seventeen years of age, of miraculous beauty, and most thrilling voice. It is needless to say she dresses admirably, as in fact we have said

From *Phoenixiana; Or, Sketches and Burlesques,* by John Phoenix, pp. 42–50. New York: D. Appleton and Co., 1856.

all we can say when we called her most truthfully, perfection. Mr. John Boots took the part of Parthenia very creditably, etc., etc.

From The Vallecetos Sentinel, *June 31st.*

MISS PELICAN.—As this lady is about to leave us to commence an engagement on the San Francisco stage, we should regret exceedingly if any thing we have said about her, should send with her a *prestige* which might be found undeserved on trial. The fact is, Miss Pelican is a very ordinary actress; indeed, one of the most indifferent ones we ever happened to see. She came here from the Museum at Fort Laramie, and we praised her so injudiciously that she became completely spoiled. She has performed a round of characters during the last week, very miserably, though we are bound to confess that her performance of King Lear last evening, was superior to any thing of the kind we ever saw. Miss Pelican is about forty-three years of age, singularly plain in her personal appearance, awkward and embarrassed, with a cracked and squeaking voice, and really dresses quite outrageously. *She has much to learn —poor thing!*

I take it the above notices are rather ingenious. The fact is, I'm no judge of acting, and don't know how Miss Pelican will turn out. If well, why there's my notice of June the 1st; if ill, then June 31st comes in play, and, as there is but one copy of the *Sentinel* printed, it's an easy matter to destroy the incorrect one; *both can't be wrong,* so I've made a sure thing of it in any event. Here follows my musical critique, which I flatter myself is of rather superior order:

THE PLAINS. ODE SYMPHONIE PAR JABEZ TARBOX.—This glorious composition was produced at the San Diego Odeon, on the 31st of June, ult., for the first time in this or any other country, by a very full orchestra (the performance taking place immediately after supper), and a chorus composed of the entire "Sauer Kraut-Verein," the "Wee Gates Association," and choice selections from the "Gyascutus" and "Pikeharmonic" societies. The solos were rendered by Herr Tuden Links, the recitations by Herr Von Hyden Schnapps, both performers being assisted by Messrs. John Smith and Joseph Brown, who held their coats, fanned them, and furnished water during the more overpowering passages.

"The Plains" we consider the greatest musical achievement that has been presented to an enraptured public. Like Waterloo among battles; Napoleon among warriors; Niagara among falls, and Peck among senators, this magnificent composition stands among Oratorios, Operas, Musical Melodramas and performances of Ethiopian Serenaders, peerless and unrivalled: *Il frappe toute chose parfaitment froid.*

"It does not depend for its success" upon its plot, its theme, its school or its master, for it has very little if any of them, but upon its soul-subduing, all-absorbing, high-faluting effect upon the audience, every member of which it causes to experience the most singular and exquisite sensations. Its strains at times remind us of those of the old master of the steamer *McKim,* who never went to sea without being unpleasantly affected;—a straining after effect he used to term it. Blair in his lecture on beauty, and Mills in his treatise on logic (p. 31), have alluded to the feeling which might be produced in the human mind, by something of this transcendentally sublime description, but it has remained for M. Tarbox, in the production of "the Plains," to call this feeling forth.

The symphonie opens upon the wide and boundless plains, in longitude 115° W., latitude 35° 21' 03" N., and about sixty miles from the west bank of Pitt River. These data are beautifully and clearly expressed by a long (topographically) drawn note from an E-flat clarionet. The sandy nature of the soil, sparsely dotted with bunches of cactus and artemisia, the extended view, flat and unbroken to the horizon, save by the rising smoke in the extreme verge, denoting the vicinity of a Pi Utah village, are represented by the bass drum. A few notes on the piccolo, calls the attention to a solitary antelope, picking up mescal beans in the foreground. The sun having an altitude of 36° 27', blazes down upon the scene in indescribable majesty. "Gradually the sounds roll forth in a song" of rejoicing to the God of Day.

> "Of thy intensity
> And great immensity
> Now then we sing;
> Beholding in gratitude
> Thee in this latitude,
> Curious thing."

Which swells out into "Hey Jim along, Jim along Josey," then *decrescendo, mas o menos, poco pocita,* dies away and dries up.

Suddenly we hear approaching a train from Pike County, consisting of seven families, with forty-six wagons, each drawn by thirteen oxen; each family consists of a man in butternut-colored clothing driving the oxen; a wife in butternut-colored clothing riding in the wagon, holding a butternut baby, and seventeen butternut children running promiscuously about the establishment; all are barefooted, dusty, and smell unpleasantly. (All these circumstances are expressed by pretty rapid fiddling for some minutes, winding up with a puff from the orpheclide, played by an intoxicated Teuton with an atrocious breath—it is impossible to misunderstand the description.) Now rises o'er the plains in mellifluous accents, the grand Pike County Chorus.

> "Oh we'll soon be thar
> In the land of gold,
> Through the forest old,
> O'er the mounting cold,
> With spirits bold—
> Oh, we come, we come,
> And we'll soon be thar.
>   Gee up Bolly! whoo, up, whoo haw!

The train now encamp. The unpacking of the kettles and mess-pans, the unyoking of the oxen, the gathering about the various camp-fires, the frizzling of the pork, are so clearly expressed by the music, that the most untutored savage could readily comprehend it. Indeed, so vivid and lifelike was the representation, that a lady sitting near us, involuntarily exclaimed aloud, at a certain passage, *"Thar, that pork's burning!"* and it was truly interesting to watch the gratified expression of her face when, by a few notes of the guitar, the pan was removed from the fire, and the blazing pork extinguished.

This is followed by the beautiful *aria:—*

> "O! marm, I want a pancake!"

Followed by that touching *recitative:—*

> "Shet up, or I will spank you!"

To which succeeds a grand *crescendo* movement, representing the flight of the child, with the pancake, the pursuit of the mother, and the final arrest and summary punishment of the former, represented by the rapid and successive strokes of the castanet.

The turning in for the night follows; and the deep and stertorous breathing of the encampment, is well given by the bassoon, while the sufferings and trials of an unhappy father with an unpleasant infant, are touchingly set forth by the *cornet à piston.*

Part Second—The night attack of the Pi Utahs; the fearful cries of the demoniac Indians; the shrieks of the females and children; the rapid and effective fire of the rifles; the stampede of the oxen; their recovery and the final repulse; the Pi Utahs being routed after a loss of thirty-six killed and wounded, while the Pikes lose but one scalp (from an old fellow who wore a wig, and lost it in the scuffle), are faithfully given, and excite the most intense interest in the minds of the hearers; the emotions of fear, admiration and delight, succeeding each other in their minds, with almost painful rapidity. Then follows the grand chorus:

> "Oh! we gin them fits,
> The Ingen Utahs.
> With our six-shooters—
> We gin 'em pertickuler fits."

After which, we have the charming recitative of Herr Tuden Links, to the infant, which is really one of the most charming gems in the performance:

> "Now, dern your skin, *can't* you be easy?"

Morning succeeds. The sun rises magnificently (octavo flute)— breakfast is eaten,—in a rapid movement on three sharps; the oxen are caught and yoked up—with a small drum and triangle; the watches, purses, and other valuables of the conquered Pi Utahs, are stored away in a camp-kettle, to a small movement on the piccolo, and the train moves on, with the grand chorus:—

> "We'll soon be thar,
> Gee up Bolly! Whoo hup! whoo haw!"

The whole concludes with the grand hymn and chorus:—

> "When we die we'll go to Benton,
> Whup! Whoo, haw!
> The greatest man that e'er land saw,
> Gee!
> Who this little airth was sent on
> Whup! Whoo, haw!
> To tell a 'hawk from a hand-saw!'
> Gee!"

The immense expense attending the production of this magnificent work; the length of time required to prepare the chorus; the incredible number of instruments destroyed at each rehearsal, have hitherto prevented M. Tarbox from placing it before the American public, and it has remained for San Diego to show herself superior to her sister cities of the Union, in musical taste and appreciation, and in high-souled liberality, by patronizing this immortal prodigy, and enabling its author to bring it forth in accordance with his wishes and its capabilities. We trust every citizen of San Diego and Vallecetos will listen to it ere it is withdrawn; and if there yet lingers in San Francisco one spark of musical fervor, or a remnant of taste for pure harmony, we can only say that the *Southerner* sails from that place once a fortnight, and that the passage money is but forty-five dollars.

The Greatest Document in American Literature

The subject for this brainy Editorial is resolved that, "Is the Song Yes We Have No Bananas the greatest or the worst Song that America ever had?"

I have read quite a lot in the papers about the degeneration of America by falling for a thing like it. Some lay it to the effects of Prohibition, some say it is the after-effects of War, that it is liable to follow every big war. I see where some have written editorials on the Song claiming that things are always in an unsettled state the year before a Presidential Election. I claim it's due to none of these causes at all; neither is it due to the French occupation of the Ruhr. I claim that it is the greatest document that has been penned in the entire History of American Literature.

From *The Illiterate Digest*, by Will Rogers, pp. 76–83. Copyright, 1923, 1924, by McNaught Syndicate, Inc.; 1924, by Albert & Charles Boni.

And there is only one way to account for its popularity, and that is how you account for anything's popularity, and that is because it has Merit. Real down to earth merit, more than anything written in the last decade. The World was just hungry for something good and when this Genius come along and got right down and wrote on a subject that every Human being is familiar with, and that was Vegetables, Bologna, Eggs and Bananas, why he simply hit us where we live. You know a War Song will only appeal to people that are interested in war, a Love Song to those who are in love, A Mammy Song to nobody at all, but when you get down and write of Cabbages, Potatoes, and Tomatoes, you just about hit on a Universal subject.

You see, we had been eating these things all our lives but no one had ever thought of paying homage to them in Words and Harmony. It opens up a new field for Song Writers. I look for an epidemic of Corned Beef, Liver and Bacon, Soup and Hash Songs to flood the Market. So more power to an originator. Did you ever stop to realize that that Song has attracted more attention than anything that has taken place in this Country since Valentino gave up the screen for a mud Face preparation?

Magnus Johnson of Wisconsin or Minnesota (they ought to put those States together; nobody can ever remember which one anything ever happens in, generally the same thing happens in both of them); well as I say, Magnus was unfortunate enough to be elected to the United States Senate at a time when Bananas was at its height. Ten thousand people can sing the song that don't know that Magnus can milk a Cow with one hand and broadcast a Political speech with the other. Millions can hum the Song that cant tell you what Lloyd George is sore at England about.

Hiram Johnson arrived from Europe a Presidential possibility, and spoke to 2 thousand people. The creator of Bananas to Music, penned one Gem of constructive thought, and spoke not to two thousand but to one hundred and ten million.

Then some Editorial Newspaper writer has the nerve to sneer at this marvelous Song, when perhaps his writings never cross the County line. Why, Italy has already made arrangements on account of his honoring their National Diet to place his name alongside of Michael Angelo, Garibaldi, and Louis Firpo. It is already bringing on International complications. England is sore because he didn't say something about Tea and Cake.

If we had had a Man like that to write our National Anthem somebody could learn it. It wouldn't take three wars to learn the words.

Mother has been done to death in Songs and not enough consideration shown her in real life. We thought when we sang about her we had paid her all the respect there was. I tell you, conditions were Just Ripe for a good fruit Song.

Geo. M. Cohan wore out more Flags than a war waving them to

music. He transferred the Flag from Cloth to Paper, he made it a two verse and Chorus affair. Now George was original. He saw an idea; he knew that a big percentage of the American people had seen the flag, so that would give him a subject to write on that people knew about. But look what a Universal subject this Bird hit on. There are thousands of Foreigners landing here daily that know Spin-ISH and HON-ions, that dont know an American Flag from a Navajo Blanket.

Did you ever just dissect the Words to some of our so-called Popular Songs? One has the words "Its not raining Rain, its raining Violets." Now can you imagine any more of a Cuckoo idea than that? You cant hardly raise the things, much less Rain em. Now which do we owe the most to, the Violet or the Banana? Even such a Genius as Geo. M. Cohan himself has a Song, "You remind me of my Mother when Mother was a Girl like you." How can any man remember his Mother when she was a girl? It's a Physical impossibility. You would have had to be born almost simultaneously with your Mother.

Now on the other hand take the Banana Classic. "We just killed a Pony so try our Bologna, It's flavored with Oats and Hay." Now that's not only good Poetry but his honesty should be rewarded. He is on the level, he is telling you just what you get. Then those History-making lines, "Our Hen Fruit have you tried em, real live Chickens inside em." Now I think in the rhyming line that is a positive Gem, and will live when Gungha Din has lost his Hot Water Bottle. That shows originality. He is not just simply going along rhyming Girl and Pearl, Beauty and Cutey, Bees and Knees.

This Boy has got the stuff. Get this one and then read all through Shakespeare and see if he ever scrambled up a mess of words like these, "Try our Walnuts and Co- CO- Nuts, there aint many nuts like They." Now just off-hand you would think that it is purely a commercial Song with no tinge of Sentiment, but dont you believe it. Read this: "And you can take home for the WIM-mens, nice juicy per-Sim-mons." Now that shows thoughtfulness for the fair sex and also excellent judgment in the choice of a Delicacy. Then there is rhythm and harmony that would do credit to a Walt Whitman, so I defy you to show me a single song with so much downright merit to it as this has.

You know, it dont take much to rank a man away up if he is just lucky in coining the right words. Now take for instance Horace Greeley, I think it was, or was it W. G. McAdoo, who said "go West, young man." Now that took no original thought at the time it was uttered. There was no other place for a man to go, still it has lived. Now you mean to tell me that a commonplace remark like that has the real backbone of this one: "Our Grapefruit I'll bet you, Is not going to wet you, we drain them out every day." Now which do you think it would take you the longest to think of, that or "Go West, Young Man."

Some other fellow made himself by saying "War is Hell." Now what was original about that? Anyone who had been in one could have told you that, and today he has one of the biggest Statues in New York. According to that, what should this Banana man get? He should be voted the Poet Lariet of America.

Now mind you, I am not upholding this man because I hold any briefs for the Songwriters. I think they are in a class with the After Dinner speakers. They should be like Vice used to be in some towns. *They should be segregated off to themselves* and not allowed to associate with people at all, *and should be made to sing these songs to each other.* That is the only way you will ever do away with the Song writing business. . . .

Evolution of a Name

The rise and fall of a mining magnate was relentlessly reflected in the salutations of the community, according to Patrick Quinn. From poor prospector he gradually became rich mine-owner, and when his gold ledge near Devil's Gate petered out he fell accordingly in public estimation. The summary of his life and fortune was contained in the way general reference was made to him. This is as he gave it to me:

> Quinn
> Pat Quinn
> C. Patrick Quinn
> Col. Cornelius Patrick Quinn
> Col. C. P. Quinn
> Patrick Quinn
> Pat Quinn
> Old Quinn

How To Be a Deckhand

. . . The Second Mate said, "Come here, stud, I wanna talk to you."

He sat down on a timberhead and watched the sunrise. He was about thirty-five years old and his face and his Grecian nose were tanned from twenty years of river weather. I liked his blond hair sticking out from under the blue Mate's cap, and better still his mouth, which seemed much more inclined to smile than to sneer. Evidently things had not yet begun to get him down. He was about six feet of Mate, with shoulders to match, and I wondered how many girls he had on the Upper Mississippi.

The deckhands went out on the barges.

"They're sending us some strange ones these days under the name of deckhands," he said, "but up to now we ain't had no college boys. What the hell's the matter with you, stud? This job is too rough even for a farm boy."

"What gives you this college boy idea?" I said.

"Why, kid, it was sticking out all over you when you come aboard."

"I suppose it was. How was it?"

"First you had on a hand-tied bow tie instead of the jazzbow model. Next your short haircut. Last, when I showed you where your bunk was at in the pigpen you says 'Thanks.' Now nobody but a college boy would be enough of a fool to say 'Thanks' for an introduction to a dirty bunk. You college boys are all the time saying 'Thanks,' 'Thanks a lot,' 'Thanks old boy,' and all that crap. If you would of growled a little bit or maybe cussed the company when you seen your luxurious sleeping accommodations, I wouldn't of been so sure, in spite of the bow tie."

I began to laugh. This bird was pretty funny.

"Well," I said, "I can let my hair grow out easy enough, throw away the bow tie, and eliminate the 'Thanks old boy.'"

"Yeah," he said. "You ought to do that. That is, if you was going to stay. But you ain't, stud, you won't be on here long enough to tell the bow from the stern."

"Oh yes I will," I said. "I'll be around for awhile. Anyway long enough for my hair to grow out."

"No you won't, kid," he said. "I hate to tell you, but the truth is, you'll never even see St. Paul. This here is the craziest life on earth, and for a guy who ain't use to misery a deckhand's life is unnecessary torture. You'll soon see there ain't no sense to it."

"I'll be here when we get to St. Paul," I said.

"No you won't. You'll be all disgusted before we get to Rock Island. By the time we get to Lynxville you'll get off, if you can crawl by that time."

"Listen, Mister," I said, "how about me going out and getting to work with the rest of the watch? If it's so damn rough I'll get off, if I like it I'll stay."

"Well, you ain't gonna like it. And on the river you don't need to call me Mister. My name is Joe."

"You're the Mate," I said. "I better not call you Joe."

"Listen stud, relax. This ain't the *Queen Mary*, just an old Upper Mississippi towboat that needs an engine overhaul. Everybody from Minneapolis to Cairo calls me Joe, so don't feel that it's a big treat."

"All right," I said.

"Your problem is gonna be keeping up with the work and trying to get enough sleep to keep alive. If you can hold out for a month without getting discouraged you might make it, if you're stubborn. . . .

"Leave me give you one little nickel's worth of bum advice, kid," he said. "I been out here on the river a long time."

"What's that?"

"If you're really set on staying here, keep pretty quiet for a while until the other deckhands get used to you. Do your work and keep your mouth shut. If they see you can hold up your end making tow in a rainstorm they'll soon forget about the college stuff. Don't try and big talk the other deckhands. Pretty soon you'll find them giving you a few pointers on the work. Watch what they do. Watch how they pick up a ratchet and set it on their shoulder. This Shorty on your watch is one of the best deckhands on the Upper River. Just study him and do like he does and someday you'll be a deckhand." He lit a cigarette and threw the match in the river. "Then you can write the president of that college and tell him the big news."

"All right," I said. "I'll do what I can."

"You can't do no more than that," Joe said. "There's one thing you can do for me, though."

"What's that?"

"Show me how to tie one of them god damn bow ties." . . .

The Folklore of Colleges

I

When she comes tripping by, stone lions will bark. A Revolutionary War cannon will fire out. Two facing statues will solemnly dismount from their pedestals, walk to the center of the courtyard, and clasp hands in congratulation. A series of boulders, delicately balanced atop each other by nature's art, will suddenly collapse. When she gazes their way, the Flattop Mountains will turn purple with rage.

On college campuses throughout the country these various signs will greet her achievement. For she will be the first virgin to graduate from the University. One report states that the teetering rocks on the University of Alabama campus did once topple to the earth, when an undefiled soul passed by. It belonged to a young man.

The variations are legion, but the theme is national, for undergraduates from Florida to Oregon inherit the same general traditions, adjusted of course to local deans and professors and coaches. We usually associate folklore with cowboys and lumberjacks, but college students also tell stories and sing songs that they learn purely by word of mouth.

Consider for instance the gags about the absent-minded or eccentric professor. Every college and university in the land possesses some odd faculty member whose behavior makes legends. At Exeter I remember hearing tales about an extremely cross-eyed Latin master, whom we

By Richard M. Dorson, in *American Mercury*, LXVIII (June, 1949), 671–677.

called "Squint" among ourselves. Enraged in class one time, Squint glared at a squirming student and roared, "Look out, I've got my eye on you!" "Which eye?" the student asked innocently. In another irate mood Squint commanded, "You in the back row, stand up," transfixing a malefactor with his wrathful gaze. Thereupon six students stood up. I always accepted these stories as gospel until recently, when I began to investigate the ways of college folklore.

At Harvard a number of anecdotes cluster around the historian, Albert Bushnell Hart, who kept pottering about the library after his retirement. Folklore says that from force of habit he took careful notes on all the books he handled each afternoon, and then tore up all the notes before going home. A curious librarian noticed him browsing in the fine-arts section for several days, and examined the books Hart had been using. Around every nude figure he found a penciled circle—proof of Hart's ever-youthful outlook. Resurrected to present a paper at the installation of a high school principal, Hart (still according to the folklore) dutifully read the speech his secretary had typed for him, including the two carbon copies she had forgotten to remove.

Everyone knows that professors live in another world, and campus yarns prove the point. A University of Texas professor of ichthyology, walking across the campus with a colleague, was greeted cordially by a student, whom he answered impersonally. "How come you don't know the name of that friendly student?" asked the colleague. "I have made it a point," replied the ichthyologist, "never to learn the names of my students. Whenever I remember a student I forget a fish."

College folklore cherishes the tale of Professor Brown's visit to Professor Smith. The evening wore on, the guest showed no signs of leaving, and finally Brown said, "Harry, I'm awfully sorry but its 2 A.M. and I must ask you to go. I have an 8 o'clock class in the morning." "Bill," said Harry, "you're in my house."

They also tell for true the story of the University of Illinois professor who invited a number of his associates to dinner. When the first guest showed up in a tuxedo, the host's wife motioned him upstairs to do a quick change into formal dress. The other guests arrived, but the host did not reappear. At length the frantic hostess excused herself and slipped up to his room. The professor snored in bed. Taking off his clothes to change, he had unconsciously put on his pajamas and gone to sleep.

II

The classic absent-minded-professor story concerns the pundit who drove his car to a destination, took a train back, and bawled out his wife for not meeting him at the station with the auto. A variation on this theme recently appeared in the *Harvard Alumni Bulletin*, which reported that Professor William J. Cunningham, holder of the chair in transportation at the Business School, had dropped his wife at a mail box and then continued on his journey. Some time later he noticed her absence and informed the police. But I have heard the same story told on a mathematics professor at the University of Michigan, whose wife went to the rest room when he stopped for gas, and came out to find him gone. Worse yet, she had newly arrived in this country and could speak no English.

Professors are important, campus-wise, chiefly because they give grades. How they arrive at their decisions, folklore alone knows. The old story, of course, is that the prof throws the bluebooks down the stairs, and gives As to those which land at the foot, Fs to those at the head. Or he throws them at the ceiling, and whichever stick receive an A. A Harvard tale has chemistry professor J. P. Cooke distributing his papers to his family; he gave the Es himself, his son-in-law the Ds, and so on up to the baby, who, being the slowest, marked the As. From way back I recall the tale of the professor who customarily placed his papers in two heaps, representing the good and the bad students. When he came across an error by a good student he disregarded it, saying, "He knows better than that." When he saw a correct answer by a poor student he marked it wrong, saying, "He couldn't have meant that."

Examinations, the source of grades, provide more folktales. Around Harvard they still talk about Robert Benchley's feat in handling a question in American diplomatic history on rights to the Newfoundland fisheries. Benchley knew nothing about the matter, so he wrote, "This question has long been discussed from the American and British points of view, but has anyone ever considered the viewpoint of the fish?" He proceeded to give it, and was awarded, appropriately enough, a C. The chairman of the University of Minnesota's history department told me of a coed who showed up at the final exam with a few cocktails under her belt. She thought the questions looked a little strange, but went at them with a will. Some weeks later she received a grade of B for a course in American political science, in which she was not enrolled, and a statement of incomplete for the course in American literature in which she belonged.

A colleague of mine claims this is gospel. He caught a student cheating on an examination, and duly reported him to the dean. Ordinarily this meant expulsion, but the student had a relative on the governing board, and was let off with a reprimand. Some years later his professor entered a bank to cash a check, and saw this youth in the front office, scrutinizing the books. He held the post of state bank examiner.

III

There is a sheaf of stories about the dumb star athlete. His coach instructs him to sit next to the class grind for the crucial exam. Forty-nine questions the two answer identically. On the fiftieth the brilliant student writes, "I don't know the answer to this," so the athlete puts down, "I don't know the answer either." Then they tell of the football star who received such encomiums in the press that the dean asked the coach, "Won't all this praise go to his head?" "No," said the coach, "he can't read."

As the prof is lowly and comical, so the coach is lofty and admired. Which college president was it whose salary was raised to make it equal that of the football coach? Anyway, tales constantly spring up of coaches' magic. For instance, Adolph Rupp, the wizard basketball coach at the University of Kentucky, lays his luck to the fact that the door to his office is exactly six feet high. If an ambitious freshman enters without stooping, Rupp doesn't even bother to stand up and shake his hand. Bernie Bierman of the University of Minnesota uses a similar technique in culling football talent. On a scouting trip he drives through a farm area until he comes to a young fellow plowing. He asks him, "Where is the University?" and if the young man points the direction with his hand, Bierman drives on. If, however, he lifts his plow to show the direction, Bierman stops to explain how attractive attendance at the University could be. This plow-lifting stunt, incidentally, is told on several European folk heroes.

Deans, too, grew into legends, and the Dean of Women leads all the rest. Her advice to new coeds echoes across the country. Never wear patent leather shoes on a date; they reflect. Never wear a red dress; it inflames. Don't eat olives; they're passion pills. Always carry along a telephone book (or a newspaper, or a copy of the Saturday Evening Post) in case your date asks you to sit on his lap. The bright street lamps erected in front of the dorms are known as Dean X's birth-control lights. A coed must turn the picture of her boy-friend to the wall before undressing at night.

In spite of these warnings, coeds do manage to have some fun. Just becoming a coed involves certain traditional procedures that the Lady Dean would be horrified to learn about. A mild one is that at Michigan State College, where a girl becomes a coed when kissed in the shadow of Beaumont Tower at the stroke of midnight. At Purdue the requirements are more demanding. Girl kisses boy under the arch of the clock tower at Havoline Hall, on the first stroke of the chimes at midnight. Then both race across campus to John Purdue's grave and commence more serious business before the last chimes strike.

Believed tales, or legends, can be found in college folklore. A macabre one that turns up in various forms is known as the Fatal Fraternity Initiation. The pledge is tied to a chair, blindfolded, and told that his arm is to be cut open. The back of the blade is pressed against his skin, while a wet towel is hung over a chair and drips into a bucket, to simulate the bleeding. The actives tell the pledge they will return later. When they come back, the boy is dead.

Sometimes the pledge is led blindfolded to the edge of a supposed cliff, and dropped two feet to die of shock. Or he is to be singed with a hot poker, which is pressed against raw meat at the same time that a piece of ice is held on the pledge's skin. He smells the burning meat, thinks it is his own flesh, and crumples up dead. In a sorority initiation, the pledge was blindfolded and told to shake the hand of a dead man. The actives thrust a pickled hand they had swiped from the laboratory into her hand, then ran out of the room and locked the door. In the morning they found their sister with snow white hair, nibbling on the pickled hand.

Campus cries form still another aspect of collegiate tradition. At Harvard "Rinehart" rallies the mob for action, and thus memorializes a lonesome alumnus. Poor Rinehart, lacking friends, would go beneath his window and call out his own name, to make the neighbors think him popular. Some say that he actually was popular. At the University of California the cry is "Pedro," and the explanations are myriad. Pedro is the ghost of a student who dropped dead from the shock of getting all As, and now assists cramming undergrads when they call him in their distress. Or he is the ghost of an Indian whose tepee was razed to build the library, and who still hangs angrily about. Or again he is the date of a girl who found herself locked out of the dorm and called after him in despair. Anyway, "Pedro" voices the soul yearnings of Berkeley bookworms on soft spring nights.

IV

Anyone who would penetrate the minds of American collegians must know their songs. The undergraduate inherits a spirited grab-bag of folksong from upperclassmen, and sings them lustily at dorm bull sessions, beer busts, fraternity and sorority parties, or any other convivial occasion. The tunes are standard Tin Pan Alley stuff latched on to parodies and originals. The texts rise up spontaneously and spread mysteriously. Some classics seem to be familiar to college students everywhere; last fall, coming back from Europe on a ship carrying fourteen hundred assorted students, I saw casual groups form on deck and join into lyric after lyric without benefit of songbooks or prompters. Most of the songs wouldn't look well in print anyway.

The *leitmotif* in college balladry is love, but not Tin Pan Alley or Hollywood brands of love. Dimpled, cherubic coeds sing the praises of an earthy, physical passion, of an insatiable sex mania. One group of their songs twines around Wicked Women and their lures: Flamin' Mamie, "a love scorcher and a human torture"; Mimi the College Widow, who taught the boys anatomy; Gumdrop Sal, the friendly Eskimo Queen, whose husband stayed out all night, in a land where the nights are six months long. But the chief beguiler, head and fins above the rest, is Minnie the Mermaid:

> Many's the night I spent with Minnie the Mermaid,
> Down at the bottom of the sea.
> She forgot her morals, down among the corals,
> Gee but she was good to me.

Many's the night when the pale moon was shining,
Down on her bungalow.
Ashes to ashes, dust to dust,
Two twin beds and only one of them mussed.

Oh it's easy to see she's not my mother,
'Cause my mother's forty-nine.
And it's easy to see she's not my sister,
'Cause I'd never give my sister such a helluva good time.

And it's easy to see she's not my sweetie,
'Cause my sweetie's too refined.
She's just a cute little kid who never knew what she did,
She's just a personal friend of mine.

In reverse plot stands the well known fate of "The Lady in Red,"
begging a night's shelter under the bar. The moral to over-ambitious
coeds: beware the ways of college men, "and how they come—and go."

The drinking songs assist men of mettle to drain their cups, stimulat-
ing them with sagas of mighty drunks, or providing due pauses for gulp-
ing purposes. Thus the popular Chug-A-Lug Song requires the rapid
downing of a mugful of beer upon the completion of each verse, while
the celebrated Whiffenpoof Song hymns a stately salute to the tavern
hall.

There are various apostrophes to beer, gin, rum and whisky, and an
epic ballad about an Irish wake:

> The night that Paddy Murphy died
> I never shall forget,
> The whole damn town got stinkin' drunk,
> And some ain't sober yet.
> The only thing they did that night
> That filled my heart with fear,
> They took the ice right off the corpse
> And put it in the beer.

> *Chorus*

> That's how they showed their respect for Paddy Murphy,
> That's how they showed their honor and their pride,
> Ho-ho-ho, that's how they showed their respect for Paddy Murphy,
> On the night that Paddy died.

> When they finished with the beer they started on the corpse.
> They took him from his coffin and put him on the porch,
> And then they went next door and stole a neighbor's pig
> And brought it back to Paddy's house and tied it on his leg.

A college story about Paddy Murphy says that he came to the States
from County Cork, spent his life cheating on, and beating up, his wife,
and died of acute alcoholism. His relatives assembled for a handsome

wake. They duly passed the body and kissed the forehead, when cousin Maureen felt a movement and screamed to Mrs. Murphy, "He's hot, he's hot!" "Hot or cold, he goes out in the morning," said the grieving widow.

At Northwestern University the alcoholic exploits of Paddy Murphy receive each fall appropriate funeral rites, sponsored by the local Sigma Alpha Epsilon chapter. A procession three blocks long files from the chapter house to the outskirts of Evanston, the marchers festooned in green and tearfully draining beer bottles as they follow the corpse, itself composed of dead beer bottles, with a red lamp bulb for a nose. Upon reaching the grave, which has been dug by pledges, the mourners light candles and break into the Paddy Murphy song. An active attired in priestly robes renders the service, paying tribute to Paddy's inspiring and heroic drunks. En route to the grave the Sigma Chis attempt to purloin the corpse, and so seriously do the SAEs defend their honor that in 1945 one circled the procession in a plane to warn his fellow-actives of the enemy's approach.

The group loyalties of college folk get expressed in odes of sentiment and corny humor to fraternities and sororities, and to the alma mater. Serious songs of love and devotion are used to serenade the newly pinned coed, or to entertain a visiting sorority. They crawl with romantic clichés. But the undergrad has no scruples about parodying himself, and will compose such a slurring "Ode by a Sigma Chi" as this:

> The girl of my dreams has bobbed her hair
> And dyed it a fiery red.
> She drinks, she smokes, and she tells dirty jokes,
> She hasn't a brain in her head.
> The girl of my dreams is a cigarette fiend,
> She drinks more booze than I.
> But the girl of my dreams is not what she seems,
> She's the sweetheart of six other guys.

One must add to the stories and songs such other folk matter as the slang of the campus, and the festivals and customs that perforate college life. The enterprising folklorist doesn't need to journey into the back hills to scoop up tradition. He can set up his recording machine in the smokeshop or the college grill.

The Fine Art of Deception

. . . [Doc Macnooder] was bumping up the stairs one afternoon, when he came to an alarmed and sudden halt. Directly opposite, from the crack of the Pink Rabbit's door, came a faint, but unmistakable odor of tobacco.

From *The Tennessee Shad*, by Owen Johnson, pp. 26–40. Copyright, 1911, by Doubleday, Page and Company. New York: A. L. Burt Company.

Now the Pink Rabbit was among the cherubim and seraphim of the school. Macnooder could hardly believe his senses. He advanced a few steps, cocked his head on one side and drew in a deep breath. The odor was strange, but distinctly of the Demon Tobacco.

Macnooder, hastily sliding around the door, beheld, in fact, the Pink Rabbit, propped up in bed, reading a novel, devouring a box of taffy, and smoking a cigarette. . . .

"For the love of Mike, Rabbit! What are you doing?" he exclaimed.

"What's the matter?" said the invalid hoarsely from his couch.

But here Macnooder suddenly sniffed the air.

"Cubebs!" he said.

"Sure."

"But that's smoking."

"Not at all. Doctor Charlie prescribed them—cure asthma, and all that sort of thing."

"Cubebs are not tobacco?" said Macnooder, who had missed the preliminary stages.

"No, you chump."

"And they're good for colds, you say."

"Hay fever and asthma."

"Well, I'll be jig-swiggered."

Macnooder continued to his room in a state of scientific speculation, halted by the window and, digging his fists into his pockets, stared out at the Circle, around which a dozen fellows were laboriously plodding in penance.

"Cubebs aren't tobacco," he repeated for the tenth time. "By the great horned spoon, there certainly is something in that idea."

That night, in the Holy of Holies, Macnooder was more silent than usual, though this time it was with a purpose.

"Doc's in love," said Shingle-Foot, suspiciously.

"I believe he is."

"He certainly acts off his feed."

This sally failed to awaken Macnooder.

"She doesn't love him."

"She loves another."

"Poor old Doc."

Macnooder calmed them with a disdainful flutter of his hand.

"I'll tell you," he said impressively, "what's been occupying me."

"Go ahead."

"I'm tired of local reputations."

"Oh, you are," said Sport McAllister critically; for he thought it was time that even Macnooder should be discouraged.

"I am."

"Indeed!—and what will satisfy you, you conceited, brassy, top-heavy squirt?"

"Nothing but an international reputation," said Macnooder, disdaining to notice the mere flight of epithets.

"You don't say so!"

"And now I've got it."

"Dear me!"

"I've got the greatest stunt that was ever pulled off in any school, at any time, in any country."

"Well, we're listening."

"I'll put it this way. What would happen if the faculty got on to the Holy of Holies?"

"I'd be guiding a plow in South Idaho," said McAllister frankly.

"The use of tobacco in any form is prohibited."

"And punishable by suspension," said Jay Gould. "So says the catalogue. Pass the coffin-nails."

"Well, this is what I propose to do," said Macnooder, "I propose to go two times around the Circle, in full sight of every master in the whole place, smoking a cigarette."

"Repeat that," said Jay Gould.

Macnooder firmly complied.

"Oh, at night!" said Tinkles Bell scornfully; "that's an easy one."

"No, in full daylight."

"And remain in the school?"

"And remain in the school."

"Repeat the whole proposition again."

"Are you a betting man?" said Sport McAllister, when Macnooder had stated the proposition the third time.

"First, last and always."

"I will bet you," said Sport McAllister, trying to still the eagerness in his voice, "I will bet you my monthly allowance from now until the close of the year. Take it, it's yours."

"I'll attend to that bet."

"What?" said McAllister, hardly believing his good fortune. "You take it?"

"The word was 'Attend.'"

"To smoke a cigarette while walking twice around the Circle in full daylight, and not get suspended."

"Exactly."

"Will you write that down?" said McAllister, who began to plan how he should enjoy the blessings of Providence.

"We have witnesses."

"When will you do it?" said Jay Gould.

"Within one week."

The next day Macnooder caught a cold which thickened considerably by the following morning. Despite this, he announced to the expectant House that the attempt would be made at one-thirty that afternoon.

Promptly at that hour Sport McAllister, Jay Gould, Tinkles and

Shingle-Foot, according to agreement, repaired to the Dickinson House, armed with opera-glasses, and spreading the great news. The word having circulated, the five Houses that bordered the Circle, as well as the long outline of the Upper, were suddenly and theatrically alive with spectators, carefully masked (also according to request) by hand-screens and window-curtains.

"Aw, he'll never dare," said Sport McAllister to the Tennessee Shad, who was furnishing the window.

"Perhaps he's been fired already."

"I'll bet there's a catch in it."

"Why, every master in the place is around now."

"Sure; he couldn't go ten yards before Robinson in the Cleve would nab him."

"Aw, he'll never dare," repeated Sport McAllister. In the misfortune of his friend, he found not only a certain pleasure, but a promised easing of the money stringency.

"What's that?"

"Where?"

"Just coming behind the trees."

"It's Macnooder!"

"No!"

"It certainly is!"

It was Macnooder, stepping briskly forward. His throat, to emphasize its delicate condition, was wrapped around with several knitted scarfs; while, besides a sweater, he wore in the warm month of October a winter overcoat.

When precisely opposite the Upper, and in full sight of the Houses, Macnooder deliberately halted and bringing forth a box, lighted a *cubeb* cigarette.

Then, puffing it forth voluminously, he started around the Circle. The nearest House was the Cleve, wherein dwelt not only the Muffin Head but Brotherly Love Baldwin, the young assistant, who had new ideas on education.

As luck would have it, at that precise moment Baldwin was on the threshold, preparing to cross the Circle.

At the sight of Macnooder, steaming briskly along his way, he stiffened one moment with horror; and the next, shot violently after the offender. He did not exactly leap forward, but there was in his advance all the growling rush of a bounding dog.

Macnooder, from the tail of his eye, beheld the sweeping approach and blew forth a particularly voluminous cloud.

"Stop!"

Macnooder came to a halt in gentle surprise.

"How dare you?" exclaimed Baldwin, almost incapable of speech.

"What's wrong, sir?" said Macnooder thickly.

Among the spectators in the Houses there was a sudden terrified craning forward.

"Throw that cigarette down! this instant—you young reprobate!"

Macnooder was seized with a fit of coughing.

"Please, sir," he said finally, "I'm trying to work off a cold. It's only a cubeb."

"A what?"

"A cubeb, sir."

Mr. Baldwin began to suspect that he had bounded into a trap. So he said with dignity:

"Were these prescribed by Dr. Jackson?"

"Oh, yes, indeed, sir. Of course, a cubeb isn't tobacco."

"But smoking is forbidden."

"Oh, no, sir."

"What!"

"Catalogue only forbids use of tobacco. Cubebs are a medicine."

Mr. Baldwin stood rubbing his chin, thoroughly perplexed. Macnooder, with serious face, waited patiently the outcome of his dilemma. Now, of course, Mr. Baldwin could have ordered him to desist from any public display so liable to misconstruction and so upsetting of discipline. But he did not; and the reason was the very human motive that actuates the oppressor and the oppressed. He had been caught, and he wanted someone else to share the ignominy.

When the spying school (who of course saw only a cigarette) actually beheld Mr. Baldwin retire and Macnooder continue on his way, smoking, a spasm of horrified amazement swept the audience, in the midst of which young Pewee Davis fell from the second story, carrying away the vines.

Nothing more happened until the first turn had been completed, when Macnooder encountered Mr. Jenkins, popularly known as Fuzzy-Wuzzy. Mr. Jenkins was near-sighted; and though he taught mathematics, his perceptions were not those of a lightning calculator.

When, on the pleasant meandering speculation of his mind, Macnooder suddenly intruded, he stopped dead, raising his hand to his spectacles to assure himself that he actually saw.

Macnooder, rounding the turn, saluted respectfully and continued his nonchalant way.

"Macnooder?"

"Yes, sir," said Macnooder, stopping at once.

"Er—er."

Macnooder inclined his head in an expectant sort of way until Mr. Jenkins was quite able to frame his words.

"Are you smoking a cigarette?" said the master slowly.

"A cubeb, sir, not tobacco," continued Macnooder; "breaks up colds, sir."

Mr. Jenkins fidgeted with his eye-glasses and stared very hard at him.

"A cubeb, sir, no tobacco," continued Macnooder, allowing the aromatic odor to drift in his direction.

"A cubeb—" repeated Mr. Jenkins slowly, pulling his beard.

"Yes, sir," said Macnooder.

He waited a moment and tipping his hat went on his way, leaving the perplexed master fairly rooted in his tracks.

Mr. Smith, the Muffin Head, the next to be encountered, was older in experience, and cannier. Likewise, he had witnessed the last encounter; so, instead of risking his reputation by rushing madly forth, he took up a book and started ostensibly for the library, carefully calculating his time and distance so as to cross Macnooder's path without seeming to have sought the meeting.

That there was a trap somewhere, he was convinced. So, carefully repressing the instinctive desire to spring upon the flaunter of the scholastic red rag, he approached all alert. A slight wind brought him the unmistakable odor of the cubeb. Now, as it happened, he, too, had suffered from bronchial affliction and was no stranger to this remedy. So, when Macnooder came to a stop, he said with a superior smile:

"Yes, what is it, Macnooder?"

"Please, sir, did you want to speak to me?" said Macnooder, himself surprised.

"About what?"

"I thought—"

"Oh, about smoking a cubeb? Not at all."

"I beg pardon, sir."

"You have a bad cold, I see."

"Yes, sir! Yes, sir!"

"That's very good for it."

The Muffin Head, chuckling with satisfaction, continued on his way. He, too, in the natural course should have sent Macnooder to his room; but again the little human strain prevented. At the entrance to Memorial, he turned and looked back to see who would fall into the trap he had evaded.

This was too much for the now utterly flabbergasted school—the Muffin Head, of all masters; the strictest of disciplinarians; the most relentless of task-masters! In rapid succession the school then beheld a dozen more masters take the bait, some fairly galloping down with rage, others suspiciously sniffing the air. By the time Macnooder had completed four rounds, there remained only Mr. Baranson, of the Griswold, who had not been tempted out to investigate.

Macnooder made one more round with his eye on the study of the Griswold, hoping against hope. Finally he said:

"Well, here goes! Someone has put him on—he's too cute to come out!"

Then, secure and triumphant, he discarded the stump of the cubeb and lit a real cigarette, completing, without mishap, twice the rounds of the Circle.

Now, Mr. Baranson, who rightly bore the title of the craftiest of the crafty, had witnessed the whole performance, chuckling hugely at the successive discomfitures of his associates, and finally guessing the explanation.

The Muffin Head, on his return from the library, hoping that he had not been seen, dropped in for an artful call; and at the proper moment paused before the window, exclaiming:

"By George, what's that!"

Mr. Baranson doubled up with laughter at the obviousness of the trap. When he had finally wiped the tears from his eyes, he said in a slightly superior manner:

"Smith, if you're going to deal with boys, you must use your imagination. You must out-think them. That's the only way, Smith; the only way. Don't walk into their traps, don't do it. Every time a master lets himself be fooled, he loses some of his authority. Imagination, Smith; imagination!"

But an hour later, at dusk, he began to consider, to weigh and to speculate; and the more he analyzed the situation, the more he began to wonder if he had seen the last curtain. He left the House and went slowly toward the road Macnooder had traveled, and his eyes were on the ground where the last cigarette stump had fallen. Suddenly behind him a voice said solicitously:

"Have you lost anything, Mr. Baranson?"

It was Macnooder.

The two stood a long moment, master and boy, the craftiest of the crafty and the ambitious Macnooder, glance to glance, one of those silent interrogatories that can not be described.

"Your cold seems to have gone," said Mr. Baranson at length, dealing out his words. Then he added, with a slightly twitching, generous smile, "I *congratulate you!*"

IX. FELONS AND FEVERS

(On the Subjects of Law and Medicine)

Introduction

The doctor and the lawyer are the butts of many folk jokes. Because both use the technical terms of their professions, they may be thought to be making their work seem more complicated than it is. Some people, for example, may jokingly accuse the doctor of using five-dollar words to describe fifty-cent ailments and ten-cent medicines so that he can charge fees commensurate with his vocabulary. And since it is extremely difficult to judge the efficacy of an internal medicine in an individual case, the doctor can frequently expect jibes about his pills.

The work of the lawyer is not so mysterious as that of the doctor, for some of his work the lawyer must perform before a crowded courtroom. The people may not understand all the language of the law, but they sometimes make folk etymologies which retain the spirit if not the letter, such as saying that they will "swear out a lie-bill" against someone. They are pleased by stories of lawyers frustrated by rambling testimony like that of Lanty Oliphant and by stories of judges nonplused by uncooperative juries like that in "A Misdirected Verdict." And they delight in stories of "mavericks" on the bench—of Roy Bean reading the "full, unexpurgated law of the great state of Texas" to be sure there was nothing in it about killing a laundryman, or of Judge Parker delivering a death sentence which began with beautiful figures and mellifluous cadences and ended in outright vituperation. Most people, though, try to stay out of court and prefer to follow Bill Arp's horse-sense dictum about arbitration: ". . . never arbytrate nuthin but a bad case. . . ."

Roy Bean Law

I guess there never was a more upstanding man in Texas, from the days of Sam Houston and Davy Crockett right down to now, than Roy Bean, judge, ex-officio coroner, *alcalde*, and all-round king of Langtry.

Somehow there's been very little written about Judge Roy Bean; perhaps because he ruled in such a lonely and wild country there, west of the Pecos.

Most of the hundreds of yarns told about him through the length and breadth of the Lone Star State are funny ones. But he was a great pioneer, just the same. Did his full share of taming and building up the wild West Texas country of the Eighties.

When the Southern Pacific first laid its rails through those untamed stretches, Roy Bean opened a saloon on the line about four-five miles due west of the Pecos on the northern bank of one of those sharp bends in the Rio Grande, though it was farther from the Pecos by the railway, which takes a sharp slant southeast after leaving Langtry, following the course of the Rio Grande till it crosses the Pecos on a high bridge a ways above the big river.

When he built his dobie hang-out there in west Val Verde County, that country wasn't noways what you'd call civilized, being mostly popu-

From *Gun Notches, The Life Story of a Cowboy-Soldier.* By Captain Thomas H. Rynning as told to Al Cohn and Joe Chisholm, pp. 125–126, 130–132. Copyright, 1931, by Frederick A. Stokes Company. A. L. Burt Company, Publishers. New York.

lated by white outlaws, renegade Mexicans and hostile Indians. Wasn't any more law in that section than in Darkest Africa.

But the railroad people soon found out that Roy Bean was holding down the wild bunch steady-like and they got him appointed justice of the peace. Right away he slapped up a big sign clear across the front of his temple of justice and tarantula juice reading:

JUSTICE OF THE PEACE—LAW WEST OF THE PECOS

Above the big sign, which was nailed across the seven posts that supported the porch roof in front of his building, he had a smaller one, right on the eaves of the porch, that said JUDGE ROY BEAN. Underneath was another: BEER ON ICE; but that was just Roy's little joke. There wasn't any ice within hundreds of miles of there, though he did keep the beer tolerable cool wrapped in wet gunnysacks.

And Judge Bean, holding court at an old desk behind the pool table at one end of the saloon, sure dealt out all kinds of law. Some of his decisions mightn't get by the United States Supreme Court, but they sure as hell was the law out there, west of the Pecos. . . .

Roy Bean's legal work was what got him his reputation amongst the waddies and rustlers as the greatest lawgiver since Moses and Daniel Webster. He had an old book of Texas statutes that dated back to somewheres round the time of Goliad and the battle of San Jacinto; but in case a difficult trial come up he didn't let that law book cramp his style none.

Once Roy's son shot and killed a laundryman because he charged too much for his laundry or something serious like that, and of course young Bean was tried before his old man. Naturally Roy wanted to give his boy as easy a deal as the law would allow, but he was a square-shooter and if his son turned out guilty of a misdemeanor or anything like that, it was a cinch he'd warp it to him just like he was a stranger.

So the Judge opened court with the usual formalities, throwing out a couple of drunks who wouldn't quit snoring during the proceedings, and started the justice mill to grinding. On account of his own kin being up for trial and all the customers watching him more interested than usual, he went about things mighty careful and legal-like.

As a rule he give his decisions right out of his deep knowledge of the law, for he'd been J. P. for a year or more then; but this time he figured he had to dig into the Unabridged Statutes of 1846, or somewheres round that date.

He hooked his spectacles onto his handsome big red nose and begun reading the law book out loud, so's everybody could see he wasn't keeping any ace in the hole. And damned if he didn't read those Texas statutes from cover to cover, cussing every cowpuncher awake that went to sleep on him and refusing to let any of them go to the bar for a drink during all that long spell of court.

When he'd waded plumb through the Texas law from murder to

cow brands, in about two hours or so, those cowpunchers and rustlers had got a darned sight more legal knowledge screwed into their skulls than lots of the tinhorn lawyers of the State ever knew. In fact, they was a plumb nuisance after that, some of them, spouting their information about Texas law by the hour every time they got drunked up and could get some unfortunate dogie to stand hitched long enough to pour it into him by the gallon.

"And there she is, gentlemen," says Roy Bean, when he'd got through. "That's the full, unexpurgated law of the great State of Texas up to 1873, and it ain't noways likely there's been any fundamental changes run into it since.

"The complete statutes of this here State, from the Alamo on ahead, and there ain't a damned line in it nowheres that makes it illegal to kill a laundryman. The defendant is discharged."

He went most justices of the peace one better in one line. Common J. P.s only held preliminary hearings in case of serious offenses, but Roy Bean would sentence them to the penitentiary just as quick as he'd fine them five dollars and costs for shooting Mexicans.

I don't remember if he ever sentenced anybody to be hung, but he'd sure as hell have done it if the case called for it.

Once, though, he run into a snag that way that made him mighty hostile. He sentenced a horse thief to twenty years in the penitentiary, but the constable come back from Huntsville and says they wouldn't hold the prisoner because the constable couldn't dig up no commitment papers.

Probably Judge Bean didn't know what the hell commitments was, anyhow, but he sent back word telling them he didn't give a dam' what they did with the sonofabitch just so long as they didn't let him commit suicide by coming back to Langtry, and they didn't.

Ordinary justices of the peace only marry people. But Roy Bean wasn't noways an ordinary J. P. He divorced them just as easy as he hooked them up.

To show what a natural legal mind he had, a fellow only has to tell about the case of the drunken cowpuncher who fell off the Southern Pacific bridge that crosses the Pecos. That's the highest railroad bridge in the world, or leastwise it was at that time. So when that waddy landed three hundred feet below he was what might be called plumb extinct.

The Pecos is the east boundary line of Val Verde County, but as the puncher landed on the west bank of the river, that brought his corpse inside Roy Bean's jurisdiction.

First Bean set as coroner and declared the late cowboy to be completely deceased. Then he went into session as judge and called attention to the fact that the corpse had in its possession two ten-dollar goldpieces and a six-shooter, and fined him twenty dollars for carrying concealed weapons.

A Misdirected Verdict

"It's a $100 in your pocket," whispered the defendant's lawyer to the juror, "if you can bring in a verdict of manslaughter in the second degree." Such proved to be the verdict, and the lawyer thanked the juror warmly as he paid him the money. "Yes," said the juror, "it was tough work, but I got there after a while. All the rest went in for acquittal."

On the Judge's Side

. . . Hon. Harry White, Judge of the Fortieth Judicial district, who is noted for his tendency to explain things to his juries, expressed in a recent case his own ideas with such force that he was surprised the jurors thought of leaving the box. They did leave it, however, and were out hours. Inquiring the trouble, the Judge was told that one of the twelve was standing out against the eleven. He summoned the jury and rebuked the recalcitrant sharply. "Your honor," said the juror, "may I say a word?" "Yes, sir," said the indignant Judge; "what have you to say?" "Well, what I wanted to say is, I'm the only fellow that's on your side."

The Law and the Constitution of Texas

The Republic was a going concern—commerce reviving, mails delivered, courts respected. A drunken lawyer was arguing a case before Three-Legged Willie.

"Where is the law to support your contention?" interrupted the judge.

The lawyer whipped out a dirk.

"There's the law," he said.

Judge Williamson dropped the muzzle of a pistol over the bench. "Yes, and there's the Constitution."

From *American Wit and Humor*, Vol. II, p. 129. Philadelphia: George W. Jacobs & Co. 1900.

From *Waifs of the Press*. Collected and Edited by Harry L. Work, p. 57. Washington: Walter Neale, Publisher. 1898.

Judge Norman Kittrell, in the Chicago *Record-Herald*, 1911, as reported by William E. Curtis. Quoted in *The Raven: A Biography of Sam Houston*, by Marquis James, p. 297. Copyright, 1929, by Marquis James. New York: Blue Ribbon Books. n.d.
Many oral versions of this story exist; in some of them the drunken lawyer waved a six-shooter and the judge placed a sawed-off shotgun on the bench.

Evasive Answers

Lawyers allege that there are four classes of witnesses—those who prove too much, those who prove too little, those of a totally negative character, and those of no character at all, who will prove anything. We have a case in point.

Far, very far away from the tall Blue mountains, at a little place called Sodom, there were upon a time three neighbours called in as arbitrators to settle a point, relative to some stolen chickens, in dispute between one Lot Corson and a "hard case" called Emanuel Allen, better known thereabout as King of the Marsh.

"Mister Constable," said one of the demi-judicials, "now call the principal witness."

"Lanty Oliphant! Lanty Olip-h-a-n-t!" bawled Dogberry. "Mosey in and be swore."

In obedience to this summons, little Lanty, whose bottle had usurped the place in his affections commonly assigned to soap and water, waddled up and was qualified, deprecating by a look the necessity of such a useless ceremony among gentlemen.

"Mister Oliphant, you are now swore. Do you know the value of an oath?" asked the senior of the board.

"Doesn't I!" rejoined Lanty, with a wink at a bystander. "Four bushel of weight wheat, the old score wiped off, and licker for the hul day throw'd in."

This matter-of-fact answer met a severe frown from the man with the red ribbon round his hat.

"Well, Mister Oliphant," continued the senior, "tell all you know about this here case. Bill M——k, *shoo* your dog off that d—d old sow."

Lanty here testified. "Feelin' a sort of outish t'other day, ses I to the old woman, ses I, I'll jist walk over to Lot's and take a nipper or two this mornin', ses I. It'll take the wind off my stomach sorter, ses I. Then the old woman's feathers riz, they did, like a porkypine's bristles, and ses she, Lanty, ses she, if you'd on'y aim more bread and meat, and drink less whisky, you wouldn't have wind on your stomach. Suse, ses I, this is one of my resarved rights, and I goes agin home industry, ses I, sort o' laughin' out o' the wrong side o' my mouth. 'Resarved rights or desarved wrongs,' ses her, 'you'r always a drinkin' and talkin' politics when you orter be at work, and there's never nothin' to eat in the house.' Well, as I was agoin over to Lot's jist fernent where the fence *was*, ses I to myself, ses I, if there isn't the old King's critters in my corn field, so I'll jist go and tell him on't. When I gets there, Good mornin', Lanty, ses he. Good mornin', old

"Lanty Oliphant in Court," by Maj. Kelly, of Louisiana, from *A Quarter Race in Kentucky and Other Sketches* . . . , edited by William T. Porter, pp. 38–40. Philadelphia: T. B. Peterson and Brothers. 1854.

hoss, ses I, and when I went in, there was a pot on the fire a cookin',
with a *great big speckled rooster* in it."

"Mister Oliphant!" here interposed one of the arbitrators. "Remember that you are on oath. How do you know that the chicken in the
pot was 'a big speckled rooster'?"

" 'Kase I *seed the feathers at the woodpile!*" promptly responded
Lanty, who then continued:

"Well, when I gits to Lot's, Good mornin', Lot, ses I. Good mornin',
Lanty, ses he. You didn't see nothin' no where of nar' a big speckled
rooster that didn't belong to nobody, did you? ses he. Didn't I? ses I.
Come, Lanty, ses he, let's take a nipper, ses he; and then I up and tells
him all about it."

"Had Mr. Allen no chickens of his own?" asked the senior.

"Sartin'," rejoined Lanty; "but there warn't a rooster in the crowd.
They was *all layin' hens!*"

"Well," inquired another of the referees, "how many of these hens
had Mr. Allen?"

This question fairly "stump'd" Lanty for a moment, but he quickly
answered:

"Why, with what was there, and what wasn't there, counting little
and big, spring chickens and all, *there was forty odd*, EXACTLY!"

No further questions were put to this witness!

Un-suitable

. . . There was a certain lawyer on the Cape a long time ago, the
only one in those 'diggin's' then, and, for aught I know, at present. He
was a man well to do in the world, and, what was somewhat surprising
in a limb of the law, averse to encouraging litigation.

One day a client came to him in a violent rage.

"Look a here, squire," said he, "that 'ere blasted shoemaker down to
Pigeon Cove has gone and sued me for the money for a pair of boots
I owed him."

"Did the boots suit you?"

"Oh! yes—I've got 'em on—fust-rate boots."

"Fair price?"

"Oh! yes."

"Then you owe him the money honestly?"

" 'Course."

"Well, why don't you pay him?"

"Why, 'cause the blasted snob went and sued me, and I want to
keep him out of the money if I kin."

"It will cost you something."

From "Concerning Crows and Cape Ann Jokers" in *Stray Subjects Arrested and
Bound Over* [by Francis A. Durivage and George P. Burnham], pp. 67–69. Philadelphia: T. B. Peterson and Brothers. 1848.

"I don't keer a cuss for that. How much money do you want to begin with?"

"Oh, ten dollars will do."

"Is that all? Well, here's a X, so go ahead," and the client went off very well satisfied with the beginning.

Our lawyer next called on the shoemaker, and asked him what he meant by commencing legal proceedings against M———.

"Why," said he, "I kept on sendin' and sendin' to him for money till I got tired. I know'd he was able to pay—and I was 'termined to make him. That's the long and short of it."

"Well," said the lawyer—"he's always been a good customer to you, and I think you acted too hastily. There's a trifle to pay on account of your proceeding——but I think you'd better take this five dollars, and call it all square."

"Certain—squire—if you say so—and darned glad to get it," was the answer.

So the lawyer forked over one V and kept the other. In a few days his client came along and asked him how he got on with his case.

"Rapidly," cried the lawyer—"we've *non-suited* him! he'll never trouble you."

"Jerusalem! that's great!" cried the client—"I'd rather a gin fifty dollars than have had him got the money for them boots!"

Going to Law: Bill Arp's Sad Experience

MR. KUMMUNS AND ET AL—GENTLEMEN:

I hav reseved your kind invitashun to address your Law school. In the situashun in which I am situated, it is onpossible for me to go. I wish I could, for I would like to tell you all I know about law bisiness myself, at this place. We are engaged in manufakturin it by holesale, and atter while it will be retaled out by the lawyers to any body that wants it. It's an esy bisiness to make law, but the greatest diffikulty is in onderstandin it atter it is made. Among the lawyers this diffikulty don't seam to lie so much in the hed as in the poket. For five dollars a lawyer can luminise sum, and more akkordin to pay. But he ortent to luminise but one side at a time. The fust case I ever had in a Justice Court I emploid old Bob Leggins, who was a sorter of a self-eddicated fool. I giv him two dollars in advanse, and he argud the case, as I thot, on two sides, and was more luminus agin me than for me. I lost the case, and found out atterwards that the defendant had employed Leggins atter I did, and gin him five dollars to lose my case. I look upon this as a warnin to all klients to pay big fees and keep your lawyer out of temtashun.

From "Bill Arp Addresses the Lebanon Law School, and Gives His Own Sad Experience," in *Bill Arp's Peace Papers*, by Bill Arp [Charles H. Smith], pp. 186–191. New York: G. W. Carleton & Co., Publishers, 1873.

My xperience in litigashun hav not been satisfaktory. I sued Sugar Black onst for the price of a lode of shuks. He sed he wanted to buy sum ruffness, and I agreed to bring him a lode of shuks for two dollers. My waggin got broke and he got tired a waitin, and sent out atter the shuks himself. When I called on him for the pay, he seemed surprised, and sed it had cost him two dollars and a half to hav the shuks hauld, and that I justly owd him a half a dollar. He were more bigger than I was, so I swallerd my bile and sued him. His lawyer pled a set-off for haulin. He pled that the shuks was unsound; that they was barred by limitashuns; that they didn't agree with his cow, and that he never got any shuks from me. He speak about a hour, and allooded to me as a swindler about 45 times. The bedevild jewry went out and brot in a verdik agin me for fifty cents, and four dollars for costs. I hain't saved many shuks on my plantashun sence, and I don't intend to til it gits less xpensiv. I look upon this as a warnin to all foaks *never to go to law about shuks,* or any other small sirkumstanse.

The next trubble I had was with a feller I hired to dig me a well. He was to dig it for 20 dollers, and I was to pay him in meat and meal, and sich like. The vagabon kep gittin along til he got all the pay, but hadn't dug nary a foot in the ground. So I made out my akkount and sued him as follers, to wit:

| Old John Hanks, to Bill Arp, | Dr. |
| To 1 well you didn't dig. | $20 |

Well, Hanks, he hired a cheep lawyer, who rared round xtensively, and sed a heep of funny things at my xpense, and finally dismissd my case for what he calld its "ridikulum abserdum." I paid those costs and went home a sadder and a wiser man. I pulld down my little kabbin and mooved it sum 300 yards nigher the spring, and I hav drunk mity little well water sence. I look upon this case as a warnin to all foaks *never to pay for enything till you git it, espeshally if it has to be dug.*

The next law case I had I ganed it all by myself, by the forse of sirkumstanses. I bot a man's note that was giv for the hire of a Negro boy, Dik. Findin he wouldn't pay me, I sued him before old Squire Maginnis, beleevin that it was sich a ded thing that the devil couldn't keep me out of a verdik. The feller pled failur of konsiderashun, and *non est faktum,* and *ignis fatuis,* and infansy, and that the Negro's name wasn't Dik, but *Richard.* The old Squire was a powerful sesesh, and hated the Yankees amazin. So, atter the lawyer had got thru his speech and finished up his readin from a book called "Greenleaf," I rose forward to a attitood. Stretchin forth my arms, ses I, "Squire Maginnis, I would ax, sur, if this is a time in the histry of our afflikted kountry when Yankee law books should be admitted in a Southern patriot's Court? Hain't we got a State of our own and a code of Georgy laws that's printed on Georgy sile? On the very fust page of the gentleman's book I seed the name of the sitty of Bosting. Yes, sur, it was ritten in Bosting, where they don't know no more about the hire of a Negro than an ox knows the man who will tan his hide." I sed sum more things that was pinted and patriotik, and closd my argyment by handin the book to the Squire. He put on his speks, and atter lookin at the book about a minit, ses he:

"Mr. Arp, you can hav a judgment, and I hope that from hense-fourth no lawyer will presoom to cum before this honerabul court with pisen dokyments to proove his case. If he do, this court will take it as an insult, and send him to jail."

I look upon this case as a warnin to all foaks who gambel in law, to hold a good hand and play it well. High jestice and patriotism are winning trumps.

My next case was about steelin a hog. Larseny from the woods, I think they call it. I didn't hav but one hog, and we had to let him run out to keep him alive, for akorns was cheeper than corn at my house. Old Romulus Ramsour sorter wanted sum fresh meat, and so he shot my shote in the woods and was catched carrying him home. He had cut off his ears and throwed em away; but we found em, with the under bit in the right and swaller fork in the left, and so Romulus was brot up square before the jewry, and his defense was that it was a wild hog. The jewry was out about two hours and brot in a verdik: "We the jewry know that shortly atter the war the kountry was scarce of provishuns, and in considerashun of the hard time our poor peepul had in maintanin their families, and the temtashuns that surrounded em, we find the defendent not guilty, but we rekommend him not to do so any more." The motto of this case is that a man ortent to keep hogs in a poor naberhood.

After this I had a diffikulty with a man by the name of Kohen, and I thot I wouldn't go to law, but would arbytrate. I had bot Tom Swil-lins' wheat at a dollar a bushel, *if he couldn't do any better,* and if he could do better he was to cum back and *giv me the prefferense.* The skamp went off and sold the wheat to Kohen for a dollar and five cents, and Kohen knowd all about his kontrak with me. Me and him lik to hav fit, and perhaps would, if I hadn't been puny; but we finally left it to Josh Billins to arbytrate. Old Josh deliberated on the thing three days and nites, and finally brot in an award that Kohen should hav the wheat and *I should hav the prefferense.* I hain't submitted no more cases to arbytration sinse, and my advise to all peepul is to arby-trate nuthin if your case is honest, for there aint no judge there to keep one man from trikkin the other. An honest man don't stan no chance nowhere xceptin in a court house with a good lawyer to back him. The motto of this case is, never to arbytrate nuthin but a bad case, and take a good lawyer to advise, and pay him fur it before you do that. . . .

Criminal

"Have you a criminal lawyer in this burg?"
"We think so but we haven't been able to prove it on him."

A Really Strict Judge

"Something was said . . . that reminded [Lincoln] of the following circumstance: 'Judge ————,' said he, 'held the strongest ideas of rigid government and close construction that I ever met. It was said of him, on one occasion, that he would hang a man for blowing his nose in the street, but he would quash the indictment if it failed to specify which hand he blew it with!' "

You Won't Be There

In the early cattle trail days, when Oklahoma was known as the Indian Territory, a certain Federal Judge, one Parker, was known for the severity of his decisions. In a cowcamp brawl of a passing trail herd, a Mexican cook shot and killed a cowboy in a dispute over a game of cards. Friends of the dead cowboy wanted to lynch the cook at once, but one of their number, the trail-herd boss, persuaded them to wait until he had seen Judge Parker about the matter. It is related that he and the Judge had several drinks together the next day in Fort Smith, Arkansas, and that the Judge readily agreed to pass sentence of death upon the Mexican according to the ideas of the trail herder. Plenty of oratory was asked for along with the sentence in order to make the proceedings entirely legal and proper. This is Judge Parker's sentence:

"José Manuel Miguel Xavier Gonzales, in a few months it will be spring, the snow of winter will flee away, the ice will vanish, and the air will become soft and balmy. In short, José Manuel Miguel Xavier Gonzales, the annual miracle of the year's awakening will come to pass, but you won't be here. The rivulet will run its purling course to the sea, the timid desert flowers will put forth their tender shoots, the glorious valleys of this imperial domain will blossom as the rose, still you won't be here. From every tree-top some wildwood songster will

From *The People, Yes,* by Carl Sandburg, p. 154. Copyright, 1936, by Harcourt, Brace and Company, Inc. New York.

From *Lincoln's Own Stories,* Collected and Edited by Anthony Gross, p. 91. Copyright, 1912, by Harper & Brothers. New York.

From "Stop-Over at Abilene," by John A. Lomax, *Southwest Review,* Vol. XXV (July, 1940), No. 4, pp. 407–418.

carol his mating song, butterflies will sport in the sunshine, the busy bee will hum happily as it pursues its accustomed vocation, the gentle breezes will tease the tassels of the wild grasses, and all nature, José Manuel Miguel Xavier Gonzales, will be glad, but you won't be here to enjoy it; for I command the sheriff or some other officer or officers of this county to lead you out to some remote spot, swing you up by the neck to a nodding bough of some sturdy oak, and there let you hang till you are dead, dead, dead. And then, José Manuel Miguel Xavier Gonzales, I command further that such officer or officers retire quietly from your swinging, dangling corpse, that the vultures may descend from the heavens upon your filthy body and pick the putrid flesh therefrom till nothing remain but the bare, bleached bones of a cold-blooded, copper-colored, bloodthirsty, chili-eating, guilty, sheep-herding, Mexican son-of-a-bitch."

Untwisting a Tangle

". . . Did you ever know," said the graybeard, resting his hands on the knob of his hickory stick, "how Patrick Henry untwisted a little love-tangle? I'll tell you. A young fellow wanted to get married without being overtaken by the law. The girl, ditto; but her parents objected. She was not of age, and the law had it all fixed that if he ran away with her and was caught, he could be sent to jail. That's where the trouble was. But the young fellow took his trouble to Patrick Henry, and Patrick said: 'You really love her, do you? How much do you love her? Do you love her better than gold? How much would you give out of pocket if you could get your sweetheart and never cast a shadow in the doorway of a jail?' 'I'd give a hundred guineas,' said his client. 'Agreed! Now do as I tell you. Go see your ladylove; request her to take a horse out of her father's stable, mount, make off, and meet you at an appointed place. You are to be on foot. You are to get on behind her. Ride to the nearest preacher's and get married. You will be arrested; but never mind that, for I shall be there to see you through.' Now we come to the second chapter—with everybody in court from five miles round. The Commonwealth's attorney said it was so plain a case that he would simply state the law and the facts, and be done with it. He did so; after which Patrick got up, and admitted that the law was just as the prosecutor had urged. But he would be better satisfied, he said, if the young woman should take the stand and give an account of the elopement. So up she went, the pretty bride, and all the men shuffled and craned, and the judges sat straight. Then she said, said she: 'I told my lover to meet me at a certain spot. I got out a good horse from my father's stable, and rode to

From *The True Patrick Henry,* by George Morgan, pp. 374–375. Copyright, 1907, by J. B. Lippincott Company. Philadelphia & London.

where he was. I took my lover up behind me, and ran away with him.' 'Did he run away with you?' said the sly old Pat. 'No, sir, I ran away with him.' 'Oh!' said Patrick, 'I see!' The court got into a side-splitting shake; the crowd roared; the Commonwealth attorney came down the persimmon-tree, and the happy chap marched off with the persimmon."

He Won By Losing

Along in the 80's a lawyer by the name of Hooper settled in one of the county-seat towns of East Texas. No one knew just where he came from or why he came to Texas, but it was rumored that he had come from Virginia. No one ever questioned Hooper about his personal history. He was dignified and aloof, and made no effort to cultivate intimacy—indeed, he kept to himself and made few friends.

But it was evident from the start that Hooper was a man of learning. He dressed in the fashion of his day, wore a Prince Albert coat, carried a gold-headed cane, and conducted himself with such decorum that he soon gained the respect, although not the friendship, of the people generally. He owned an excellent library and at times he quoted Latin and Greek authors. He rode in a fine carriage and was generally attended by a Negro footman. What with his aristocratic bearing and cool courtesy, it soon became apparent to the people that Hooper was haughty and that he disdained the common run of folks.

Without doubt Hooper's attainments were such that he could have been popular had he so desired, but he evidently did not want popularity. He had a passion for attending to his own business and leaving other people to theirs. He was in fact a stoic, if not a cynic. In a small county-seat town he did the unusual thing of confining his practice to civil matters. He simply would not take a criminal case. Neither would he take small civil cases; that is, he would not practise in the justice courts. But such was his learning and skill as a technical civil lawyer that he soon enjoyed a large practice. It was he, you might say, that introduced in his section the custom of appealing to the higher courts. When he was defeated in the local courts, he nearly always appealed and in most instances he succeeded in reversing the judgments of the lower courts. Such was his success that it was not long until he represented almost all of the monied clients in his county.

As Hooper became more independent financially, he became more independent in his views and bolder in expressing them. For instance, one day in arguing a motion for rehearing before a judge who had

From "Anecdotes about Lawyers," by Lloyd E. Price, in *Backwoods to Border*, edited by Mody C. Boatright and Donald Day, pp. 208–212. Texas Folk-Lore Society Publications, Number XVIII, J. Frank Dobie, General Editor. Copyright, 1943, by the Texas Folk-Lore Society. Austin and Dallas: Texas Folk-Lore Society and University Press in Dallas, Southern Methodist University.

held against him more from political than from legal reasons, Hooper
said in the course of his argument, "It was plain to the honest and
fearless statesmen who founded this nation, as it is plain to intelligent
people of this day, that the greatest danger to the institutions of
America lies in the uneducated masses of people when led by self-seek-
ing politicians and demagogues." He also said that when America was
destroyed it would be destroyed by some power-loving demagogue
with the howling majority behind him. He said that unless officials,
including judges, stood up to their oaths and obligations the country
would eventually disintegrate.

It was only natural that Hooper should be unpopular.

One of Hooper's best clients was the largest bank in the town where
he practised. One fall that bank was sued out in one of the rural Justice of the Peace Courts for $100 by a tenant farmer. Now Hooper
decided that he wanted to represent his bank in all its business, and
so he decided to make an exception to his rule. As the plaintiff was
represented by a popular young orator who had political ambitions,
Hooper expected hard sledding in the rural court out where the plaintiff lived.

But Hooper faced the music. On the day of the trial he dressed
more immaculately than usual and drove out to the precinct court in
his rubber-tired carriage. The Justice of the Peace convened court in
the lower story of an old frame lodge building. There were an old
pine table and a few chairs with cow-hide bottoms. The jury of six
men were close neighbors and friends of the plaintiff and no doubt
had prejudged the case in his favor before court convened. Hooper
did not ask the jury a question, and made no objections whatever.
Both the old Justice of the Peace and the members of the jury were
dressed in their ordinary work clothes, and their appearance con-
trasted strongly with that of the spic and span Lawyer Hooper. As
the young lawyer for plaintiff put on his evidence, the jury squirted
long streams of tobacco juice on the floor. At times they glared ominously at Hooper who sat there in splendid isolation with not a single
representative of his client present save himself, and without a single
defendant witness.

When the plaintiff had made his case against the bank and rested,
Hooper arose and curtly announced, "No evidence for defendant will
be offered."

The plaintiff's lawyer then addressed the jury and you may be sure
that he castigated the bank. Dramatically, he depicted the plaintiff as
a hard-working, honest man who made his living by the sweat of his
brow working in the field from sun-up to sun-down, while the defendant was a rich, greedy, soulless corporation that increased its wealth
by feeding on the meagre earnings of men like the plaintiff. He concluded by comparing the defendant bank to the greedy money-
changers whom Christ drove out of the temple. By the time he had

finished the jury was as mad as biting sows and at times cast sullen glances at the cool and immaculate Hooper, who sat there as the sinister representative of corporate wealth and greed.

Hooper arose to speak but before saying a word he first flecked some dust from his tailored coat and then addressed the jury, "Gentlemen of the jury, if I may call you such, there never was a bigger lie ever told on earth than by old Tom Jefferson when he said that all men are created equal. Why, look at me and then look at you; here I stand, well-educated and well-dressed—bathe every day while there you sit with snuff and tobacco all over you. Some of you haven't bathed in weeks; there you sit with your cheap breeches held up by one suspender prong fastened by a shingle nail. Yes, I assert there never was a bigger lie ever told on earth than that by Jefferson when he said that all men are created equal."

The Justice of the Peace was too astonished to remonstrate and the jury from some cause seemed determined to listen to the end.

"I know," said Hooper, "exactly what you're going to do. You are prejudiced against my bank and you are going to bring in a judgment in favor of your friend, the plaintiff, and that is just what I want you to do. The defendant bank has plenty of money, it has already paid me one good fee to come down here; and it is able to pay me several more fees in this case. When you decide against me here, I will appeal right away to the county court and that will mean another good fee for me—more money for Hooper. [At this point he tapped his breast significantly.] The county court is some little better than this court, but even if I am defeated there I shall appeal to the Supreme Court of Texas, which, for your information, is a court composed of three scholars and gentlemen who know the law, and incidentally, that appeal will mean another fee for me—more money for Hooper. At last in the Supreme Court we will get justice and that court will reverse the lower judgments and this plaintiff will get nothing except that he will get all the costs of every court taxed against him. Now go ahead, and do what you want to do."

One husky juror looked as if he were about to lunge at the offending lawyer, and Hooper squared himself, but the bailiff interfered and commanded the jury to retire to make up their verdict, which they did.

In just a few minutes they returned and their foreman read their verdict which went like this:

"We, the jury, find against the plaintiff and in favor of the defendant bank."

Subsequently the plaintiff's lawyer asked the foreman just why they had brought in such a verdict. The foreman said, "Why that old devil Hooper would do just what he threatened, and we did not want him to get another damned cent out of this case."

No Brainer

One time dare was a man studyin' to be a minister and he brain went bad. So he go to de doctor. De doctor 'vised dat he see a speshlist. De speshlist say dat he need a brain operation. He say dat de brain got to come out and be scraped and retimed. So de man he left de brain dare and went away. He 'sposed to come back in a few days for the brain, but he never come back. Few days later de speshlist see de man on de streets weavin' back an' fo'th. So de speshlist ast him why he never come back for he brain. Say it been ready for days now. De man say that he could keep it. Say when he come in with de bad brain he was studyin' to be a minister and he needed he brain, but now he's 'cided to be a doctor and he won't need it.

Doesticks: The New Patent Medicine Man

As I too desire to have a mansion on the Fifth Avenue, like the Medical Worthy of Sarsaparilla memory, and wished like him to be able to build a patent medicine palace, with a private chapel under the back-stairs, and a conservatory down-cellar, I cast about me for some means whereby the requisite cash might be reputably accumulated.

I feared that the Panacea and Cure-Everything trick had been played too often, but I determined to make one big try, and I think that at last my fortune is made.

Congratulate me—I am immortalized, and I've done it myself. My name will be handed down to posterity as that of a universal benefactor. The hand which hereafter writes upon the record of Fame, the names of Ayer, Sands, Townsend, Moffat, Morrison, and Brandreth, must also inscribe, side by side with these distinguished appellations, the no less brilliant cognomen of the undying Doesticks.

Emulous of the deathly notoriety which has been acquired by the medicinal worthies just mentioned, *I* also resolved to achieve a name and a fortune in the same reputable and honest manner.

Bought a gallon of tar, a cake of beeswax, and a firkin of lard, and in twenty-one hours I presented to the world the first batch of *"Doesticks' Patent, Self-Acting, Four-Horse Power Balsam,"* designed to cure all diseases of mind, body, or estate, to give strength to the weak, money to the poor, bread and butter to the hungry, boots to the bare-

From "Negro Folktales from Alabama," by Ray B. Browne, in *Southern Folklore Quarterly*, Vol. XVIII (June, 1954), No. 2, pp. 129–133.

From *Doesticks' Letters, and What He says, . . .* , by Q. K. Philander Doesticks, P. B. [pseudonym of Mortimer Thompson], pp. 84–91. Philadelphia: T. B. Peterson and Brothers. [1855?]

foot, decency to blackguards, and common sense to the Know-Nothings. It acts physically, morally, mentally, psychologically, physiologically, and geologically, and it is intended to make our sublunary sphere a blissful paradise, to which Heaven itself shall be but a side-show.

I have not yet brought it to absolute perfection, but even now it acts with immense force, as you will perceive by the accompanying testimonials and records of my own individual experience. You will observe that I have not resorted to the usual manner of preparing certificates: which is, to be certain that all those intended for Eastern circulation shall seem to come from some formerly unheard-of place in the West, while those sent to the West shall be dated at some place forty miles east of sun-rise. But I send to *you*, as representing the western country, a certificate from an Oregon farmer.

DEAR SIR: The land composing my farm has hitherto been so poor that a Scotchman couldn't get his living off it; and so stony that we had to slice our potatoes and plant them edgeways; but, hearing of your balsam, I put some on the corner of a ten-acre lot, surrounded by a rail-fence, and in the morning I found the rocks had entirely disappeared—a neat stone wall encircled the field, and the rails were split into ovenwood and piled up symmetrically in my back yard.

Put half an ounce into the middle of a huckleberry swamp—in two days it was cleared off, planted with corn and pumpkins, and had a row of peach trees in full bloom through the middle.

As an evidence of its tremendous strength, I would state that it drew a striking likeness of my eldest daughter—drew my youngest boy out of the mill-pond—drew a blister all over his stomach—drew a load of potatoes four miles to market, and eventually drew a prize of ninety-seven dollars in the State Lottery.

And the effect upon the inhabitants hereabout has been so wonderful, that they have opened their eyes to the good of the country, and are determined to vote for a Governor who is opposed to frosts in the middle of June, and who will make a positive law against freshets, hail-storms, and the seventeen-year locusts.

There, isn't that *some?*

But I give one more from a member of the senior class in a western college, who, although misguided, neglected, and ignorant, is, undoubtedly, as honest and sincere as his Prussianized education will admit of.

I have corrected the orthography, and revised some grammatical inaccuracies; but, besides attending to these trifles, inserting marks of punctuation, and putting the capitals in the right places, I assure you I have made no alteration.

SALL HARBOR, JUNE 31, 1854.

MY DEAR DOCTOR. [You know I attended medical lectures half a winter, and once assisted in getting a crooked needle out of a baby's leg; so I understand perfectly well the theory and practice of medicine, and the *Doctor* is perfectly legitimate under the Prussian system.] By the incessant study required in this establishment, I had become worn down so thin that I was obliged to put on an overcoat to cast a shadow—but accidentally hearing of your Balsam, I obtained a quantity, and, in obedience to the Homœopathic principles of this Institution, took an *infinitesimal* dose only; in four days I measured one hundred and eighty-two inches round the waist; could chop eleven cords of hickory wood in two hours and a half; and, on a bet, carried a yoke of oxen two miles and a quarter in my left hand, my right being tied behind me, and if any one doubts the fact, the oxen are still to be seen.

About two weeks after this, I had the pleasure of participating in a gunpowder explosion, on which occasion my arms and legs were scattered over the village, and my mangled remains pretty equally distributed throughout the entire county.

Under these circumstances my life was despaired of, and my classmates had bought a pine coffin, and borrowed whole shirts to attend the funeral in; when the invincible power of your four horse-power balsam (which I happened to have in my vest pocket) suddenly brought together the scattered pieces of my body—collected my limbs from the rural districts—put new life into my shattered frame; and I was restored, uninjured to my friends, with a new set of double teeth.

I have preserved the label which enveloped the bottle, and have sewed it into the seat of my pantaloons, and I now bid grim death defiance, for I feel that I am henceforth unkillable, and in fact I am even now generally designated the '*Great Western Achilles.*'

Yours entirely   Ski Hy.

I feel that after this, I need give you no more reports of third persons, but will detail some of my own personal experience of the article.

I caused some to be applied to the Washtenaw Bank after its failure, and while the Balsaam lasted the Bank redeemed its notes with specie.

The cork of one of the bottles dropped upon the head of a childless widow, and in six weeks she had a young and blooming husband.

Administered some to a hack-driver in a glass of gin and sugar, and that day he swindled but seven people, and only gave two of them bad money in change.

Gave a few drops gratis to a poor woman who was earning a precarious subsistence by making calico shirts with a one-eyed needle, and the next day she was discovered to be heir to a large fortune.

Gave some to an up-town actor, and that night he said "damned" only twenty-one times.

One of the daily papers got the next dose, and in the next edition but one there were but four editorial falsehoods, seven indecent advertisements, and two columns and a half of home-made "Foreign Correspondence."

Caused fifteen drops to be given to the low comedian of a Broadway Theatre, and that night he was positively dressed more like a man than a monkey, actually spoke some lines of the author, made only three inane attempts at puerile witticisms—only twice went out of his way to introduce some grossly indelicate line into his part, and for a wonder, lost so much of his self-conceit that for a full half-hour he did not believe himself the greatest comedian in the world.

Gave some to a news-boy, and he manufactured but three fires, a couple of murders, and one horrible rail-road accident, in the next thirty minutes.

Put some on the outside of the Crystal Palace and the same day the stock went from 22 up to 44.

Our whole Empire City is entirely changed by the miraculous power of "Doesticks' Patent Self-Acting Four Horse Power Balsam." The gas is lighted on the dark nights, instead of on the moonlight evenings—there are no more highway robberies in the streets, or, if there are, the offenders, when arrested, are instantly discharged by the police magistrate. No more building materials on the sidewalks; no more midnight murders; no more Sunday rows; no more dirty streets; no more duels in Hoboken, and no more lies in the newspapers.

Broadway is swept and garnished: the M. P.'s are civil, and the boys don't steal any more dogs. In fact, so well content are we now with our City, that we feel, as the Hibernian poet so beautifully says:

> "O, if there be an Elysium on earth,
> It is this—it is this."

Orders for my Balsam, *accompanied by the money*, will be immediately attended to; otherwise not, for my partner and I have resolved to sell for cash only feeling as did Dr. Young, who appropriately and feelingly remarks—

> "We take no notes on Time."

Bull Dogge says I have piled it up too strong, and that no one will believe what he calls "that humbug about the newspapers, and the preposterous nonsense concerning the Broadway Actor." I am aware that in these instances my medicine has performed a modern miracle, but the facts remain "no less true than strange."

If I fail to accumulate a "pile" in this speculation, I shall start a Know-Nothing Newspaper, run it a month, and then fail and swindle the subscribers; get an overgrown woman or a whiskered lady, and exhibit her for twenty-five cents a head, or get up a Grand Gift Enterprise, with $20,000 prizes.

Overture to an Operation

. . . Having always . . . enjoyed perfectly riotous and absolutely unbridled health, never feeling weak and distressed unless dinner happened to be ten or fifteen minutes late, I was green regarding physicians and the ways of physicians. But I knew Doctor X slightly, having met him last summer in one of his hours of ease in the grand stand at a ball game, when he was expressing a desire to cut the umpire's throat from ear to ear, free of charge; and I remembered his name, and remembered, too, that he had impressed me at the time as being a person of character and decision and scholarly attainments.

He wore whiskers. Somehow in my mind whiskers are ever associated with medical skill. I presume this is a heritage of my youth, though I believe others labor under the same impression. As I look back it seems to me that in childhood's days all the doctors in our town wore whiskers.

I recall one old doctor down there in Kentucky who was practically lurking in ambush all the time. All he needed was a few decoys out in front of him and a pump gun to be a duck blind. He carried his calomel about with him in a fruit jar, and when there was a cutting job he stropped his scalpel on his bootleg.

You see, in those primitive times germs had not been invented yet and so he did not have to take any steps to avoid them. Now we know that loose, luxuriant whiskers are unsanitary, because they make such fine winter quarters for germs; so, though the doctors still wear whiskers, they do not wear them wild and waving. In the profession bosky whiskers are taboo; they must be landscaped. And since it is a recognized fact that germs abhor orderliness and straight lines they now go elsewhere to reside, and the doctor may still retain his traditional aspect and yet be practically germproof. Doctor X was trimmed in accordance with the ethics of the newer school. He had trellis whiskers. So I went to see him at his offices in a fashionable district, on an expensive side street.

Before reaching him I passed through the hands of a maid and a nurse each of whom spoke to me in a low, sorrowful tone of voice, which seemed to indicate that there was very little hope.

I reached an inner room where Doctor X was. He looked me over, while I described for him as best I could what seemed to be the matter with me, and asked me a number of intimate questions touching on the lives, works, characters and peculiarities of my ancestors; after which he made me stand up in front of him and take my coat off, and he punched me hither and yon with his forefinger. He also knocked repeatedly on my breastbone with his knuckles, and each time, on

From *"Speaking of Operations, —"* by Irvin S. Cobb, pp. 16–21. Copyright, 1915, by George H. Doran Company. New York.

doing this, would apply his ear to my chest and listen intently for a spell, afterward shaking his head in a disappointed way. Apparently there was nobody at home. For quite a time he kept on knocking, but without getting any response.

He then took my temperature and fifteen dollars, and said it was an interesting case—not unusual exactly, but interesting—and that it called for an operation.

From the way my heart and other organs jumped inside of me at that statement I knew at once that, no matter what he may have thought, the premises were not unoccupied. Naturally I inquired how soon he meant to operate. Personally I trusted there was no hurry about it. I was perfectly willing to wait for several years, if necessary. He smiled at my ignorance.

"I never operate," he said; "operating is entirely out of my line. I am a diagnostician."

He was, too—I give him full credit for that. He was a good, keen, close diagnostician. How did he know I had only fifteen dollars on me? You did not have to tell this man what you had, or how much. He knew without being told.

No Doctor to Blame

There may have been more truth than unintended humor in the answer of a frontier Negro to the question as to what doctor had attended his lately deceased brother: "Bill didn't have no doctah, he died a natural death."

Needling the Doctor

In 1858 [Lincoln] had an appointment in Cumberland County, and after he had spoken, a Dr. Hamburgher (a bitter Democrat) imprudently jumped up and said he would reply. So Lincoln took a seat on the outer edge of the plank seat and listened.

Hamburgher presently got violent and insulting, when a little, insignificant-looking lame man jumped up to Lincoln and said: "Don't mind him; I know him; I live here; I'll take care of him; watch me." . . . When Hamburgher concluded, the little lame man was on the platform and at once commenced a reply, and had proceeded but a short time when Hamburgher roared out: "That's a lie." "Never mind," retorted the lame man, patronizingly, "I'll take that from you —in fact, I'll take anything from you except your pills." This cut the

From *Texas Tradition*, by Ross Phares, p. 160. Copyright, 1954, by Ross Phares. New York; Henry Holt and Company, Publishers.

From *Lincoln's Own Stories*, Collected and Edited by Anthony Gross, pp. 55–56. Copyright, 1912, by Harper & Brothers. New York.

doctor to the raw. "You scoundrel!" exclaimed he, "you know I've quit practising medicine." The little lame man instantly dropped down on his sound knee and, raising his hands in mock worship, exclaimed: "Then, thank God, the country is safe!"

X. THE UNHUMAN COMEDY
(About Critters and Varmints)

Introduction

The only consistent feeling man has had about the birds and beasts is that they are all inferior to him, but from time to time he experiences various other emotions. When he is not petting them with affection, hunting them for food or sport, running from them in fear, or thrashing them in anger, man be laughing at the lower animals. Some amuse him simply because he thinks they look funny. The child on his first trip to the zoo may say that the elephant is a big animal with a tail on each end and the zebra is a mule with clothes like those of Uncle Fred, who works for the state. His forefathers probably felt the same sort of surprise when they first saw mules and jackrabbits, which are in a sense comic caricatures, for their ears and legs are too long for animals of their general kind. And they may have wondered at the split personality of the rattlesnake, with gaiety on one end and sorrow on the other.

The people have always enjoyed stories of animals so large, so strong, or so fierce that they placed man at a disadvantage. They have laughed at Mark Twain, for example, who was forced to admit that the "genuine Mexican plug" was too much for him, and at Nat Straw astride a strange bear, who did not need to admit anything. If the birds, beasts, or bugs were not large enough, the storyteller simply increased their size for them until mosquitoes were so big and strong that "two of them could whip a dog and four of them could hold a man down."

Animals also serve man as a source of humor because the members of the human species try to project into them human emotions and thought processes. We delight in archy, the typewriting cockroach, and mehitabel the cat, whose favorite motto was *"toujours gai,"* in bedbugs ingenious enough to walk stilts across tar, in talking horses, mules, and dogs. But just as we become convinced that an animal is going to act like an intelligent human being, he acts like an animal, and we immediately decide that he is dumb, perverse, and capricious. The mule, for instance, has had a very bad reputation for dumbness and perversity, but Judge Lamm proved by close legal reasoning that the mule hardly deserved to keep that reputation.

archy and mehitabel

i the coming of archy

Dobbs Ferry possesses a rat which slips out of his lair at night and runs a typewriting machine in a garage. Unfortunately, he has always been interrupted by the watchman before he could produce a complete story.

It was at first thought that the power which made the typewriter run was a ghost, instead of a rat. It seems likely to us that it was both a ghost and a rat. Mme. Blavatsky's ego went into a white horse after she passed over, and someone's personality has undoubtedly gone into this rat. It is an era of belief in communications from the spirit land.

And since this matter had been reported in the public prints and seriously received we are no longer afraid of being ridiculed, and we do not mind making a statement of something that happened to our own typewriter only a couple of weeks ago.

We came into our room earlier than usual in the morning, and discovered a gigantic cockroach jumping about upon the keys.

He did not see us, and we watched him. He would climb painfully upon the framework of the machine and cast himself with all his force upon a key, head downward, and his weight and the impact of the blow were just sufficient to operate the machine, one slow letter after another. He could not work the capital letters, and he had a great deal of difficulty operating the mechanism that shifts the paper so that a fresh line may be started. We never saw a cockroach work so hard or perspire so freely in all our lives before. After about an hour of this frightfully difficult literary labor he fell to the floor exhausted, and we saw him creep feebly into a nest of the poems which are always there in profusion.

Congratulating ourself that we had left a sheet of paper in the machine the night before so that all this work had not been in vain, we made an examination, and this is what we found:

> expression is the need of my soul
> i was once a vers libre bard
> but i died and my soul went into the body of a cockroach
> it has given me a new outlook upon life
> i see things from the under side now

From *archy and mehitabel*, by don marquis, pp. 1–9. copyright, 1927, by double-day, page & company. garden city, new york.

thank you for the apple peelings in the wastepaper basket
but your paste is getting so stale i cant eat it
there is a cat here called mehitabel i wish you would have
removed she nearly ate me the other night why dont she
catch rats that is what she is supposed to be for
there is a rat here she should get without delay

most of these rats here are just rats
but this rat is like me he has a human soul in him
he used to be a poet himself
night after night i have written poetry for you
on your typewriter
and this big brute of a rat who used to be a poet
comes out of his hole when it is done
and reads it and sniffs at it
he is jealous of my poetry
he used to make fun of it when we were both human
he was a punk poet himself
and after he has read it he sneers
and then he eats it

i wish you would have mehitabel kill that rat
or get a cat that is onto her job
and i will write you a series of poems showing how things look
to a cockroach
that rats name is freddy
the next time freddy dies i hope he wont be a rat
but something smaller i hope i will be a rat
in the next transmigration and freddy a cockroach
i will teach him to sneer at my poetry then
dont you ever eat any sandwiches in your office
i havent had a crumb of bread for i dont know how long
or a piece of ham or anything but apple parings
and paste leave a piece of paper in your machine
every night you can call me archy

ii mehitabel was once cleopatra

boss i am disappointed in
some of your readers they
are always asking how does
archy work the shift so as to get a
new line or how does archy do
this or do that they
are always interested in technical
details when the main question is
whether the stuff is
literature or not
i wish you would leave
that book of george moores on
the floor

mehitabel the cat and i want to
read it i have discovered that
mehitabel s soul formerly inhabited a
human also at least that
is what mehitabel is claiming these
days it may be she got jealous of
my prestige anyhow she and
i have been talking it over in a
friendly way who were you
mehitabel i asked her i was
cleopatra once she said well i said i
suppose you lived in a palace you bet
she said and what lovely fish dinners
we used to have and licked her chops

mehitabel would sell her soul for
a plate of fish any day i told her i thought
you were going to say you were
the favorite wife of the emperor
valerian he was some cat nip eh
mehitabel but she did not get me
                                archy

iii the song of mehitabel

this is the song of mehitabel
of mehitabel the alley cat
as i wrote you before boss
mehitabel is a believer
in the pythagorean
theory of the transmigration
of the soul and she claims
that formerly her spirit
was incarnated in the body
of cleopatra
that was a long time ago
and one must not be
surprised if mehitabel
has forgotten some of her
more regal manners

i have had my ups and downs
but wotthehell wotthehell
yesterday sceptres and crowns
fried oysters and velvet gowns
and today i herd with bums
but wotthehell wotthehell
i wake the world from sleep
as i caper and sing and leap
when i sing my wild free tune
wotthehell wotthehell
under the blear eyed moon

i am pelted with cast off shoon
but wotthehell wotthehell

do you think that i would change
my present freedom to range
for a castle or moated grange
wotthehell wotthehell
cage me and i d go frantic
my life is so romantic
capricious and corybantic
and i m toujours gai toujours gai

i know that i am bound
for a journey down the sound
in the midst of a refuse mound
but wotthehell wotthehell
oh i should worry and fret
death and i will coquette
there s a dance in the old dame yet
toujours gai toujours gai

i once was an innocent kit
wotthehell wotthehell
with a ribbon my neck to fit
and bells tied onto it
o wotthehell wotthehell
but a maltese cat came by
with a come hither look in his eye
and a song that soared to the sky
and wotthehell wotthehell
and i followed adown the street
the pad of his rhythmical feet
o permit me again to repeat
wotthehell wotthehell

my youth i shall never forget
but there s nothing i really regret
wotthehell wotthehell
there s a dance in the old dame yet
toujours gai toujours gai

the things that i had not ought to
i do because i ve gotto
wotthehell wotthehell
and i end with my favorite motto
toujours gai toujours gai

boss sometimes i think
that our friend mehitabel
is a trifle too gay

A Mosquito Policy

. . . A Mr. H. furnished some minor details of fact concerning this region which I would have hesitated to believe, if I had not known him to be a steamboat mate. He was a passenger of ours, a resident of Arkansas City, and bound to Vicksburg to join his boat, a little Sunflower packet. He was an austere man, and had the reputation of being singularly unworldly, for a river man. Among other things, he said that Arkansas had been injured and kept back by generations of exaggerations concerning the mosquitoes there. One may smile, said he, and turn the matter off as being a small thing; but when you come to look at the effects produced, in the way of discouragement of immigration and diminished values of property, it was quite the opposite of a small thing, or thing in any wise to be coughed down or sneered at. These mosquitoes had been persistently represented as being formidable and lawless; whereas "the truth is, they are feeble, insignificant in size, diffident to a fault, sensitive"—and so on, and so on; you would have supposed he was talking about his family. But if he was soft on the Arkansas mosquitoes, he was hard enough on the mosquitoes of Lake Providence to make up for it—"those Lake Providence colossi," as he finely called them. He said that two of them could whip a dog, and that four of them could hold a man down; and except help come, they would kill him—"butcher him," as he expressed it. Referred in a sort of casual way—and yet significant way, to "the fact that the life policy in its simplest form is unknown in Lake Providence —they take out a mosquito policy besides." He told many remarkable things about those lawless insects. Among others, said he had seen them try to *vote*. Noticing that this statement seemed to be a good deal of a strain on us, he modified it a little; said he might have been mistaken as to that particular, but knew he had seen them around the polls "canvassing." . . .

The Owl-Critic

A LESSON TO FAULT-FINDERS.

"Who stuffed that white owl?" No one spoke in the shop:
The barber was busy, and he couldn't stop;
The customers, waiting their turns, were all reading
The "Daily," the "Herald," the "Post," little heeding

From *Life on the Mississippi*, by Samuel L. Clemens, Ch. XXIV. Copyright, 1874, 1875, by H. O. Houghton and Company; 1883, 1889, 1903, by Samuel L. Clemens; 1911 by Clara Gabrilowitsch. New York and London: Harper and Brothers.

From *Ballads and Other Verses*, by James T. Fields, pp. 7–11. Boston: Houghton, Mifflin and Company. 1881. [First published circa 1860.]

The young man who blurted out such a blunt question;
Not one raised a head, or even made a suggestion;
      And the barber kept on shaving.

"Don't you see, Mister Brown,"
Cried the youth, with a frown,
"How wrong the whole thing is,
How preposterous each wing is,
How flattened the head is, how jammed down the neck is—
In short, the whole owl, what an ignorant wreck 't is!
I make no apology;
I've learned owl-eology.
I've passed days and nights in a hundred collections,
And cannot be blinded to any deflections
Arising from unskilful fingers that fail
To stuff a bird right, from his beak to his tail.
Mister Brown! Mister Brown!
Do take that bird down,
Or you'll soon be the laughing-stock all over town!"
      And the barber kept on shaving.

"I've *studied* owls,
And other night fowls,
And I tell you
What I know to be true:
An owl cannot roost
With his limbs so unloosed;
No owl in this world
Ever had his claws curled,
Ever had his legs slanted,
Ever had his bill canted,
Ever had his neck screwed
Into that attitude.
He can't *do* it, because
'Tis against all bird-laws.
Anatomy teaches,
Ornithology preaches
An owl has a toe
That *can't* turn out so!
I've made the white owl my study for years,
And to see such a job almost moves me to tears!
Mister Brown, I'm amazed
You should be so gone crazed
As to put up a bird
In that posture absurd!

To *look* at that owl really brings on a dizziness;
The man who stuffed *him* don't half know his business!"
>   And the barber kept on shaving.

"Examine those eyes.
I'm filled with surprise
Taxidermists should pass
Off on you such poor glass;
So unnatural they seem
They'd make Audubon scream,
And John Burroughs laugh
To encounter such chaff.
Do take that bird down;
Have him stuffed again, Brown!"
>   And the barber kept on shaving.

"With some sawdust and bark
I could stuff in the dark
An owl better than that.
I could make an old hat
Look more like an owl
Than that horrid fowl,
Stuck up there so stiff like a side of coarse leather.
In fact, about *him* there's not one natural feather."

Just then, with a wink and a sly normal lurch,
The owl, very gravely, got down from his perch,
Walked round, and regarded his fault-finding critic
(Who thought he was stuffed) with a glance analytic,
And then fairly hooted, as if he should say:
"Your learning's at fault *this* time, any way;
Don't waste it again on a live bird, I pray.
I'm an owl; you're another. Sir Critic, good-day!"
>   And the barber kept on shaving.

The Boomer Fireman's Fast Sooner Hound

A boomer fireman is never long for any one road. Last year he may
have worked for the Frisco, and this year he's heaving black diamonds
for the Katy or the Wabash. He travels light and travels far and doesn't
let any grass grow under his feet when they get to itching for the
greener pastures on the next road or the next division or maybe to hell
and gone on the other side of the mountains. He doesn't need furniture

By Jack Conroy. From "Chicago Industrial Folklore." Manuscripts of the Federal
Writers' Project of the Works Progress Administration for State of Illinois.

and he doesn't need many clothes, and God knows he doesn't need a family or a dog.

When the Boomer pulled into the roadmaster's office looking for a job, there was that sooner hound of his loping after him. That hound would sooner run than eat and he'd sooner eat than fight or do something useful like catching a rabbit. Not that a rabbit would have any chance if the sooner really wanted to nail him, but that crazy hound dog didn't like to do anything but run and he was the fastest thing on four legs.

"I might use you," said the roadmaster. "Can you get a boarding place for the dog?"

"Oh, he goes along with me," said the Boomer. "I raised him from a pup just like a mother or father and he ain't never spent a night or a day or even an hour far away from me. He'd cry like his poor heart would break and raise such a ruckus nobody couldn't sleep, eat or hear themselves think for miles about."

"Well, I don't see how that would work out," said the roadmaster. "It's against the rules of the road to allow a passenger in the cab, man or beast, or in the caboose and I aim to put you on a freight run so you can't ship him by express. Besides, he'd get the idea you wasn't nowhere about and pester folks out of their wits with his yipping and yowling. You look like a man that could keep a boiler popping off on an uphill grade, but I just don't see how we could work it if the hound won't listen to reason while you're on your runs."

"Why, he ain't no trouble," said the Boomer. "He just runs along-side, and when I'm on a freight run he chases around a little in the fields to pass the time away."

> "That may be so, I do not know;
> It sounds so awful queer.
> I don't dispute your word at all,
> But don't spread that bull in here,"

sang the roadmaster.

"He'll do it without half trying," said the Boomer. "It's a little bit tiresome on him having to travel at such a slow gait, but that sooner would do anything to stay close by me, he loves me that much."

"Go spread that on the grass to make it green," said the roadmaster.

"I'll lay my first paycheck against a fin [1] that he'll be fresh as a daisy and his tongue behind his teeth when we pull into the junction. He'll run around the station a hundred times or so to limber up."

"It's a bet," said the roadmaster.

On the first run the sooner moved in what was a slow walk for him. He kept looking up into the cab where the Boomer was shoveling in the coal.

---

[1] Five dollar bill.—J. C.

"He looks worried," said the Boomer. "He thinks the hog law [2] is going to catch us, we're making such bad time."

The roadmaster was so sore at losing the bet that he transferred the Boomer to a local passenger run and doubled the stakes. The sooner speeded up to a slow trot, but he had to kill a lot of time, at that, not to get too far ahead of the engine.

Then the roadmaster got mad enough to bite off a drawbar. People got to watching the sooner trotting alongside the train and began thinking it must be a mighty slow road. Passengers might just as well walk; they'd get there just as fast. And if you shipped a yearling calf to market, it'd be a bologna bull before it reached the stockyards. Of course, the trains were keeping up their schedules the same as usual, but that's the way it looked to people who saw a no-good mangy sooner hound beating all the trains without his tongue hanging out an inch or letting out the least little pant.

It was giving the road a black eye, all right. The roadmaster would have fired the Boomer and told him to hit the grit with his sooner and never come back again, but he was stubborn from the word go and hated worse than anything to own up he was licked.

"I'll fix that sooner," said the roadmaster. "I'll slap the Boomer into the cab of the Cannon Ball, and if anything on four legs can keep up with the fastest thing on wheels I'd admire to see it. That sooner'll be left so far behind it'll take nine dollars to send him a post card."

The word got around that the sooner was going to try to keep up with the Cannon Ball. Farmers left off plowing, hitched up, and drove to the right of way to see the sight. It was like a circus day or the county fair. The schools all dismissed the pupils, and not a factory could keep enough men to make a wheel turn.

The roadmaster got right in the cab so that the Boomer couldn't soldier on the job to let the sooner keep up. A clear track for a hundred miles was ordered for the Cannon Ball, and all the switches were spiked down till after that streak of lightning had passed. It took three men to see the Cannon Ball on that run: one to say, "There she comes," one to say, "There she is," and another to say, "There she goes." You couldn't see a thing for steam, cinders and smoke, and the rails sang like a violin for a half hour after she'd passed into the next county.

Every valve was popping off and the wheels three feet in the air above the roadbed. The Boomer was so sure the sooner would keep up that he didn't stint the elbow grease; he wore the hinges off the fire door and fifteen pounds of him melted and ran right down into his shoes. He had his shovel whetted to a nub.

The roadmaster stuck his head out of the cab window, and—whosh! —off went his hat and almost his head. The suction like to have jerked

---

[2] Rule forbidding excessive over time.—J. C.

his arms from their sockets as he nailed a-hold of the window seat.

It was all he could do to see, and gravel pinged against his goggles like hailstones, but he let out a whoop of joy.

"THE SOONER! THE SOONER!" he yelled. "He's gone! He's gone for true! Ain't *nowhere* in sight!"

"I can't understand that," hollered the Boomer. "He ain't *never* laid down on me yet. It just ain't like him to lay down on me. Leave me take a peek."

He dropped his shovel and poked out his head. Then he whooped even louder than the roadmaster had.

"He's true blue as they come!" the Boomer yelled. "Got the interests of the company at heart, too. He's still with us."

"Where do you get that stuff?" asked the roadmaster. "I don't see him nowhere. I can't see hide nor hair of him."

"We're going so fast half the journal boxes are on fire and melting the axles like hot butter," said the Boomer. "The sooner's running up and down the train hoisting a leg above the boxes. He's doing his level best to put out some of the fires. That dog is true blue as they come and he's the fastest thing on four legs, but he's only using three of them now."

A Beat Dog

The small-town man of Arkansas places great stock in his knowledge of animals and their ways. Norris Goff tells of the time Ezra Seestrunk got lost in the woods, far from town. Ezra had his dog with him and after hours of wandering hit upon a scheme for finding his way back to town. He cut himself a switch from a tree and began to whip the dog. The dog lit out through the woods, running about half a mile, then stopping to wait for Ezra. When Ezra would catch up, he'd beat the dog some more with the switch and the animal would run another half mile. Before long Ezra and dog were home. "A beat dog," said Ezra, "will head for home ever' time."

Country Dogs *vs.* City Dogs

. . . But I dident start to tell you a dog story—only now, since I've mentioned him, I must tell you a circumstance about Cees. He was a middlin size broot, with fox ears and yaller spots over his eyes and could out bark and out brag all creation when he was inside the yard. If another dog was goin along he'd run up and down the palins and bark and take on like he'd give the world if that fence wasent there.

From *The World, The Flesh, and H. Allen Smith,* edited with an introduction by Bergen Evans, pp. 248–249. Copyright, 1954, by Hanover House. Garden City, New York.

From *Peace Papers,* by Bill Arp [Charles H. Smith], pp. 226–228. New York: G. W. Carleton & Co., Publishers, 1873.

So one day when he was showin off in that way I caught him by the nap of the neck as he run by me and jest histed him right over and drapped him. He struck the ground like an injun rubber ball, and was back agin on my side in a jiffy. If he had ever jumped that fence before I dident know it. The other dog run a quarter of a mile without stoppin. Now, that's the way with sum foaks. If you want to hear war tawk jest put a fence between em; and if you want it stopped, jest take the fence away. Dogs is mighty like peepul anyhow. They've got karacter. Sum of em are good honest trusty dogs that bark mity little, and bite at the right time. Sum are good pluk, and will fite like the dickens when their masters is close by to back em, but aint worth a cent by themselves. Sum make it a bizness to make other dogs fite. You've seen these little fices a runnin around growlin and snappin when two big dogs cum together. They are jest as keen to get up a row and see a big dog fite as a store clerk or a shoemaker, and seem to enjoy it as much. And then, there's them mean yaller eyed bull terriers that don't care who they bite, so they bite sumbody. They are no respekter of persons, and I never had much respekt for a man who kept one on his premises. But of all mean, triflin, contemptbile dogs in the world, the meanest of all is a mean country houn—one that will kill sheep, and suck eggs, and lick the skillet, and steal evrything he can find, and try to do as nigh like his master as possibul. Sum dogs are filosofers, and study other dog's nature, just like foaks study foaks. It's amazin to see a town dog trot up to a country dog and interview him. How quick he finds out whether it will do to attack him or not. If the country dog shows fite jest notis the consequential dignity with which the town dog retires. He goes off like there was a sudden emergency of bisness a callin him away. Town dogs sumtimes combine agin a country dog, jest like town boys try to run over country boys. I wish you could see Dr. Miller's dog Cartoosh. He jest lays in the piazzer all day watchin out for a stray dog, and as soon as he sees him he goes for him, and he can tell in half a minit whether he can whip him or run him, and if he can, he does it instanter, and if he can't, he runs to the next yard where there's two more dogs that nabor with him, and in a minit they all cum a tarin out together, and that country dog has to run or take a whippin, shore. I've seen Cartoosh play that game many a time. . . .

The Dog Who Paid Cash

While I didn't have anything else to do, I got to watching an old spotted dog. He was just an ordinary dog, but when I looked at him

From *The Autobiography of Will Rogers*, selected and edited by Donald Day, with a foreword by Bill and Jim Rogers, pp. 9–10. Copyright, 1926, 1927, 1928, 1929, 1932, by the Curtis Publishing Company; 1921, 1922, 1923, 1924, 1925, 1926, 1927, 1928, 1929, 1930, 1931, 1932, 1933, 1934, 1935, 1949, by Rogers Company.

close, he was alert and friendly with every one. Got to inquiring around and found out he'd been bumped off a freight train and seemed to have no owner. He made himself at home and started right in business. When a crowd of cowboys would go into a saloon, he would follow 'em in and begin entertaining. He could do all kinds of tricks—turn somersaults, lay down and roll over, sit up on his hind feet, and such like.

He would always rush to the door and shake hands with all the newcomers. The boys would lay a coin on his nose, and he'd toss it high in the air and catch it in his mouth and pretend to swallow it. But you could bet your life he dident swallow it—he stuck it in one side of his lip and when he got a lip full of money, he'd dash out the back door and disappear for a few minutes. What he really done was hide his money. As soon as he worked one saloon, he would pull out and go to another place.

I got to thinking while watching this old dog, how much smarter he is than me. Here I am out of a job five hundred miles from home, and setting around and can't find a thing to do, and this old dog hops off a train and starts right in making money, hand over fist.

Me and some boys around town tried to locate his hidden treasure, but this old dog was too slick for us. He never fooled away no time on three or four of us boys that was looking for work. He seemed to know we was broke, but he was very friendly. As he was passing along by me, he'd wag his tail and kinda wink. I musta looked hungry and forlorn. I think he wanted to buy me a meal.

When times was dull and he got hungry, he would mysteriously disappear. Pretty soon he'd show up at a butcher shop with a dime in his mouth and lay it on the counter and the butcher would give him a piece of steak or a bone. He always paid for what he got in the line of grub. Pretty soon he seemed to get tired of the town, and one morning he was gone. A railroad man told us later that he seen this same dog in Trinidad, Colorado.

A Sure Cure for Fleas

The following recipe from the writings of Miss Hannah More, may be found useful to your readers:

In a climate where the attacks of fleas are a constant source of annoyance, any method which will alleviate them becomes a *desideratum*. It is, therefore, with pleasure I make known the following recipe, which I am assured has been tried with efficacy.

Boil a quart of tar until it becomes quite thin. Remove the clothing, and before the tar becomes perfectly cool, with a broad flat

"Antidode for Fleas" from *Phoenixiana* . . . , by John Phoenix [George H. Derby], pp. 71–72. New York: D. Appleton & Company, 1856.

brush, apply a thin, smooth coating to the entire surface of the body and limbs. While the tar remains soft, the flea becomes entangled in its tenacious folds, and is rendered perfectly harmless; but it will soon form a hard, smooth coating, entirely impervious to his bite. Should the coating crack at the knee or elbow joints, it is merely necessary to retouch it slightly at those places. The whole coat should be renewed every three or four weeks. This remedy is sure, and having the advantage of simplicity and economy, should be generally known.

So much for Miss More. A still simpler method of preventing the attacks of these little pests, is one which I have lately discovered myself;—in theory only—I have not yet put it into practice. On feeling the bite of a flea, thrust the part bitten immediately into boiling water. The heat of the water destroys the insect and instantly removes the pain of the bite. . . .

The Rip Van Winkle Bug

A few evenings since, in the "private crib" of one of our exchanges, there was a learned dissertation, subject, "Bed-bugs, and their Remarkable Tenacity of Life." One asserted of his own knowledge that they could be boiled, and then come to life. Some had soaked them for hours in turpentine without any fatal consequences. Old Hanks, who had been listening as an outsider, here gave in his experience in corroboration of the facts. Says he, "Some years ago I took a bed-bug to an iron-foundry, and dropping it into a ladle where the melted iron was, had it run into a skillet. Well, my old woman used that skillet pretty constant for the last six years, and here the other day it broke all to smash; and what do you think, gentlemen, that 'ere insect just walked out of his hole, where he'd been layin' like a frog in a rock, and made tracks for his old roost upstairs! But," added he, by way of parenthesis, "he looked mighty pale."

In Defense of Crumbs

Paul Bunyan was all right in his time, but he didn't have the big shots of today to deal with—and he never was able to get rid of the crumbs. It was the Wobblies—and you got to give 'em credit for it—that really done something about the crumbs. That was one of their big fights.

In Bunyan's day the camps was crummy, the bunks was crummy, and the men were so used to being crummy that they wouldn't of

From *The American Joe Miller*, A Collection of Yankee Wit and Humor, compiled by Robert Kempt, pp. 8–9. London: Adams and Francis. 1865.

By Wayne Walden. Manuscripts of the Federal Writers' Project of the Works Progress Administration in New York City.

knowed what to do without 'em. After the Wobs began to have some say-so on the jobs they begun to holler for clean bedding, and that sort of put the skids under the crumbs—a lot of 'em anyway.

A crumb is what you'd call a louse. They was called "cooties" by the soldiers during the war, but they're the same thing; we always called 'em crumbs. Anyhow, as I was going to say, one time when one of the big shots come out to look things over, he stuck his head in one of the bunkhouse doors. Before he could duck back again he heard a bunch of voices yelling at him, "Hello, Brother." It kinda puzzled him. After a while, when he seen that the crumbs were coming to meet him, and was actually calling him their brother, the boss got mad. He figured that that was an insult to his dignity, you see.

"What do you mean by calling me your brother?" he says to them. "Well, we are, ain't we?" they says. "We don't need no interpreter," they says, "we may be a little different looking on the outside, but we got the same souls, ain't we?" they says to him. "We get our living from the same source, don't we?" they says. "It's the blood of the guys you got working for you," they says. "You bleed 'em by day, and we bleed 'em by night," they says, "that makes you and us blood-brothers," they says to the boss.

"Yeah?" says the boss, "well, as you weaken 'em and rob 'em of some of their energy, I'm going to kill you," the boss says to the crumbs.

"All right," says the crumbs, "hop to it; but you'll lose the best ally you got, or ever had."

"How so?" says the boss.

"Well," says the crumbs, "ain't it our gouging into the hides of your slaves that keeps 'em so busy scratching they can't do any thinking? And as long as they can't think," they says, "your slaves won't bother to organize," they says. "They won't demand any improvements," they says. . . .

And, well, by that time, I was kinda tired of listening to their damned propaganda.

Bill Me Later

I was lying in bed one night after lights out sounded, when I heard a whining hum and a huge mosquito bit me on the arm. I pulled my blanket over me and tried to go to sleep. But the same mosquito came back and bit me again, right through the blanket.

"That's going too far," I said, and I covered myself with two blankets. But the mosquito bit through both of them. He also bit through a third. When I put a fourth blanket on me, however, that stopped him.

From *Tall Tales They Tell in the Services*, Edited by Sgt. Bill Davidson, p. 34. Copyright, 1943, by Thomas Y. Crowell Company, 1943. New York.

But not completely.

I heard a commotion, put on the light, and looked up. There was that damned mosquito sitting on a rafter. He was working away furiously with a pipe wrench—changing bills.

Bugs on Stilts

. . . "You see, I went to bed pretty all-fired used up, after a hull day on the old road before the plank was laid, calkalatin' on a good snooze. Waal, just as the shivers began to ease off, I kinder felt suthin' tryin' to pull off my shirt, and diggin' their feet into the small of my back to get a good hold. Wiggled and twisted, and doubled and puckered—all no use—kept agoin' it like all sin. Bimeby got up and struck a light to look round a spell—found about a peck of bed-bugs scattered around, and more droppin' off my shirt and runnin' down my legs every minnit. Swept off a place on the floor, shook out a quilt, lay down and kivered up in it for a nap. No use—mounted right on to me like a passel of rats on a meal tub, dug a hole through the kiver-lid, and crawled through and give me fits for trying to hide. Got up agin, went down stairs, and got the slush bucket from the wagon. Brought it up and made a circle of tar on the floor, lay down on the floor in the inside, and felt comfortable that time, any how. Left the light burnin' and watched 'em. See 'em get together and have a camp meeting 'bout it; and then they went off in a squad, with an old grey-headed he one at the top, right up the wall, out on the ceiling, till they got to the right spot, then dropped right plump into my face—fact, by thunder. Waal, I swept 'em up again and made a circle of tar on the ceiling too. Thought I had 'em foul that time; but I swan to man, if they didn't pull straws out of the bed and build a reg'lar bridge over it!" Seeing an incredible expression on our visage, he clinched the story thus: "It's so, whether you believe it or not, and some of 'em *walked across on stilts.* Bed-bugs are curus critters, and no mistake—'specially the Kalamazoo kind."

The Foxy Wolves

One day when hunting for fur-bearing animals along a certain river, [Jim Bridger] was suddenly taken upon by a pack of wolves. The

---

From *A Plate of Chowder* [on front cover and in running page heads, but not on title page], *The Book of 1000 Comical Stories; an Endless Repast of Fun, A Rich Banquet for Every Day of the Year, with Several Courses, and a Dessert . . . Bill of Fare . . . ,* by the Author of "Mrs. Partington's Carpet-Bag of Fun" (Samuel P. Avery), pp. 34–35. New York: Dick and Fitzgerald, Publishers. 1859.

From *Foolish Questions, Yellowstone National Park,* by Jack Chaney, p. 55. Copyright, 1924, by Jack Chaney. [Lincoln, Nebraska.]

incident caught him rather unawares, so he ran for the nearest tree and climbed out of reach. The wolves waited at its base for about two hours, when finally all departed except one and that one remained on guard. In about half an hour the pack returned with a beaver to chew down the tree.

Nat Straw and His Saddlebear

To know old Nat Straw, that famous bear hunter of the Rockies, "were as good a deed as to drink when man's a-hungry" . . . If anybody from David Crockett on down has ever, *ever* told a better bear story than the one Nat Straw tells about his saddle bear, I haven't heard it.

"The best b'ar I ever owned or ever saw was a half-grown one I captured and gentled. He was so intelligent and gentle-natured and powerful that I broke him to ride. Then purty soon I got him trained to help me hunt other b'ars. Meantime he grew up to be a regular monster in size. Generally I rode with a hackamore (a halter) on him and reins, but really he didn't need any, he was so easy to turn, and I never did use a saddle. Just rode bareback. He had a soft-cushioned back that was as comfortable as a rocking chair. On account of him being so cunning and such a good trailer, I named that b'ar Geronimo.

"I didn't need no dogs after me when Geronimo and me got to working together. He'd wind a trail, and then about the time it got real hot, I'd slip off and crawl along next to Geronimo's side so that the b'ar we were hunting could not see me, and of course it would not run from another b'ar. Then when we got up close, I'd take aim under Geronimo's belly and kill the b'ar.

"Well, one day I rode out without a gun. I never had any idea of needing one. I was just riding Geronimo around kinder for exercise when we struck about as big a b'ar as you ever heard of. I shore didn't want to let it go, and right there Geronimo showed his sense. He seemed to know that I didn't have a gun and that I wanted that big b'ar.

"I slipped the hackamore off his head right quick and told him to shoot has wad. He just waddled on up to the stranger as if he wanted to talk with him, me being off there behind some bushes. Then when everything was set right, he gave that other b'ar a slap and a hug, and I don't know what happened next. That strange b'ar was a fighter from Bitter Creek. The two clinched and cuffed and bellered and wallered, and the fur was flying so thick and the bushes was cracking so

From "Great Liars of the Golden West," by J. Frank Dobie; *Vanity Fair*, Vol. 38 (March, 1932), No. 1, p. 30. Copyright, 1932, by the Conde Nast Publications, Inc. New York.

loud that I couldn't see or hear straight. I did see though that they was almost the same size and color and everything.

"But d'reckly it appeared to me that Geronimo was getting the worst of the tussle—and there I was without a thing to take up for him with . . . I was a-thinking hard what to do. Then it came to me that Geronimo would obey me if I gave him an order. I decided right there to call him off, jump astraddle of him, and ride him home.

"Well, I yelled out 'Geronimo.' At this the b'ars kinder slacked their holts. I yelled 'Geronimo' a second time, loud like. He turned towards me, and then I saw on his face a fierce expression I'd never seen before. I didn't see it long, though. I just glanced at it. I made a leap for his back like a buck deer a-hitting the brush in rutting season, and, roweling his off-side with my spur, yelled for him to git. There wan't no time for putting the hackamore back on him. By golly, you ought to have seen that b'ar leave Cheyenne.

"We went tearing through oak brush and and under scrub junipers and over fallen pine logs as if they was nothing but weeds. It was all I could do to stay on that b'ar and not hardly any of my skin was staying on me. I'd a-jumped off, but from the sounds going on, I judged the other b'ar was a-tearing after us. I didn't have time to look back to see. I've heard about the clatter wheels of hell being noisy, but I tell you the landslide we made was noisier than any kind of clatter wheels ever invented. I just hadn't any idea that Geronimo could be so reckless. I tried talking to him to hold him up, but it seemed the more I talked the wilder he got.

"Then I tried reaching over and catching him by the right ear. When I did I seen that about half of it was gone, not from any recent fight, either. The skin was haired over. Well, sir, right then the facts dawned on me. Geronimo wasn't gotched in the ear at all. I had mounted the wrong bear and had ridden him a mile down Cienega Canyon. I didn't wait till he stopped to get off. I just fell off.

"I'd had such a bait of b'ar-riding that I never did mount old Geronimo after that. He come into camp all right and lived with me for years after that. But somehow I had lost all confidence in him as a saddle animal and he was the last b'ar I ever trained to ride."

Crockett and the Talking 'Coon

Almost every boddy that knows the forrest, understands parfectly well that Davy Crockett never loses powder and ball, havin' ben brort up to blieve it a sin to throw away amminition, and that is the bennefit of a vartuous eddikation. I war out in the forrest won arternoon, and had jist got to a plaice called the grate gap, when I seed a rak-

From *Mince Pie for the Million*. Philadelphia and New York: Turner & Fisher. 1846.

koon setting all alone upon a tree. I klapped the breech of Brown Betty to my sholder, and war jist a going to put a piece of led between his sholders, when he lifted one paw, and sez he, "Is your name Crockett?"

Sez I, "You are rite for wonst, my name is Davy Crockett."

"Then," sez he, "you needn't take no further trubble, for I may as well cum down without another word"; and the cretur wauked rite down from the tree, for he considered himself shot.

I stoops down and pats him on the head, and sez I, "I hope I may be shot myself before I hurt a hare of your head, for I never had sich a kompliment in my life."

"Seeing as how you say that," sez he, "I'll jist walk off for the present, not doubting your word a bit, d'ye see, but lest you should kinder happen to change your mind."

Dat Mule Is Talkin'

Ole feller one time had uh mule. His name wuz Bill. Every mornin' de man go tuh ketch 'im he say, "Come round, Bill!"

So one mornin' he slept late, so he decided while he wuz drinkin' some coffee he'd send his son tuh ketch Ole Bill.

Told 'im say, "Go down dere, boy, and bring me dat mule up here."

Boy, he sich a fast Aleck, he grabbed de bridle and went on down tuh de lot tuh ketch Ole Bill.

He say, "Come round, Bill!"

De mule looked round at 'im. He told de mule, "Tain't no use you rollin' yo' eyes at *me*. Pa want yuh dis mawnin'. Come on round and stick yo' head in dis bridle."

Mule kept on lookin' at 'im and said, "Every mornin' it's 'Come round. Bill! Come round, Bill!' Don't hardly git no night rest befo' it's 'Come round, Bill!' "

De boy throwed down dat bridle and flew back tuh de house and told his Pa, "Dat mule is talkin'."

"Ah g'wan, boy, tellin' yo' lies! G'wan ketch dat mule."

"Naw suh, Pa, dat mule's done gone tuh talkin'. You hatta ketch dat mule yo' ownself. Ah ain't gwine."

Ole man looked at ole lady and say, "See whut uh lie dat boy is tellin'?"

So he gits out and goes on down after de mule hisself. When he got down dere he hollored, "Come round, Bill!"

Ole mule looked round and says, "Every mornin' it's come round, Bill!"

De old man had uh little fice dog useter foller 'im everywhere he go,

From *Mules and Men*, by Zora Neale Hurston, pp. 217–218. Copyright, 1935, by Zora Neale Hurston. Philadelphia and London: J. B. Lippincott Company.

so he lit out wid de lil fice right behind 'im. So he told de ole lady, "De boy ain't told much of uh lie. Dat mule *is* talkin'. Ah never heered uh mule talk befo'."

Lil fice say, "Me neither."

De ole man got skeered agin. Right through de woods he went wid de fice right behind 'im. He nearly run hisself tuh death. He stopped and commenced blowin' and says, "Ah'm so tired Ah don't know whut tuh do."

Lil dog run and set down in front of 'im and went to hasslin' and says, "Me too."

Dat man is runnin' yet.

The Missouri Mule: A Legal Opinion

But it must be allowed as a sound psychological proposition that haltering his head or neck can in nowise control the mule's thoughts or control the hinder parts affected by those thoughts. So much, I think, is clear and is to be said of the Missouri mule, whose bones, in attestation of his activity and worth, lie bleaching from Shiloh to Spion Kop, from San Juan to Przemysl (pronounced, I am told by a scholar, as it is spelled).

(1) There are sporadic instances of mules behaving badly. That one that Absalom rode and "went from under" him at a crisis in his fate, for instance. So it has been intimated in fireside precepts that the mule is *unexpected* in his heel action, and has other faults. In Spanish folklore it is said: He who wants a mule without fault must walk. So, at the French chimney-corner the adage runs: The mule long keeps a kick in reserve for his master. "The mule don't kick according to no rule," saith the American Negro. His voice has been a matter of derision and there are those who put their tongue in their cheek when speaking of it. Witness the German proverb: Mules make a great fuss about their ancestors having been asses. And so on, and so on. But none of these things are factors in the instant case; for here was no kicking and no braying standing in relation of *causa causans* to the injury of the wheel.

Moreover, the rule of logic is that induction which proceeds by merely citing instances is a childish affair and, being without any certain principle of inference, it may be overthrown by contrary instances. Accordingly the faithfulness, the dependableness, the surefootedness, the endurance, the strength and good sense of the mule, all matters of common knowledge, may be allowed to stand over against his faults and create either an equilibrium or a preponderance in the scales in his favor. He, then, as a domestic animal is entitled to the

From the opinion of Judge Henry Lamm of the Missouri Supreme Court in *Lyman vs. Dale,* 262 Mo. 353.

doctrine that if he become vicious, guilty knowledge (the *scienter*) must be brought home to his master, precisely as it must be on the dog or ox. The rule of the master's liability for acts of the ox is old (Ex. 21:29). That for the acts of the dogs is put this way: The law allows the dog his first bite. Lord Cockburn's dictum covers the master's liability on a kindred phase of liability for sheep-killing, to-wit: Every dog is entitled to at least one worry. So with this mule. Absent proof of the bad habit of "spreading" when led and the *scienter*, liability did not spring from the mere fact his hind leg (he being scared) got over the wheel while he was led by a five-foot halter rope; for it must be held that a led mule is not a nuisance per se, unless he is to be condemned on that score out-and-out because of his ancestry and some law of heredity, some asinine rule, so to speak, a question we take next.

(2) Some care should be taken not to allow such scornful remarks as that "the mule has no pride of ancestry or hope of posterity" to press upon our judgment. He inherits his father's ears, but what of that? The ass's ears, presented by an angry Apollo, were an affliction to King Midas, but not to the mule. He is a hybrid, but that was man's invention centuries gone in some province of Asia Minor, and the fact is not chargeable to the mule. So, the slowness of the domestic ass does not descend as a trait to the Missouri mule. It is said that a thistle is a fat salad for an ass's mouth. Maybe it is also in a mule's, but be it so, surely his penchant for homely fare cannot so far condemn him that he does not stand *rectus in curia*. Moreover, if his sire stands in satire as an emblem of sleepy stupidity, yet that avails naught; for the authorities (on which I cannot put my finger at this moment) agree that the Missouri mule takes after his dam and not his sire in that regard. All asses are not four-footed, the adage saith, and yet to call a man an "ass" is quite a different thing than to call him "mulish" (*vide,* the lexicographers).

Furthermore, the very word jack-ass is a term of reproach everywhere, as in the literature of the law. Do we not all know that a certain phase of the law of negligence, the humanitarian rule, first announced, it has been said, in a donkey case (Davies v. Mann, 10 Mees. & Wels. 545) has been called, by those who deride it, the "jackass doctrine"? This on the doctrine of the adage: Call a dog a bad name and then hang him. But, on the other hand, to sum up fairly, it was an ass that saw the heavenly vision, even Balaam, the seer, could not see and first raised a voice against cruelty to animals. (Num. 22:23 et seq.) So, did not Sancho Panza by meditation gather the sparks of wisdom while ambling along on the back of one, that radiated in his wonderful judgments pronounced in his decision by the common-sense rule of knotty cases in the Island of Barataria? Did not Samson use the jawbone of one effectually on a thousand Philistines? Is not his name imperishably preserved in that of the fifth proposition of the first book of Euclid—the *pons asinorum?* But we shall pursue the subject no further. Enough has been said to show that the ass is not without some rights in the courts even on sentimental grounds; *ergo*, if his hybrid son, tracing his lineage as he does to the Jacks of Kentucky and Andalusia, inherits some of his traits he cannot be held bad *per se. Q.E.D.*

It is meet that a five-dollar case, having its tap root in anger (and possibly in liquor), should not drag its slow lengths through the courts for more than five years, even if it had earned the *sobriquet* of "the celebrated mule case."

The Mule: Josh Billings' Opinion

The mule is haf hoss and haf Jackass, and then kums tu a full stop, natur diskovering her mistake.

Tha weigh more, akordin tu their heft, than enny other kreetur, except a crowbar.

Tha kant hear enny quicker, nor further than the hoss, yet their ears are big enuff for snow shoes.

You kan trust them with enny one whose life aint worth enny more than the mules. The only wa tu keep the mules into a paster, is tu turn them into a medder jineing, and let them jump out.

Tha are reddy for use, just as soon as they will du tu abuse.

Tha haint got enny friends, and will live on huckle berry brush, with an ockasional chanse at Kanada thistels.

Tha are a modern invenshun, i dont think the Bible deludes tu them at tall.

Tha sel for more money than enny other domestik animile. Yu kant tell their age by looking into their mouth, enny more than you kould a Mexican cannons. Tha never hav no disease that a good club wont heal.

If tha ever die tha must kum rite tu life agin, for i never herd noboddy sa "ded mule."

Tha are like sum men, verry korrupt at harte; ive known them tu be good mules for 6 months, just tu git a good chanse to kick sumbody.

I never owned one, nor never mean to, unless thare is a United Staits law passed, requiring it.

The only reason why tha are pashunt, is bekause tha are ashamed ov themselfs.

I have seen eddikated mules in a sirkus.

Tha kould kick, and bite, tremenjis. I would not sa what I am forced tu sa again the mule, if his birth want an outrage, and man want tu blame for it.

From *Josh Billings* [Henry W. Shaw]: *His Works Complete,* pp. 163–164. New York: G. W. Dillingham, Publisher. Copyright, 1876, G. W. Carleton & Co.

Enny man who is willing tu drive a mule, ought to be exempt by law from running for the legislatur.

Tha are the strongest creeturs on earth, and heaviest ackording tu their sise; I herd tell ov one who fell oph from the tow path, on the Eri kanawl, and sunk as soon as he touched bottom, but he kept rite on towing the boat tu the nex stashun, breathing thru his ears, which stuck out ov the water about 2 feet 6 inches; i didn't see this did, but an auctioneer told me ov it, and i never knew an auctioneer tu lie unless it was absolutely convenient.

The Horse Who Sat on Eggs

Sally had walked over and put her arm around the horse's neck. "Did you ever hear the story," she asked, "about the horse who sits on eggs?"

"No," said Charlie with a grin.

"Well," replied Sally, "this is that horse. One day a stranger came round here wanting to buy a horse—a city fellow like you—only much older—sort of a bank president—very dignified. Well, anyway, he wanted to buy my horse—and pappy was just crazy enough to sell him—but he says to the stranger, just before he closed the deal, 'I think I ought to tell you about this horse before you take him,' and the gentleman says, 'That's mighty nice of you, and what is it you wish to tell me about this horse? Come, my man, speak up.'

" 'Well,' says pappy, 'this here horse sits on eggs.'

" 'What?' says the gentleman. 'Sits on what?''

" 'Eggs,' replies pappy.

" 'Sits on eggs?' says the gentleman, blinking.

" 'That's right,' says pappy. 'Sits on eggs.'

" 'Well,' says the gentleman. 'That's very interesting. But I want this horse very badly and I generally get what I want.'

"So pappy hitched the horse up and off drove the gentleman, sitting very straight. And sure enough, before long, he came to a farmhouse where there was a basket of eggs out in the front yard, and what did Beautiful Joe do but try to climb over the fence and sit down on those eggs because that's the kind of a horse he is.

" 'Whoa!' yelled the gentleman, and a farmer come running out of the house and together, between the both of them, they grabbed Beautiful Joe and got him away from the eggs and out into the road again and the gentleman thanked the farmer and gave him a five dollar bill and drove on.

"Well, he must have drove a mile further and then suddenly he came to a small creek where there was a bridge over the creek and

From *The Crazy Fool*, by Donald Ogden Stewart, pp. 148–151. Copyright, 1925, by Albert & Charles Boni, Inc. New York.

right in the middle of that bridge Beautiful Joe stopped and what did he do but jump over the bridge and sit down in the creek.

"Well, that made the gentleman very angry, indeed, because he had been thrown out of the buggy and had got all wet, and broken his left arm in two places, and he was late, anyway, so when he got Joe finally out of the creek, he drove on to the next town and right away he called pappy up on the telephone.

" 'Say,' he said, talking very loud, 'about that horse you sold me.'

" 'Yeh,' says pappy.

" 'You said that horse sits on eggs,' screamed the gentleman.

" 'Yes,' says pappy, 'that's right. Sits on eggs.'

" 'Well,' says the gentleman. 'I was driving along the Sunbury pike and we came to a bridge and right in the middle of the bridge that blankety blank horse jumped over and—'

" 'Oh my gosh,' says pappy. 'Oh my *gosh*. I forgot to tell you. He sits on fish, *too*.' "

Author's Acknowledgment. The story about the horse who sits on eggs is not mine. I wish it were. Also the horse. D.O.S.

A Genuine Mexican Plug

I resolved to have a horse to ride. I had never seen such wild, free, magnificent horsemanship outside of a circus as these picturesquely clad Mexicans, Californians, and Mexicanized Americans displayed in Carson streets every day. How they rode! Leaning just gently forward out of the perpendicular, easy and nonchalant, with broad slouch-hat brim blown square up in front, and long riata swinging above the head, they swept through the town like the wind! The next minute they were only a sailing puff of dust on the far desert. If they trotted, they sat up gallantly and gracefully, and seemed part of the horse; did not go jiggering up and down after the silly Miss-Nancy fashion of the riding-schools. I had quickly learned to tell a horse from a cow, and was full of anxiety to learn more. I was resolved to buy a horse.

While the thought was rankling in my mind, the auctioneer came scurrying through the plaza on a black beast that had as many humps and corners on him as a dromedary, and was necessarily uncomely; but he was "going, going, at twenty-two!—horse, saddle and bridle at twenty-two dollars, gentlemen!" and I could hardly resist.

A man whom I did not know (he turned out to be the auctioneer's brother) noticed the wistful look in my eye, and observed that that was a very remarkable horse to be going at such a price; and added that the saddle alone was worth the money. It was a Spanish saddle, with

From *Roughing It*, by Samuel L. Clemens, Vol. I, pp. 168–171. Entered . . . , 1871, by the American Publishing Company. Copyright, 1899, by Samuel L. Clemens. New York and London: Harper & Bros., Publishers.

ponderous *tapidaros,* and furnished with the ungainly sole-leather covering with the unspellable name. I said I had half a notion to bid. Then this keen-eyed person appeared to me to be "taking my measure"; but I dismissed the suspicion when he spoke, for his manner was full of guileless candor and truthfulness. Said he:

"I know that horse—know him well. You are a stranger, I take it, and so you might think he was an American horse, maybe, but I assure you he is not. He is nothing of the kind; but—excuse my speaking in a low voice, other people being near—he is, without the shadow of a doubt, a Genuine Mexican Plug!"

I did not know what a Genuine Mexican Plug was, but there was something about this man's way of saying it, that made me swear inwardly that I would own a Genuine Mexican Plug, or die.

"Has he any other—er—advantages?" I inquired, suppressing what eagerness I could.

He hooked his forefinger in the pocket of my army shirt, led me to one side, and breathed in my ear impressively these words:

"He can out-buck anything in America!"

"Going, going, going—at *twent-ty*-four dollars and a half, gen—"

"Twenty-seven!" I shouted, in a frenzy.

"And sold!" said the auctioneer, and passed over the Genuine Mexican Plug to me.

I could scarcely contain my exultation. I paid the money, and put the animal in a neighboring livery stable to dine and rest himself.

In the afternoon I brought the creature into the plaza, and certain citizens held him by the head, and others by the tail, while I mounted him. As soon as they let go, he placed all his feet in a bunch together, lowered his back, and then suddenly arched it upward, and shot me straight into the air a matter of three or four feet! I came as straight down again, lit in the saddle, went instantly up again, came down almost on the high pommel, shot up again and came down on the horse's neck—all in the space of three or four seconds. Then he rose and stood almost straight up on his hind feet, and I, clasping his lean neck desperately, slid back into the saddle, and held on. He came down, and immediately hoisted his heels into the air, delivering a vicious kick at the sky, and stood on his forefeet. And then down he came once more, and began the original exercise of shooting me straight up again.

The third time I went up I heard a stranger say: "Oh, don't he buck, though!"

While I was up, somebody struck the horse a sounding thwack with a leathern strap, and when I arrived again the Genuine Mexican Plug was not there. A Californian youth chased him up and caught him, and asked if he might have a ride. I granted him that luxury. He mounted the Genuine, got lifted into the air once, but sent his spurs home as he descended, and the horse darted away like a telegram. He soared over three fences like a bird, and disappeared down the road toward the Washoe Valley.

I sat down on a stone with a sigh, and by a natural impulse one of my hands sought my forehead, and the other the base of my stomach. I believe I never appreciated, till then, the poverty of the human machinery—for I still needed a hand or two to place elsewhere. Pen cannot describe how I was jolted up. Imagination cannot conceive how disjointed I was—how internally, externally, and universally I was unsettled, mixed up, and ruptured. There was a sympathetic crowd around me, though.

One elderly-looking comforter said:

"Stranger, you've been taken in. Everybody in this camp knows that horse. Any child, any Injun, could have told you that he'd buck; he is the very worst devil to buck on the continent of America. You hear *me*. I'm Curry. *Old* Curry. Old *Abe* Curry. And moreover, he is a simon-pure, out-and-out, genuine d——d Mexican plug, and an uncommon mean one at that, too. Why, you turnip, if you had laid low and kept dark, there's chances to buy an *American* horse for mighty little more than you paid for that bloody old foreign relic."

I gave no sign; but I made up my mind that if the auctioneer's brother's funeral took place while I was in the territory I would postpone all other recreations and attend it.

The Yellow Horse

I don't really believe a yellow horse is any worse by nature than a bay horse, or a white horse, or a horse of any color or combination of colors; but our judgment of things in this world is often liable to be influenced by our prejudices. For this reason, perhaps, I cannot look upon a yellow horse with any feelings of delight.

A yellow horse was standing at the depot in Washington the time I came down the Shepaug road. Looking at the animal as he felt around casually with his hind foot for his owner's brains, my mind receded back to the home of my childhood.

It seemed so blessed to lean back in the seat, and with partly closed eyes give myself up to reveries retrospective.

I remember quite distinctly the day my parent brought home a yellow horse; in fact, I can without much difficulty pick out any day of the eight which that animal passed in our society. He was a comely beast, with long limbs, a straight body, and eyes that would rival those of an eagle in looking hungry.

When he came into the yard we all went out to look at him. It was an evening—clear, bright, and beautiful. My parent stood near the

From *Life in Danbury*, by James M. Bailey, "The Danbury News Man," pp. 90–95. Entered . . . , 1873, by Shepard & Gill, in the Office of the Librarian of Congress at Washington. Boston: Shepard and Gill.

well holding the animal by a halter. We had a dog, a black and white, and if there ever was a dog who thought he had a head stowed full of knowledge it was that dog.

How plainly I can see him approach that yellow horse, to smell of his heels. He ought to have got more of a smell than he did, considering that he lost the greater part of one ear in the attempt. It was done so quick that it is possible we would not have known anything about it, had the dog not spoken of it himself.

He never smelt of that yellow horse again. The flavor wasn't what he had been used to, I think.

Three days later when he was turning around, to speak to a flea near his tail, as is customary with dogs, that yellow horse unexpectedly reached down, and took a mouthful of spinal joints out of the dog's back, and the mortification from being thus caught preyed so heavily upon the dog's mind that he died in a minute or two.

That evening mother interested father with an account of Caper's death while he was waiting for her to replace the collar the yellow horse that afternoon had snatched from his best coat.

And thus time passed. But the horse lost none of it. There wasn't a neighbor within a half mile of our house but bore some mark of that animal's friendship. Like death he was no respecter of persons. He never stopped to inquire whether a man was worth a million dollars or ten cents when reaching for him. He may have had some curiosity about it afterwards, but he never showed it.

Finally people came to avoid him when they met him on the street. I don't think they did it purposely, but it seemed to come natural to them to rush through the first doorway or over the most convenient fence when they saw him approach. This inexplicable dread communicated itself to the very dogs on the street, but before they had come fairly to understand him, he had succeeded in reducing the price of a winter-breakfast luxury to almost a mere song.

After that they looked up to him with the respect exacted by a Hindoo god with two changes of underclothes, and no dog within three blocks of us would think of going to sleep at night without first coming over to see if that horse was locked up. It was instinct, probably.

My parent never enjoyed a single day of the eight he was the sole possessor of the animal. He nipped away some portion of him every once in a while. My parent was not a profane man, but he was sorely tempted to be every hour in the day. The man who lived next to us was a profound swearer. He owned a horse that was a model of goodness in every respect—as gentle as a lamb, and as lovable as a girl of sixteen. My father could never understand this. He always spoke of it as one of the inscrutable ways of providence.

There was only one person that had anything to do with the animal who came out of that fiery ordeal unscathed. He was the hired man, and he owed his salvation to a misfortune. He was cross-eyed. He was a great source of misery to that yellow horse. The misformation of his eyes was calculated to deceive even smarter beings. The beast kicked at him a few times when he was evidently looking the other way, but that was just the time he was bearing one eye strongly on him, and he missed; and when he really was not looking was just the time the beast thought he was, and so it went through the entire eight days, both stomach and heels yearning for a morsel of him, but never getting it.

I am sure there never was another such horse to kick and bite. He did it so unexpectedly, too. He would be looking a stranger square in the face, apparently about to communicate some information of value, and then suddenly lift his hind foot, and fetch the unsophisticated man a rap on the head that would make him see seventy-five dollars' worth of fire works in a minute.

He would bite at anything whether he reached it or not; but in kicking, he rarely missed. He could use any leg with facility, but prided himself mainly on the extraordinary play of the left hind leg. With that limb he would break up a political meeting in five minutes and kick over the entire plan of the campaign before the last man got to the door.

The very air about our place was impregnated with camphor and the various new kinds of liniments. The neighbors came around after dark, and howled for the blood of that yellow horse like so many Indians clamoring for a pint of New England potash.

Matters commenced to assume a critical form. The people wanted the animal killed, and cut open so they could get back their things.

And so my parent determined to shoot the beast, but at the last moment his heart failed him. Pity triumphed, and he sold him to a man from a distance, and it was such a great distance that none of us were able to attend his funeral two weeks later, although earnestly invited to do so. He left a wife and three interesting children, and was struck just above the right temple, I believe.

Razorback Toughness

The razorback has been as distinctive of the Southern swamps and pine barrens as the long-horned steer has been of Texas. He was a principal support of life in the region of the Dismal Swamp when Byrd and his party ran the dividing line, and he has been an important economic and social factor in the region ever since. Nothing tougher ever ran on four legs. The razorback may lack the speed of

From "There's a Geography of Humorous Anecdotes," by Charles F. Arrowood, *In the Shadow of History*, edited by J. Frank Dobie, Mody C. Boatright, and Harry H. Ransom, pp. 80–81. Texas Folklore Society Publications, Number XV. Copyright, 1939, by the Texas Folk-Lore Society. Austin.

the wolf, the fighting equipment of a wildcat, the strength of a bear, but no wolf, cat or bear can exceed him in ability to absorb punishment and come back for more.

A farmer was clearing a new ground—grubbing up the stumps laboriously, by hand. A county demonstration agent came by and showed him how easily and cheaply the stumps could be removed by the use of dynamite. The farmer was delighted. He went to the store, bought dynamite, fuse, and caps. Coming home, he dug a hole by a big white oak stump, set a charge of dynamite under it, lighted the fuse, and went to his house for supper. The fuse went out, but by that time the farmer was clear of the new ground; so he decided to wait until the next morning before lighting it again.

The next morning, early, the farmer's big razorback hog got up and went foraging. He found that stick of dynamite and ate it. Then he saw the farmer about the barn lot and hustled up to see if he could steal a little corn from the mule's breakfast. He broke into the mule's stall, and made for the feed trough. The mule, naturally, kicked at him, and, for the first and last time in his life, connected. The dynamite, at last, went off.

A neighbor heard the explosion and hurried over. He found the owner leaning over the fence of his barn lot, viewing the ruins.

The neighbor heaved a sympathetic sigh. "It looks pretty bad, friend," he said, "pretty bad."

"Yes," said the victim, "it is bad. Killed my mule, wrecked my barn, broke every window out of one side of my house, and, brother, I've got an awful sick hog."

The Lazy Indian and His Pet Trout

. . . It is a likely story enough, as such things go, but there are points about it here and there which seem to require confirmation. I am told that it is a story well known and often repeated in Nova Scotia, but even that cannot be accepted as evidence of its entire truth. Being a fish-story it would seem to require something more. This is the tale as Charlie told it.

"Once there was a half-breed Indian," he said, "who had a pet trout named Tommy, which he kept in a barrel. But the trout got pretty big and had to have the water changed a good deal to keep him alive. The Indian was too lazy to do that, and he thought he would teach the trout to live out of water. So he did. He commenced by taking Tommy out of the barrel for a few minutes at a time, pretty often, and then he took him out oftener and kept him out longer, and by and by Tommy got so he could stay out a good while if he was in the

From *Angling in America* by Charles Eliot Goodspeed, pp. 315–316. Copyright, 1939, by Charles E. Goodspeed. Boston: Houghton Mifflin Company.

wet grass. Then the Indian found he could leave him in the wet grass all night, and pretty soon that trout could live in the shade whether the grass was wet or not. By that time he had got pretty tame, too, and he used to follow the Indian around a good deal, and when the Indian would go out to dig worms for him, Tommy would go along and pick up the worms for himself. The Indian thought everything of that fish, and when Tommy got so he didn't need water at all, but could go anywhere—down the dusty road and stay all day out in the hot sun—you never saw the Indian without his trout. Show people wanted to buy Tommy, but the Indian said he wouldn't sell a fish like that for any money. You'd see him comming to town with Tommy following along in the road behind, just like a dog, only of course it traveled a good deal like a snake, and most as fast.

"Well, it was pretty sad the way that Indian lost his trout, and it was curious, too. He started for town one day with Tommy coming along behind, as usual. There was a bridge in the road and when the Indian came to it he saw there was a plank off, but he went on over it without thinking. By and by he looked around for Tommy and Tommy wasn't there. He went back a ways and called, but he couldn't see anything of his pet. Then he came to the bridge and saw the hole, and he thought right away that maybe his trout had got in there. So he went to the hole and looked down, and sure enough, there was Tommy, floating on the water, bottom-side up. He'd tumbled through that hole into the brook and drowned."

Rattlers Ain't Pizen?

"Some say rattlers ain't pizen," said Buckskin Williams, an old freighter, "but I know different. I'm pullin' out of Milk River one day with 14, when I notice my line hoss swing out an' every hoss on the near side crowds the chain. My near wheel hoss, that I'm ridin', rares up an' straddles the tongue. It's then I see what the trouble is— a big rattler has struck, misses my hoss an' hits the tongue. The tongue starts to swell up. I have to chop it off to save the wagon, an' I'm damn quick doin' it, too!"

The Cayote

. . . Along about an hour after breakfast we saw the first prairie-dog villages, the first antelope, and the first wolf. If I remember

From *Trails Plowed Under*, by Charles M. Russell, pp. 191–194. Copyright, 1927, by Doubleday, Page & Company. Garden City, New York.

From *Roughing It*, by Samuel L. Clemens, Vol. I, Ch. V. Entered . . . , 1871, by The American Publishing Company; copyright, 1899, by The American Publishing Company; 1899, by Samuel L. Clemens.

rightly, this latter was the regular *cayote* (pronounced ky-*o*-te) of the farther deserts. And if it *was*, he was not a pretty creature, or respectable either, for I got well acquainted with his race afterward, and can speak with confidence. The cayote is a long, slim, sick and sorry-looking skeleton, with a gray wolf-skin stretched over it, a tolerably bushy tail that forever sags down with a despairing expression of forsakenness and misery, a furtive and evil eye, and a long, sharp face, with slightly lifted lip and exposed teeth. He has a general slinking expression all over. The cayote is a living, breathing allegory of Want. He is *always* hungry. He is always poor, out of luck and friendless. The meanest creatures despise him, and even the fleas would desert him for a velocipede. He is so spiritless and cowardly that even while his exposed teeth are pretending a threat, the rest of his face is apologizing for it. And he is *so* homely!—so scrawny, and ribby, and coarse-haired, and pitiful. When he sees you he lifts his lip and let a flash of his teeth out, and then turns a little out of the course he was pursuing, depresses his head a bit, and strikes a long, soft-footed trot through the sage-brush, glancing over his shoulder at you, from time to time, till he is about out of easy pistol range, and then he stops and takes a deliberate survey of you; he will trot fifty yards and stop again—another fifty and stop again; and finally the gray of his gliding body blends with the gray of the sage-brush, and he disappears. All this is when you make no demonstration against him; but if you do, he develops a livelier interest in his journey, and instantly electrifies his heels and puts such a deal of real estate between himself and your weapon, that by the time you have raised the hammer you see that you need a minie rifle, and by the time you have got him in line you need a rifled cannon, and by the time you have "drawn a bead" on him you see well enough that nothing but an unusually long-winded streak of lightning could reach him where he is now. But if you start a swift-footed dog after him, you will enjoy it ever so much—especially if it is a dog that has a good opinion of himself, and has been brought up to think he knows something about speed. The cayote will go swinging gently off on that deceitful trot of his, and every little while he will smile a fraudful smile over his shoulder that will fill that dog entirely full of encouragement and worldly ambition, and make him lay his head still lower to the ground, and stretch his neck further to the front, and pant more fiercely, and stick his tail out straighter behind, and move his furious legs with a yet wilder frenzy, and leave a broader and broader, and higher and denser cloud of desert sand smoking behind, and marking his long wake across the level plain! And all this time the dog is only a short twenty feet behind the cayote, and to save the soul of him he cannot understand why it is that he cannot get perceptibly closer; and he begins to get aggravated, and it makes him madder and madder to see how gently the cayote glides along and never pants or sweats or ceases to smile; and he grows still more and more incensed to see how shamefully he has been taken in by an entire stranger, and what an ignoble swindle that long, calm, soft-footed trot is; and next he notices that he is getting fagged, and that the cayote actually has to slacken speed a little to keep from running away from him—and *then* that town-dog is mad in earnest, and he begins to strain and weep and swear, and paw the sand higher than ever, and reach for the cayote with concentrated and desperate energy. This "spurt" finds him six feet behind the gliding enemy, and two miles from his friends. And then, in the instant that a wild new hope is lighting up his face, the cayote turns and smiles blandly upon him once more, and with a something about it which seems to say: "Well, I shall have to tear myself away from you, bub—business is business, and it will not do for me to be fooling along this way all day"—and forthwith there is a rushing sound, and the sudden splitting of a long crack through the atmosphere, and behold that dog is solitary and alone in the midst of a vast solitude!

It makes his head swim. He stops, and looks all around; climbs the nearest sand-mound, and gazes into the distance; shakes his head reflectively, and then, without a word, he turns and jogs along back to his train, and takes up a humble position under the hindmost wagon, and feels unspeakably mean, and looks ashamed, and hangs his tail at half-mast for a week. And for as much as a year after that, whenever there is a great hue and cry after a cayote, that dog will merely glance in that direction without emotion, and apparently observe to himself, "I believe I do not wish any of the pie."

The cayote lives chiefly in the most desolate and forbidding deserts, along with the lizard, the jackass-rabbit and the raven, and gets an uncertain and precarious living, and earns it. He seems to subsist almost wholly on the carcasses of oxen, mules, and horses that have dropped out of emigrant trains and died, and upon windfalls of carrion, and occasional legacies of offal bequeathed to him by white men who have been opulent enough to have something better to butcher than condemned army bacon. He will eat anything in the world that his first cousins, the desert-frequenting tribes of Indians, will, and they will eat anything they can bite. It is a curious fact that these latter are the only creatures known to history who will eat nitro-glycerine and ask for more if they survive.

The cayote of the deserts beyond the Rocky Mountains has a peculiarly hard time of it, owing to the fact that his relations, the Indians, are just as apt to be the first to detect a seductive scent on the desert breeze, and follow the fragrance to the late ox it emanated from, as he is himself; and when this occurs he has to content himself with sitting off at a little distance watching those people strip off and dig out everything edible, and walk off with it. Then he and the waiting ravens explore the skeleton and polish the bones. It is considered that the cayote, and the obscene bird, and the Indian of the desert, testify their blood kinship with each other in that they live together in the waste places of the earth on terms of perfect confidence and friendship, while hating all other creatures and yearning to assist at their funerals. He does not mind going a hundred miles to breakfast, and a hundred and fifty to dinner, because he is sure to have three or four days between meals, and he can just as well be traveling and looking at the scenery as lying around doing nothing and adding to the burdens of his parents.

We soon learned to recognize the sharp, vicious bark of the cayote as it came across the murky plain at night to disturb our dreams among the mail-sacks; and remembering his forlorn aspect and his hard fortune, made shift to wish him the blessed novelty of a long day's good luck and a limitless larder the morrow.

Rabbits Is Rabbits

"I, myself, [said Colonel John R. Stingo] in an anterior period of my life, had devoted time, if not money, to the promotion of an enterprise known as the Mid-Continental Chinchilla Rabbitry, under the aegis of a figurator named Kelly Mason, who had become entranced by the multipular possibilities of those rodents. In Kelly's mind it presented an aspect of a progressive bet, or endless winning parlay. He had read in some newspaper, doubtless discarded by somebody else on the seat adjoining Kelly's in a race train, for he himself never purchased anything but the racing form, that the air and track conditions in Kansas were so favorable to rabbits that the state was spending thousands of dollars in the form of bounties for their extirpation. 'That,' he said to himself, 'is of a surety the place to breed rabbits.' He had seen two of these animals in a pet-shop window, marked fifty cents apiece. Further inquiry instructed him that rabbit pelts were used in the manufacture of hatter's felts and a fur called royal seal,—there was a market for them as illimitable as for four to one against Roseben.

"He leased a farm of twenty-two acres near Wichita, Kansas, after asking the yokel who leased it to him specifically whether it was good rabbit ground. He installed hatches, a kind of coop covered with earth to make the rabbits feel at home. They are so denominated, I suppose, because the rabbits hatch their young therein. The rabbits needed little encouragement; they spawned monstrously. Kelly made contacts with furriers in Kansas City, Missouri and with hatmakers in Danbury, Connecticut to take all his output, but as the production in-

From *The Honest Rainmaker, The Life and Times of Colonel John R. Stingo*, by A. J. Liebling, pp. 250–254. Copyright 1952, 1953, by A. J. Liebling. Garden City, New York: Doubleday & Company, Inc. 1953.

creased, like a mighty gusher of oil it proves impossible to cap, he had to sell farther afield, his operations reaching the Brunswick-Balke-Collender Company, manufacturers of billiard tables, which are of course felt-covered, and also Luchow's Restaurant, the Blue Ribbon, Hans Jaeger's and the Hofbrau, New York; the Golden Ox, Chicago; and the Techau Tavern, San Francisco, all manufacturers of *hasen-pfeffer.*

"Things began to look so good that Kelly sent for me to undertake a campaign of national promotion, but on the very day of my arrival we were visited by a representative of a newspaper who demanded Kelly buy a full-page ad, reading simply, 'Compliments of a Friend.' I remonstrated that this did not seem to me the type of pulling copy we needed. It said nothing about our wares. 'It better not,' the small town newspaperman said, 'since there is a state law that makes it a misdemeanor to raise rabbits in the state of Kansas, imposing a fine of five dollars, or three days in jail for each rabbit so produced. You probably owe about sixty thousand dollars now, if anyone wanted to get tough about it.' We took the ad, and business went on as usual for a couple of weeks when another dumb rural newsman appeared from the sheet published in the seat of the adjoining county. He said they were getting out their annual centennial edition. Every year is the centennial of something, he said. He wanted two pages of complimentary advertising. So we gave him that.

"After awhile the sheriff came over for a contribution to his campaign fund, and then the fellow who was running against him, and a committee of ladies from a X Congregational Church, who said it was so nice having us in the area, they knew we would be glad to donate five hundred dollars to build new pews. Then eventuated delegations from the Campbellites, and the River Brethren and the Methodists and the Greek Orthodox. They were all on the shake. Even the WCTU got us for a grand." The Colonel looked glum. "Even a stick-up man will let you keep coffee-money," he said, "but not a woman engaged in God's work.

"The reason for the ban, we learned, was that rabbits are prone to escape,—they become stir-crazy, although not, like the poor souls at Alcatraz, sexually deprivated. It is a wonder to me," the Colonel said, "that they had any energy left. Having escaped, they would proliferate extramurally, thus nullifying the efforts of the state to exterminate them. They were a menace to the great universal granary, the Kansas wheat fields. They cost more than Professor Hatfield with his Gatling gun.

"Our rabbits kept right on breeding," he said, "unaware that their activities were without legal sanction, and Kelly continued to market the pelts, because he had a bite to meet every time a strange Ford honked at the gate. He figurated by now if anybody sang he was in for a million and a half dollars in fines, nine hundred thousand days in durance laborious. 'I haven't the heart to think of it in years,' he said, 'but it's a long rap.'

"Eventually the rube who was renting him the place came around and told him he had broken the lease by conducting illegal activities, but it would be all right if Kelly and I cut him in for fifty per cent.

"That was the day before the night Kelly got drunk with the husband of the president of the WCTU and they turned all the rabbits loose.

" 'I don't want any incriminating evidence left on the place when the law comes,' Kelly told this good old countryman, so after they had run a tractor through the wire fence that surrounded the Mid-Continental Chinchilla Rabbitry they loosed a pack of beagles on the property. Next morning there wasn't a chinchilla left on the farm.

" 'Here is something for your wife,' Kelly said to the benevolent rustic as we climbed into our Winton racer to depart, and he handed him a sawed-off shotgun loaded with deer slugs. The old fellow looked as pleased as a ballplayer accepting a free automobile. He promised to give it an early trial. Within the next year the state of Kansas had to pay out $723,000 additional bounty in that county alone."

The Colonel paused.

"The moral of Mr. Mason's adventure," he said, "if any, may be expressed: 'Never enter a race without reading the condition book carefully.' "

XI. THERE'S NO PLACE LIKE HOME
(Aspects of Love, Marriage, and Family Life)

Introduction

Most Americans relish a humorous story or remark about courtship, marriage, and family life. The people tell about tricks played in winning a girl, such as the fellow's offering to take her to a carnival at the opportune moment or his borrowing a fine calf to make himself look more prosperous, and they laugh about the "one that got away" or about the man's chasing the woman until she caught him. They have humorous stories, too, about the marriage ceremony, the burning of the last bridge: about eloping, branding the bride, or jumping the broomstick, about fake weddings, quickie weddings, and shotgun weddings. Whatever the type of ceremony, the romance of moonlight and roses is likely to disappear shortly after the vows are pronounced unless one can see the moon through the dust of housecleaning and smell the roses through the odor of burnt toast. There are sorrows in making a home and rearing a family, of course, but there are also the joys of watching children grow up, trying like Penrod to learn the difference between imagination and reality.

But love is a many-splintered thing, and all love stories do not end with boy getting girl. The men who fail to convince the lady may, like Sut Lovingood, express their resentment, but few would go so far as to turn a wedding feast into pandemonium with the help of a bull and a hive of bees. Or the disappointed lover may take refuge in some biting comparison like that of Sugar, "the standing candidate": "I've allays thort since then, boys, that *wimin* wur a good deal like *licker,* ef you love 'em too hard thar sure to throw you some way. . . ."

Cotching Is What Counts

Noty Benny.—Pleas give my compliments to Mister Boston, of Batten Roosh, and tell him I would be glad to cum up and see him if they hadn't the Legislatur up thar. You see, sum year or two ago, I was travelin for my helth, and stopt two or three days whar thar was a legislatur a settin. They was actin on a bill to punish seducin people, and I tuk notis of one chap takin a great intrest in the bill. Bymeby the clerk read a sekshun which sed "if enny man by makin false promises, shall seduce eny chasd female," &c&c. When he cum to that part, the chap I noticed gets up and ses—"Mister speaker, I move to mend this secshun by insertin the words, 'an cotched,' after the word 'chasd,' cause it stands to reason that a fellow may chase a female all day, and if he dont cotch her, thar aint no harm done."

They kicked up the tarnalest rakit I ever heard, and I aint been to see no legislaturs since.

Why Sugar Never Got Married

. . . The speaking being done, candidates and hearers gathered around old *Sugar,* to hear his comments upon the speeches, and to many inquiries of how he liked them, the old man answered:—

"They were all pooty good, but that tall fellar they call Tom, from St. Louis; *you,* I mean, *stranger,*" pointing at the same time to the candidate, "you jest scart up my feelin's to the right pint—you jest made

By "Cap'n Bender." From The New Orleans *Weekly Delta,* Vol. IV, No. 30 (May 7, 1849), p. 237.

From *Streaks of Squatter Life, and Far-West Scenes,* by John S. Robb, pp. 97-100. Copyright, 1843, by Carey & Hart, Philadelphia. Republished, 1858, by T. B. Peterson and Brothers, Philadelphia, as a part of *The Swamp Doctor's Adventures in the South-West,* by "Madison Tensas," M.D., and "Solitaire" (John S. Robb, of St. Louis, Mo.).

me feel wolfish as when I and old dad war arter the red varmints; and now what'll *you* take? I'm goin' to publicly *de*cline in your favor."

Pouring out a tin full of the liquor, and stirring it as before, he stood upright upon the stump, with a foot on each side of his kegs, and drawing off his cap, toasted:—

"The memory of the western *pioneers!*"

A shout responded to his toast, which echoed far away in the depths of the adjoining forest, and seemed to awaken a response from the spirits of those departed heroes.

"That's the way to sing it out, boys," responded old *Sugar*, "sich a yell as that would *scar* an inimy into ager fits, and make the United States Eagle scream 'Hail Columby.'"

"While you're up, *Sugar*," said one of the crowd, "give us a stump speech, yourself."

"Bravo!" shouted an hundred voices, "a speech from *Sugar*."

"Agreed, boys," said the old man, "I'll jest gin you a few words to wind up with, so keep quiet while your daddy's talkin'

> 'Sum tell it out just like a song,
> I'll gin it to you sweet and strong.'

"The ony objection ever made to me in this arr county, as a legislatur', was made by the *wimin*, 'cause I war a *bachelor*, and I never told you afore why I *re*-mained in the state of number *one*—no fellar stays single *pre*-meditated, and, in course, a hansum fellar like me, who all the gals declar' to be as enticin' as a jay bird, warn't goin' to stay alone, ef he could help it. I did see a creatur' once, named *Sofy Mason,* up the Cumberland, nigh onto Nashville. Tenne*see,* that I tuk an orful hankerin' arter, and I sot in to lookin' anxious fur matrimony, and gin to go reglar to meetin', and tuk to dressin' tremengeous finified, jest to see ef I could win her good opinion. She did git to lookin' at me, and one day, cumin' from meetin', she was takin' a look at me a kind of shy, jest as a hoss does at suthin' he's scart at, when arter champin' at a distance for awhile, I sidled up to her and blarted out a few words about the sarmin'—she said yes, but cuss me ef I know whether that wur the right answer or not, and I'm a thinkin' she didn't know then, nuther! Well, we larfed and talked a leetle all the way along to her daddy's, and thar I gin her the best bend I had in me, and raised my bran new hat as peert and *per*lite as a minister, lookin' all the time so enticin' that I sot the gal tremblin'. Her old daddy had a powerful numerous lot of healthy slaves, and lived right adjinin' my place, while on tother side lived Jake Simons—a sneakin', cute varmint, who war wusser than a miser fur stinginess, and no sooner did this cussed sarpint see me sidlin' up to Sofy, than he went to slickin' up, too, and sot himself to work to cut me out. That arr wur a struggle ekill to the battle of Orleans. Furst sum new fixup of Jake's would take her eye, and then I'd sport suthin' that would outshine him, until Jake at last gin in tryin' to outdress me, and sot to thinkin' of suthin' else. Our farms wur jest the same num-ber of acres, and we both owned three niggers apiece. Jake knew that Sofy and her dad kept a sharp eye out fur the main chance, so he thort he'd clar me out by buyin' another nigger; but I jest follor'd suit, and bought one the day arter he got his, so he had no advantage thar; he then got a *cow*, and so did I, and jest about then both on our *pusses* gin out. This put Jake to his wits' eend, and I war a wunderin' what in the yearth he would try next. We stood so, hip and thigh, fur about two weeks, both on us talkin' sweet to Sofy, whenever we could git her alone. I thort I seed that Jake, the sneakin' cuss, wur gittin' a mite ahead of me, 'cause his tongue wur so iley; howsever, I didn't let on, but kep a top eye on him. One Sunday mornin' I wur a leetle mite late to meetin', and when I got thar the furst thing I seed war Jake Simons, sittin' close bang up agin Sofy, in the same pew with her daddy! I biled a spell with wrath, and then tarned sour; I could taste myself! Thar they wur, singin' *himes* out of the same book. Je-e-eminy, fellars, I war so *enormous* mad that the new silk handkercher round my neck lost its color! Arter meetin' out they walked, linked arms, a smilin' and lookin' as pleased as a young couple at thar furst christenin', and Sofy tarned her 'cold shoulder' at me so orful pinted, that I wilted down, and gin up right straight—Jake had her, thar wur no disputin' it! I headed toward home, with my hands as fur in my trowsers pockets as I could push 'em, swarin' all the way that she wur the last one would ever git a chance to rile up my feelin's. Passin' by Jake's plantation I looked over the fence, and thar stood an explanation of the marter, right facin' the road, whar every one passin' could see it—his consarned *cow* was tied to a stake in the gardin', *with a most promisin' calf alongside of her!* That *calf* jest soured my milk, and made Sofy think, that a fellar who war allays gittin' ahead like Jake, wur a right smart chance for a lively husband!"

A shout of laughter here drowned *Sugar's* voice, and as soon as silence was restored he added, in a solemn tone, with one eye shut, and his forefinger pointing at his auditory:—

"What is a cussed sight wusser than his gittin' Sofy war the fact, that he *borrowed that calf the night before from Dick Harkley!* Arter the varmint got Sofy hitched, he told the joke all over the settle*ment*, and the boys never seed me arterwards that they didn't *b-a-h* at me fur lettin' a *calf* cut me out of a gal's affections. I'd a shot Jake, but I thort it war a free country, and the gal had a right to her choice without bein' made a widder, so I jest sold out and travelled! I've allays thort sence then, boys, that *wimin* wur a good deal like *licker*, ef you love 'em too hard thar sure to throw you some way:

'Then here's to *wimin*, then to *licker*,
Thar's nuthin' swimmin' can be slicker!"

Common Consent

. . . One day a wagon with several occupants drew up in front of the county courthouse. A young man got out and came into the office of the county clerk.

"Is this the place where a feller comes to git a license to git married?" he asked.

"Yes, sir," answered the clerk. "You surely have come to the right place."

"Well, make me out a license so that John Brown can marry Samathy Smith."

"Are you John Brown?"

"Yes, I'm John Brown."

"And is the young lady of age?"

"Naw, she ain't."

"Then I suppose you have her father's permission to marry her?"

"Well, I guess I have. See that old man a-settin' out there in that wagon with a shotgun across his lap? Well, that's her father."

How He Won His Bride

"Nathan, you are married, I understand," said the Governor of Tennessee, addressing a hillside constituent.

"Yes, sir, captured the best-looking girl in the whole community. Old Lige Peterson's daughter, Rose. You knowed her, I reckon."

"Yes, but I thought that she was engaged to Sam Parker."

"She was, but I got ahead of him. Tell you how it was. She loved Sam powerful, for he is the best circuit rider we have ever met. I loved Rose and was might'ly downcast, for I thought thar wa'nt no use buckin' agin him. Well, the day for the marriage was set, and a passul of us come to see the weddin', for Rose 'lowed that she wanted to be married in town, and then take the cars for home, thereby getting a ten-mile bridal tower. When we got up to town lo and behold, there was a circus, with mo' horses than a strong man could shake a pole at. Rose was mighty keen to go to the show, but Sam says, says he, 'Rose, you know it's agin my religion, an' therefo' we can't go. Stay here till I go an' git the license.' Rose's under jaw drapped. When Sam was gone I says, says I, 'Rose, wouldn't you like to go to that show?'

" 'Yes, but Sam won't take me.'

" 'That's bad, Rose, for they've got a world of hosses.'

From *Folk Laughter on the American Frontier*, by Mody C. Boatright, p. 105. New York: The Macmillan Company, 1949.

From *New Yarns & Funny Jokes comprising Original and Selected American Humor* . . . , p. 38. New York: Excelsior Publishing House. 1890.

"Then she tuned up and began to cry. 'Rose,' says I, 'if you marry Sam you kan't go to the show; that's certain, but if you marry me I'll take you.' She studied awhile and says, says she, 'an' let me stay to the concert airter the big show's over?'

" 'Yes.'

" 'An' let me look at the monkeys all I want to?'

" 'Tibby sho'.'

" 'An' won't pull an' haul me aroun' when I get interested?'

" 'No, sw'ar I won't.'

" 'An' when the show's all over will you let me look at the monkeys again?'

" 'Yes.'

" 'Nath,' she said, puttin' her hand mighty lovin'ly on my arm. 'I'm yourn.' Then I jumped up, popped my heels together, an' in less'n a half hour we was done married an' a-lookin' at the monkeys. That's the way I won that jewel, governor."—*Arkansaw Traveler*

Old Hoss, You're Too Late!

. . . This is a great country for jokes, and we have just heard one that is too good to keep. Early this morning there were added to our company of travellers a pair who looked very like runaways; the gentleman a tall, raw-boned specimen of the "half horse, half alligator" class, and the lady a fair match for him. Among the passengers from Napoleon is a solemn-looking gentleman, who has all along been taken for a preacher. About nine o'clock last night I was conversing with the "reverend" individual, when a young man stepped up, and addressing him, remarked: "We are going to have a wedding, and would like to have you officiate." "All right, sir," he replied, laughingly, and we stepped into the ladies' cabin, where, sure enough, the couple stood waiting. There had been several "kissing games" and several mock marriages gone through with during the evening, and I supposed that this was merely a continuation of the sport; and so thought the preacher, who, I could see, had a good deal of humor in him, and was inclined to promote general good feeling and merriment. The couple stood up before him—a good deal more solemn than was necessary in a mock marriage, I thought—and the "preacher" asked the necessary questions; and then, proceeding in the usual way, announced them "husband and wife." There was a good deal of fun afterward, and when it was over I left the cabin and so did the "preacher," who remarked to me that he liked to see young folks enjoying themselves, and took a good deal of

From *A Plate of Chowder* [on front cover and in running page heads, but not on title page] *The Book of 1000 Comical Stories; an Endless Repast of Fun, A Rich Banquet for Every Day of the Year, with Several Courses, and a Dessert . . . Bill of Fare . . .* , by the Author of "Mrs. Partington's Carpet-Bag of Fun" (Samuel P. Avery), pp. 67–68. New York: Dick and Fitzgerald, Publishers. 1859.

pleasure in contributing to their fun—but he did not understand why they selected him to act as preacher. Just then some one called me aside, and the old gentleman stepped into his state-room, which was next to mine. When I returned, the door stood open, and the "preacher" stood just inside, with his coat and vest off, and one boot in his hand, talking with the gentleman who had played the "attendant," and who, as I came up, remarked: "Well, if that's the case, it *is* a good joke, for they are in dead earnest, and are gone to the same state-room." The old gentleman raised both hands, as he exclaimed: "Good heavens! you don't tell me so!" and rushing just as he was, boot in hand, to the state-room indicated, commenced an assault on the door, as if he would break it down, exclaiming, at each lick:

"For heaven's sake don't! I aint a preacher!"

The whole cabin was aroused. Every state-room flying open with a slam, when the door opened, and the "Arkansas traveller," poking out his head, coolly remarked:

"Old hoss, you're too late!"

The Wedding Brand

Dr. R. B. Buckner told of performing a ceremony for a young Negro man and woman, which seemingly inspired another couple in the audience to take the same step without delay. The would-be groom came to Dr. Buckner and asked him if it would be all right for him to borrow the license of the newly wedded couple and bring his sweetheart and get married without further bother.

The story is told of another couple that came to a minister late one Saturday night without a license. The minister told them that he could not marry them then—telling them to come back Monday. The young fellow asked: "Couldn't you just say a few words to tide us over the week end?"

Stanley Vestal tells of a cowboy who fell in love with a nester's daughter who was willing to marry him, but insisted upon a proper wedding. No preacher was within a day's ride. So the boys got together, organized, and elected one of their number justice of the peace. "In the cow-camp, there was no book but the brand book, but the J. P. was undaunted. Using the brand book as a Bible, he improvised a ceremony to the satisfaction of all concerned. The cowboy 'put his brand' on his bride, and the two were 'hitched to run in double harness.'"

From *Texas Tradition,* by Ross Phares, p. 17. Copyright, 1954, by Ross Phares. New York: Henry Holt and Company, Publishers.

Sicily Burns's Wedding

"Hey Ge-orge!" rang among the mountain slopes; and looking up to my left, I saw "Sut," tearing along down a steep point, heading me off, in a long kangaroo lope, holding his flask high above his head, and hat in hand. He brought up near me, banteringly shaking the half-full "tickler," within an inch of my face.

"Whar am yu gwine? take a suck, hoss? This yere truck's *ole*. I kotch hit myse'f, hot this mornin frum the still wum. Nara durn'd bit ove strike-nine in hit—I put that ar piece ove burnt dried peach in myse'f tu gin hit color—better nur ole Bullen's plan: he puts in tan ooze, in what he sells, an' when that haint handy, he uses the red warter outen a pon' jis' below his barn;—makes a pow'ful natral color, but don't help the taste much. Then he correcks that wif red pepper; hits an orful mixtry, that whisky ole Bullen makes; no wonder he seed 'Hell-sarpints.' He's pisent ni ontu three quarters ove the b'levin parts ove his congregashun wif hit, an' tuther quarter he's sot intu ruff stealin an' cussin. Ef his still-'ous don't burn down, ur he peg out hisse'f, the neighborhood am ruinated a-pas' salvashun. Haint he the durndes sampil ove a passun yu ever seed enyhow?

"Say George, du yu see these yere well-poles what I uses fur laigs. Yu sez yu sees em, dus yu?"

"Yes."

"Very well; I passed 'em a-pas' each uther tuther day, right peart. I put one out a-head jis' so, an' then tuther 'bout nine feet a-head ove hit agin jis' so, an' then kep on a-duin hit. I'll jis' gin yu leave tu go tu the devil ha'f hamon, ef I didn't make fewer tracks tu the mile, an' more tu the minit, than were ever made by eny human man body, since Bark Wilson beat the saw-log frum the top ove the Frog Mountin intu the Oconee River, an' dove, an' dodged hit at las'. I hes allers look'd ontu that performince ove Bark's as onekel'd in histery, allers givin way tu dad's ho'net race, however.

"George, every livin thing hes hits pint, a pint over sum sort. Ole Bullen's pint is a durn'ed fust rate, three bladed, dubbil barril'd, warterproof, hypockracy, an' a never-tirein appertite fur bal'-face. Sicily Burns's pint am tu drive men folks plum crazy, an' then bring em too agin. Gin em a rale Orleans fever in five minits, an' then in five minits more, gin em a Floridy ager. Durn her, she's down on her heels flat-footed now. Dad's pint is tu be king over all durn'd fools, ever since the day ove that feller what cribb'd up so much co'n down in Yegipt, long time ago, (he run outen his coat yu minds). The Bibil tells us hu wer the

From *Sut Lovingood* . . . , by . . . [George W. Harris], pp. 86–97. New York: Dick & Fitzgerald. 1867.

stronges' man—hu wer the bes' man—hu were the meekis' man, an' hu
the wises' man, but leaves yu tu guess hu wer the bigges' fool.

"Well, eny man what cudent guess arter readin that ar scrimmage
wif an 'oman 'bout the coat, haint sense enuf tu run intu the hous', ef
hit wer rainin ded cats, that's all. Mam's pint am in kitchen insex, bakin
hoe-cake, bilin greens, an' runnin bar laiged. My pint am in takin aboard
big skeers, an' then beatin enybody's hoss, ur skared dorg, a-runnin
frum onder em agin. I used tu think my pint an' dad's were jis' the
same, sulky, unmix'd king durn'd fool; but when he acted hoss, an'
mistook hossflies fur ho'nets, I los' heart. Never mine, when I gits his
'sperence, I may be king fool, but yet great golly, he gets frum bad tu
wus, monstrus fas'.

"Now ef a feller happens tu know what his pint am, he kin allers git
along, sumhow, purvided he don't swar away his liberty tu a temprins
s'ciety, live tu fur frum a still-'ous, an' too ni a chu'ch ur a jail. Them's
my sentimints on 'pints,'—an' yere's my sentimints ontu folks: Men wer
made a-purpus jis' tu eat, drink, an' fur stayin awake in the yearly part
ove the nites: an' wimen wer made tu cook the vittils, mix the sperits,
an' help the men du the stayin awake. That's all, an' nuthin more, on-
less hits fur the wimen tu raise the devil atwix meals, an' knit socks
atwix drams, an' the men tu play short kerds, swap hosses wif fools, an'
fite fur exersise, at odd spells.

"George, yu don't onderstan life yet scarcely at all, got a heap tu larn,
a heap. But 'bout my swappin my laigs so fas'—these yere are very par ove
laigs. I hed got about a fox squirril skin full ove biled co'n juice packed
onder my shut, an' onder my hide too, I mout es well add, an' were
aimin fur Bill Carr's on foot. When I got in sight ove ole man Burns's,
I seed ni ontu fifty hosses an' muels hitch'd tu the fence. Durnashun!
I jis' then tho't ove hit, 'twer Sicily's wedding day. She married ole
Clapshaw, the suckit rider. The very feller hu's faith gin out when he
met me sendin sody all over creashun. Suckit-riders am surjestif things
tu me. They preaches agin me, an' I hes no chance tu preach back at
them. Ef I cud I'd make the institushun behave hitsef better nur hit
dus. They hes sum wunderful pints, George. Thar am two things nobody never seed: wun am a dead muel, an' tuther is a suckit-rider's
grave. Kaze why, the he muels all turn into old field school-masters, an'
the she ones intu strong minded wimen, an' then when thar time cums,
they dies sorter like uther folks. An' the suckit-riders ride ontil they
marry; ef they marrys money, they turns intu store-keepers, swaps hosses,
an' stas away ove colleckshun Sundays. Them what marrys, an' by sum
orful mistake *misses the money,* jis' turns intu polertishuns, sells 'ile
well stock,' an' dies sorter in the human way too.

"But 'bout the wedding. Ole Burns hed a big black an' white bull,
wif a ring in his snout, an' the rope tied up roun his ho'ns. They rid
'im tu mill, an' sich like wif a saddil made outen two dorgwood forks,
an' two clapboards, kivered wif a ole piece ove carpet, rope girth, an'

rope stirrups wif a loop in hit fur the foot. Ole 'Socks,' es they call'd
the bull, hed jis' got back frum mill, an' wer turn'd intu the yard, saddil
an' all, tu solace hissef a-pickin grass. I wer slungin roun the outside
ove the hous', fur they hedn't hed the manners tu ax me in, when they
sot down tu dinner. I wer pow'fully hurt 'bout hit, an' happen'd tu
think—SODY. So I sot in a-watchin fur a chance tu du sumthin. I fus'
tho't I'd shave ole Clapshaw's hoss's tail, go tu the stabil an' shave Sicily's
mare's tail, an' ketch ole Burns out, an' shave his tail too. While I wer
a-studyin 'bout this, ole Sock wer a-nosin 'round, an' cum up ontu a
big baskit what hilt a littil shattered co'n; he dipp'd in his head tu git
hit, an' I slipp'd up an' jerked the handil over his ho'ns.

"Now, George, ef yu knows the nater ove a cow brute, they is the
durndes' fools amung all the beastes, ('scept the Lovingoods;) when
they gits intu tribulashun, they knows nuffin but tu shot thar eyes,
beller, an' back, an' keep a-backin. Well, when ole Sock raised his head
an' foun hissef in darkness, he jis' twisted up his tail, snorted the shatter'd co'n outen the baskit, an' made a tremenjus lunge agin the hous'.
I hearn the picters a-hangin agin the wall on the inside a-fallin. He
fotch a deep loud rusty beller, mout been hearn a mile, an' then sot
intu a onendin sistem ove backin. A big craw-fish wif a hungry coon
a-reachin fur him, wer jis' nowhar. Fust agin one thing, then over anuther, an' at las' agin the bee-bainch, knockin hit an' a dozen stan ove
bees heads over heels, an' then stompin back'ards thru the mess. Hit
haint much wuf while tu tell what the bees did, ur how soon they sot
intu duin hit. They am pow'ful quick-tempered littil critters, enyhow.
The air wer dark wif 'em, an' Sock wer kivered all over, frum snout tu
tail, so clost yu cudent a-sot down a grain ove wheat fur bees, an' they
wer a-fitin one anuther in the air, fur a place on the bull. The hous'
stood on sidelin groun, an' the back door were even wif hit. So Sock
happen tu hit hit plum, jis' backed intu the hous' onder 'bout two hundred an' fifty pouns ove steam, bawlin orful, an' every snort he fotch
he snorted away a quart ove bees ofen his sweaty snout. He wer the
leader ove the bigges' an' the madest army ove bees in the worild. Thar
wer at leas' five solid bushels ove 'em. They hed filled the baskit, an'
hed lodged ontu his tail, ten deep, ontil hit wer es thick es a waggin
tung. He hed hit stuck strait up in the air, an' hit looked adzackly like a
dead pine kivered wif ivey. I think he wer the hottes' and wus hurtin'
bull then livin; his temper, too, seemed tu be pow'fully flustrated. Ove
all the durn'd times an' kerryins on you *ever* hearn tell on wer thar an'
thar abouts. He cum tail fust agin the ole two story Dutch clock, an'
fotch hit, bustin hits runnin geer outen hit, the littil wheels a-trundlin
over the floor, an' the bees even chasin them. Nex pass, he fotch up
agin the foot ove a big dubbil injine bedstead, rarin hit on aind, an'
punchin one ove the posts thru a glass winder. The nex tail fus' exper-
dishun wer made aginst the caticorner'd cupboard, outen which he
made a perfeck momox. Fus' he upsot hit, smashin in the glass doors,

an' then jis' sot in an' stomp'd everything on the shelves intu giblits, a-tryin tu back furder in that direckshun, an' tu git the bees ofen his laigs.

"Pickil crocks, perserves jars, vinegar jugs, seed bags, yarb bunches, paragorick bottils, aig baskits, an' delf war—all mix'd dam permiskusly, an' not worth the sortin', by a duller an' a alf. Nex he got a far back acrost the room agin the board pertishun; he went thru hit like hit hed been paper, takin wif him 'bout six foot squar ove hit in splinters, an' broken boards, intu the nex room, whar they wer eatin dinner, an' rite yere the fitin becum gineral, an' the dancin, squawkin, cussin, an' dodgin begun.

"Clapshaw's ole mam wer es deaf es a dogiron, an' sot at the aind ove the tabil, nex tu whar ole Sock busted thru the wall; tail fus' he cum agin her cheer, a-histin her an' hit ontu the tabil. Now, the smashin ove delf, an' the mixin ove vittils begun. They hed sot severil tabils tugether tu make hit long enuf. So he jis' rolled 'em up a-top ove one anuther, an' thar sot ole Missis Clapshaw, a-straddil ove the top ove the pile, a-fitin bees like a mad wind-mill, wif her calliker cap in one han, fur a wepun, an' a cract frame in tuther, an' a-kickin, an' a-spurrin like she wer ridin a lazy hoss arter the doctor, an' a-screamin rape, fire, an' murder, es fas' es she cud name 'em over.

"Taters, cabbige, meat, soup, beans, sop, dumplins, an' the truck what yu wallers 'em in; milk, plates, pies, puddins, an' every durn fixin yu cud think ove in a week, wer thar, mix'd an' mashed, like hit had been thru a thrashin-meesheen. Ole Sock still kep a-backin, an' backed the hole pile, ole 'oman an' all, also sum cheers, outen the frunt door, an' down seven steps intu the lane, an' then by golly, turn'd a fifteen hundred poun summerset hissef arter em, lit a-top ove the mix'd up mess, flat ove his back, an' then kicked hissef ontu his feet agin. About the time he ris, ole man Burns—yu know how fat, an' stumpy, an' cross-grained he is, enyhow—made a vigrus mad snatch at the baskit, an' got a savin holt ontu hit, but cudent *let go quick enuf;* for ole Sock jis' snorted, bawled, an' histed the ole cuss heels fust up intu the air, an' he lit on the bull's back, an' hed the baskit in his han.

"Jis' es soon es ole Blackey got the use ove his eyes, he tore off down the lane tu out-run the bees, so durn'd fas' that ole Burns wer feard tu try tu git off. So he jis' socked his feet intu the rope loops, an' then cummenc'd the durndes' bull-ride ever mortal man ondertuck. Sock run atwix the hitched critters an' the rail-fence, ole Burns fust fitin him over the head wif the baskit tu stop him, an' then fitin the bees wif hit. I'll jis' be durn'd ef I didn't think he hed four ur five baskits, hit wer in so meny places at onst. Well, Burns, baskit, an' bull, an' bees, skared every durn'd hoss an' muel loose frum that fence—bees ontu all ove 'em, bees, by golly, everywhar. Mos' on 'em, too, tuck a fence rail along, fas' tu the bridil reins. Now I'll jus' gin yu leave tu kiss my sister Sall till she squalls, ef ever sich a sight wer seed ur sich nises hearn, es filled up that long lane. A heavy cloud ove dus', like a harycane hed been blowin, hid all the hosses, an' away abuv hit yu cud see tails, an' ainds ove fence-rails a-flyin about; now an' then a par ove bright hine shoes wud flash in the sun like two sparks, an' away ahead wer the baskit a-sirklin roun an' about at randum. Brayin, nickerin, the bellerin ove the bull, clatterin ove runnin hoofs, an' a mons'ous rushin soun, made up the noise. Lively times in that lane jis' then, warnt thar?

"I swar ole Burns kin beat eny man on top ove the yeath a-fitin bees wif a baskit. Jis' set 'im a-straddil ove a mad bull, an' let thar be bees enuf tu exhite the ole man, an' the man what beats him kin break me. Hosses an' muels wer tuck up all over the county, an' sum wer forever los'. Yu cudent go eny course, in a cirkil ove a mile, an' not find buckils, stirrups, straps, saddil blankits, ur sumthin belongin tu a saddil hoss. Now don't forgit that about that hous' thar wer a good time bein had ginerally. Fellers an' gals loped outen windows, they rolled outen the doors in bunches, they clomb the chimleys, they darted onder the house jis' tu dart out agin, they tuck tu the thicket, they rolled in the wheat field, lay down in the krick, did everything but stan still. Sum made a strait run *fur* home, an' sum es strait a run *frum* home; livelyest folks I ever did see. Clapshaw crawled onder a straw pile in the barn, an' sot intu prayin—yu cud a-hearn him a mile—sumthin 'bout the plagues ove Yegipt, an' the pains ove the secon death. I tell yu now he lumbered.

"Sicily, she squatted in the cold spring, up tu her years, an' turn'd a milk crock over her head, while she wer a drownin a mess ove bees onder her coats. I went tu her, an' sez I, 'Yu hes got anuther new sensashun haint yu?' Sez she—

" 'Shet yer mouth, yu cussed fool!'

"Sez I, 'Power'ful sarchin feelin bees gins a body, don't they?'

" 'Oh, lordy, lordy, Sut, these yere 'bominabil insex is jis' burnin me up!'

" 'Gin 'em a mess ove SODY,' sez I, 'that'll cool 'em off, an' skeer the las' durn'd one ofen the place.'

She lifted the crock, so she cud flash her eyes at me, an' sed, 'Yu go tu hell!' *jis es plain.* I thought, takin all things tugether, that p'raps I mout es well put the mountin atwix me an' that plantashun; an' I did hit.

"Thar warnt an' 'oman, ur a gal at that weddin, but what thar frocks, an' stockins wer too tite fur a week. Bees am wus on wimen than men, enyhow. They hev a farer chance at 'em. Nex day I passed ole Hawley's, an' his gal Betts wer sittin in the porch, wif a white hankerchef tied roun her jaws; her face wer es red es a beet, an' her eyebrows hung 'way over heavy. Sez I, 'Hed a fine time at the weddin, didn't yu?' 'Yu mus' be a durn'd fool,' wer every word she sed. I hadent gone a hundred yards, ontil I met Missis Brady, her hans fat, an' her ankils swelled ontil they shined. Sez she,—

" 'Whar yu gwine, Sut?'

" 'Bee huntin,' sez I.

" 'Yu jis' say bees agin, yu infunel gallinipper, an' I'll scab yer head wif a rock.'

"Now haint hit strange how tetchus they am, on the subjick ove bees?

"Ove all the durn'd misfortinit weddins ever since ole Adam married that heifer, what wer so fon' ove talkin tu snaix, an' eatin appils, down ontil now, that one ove Sicily's an' Clapshaw's wer the worst one fur noise, disappintment, skeer, breakin things, hurtin, trubbil, vexashun ove spirrit, an' gineral swellin. Why, George, her an' him cudent sleep tugether fur ni ontu a week, on account ove the doins ove them ar hot-footed, 'vengeful, 'bominabil littil insex. They never will gee tugether, got tu bad a start, mine what I tell yu. Yu haint time now tu hear how ole Burns finished his bull-ride, an' how I cum tu du that lofty, topliftical speciment ove fas' runnin. I'll tell yu all that, sum uther time. Ef eny ove 'em axes after me, tell 'em that I'm over in Fannin, on my way tu Dahlonega. They is huntin me tu kill me, I is fear'd.

"Hit am an orful thing, George, tu be a natral born durn'd fool. Yu'se never 'sperienced hit pussonally, hev yu? Hits made pow'fully agin our famerly, an all owin tu dad. I orter bust my head open agin a bluff ove rocks, an' jis' wud du hit, ef I warnt a cussed coward. All my yeathly 'pendence is in these yere laigs—d'ye see em? Ef they don't fail, I may turn human, sum day, that is sorter human, enuf tu be a Squire, ur school cummisiner. Ef I wer jis' es smart es I am mean, an' ornary, I'd be President ove a Wild Cat Bank in less nor a week. Is sperrits plenty over wif yu?"

A Perfect Woman

". . . The President told of a Southern Illinois preacher who, in the course of his sermon, asserted that the Saviour was the only perfect man who had ever appeared in this world; also, that there was no record in the Bible, or elsewhere, of any perfect woman ever having lived on the earth. Whereupon there arose in the rear of the church a persecuted-looking personage who, the parson having stopped speaking, said '*I* know a perfect woman, and for the last six years.' 'Who was she?' asked the minister. 'My husband's first wife,' replied the afflicted female."

From *Abraham Lincoln, The War Years,* by Carl Sandburg, Vol. IV, p. 118. Copyright 1939 by Carl Sandburg. New York: Harcourt, Brace and Company. (Originally from the diary of Col. James Grant Wilson, March 15, 1865.)

You Tell Um

The government inspector at the Indian reservation was telling the tribal chieftain that it was a violation of the law to have more than one wife.

"Now, I want you to tell all of your wives except one that they can no longer look upon you as a husband," he warned.

"You tell um," suggested the chief.

Taught Him a Lesson

An Indiana man bet ten dollars that he could ride a fly-wheel in a saw mill, and as his widow paid the bet, she remarked: "William was a kind husband, but he didn't know much about fly-wheels."

He Forgot Somethin'

The following story is told: "I say, cap'n!" cried a little keen-eyed man, as he landed from a steamer at Natchez; "I say, cap'n, these here aren't all. I've left somethin' on board, that's a fact." "Them's all the plunder you brought on board, anyhow," answered the captain. "Wal, I see now; I grant it's O. K. accordin' to list: four boxes, three chests, two band-boxes, and portmanty; two hams, one part cut, three ropes of inyens, and a tea-kettle. But, see, cap'n, I'm dubersome; I feel there's somethin' short, tho' I've counted um nine times over, and never took my eyes off um while on board; there's somethin' not right, somehow." "Wal, stranger, time's up; thems all I knows on; so just fetch your wife and five children out of the cabin, cos I'm off." "*Them's um!* Darn it, thems um! I know'd *I'd forgot somethin'!*"

Home Made Sausage

Hog killing is over at last. We had about made up our minds, to kill one at a time as we needed them and not cure any for bacon but the

From *Rocky Mountain Life,* Vol. 2 (December, 1948), No. 10, p. 45.

From *American Wit and Humor,* Vol. II, p. 119. Philadelphia: George W. Jacobs & Co. 1900.

From *Flashes and Sparks of Wit and Humor by Our American Humorists* . . . , p. 35. New York: M. J. Ivers & Co. 1880.

"Making Sausage," from *Bill Arp's Scrap Book, Humor and Philosophy* . . . , by Bill Arp [Charles H. Smith], pp. 213–214. Atlanta: Jas. P. Harrison & Co., Publishers. 1884.

weather got right and the moon was on the increase, and so we slayed them. I don't care anything about the moon myself, but there are some old family superstitions that the meat will shrink in the pot if the moon is on the wane when you kill it. The new moon is quite level this time, which is a sure sign that it will rain a good deal this month, or that it wont. We have pretty well disposed of this greasy business. The little boys had a good time frying liver on the hot rocks and roasting tails in the ashes and blowing up balloons, and now if we had a few darkeys to coog up the heads and clean the feet and fix up the skins for sausages and make a nice lot of souse, we could live like princes, but it's trouble-some work and costs more than it comes to if we have to do it ourselves.

I am very fond of sausage—home made sausage such as Mrs. Arp knows how to make, and so she delicately informed me that the meat was all chopped and ready for the machine, and said something about my every day clothes and one of her old aprons. She further remarked that when it was all ground up she would come down and show me how much salt and pepper and sage to put in and how to mix it all up together. Well, I dident mind the machine business at all, but I re-membered seeing her work mighty hard over that mixing of the salt and pepper and sage, and frying a little mess on the stove and tasting it, and then putting in more salt and work it over again, and cooking another mess and tasting it again, and then putting in more pepper and more sage, and after the job was all over, heard her declare there wasn't enough of anything in it, and so I conjured up a bran new idea, and sprinkled about a hatful of salt and a quart of black pepper and a pint of cayenne and all the sage that was on the premises all over the meat before I ground it. Then I put it through the machine, and cooked and tasted it myself. Well, it was a little hot—that's a fact—and a little salty, and a right smart sagey, but it was good, and a little of it satisfied a body quicker than a good deal of the ordinary kind, and the new plan saved a power of mixing. I took a nice little cake of it up to Mrs. Arp to try, which she did with some surprise and misgiving. By the time she had sneezed four times and coughed the plate out of her lap, she quietly asked me if it was all like that. "All," said I, solemnly. "Do you like it?" said she. "Pretty well, I think" said I; "I wanted to save you trou-ble, and maybe I have got it a leetle too strong." She never replied, but the next day she made up the little cloth bags and stuffed 'em and hung all overhead in the kitchen, and remarked as she left, "Now, chil-dren, that's your pa's sausage. It's a pity he hadn't stayed away another day." . . .

Home Hints

Next to a thoroughbred mother-in-law, a fire is the most dangerous thing to have about the house. The latter can be put out if you are lively, the former cannot, except upon occasions. Dropping the former features, which are often harsh and disagreeable, we turn to the fire for warmth and cheerfulness.

Should a fire break out in the daytime, obtain as much ice water as possible and throw it on the flames. This has more effect than warm water. Buy a rope that will reach within eleven feet from your room to the ground, in case of a fire in the night, tie one end about your bed post, the other end around your neck, and jump from the window.

To MAKE A TOOTHPICK.—To make a durable family toothpick, purchase a 3 x 4 joist and whittle it down to the requisite size. Then pick.

To MAKE A SCRAP BOOK.—Take a handsomely bound book, tear the pages into small bits and there's your scrap book. . . .

To RAISE BREAD.—Get trusted for a few loaves at the nearest bakers.

IN CASE OF SUNSTROKE pick the patient up carefully and place him on the cool side of the house in a snowbank, run icicles down his neck, fill his shoes with snow and hang him over a clothes line.

To PRESS WILD FLOWERS.—Gather the flowers after cutting them down with a lawn mower. Pick them carefully and press them in a hay press or under a fat man in church. Frame them and hang the horror in the attic.

To CLEAN A STOVEPIPE.—Take down the pipe with as little jar as possible. Carry it out in the backyard, hold it above your head so you can see through it, have your wife beat the pipe and you will be thoroughly sooted.

To PARE APPLES.—Place them in couples.

To APPLE PEARS.—It can't be done, dear reader.

To LAY A CARPET.—Either do it yourself or send for someone else; anybody but a hen.

To PAPER A ROOM.—Ascertain the size of the room by multiplying the size of the room by the number of days required to do the job. Square the base boards. Put it on with buckwheat cake batter, with a freize of maple syrup.

To TELL A BAD EGG.—This depends entirely on what you wish to tell the egg. If it be bad news, break it gently—this applies both to the communication and the fruit. The former had better be made by telephone, with the safety plug in position. . . .

While satisfied that the readers of this work know a good thing when they see it, from the fact that they have purchased the book, there may

From *The Berkshire News Comic Cook Book and Dyspeptics Guide to the Grave,* by Fred H. Curtiss, pp. 63–65; 67–68. Copyright, 1890, by Douglas Bros., Publishers. Great Barrington, Massachusetts.

be a few—very few—things that they don't know, and which may be found in this department, which is the result of many years of careful research among the standard authorities on many subjects. The first one is a receipt for:

CLEANING POSTAGE STAMPS.—It is a well-known fact that when you cancel a stamp you can't sell it, and when you can sell it, the postal authorities also cancel it. To economize, stamps may be used a second time by cleaning them with a weak solution of something or other. The first time, the stamps cost their face value, the second time the government charges a cool fifty dollars in the shape of a fine, which, by the way, is not at all fine.

To BUILD A FIRE.—Load up a stove with kindling wood, etc., with plenty of the etc., pour on a yard or two of kerosene, applying a match while so doing. It is well to have an aperture made in the roof of the kitchen as a sort of fire escape, to expedite the hired girl's journey up the golden stairs. The following epitaph suggests itself:

> She used kerosene to light the fire,
> And now, alas, she has gone up higher

To BREAK A COLT.—Hit him across the back with a sledge hammer. One blow should be sufficient to break him—or at least, break his back.

To REMOVE SUPERFLUOUS HAIR.—Get married. This prescription is intended for gentlemen whose heads are crowned with a superabundance of capillary fringe.

To MAKE ICE-WATER LAST.—Prepare everything else first.

Penrod Perplexed

Next day, Penrod acquired a dime by a simple and antique process which was without doubt some times practised by the boys of Babylon. When the teacher of his class in Sunday-school requested the weekly contribution, Penrod, fumbling honestly (at first) in the wrong pockets, managed to look so embarrassed that the gentle lady told him not to mind, and said she was often forgetful herself. She was so sweet about it that, looking into the future, Penrod began to feel confident of a small but regular income.

At the close of the afternoon services he did not go home, but proceeded to squander the funds just withheld from China upon an orgy of the most pungently forbidden description. In a Drug Emporium, near the church, he purchased a five-cent sack of candy consisting for the most part of the heavily flavoured hoofs of horned cattle, but undeniably substantial, and so generously capable of resisting solution that the purchaser must needs be avaricious beyond reason who did not realize his money's worth.

From *Penrod*, by Booth Tarkington, pp. 51–57. Copyright, 1914, by Doubleday, Page and Company. Garden City, New York.

Equipped with this collation, Penrod contributed his remaining nickel to a picture show, countenanced upon the seventh day by the legal but not the moral authorities. Here, in cozy darkness, he placidly insulted his liver with jaw-breaker upon jaw-breaker from the paper sack, and in a surfeit of content watched the silent actors on the screen.

One film made a lasting impression upon him. It depicted with relentless pathos the drunkard's progress; beginning with his conversion to beer in the company of loose travelling men; pursuing him through an inexplicable lapse into evening clothes and the society of some remarkably painful ladies, next, exhibiting the effects of alcohol on the victim's domestic disposition, the unfortunate man was seen in the act of striking his wife and, subsequently, his pleading baby daughter with an abnormally heavy walking-stick. Their flight—through the snow—to seek the protection of a relative was shown, and finally, the drunkard's picturesque behaviour at the portals of a madhouse.

So fascinated was Penrod that he postponed his departure until this film came round again, by which time he had finished his unnatural repast and almost, but not quite, decided against following the profession of a drunkard when he grew up.

Emerging, satiated, from the theatre, a public timepiece before a jeweller's shop confronted him with an unexpected dial and imminent perplexities. How was he to explain at home these hours of dalliance? There was a steadfast rule that he return direct from Sunday-school; and Sunday rules were important, because on that day there was his father, always at home and at hand, perilously ready for action. One of the hardest conditions of boyhood is the almost continuous strain put upon the powers of invention by the constant and harassing necessity for explanations of every natural act.

Proceeding homeward through the deepening twilight as rapidly as possible, at a gait half skip and half canter, Penrod made up his mind in what manner he would account for his long delay, and, as he drew nearer, rehearsed in words the opening passage of his defence.

"Now see here," he determined to begin; "I do not wish to be blamed for things I couldn't help, nor any other boy. I was going along the street by a cottage and a lady put her head out of the window and said her husband was drunk and whipping her and her little girl, and she asked me wouldn't I come in and help hold him. So I went in and tried to get hold of this drunken lady's husband where he was whipping their baby daughter, but he wouldn't pay any attention, and I *told* her I ought to be getting home, but she kep' on askin' me to stay—"

At this point he reached the corner of his own yard, where a coincidence not only checked the rehearsal of his eloquence but happily obviated all occasion for it. A cab from the station drew up in front of the gate, and there descended a troubled lady in black and a fragile little girl about three. Mrs. Schofield rushed from the house and enfolded both in hospitable arms.

They were Penrod's Aunt Clara and cousin, also Clara, from Dayton, Illinois, and in the flurry of their arrival everybody forgot to put Penrod to the question. It is doubtful, however, if he felt any relief; there may have been even a slight, unconscious disappointment not altogether dissimilar to that of an actor deprived of a good part.

In the course of some really necessary preparations for dinner he stepped from the bathroom into the pink-and-white bedchamber of his sister, and addressed her rather thickly through a towel.

"When'd mamma find out Aunt Clara and Cousin Clara were coming?"

"Not till she saw them from the window. She just happened to look out as they drove up. Aunt Clara telegraphed this morning, but it wasn't delivered."

"How long they goin' to stay?"

"I don't know."

Penrod ceased to rub his shining face, and thoughtfully tossed the towel through the bathroom door. "Uncle John won't try to make 'em come back home, I guess, will he?" (Uncle John was Aunt Clara's husband, a successful manufacturer of stoves, and his lifelong regret was that he had not entered the Baptist ministry.) "He'll let 'em stay here quietly, won't he?"

"What *are* you talking about?" demanded Margaret, turning from her mirror. "Uncle John sent them here. Why shouldn't he let them stay?"

Penrod looked crestfallen. "Then he hasn't taken to drink?"

"Certainly not!" She emphasized the denial with a pretty peal of soprano laughter.

"Then why," asked her brother gloomily, "why did Aunt Clara look so worried when she got here?"

"Good gracious! Don't people worry about anything except somebody's drinking? Where did you get such an idea?"

"Well," he persisted, "you don't *know* it ain't that."

She laughed again, whole-heartedly. "Poor Uncle John! He won't even allow grape juice or ginger ale in his house. . . . Now what in the name of the common sense put it into your head that Uncle John had taken to—"

"Oh, nothing." He turned lifelessly away and went downstairs, a newborn hope dying in his bosom. Life seems so needlessly dull sometimes.

———

XII. ANOTHER DAY, ANOTHER DOLLAR
(Work and Workers' Hero Stories)

Introduction

The American worker realizes the monotony of his task, but he accepts the day-to-day dullness with confident laughter: "Another day, another dollar; a million days, a million dollars." Some workers lighten the dullness of their daily labor by creating an occupational hero, a demigod, who could do the job faster and easier. Unlike the demigods of other peoples, the demigods of the Americans are comic, not serious. They were patently created for entertainment, not worship.

The lumberjack has Paul Bunyan, who could log land by sections with the aid of Babe, the blue ox which could "pull anything with two ends to it." The cowboy has Pecos Bill, who "invented most of the things connected with the cattle business," but did not invent cow-stealing, for that "was discovered by King David in the Bible, but Bill improved on it." The bartender can tell of Hank, who mixed "specials" for almost any complaint, and the sign-painter can brag of the exploits of Slappy Hooper, who could paint signs on the sky.

Some occupations do not have a cycle of stories clustered around a hero, but do have a few stories about a great workman—often unidentified—who could do the job extremely well. Such is the story of the man who built a fireplace that would suck a cat up the chimney. Other occupations have stories about the roughness and toughness of a group of workmen like the men in the rock quarries of Hardscrabble County.

Paul Bunyan Tales

I. BABE, THE BIG BLUE OX

Babe, the big blue ox constituted Paul Bunyan's assets and liabilities. History disagrees as to when, where and how Paul first acquired this bovine locomotive but his subsequent record is reliably established. Babe could pull anything that had two ends to it.

Babe was seven axehandles wide between the eyes according to some authorities; others equally dependable say forty-two axehandles and a plug of tobacco. Like other historical contradictions this comes

From *The Marvelous Exploits of Paul Bunyan* . . . , text and illustrations by W. B. Laughead, pp. 7–13. Third edition, 1924. Minneapolis, Minn.: The Red River Lumber Company.

from using different standards. Seven of Paul's axehandles were equal to a little more than forty-two of the ordinary kind.

When cost sheets were figured on Babe, Johnny Inkslinger found that upkeep and overhead were expensive but the charges for operation and depreciation were low and the efficiency was very high. How else could Paul have hauled logs to the landing a whole section (640 acres) at a time? He also used Babe to pull the kinks out of the crooked logging roads and it was on a job of this kind that Babe pulled a chain of three-inch links out into a straight bar.

They could never keep Babe more than one night at a camp for he would eat in one day all the feed one crew could tote to camp in a year. For a snack between meals he would eat fifty bales of hay, wire and all and six men with picaroons were kept busy picking the wire out of his teeth. Babe was a great pet and very docile as a general thing but he seemed to have a sense of humor and frequently got into mischief. He would sneak up behind a drive and drink all the water out of the river, leaving the logs high and dry. It was impossible to build an ox-sling big enough to hoist Babe off the ground for shoeing, but after they logged off Dakota there was room for Babe to lie down for this operation.

Once in a while Babe would run away and be gone all day roaming all over the Northwestern country. His tracks were so far apart that it was impossible to follow him and so deep that a man falling into one could only be hauled out with difficulty and a long rope. Once a settler and his wife and baby fell into one of these tracks and the son got out when he was fifty-seven years old and reported the accident. These tracks, today form the thousands of lakes in the "Land of the Sky-Blue Water."

II. Benny, the Little Blue Ox

Because he was so much younger than Babe and was brought to camp when a small calf, Benny was always called the Little Blue Ox although he was quite a chunk of an animal. Benny could not, or rather, would not haul as much as Babe nor was he as tractable but he could eat more.

Paul got Benny for nothing from a farmer near Bangor, Maine. There was not enough milk for the little fellow so he had to be weaned when three days old. The farmer only had forty acres of hay and by the time Benny was a week old he had to dispose of him for lack of food. The calf was undernourished and only weighed two tons when Paul got him. Paul drove from Bangor out to his headquarters camp near Devil's Lake, North Dakota that night and led Benny behind the sleigh. Western air agreed with the little calf and every time Paul looked back at him he was two feet taller.

When they arrived at camp Benny was given a good feed of buffalo milk and flapjacks and put into a barn by himself. Next morning the barn was gone. Later it was discovered on Benny's back as he scampered over the clearings. He had outgrown his barn in one night.

Benny was very notional and would never pull a load unless there was snow on the ground so after the spring thaws they had to white wash the logging roads to fool him.

Gluttony killed Benny. He had a mania for pancakes and one cook crew of two hundred men was kept busy making cakes for him. One night he pawed and bellowed and threshed his tail about till the wind of it blew down what pine Paul had left standing in Dakota. At breakfast time he broke loose, tore down the cook shanty and began bolting pancakes. In his greed he swallowed the red-hot stove. Indigestion set in and nothing could save him. What disposition was made of his body is a matter of dispute. One oldtimer claims that the outfit he works for bought a hind quarter of the carcass in 1857 and made corned beef of it. He thinks they have several carloads of it left.

Another authority states that the body of Benny was dragged to a safe distance from the North Dakota camp and buried. When the earth was shoveled back it made a mound that formed the Black Hills in South Dakota.

III. BRIMSTONE BILL

The custodian and chaperon of Babe, the Big Blue Ox, was Brimstone Bill. He knew all the tricks of that frisky giant before they happened.

"I know oxen," the old bullwhacker used to say, "I've worked 'em and fed 'em and doctored 'em ever since the ox was invented. And Babe, I know that pernicious old reptyle same as if I'd abeen through him with a lantern."

Bill compiled "The Skinner's Dictionary," a hand book for teamsters, and most of the terms used in directing draft animals (except mules) originated with him. His early religious training accounts for the fact that the technical language of the teamster contains so many names of places and people spoken of in the Bible.

The buckskin harness used on Babe and Benny when the weather was rainy was made by Brimstone Bill. When this harness got wet it would stretch so much that the oxen could travel clear to the landing and the load would not move from the skidway in the woods. Brimstone would fasten the harness with an anchor Big Ole made for him and when the sun came out and the harness shrunk the load would be pulled to the landing while Bill and the oxen were busy at some other job.

The winter of the Blue Snow, the Pacific Ocean froze over and Bill kept the oxen busy hauling regular white snow over from China. M. H. Keenan can testify to the truth of this as he worked for Paul on the Big Onion that winter. It must have been about this time that Bill made the first ox yokes out of cranberry wood.

IV. Bunyan's Complicated Cooking

Feeding Paul Bunyan's crews was a complicated job. At no two camps were conditions the same. The winter he logged off North Dakota he had 300 cooks making pancakes for the Seven Axemen and the little Chore-boy. At headquarters on the Big Onion he had one cook and 462 cookees feeding a crew so big that Paul himself never knew within several hundred either way, how many men he had.

At Big Onion camp there was a lot of mechanical equipment and the trouble was a man who could handle the machinery cooked just like a machinist too. One cook got lost between the flour bin and the root cellar and nearly starved to death before he was found.

Cooks came and went. Some were good and others just able to get by. Paul never kept a poor one, very long. There was one jigger who seemed to have learned to do nothing but boil. He made soup out of everything and did most of his work with a dipper. When the big tote-sled broke through the ice on Bull Frog Lake with a load of split peas, he served warmed up lake water till the crew struck. His idea of a lunch box was a jug or a rope to freeze soup onto like a candle. Some cooks used too much grease. It was said of one of these that he had to wear calked shoes to keep from sliding out of the cook-shanty and rub sand on his hands when he picked anything up.

There are two kinds of camp cooks, the Baking Powder Bums and the Sourdough Stiffs. Sourdough Sam belonged to the latter school. He made everything but coffee out of Sourdough. He had only one arm and one leg, the other members having been lost when his sourdough barrel blew up. Sam officiated at Tadpole River headquarters, the winter Shot Gunderson took charge.

After all others had failed at Big Onion camp, Paul hired his cousin Big Joe who came from three weeks below Quebec. This boy sure put a mean scald on the chuck. He was the only man who could make pancakes fast enough to feed the crew. He had Big Ole, the blacksmith, make him a griddle that was so big you couldn't see across it when the steam was thick. The batter, stirred in drums like concrete mixers, was poured on with cranes and spouts. The griddle was greased by colored boys who skated over the surface with hams tied to their feet. They had to have colored boys to stand the heat.

At this camp the flunkeys wore roller skates and an idea of the size of the tables is gained from the fact that they distributed the pepper with four-horse teams.

Sending out lunch and timing the meals was rendered difficult by the size of the works which required three crews—one going to work, one on the job and one coming back. Joe had to start the bull-cook out with the lunch sled two weeks ahead of dinner time. To call the men who came in at noon was another problem. Big Ole made a dinner horn so big that no one could blow it but Big Joe or Paul himself. The first time Joe blew it he blew down ten acres of pine. The Red River people wouldn't stand for that so the next time he blew straight up but this caused severe cyclones and storms at sea so Paul had to junk the horn and ship it East where later it was made into a tin roof for a big Union Depot.

When Big Joe came to Westwood with Paul, he started something. About that time you may have read in the papers about a volcanic eruption at Mt. Lassen, heretofore extinct for many years. That was where Big Joe dug his bean-hole and when the steam worked out of the bean kettle and up through the ground, everyone thought the old hill had turned volcano. Every time Joe drops a biscuit they talk of earthquakes.

It was always thought that the quality of the food at Paul's Camps had a lot to do with the strength and endurance of the men. No doubt it did, but they were a husky lot to start with. As the feller said about fish for a brain food, "It won't do you no good unless there is a germ there to start with."

There must have been something to the food theory for the chipmunks that ate the prune pits got so big they killed all the wolves and years later the settlers shot them for tigers.

A visitor at one of Paul's camps was astonished to see a crew of men unloading four-horse logging sleds at the cook shanty. They appeared to be rolling logs into a trap door from which poured clouds of steam.

"That's a heck of a place to land logs," he remarked.

"Them ain't logs," grinned a bull-cook, "them's sausages for the teamsters' breakfast."

At Paul's camp up where the little Gimlet empties into the Big Auger, newcomers used to kick because they were never served beans. The bosses and the men could never be interested in beans. E. E. Terrill tells us the reason:

Once when the cook quit they had to detail a substitute to the job temporarily. There was one man who was no good anywhere. He had failed at every job. Chris Crosshaul, the foreman, acting on the theory that every man is good *somewhere*, figured that this guy must be a cook, for it was the only job he had not tried. So he was put to work and the first thing he tackled was beans. He filled up a big kettle with beans and added some water. When the heat took hold the beans swelled up till they lifted off the roof and bulged out the walls. There was no way to get into the place to cook anything else, so the whole crew turned in to eat up the half cooked beans. By keeping at it steady they cleaned them up in a week and rescued the would-be-cook. After that no one seemed to care much for beans.

It used to be a big job to haul prune pits and coffee grounds away from Paul's camps. It required a big crew of men and either Babe or Benny to do the hauling. Finally Paul decided it was cheaper to build new camps and move every month.

The winter Paul logged off North Dakota with the Seven Axemen, the Little Chore Boy and the 300 cooks, he worked the cooks in three shifts—one for each meal. The Seven Axemen were hearty eaters; a portion of bacon was one side of a 1600-pound pig. Paul shipped a stern-wheel steamboat up Red River and they put it in the soup kettle to stir the soup.

Like other artists, cooks are temperamental and some of them are full of cussedness but the only ones who could sass Paul Bunyan and get away with it were the stars like Big Joe and Sourdough Sam.

The lunch sled,—most popular institution in the lumber industry! Its arrival at the noon rendezvous has been hailed with joy by hungry men on every logging job since Paul invented it. What if the warm food freezes on your tin plate, the keen cold air has sharpened your appetite to enjoy it. The crew that toted lunch for Paul Bunyan had so far to travel and so many to feed they hauled a complete kitchen on the lunch sled, cooks and all.

Hank's Bar Specials

As a bartender, Hank was much more of an artist. The usual Tom Collins, dry Martinis and such stuff were child's play. Likewise the Mickey Finn. His specialty was sizing up a customer and prescribing the proper drink. His specials were good for any ailment. When a customer came in with the blues, the gout or the pip, Hank would study him a minute and then turn to the back bar. Nobody knew just what he did and he never told what went into his concoctions because all the other bartenders were jealous. His specials were things that nobody but Hank could make.

He'd run his eye over the bottles on the back bar, take a little of this and a little of that, hold it up to the light, sniff it, taste it, and then add a little something else. And whatever it was it was always right. Hank got to curing so many human ills that he got the doctors down on him and they threatened to have him pinched for practicing medicine without a license. So Hank, being a good union man, gave up curing people's ills and turned to other fields.

Hank got to be pretty popular with his fancy drinks. He worked all over the country for somebody was always jealous of his popularity and luring him away to a better job. He knew some of the best people.

There was a little wop used to come to a place where Hank worked in New York. The wop was always broke and downhearted. One night he said to Hank: "Jeez, if I could only sing. Maka lotsa dough in da opera." So Hank thought it over and turned to the back bar. He mixed something slowly and carefully and pushed it over the bar like

By J. D. Stradling. From "Chicago Folkstuff." Manuscripts of the Federal Writers' Project of the Works Progress Administration for the State of Illinois.

it was holy communion. "Here, try this," he said. Maybe you remember Caruso. He was one of Hank's best friends.

Hank was out West one time. Somebody had been selling booze and guns to the Sioux. There was a young lad by the name of William Hickok in the saloon when the Indians hit town loaded with booze. After a couple of Hank's specials, young Bill was seeing double, so he shot two redskins with each bullet and had a couple left over. That was how Wild Bill got his start.

Sometimes Hank's specials were not so lucky. Joe, a baldheaded man, had been having trouble with his wife. He was feeling pretty low. "Here, try this. It'll grow hair on your chest," said Hank. It gave Joe a sudden idea. "By golly," he said, "I've tried everything else on my head, I might as well try this, too." So he took a bottle home. His wife saw him fixing to put booze on his head and knew he had been drinking again, so she beat him up and threw the bottle out the window into a crick that ran behind the house. Come Saturday, Joe went down to the crick to take a bath. Hair sprouted all over him so fast that he was shot by mistake for a grizzly before he could reach his clothes.

One night Hank was mixing up something for experiment. A few drops fell on the floor. There was a mouse running around under the bar. Suddenly the mouse rared up on its hind legs, roared like a lion, and chased Hank and the bouncers right out of the place.

Not long after, a pale little man with a worried look asked Hank for a pick-me-up. Hank looked at the customer and remembered the mouse. He ran his eye over the array of bottles trying to remember what he had used. He took a little of this and a little of that with the air of an artist and the care of a drug clerk. "Try this," he said.

But Hank never made that again. The little man coughed, whooped, turned a back somersault off the stool and got up fighting mad. "Where's that cop?" he yelled and went out looking for the man on the beat. Soon the riot squad was out and when he finished up with them, the customer looked around, brushed his hands, and said: "Now where can I find them damn Marines?"

Hank saw he might be accessory to murder so he went to work in the opposite direction. A husky longshoreman came in looking for trouble. He was too big and tough for three bartenders so the boss said to slip him a Mickey. But Hank slipped him his new special. The tough egg was mighty surprised to find wings sprouting out on his shoulders. He broke out in a hymn and went out looking for a soap box to start preaching. Hank thought it was a good idea and mixed his special for a lot more. But it got the preachers down on him. There were revival meetings on every corner. The preachers threatened to close the saloon if Hank did any more so the boss told Hank to lay off.

Lots of times Hank's specials were too good. There was the young lady who tipped off Hank in advance that her sweetheart didn't love her any more. Hank studied hard on the problem and when she brought her fiance in, Hank was all ready for him. But it didn't work out right. She was nearly raped right there in the saloon and the last they saw of her, she was heading down the street as fast as she could go, screaming bloody murder, with the boy friend two jumps behind with fire in his eye.

Mose, the old darky who was swamper in the saloon, was known as a good man among the colored folks. He always had wenches dropping around to walk home with him after hours. Old Mose was ailing and Hank thought he looked worn and peaked. Hank asked Mose if he would like to have one of those specials. But old Mose just shook his head sadly and said: "No suh, boss. If ah got mah druthers, ah'd ruther not."

A couple of firemen got to arguing one night over which was best at the job. One fired for the Rock Island and the other for the Q. There were some other trainmen in the saloon and they took up the argument. It began to spread so far that finally the two roads agreed on a race. They decided on Chicago to Kansas City with tracks cleared all the way.

Just before the race, young Newt, who fired for the Q. dropped in for one of Hank's specials. He was feeling pretty low because betting was seven to five and he was on the five end. Hank thought for a few minutes and then mixed up something that cheered Newt so much he decided to take along a bottle.

The race got under way and Newt was soon feeling so good he had even the drivers red hot. When he finished the last of the bottle, he carelessly threw it into the firebox. The engine let out one shriek of the whistle and all Newt could do was grab hold of a stanchion and hang on.

The Rock Island was due in K. C. at 8:30 and rolled in at 7:45. There was no sign of the Q. Pretty soon they got a wire from Newt asking what time the R. I. got in. The dispatcher wired back: "R. I. in forty five minutes ahead of schedule. Where are you broke down?" But Newt wired back: "Broke down, Hell. We just got her stopped in Colorado."

Hank was very sad when Prohibition came along for he couldn't do very much with white mule and bathtub gin. Folks had lost all appreciation of real art. They were drinking their dynamite raw and thinking it quite an accomplishment. Those were the days when a customer would down a green jolt, turn a couple of somersaults, get up, push his eyes back in his head, and say: "Gosh, that was good!"

But Hank never gave up and kept on experimenting. One day he was mixing up something from bootleg hootch. He got up the courage to try it himself. Everything was all right for a minute and then something went Wham. Hank was never seen again. Seems the ingredients

of that one were all right while they were iced but when they got
warmed up inside Hank they exploded.

A lot of saloons and speakeasies claimed that Hank had worked
for them. Once he was gone, they all tried to cash in on his popularity.
But the meanest of all was a speakeasy in St. Louis that had a large
brown spot on the ceiling. Whenever anyone would say: "I wonder
what became of Hank?" they'd point to the ceiling and say: "See that
big grease spot up there with arms and legs like a man? Well, that's
Hank."

Slappy Hooper, Sign Painter

Slappy Hooper wasn't big because he was six foot nine and wide
between the eyes, no more than he weighed three hundred pounds
without his cap on or his bucket in one hand and his brush in the
other. It was just that there wasn't no job any too big for Slappy, and
he never wanted a helper to mess around with.

Even when he was painting a high stack, he didn't want any rube
staggering and stumbling around the lines to his bosun's chair. He
knew too well that lots of times a helper can be more trouble than he's
worth. He'll yawn and gape around or send up the wrong color or the
wrong brush, or he'll throw rocks at birds, or he'll make goo-goo eyes
at dames passing by. Like as not, he'll foul the lines or pull the wrong
one and send you butt over appetite to kingdom come.

At any rate, a helper keeps a man uneasy, and when a man's uneasy
he ain't doing his best work. They ought to make it a penitentiary
act for a helper "gapering, mopering, and attempting to gawk." Slappy
said his life was too short to take a helper to raise up. He could let himself up and down as fast as a monkey could skin up a cocoanut tree or
a cat lick its hind leg with its leg up and its tongue out. Anything
Slappy wanted on the ground he could lasso with his special long and
tough rawhide lariat and pull it up to where he was working.

Slappy done some big jobs in his day, and he done them right and
fast. He says if there ever was a crime against nature it's this way they
got here of late of blowing paint on with a spray gun like you was
slaying cockroaches or bedbugs or pacifying a cow to keep the flies off
her until she can get milked. Slappy liked to splash it on with a good
old eight-inch brush, and he never was known to leave a brush lap
or a hair on the surface when the job was finished. Slapping it on up
and down or slapping it on crossways or anti-goggling [1] you couldn't
tell the difference. It was all of a solid sheet.

With all these new inventions like smoke-writing from airplanes

---

By Jack Conroy. From "Chicago Industrial Folklore." Manuscripts of the Federal
Writers' Project of the Works Progress Administration for the State of Illinois.

[1] Slantwise, or crooked.—J. C.

and painting signs from a pounce [1] (even pictures they do that way), it's hard to appreciate an old-timer like Slappy.

He used to get jobs of lettering advertising on the sky, and it didn't fade away in a minute like smoke that pours out of a plane and gets torn to pieces by the wind before you can hardly spell out what it says. It was all pretty and fancy colors, too; any shade a man's heart could wish for, and it'd stay right there for days if the weather was fair. Of course, birds would fly through it, and when it'd rain the colors would all run together and when the clouds rolled by, there'd be what folks got to calling a rainbow. It really was nothing but Slappy Hooper's sky-writing all jumbled together. It seems that no man, woman, child or beast, alive or dead, was ever able to invent waterproof sky paint. If it could have been done, Slappy would have done it.

His biggest job was for the Union Pacific Railroad, and stretched from one end of the line to the other. The only way you could read it all was to get on a through train and look out of the window and up at the sky all the time. Everybody got stiff necks, of course, so Slappy had the bright idea of getting Sloan's Liniment to pay him for a big sign right at the end of the Union Pacific sign.

Nobody ever did understand how Slappy managed to do the sky-painting. He'd have been a chump to tell anybody. He always used to say when people asked him: "That's for me to know and you to find out," or, "If I told you that, you'd know as much as I do."

The only thing people was sure of was that he used skyhooks to hold up the scaffold. He used a long scaffold instead of the bosun's chair he used when he was painting smokestacks or church steeples. When he started in to fasten his skyhooks, he'd rent a thousand acre field and rope it off with barbed wire charged with electricity. He never let a living soul inside, but you could hear booming sounds like war times and some folks figured he was firing his skyhooks out of a cannon and that they fastened on a cloud or some place too high for mortal eyes to see or mortal minds to know about. Anyways, after a while—if you took a spy glass—you could see Slappy's long scaffold raising up, up, up in the air and Slappy about as big as a spider squatting on it.

But that played out, somehow. It wasn't that people didn't like his skypainting any more, but the airplanes got to buzzing around as thick as flies around a molasses barrel and they was always fouling or cutting Slappy's lines, and he was always afraid one would run smack into him and dump over his scaffold and spill his paint if nothing worse. Besides, he said, if advertisers was dumb enough to let a farting air-

---

[1] Perforated outline or stencil for painters unable to do freehand work efficiently. Derived from the bag of chalk, or pounce, used to pat the stencil onto the billboard or sign. Sometimes the outline is transferred by blowing powdered chalk against the . . . I. C.

hood days in west Texas I first heard of Bill, and in later years I have often listened to chapters of his history told around the chuck-wagon by gravely mendacious cow-boys.

The stranger in cattle-land usually hears of Bill if he shows an incautious curiosity about the cow business. Some old-timer is sure to remark mournfully:

"Ranchin' ain't what it was in the days Bill staked out New Mexico."

If the visitor walks into the trap and inquires further about Bill, he is sure to receive an assortment of misinformation that every cow-hand delights in unloading on the unwary.

Although Bill has been quoted in a number of Western stories, the real history of his wondrous deeds has never been printed. I have here collected a few of the tales about him which will doubtless be familiar to cow-men, but deserve to be passed on to a larger audience.

Bill invented most of the things connected with the cow business. He was a mighty man of valor, the king killer of the bad men, and it was Bill who taught the broncho how to buck. It is a matter of record that he dug the Rio Grande one dry year when he grew tired of packin' water from the Gulf of Mexico.

According to the most veracious historians, Bill was born about the time Sam Houston discovered Texas. His mother was a sturdy pioneer woman who once killed forty-five Indians with a broom-handle, and weaned him on moonshine liquor when he was three days old. He cut his teeth on a bowie-knife, and his earliest playfellows were the bears and catamounts of east Texas.

When Bill was about a year old, another family moved into the country, and located about fifty miles down the river. His father decided the place was gettin' too crowded, and packed his family in a wagon and headed west.

One day after they crossed the Pecos River, Bill fell out of the wagon. As there were sixteen or seventeen other children in the family, his parents didn't miss him for four or five weeks, and then it was too late to try to find him.

That's how Bill came to grow up with the coyotes along the Pecos. He soon learned the coyote language, and used to hunt with them and sit on the hills and howl at night. Being so young when he got lost, he always thought he was a coyote. That's where he learned to kill deer by runnin' them to death.

One day when he was about ten years old a cow-boy came along just when Bill had matched a fight with two grizzly bears. Bill hugged the bears to death, tore off a hind leg, and was just settin' down to breakfast when this cow-boy loped up and asked him what he meant by runnin' around naked that way among the varmints.

"Why, because I am a varmint," Bill told him. "I'm a coyote."

The cow-boy argued with him that he was a human, but Bill wouldn't believe him.

"Ain't I got fleas?" he insisted. "And don't I howl around all night, like a respectable coyote should do?"

"That don't prove nothin'," the cow-boy answered. "All Texans have fleas, and most of them howl. Did you ever see a coyote that didn't have a tail? Well, you ain't got no tail; so that proves you ain't a varmint."

Bill looked, and, sure enough, he didn't have a tail.

"You sure got me out on a limb," says Bill. "I never noticed that before. It shows what higher education will do for a man. I believe you're right. Lead me to them humans, and I'll throw in with them."

Bill went to town with this cow-hand, and in due time he got to enjoyin' all the pleasant vices of mankind, and decided that he certainly was a human. He got to runnin' with the wild bunch, and sunk lower and lower, until finally he became a cow-boy.

It wasn't long until he was famous as a bad man. He invented the six-shooter and train-robbin' and most of the crimes popular in the old days of the West. He didn't invent cow-stealin'. That was discovered by King David in the Bible, but Bill improved on it.

There is no way of tellin' just how many men Bill did kill. Deep down he had a tender heart, however, and never killed women or children, or tourists out of season. He never scalped his victims; he was too civilized for that. He used to skin them gently and tan their hides.

It wasn't long before Bill had killed all the bad men in west Texas, massacred all the Indians, and eat all the buffalo. So he decided to migrate to a new country where hard men still thrived and a man could pass the time away.

He saddled up his horse and hit for the West. One day he met an old trapper and told him what he was lookin' for.

"I want the hardest cow outfit in the world," he says. "Not one of these ordinary cow-stealin', Mexican-shootin' bunches of amateurs, but a real hard herd of hand-picked hellions that make murder a fine art and take some proper pride in their slaughter."

"Stranger, you're headed in the right direction," answers the trapper. "Keep right on down this draw for a couple of hundred miles, and you'll find that very outfit. They're so hard they can kick fire out of a flint rock with their bare toes."

Bill single-footed down that draw for about a hundred miles that afternoon; then he met with an accident. His horse stubbed his toe on a mountain and broke his leg, leavin' Bill afoot.

He slung his saddle over his shoulder and set off hikin' down that draw, cussin' and a-swearin'. Profanity was a gift with Bill.

All at once a big ten-foot rattlesnake quiled up in his path, set his tail to singin', and allowed he'd like to match a fight. Bill laid down his saddle, and just to be fair about it, he gave the snake the first three bites. Then he waded into that reptile and everlastingly frailed the pizen out of him.

By and by that old rattler yelled for mercy, and admitted that when it came to fightin', Bill started where he let off. So Bill picked up his saddle and started on, carryin' the snake in his hand and spinnin' it in short loops at the Gila monsters.

About fifty miles further on, a big old mountain-lion jumped off a cliff and lit all spraddled out on Bill's neck. This was no ordinary lion. It weighed more than three steers and a yearlin', and was the very same lion the State of Nuevo León was named after down in old Mexico.

Kind of chucklin' to himself, Bill laid down his saddle and his snake and went into action. In a minute the fur was flyin' down the cañon until it darkened the sun. The way Bill knocked the animosity out of that lion was a shame. In about three minutes that lion hollered:

"I'll give up, Bill. Can't you take a joke?"

Bill let him up, and then he cinched the saddle on him and went down that cañon whoopin' and yellin', ridin' that lion a hundred feet at a jump, and quirtin' him down the flank with the rattlesnake.

It wasn't long before he saw a chuck-wagon with a bunch of cow-boys squattin' around it. He rode up to that wagon, splittin' the air with his war-whoops, with that old lion a-screechin', and that snake singin' his rattles.

When he came to the fire he grabbed the old cougar by the ear, jerked him back on his haunches, stepped off him, hung his snake around his neck, and looked the outfit over. Them cow-boys sat there sayin' less than nothin'.

Bill was hungry, and seein' a boilerful of beans cookin' on the fire, he scooped up a few handfuls and swallowed them, washin' them down with a few gallons of boilin' coffee out of the pot. Wipin' his mouth on a handful of prickly-ear cactus, Bill turned to the cow-boys and asked:

"Who the hell is boss around here?"

A big fellow about eight feet tall, with seven pistols and nine bowie-knives in his belt, rose up and, takin' off his hat, said:

"Stranger, I was; but you be."

Bill had many adventures with this outfit. It was about this time he staked out New Mexico, and used Arizona for a calf-pasture. It was here that he found his noted horse Widow-Maker. He raised him from a colt on nitroglycerin and dynamite, and Bill was the only man that could throw a leg over him.

There wasn't anythin' that Bill couldn't ride, although I have heard of one occasion when he was thrown. He made a bet that he could ride an Oklahoma cyclone slick-heeled, without a saddle.

He met the cyclone, the worst that was ever known, up on the

Kansas line. Bill eared that tornado down and climbed on its back. That cyclone did some pitchin' that is unbelievable, if it were not vouched for by many reliable witnesses.

Down across Texas it went sunfishin', back-flippin', side-windin', knockin' down mountains, blowin' the holes out of the ground, and tyin' rivers into knots. The Staked Plains used to be heavily timbered until that big wind swiped the trees off and left it a bare prairie.

Bill just sat up there, thumbin' that cyclone in the withers, floppin' it across the ears with his hat, and rollin' a cigarette with one hand. He rode it through three States, but over in Arizona it got him.

When it saw it couldn't throw him, it rained out from under him. This is proved by the fact that it washed out the Grand Cañon. Bill came down over in California. The spot where he lit is now known as Death Valley, a hole in the ground more than one hundred feet below sea-level, and the print of his hip-pockets can still be seen in the granite.

I have heard this story disputed in some of its details. Some historians claim that Bill wasn't thrown; that he slid down on a streak of lightnin' without knockin' the ashes off his cigarette. It is also claimed that the Grand Cañon was dug by Bill one week when he went prospectin'; but the best authorities insist on the first version. They argue that that streak of lightin' story comes from the habit he always had of usin' one to light his cigarette.

Bill was a great roper. In fact, he invented ropin'. Old-timers who admit they knew him say that his rope was as long as the equator, although the more conservative say that it was at least two feet shorter on one end. He used to rope a herd of cattle at one throw.

This skill once saved the life of a friend. The friend had tried to ride Widow-Maker one day, and was thrown so high he came down on top of Pike's Peak. He was in the middle of a bad fix, because he couldn't get down, and seemed doomed to a lingerin' death on high.

Bill came to the rescue, and usin' only a short calf-loop, he roped his friend around the neck and jerked him down to safety in the valley, twenty thousand feet below. This man was always grateful, and became Bill's horse-wrangler at the time he staked out New Mexico.

In his idle moments in New Mexico Bill amused himself puttin' thorns on the trees and horns on the toads. It was on this ranch he dug the Rio Grande and invented the centipede and the tarantula as a joke on his friends.

When the cow business was dull, Pecos Bill occasionally embarked in other ventures; for instance, at one time he took a contract to supply the S. P. Railroad with wood. He hired a few hundred Mexicans to chop and haul the wood to the railroad line. As pay for the job, Bill gave each Mexican one fourth of the wood he hauled.

These Mexicans are funny people. After they received their share of the wood they didn't know what to do with it; so Bill took it off their hands and never charged them a cent.

On another occasion Bill took the job of buildin' the line fence that forms the boundary from El Paso across to the Pacific. He rounded up a herd of prairie-dogs and set them to dig holes, which by nature a prairie-dog likes to do.

Whenever one of them finished a nice hole and settled down to live in it, Bill evicted him and stuck a fence-post in the hole. Everybody admired his foresight except the prairie-dogs, and who cares what a prairie-dog thinks?

Old Bill was always a very truthful man. To prove this, the cowboys repeat one of his stories, which Bill claimed happened to him. Nobody ever disputed him; that is, no one who is alive now.

He threw in with a bunch of Kiowa Indians one time on a little huntin'-trip. It was about the time the buffalo were getting scarce, and Bill was huntin' with his famous squatter-hound named Norther.

Norther would run down a buffalo and hold him by the ear until Bill came up and skinned him alive. Then he would turn it loose to grow a new hide. The scheme worked all right in the summer, but in the winter most of them caught colds and died.

The stories of Bill's love-affairs are especially numerous. One of them may be told. It is the sad tale of the fate of his bride, a winsome little maiden called Slue-Foot Sue. She was a famous rider herself, and Bill lost his heart when he saw her riding a catfish down the Rio Grande with only a surcingle. You must remember that the catfish in the Rio Grande are bigger than whales and twice as active.

Sue made a sad mistake, however, when she insisted on ridin' Widow-Maker on her weddin'-day. The old horse threw her so high she had to duck her head to let the moon go by. Unfortunately, she was wearin' her weddin'-gown, and in those days the women wore those big steel-spring bustles.

Well, when Sue lit, she naturally bounced, and every time she came down she bounced again. It was an awful sad sight to see Bill implorin' her to quit her bouncin' and not be so nervous; but Sue kept right on, up and down, weepin', and throwin' kisses to her distracted lover, and carryin' on as a bride naturally would do under those circumstances.

She bounced for three days and four nights, and Bill finally had to shoot her to keep her from starvin' to death. It was mighty tragic. Bill never got over it. Of course he married lots of women after that. In fact, it was one of his weaknesses; but none of them filled the place in his heart once held by Slue-Foot Sue, his bouncin' bride.

There is a great difference of opinion as to the manner of Bill's demise. Many claim that it was his drinkin' habits that killed him. You see, Bill got so that liquor didn't have any kick for him, and he fell into the habit of drinkin' strychnine and other forms of wolf pizen.

Even the wolf bait lost its effect, and he got to puttin' fish-hooks and barbed wire in his toddy. It was the barbed wire that finally killed him. It rusted his interior and gave him indigestion. He wasted away to a mere skeleton, weighin' not more than two tons; then up and died, and went to his infernal reward.

Many of the border bards who knew Pecos Bill at his best have a different account of his death.

They say that he met a man from Boston one day, wearing a mail-order cow-boy outfit, and askin' fool questions about the West; and poor old Bill laid down and laughed himself to death.

Hardscrabblers

The men that work in the rock quarries of Hardscrabble County are so tough they crack great big rocks just by spitting on them. The farther you go west in the county the tougher the men get, and the rock quarries are right on the western boundary line. When they set off a blast, those bullies are right out there with ten-year-old white oaks in their hands batting those big boulders around, or else they're playing catch without any gloves.

When they get constipated in the rock quarry camp they never use anything but blasting powder, and they whip their children with barb wire until the kids get to be ten years old and then they thresh their parents.

Strangers almost never travel into the rock quarry country, because no man, woman, beast or child that dared to try it ever returned to tell about it no more than any soul ever fetched back a report from hell.

When the quarrymen leave their camp, everybody but invalids, little children, and cripples take to the hills till danger's past. It's lucky that they usually come in a drove, and you can see their dust for miles away and hear their fearsome blackguarding and whooping for a good hour and a half before they strike the city limits.

Gentlemen, it's no lie nor fairy tale when I tell you that those Hardscrabble County quarrymen are enough to plague a saint. They use them in the farm villages to scare little children and make them behave, but the grownups are even scareder than the young ones.

One day a lone wolf got right into town before anybody knew he was on the way. He came riding two snapping, snarling panthers, straddling them with a foot on each, and he was lashing them into a lather with a whip made of three six-foot rattlesnakes knotted together.

This fellow was a sight to behold, and everybody knew in a minute

By Jack Conroy. From "Chicago Industrial Folklore." Manuscripts of the Federal Writers' Project of the Works Progress Administration for the State of Illinois.

that he was a quarryman. He stood a good eight feet without tiptoe-
ing, and not enough fat on him to grease a one-egg skillet. That man
was muscled like a draft mule, and he moved around like a bolt of
lightning on its holiday.

First thing off he went to the shoe store and bought him a pair of
brogans. Then he got a nickel's worth of stout roofing nails from the
hardware store and asked for the loan of a hammer. He drove these
roofing nails right through the soles and heels of the shoes and put
the shoes back on his feet. He wore a size fifteen, broad last.

"That's the way I like it," he said. "It gives you a good grip and all
you got to do when your foot itches is to wiggle it around a little.

"I want to get prettied up a little," the quarryman said, and went
into the barber shop. The barber took the edge off his shears when
he tried to cut his hair.

"Ain't you got no tinsmiths in this town?" asked the quarryman.
"Get a pair of tinsnips, extra large. And fetch a blowtorch from the
plumber's. I ain't had a decent shave for a month of Sundays."

He dropped in the Blue Moon Saloon then and asked for a good
stiff drink, talking as polite as chips. The bartender planked down a
bottle of his strongest brand of fortyrod. Some of it sloshed over and
ate a spot of varnish off the bar the size of a five-dollar bill. The
quarryman lost his temper then, and snorted and fumed fit to kill.

"None of that bellywash for me! I'd as soon have a pinky, sticky ice
cream sody with a cherry on it."

"What sort of a charge do you crave, stranger?" asked the bartender, his false choppers almost shaking out of his mouth.

"Gimme a prussic acid cocktail with a little sulphuric for a chaser,"
ordered the quarryman, "and see that you don't go diluting it with no
carbolic, neither. What are you, anyway? One of them temperance
cranks? You must think I'm a plumb teetotaler!"

The bartender dashed out the back way and hotfooted it to the
drug store and got the stuff for the drinks. The quarryman got in a
little better humor then, and began passing the time away by spitting
on the floor and burning holes right through to the ground underneath.

"Not bad!" he said. "A little weak. Only trouble with this tipple is
that it's hell on underwear. Every time you break wind it burns a
hole in them."

"I guess you aim to get back to the quarries before nightfall, don't
you, stranger?" said the bartender, hoping to God it was so.

"No, no!" answered the quarryman, shaking his head kind of sad.
"I don't reckon I'll ever go back."

He grabbed a can of tomatoes off the shelf behind the bar and
gulped it down without chewing it open.

"Don't it lay heavy on your stomach, stranger?" asked the bartender,
terribly put out that the quarryman wasn't leaving that night.

"Not long," answered the quarryman. "I soon digest the can from around the tomatoes. It's easy. A doorknob is harder, but I can do it easy as pie when I set my head to it."

"You aim to make your home in our little Magic City?" asked the bartender, still hoping he had heard wrong.

"Hell's fire and damnation no, man!" said the quarryman, so riled he bit a foot long chunk out of the mahogany bar and spat it right in the bartender's face. "I wouldn't live here for love nor money. I wouldn't be caught dead here."

"Well, then," said the bartender, getting a little bolder, "why did you leave the quarries?"

"Aw, I didn't *want* to," answered the quarryman. "I had to."

"You had to? Why? Get in a fight or some kind of trouble there?"

"A fight? Are you plumb stark, staring looney, man? Whoever heard of a man getting into trouble over fighting in the Hardscrabble County rock quarries?"

"Why did you have to leave then?"

"Well," said the quarryman, looking like a sheepkilling dog. "They chased me out because they said I was a sissy."

Rival Divers

You ask me why I'm all bunged up this way, going on crutches, both arms busted and what may still be a fractured skull. The doctor ain't sure about that yet. I'll live, I guess, but I don't know what for. I can't never be a high diver any more. I'll go to selling razor blades, like as not, and there's plenty doing that already.

Eddie La Breen is to blame for it all. High diving was an easy and high-paying profession before he tried to root me and every other performer out of it. I would go traveling in the summer with a carnival company, and my high dive would be a free feature attraction. The local merchants would kick in for signs to put on my ladder and advertise their goods. Sometimes I'd make a little spiel from the top of the ladder just before I dived off into the tank.

Eddie La Breen called himself "The Human Seal." He bragged that he could dive higher into shallower water than any man alive. I was pretty good myself, being billed as Billie the Dolphin, spectacular and death-defying high diver extraordinary.

I'm doing all right with Miller's Great Exposition Shows, using a twenty-five foot ladder and diving into a ten-foot tank. Big crowds of people would come from miles around to see me, and not a soul ever seemed dissatisfied until we happen to be playing Omaha on a lot over ten blocks away from where Eddie La Breen is playing with Barker's World's Fair Shows.

By Jack Conroy. From "Chicago Industrial Folklore." Manuscripts of the Federal Writers' Project of the Works Progress Administration for the State of Illinois.

Just when I come up out of the tank and start to take a bow one night I hear somebody say: "That ain't *nothing*. You ought to see Eddie La Breen over on Farnum Street diving twice as high into water half as deep."

I found out it's so. Eddie has been diving into five feet of water from a fifty-foot ladder, and Mr. Miller threatens to let me go if I can't do as well.

It sure looked high when I got up there and I could feel my nose scraping on the bottom of the tank just as I made the upturn. But I'm no slouch at the high dive myself, and Eddie La Breen ain't going to outdo me if I can help it.

I added the fire act to my dive, too, and most of the time I could hardly see where to dive. For the fire act you have a little bit of gasoline pouring into the tank. It stays right on top of the water and when you fire it it makes a fearful sight, splashing fire in every direction when you hit the water.

Eddie sends me word that I might as well give up. "I'm going to dive next from a thousand feet into a tank of solid concrete," he says, "and I'll do it while playing the ukulele, eating raw liver, and keeping perfect time. Why, when I was a kid of ten or so I could dive off a silo onto the dew in the grass, bellybuster, and never even grunt when I lit."

He didn't do quite that, but he did enough. He raised his ladder to a hundred feet, and kept only two and a half feet of water in the tank.

I practised and practised and got a few bruises, but I cut that depth to two feet and I raised my ladder to a hundred and fifty feet.

By this time Eddie sent word he was good mad, and he's going to call himself the Minnow. "You know how a minnow just skitters along on top of a pond," he says. "Well, that's the way I'll light on that tank. From two hundred feet I'll dive into six inches of water and just skim off without hardly making a bubble."

If ever a man practised hard to make a shallow dive, that was me. I did that minnow dive in four inches of water from a height of 250 feet, lit right on my feet after barely touching the water, and didn't even muss my hair.

When Eddie makes it from 300 feet into three inches, I'm a little put out but I don't give up. I tell Miller to get me a good heavy bath mat and soak it good all day. First time I hit that bath mat it sort of knocked me dizzy. You know how it is when you have the breath knocked out of you and all you do is croak like a frog. But I got better and better at it until I hardly puffed at all.

I beat Eddie La Breen fair and square, but he wasn't man enough to admit it or take it like a man. He showed that he was rotten to the core and treacherous from the word go.

We were playing Sheboygan, Wisconsin, and I had no idea that

Eddie was anywhere within miles. I had heard that Barker had told him to pack his keister and get out when I bested him.

When I hit that bath mat that night I thought my time had come. That was six months ago, and look at me now. Still on crutches, and lucky if I ever get off of them.

Well, sir, I don't know anybody but Eddie who wanted to have done me that dirt. They had soaked my heavy bath mat in water, all day, the same as usual, but they must have let it get out of their sight some time or other, because some one had wrung it out practically dry.

That's the way I had it done to me. I heard somebody say later that a man answering to the description of Eddie La Breen had been seen lurking around the show grounds that evening.

And if he didn't do it, who did?

Not So Hot Rod

The Governor of Michigan was invited as honor guest to the factory of a certain automobile company. And in the presence of the Governor, the company assembled a completed car in exactly two minutes. The newspapers gave the story plenty of space—how the car, in honor of the Governor, was assembled in two minutes. A month later, a fellow called up the auto factory and said, "Is it true what I read in the papers—that, in honor of the Governor, your factory assembled an automobile in two minutes?" "Absolutely true," came the reply. "Damn your hides," shot back the irate citizen, "I'VE GOT THAT CAR."

A Real Fireplace

I told the contractor that I wanted the house built . . . around a fireplace of limestone and firebrick. He was very eager to begin; this was in 1932, and my contractor was worried. He said that it was "a hell of a thing that a depression would come along durin' sich hard times," and he thought that if he had not received the contract to build my little house, he might resort to eating "Hoover hogs," which was the name given to rabbits by the valley farmers.

"This fireplace business is serious," I said . . . "I want a real fireplace; one that will draw; one that will work. I want the house sorta built around the fireplace—see what I mean?"

"Sure," he said, "I know; I been buildin' the goddam things for years, and they ain't ary one of 'em I ain't proud of—I'd be 'shamed

From *Now I'll Tell One,* by Harry Hershfield, p. 19. Copyright, 1938, by Greenberg: Publisher, Inc. New York.

From *Talking to the Moon,* by John Joseph Mathews, pp. 6–7. Copyright, 1945, by The University of Chicago Press. Chicago.

to show to a man." He picked up a twig from the tree and began
cutting it into little sections, using his flat, calloused thumb as a stop
for the blade of his knife.

"Well," I said, slightly annoyed with his assurance. "I just wanted
you to know what I expect in the way of a fireplace; I am sure you
can build one or I shouldn't have asked you . . ."

I continued: "You see, men have been building fireplaces for centuries, and still they have not perfected the art . . . A man can build
a house and say it's good, but it seems to me when he builds a fireplace, he is gambling—not even he knows whether it will work—no
draft, throat out of dimension with the depth, or something."

He looked at me steadily. He feigned slight annoyance, to indicate
the uselessness of attempting to impress on me, who apparently knew
little about anything, that he could build a fireplace or anything else
that pertained to the building trade. He changed his tobacco to the
other side of his mouth, spread his hands with the twig in one and the
knife in the other, and spat straight out between them. He looked
straight into my eyes, then said:

"You got ary cat?"

"No," I answered, "wouldn't have one on the place—why?"

He looked back at the twig and cut two more sections before he
answered, perhaps for dramatic effect.

"I was jist figgerin'; when I git that fa'r place built, she'll work,
and if you had ary cat that you thought right smart about, you'd
better keep the sonofabitch away from that fa'r place er it'ud suck
'im up."

Curing a Smoky Chimney

There lives in New Hampshire a man called Joe, a fellow noted
for the tough lies he can tell. A correspondent informs us that Joe
called in at Holton's lately, and found him almost choked with smoke,
when he suggested, "You don't know as much about managing smoky
chimneys as I do, squire, or you'd cure 'em." "Ah!" said Holton, with
interest, "did you ever see a smoky chimney cured?" "Seen it?" said old
Joe, "I think I have. I had the worst one in Seaboard county once, and
I cured it a little too much." "How was that?" asked Holton. "Why,
you see," said Joe, "I built a little house out yonder, at Wolf Hollow,
10 or 12 years ago. Jim Bush, the fellow that built the chimneys, kept
blind drunk three quarters of the time, and crazy drunk the other. I
told him I thought he'd have something wrong; but he stuck to it and
finished the house. Well, we moved in and built a fire the next morning to boil the tea-kettle. All the smoke came through the room and

From *Flashes and Sparks of Wit and Humor by Our American Humorists* . . . ,
pp. 34–35. New York: Excelsior Publishing House. 1883.

went out of the windows; not a bit went up the flues. We tried it for two or three days and it got worse and worse. By and by it came on to rain, and the rain began to come down the chimney. It put the fire out in a minute, and directly it came down by the pailful. We had to get baby off the floor as soon as we could, or it would have been drowned. In fifteen minutes the water stood knee-deep on the floor. I pretty soon saw what was the matter. The drunken cuss had put the chimney wrong end up, and it drawed downward. It gathered all the rain within a hundred yards, and poured it down by bucketfuls." "Well, that was unfortunate," remarked Holton, "but what in the world did you do with the house? Surely you never cured that chimney?" "Didn't I, though?" answered old Joe; "yes I did." "How?" asked Holton. "Turned it the other end up," said the incorrigible, "and then you ought to have seen it draw. That was the way I cured it too much." "Drew too much?" asked Holton. "Well, squire, you may judge for yourself," said old Joe. "Pretty soon after we got the chimney down the other end up I missed one of the chairs out of the room, and directly I see'd another of 'em shooting toward the fireplace. Next the table went, and I see the blacklog going up. Then I grabbed the old woman under one arm and the baby under t'other, and started; but just as I got to the door I see'd the cat going across the floor backward, holding on with her claws to the carpet, yelling awfully. It wasn't no use. I just see her going over the top of the chimney, and that was the last of her." "Well, what did you do then?" asked Holton; "of course you could not live in such a house?" "Couldn't I, though?" said Joe; "but I did; I put a poultice on the jamb of the fireplace, and that drawed t'other way, so we had no more trouble."

Part of the Job

"After you get through banging them dishes together in the dishpan you can start on your beds."

"Nobody down there at St. Louis tole me I hadda make no beds on this here job."

"My that makes me sad to hear that."

"They never said nothing about no beds."

"Ain't there a nice novelty to it though? I don't suppose you got beds down in Gasconade County."

"The hell we ain't. We got three beds right in our own house."

"My, my; you must be the rich folks in town."

"We don't live in no town. We live out on the branch, right near Gilberts Bridge."

From *A Stretch on the River*, by Richard Bissell, p. 90. Copyright, 1950, by Richard Bissell. An Atlantic Monthly Press Book printed by Little, Brown and Company. Boston.

"Leave me know when you're ready, and I'll show you just one more time how to make up them beds."

"They never said nothing about beds. I got half a notion to quit."

"Get another half notion and you'll have a whole one, and you can end your travels right up around the bend."

"Aw."

PART THREE

The Dessert

I. SNIPES AND LEFT-HANDED MONKEY WRENCHES

(Practical Jokes)

Introduction

Snipe hunts, exploding cigars, April Fool wallets, fake murders, and all the hundreds of other practical jokes arise from youthful, even adolescent, high spirits, although they may be perpetrated by sexagenarians. The high-spirited individual may spend days planning a joke that will give only ten minutes of discomfort to the jokee, but if he has worked the prank well, he will have a good story to tell for the remainder of his days. The joke may be on a greenhorn, as in "The Cow's Upper Teeth," on a "city slicker," as in "Taking the Starch Out of Him," or on a gullible member of one's own group, as in the three stories about "going to see the widow." These last three stories, by the way, indicate how thoroughly folk humor is diffused through all of America and through all social and economic classes, for basically the same practical joke is reported from South Carolina, Wisconsin, and New York City and from different socio-economic classes.

Stories about practical jokes which succeed are only mildly amusing, for the perpetrators have all the cards stacked in their favor, but stories of pranks which backfire delight Americans, for we are lovers of the underdog as well as fun-lovers who like unexpected twists. We are happy to learn of P. T. Barnum's success in winning Old Darrow's trick bet about a "whole shirt" and of the fun and profit Nicodemus Dodge and Bull Runnels had at the expense of practical jokers who thought they were dealing with fellows who were little better than half-wits.

Taking the Starch out of Him

A knot of idlers stood upon the end of a pier which runs out into the Hudson River, in one of the small towns near Albany, a few days ago, amusing themselves with hurling stones into the broad stream, each vieing with his neighbor in the endeavor to pitch a missile at the farthest distance from the shore; when a tall, rugged-built Vermonter, direct from the Green Hills, suddenly made his appearance in their midst, and for a while remained a quiet observer of their movements.

He was a brawny, strong-looking Yankee, and was very decently clad. The efforts of the little party had been exhibited over and over again, when the stranger quietly picked up half a brick which lay near him, and, giving it a jerk, it fell in the water a long way beyond the line which had as yet been reached by the foremost of the crowd. At the conclusion of this feat a loud "bravo!" went up from half a dozen voices around him.

It was a cold, clear day in October, and the men, determined not to be outdone, renewed their attempts; but the Vermonter, without saying a syllable to any one, continued to pitch the pebbles far out into the stream, which seemed to annoy one of them, in a green jacket, the apparent leader of the gang, who declared he wouldn't be beaten by a "feller right strait out o' the woods, no how"; and, sidling up to the stranger, he determined to make his acquaintance.

"Where do you come from, neighbor?" inquired the other.

"*Me?* Wal, I hails from Varmount, jes' naow, friend."

"Haint been in these parts long, I reck'n."

"Wal, no. Not edzackly *here,* but up and daown, sorter."

"Yis, so I s'posed."

"Yaas," continued the green 'un, carelessly, and seizing a big billet of wood he twirled it over his head, and it landed several rods from the shore in the water.

"You've a little strength in your arms, neighbor."

"*Some* 'pun'kins' is them flippers, stranger. Up in aour taown, more'n a munth ago, I druv them are knuckles rite strut thru a board more'n a ninch-n-'aff thick!"

"Haw, haw!" shouted his hearers; the man in the green jacket laughing loudest.

"Maybe yeu don't b'lieve it."

"Not much," answered the crowd.

"We aint *very* green down here in York, *we* aint," said the fellow in the green jacket; "we've been about, you see."

From *Gleanings from The Portfolio of the "Young 'Un"* [G. P. Burnham], pp. 66–70. Boston: R. B. Fitts & Co. 1849.

"Wal, jes yeu look yere, friend," continued the Vermonter, in the most plausible manner; "up in aour kaounty we've a purty big river considerin', Inyun river, it's called, and maybe you've heern on it. Wal, I hove a man clean across that river t' other day, and he came daown fair and square on t' other side!"

"Ha, ha, *ha!*" yelled his auditors.

"Wal, naow, yeu may laff, but I kin dew it agin."

"Do what?" said the green-jacket, quickly.

"I kin take and heave yeu across that river yender, jest like open and shet."

"Bet you ten dollars of it."

"Done," said the Yankee; and drawing forth an X, (upon a broken down-east bank!) he covered the braggart's shinplaster.

"Kin yeu swim, feller?"

"Like a duck," said green-jacket; and, without further parley, the Vermonter seized the knowing Yorker stoutly by the nape of the neck and the seat of his pants, jerked him from his foothold, and with an almost superhuman effort dashed the bully heels over head from the end of the dock some ten yards out into the Hudson river.

A terrific shout rang through the crowd, as he floundered into the water, and, amidst the jeers and screams of his companions, the ducked bully put back to the shore and scrambled up the bank, half frozen by his sudden and involuntary cold-bath.

"I'll take that ten-spot, if you please," said the shivering loafer, advancing rapidly to the stakeholder. "You took us for green-horns, eh? We'll show you how *we* do things down here in York"—and the fellow claimed the twenty dollars.

"Wal, I reck'n you wunt take no ten-spots jes' yit, cap'n."

"Why? You've lost the bet."

"Not edzactly. I didn't calkilate on dewin' it *the fust time*—but I tell yeu I kin *dew* it,"—and again, in spite of the loafer's utmost efforts to escape him, he seized him by the scruff and the seat of his overalls, and pitched him three yards farther into the river than upon the first trial.

Again the bully returned amid the shouts of his mates, who enjoyed the sport immensely.

"Third time never fails," said the Yankee, stripping off his coat; "I kin dew it, I tell ye."

"Hold on!" said the almost petrified victim.

"And I *will* deu it, *ef I try till to-morrer mornin'.*"

"I give it up!" shouted the sufferer between his teeth, which now chattered like a mad badger's—"take the money."

The Vermonter very coolly pocketed the ten-spot, and, as he turned away, remarked—

"We aint much acquainted with yeu smart folks daoun here 'n York, but we sometimes 'take the starch aout of 'em' up aour way, and p'raps yeu wont try it on tu strangers again. I *reck'n* you wunt," he continued, and putting on a broad grin of good humor, he left the company to their reflections.

A Message to the Pope

When the railroad built into Tucson in 1879, Pete [Kitchin] and some of his old side-kicks was terrible proud of the fact. They was in Fred Maish's Palace Saloon h'isting them regular, blowing about what a hell of a great town they lived in, and how New York and Frisco wouldn't ever amount to much, being so far away from Tucson. After a while they got the notion that maybe there was an outside chance that some unfortunate people in the world mightn't know the railroad had sure enough reached the great Arizona settlement on the Santa Cruz. They figured they ought to fix that up by sending a few telegrams.

Some maverick thought they'd better send the President of the United States a wire, but Pete says if the main boss of the U. S. A. didn't already know about it he was sure too dumb to be wasting telegrams on.

Then finally Pete got the reasonable idea that maybe the Pope, being so far away in Europe or wherever he hung out, mightn't have heard of it yet. Nobody knew where the hell the Pope lived, but Pete's Mexican wife, Doña Anna, was a good Catholic and Pete says it's a cinch she'd know the old boy's address.

So they sent a boy out to the ranch and Doña Anna sent back word that the Pope lived in a town called Rome. They used up about twenty telegraph blanks doping out the important message and finally got her fixed up reading:

Tucson, Arizona Territory,
May 15, 1879.

Pope Leo XIII,
Rome City, Europe.

The railroad has done reached Tucson.
Pete Kitchin

Then they had a few more drinks to brace them up after all that heavy brain work and waited round speculating about how long it would be before they'd be like to get an answer.

They'd been playing seven-up for the drinks and shaking the dice for nearly two hours and was beginning to get mighty anxious, afraid that perhaps the telegram had got wore out before it got to Rome,

From *Gun Notches, The Life Story of a Cowboy-Soldier.* By Captain Thomas H. Rynning as told to Al Cohn and Joe Chisholm, pp. 120–122. Copyright, 1931, by Frederick A. Stokes Company. New York: A. L. Burt Company, Publishers.

going all that distance across the country and through the Atlantic
Ocean, when the young Mexican who worked round the telegraph
office come busting into the Palace and handed Pete the reply.

Everybody held their breaths while Pete opened her up and closed
one eye to cipher it out. Then he looked sour as a horn toad as he
handed it over to the barkeep to read it out loud. The message was:

> Rome, Italy,
> May 15, 1879.
>
> Pete Kitchin,
> Tucson, Arizona Territory,
>
> Mr. Kitchin I am plumb glad to know the
> railroad has reached you, but where in hell
> is Tucson?
>
> > Pope Leo XIII.

Of course the boys had captured and bribed the messenger on his
way to the telegraph office with Pete's telegram and wrote the phony
one that Kitchin got a couple hours afterward. But old Pete thought
it was on the square up to the day he died, for when they saw how sore
he was, the jobbers was afraid to give their dirty work away. So the
old boy held a grudge for the Pope as long as he lived for not knowing where Tucson was.

Going to See the Widow

Folklorists recognize the practical joke as a source of amusement of
a rather crude and active type often motivated by a desire on the part
of the group to punish an enemy or deflate a braggart, or to test or
initiate a newcomer or tenderfoot. The "snipe hunt" is a relatively
wide-spread and harmless prank of this kind. Frequently, however,
practical jokes are more complex and violent. A joke known in eastern
South Carolina as "taking someone to see the widow" is an example of
this type.

The ideal victim is a newcomer to the community given to boasting
about his sexual capabilities and exhibiting an inordinate interest in
women. He is led by the pranksters to believe that a certain widow
who lives a few miles from town, a woman of unquestionable charm
but doubtful virtue, is interested in making his acquaintance. Furthermore, he is told that it can be arranged for him to meet her. He is
warned, however, that the widow has an ardent suitor whose jealousy
has been inflamed by rumors concerning her conduct. In due time a
meeting is arranged and the victim agrees to visit the widow in the
company of one of the men in on the joke. Before the appointed hour

By Hennig Cohen, in *The Journal of American Folklore*, LXIV (April-June, 1951),
p. 223.

he is told further tales which serve to convince him of the attractions of the widow and his own prowess as a lover.

On the designated evening, the victim and his companion drive several miles into the country before stopping at an isolated farmhouse. They get out of their car and walk up to the house. As they start up the steps a woman opens the door, calls out a warning and rushes back inside. A series of blasts from a shotgun ring out in the darkness, followed by shouts and threats. The victim's companion runs and then pretends to fall wounded.

Usually the victim is utterly terrified and runs down the road. Other participants in the joke are hidden at intervals along the road and speed the victim's flight by further shouting and firing. Eventually the victim is overtaken and the joke is explained to him. If he shows that he is a "good sport," the success of the prank is celebrated by drinks and general expressions of friendship, and his acceptance into the group is assured.

This practical joke is no doubt practiced in other parts of the South, but as far as the writer knows it is unknown elsewhere. To the writer's knowledge, it has been staged in various parts of South Carolina for at least thirty years, but its date of origin is probably in the distant past.

Wisconsin Pastimes

... "Going to See the Widow" reminded me of a relative's experiences in the old logging days when he worked on 'drives' and in lumber camps from 1897 to 1910 in Oconto County. On the first Saturday night in camp, older fellows who had been in camp before would clean up and shave. When asked by a newcomer if they were going somewhere, they would reply, "Oh, we're going to Callahan's Dance." Of course, he would ask to go along. Meanwhile, several men had started out ahead, a few with rifles. By the time the others had come along with the newcomer, they would hear a loud howling like a pack of wolves, and Indian war whoops. Then a shot would ring out and one of the fellows would yell, "They got me," and drop to the ground. Finally, several were lying on the 'tote' road that the newcomer and the others were walking on. By this time he was terrified and would usually start back to camp yelling, "Let me in, let me in." On the path to the bunkhouse, those who had remained in camp had placed pots and pans over which he would stumble in his frantic haste to reach the door. As he opened the door he would fall into a tub of water. This completed the initiation. One night, a fellow took off in the wrong direction and got lost. They searched for him all night and most of the next day until they found him. The camp boss said, "No

By Mrs. Morton H. Starr, in *The Journal of American Folklore*, Vol. LXVII (April-June, 1954), No. 264, p. 184.

more Callahan's Dance around here from now on. Why, that would
have been a state's prison offense for sure if that boy would'a died
from cold and fright."

'Snipe Hunt' was known among lumberjacks and hunters in northern Wisconsin. The new recruit would be given a large bag or gunny-
sack and told to wait at a certain spot while the others drove the
snipes in his direction. They would fire a few shots when they were
out of sight, just to make it look good. After an hour or two of 'holding the bag' he would finally realize that it was all a joke and would
start back for camp with murder in his heart! A variant of this from
Ladysmith stations the newcomer in the middle of a bridge while the
others are to drive the snipes from both sides of the bridge. "You
just can't miss 'em that way!"

'Seeing stars in the daytime' was popular years ago among Oconto
County children. A visitor or new resident in the neighborhood would
be asked if he or she would like to see stars in the daytime. The answer was, usually, "yes." He would be taken to the woodshed or
down in the cellar or other dark place, and the armhole of a coat
sleeve would be fitted over his face. He would then be asked, "Do you
see the stars yet?" The answer would be, "no." "Then close your eyes
and open them real quick." At that, a cup of cold water would descend into the blinking eyes to the utter discomfort of the victim who
wouldn't rest until he found someone who "wanted to see the stars."

The Trainman's Daughter

You would never believe me if I told you the names of the real big
guys in show biz who fell for "the trainman's daughter"! It was usually worked from Wolpin's and Lindy's restaurants. The gag was to
tell the "fall guy" about a beautiful gal on the West Side, who was
the daughter of a trainman who worked nights. All you had to do
was to bring her a strawberry pie (or any messy pie in season) and
you'd have a date. It was all done in an offhand manner by expert
ribbers. The victim would buy the pie, which was carried by his guide,
and would be taken to a certain tenement on the West Side that had
small gas lights in the halls. As they got to the top floor, he would
call "Anna. Anna." At this moment one of the boys planted on the
top floor would look over the banister and yell, "So you are the So-
and-Sos who are ruining my Anna! I'll kill you!" With that he would
throw an old electric bulb, which would explode and sound like a
shot from a gun. By now both guys were racing down the steps, and
the guide would manage in the excitement to throw the gooey pie
into the victim's face, and as they ran up the street, the fellows in on
the gag, who were hidden in doorways, would keep throwing bulbs.

From *Vaudeville: From the Honky-Tonks to the Palace,* by Joe Laurie, Jr., p. 260.
Copyright, 1953, by Joe Laurie, Jr. New York: Henry Holt & Co.

Both guys would run back to Wolpin's or Lindy's with the victim scared to death and the victim's face covered with pie! When I tell you that a "smarty" like the late Wilson Mizner (the wisest of all wise guys) went for this, you can imagine how the other un-smarties went for it. It got so bad that the police of the West Forty-seventh Street station gave orders to quit it. (They were in on it for years and got many a laugh out of the gag.)

The Cows' Upper Teeth

. . . When a greenhorn comes into a range he will have all sorts of impositions practiced on him until he cuts his eye-teeth. Never anything very serious but sometimes very annoying . . . unless one is very genial and accepts it as part of his training . . . A young man moved into a good range and after looking round bought a bunch of cattle of a ranchman who lived some five miles from where he was stopping. He drove over a nice bunch of young cattle and gave them some salt. In the meantime several of the boys gathered on the cow-yard. By and by one of them broke out laughing; the rest of the boys knew it was a joke and began laughing also. The young fellow looked puzzled and asked an explanation. After enjoying the laugh, the one who had started it said, "Bob, if I wasn't your friend I wouldn't tell you, but you have allowed that fellow to swindle you." "In what way?" asked the astonished boy. "Why, those cattle are the remnant of an old stock that fellow has been working off on greeners for some time; they are an old rundown stock and are so near run out that they have no front teeth in their upper jaw.[1] The looks of the youngster would have been a study for an artist. It was a combination of surprise, chagrin and incredulity. All the boys chimed in to verify the statement, and to prove it to him roped several head of the cattle and let him see for himself. He finally became very angry, and when some of the boys proposed to help him drive them back and see that he got justice he readily consented, drove them back and demanded his money. The man of whom he got them, in order to carry out the joke, agreed to rue the bargain. After dinner was over they explained it to him, and he enjoyed the joke as much as anyone, drove the cattle home, and in a few years became as good a judge of a cow as any of the boys. He always knew the ones that had no teeth after that.

From *Cow-Boy Life in Texas, or 27 years a Maverick. A Realistic and True Recital of Wild Life on the Boundless Plains of Texas, being the Actual Experience of Twenty-seven Years in the Exciting Life of a Genuine Cow-boy, Among the Roughs and Toughs of Texas*, by W. S. James, pp. 137-138. Chicago: M. A. Donohue & Co. 1893.

[1] The author takes it for granted that his readers will know that cows do not have upper front teeth.

Again and Again and Again

On one occasion Whisky Jack's raft was tied to the bank at Richland City, a once thriving Wisconsin River town, but now off the map or largely in the river bed. The crew were mighty thirsty, but they had no money with which to buy drinks. This was a serious dilemma. Finally, one of the men took a bundle of lath from the raft and walked to the tavern. The tavernkeeper was willing to trade drinks for the lath. He told the raftsman to place the bundle outside the rear door of the tavern. When the man left by this door he picked up the lath and handed it to another member of the crew who was coming up. This man also traded the lath for drinks, leaving the bundle outside the door for another raftsman when he departed. This process was repeated again and again until every member of the raft crew had been served with drinks. When all had gone the tavernkeeper looked out of the rear door and was greatly disappointed to find but one bundle of lath instead of the several dozen bundles he expected to see there.

The Great Lunch Mystery

William Milburn, a gentleman of many qualifications in the newspaper business . . . had been a printer on Bennett the Elder's *New York Herald*, on Bennett the Younger's *Evening Telegram*, and on William Cullen Bryant's *New York Evening Post*.

Milburn was one of the older Bennett's few favorites, largely on account of a prank he had played on Horace Greeley. Greeley, it appears, was gloriously absent-minded, but vehemently denied that failing. References in rival newspapers as to his mental lapses made his whiskers curl.

Uncle Horace, when snipping paragraphs from other publications for editorial reference, had a habit of pinning them to his lapel. Thus he wouldn't be so apt to mislay his cuttings during a spell of woolgathering. Often he took such work to Hitchcock's restaurant, near the old *Tribune* building in Park Row, later emerging from a repast, his lapel decked with so many paper ribbons that he resembled a heavy winner in a dog show.

Milburn and other *Herald* men were eating at Hitchcock's one noon

From *Whisky Jack Yarns,* Short Tales of the Old Time Lumber Raftsmen of the Wisconsin River and their Mythical Hero, Raft and River Bank Tales, by Charles E. Brown, page 2. Madison, Wisconsin: Wisconsin Folklore Society. 1940.

From *Timberline, a Story of Bonfils and Tammen,* by Gene Fowler, p. 96. Copyright, 1933, by Gene Fowler. Garden City Reprint Edition, 1951, by special arrangement with Crown Publishers.

when Horace and his work got together at the table. Now, in that era it was customary at Hitchcock's for a patron to be seated and served without ordering. The meals were "as is" for the day: soup, beans, bread, potatoes, coffee and apple pie. A patron paid on his way out. This day Horace was over-busy with his shears. The waiter brought his viands, but the eminent clipster didn't attend them at once; he just kept on clipping, pinning the cuttings to his lapels for safe-keeping.

Milburn and his cronies stealthily appropriated Horace's food and drink for themselves. At length the hard-working Greeley was ready to refresh his editorial duodenum. He seemed mildly astonished at the sight of the empty plates and drained cup. He studied the ceiling, as though reading the stars, pursed his lips, then sighed, dabbed his mouth with a napkin, rose and went out, paying his tab.

Milburn wrote an account of this absent-mindedness for the *Herald*. Greeley was outraged. He penned in self-defense that it was "a shame and a vicious libel, this canard concerning my alleged absorption in work to the exclusion of mundane needs," and added: "I solemnly aver that I not only ate my full meal at Hitchcock's, as any other normal citizen might, but actually *ordered and enjoyed a second portion of beans.*" Next day, the *Herald* contained a facsimile of affidavits sworn to by Milburn and his cronies . . .

The Yank Kicked First

Few men of his age have written so much and so well as Mr. Field, whose contributions to the press, under the signatures of "Straws," "Everpoint," etc., etc., would make a large and most amusing series of pen and ink sketches. His facility of composition is not less surprising than his industry, for he has been for years either engaged in the laborious profession of the stage, or writing for a daily newspaper.

A very handsome friend of ours, who a few weeks ago was *poked* out of a comfortable office up the river, has betaken himself to Bangor, for a time, to recover from the wound inflicted upon his feelings by our "unprincipled and immolating administration."

Change of air must have had an instantaneous effect upon his spirits, for, from Galena, he writes us an amusing letter, which, among other things, tells us of a desperate quarrel that took place on board of the boat between a real live dandy tourist, and a real live Yankee settler. The latter trod on the toes of the former; whereupon the former threatened to "Kick out of the cabin" the latter.

"You'll kick me out of this cabing?"

"Kicking a Yankee," by Jos. M. Field, Esq., of the St. Louis *Reveille*, from *A Quarter Race in Kentucky and Other Sketches*, edited by William T. Porter, pp. 161–164. Philadelphia: T. B. Peterson & Brothers. 1858. First published in the St. Louis *Reveille*.

"Yes, sir, I'll kick you out of this cabin!"

"You'll kick *me*, Mr. *Hitchcock*, out of this cabing?"

"Yes, sir, I'll kick *you*, Mr. Hitchcock!"

"Wal, I guess," said the Yankee, very coolly, after being perfectly satisfied that it was himself who stood in such imminent peril of assault—"I guess, since you talk of kicking, you've never heard me tell about old Bradley and my mare, there, to hum?"

"No, sir, nor do I wish——"

"Wal, guess it won't set you back much, any how, as kicking's generally best to be considered on. You see old Bradley is one of these sanctimonious, long-faced hypocrites, who put on a religious suit every Sabbath morning, and with a good deal of screwing, manage to keep it on till after sermon in the afternoon; and as I was a Universalist, he allers picked me out as a subject for religious conversation—and the darned hypocrite would talk about heaven, hell, and the devil—the crucifixion and prayer, without ever winking. Wal, he had an old roan mare that would jump over any fourteen-rail fence in Illinois, and open any door in my barn that hadn't a padlock on it. Tu or three times I found her in my stable, and I told Bradley about it, and he was 'very sorry'—'an unruly animal'—'would watch her,' and a hull lot of such things, all said in a very serious manner, with a face twice as long as old Deacon Farrar's on Sacrament day. I knew all the time he was lying, and so I watched him and his old roan tu; and for three nights regular, old roan came to my stable about bedtime, and just at daylight Bradley would come, bridle her, and ride off. I then just took my old mare down to a blacksmith's shop, and had some shoes made with 'corks' about four inches long, and had 'em nailed on to her hind feet. Your heels, mister, aint nuthing tu 'em. I took her home, give her about ten feet halter, and tied her right in the centre of the stable, fed her well with oats about nine o'clock, and after taking a good smoke, went to bed, knowing that my old mare was a truth-telling animal, and that she'd give a good report of herself in the morning. I hadn't got fairly to sleep before the old 'oman hunched me and wanted to know what on airth was the matter out at the stable. Says I, 'Go tu sleep, Peggy, it is nothing but Kate—she is kicking off flies, I guess!' Purty soon she hunched me agin, and says she, 'Mr. Hitchcock, du git up and see what in the world is the matter with Kate, for she is kicking most powerfully.' 'Lay still, Peggy, Kate will take care of herself, I guess.' Wal, the next morning, about daylight, Bradley, with bridle in hand, cum to the stable, as true as the book of Genesis; when he saw the old roan's sides, starn, and head, he cursed and swore worse than you did, mister, when I came down on your toes. Arter breakfast that morning Joe Davis cum to my house, and says he, 'Bradley's old roan is nearly dead—she's cut all to pieces and can scarcely move.' 'I want to know,' says I, 'how on airth did it happen?' Now Joe Davis was a member of the same church with Bradley, and whilst we were talking, up cum that everlastin' hypocrite, and says he, 'Mr. Hitchcock, my old roan is ruined!' 'Du tell,' says I. 'She is cut all to pieces,' says he; 'do you know whether she was in your stable, Mr. Hitchcock, last night?' Wal, mister, with this I let out: 'Do I *know* it?'—(the Yankee here, in illustration, made a sudden advance upon the dandy, who made way for him unconsciously, as it were)—'Do I know it, you no-souled, shad-bellied, squash-headed, old night-owl you!—you hay-hookin', corn-cribbin', fodder-fudgin', cent-shavin', whitlin'-of-nuthin' you!—Kate kicks like a mere dumb beast, but I've reduced the thing to a *science!*'" The Yankee had not ceased to advance, or the dandy, in his astonishment, to retreat; and now, the motion of the latter being accelerated by an apparent demonstration on the part of the former to "suit the action to the word," he found himself in the "social hall," tumbling backwards over a pile of baggage, and tearing the knees of his pants as he scrambled up, a perfect scream of laughter stunning him from all sides. The defeat was total:—a few moments afterwards he was seen dragging his own trunk ashore, while Mr. *Hitchcock* finished his story on the boiler deck.

On a Wrong Cent

About 1836, on visiting Bridgeport, I became acquainted with a number of business men, and in the course of social conversation at the hotel one evening a man about sixty years of age with gray hair and whiskers came into the room.

The gentlemen all received him cordially and introduced him to me as "Old Darrow." The old man took a seat and soon proved a jolly companion. It seems that he kept the tool-bridge over the Pequonnock River near the hotel, and was known for miles around as an inveterate joker. He would limp into the hotel every morning about 11 o'clock, take a drink and a cigar, and if a stranger happened to be present he would be sure to play some trick upon him.

For instance, he would step up to the man and say, "Stranger, I want to show you a curious scientific experiment, and with that he would drop an old-fashioned copper cent on the floor and say, "Now look at the sole of my boot and see that there is nothing stuck to it; I now put my foot on that cent, and by pressing heavily and turning my foot swiftly several times, it will exclude the air, so that the cent will adhere to the sole of my boot."

He would then begin his experiment, and while twisting his foot very earnestly, he would look another way, and his foot would slip off from the cent apparently without his knowledge.

From *Funny Stories* told by Phineas T. Barnum. pp. 79–80. Copyright, 1890, by Phineas T. Barnum. New York: George Routledge and Sons, Ltd.

The stranger, if he had any humor about him, would pick up the cent and put it in his pocket. Old Darrow would then lift up his foot and put it on top of the other foot.

"There, Stranger," he would say, "now you see I have got a cent between my two feet."

"What will you bet?" the knowing stranger would inquire.

"Well, I will bet a treat for the company that the cent is between my two feet."

The bet would be taken.

Darrow would then pull off his boot and empty out a cent which he had put there when dressing himself in the morning. The company would decide that he had the cent between his two feet, and of course the stranger would have to pay the bet. But on one occasion he lost his bet; much to his astonishment, the cent wasn't there, having slipped from a hole in his boot.

The Shirt Trick

[Old Darrow] had a variety of similar tricks which he delighted in playing upon any person whom he could take in. On one occasion . . . Darrow, who stuttered, made a final trial as follows:—

"Come, Barnum, I'll make you another proposition. I'll bet you ha'n't got a whole shirt on your back."

The catch consists in the fact that generally only one-half of that convenient garment is on the back; but I had anticipated the proposition—in fact I had induced a friend, Mr. Hough, to put Darrow up to the trick—and had folded a shirt nicely upon my back, securing it there with my suspenders. The bar-room was crowded with customers, who thought that if I made the bet I should be nicely caught, and I made a pretence of playing off, and at the same time stimulated Darrow to press the bet by saying:—

"That is a foolish bet to make; I'm sure my shirt is whole, because my shirt is nearly new; but I don't like to bet on such a subject."

"A good reason why," said Darrow in great glee; "it's ragged. Come, I'll bet you a treat for the whole company that you ha'n't got a whole shirt on your b-b-b-back!"

"I'll bet my shirt is cleaner than yours," I replied.

"That's nothing to do w-w-with the case; it's ragged, and y-y-you know."

"I know it is not," I replied, with pretended anger, which caused the crowd to laugh heartily.

"You poor ragged f-f-fellow, come down here from D-D-Danbury, I'm sorry for you," said Darrow, tantalizingly.

"You would not pay if you lost," I remarked.

Ibid., pp. 81–83.

"Here's f-f-five dollars I'll put in Captain Hinman's [the landlord's] hands. Now b-b-bet if you dare, you ragged c-c-creature, you."

I put five dollars in Captain Hinman's hands, and told him to treat the company from it if I lost the bet.

"Remember," said Darrow, "I b-b-bet you ha'n't got a whole shirt on your back!"

"All right," said I, taking off my coat and commencing to unbutton my vest. The whole company, feeling sure I was caught, began to laugh heartily. Old Darrow fairly danced with delight, and as I laid my coat on a chair he came running up in front of me, and slapping his hands together, exclaimed:—

"You needn't t-t-take off any more c-c-clothes, for if it ain't all on your b-b-back, you've lost it."

"If it is, I suppose you have!" I replied, pulling the whole shirt off from my back!

Such a shriek of laughter as burst forth from the crowd I scarcely ever heard, and certainly such a blank countenance as old Darrow exhibited it would be hard to conceive. Seeing that he was most incontinently "done for," and perceiving that his neighbor Hough had helped to do it, he ran up to him in great anger, and shaking his fist in his face, exclaimed:—

"H-H-Hough, you infernal r-r-rascal, to go against your own neighbour in favour of a D-D-Danbury man. I'll pay you for that some time, you see if I d-d-don't."

All hands went up to the bar and drank with a hearty good will, for it was seldom that Darrow got taken in, and he was so inveterate a joker they liked to see him paid in his own coin. . . .

Barnum's Wood-Chopper Story

A cord of hickory wood lay in front of my grandfather's door; and as he and Squire Ben Hoyt stood by, a wood-chopper, axe in hand, came along. Always ready for a joke, the old gentleman said:—

"Ben, how long would it take me to cut all that wood in lengths suitable for my fireplace?"

"About five hours, I should say."

"I think I could do it in four hours and a half."

"Doubtful; hickory is very tough wood."

"I could do it in four hours," said the wood-chopper.

"I don't believe it," Ben Hoyt said. "I don't think any man could cut that wood in four hours."

"I'll bet you a quart of rum that this man can," said my grandfather; and Ben, who now saw the joke, at once took the bet.

The now interested wood-chopper took off his coat and inquiring

Ibid., pp. 68–70.

the time o' day—it was just nine o'clock—he said to my grandfather:—

"If I get it chopped by one o'clock you win your bet." And at it he went, and the chips flew fast.

By this time several neighbours assembled, and took sides as to who would win the bet. At eleven o'clock more than half the wood was cut, and to stimulate the zealous chopper my grandfather gave him a glass of Santa Cruz [rum]. Hoyt professed to think that the woodchopper was beginning to give out, while my grandfather insisted that he should win the bet. These remarks, intended for the chopper's ear, had the desired effect. He rapidly diminished the pile, the spectators cheered him, and at half-past twelve only a few sticks remained uncut.

All at once he stopped as suddenly as if he had been shot. A serious thought struck him. Resting on his axe he addressed my grandfather:—

"Look here! who's going to pay me for cutting this wood?"

"Oh, I don't know anything about that," said the old gentleman, with great gravity.

"Thunder! you don't expect me to cut a cord of wood for nothing, do you?" exclaimed the indignant wood-chopper.

"That's no affair of mine; but really I hope you won't waste your time now, or I shall lose my bet."

"Go to blazes with your bet!" And the now thoroughly angry wood-cutter threw his axe on the ground, and sat on the pile till the neighbors had had their fun out of him, and my grandfather paid his demands.

"All right!" said the chopper; "but I guess I shall know who employs me before I begin on the next cord of wood."

Nicodemus Dodge

When I was a boy in a printing office in Missouri, a loose-jointed, long-legged, tow-headed, jeans-clad, countrified cub of about sixteen lounged in one day, and without removing his hands from the depths of his trowsers pockets or taking off his faded ruin of a slouch hat, whose broken brim hung limp and ragged about his eyes and ears like a bug-eaten cabbage leaf, stared indifferently around, then leaned his hip against the editor's table, crossed his mighty brogans, aimed at a distant fly from a crevice in his upper teeth, laid him low, and said with composure,

"Whar's the boss?"

"I am the boss," said the editor, following this curious bit of architecture wonderingly along up to its clock-face with his eye.

"Don't want anybody fur to learn the business, 't ain't likely?"

From *A Tramp Abroad*, by Samuel L. Clemens, pp. 224–229. Hartford, Conn., American Publishing Company, 1880.

"Well, I don't know. Would you like to learn it?"

"Pap's so po' he caint run me no mo', so I want to git a show somers if I kin, 'taint no diffunce what—I'm strong and hearty, and I don't turn my back on no kind of work, hard nur soft."

"Do you think you would like to learn the printing business?"

"Well, I don't re'ly k'yer a durn what I *do* learn, so's I git a chance fur to make my way. I'd jist as soon learn print'n 's anything."

"Can you read?"

"Yes,—middlin'."

"Write?"

"Well, I've seed people could lay over me thar."

"Cipher?"

"Not good enough to keep store, I don't reckon, but up as fur as twelve-times-twelve I ain't no slouch. 'Tother side of that is what gits me."

"Where is your home?"

"I'm f'm old Shelby."

"What is your father's religious denomination?"

"Him? O, he's a blacksmith."

"No, no,—I don't mean his trade. What's his *religious* denomination?"

"*O*,—I didn't understand you befo'. He's a Freemason."

"No—no, you don't get my meaning yet. What I mean is, does he belong to any *church?*"

"*Now* you're talkin'! Couldn't make out what you was a tryin' to git through yo' head no way. B'long to a *church!* Why boss he's ben the pizenest kind of a Free-will Babtis' for forty year. They ain't no pizener ones 'n' what *he* is. Mighty good man, pap is. Everybody says that. If they said any diffrunt they wouldn't say it whar *I wuz*—not *much* they wouldn't."

"What is your own religion?"

"Well, boss, you've kind o' got me, thar—and yit you hain't got me so mighty much, nuther. I think't if a feller he'ps another feller when he's in trouble, and don't cuss, and don't do no mean things, nur noth'n' he ain' no business to do, and don't spell the Savior's name with a little g, he ain't runnin' no resks,—he's about as saift as if he b'longed to a church."

"But suppose he did spell it with a little g,—what then?"

"Well, if he done it a-purpose, I reckon he wouldn't stand no chance,—he *oughtn't* to have no chance, anyway, I'm most rotten certain 'bout that."

"What is your name?"

"Nicodemus Dodge."

"I think maybe you'll do, Nicodemus. We'll give you a trial, anyway."

"All right."

"When would you like to begin?"

"Now."

So, within ten minutes after we had first glimpsed this nondescript he was one of us, and with his coat off and hard at it.

Beyond that end of our establishment which was furthest from the street, was a deserted garden, pathless, and thickly grown with the bloomy and villainous "jimpson" weed and its common friend the stately sunflower. In the midst of this mournful spot was a decayed and aged little "frame" house with but one room, one window, and no ceiling,—it had been a smokehouse a generation before. Nicodemus was given this lonely and ghostly den as a bed chamber.

The village smarties recognized a treasure in Nicodemus, right away,—a butt to play jokes on. It was easy to see that he was inconceivably green and confiding. George Jones had the glory of perpetrating the first joke on him: he gave him a cigar with a fire-cracker in it and winked to the crowd to come; the thing exploded presently and swept away the bulk of Nicodemus's eyebrows and eyelashes. He simply said,—

"I consider them kind of seeg'yars dangersome,"—and seemed to suspect nothing. The next evening Nicodemus waylaid George and poured a bucket of ice-water over him.

One day, while Nicodemus was in swimming, Tom McElroy "tied" his clothes. Nicodemus made a bonfire of Tom's, by way of retaliation.

A third joke was played upon Nicodemus, a day or two later,—he walked up the middle aisle of the village church, Sunday night, with a staring hand-bill pinned between his shouders. The joker spent the remainder of the night, after church, in the cellar of a deserted house, and Nicodemus sat on the cellar door till toward breakfast time to make sure that the prisoner remembered that if any noise was made, some rough treatment would be the consequence. The cellar had two feet of stagnant water in it, and was bottomed with six inches of soft mud.

. . . Before a very long time had elapsed, the village smarties began to feel an uncomfortable consciousness of not having made a very shining success out of their attempts on the simpleton from "old Shelby." Experimenters grew scarce and chary. Now the young doctor came to the rescue. There was delight and applause when he proposed to scare Nicodemus to death, and explained how he was going to do it. He had a noble new skeleton,—the skeleton of the late and only local celebrity, Jimmy Finn, the village drunkard,—a grisly piece of property which he had bought of Jimmy Finn himself, at auction, for fifty dollars, under great competition, when Jimmy lay very sick in the tan-yard a fortnight before his death. The fifty dollars had gone promptly for whisky and had considerably hurried up the change of ownership in the skeleton. The doctor would put Jimmy Finn's skeleton in Nicodemus's bed!

This was done,—about half past ten in the evening. About Nicodemus's usual bedtime—midnight,—the village jokers came creeping stealthily through the jimpson weeds and sunflowers toward the lonely frame den. They reached the window and peeped in. There sat the long-legged pauper, on his bed, in a very short shirt, and nothing more; he was dangling his legs contentedly back and forth, and wheezing the music of "Camptown Races" out of a paper-overlaid comb which he was pressing against his mouth; by him laid a new jew's-harp, a new top, a solid india-rubber ball, a handful of painted marbles, five pounds of "store" candy, and a well-gnawed slab of ginger-bread as big and as thick as a volume of sheet music.

He had sold the skeleton to a traveling quack for three dollars and was enjoying the result!

Swallowing an Oyster Alive

At a late hour, the other night, the door of an oyster house in our city was thrust open, and in stalked a hero from the Sucker state. He was quite six feet high, spare, somewhat stooped, with a hungry, anxious countenance, and his hands pushed clear down to the bottom of his breeches pockets. His outer covering was hard to define, but after surveying it minutely, we came to the conclusion that his suit had been made in his boyhood, of a dingy yellow linsey-woolsey, and that, having sprouted up with astonishing rapidity, he had been forced to piece it out with all colours, in order to keep pace with his body. In spite of his exertions, however, he had fallen in arrears about a foot of the necessary length, and consequently, stuck that far through his inexpressibles. His crop of hair was surmounted by the funniest little seal-skin cap imaginable. After taking a position, he indulged in a long stare at the man opening the *bivalves,* and slowly ejaculated— "Isters?"

"Yes, sir," responded the attentive operator,—"and fine ones they are, too."

"Well, I've heard of isters afore," says he, "but this is the fust time I've seed 'm, and *pre-haps* I'll know what *thar* made of afore I git out of town."

Having expressed this desperate intention, he cautiously approached the plate and scrutinized the uncased shell-fish with a gravity and interest which would have done honour to the most illustrous searcher

---

From *The Big Bear of Arkansas, and Other Sketches,* Illustrative of Characters and Incidents in the South and South-West, edited by William T. Porter, pp. 80–86. Entered, according to Act of Congress, in the year 1845, by Carey & Hart, in the Clerk's Office of the District Court of the United States, of the Eastern District of Pennsylvania. Philadelphia.

into the hidden mysteries of nature. At length he began to soliloquize on the difficulty of getting them out, and how queer they looked when out.

"I never seed any thin' hold on so—takes an amazin' site of screwin, hoss, to get 'em out, and aint they slick and slip'ry when they does come? Smooth as an eel! I've a good mind to give that feller lodgin', jist to realize the effects, as uncle Jess used to say about speckalation."

"Well, sir," was the reply, "down with two bits, and you can have a dozen."

"Two bits!" exclaimed the Sucker, "now come, that's stickin' it on rite strong, hoss, for *isters*. A dozen on 'em aint nothin' to a chicken, and there's no gettin' more'n a picayune a piece for *them*. I've only realized forty-five picayunes on my first ventur' to St. Louis. I'll tell you what, I'll gin you two chickens for a dozen, if you'll conclude to deal."

A wag, who was standing by indulging in a dozen, winked to the attendant to shell out, and the offer was accepted.

"Now mind," repeated the Sucker, "all fair—two chickens for a dozen—you're a witness, mister," turning at the same time to the wag; "none of your tricks, for I've heard that your city fellers are mity slip'ry coons."

The bargain being fairly understood, our Sucker squared himself for the onset; deliberately put off his seal-skin, tucked up his sleeves, and, fork in hand, awaited the appearance of No. 1. It came—he saw—and quickly it was bolted! A moment's dreadful pause ensued. The wag dropped his knife and fork with a look of mingled amazement and horror—something akin to Shakespeare's Hamlet on seeing his daddy's ghost—while he burst into the exclamation—

"Swallowed alive, as I'm a Christian!"

Our Sucker hero had opened his mouth with pleasure a moment before, but now it *stood* open. Fear—a horrid dread of he didn't know what—a consciousness that all wasn't right, and ignorant of the extent of the wrong—the uncertainty of the moment was terrible. Urged to desperation, he faltered out—

"What on earth's the row?"

"Did you swallow it alive?" inquired the wag.

"I swallowed it jest as he gin it to me!" shouted the Sucker.

"You're a dead man!" exclaimed his anxious friend, "the creature is alive, and will eat right through you," added he, in a most hopeless tone.

"Get a pizen pump and pump it out!" screamed the Sucker, in a frenzy, his eyes fairly starting from their sockets. "O gracious!—what 'ill I do?—It's got holds of my innards already, and I'm dead as a chicken!—do somethin' for me, do—don't let the infernal sea-toad eat me afore your eyes."

"Why don't you put some of this on it?" inquired the wag, pointing to a bottle of strong pepper-sauce.

The hint was enough—the Sucker, upon the instant, seized the bottle, and desperately wrenching out the cork, swallowed half the contents at a draught. He fairly squealed from its effects, and gasped and blowed, and pitched, and twisted, as if it were coursing through him with electric effect, while at the same time his eyes ran a stream of tears. At length becoming a little composed, his waggish adviser approached, almost bursting with suppressed laughter, and inquired,—

"How are you now old fellow—did you kill it?"

"Well, I did, hoss'—ugh, ugh o-o-o my innards. If that *ister* critter's dyin' agonies didn't stir a 'ruption in me equal to a small arthquake, then 'taint no use sayin' it—it squirmed like a sarpent, when that killin' stuff touched it; hu' "—and here with a countenance made up of suppressed agony and present determination, he paused to give force to his words, and slowly and deliberately remarked, "If you git two chickens from me for that live animal, I'm d—d—!" and seizing his seal-skin he vanished.

The shout of laughter, and the contortions of the company at this finale, would have made a spectator believe that they had all been *swallowing oysters alive*.

A Real Hunk of Dreaming

Everybody said Bull Runnels had ought to be bored for the simples.

First time they said it, he was still just a young'un, about fourteen year old but even then as big as a man. People got to noticing how he clumb to the top of every tall tree he come around and would set up there for minutes at a time craning his neck in all directions.

"What on earth are you doing, boy?" they asked.

"A-looking at the weather," says he. "You can see heap more of it up here."

So they shaken their heads and started saying, "That Runnels boy ought to be bored for the simples!"

Looked like that boy just never did aim to stop growing. Why, when he was eighteen he was easy the biggest man in town. He could tote a bigger load and do more downright back-breaking work than any two work horses in the country. His real name was Willie, but who's going to call a big strappling six-foot-four two-hundred-pounder a name like *Willie?* No, it was Bull Runnels—had to be Bull, that's all.

Ben Canada was the blacksmith and he kept sprying his eyes after

By James R. Aswell. From *God Bless the Devil! Liars' Bench Tales,* by James R. Aswell, Julia Willhoit, Jennette Edwards, E. E. Miller, and Lena E. Lipscomb, of the Tennessee Writers' Project, pp. 11–24. Copyright, 1940, by the University of North Carolina Press, Chapel Hill.

Bull Runnels. "Look at them shoulders!" says he. "Look at them arm muscles a-working like a mess of eels! He'll make a master blacksmith, that boy!" So Ben Canada taken Bull Runnels on to be his helper and started training him.

Nobody ever saw his beat when he got started. He made that old anvil ring till it shaken every window in town and sounded like a steeple full of big iron bells. When he got busy bending horseshoes or hammering out wagon springs or axles, the inside of that blacksmith shop looked like hell on a busy day, with flames shooting every which way and sparks flying like red-hot sleet.

Bull was too busy now to climb trees and look at the weather. When he wasn't hammering hot iron, he was sleeping or setting on his heels out behind Ben Canada's shop in the chicken yard listening to the hens.

"I got a theery," he says, "and it's about chickens. Now, chickens is clever if you get to know them good. I figger they can talk like anybody else, only we can't make it out. I got a theery if I just [set] around the coop a-listening long enough I'll get to where I can understand them. Now, that would be a reel novelty!"

So people said they *knowed* Bull Runnels had ought to be bored for the simples.

Bull never could get the hang of chicken talk, so he give it up, and pretty soon something else was working on his mind.

"I hear folks all the time talking about dreaming," says he, "but me now, I ain't never had one of them things. Don't even know what one feels like. Just close my eyes and—*pop!*—I'm a goner. Next thing I know it's time to go to work again. Nothing happens but plain nothing in between. Now, I sure would like to have one of them things just once, just so's I could say I'd had it."

Ben Canada says, "Shucks, Bull, dreams don't amount to so much. Some's good and some's bad, but mostly they're bad."

Was always two or three men hanging around the shop to watch Bull work and somebody'd say, "Aw shoot, Ben, you know that ain't so. Don't listen to him, Bull."

Bull would lay his hammer down and push the long hair out of his eyes and say, "Now looky-here, boys! Don't you go short-talking Mister Ben like that. I'll tromp somebody's britches if you don't watch out, now!"

"Calm down there, Bull," they'd say, ready to cut and run if a mean streak hit him. "We don't mean no harm. We was aiming to say they're a lot of dreams that's gay to have."

"Says which?" Bull would get all interested.

"Well," they'd tell him, "some eating dreams is first rate. Maybe you dream all night you're eating. Maybe it's spare-ribs and beaten biscuit, buttermilk, and gravy and peach dumplings."

"How about chittlins, now?"

"Chittlins, too. Just anything. You eat all night and never get full. A big fat waiter always ready to heap the grub on your plate! Ice cream and pie and stripe candy—the more you eat, the more they feed you when you're dreaming."

Bull would set down and put his head in his hands. "Aw me! I sure wish I could have a dream, now! I sure do, now!"

"That ain't all, neither," they'd say. "You dream about pretty gals, too."

"Sure enough?" Bull says. He was awful timid around the ladies, Bull was. All he could do was stand and blush and grin around them. So now he looked sly and says, "What *kind* of gal dreams?"

"Aw," they told him, "you know. All the pretty gals love you and you hug them all and buss them good. Stuff like that."

"*Whoo-ee!*" says Bull, jumping up and grabbing a hot bar of iron out of the charcoal furnace and banging it with his hammer till the anvil danced a jig. "I sure would like to have one of them gal dreams, now!"

Slim Loggins—Lawyer Loggins, his boy Slim—was the ring-leader when it come to telling Bull about dreaming. He had a gift for it. He could tell a dream to where it sounded better than heaven's rest to a damned soul.

"Yes sir, Bull," he'd say, "everything you've ever wanted to do, don't matter what it is, you do it when you dream. The whole world's yours. All you have to do is reach out and grab it. Say you dream of money. Why, man, you find it in piles! Yes sir, big stacks of bright shiny dollars! You can just rake it in, shovel it in a wagon, and haul it away."

"Can you keep the money?" says Bull.

"Sure you can."

"Aw me!" moans Bull. "And I can't dream nohow at all. Aw me!"

Everybody in town knew how hard Bull Runnels was trying to dream. Ben Canada's old woman told about it. Bull lived in the Canadas' back room and they heard him at it.

"With him grunting and groaning and doing around like he does," says old Mrs. Canada, "we don't get any rest hardly, me and Ben. First he bounces up and down till it sounds like the bed's going to fall to pieces. Then he quiets down some and just about the time we're dropping off he lets out a snort and says, 'Dad-fetch it, start a-going, dreams!'

"Then he starts a-mumbling and saying, 'Aw me! Aw me!' and bouncing and blowing till we think he ain't never liable to quit. It goes on and on like that. All of a sudden, along about midnight, he bubbles two or three times and starts snoring peaceful as a baby. Me and Ben don't get a wink till then, neither."

Slim Loggins tells Bull, "Trouble is, you got too good a digestion. If you eat nails, they wouldn't bother you."

"I never et no nails that I know of," Bull says.

"What I mean," Slim tells him, "is that you ought to eat something that will give your stummick fits. That's the best way to have a dream."

Bull would scratch an ear and ask, "What ought I to eat, then? I eat everything a-going now, but I don't never have no dreams."

"Well," says Slim, "why don't you eat some pig knuckles, chittlins, and sourkraut with plenty of vinegar. Then eat a mess of catfish and some bananas and ice cream and mince pie. Eat lots of each thing and see what happens."

"Reckon I'll have one of them gal dreams?" says Bull.

"You ought to have some kind," Slim says.

Bull kind of twists his blacksmith's apron and grins. "You mind if I dream about your gal, Slim? I mean Birdie, now."

Slim looked funny. Birdie was Doc Nugent's daughter and the prettiest bouncing blue-eyed gal in town. But he says, "Why, naw. You go ahead and dream about whoever you want to."

"I sure thank you," says Bull. "I sure do, now."

So Bull went and eat slathers of all that stuff and went home and slept like a log. He didn't dream a thing.

Next day he told the boys, "It just ain't any use. 'Tain't in me to have one of them things. Aw me!"

Slim Loggins got all the boys together at Sneed's drugstore one night. He says, "I figger it's high time to do something about Bull Runnels."

"What can anybody do about Bull Runnels?" they said.

"Hold quiet and I'll tell you. I'll get Birdie to slip out one of Doc's prescription blanks. I'll write some scratchy-looking stuff all over it and tell Bull it's for medicine that will make him dream sure. When Bull brings it over, Doc Sneed here will give him a bottle of baby-soother—you game, Doc?"

Doc Sneed says, "Reckon so, sure. No harm, I reckon."

"All right. Well, Bull will go home and drink the whole bottle and lay down to dream. That baby-soother will work on him. When he's helpless, we'll just slip in his window, all dressed in sheets, and tie him up, heist him out the window, and carry him over into the woods.

"Then we'll really fix him up, boys! Nothing that'll really damage him, of course. Nope, just a regular little old initiation like we give at the lodge. He'll be so dope-headed with that soothing syrup he won't hardly know what's happening. We'll lay it to him to a fare-you-well, then take him home. In the morning he'll be sore behind and scared in the head. I'm willing to bet good money he won't want no more dreams. And what's more, he'll quit this everlasting talk about it. How's it strike everybody?"

They all said the idea was a ripper. So they set around laughing and planning out just what they aimed to do to Bull Runnels to cure him from craving a dream.

"One thing, though," says Slim. "Don't nobody ever let on to Bull about what really happened. He gets tempered up easy and when that happens he'll crack bones like kindling wood. The man that gives us away will have the rest of us to whip as well as Bull."

In a day or two Slim Loggins and some of the boys went down to the blacksmith shop. They told Bull Runnels about this sure-fired dream medicine Doc Nugent was putting out.

"If you want to try it," says Slim, pulling out the blank he'd hen-scratched all over, "here's the prescription. Doc Sneed can fill it for you."

Bull dropped his hammer to the ground and reached for that piece of paper. He held it up and admired it like he was seeing visions already.

"Slim," he says, "do you reckon it will reelly work, now? Reckon if I take it I'll have one of them dreams, sure enough?"

"Why," Slim tells him, "can't be no doubt about it! Do you think a fine man like Doc Nugent would go passing out medicine that won't work?"

Bull scratched his ear and says no, that wasn't likely because Doc was a mighty fine man. Then he grinned and looked sly. "Doc sure has got one more pretty gal! Birdie's a reel baby doll, now!"

Slim didn't like that. He looked cross and says, "You'll have a real hunk of a dreaming, Bull. I garntee *that!*"

When it was good dark, Slim and the boys got together and waited around till by their judgment the baby-soother had got in its licks. Everybody well knowed that Bull Runnels bedded early.

About a little after eight Slim says, "Well, let's go. Bull's pounding it hard by now."

With him leading, the boys stole around behind Ben Canada's house, all trying to keep from busting out with the heehaws.

Life is a funny place sometimes. Most anybody who'd drunk that whole bottle of baby-soother would have been dead to the world. But, somehow, it didn't operate to amount to much on Bull Runnels. No, he was just laying on his back in bed feeling a little drowsy and faraway.

"Maybe," says he, "this is the way you feel when you're a-fixing to dream. Maybe I'm just before fetching out one of them things, now."

He rolled over facing to the window. Then he blinked his eyes. "Here she starts, sure enough!" he thinks.

Coming through the window he sees some white floppy things. "Must be a dream," he thinks, "because I've been a-living all my life and ain't never laid eye on nothing like that. Well, now I'm a-dreaming, I might as well start in."

So he hopped out of bed in his nightshirt and grabbed hold of the white things and chucked them out the window. "Go way," says he.

"I ain't studying to dream about old white nothings like you! It's eating dreams and gal and money dreams I'm after."

Sheets with two pair of legs each were flying every which way when Bull Runnels clumb out his window in his nightshirt. "I reckon," says he, watching them go in the dimmishness, "that them is what you call nightmares."

By the time Bull got out in front of the house, not a sheet could he see. Pretty scared, they'd scattered to their own houses. Slim Loggins was mad enough to destroy creation, but he knowed better than face Bull Runnels. So he throwed his sheet away and stomped over to set awhile with Birdie.

Bull Runnels didn't know what to do next. He stood in the middle of the road scratching his ear and wool-gathering. "Dad-fetch it, now!" he says. "Ain't hardly reasonable for me to have them three kinds of dreams at once. Couldn't get much reel satisfaction out trying to eat and buss a pretty gal and pick up money at the same time. It would be a mess, if you ask me. All right then, we'll see, now."

He picked up a flat rock and spit on it. He called that side heads and the dry side tails and flipped it to see which way to take his dreams.

"Eats first," says he, "then money, then the pretty gal dream."

Straight away he loped down to the square in his bare feet with his nightshirt switching around his big hairy legs. He made for Tom's Dandy Eats, the best place in town to get a meal.

It was late and wasn't a soul in Tom's Dandy Eats except Tom himself. Tom lets out a howl when Bull comes in. "Bull Runnels!" he says. "What the devil ails you?"

Bull looked him in the eye and pointed his finger. "Don't give me no trouble, Mister Tom," he says, "or I'll churn your head. I'm having a dream of eating and the mouth juice is about to choke me, now. So hump yourself, Mister Tom. Whatever you got that's hot. Don't matter. Just so's they's a plenty of it."

"Who's going to pay? I ask you, Bull Runnels?"

"Why, don't act so crazy, Mister Tom!" says Bull. "This is a dream. Everything's free in a dream. Make haste, now. They's piles of silver dollars and a pretty little gal a-waiting to be dreamt."

Here's the way it was. Tom had heard some talk when the boys were eating with him. So he figgered it out in a wink and vowed to himself he'd make them pay for whatever Bull put away. So he just loaded the table down.

Bull slapped his stomach, grabbed a knife, and started shoveling. Eat two pounds of steak and half a ham butt. Eat four helpings of fried potatoes, a plate of brains and eggs, some cabbage and turnip greens, some batter cakes and sorghum-lasses and butter, soda biscuits, corn pone, lamb fries, and washed it all down with sweetmilk and coffee.

In about an hour he pushed back his chair and wiped his mouth on his nightshirt tail. "Ah Lordy!" says he. "I sure dreampt a good un!"

Next Bull tried to get into the bank but couldn't. "Doggone!" he says. "They didn't tell me you had locks in dreams! But they sure got them on the bank."

So then he cut over to Doc Sneed's drugstore and walked in.

When Doc viewed him he got scared, thought Bull was coming after him for being in on the joke. He backed up against the wall and pled, "Don't do it, Bull! I didn't mean nothing by it! Swear to God I didn't, Bull!"

Bull just gawped at him. "Doc," he says, "you sure act funny in a dream. I wish you'd quit shaking and come over here and show me how to open this cash register. I push these little stickout things?"

"Aw, you ain't going to raid the till, Bull!"

"Why no," says Bull, filling a sack with change and bills. "I'm just having my money dream, now."

It was fair killing Doc Sneed to watch it. Must've been anyhow fourteen or fifteen dollars in the till. But he knowed better than tell Bull it was a joke. If he believed it, Bull might've wrecked the place pretty near. Doc was madder than Tucker the day his dog died, but he couldn't do a thing about it.

"Thank you kindly, Doc," says Bull. "Much obliged for the money dream."

And then he went back to Ben Canada's and clumb in the back window and stashed the sack of change and bills.

"Now," says he, "for the pretty gal dream! *Whoo-ee!*" He poured half a bottle of sweet hair oil over his bushy head, clumb out the window, and started for Birdie Nugent's house. He was in a big way, feeling mighty bobbish, and he walked like a man stepping over cornstalks, with his head in the air and his nightshirt waving around his legs.

So happened that old Doc Nugent was away from home on a night call and his old lady had gone to bed. Slim Loggins and Birdie were sweethearting on the sofa in the parlor.

Bull come up on the piazza in his quiet bare feet. He stood there peeking in, grinning, and clucking. "Ah Lordy!" says he, "that Birdie! Pretty as a spotted pup!"

First thing Slim or Birdie knowed, Bull had hauled off and come bulging in the front door. "Hi there, Miss Birdie!" says he.

Birdie screeched and Slim near swallowed his neck-bean. Slim jumped behind the sofa in a sweat panic. Birdie stood up, pale as death, and her knees about to jack-knife under her.

"Here I am, little hossfly!" says Bull. Then he picks Birdie up like a baby and sets on the sofa with her on his knee. But Birdie didn't know about it. She gave a little cheep and then she mere fainted away.

"Buss me, hossfly," says Bull, and he gave her a big old smack right square on the mouth. *"Whoo-ee!"* says he. "You're good enough to eat, now!"

He started patting her head with his big hand like you'd pat the flank of a horse. He didn't notice a thing—neither that Birdie'd swooned out or that Slim Loggins was crawling on his belly over by the wall towards the grate. Didn't see Slim get the poker.

"Little Birdie gal," says Bull, "a man couldn't want no better dream than you. Buss me again, little pistol."

So Bull didn't see Slim behind the sofa, gritting his jaws like he could chew the edge off a cold chisel. He didn't see that poker in both Slim's hands and blood in Slim's eye. Didn't see it coming down like a jag of blue lightning.

The poker landed so hard it just jarred the house. Bull Runnels started leaning over sort of slow. Slim caught up Birdie, and Bull slid out on the floor, dead to the world.

After rolling Bull out on the piazza, Slim brought Birdie to. He got some of the boys and they toted Bull home and dumped him in bed.

Next morning Slim and the boys drifted down to the blacksmith shop. Doc Sneed come along too. They were all kind of worried, scared Slim had maybe damaged Bull's head with the poker.

But no Lord! There was Bull hard at it bending horseshoes and making that old anvil ring like a steeple full of big iron bells.

Bull let out a bellow when he noticed the boys edging through the door. "Boys," says he, "it done the trick! That medicine give me a sure enough reel hunk of dreaming, now! I had a gal dream the sweetest ever!" Bull smacked his lips and rolled his eyes.

"Yep," says Bull, "made me fifteen dollars and seventy-seven cents in my money dream, and I won't never forget the eating dream. I'm satisfied now, though. Don't want to dream no more ever, now. It gives you too big a headache when you wake up."

So everybody just looked at him. Doc Sneed was out his money. Slim had had his best gal bussed, and the lot of them had to chip in and pay a big feed bill at Tom's Dandy Eats.

So Slim Loggins cocked his eye at the roof and stuck his hands in his pockets. "Boys," says he, "I ain't so sure about *who* ought to be bored for the simples now."

The Hen's Revenge

An Essex Street man killed a hen that belonged to a neighbor because it flew into his yard. The neighbor made no demonstration. But he went around among the juveniles, and told them that the one among them who could say "Shoes and socks shock Susan" four times running, without mistake, would receive two dollars from the hen killer. So they went up to his house, in the guilelessness of childhood, and filled the hall and the stoop, and crowded the yard, and made up their minds they would earn that two dollars or die. And they sailed in, and the man tried to drive them off, but couldn't, and then he went up stairs, but they followed him. The air resounded with "Shuwack snoozen socker" with hideous variations in the shrillest of voices keyed to the highest of pitches. In vain the victim appealed for mercy with ink bottles, and hot water, and mustard boxes. His arguments were unheeded and his cries were unheard, and he finally scaled a fence and fled, pursued by what he was firmly convinced were a score of demons. The hen was avenged.

Pike Sellers' Whizzer

Typical adjunct to life in the hell-roarin' days of the Argonauts when camps reeked gold and the humors of men were raw as new-plowed prairie land, was that effervescent phenomenon known as the Whizzer.

The Whizzer was the high ace in the deck of life as it was dealt over gravel bar and auriferous stream bank. Individuals and towns reaped fame by it. A successful Whizzer not only crowned its originator and perpetrator with glory, but shed an enviable light upon the entire community that witnessed—or suffered—its execution. Whizzers of superlative merit have been embalmed in the memories of very old men who still sun themselves in the ghost towns of gold and who can be led, with much chuckling, to recount them. In a few rare volumes of reminiscences long out of print you'll find samples of this long extinct genus pinned like gorgeous butterflies to the pages.

A noteworthy swindle, a practical joke, a brilliant hoax: these were the magic components of which the Whizzer was made. They were of two classes, the plain and the bald-headed. A bald-headed Whizzer was one so adroitly built upon a human foible or frailty, so carefully exploited by its author as to bring a whole community into the arena

From *Life in Danbury* . . . , by James M. Bailey, "The Danbury News Man . . . ," pp. 139–140. Boston. Shepard and Gill, 1873.

From *The Hell-Roarin' Forty-Niners,* by Robert Welles Ritchie, pp. 233–237. Copyright, 1928, by J. H. Sears & Co., Incorporated. New York.

of mocking laughter. The distinction between the two varieties was comparative; the gage, you might say, of genius.

One of the earliest Whizzers of the gold diggin's to gain immortality was that one perpetrated by a genius whose name comes down as Pike Sellers—undoubtedly one of the Wild Missouri hellions generically lumped as "Pikes," in the vocabulary of the mines. This Pike had an imagination and a devilishly sly humor which would qualify him to-day for one of our highly specialized lines of salesmanship.

It was in the spring of '50 when word of the incredible richness of Downie's Flat, away up near the headwaters of Yuba's north fork, swept downstream and set a crowd of wild-eyed boomers hurrying thither. Original discoverers of Downie's Flat were digging a pound of gold a day to the man out of crevices under the rim rock with the point of a butcher knife. Major Downie himself had sifted downstream to Bullard's Bar with $3000 in nuggets, result of three days' work! So rumor exploded.

When the first of the rush commenced to lower themselves hand over hand down the precipitous wall of the gorge to Downie's camp on the forks of white water they were not very cordially received by the ten or a dozen original discoverers who'd spent a hard winter there. It was, in fact, quite true that Downie and his associates had been hitting raw gold out of the bank with butcher knives and iron spoons over several months; and they did not welcome a division of riches.

Then it was that Pike Sellers had his inspiration.

He was working away at the soft dirt of the stream bank one day when he saw one of the boomers, pack on back, crawling precariously down trail. Pike, unseen himself, scrambled up out of the stream bed and commenced furiously prying with his long knife at the bark slabs on a jack-pine. Just as the stranger came up one of the rough shags of bark became loosened. Pike pushed two fingers behind it and withdrew a fat gold nugget.

Eyes of the stranger popped. Pike tackled another bark slab without so much as a glance over shoulder at the fascinated onlooker. By a simple trick of legerdemain that hunk yielded a second alluring gold pebble.

"My Gawd!"—from the tenderfoot. "I hearn ye was digging' the yaller stuff outa cracks in the rocks, but I didn't know she grew on trees."

"Gits lodged thar when th' tree's pushing up through th' soil," indifferently from Pike. "Most of th' nuggets is up higher, but too dam'd much trouble to shin up th' trees. Me, I'm jist satisfied to peck round nigh th' ground."

Under the believing eyes of the newcomer Pike found a couple more nuggets. Then the former whipped out his bowie-knife and started to work on a near-by jack-pine.

"Hold on thar!" commandingly from the Sellers person. "Yo're on my claim. Rule in this camp ev'ry fella's entitled to ten gold bearin' pines; that thar one belongs to me."

The boomer wanted to know in an excited whine where he could stake himself to a tree. Reluctantly Pike Sellers abandoned his work to stride through the forest to where a jack-pine of smaller growth reared.

"Like I said, she's richest nigh th' top. Ye can climb this one 'thout a ladder iffen yo're so minded." Pike showed a commendable interest in seeing the newcomer make his first strike of jack-pine gold. The latter dropped his pack and, bowie in teeth, commenced to shin up the rough trunk.

"Higher up's better," bawled Pike when his protege had come to the first limbs. "Nothin' but flake gold low down mostly."

Up went the avid tenderfoot, before his eyes the vision of a man prying nuggets from beneath tree bark. Pike let him risk his neck until the luckless light-wit was fifty or sixty feet from the ground.

"That's a likely 'nough place to begin on. Only be mighty keerful not to drop any nuggets. I kain't be held responsible fer losses like that."

The searcher after tree gold began to attack the bark with his bowie knife. Pike Sellers sifted back to the stream bed to bring an audience for the farce comedy he had staged. Thereafter "jack-pine gold" became a synonym through all the Northern Mines.

Pike Sellers reaped enduring fame as the father of a Whizzer.

II. SPREAD, EAGLE, SPREAD
(Tall Tales)

Introduction

Tall tales are not really lies, for they are told for fun rather than profit. The teller of such tales is a literary and dramatic artist who is giving a demonstration of the fun of being imaginative. He is not trying to sell you stock in a company to make and sell "windwagons" to sail the prairies; he is only telling you about such wagons. Some tall tales are near enough to the truth that they may be believed by the greenhorn, but they have in them indicators to let the initiates know that they are fancy rather than fact. Most tall tales, however, are so far from the truth that no one would be misled; they are meant to be enjoyed rather than believed. Our enjoyment comes from the literary art which makes the unbelievable at least partially believable (just as does the art of the ghost story) and from the imaginative combination of details.

In order to make the exaggerations of the tale more nearly credible, the narrator maintains at all times an air of truthfulness. He talks gravely and seriously, becoming even more grave as the tale gets more exaggerated. He also gives the appearance of being extremely careful with details, giving the exact day and the exact spot where an event occurred and occasionally stopping to correct himself about the day, the year, or the names of the people who were in the party at the time. Paradoxically, some of the art of the tall tale lies in using inconsistent details, for the narrator wants to be interrupted so that he can explain or defend the inconsistency. In his account of his buffalo hunt, for example, Bemis first described the hunt on a treeless plain, but when it became absolutely necessary, he climbed a tree. The tale-teller is almost always prepared to offer some "proof" of his veracity, although the listeners are free to see that the evidence is not very conclusive. He may display a chip of wood from the wagon, pull out the knife used in killing the bear, or, like Bemis, offer merely negative evidence:

"Proofs! Did I bring back my lariat?"
"No."
"Did I bring back my horse?"
"No."
"Did you ever see the bull again?"
"No."
"What more do you want?"

But one of the neatest tricks to use in demonstrating one's veracity is to approach an obviously good place to exaggerate and then retreat from it. The narrator is thus indirectly saying, "A liar would 'go the whole hog' here, but I prefer to stay with the truth." Bill Dean, for example, told of running along behind a grass fire, holding his horse meat over the flame to cook it, but when he was asked whether the meat was well cooked, he admitted that it was "just crusted over a little." And "Kit Carson," in the midst of a series of delightfully wild exaggerations, stopped to say to Joe, "If I told you that the old Southern gentleman was my grandfather, you wouldn't believe me, would you?" When Joe replied that he might, Kit refused to go that far, saying, "Well, it so happens he wasn't. Would have been romantic if he had been, though."

The Fast-Running Double-Action Dog

Fox-hunting was a favorite sport with many; indeed, all loved it, but only a few kept hounds and gave chase to mischievous Reynard. Foxes were quite plenty, and renowned for deeds of daring. The women hated hounds most cordially, yet they would endure them for the sake of their fowls. If their fowls were destroyed, they could neither make soup nor their rich pot-pies, both of which were much admired. Wylie Franklin was a great favorite with chicken-raisers, for if a hen-roost was invaded a *hint* to him was all that was needed, and the marauder was soon taken. The compositions of Mozart, Handel, and Haydn were no music to these fox-hunters compared with the voice of hounds in the chase. Sometimes there would be a great rally of fox-hunters at some point to have a united chase, to see who had the fastest and the toughest hound. This must be kept in view in reading the story of Larkin's fast-running dog.

"You see," said Larkin, "a passel uv fellers cum frum 'bout Rockford, Jonesville, and the Holler to have a fox-hunt, and kep' a-boastin' uv thar fast dogs. I told 'um my little dog Flyin'-jib could beat all thar dogs, and give 'um two in the game. I called him up and showed him to 'um, and you mout a hearn 'um laugh a mile, measured with a 'coonskin and the tail throwed in. I told 'um they'd laugh t'other side o' thar mouths afore it were done. They hooted me.

"We went out with 'bout fifty hounds, and, as good luck would hev it, we started a rale old Virginny red fox, 'bout three hours afore day, on the west side uv Skull Camp Mountin. He struck right off for the Saddle Mountin, then whirled round over Scott's Knob, then to Cedar Ridge, up it, and over Fisher's Peak, round back uv the Blue Ridge, then crossed over and down it at Blaze Spur, then down to and over Round Peak, then Down Ring's Creek to Shipp's Muster-ground, and on agin to'ads Skull Camp. Not fur from Shipp's Muster-ground they passed me, and Flyin'-jib were 'bout half a mile ahead on 'um all, goin' fast as the report of a rifle gun. Passin' through a meader whar thar were a mowin'-scythe with the blade standin' up, Flyin'-jib run chug against it with sich force that it split him wide open frum the eend uv his nose to the tip uv his tail. Thar he lay, and nuver whimpered, tryin' to run right on. I streaked it to him, snatched up both sides uv him, slapped 'um together, but were in sich a hurry that I put two feet down and two up. But away he went arter the fox, scootin' jist in that fix. You see, when he got tired runnin' on two feet on one side, he'd whirl over, quick as lightnin', on t'other two, and it seemed ruther to hev increased his

From *Fisher's River* (North Carolina). Scenes and Characters by "Skitt" [H. E. Taliaferro] "who was raised thar." Pp. 149–151. New York: Harper & Brothers, Publishers, 1859.

verlocity. He cotch the fox on the east side uv Skull Camp, a mile ahead uv the whole kit uv 'um.

"Now when the fellers cum up, and seen all thar dogs lyin' on the ground pantin' fur life, and Flyin'-jib jist gittin' his hand in, they was mighty low down in the mouth, I warrant you. All the conserlation they had was seein' my dog in sich a curious fix. But I jist kervorted, and told 'um that were the way fur a dog to run fast and long, fust one side up, then t'other—it rested him."

Mule in Sheep's Clothing

While our outfit was on maneuvers in Louisiana last year, we lost most of our motor transportation. To move our supplies, we had to hire a white mule named Bessie from one of the farmers in the neighborhood.

Bessie was a good mule, but one day we found her lying peacefully on the ground. We tried to revive the old girl, but it was no use. So instead of taking a total loss on the mule, we skinned her and turned the hide over to the farmer.

This year we ended up in the same maneuver area and stopped by to pay the farmer a visit. He looked at us for a minute, then gravely shook his head. "You know, boys," he said, "when I hired out old Bessie to you last year, I plumb forgot to tell you that when she went to sleep, nothing could get her awake till she had her sleep out. She wasn't dead when you skinned her—just sleeping.

"Later that day, after you fetched her hide back to me, she came walking home. I had just butchered a few sheep, so I right away covered her with sheep skins and fastened them with blackberry thorns.

"You know, boys, that old mule came out just fine. This year—besides having Bessie to work—I sheared 140 pounds of wool and my wife picked 55 quarts of blackberries off her."

A Midget Weighing Thirty-Nine Pounds

[*An old man who looks as if he might have been Kit Carson at one time walks in importantly, moves about, and finally stands at* JOE'S *table.*]

KIT CARSON. Murphy's the name. Just an old trapper. Mind if I sit down?

JOE. Be delighted. What'll you drink?

From *Tall Tales They Tell in the Services,* Edited by Sgt. Bill Davidson, p. 11. Copyright, 1943, by Thomas Y. Crowell Company. New York.

From *The Time of Your Life,* by William Saroyan, Act Two. Copyright, 1939, by Harcourt, Brace and Company, Inc. New York.

KIT CARSON (*sitting down.*) Beer. Same as I've been drinking. And thanks.

JOE (*to* NICK). Glass of beer, Nick.

[NICK *brings the beer to the table,* KIT CARSON *swallows it in one swig, wipes his big white mustache with the back of his right hand.*]

KIT CARSON (*moving in*). I don't suppose you ever fell in love with a midget weighing thirty-nine pounds?

JOE (*studying the man*). Can't say I have, but have another beer.

KIT CARSON (*intimately*). Thanks, thanks. Down in Gallup, twenty-years ago. Fellow by the name of Rufus Jenkins came to town with six white horses and two black ones. Said he wanted a man to break the horses for him because his left leg was wood and he couldn't do it. Had a meeting at Parker's Mercantile Store and finally came to blows, me and Henry Walpal. Bashed his head with a brass cuspidor and ran away to Mexico, but he didn't die.

Couldn't speak a word. Took up with a cattle-breeder named Diego, educated in California. Spoke the language better than you and me. Said, "Your job, Murph, is to feed them prize bulls." I said, "Fine, what'll I feed them?" He said, "Hay, lettuce, salt, beer, and aspirin." Came to blows two days later over an accordion he claimed I stole. I had *borrowed* it. During the fight I busted it over his head; ruined one of the finest accordions I ever saw. Grabbed a horse and rode back across the border. Texas. Got to talking with a fellow who looked honest. Turned out to be a Ranger who was looking for me.

JOE. Yeah. You were saying, a thirty-nine-pound midget.

KIT CARSON. Will I ever forget that lady? Will I ever get over that Amazon of small proportions?

JOE. Will you?

KIT CARSON. If I live to be sixty.

JOE. Sixty? You look more than sixty now.

KIT CARSON. That's trouble showing in my face. Trouble and complications. I was fifty-eight three months ago.

JOE. That accounts for it, then. Go ahead, tell me more.

KIT CARSON. Told the Texas Ranger my name was Rothstein, mining engineer from Pennsylvania, looking for something worth while. Mentioned two places in Houston. Nearly lost an eye early one morning, going down the stairs. Ran into a six-footer with an iron claw where his right hand was supposed to be. Said, "You broke up my home." Told him I was a stranger in Houston. The girls gathered at the top of the stairs to see a fight. Seven of them. Six feet and an iron claw. That's bad on the nerves. Kicked him in the mouth when he swung for my head with the claw. Would have lost an eye except for quick thinking. He rolled into the gutter and pulled a gun. Fired seven times. I was back upstairs. Left the place an hour later, dressed in silk and feathers, with a hat swung around

over my face. Saw him standing on the corner, waiting. Said, "Care
for a wiggle?" Said he didn't. I went on down the street and left
town. I don't suppose you ever had to put a dress on to save your
skin, did you?

JOE. No, and I never fell in love with a midget weighing thirty-nine
pounds. Have another beer?

KIT CARSON. Thanks. (*Swallows a glass of beer.*) Ever try to herd cattle
on a bicycle?

JOE. No. I never got around to that.

KIT CARSON. Left Houston with sixty cents in my pocket, gift of a girl
named Lucinda. Walked fourteen miles in fourteen hours. Big
house with barb wire all around, and big dogs. One thing I never
could get around. Walked past the gate, anyway, from hunger and
thirst. Dogs jumped up and came for me. Walked right into them,
growing older every second. Went up to the door and knocked. Big
Negress opened the door, closed it quick. Said, "On your way, white
trash." Knocked again. Said, "On your way." Again. "On your way."
Again. This time the old man himself opened the door, ninety, if
he was a day. Sawed-off shotgun, too. Said, "I ain't looking for
trouble, Father. I'm hungry and thirsty, name's Cavanaugh." Took
me in and made mint juleps for the two of us. Said, "living here
alone, Father?" Said, "Drink and ask no questions. Maybe I am and
maybe I ain't. You saw the lady. Draw your own conclusions." I'd
heard of that, but didn't wink out of tact. If I told you that old
Southern gentleman was my grandfather, you wouldn't believe me,
would you?

JOE. I might.

KIT CARSON. Well, it so happens he wasn't. Would have been romantic
if he had been, though.

JOE. Where did you herd cattle on a bicycle?

KIT CARSON. Toledo, Ohio, 1918.

JOE. They don't herd cattle in Toledo.

KIT CARSON. They don't any more. They did in 1918. One fellow did,
leastaways. Bookkeeper named Sam Gold. Straight from the East
Side, New York. Sombrero, lariats, Bull Durham, two head of cattle
and two bicycles. Called his place The Gold Bar Ranch, two acres,
just outside the city limits. That was the year of the war, you'll remember.

JOE. Yeah, I remember, but how about herding them two cows on a
a bicycle? How'd you do it?

KIT CARSON. Easiest thing in the world. Rode no hands. Had to, otherwise couldn't lasso the cows. Worked for Sam Gold till the cows
ran away. Bicycles scared them. They went into Toledo. Never saw
hide nor hair of them again. Advertised in every paper, but never
got them back. Broke his heart. Sold both bikes and returned to
New York. Took four aces from a deck of red cards and walked to

town. Poker. Fellow in the game named Chuck Collins, liked to gamble. Told him with a smile I didn't suppose he'd care to bet a hundred dollars I wouldn't hold four aces the next hand. Called it. My cards were red on the blank side. The other cards were blue. Plumb forgot all about it. Showed him four aces. Ace of spades, ace of clubs, ace of diamonds, ace of hearts. I'll remember them four cards if I live to be sixty. Would have been killed on the spot except for the hurricane that year.

JOE. Hurricane?

KIT CARSON. You haven't forgotten the Toledo hurricane of 1918, have you?

JOE. No. There was no hurricane in Toledo in 1918, or any other year.

KIT CARSON. For the love of God, then what do you suppose that commotion was? And how come I came to in Chicago, dream-walking down State Street?

JOE. I guess they scared you.

KIT CARSON. No, that wasn't it. You go back to the papers of November 1918 and I think you'll find there was a hurricane in Toledo. I remember sitting on the roof of a two-story house, floating northwest.

JOE (seriously). Northwest?

KIT CARSON. Now, son, don't tell me you don't believe me, either?

JOE (Pause. Very seriously, energetically and sharply). Of course I believe you. Living is an art. It's not bookkeeping. It takes a lot of rehearsing for a man to get to be himself.

KIT CARSON (thoughtfully, smiling, and amazed). You're the first man I've ever met who believes me.

JOE (seriously). Have another beer.

Windwagon Smith

I

Windwagon Smith had a face like any other man, and two legs to walk on, but the morning he rode into Westport the quietest mule in

From "Windwagon Smith," by Wilbur L. Schramm, *Atlantic Monthly*, Vol. 168 (July, 1941), No. 1, pp. 26–35. Copyright, 1941, by the Atlantic Monthly Company, Boston, Massachusetts. All rights reserved.

Compare "Sailing the Prairies" by Stanley Vestal, *Southwest Review*, Vol. XXIII (July, 1938), No. 4, pp. 432–435. Reprinted under title "Windwagon Thomas," *A Treasury of Western Folklore*, edited by B. A. Botkin (New York: Crown Publishers, Inc., 1951); "Windwagon Smith," *Tall Tale America*, by Walter Blair (New York: Coward-McCann, 1944); "How to Write Folklore," by H. Allen Smith, *The World, the Flesh, and H. Allen Smith*, pp. 111–114 (Garden City, New York: Hanover House, 1954).

The first printed version of this American folktale, as far as it has been traced, appeared as a newspaper feature entitled "Westport's Dry-Land Navy," in the Kansas City *Star*, August 5, 1906.

town jumped sixteen feet. And some men would have flown like bald eagles that day, if they could.

That was when Westport was the great city of the prairie. Now it is only a far corner of Kansas City and smells like gasoline and coal smoke, but in those days it smelled of prairie grass and clean wind, and was on every road west. No matter where you were going beyond the Missouri, you started at Westport. You followed a rutted trail twenty miles from town to a meadow where Jake Shafer's Negro boy had nailed a box top to a runt cottonwood and painted on it, 'Rode to Oregon.' There the families for Oregon turned north, and the wagons from Santa Fe and the Spanish cities southwest. West of the crossing, two hundred miles of grass rolled away to the sky, waist-high, blowing black and green and yellow. Your shoes got slick as lard in that grass. Then you came out into the sagebrush, and the grit chewed off your soles and left you barefoot. And about that time the Comanches would come yelling out of the sand hills. All the way across a thousand miles of empty prairie you would wish you were back in Westport, sitting in Punch Dunkelberger's Star of the West saloon, listening to Jake Shafer tell how Davy Crockett could grin the bark off a tree.

Westport could have been the greatest city in the United States. It could have been Boston and New York and Detroit pressed into one and set down in the middle of the prairie, if it hadn't made one mistake. That was about Windwagon Smith.

The morning Windwagon came, Punch Dunkelberger's hound dog woke up bristling like a hairbrush. That dog always slept until noon under his master's hat peg in the Star of the West; he had slept through a cyclone and seven street fights. But that morning he woke up about ten o'clock, waved his nose in the air, howled a long quaver, and slunk into a closet. Two Pawnees in the Star looked at the dog and blew away like smoke. Jake Shafer changed his seat and drew a bead on the door. The door opened slowly. But only Shelby Foster glided in, with his apologetic way, giving a little bow before speaking, because he was from the East and knew manners. When he tried to talk he was so excited he couldn't squeeze the words out, and stood there with his mouth mostly open, his eyes big as soap kettles, and a silly polite look on his face, waving his hands toward the street as though he were batting gnats.

'I never hoped to see the Missouri flow juleps,' said Jake Shafer, 'or a gopher running a coyote, or Foster without anything to say.'

Foster looked behind him and croaked and skipped aside, and there was a crash, and the head and shoulders of Jake's mule Martha appeared in the doorway. The doors slammed back and caught the mule's neck in a pincers, and there she stood like a moose head on the wall rolling her eyes.

'I can stand bugs in the beer,' bellowed Jake in his big barrel voice, 'but when the draft animals come in I go out.'

When they went out, there was Windwagon Smith.

All they saw at first was a Conestoga wagon coming down the street between the log houses. It was like any other Conestoga wagon, sway-backed, with a horseshoe canvas top. Except for one thing: there was nothing in front of it.

No oxen, no mules, no horses. Nothing. The wagon was just coming down the street.

The Pawnees were peeking from behind trees, eyes bulging like hard-boiled eggs. The dogs were barking, and the ponies that hadn't run away were pulling at their hackamores.

'He's got a sail,' said Punch suddenly.

A pole stuck up out of the wagon like a ship's mast, and on it a square of canvas turned half sideways to catch the quartering wind.

A little man in blue denim was riding on the wagon seat. He furled the sail in quick movements, locked the wagon wheel, and came to a stop exactly where Jake's mule had been. When he hopped down from the wagon he walked with a sailor's roll and sway. The dogs quit barking and balanced on their hind legs, ready to go either way. It was so quiet you could hear the stranger's feet crunch in the dust and sand.

'Ahoy!' he said out of the silence. 'Think I'll drop anchor and come ashore for a bit of refreshment.'

His voice was deep and rolling, with something about it that prolonged the r's and clipped the consonants like axebites in an oak tree.

'My name's Smith,' he explained. 'I'm the master, the crew, and most of the cargo of this ship, and I aim to do a lot of sailing on the prairie.' There was never so much r in prairie until he said it.

It was Painted Dog, a Pawnee, who really named him. Painted Dog had been behind the nearest tree when Jake's mule jumped into the saloon. 'Mule be there,' he explained later, 'door there. Windwagon blow down street. Whoosh! Mule: here, there!' So they called the stranger Windwagon, for he was the kind of person who had to have a shinier name than Smith.

The whole town followed the stranger to the Star. They made a circle around his table, then circles around that circle, like winding up a ball of yarn, until the room was full. Those who were near passed word over their shoulders to those who were not, so that bulletins would slide outward like waves when you throw a stone in a pond: 'He's sitting down'—'sitting down'—and finally, at farthest remove, the Pawnees would hear the news and pass it on: 'Sittum down'—'sittum.'

The stranger savored his drink like a man who had been long away from the good things. He was one of those old youngsters, anywhere between thirty and fifty. His face was burned and lined, his sandy hair had been tumbled and tousled by many a wind, and his eyes had the perpetual squint that a sailor gets from peeking all day at horizons. People looked mostly at his eyes: they burned like a tent preacher's. When he began to talk, he wasn't bashful or brash, just quiet and sure, and convincing, his big burry voice rolling like the tide. He told how the prairies were going to look tomorrow, speckled with mansions and factories and towns, wealthier than India. But he said people needed one great thing before they could have any of those things. They needed a way to move fast, a way to carry goods from town to town; to build this new prairie of tomorrow they had to have the speed of the wind! Then he talked about his wagon, how it would sail any place on the prairie ten times as fast as a draft animal, yet, without animals to buy or feed, it didn't need to follow crooked trails along rivers, and it would always have free power because the wind never stops on the prairie.

Jake Shafer nodded his head at that, and the circle behind him nodded, and two minutes later the Pawnees were nodding their heads, too; they knew that prairie wind. Then the stranger looked Jake straight in the eye and said he wanted the men of Westport to ante in some money and build a fleet of big sail wagons, like his little one, for the Santa Fe trade. For a minute everybody stared at him. Then somebody snickered, and somebody laughed, and everybody around began to laugh, and the room shook, and mirth rippled outward until the farthest Pawnee was holding his belly and gurgling *ug-ug-ug* in his throat.

When the room was quiet again, the stranger said he had thought they might feel that way. He would be back in a few days; they should think it over. Then he climbed back into his wagon, unfurled the sail, and rumbled away in a great arc toward the west.

II

For the next few days they talked of nothing except Windwagon Smith. Jake Shafer said that he didn't hand over any chips until he saw the cards on the table, and everybody agreed that was sage. Shelby Foster, who had just graduated from a New England college, said that the kind of mathematics they taught in New England colleges proved that such a big wagon couldn't run, and only a fool would invest money in it. Foster had come out to write a book like Francis Parkman's about the Oregon Trail, and went around looking at people and writing in his notebook. And as soon as Foster came out against windwagons people began to look at them more favorably. Jake's daughter Rosalie, who was as sweet as clover honey, said that maybe this was one of the things you just have to believe in—like boats, the first time you see one. Someone suggested that maybe Smith had gone to St. Joe, Westport's rival town, and St. Joe would build windwagons and take over the whole trade; and everybody spent a bad day imagining St. Joe full of millionaires. But a rider from St. Joe said Smith hadn't been up there.

And when he hadn't come back in four days, Westport gave him up and thought of other things.

When Windwagon Smith had been gone six days, a trapper came to Westport with a strange story. He had been riding about ten miles from town when he saw a white streak on the prairie. The streak turned out to be an old cow, sticking its head between its legs and uncoiling with ten-foot jumps, stringing its tail out behind like a fence rail. Before he could think what to do about the cow, it sailed past him and disappeared in a funnel of dust. He pondered whether he should catch the cow and race it against all comers, but he didn't know that he *could* catch it; it was the fastest cow he ever saw.

That same day a caravan that had just started west passed back through Westport, headed *east*. The men of the caravan held tight to their guns and kept their mouths shut. One woman who was a little hysterical said they weren't afraid of the Sioux or the Mormons, but they weren't going out on the prairie among the *spirits*. They were going back to Ohio where bodies stayed in their graves!

Punch Dunkelberger and Jake Shafer talked of these events in the Star, Doctor Jackson told his patients about them while he prescribed calomel and mustard plasters, Shelby Foster discussed them with Rosalie Shafer while they looked at the moon. But the meaning was not fully comprehended until the next morning, when the dogs waved their noses in the air again and slunk away, all the ponies that could jump leaped the corrals and started east, and the Indians began to glide around, looking for wide trees. And soon Windwagon sailed down the street, waving to everyone.

'Ahoy!' he said. 'I'd have been back yesterday, but came on a caravan and maybe scared them, so I took a long swing off the trail and waited until I was sure they were out of the way.'

The town followed him into the Star again, and he showed a stone that was as good as an affidavit for where he had been. It was jagged and black, and still warm from lying in a little gully beyond Council Grove where all the wind blows straight up, hot as Mexican pepper. That gully is one of the side doors to hell, people think. The Doctor worked long division on a table top, and calculated that the windwagon had made nearly seventy miles a day. An ox team was lucky to make fifteen. When Windwagon said he thought he might go to St. Joe, Jake looked at the faces around him and then jumped up and banged the table and said, 'By God, we'll form a company *here!*' A great whoop went up behind him, and undulated outward, and in a little while the Pawnees were screaming and dancing in the street, the dogs snapping at their heels.

That is how the Westport Prairie Clipper Company was formed. You can see it in the company's minute book. Jake Shafer was elected president; Punch Dunkelberger, vice president; the Doctor, secretary and treasurer. Windwagon could have had any office he wanted, but he wanted only to be Navigator—Navigator of the Prairies, he said with a faraway look in his eyes. He said you had to believe in the future. Columbus had to believe; Dan Boone had to believe in Kentucky before he cut the Wilderness Road; Fulton had to believe that a little engine could push a big boat. Every time progress is made it's because people believe enough in something to take a chance. He said that pretty soon the prairie would be white with sails. The clippers would cruise past the oxen like coyotes past snails. Every day a clipper would dock in Westport with its hold full of gold and spices and blankets, and every day in the Spanish cities (ports, he called them) they would shout, 'Make way for the Westport Prairie Clipper!'

Punch Dunkelberger was so near to tears he made the mistake of setting up the whole crowd.

They were slow in starting to build the clippers, because Windwagon was particular. He wanted white oak and hickory for the bed, so it could be curved just right to hold the cargo on slopes; and long-seasoned ash for the spokes and the tillers and all the moving parts that weren't iron. The iron had to be beaten just enough. When Jake saw what a job it was going to be, he said they would build one clipper and try it out before building the others. Windwagon looked a little hurt, but he put the measurements on paper and sent riders to St. Joe and Independence to see what materials they could collect. Some things had to be ordered from St. Louis and Pittsburgh.

While the clipper was building, Windwagon had plenty of time to talk. He was ever one to talk grandly—not boastfully, just grandly. As soon as he got a dozen wagons promised, he began to talk of a hundred-wagon fleet. And one evening he said, 'It'll never do any good to have ships unless we have sailors. We've got to build crews at the same time we build clippers. If you are going to be the first captains in the Santa Fe voyage, you've got to learn to pilot.'

So Jake climbed into Smith's little wagon one day, with his jaw set firm and his hands holding tight, and Windwagon sat beside him and explained how the sail worked. He let Jake try to steer, and they staggered over the prairie for a while. When they came back, Jake climbed out quickly with the sweat running down his face and said he'd rather drive a runaway bull team than handle a 6 x 6 sail. One by one the other members of the Company began to go out for sailing lessons. They would swell out their muscles and hold on to the tiller as though they were driving a twelve-mule span, and tug at the tiny sail like wrestling a steer. Windwagon would shake his head in despair and take the tiller from them, and make the wagon glide this way and that. When Windwagon steered it was as though the man, the wagon, and the wind were all one will. But when Jake, or Punch, or the Doctor steered, the wagon would stagger and hesitate and groan in its joints. And when the lesson was over, the pupil would climb out as quickly as possible and go into the Star for a long drink.

Windwagon explained that a captain must also know how to navigate. Foster snorted at that; he said that to navigate you need to know the kind of elevated mathematics that is taught only in New England colleges, but Windwagon said that for a man of sense it wasn't necessary to go to college, and he began to teach Westport the common rules about the stars and directions and estimating distances.

Jake Shafer ordered a sextant from Baltimore, and Windwagon nearly cried when he saw it. It reminded him of the sea, and he spent a whole afternoon telling how it feels to skid before a salt breeze, and how the mountains come to the bay at Naples, and how in a few weeks the first clipper would be sailing into Santa Fe.

One day Punch Dunkelberger appeared wearing a captain's cap he had ordered from St. Louis. It was bright blue with silver braid, and Punch looked like baked ham with birthday candles. But in a few weeks everyone had a blue cap. Each new one seemed to have more trimming than the one before, until Punch got ashamed of his and talked of putting a red turkey feather on it. The town was no longer interested in the things it had been. A caravan could hardly buy a mule or an ox in the village. The blacksmith was working on the clipper and had no time to shoe animals or repair wheels. Most of the business men closed up shop, hid their leathery faces under blue caps, sighted through the sextant, and tried to walk and talk like Windwagon. It was wonderful to hear them go on about tacking and hauling, port and starb'd.

Sometimes a man would look at himself in his wife's mirror or calculate how much money the experiment was costing him. Then he would go to Windwagon, clear his throat and furrow his brow, and try to say his worries. Always Windwagon would soothe him and tell him about Tomorrow and send him away figuring how much money could be made on one trip to Santa Fe. You couldn't doubt a man who believed as hard as Windwagon.

Shelby Foster was the only man in Westport that Windwagon couldn't convince. Foster stood around and wrote in his notebook and groused. He said he had learned in college how another damned fool once wanted to make a machine that would fly on the wind—somebody named Darius Green, he said. That led to Foster's quarrel with Rosalie Shafer. When Foster had come to Missouri he had tried once to ride a pony and taken one look at Rosalie, and decided to write his book in Westport rather than on the Trail. Before that, Rosalie hadn't had any beau except on Sunday nights when Punch would come over and sit beside her and talk about the mule business with Jake. She said Punch lacked imagination. Foster would kiss her hand and tell her she was a flower. They would sit close together and he would read poetry to her, the kind they learn in the New England colleges, about skylarks. But sometimes they talked about Windwagon Smith, and Foster said sensible men would lock Windwagon up, and Rosalie called Foster a coward and said he too lacked imagination, and they would sit at opposite ends of the bench and look at the moon individually.

Windwagon had imagination, Rosalie said. And finally she teased him into giving her a sailing lesson, and after that he went out often with her late in the afternoon, when the sun would glint like a Sioux bonfire on Rosalie's hair, and Foster would sit in front of the Star, looking as though he were chewing pickled nails. Rosalie might become a good sailor, Windwagon said; she had sea sense. But that's all he said about her. Foster still went to see her six nights a week, and Punch on Sunday nights, but Punch said she didn't act so interested in the mule business any more.

III

When two caravans wanted to buy windwagons, the men of Westport began to see what kind of business they were in.

'There's no end to it,' Windwagon said. 'When we build our fleet of a hundred we can squeeze almost everybody else off the trail. When we build a thousand we can take over the whole trade. Then we can build a thousand more and spread out into Iowa and Illinois and maybe start a water-level route beside the Lakes as far east as New York State. Then we'll build a million little wagons and sell them to the Oregon settlers. We'll keep the Santa Fe route to ourselves. We'll have our shipyards over there in the bottom by the creek, and start branches in St. Joe and Independence. We'll train other captains, and become admirals and have fleets under us.'

The Doctor calculated they could make two hundred thousand dollars the first year and six million the second. They got so tangled figuring what the income might be the fourth year that Windwagon forgot Rosalie's sailing lesson, and Foster sneaked over and read Milton to her.

One day half a dozen business men came up on the boat from St. Louis, looked at the wagon, and offered a thousand dollars cash for it; said they didn't know whether Windwagon was crazy or a genius, but they liked to gamble. Jake laughed at them. They talked to Windwagon a while and offered ten thousand, but Jake told them to go home and dig up some real money.

Foster said Westport contained seven kinds of fools, all bad.

A company of soldiers marched down from Leavenworth one day. They had heard that cannons were being mounted in the wagons to conquer an empire in the Southwest, like Aaron Burr's. There weren't any cannons. Some people thought Windwagon looked a little crestfallen; it was the only thing he hadn't thought of. The soldiers poked around and talked impressively about military possibilities.

Jim Bridger himself came in one day and spent a long time studying the wagon. He looked sad, as though he saw the old West changing. And Kit Carson came up, with his Indian wife, and talked a long time to Windwagon like a brother, and said he wished he were thirty years younger.

Westport was becoming a tourist town. The store stopped carrying powder and stocked little windwagons carved from soft wood. The print shop at St. Joe put out a souvenir booklet all about Windwagon Smith, saying that he had once been an admiral in the Scotch navy, had captured the Sandwich Isles from the cannibals, and had twice sailed around the world. Foster sneered that if the truth were known he'd bet Windwagon had a past a lot different from that. Rosalie said Foster had less imagination than Punch. Windwagon just laughed.

When the windwagon was done, it seemed that the whole population of the western territories came into Westport to see it. You could hardly shuffle your feet without stepping on a dog or baby. The windwagon was ten times as large as a Conestoga wagon, and built with two decks. Passengers could shoot buffalo from the upper deck when regular service started, Windwagon said. When the windwagon service was extended to Africa, they could shoot lions. It had a mainsail as big as a house, and the wheels were a foot wide and tired with iron. Yet, big as it was, it was so beautifully fitted and greased that it moved with hardly a push of the hand. Some were in favor of painting it red, white, and blue, like most of the wagons, but Windwagon said this must have dignity; this wasn't a wagon, it was a clipper ship. They made it blue with silver trimmings, and red spokes in the wheels.

The day before the first trip, the manager of an Eastern railroad said that he didn't think the ship would run but was willing to offer twenty-five thousand for complete rights. Jake was pretty uncertain for a while, and then talked to Windwagon, and came back and laughed and said they wouldn't take a million dollars for the clipper. He talked almost as convincingly as Windwagon.

The Westport Prairie Clipper Company invited the President of the United States to dedicate the new ship, but he regretted. However, two top-hatted men walked into the Star, and when Punch went up to them and said in the new grand manner, 'I am Captain Dunkelberger. I don't believe I have the pleasure of your acquaintance,' they looked at him oddly and one said he was the Secretary of the Navy and the other the Secretary of War. Then they borrowed ten dollars from him.

The prairie clipper was rolled out to the edge of town, and Rosalie Shafer broke a bottle of corn whiskey right prettily over one front wheel. Everybody yelled for a speech from Windwagon, everybody except Shelby Foster. Windwagon climbed up on the upper deck, blew his nose, hawked his throat, and began to talk with that faraway shine in his eyes.

'Ladies and gents,' he said, 'and them of you as has come a long way to see us today. I want to welcome you to the port of the prairie. And I thank you for coming to see our little ship, the first clipper ever built for trans-prairie shipping in America. And I wish I could tell you what this is going to mean to you. I wish I could paint a picture the way this prairie is going to look in five years. This ship you see here today is only a pack rat compared to the ships you are going to see tied up in this port. There'll be passenger ships and freighters big enough to carry this one on the poop deck, big enough to carry a whole caravan or a whole army. And there'll be little windwagons. Where there's big ones, there's usually little ones, you know. (*Long laughter.*) We'll make so many they won't cost much. And every one of you'll have a little wind-wagon in your barn, and you can get in it and go anywhere you want on the prairie just as easy as you put a chicken in a pot. This clipper shows that all you have to do is believe in these things and they'll come true. This is just like the sunrise on a new day, only you and me are helping to pull up the sun!'

In was the best speech Windwagon ever made, but he never made a bad speech.

IV

The maiden voyage, Windwagon called it, and said that only the real charter members of the company should go—and the Secretary of War and the Secretary of the Navy, if they were sober. The President could have gone, too, if he had come. But nobody else. Not even Rosalie, who almost bawled in front of everybody when Jake told her no. The passengers boarded the ship and waved their caps. Punch had a red feather in his. Then Windwagon climbed up to the seat he called the bridge, grabbed the tiller, and yelled, 'Cast off!' Jake's Negro boy took a block from under one of the wheels, and the clipper began to move.

There wasn't much jerk when they started, for Windwagon payed out the sail slowly, but in a minute Westport was a quarter mile away and the grass under wheel like a green rug. Punch said so later. In two minutes they could hardly see the ponies and the crowd, and Shelby Foster out in front in his red shirt, looking as though he were balancing the family tree on his nose.

They all said they had never felt anything like that ride. It was airy, like flying. This is the way a hawk feels, they guessed. This is the way it feels to scud in a three-master before the trade winds. The clipper swished past an ox team as though it were standing still. A Pawnee on a painted pony tried to race, but was left so far behind he got off his horse and gave the sacred salute of one thumb and four fingers.

Under full sail, the clipper rushed across the prairie. Occasionally it struck a gully or a dry creek bed, and then the body bounced on the springs, and the passengers bounced in their seats. Sometimes it swayed sharply as it hurried down a prairie swell. But the swaying and bouncing were mostly in the body. The great wheels rolled true and straight where the tiller pointed them.

'It runs like a flagship,' shouted Windwagon over the whine of the wind. 'It'll run to Santa Fe in a week.'

He had to give his attention immediately to steering over an acre of badlands. That was when Punch Dunkelberger bounced into the lap of the Secretary of War. Punch weighed three hundred pounds.

'I say,' said the Secretary, 'don't you think we are going rather fast? For a maiden voyage?' he added.

The Secretary of the Navy looked at the grass swirling past, then looked hastily away from it.

'Go up and talk to him,' the Doctor said to Jake.

Jake crawled to the front.

'Don't you think we are going a bit fast?' he said in Windwagon's ear. 'Confidentially, some of the passengers who aren't so used to this as we are seem to be getting a little frightened.'

Windwagon laughed. He threw back his head and laughed from his toes up, as free as the wind, happy as a child.

'This is just crawling,' he said. 'Tomorrow we'll be going over this prairie so fast we'll hardly need to touch the ground.'

Jake crawled back to his seat and closed his eyes.

'The man is mad,' said the Doctor.

'Knock him over the head,' said Punch.

'Then who'll steer and stop this thing?' asked Jake.

'True,' said the Doctor.

Windwagon looked back over his shoulder. 'Would you gentlemen from Washington like to ask any questions?' he called.

'Us? No,' grunted the Secretary of War weakly.

The sail thumped like a drum in the wind, and the stench of hot axle grease rose inside the wagon.

'What if we hit something at this speed?' said Jake.

'Or turn over?' said the Secretary of War.

'Don't worry,' said Windwagon.

'Can you pull the brake?' asked the Doctor.

'I think I'd better,' said Jake. He crawled forward until he could reach the lever.

When the brake caught, the wagon skidded, groaned, began to turn almost at a right angle. It leaned dangerously on its springs. The sail strained and the hickory mast trembled. The wagon came around, grandly, thrillingly. But it didn't stop, and it didn't come out of the turn. It shuddered, hesitated, then swung around so that it was running backwards, slowly at first, then faster and faster.

They said Windwagon gave one slow look at Jake. He didn't say anything. One slow look, more sad than angry, but Jake shriveled under it. And then Windwagon laughed again, that same free laugh from his toes to his mouth, but more rueful. He laughed and turned back and worked with the sail.

Later they knew what had happened. A brake on one wheel will stop a wagon going slow, but not a prairie clipper at full speed. The brake held just long enough to throw the clipper into a sharp turn and lock the steering gear. The sail turned on the mast and twisted its rope beyond chance of furling.

Far back, the crowd watched admiringly as the wagon bore down stern-first upon them, cutting a wide arc over the waves of prairie grass. Not until it was two hundred yards away did they stop cheering. When it was a hundred yards away, they scattered like a buffalo stampede. The prairie streamed pintos.

There were three little gullies in the path of the circle. Every twenty seconds the wagon hit a gully and the passengers bounced around like popcorn. About the tenth gully, the Secretary of War bounced out. He lit in a ball and rolled like a tumbleweed. Then he got up and ran like a jack rabbit away from the path of the wagon. 'Stop the ship!' shouted Jake. 'Stop the ship at once! We've lost His Honor!'

'You stop it,' Punch suggested.

'Excuse me,' said the Secretary of the Navy, and jumped. He yelled and sprang up and began to pick things out of his pants.

'Dwarf cactus,' observed Punch.

'Gentlemen,' said the Doctor, 'I know the consequences of broken bones. I do not advise jumping.'

Two more passengers jumped, and then another, and finally the Doctor himself. That left Windwagon and Jake and Punch.

'Father,' said a sweet voice in the wagon.

Jake covered his eyes with his hands. 'Did you ever hear of the voices of your beloved speaking to you just before death?' he asked Punch. Punch held tight and groaned. 'Speaking to me, too,' he moaned.

'Father,' said someone again.

Jake looked toward the back of the wagon.

'Rosalie!' he bellowed.

Rosalie was just climbing out of the compartment Windwagon had designed to hold liquids and pottery on the Santa Fe run.

'Rosalie!' said Punch Dunkelberger, between bounces.

'Miss Shafer!' said Windwagon, looking around quickly.

'What are you doing here?' Jake thundered.

'You know this is a very great thing,' yelled Windwagon above the roar of wind and wagon. 'Miss Shafer is the first stowaway in the history of prairie clippers.' He went back to working with the sail. They said he was just as calm as though this were a box social in the schoolhouse.

Jake said some short ugly words.

'You'd better jump,' Punch advised her.

'Don't you dare jump,' said Windwagon over his shoulder. 'You might get killed.'

'I'll take care of you,' offered Punch.

'You need a spanking,' said Jake.

'I don't need taking care of,' Rosalie said to Punch. She looked Jake in the eye.

'You pulled the brake, didn't you?' she said, low and hard.

Jake stared at her.

'You couldn't believe in Windwagon. You couldn't put your chips down and take a chance. You got scared. You pulled the brake.'

Jake made gurgling noises.

'I'm going up and sit with Windwagon,' Rosalie said. Once she looked back at her father and Punch, who was staring at the nearest exit.

'Don't give up the ship, Captain Dunkelberger,' she said sweetly.

The wagon whirled in its circle, the wind shrieking.

'There went Jake!' yelled Punch. Then Punch went.

He said he hit the ground unanimously, every square inch of him. He pulled himself out of the track and watched the windwagon. There was something beautiful about it even going backwards, something ship-like, birdlike, not wagonlike, with the wind filling out the sail blue-white against the blue-green grass. But he could see something from the ground he couldn't from the clipper: every circle was carrying it farther west. Already at its most distant point it was out of sight behind the swell of the prairie.

'Catch it! Catch it!' yelled Jake, limping along.

'Stop them!' yelled Shelby Foster, bouncing along on a borrowed pony, holding tight to the saddle horn.

The windwagon changed its circles into ovals, its ovals into a pattern that couldn't be made out because it was so far away. The last time anybody saw it, it was scudding backwards into the west, with Shelby Foster after it, far behind, occasionally taking one hand off the saddle horn to shake his fist. Rosalie and Windwagon were sitting close. Whenever they hit a gully they held to each other.

V

The Secretary of the Navy had to walk all the way back to town because he couldn't sit. The others rode back on borrowed ponies, each jog showing up a fresh bruise. In Westport it was like a picnic breaking up after everyone had got indigestion and poison ivy. Shelby Foster came into the Star and said politely, 'Good evening, Captain Dunkelberger,' and Punch chased him halfway into Independence. Punch had a bandage around his head and was pale as whitewash, but full of fight. It took the Doctor two hours to pick all the cactus spines out of the Secretary of the Navy. Then the secretaries stole two horses and gave a sort of generalized scowl at all of Westport before they rode away.

The town went back into the mule, powder, and bacon business, trying not to hear a tide of scornful laughter that rose in St. Joe and spread and bounced back and forth between the Rockies and the Appalachians. But history seemed to be moving past Westport. The wagons began to go farther north, and when the railroads came in they chose other towns. Westport shrank and Kansas City grew, and after a while Ka̶n̶ swallowed Westport and put its street railwa̶y̶

the Star had stood and built its municipal airport on the very land where the windwagon had begun its maiden voyage.

They never saw the windwagon again, although they searched the prairie as far as Council Grove. Of course, there were stories. Every once in a while a bullwhacker would be picked up barefoot and half-dead from thirst, and tell how his draft animals had suddenly reared up at a dust cloud and run away like antelope; and the worst drinker in Independence swore off and became an elder in the Lutheran church because he saw the ghost of a Conestoga wagon floating on the wind near the Pueblo. But that man was always seeing things.

Many a man saw Windwagon Smith after he left Westport, though. He was in the pilot house, he and a beautiful red-haired woman, when the first steamboat came up the Yellowstone, and they swear that nobody but Windwagon Smith held the golden spike when the two railroads came together at Promontory Point. And not long ago when the first transcontinental airplane roared out of Kansas City a little sandy-haired man closed the plane's door and waved the pilot on. The little man walked like a sailor, they said. His eyes seemed to burn, and he had the perpetual squint that comes from looking always at horizons.

The Sneaky Eels

"Now, you see, while I were keepin' Mr. Easley's mill," said Larkin, squinting his eyes and features, showing the remains of his little round teeth, nearly worn to the gums chewing tobacco, "I planted me a track patch near the bank uv the river, jist below the mill-dam. I knowed I could work it at odd spells, while the water were low and the mill ran slow, and I jist filled it with all sorts o' things and notions. But as all on us, the old Quilt (his wife), childering and all, was mighty fond o' peas, I were mighty pertic'ler to plant a mighty good share uv them; and to make a bully crap o' Crowders and all other sorts o' peas uver hearn on, I pitched them in the best spot uv the little bit uv yeth, near the river, clost on the bank.

"We, the old Quilt and I, spilt sevrul galluns uv humin grease workin' on 'um, and they growed monstus nice. We was a-congratterlatin' ourselves on the monstus crap we'd make, when we seed suthin' kept crappin' 'um, pertic'ler right on the bank uv the river. Uvry mornin' it was wuss and wuss. I soon seen the thing would be out wi' my peas ef thar warn't a stop put to it, fur thar wouldn't a bin a Crowder to sweeten our teeth with. I kept watchin' and watchin', but couldn't make the least 'scuvry. The fence were allers up good, the gate shot, and not the track of varmunts could be seen nur smelt, har nur hide. I were

―――――― Fisher's River (North Carolina), Scenes and Characters by "Skitt" [H. E. ―――ned thar." Pp. 142-148. New York: Harper & Brothers, Pub-

mighty low down in the mouth, I tell you. Starvation huv in sight; my sallet were meltin' away mighty fast.

"I were so mightily taken down 'bout it I couldn't sleep a wink; so I thort I mout as well watch. I sneaked along down to the bank uv the river through my pea-patch.

"The moon were shinin' mighty bright, and what do you think I seen? I seen 'bout five hundred big maulbustin eels dart into the river out'n my pea-patch. I soon seen through the dreadful 'vastation uv my black-eyed Crowders; the pesky eels had done it."

"Dang it, Larkin," said Dick Snow, "whar did sich a gullbustin chance uv eels cum from?"

"Eels, you see," continued Larkin, "ef you knowed the natur on 'um, are mighty creeturs to travel, and they'd cum up—a host on 'um—fur as the mill-dam, and couldn't git no furder. They had to live, and they'd cotched uvry minner, and had eat up uvry thing in the river about thar, and they moseyed out on my pea-patch.

"Now I were fur from lettin' them eat up my crap, so I put on my studyin' cap to find out the best plan to make a smash uv the whole bilin' on 'um. I soon hit the nail on the head, and fixed on the plan.

"You see thar were but one place whar they could git out'n the river inter my patch uv Crowders, and that were a narrer place, 'bout three foot wide, that crossed the river. I knowed it warn't wuth while to try to hold the creeters, they was so slickery; so, you see, I sot a big, whoppin bar'l near the river whar they cum out, near thar path. I told the old Quilt to fill it full uv dry ashes durin' the day while I were grindin', which she done, fur the old creetur thought a mighty sight uv her pea-patch.

"Now when night cum on, and a dark one too—a good night fur eels to graze, and when I thort all on 'um was out a-grazin', I sneaked along by the bank uv the river, mighty sly, I tell you, till I got to the bar'l. I then listened, and hearn 'um makin' the peas wake; so I jist turned the bar'l over right smack in thar path, and filled it chug full uv the dry ashes fur ten steps, I reckon. I then went up in the patch above 'um, gin a keen holler, and away they went, scootin' fur the river. You nuver hearn sich a rippin' and clatteration afore, I reckon. I knowed I had 'um; so, you see, I called fur a torchlight to see my luck. Now when the old Quilt and the childering brought the light, hallaluyer! what a sight. Sich a pile on 'um, all workin' up together in the dry ashes, like maggits in carron. The ashes were the very thing fur 'um, fur they soon gin up the ghost.

"I soon, you see, 'cided what to do with 'um. We went to work and tuck out'n the ashes five hundred and forty-nine, some uv 'um master eels. All the next day we was a-skinnin', cleanin', and barrelin' on 'um up. They'd got fat out'n my peas, but we got good pay out'n 'um fur it. The fryin'-pan stunk fur months with fat eels, and we all got fat and sassy. So I were troubled no more with eels that year; fur I think, you see, we shucked out the whole river."

The Jackpot Shot

This guy was huntin' and the gun he used was one of these muzzle loaders—you have to put your powder in, then your wad in, and then your shot. All right. He had plenty of powder, and he only had enough lead to load one time. So he looked and he could see a turkey settin' up on a limb. So he loaded his gun with this last load; then he looked back—beneath the limb stood a deer. Heard a racket down under his feet—was a rattlesnake. So he was settin' near a stream and he finally decided to shoot the turkey and take chances on the rattlesnake bitin'. So he was kinda nervous when he drew his gun. He shot a little too low. Part of his load went into the turkey, the other part went in the limb. The limb fell on the deer and killed him, ramrod fell out of his gun killed the rattlesnake. The gun kicked him backwards into the stream and when he came up he had his short tail full of fish. So he carried home deer, turkey, and fish.

High Tale

Two brothers I knew, who were pilots in World War I, were out on a reconnaissance mission together, when they ran into a formation of eight German Fokkers. They shot down all eight German planes, but one of the Heinies fell so close to the younger brother's plane that the flames fired the American's right wing tip.

"In a few minutes," says the older brother, "the kid's plane might have been a mass of flames. But without thinking, I started blazing away with my machine gun and cut about three feet of the burning right wing clear off. That took care of the flames—but the unbalanced wings then threw the kid's plane into a spin. This time it looked as if he were *really* finished. I followed him down. Then I got an idea. As soon as the other wing hove into view, I let go with my machine gun again, and cut three feet off the *left* side. That balanced things up. The kid pulled out of the spin and headed for home.

"The very next day the kid evened the score. A shell blasted the tail off my plane. He flew right underneath and held up the stub of my tail with his wing, while I climbed off into his cockpit."

From "Tales of a Mississippi Soldier," by Lt. Herbert Halpert. Told by Corp. Thomas W. Newell, of Richton, Perry County, Miss. *Southern Folklore Quarterly*, Vol. VIII (June, 1944), p. 112.

From *Tall Tales They Tell in the Services*, Edited by Sgt. Bill Davidson, p. 59. Copyright, 1943, by Thomas Y. Crowell Company. New York.

Brain Work

"Hey, I remember one time back in 1840, and pap, he sent me out huntin to git a hide for to make a pair of shoes. He counted the bullets and measured out the powder and I had to fetch a hide for every bullet or I got a tannun. Well, I hunted all day and didn't see nothin to shoot at except a few squirrels. So long about sundown I reckoned I'd kill a squirrel but every time I'd go to shoot at them dad-burned things they'd hide behind a tree and I couldn't see nothin but the head and I didn't want to shoot the head for pap warned me to bring the brains of anything I killed to tan the hide with. Well, I finally got mad and shot one in the head and I just about blowed all the brains out. That made me feel pretty bad. Well, I was in for a wallopun when I happened to remember there was a settlement of Missourians over the hill just about as far as I could see and twice as far as I could holler. Well, so I decided to go down there and shoot one them-there Missourians for some brains to tan that squirrel hide with."

"Oh, the heck you did," said one of the men.

"Yes, and I did," said Jack. "But that ain't the worst of it. Say, you know I had to kill nine of them-there Missourians to get enough brains to tan that hide?"

Better Than Heaven

An honest man died and soon was knocking on the Pearly Gates. Saint Peter opened his register: "Where are you from, my friend?"

"I'm a Southwesterner, Sir. Born and raised on the Mexican frontier."

"The sunny Southwest, eh?" The good saint was hesitant, but finally opened the gates. "Well, come on in. But you won't like it."

What a Whirl!

"I was on the gunboat Barracot, down Wilmington way," said the old mariner. "She was a light-draft boat, an' one day orders came from the flagship to take the Barracot an' go up a river there an' see if there were any rebs about. We went, an' we found the rebs, too.

From *Idaho, A Guide in Word and Picture*, prepared by the Federal Writers' Project of the Works Progress Administration, Vardis Fisher, State Director, pp. 395–396. Copyright, 1937, by Franklin Girard, Secretary of State of Idaho; Ira H. Masters, Secretary of State of Idaho. Sponsored by the Secretary of State. Caldwell, Idaho: The Caxton Printers, Ltd. Copyright, 1937, 1950, by Oxford University Press, Inc.

From *Sun in Your Eyes*, New Light on the Southwest, by Oren Arnold, p. 217. Copyright, 1947, by the University of New Mexico Press. Albuquerque.

From *Waifs of the Press*. Collected and Edited by Harry L. Work, pp. 188–189. Washington: Walter Neale, Publisher. 1898.

"The river was shallow, an' we had to take soundin's all the time. I was sent forward in the chains with the lead line an' was callin' off the deeps an' marks all nice an' easy when the dad-blamed rebels opened fire on us. A lot of sharpshooters was up on a hill, an' they got our range first-rate, an' the fust thing I knew I an' the man at the wheel was the only ones left on deck. All the rest of the crew had business below. Well, the steersman managed to shelter himself all right, but thar I was, way out on her bow an' no way to get under cover except I expose myself more doin' it.

"Well, the rebs got onto me quick enough an' begun firin' in my direction. I heard the first bullets fly by me, an', thinks I, it's about time to get under cover. I didn't know what else to do, so I begins whirlin' the lead line around my head. Well, I whirled that lead so fast that there wasn't no chance for a bullet to hit me. It was just like I had a solid shield in front of me, an' when we got out of range there was at least a pound of rebel lead stuck in the ship's lead where the bullets hit."

"Why didn't you keep that lead for a souvenir?"

"Well, I s'pose I ought to. But, say, them rebels made me so darn mad firin' at me that way that when we got safe out of range I just gave that ole lead line an extra whirl an' let her go, an' dad blame me if she didn't fly clean back an' kill three of the Johnnies. Yes, sir, that's a fact."

Lead Go

It happened down in the brush country. Two genuine Texas frontiersmen got into a difficulty and decided to shoot it out. They were both for a strictly ethical duel. Each had a long rifle. They met in a little opening, stood back to back, and then each took ten long steps straight out from the other. Simultaneously each turned around and with his right eye drew a bead on his opponent's left eye. Such precision was never seen even in the army. It wasn't considered sportsman-like to shoot out the other man's right eye, and thus spoil his aim. So, as has been said, each shooter aimed at the other's left eye.

"Well, they fired at the same instant, and much to their surprise, and to the surprise of several men who were watching, neither bullet took effect. They shot a second time. The result was the same. To make a long story short, they stood there, reloading and aiming and firing until they had shot ten rounds.

"By grabs, there's something spooky about this," one of them finally said.

"There shore is," the other replied. "Speerits in the air or something."

From "Great Liars of the Golden West," by J. Frank Dobie, *Vanity Fair*, Vol. 38 (March, 1932), No. 1, p. 31. Copyright, 1932, by the Conde Nast Publications, Inc. New York.

"I'm just about ready to shake hands," announced the first speaker.

"Shake. Here's mine," agreed the other.

The two men advanced, each of them taking ten long steps, so that they met face to face exactly where they had parted back to back. After they had shaken hands and each had bit a chew off one plug of tobacco to pledge their good will, one of them happened to look on the ground.

"Shades of Jericho!" he exclaimed, "what is that?"

"Lead, by grabs, and still hot."

In fact, the ground was spatted with a pile of melted lead. So accurate had been the aim of the frontiersmen, each sighting his long rifle at the left eye of his opponent, and both firing simultaneously, that the two hot lead balls had met midway, stopped each other, and melted down to the ground.

The Water of the Mississippi

. . . When I went up to my room, I found there the young man called Rogers, crying. Rogers was not his name; neither was Jones, Brown, Dexter, Ferguson, Bascom, nor Thompson; but he answered to either of these that a body found handy in an emergency; or to any other name, in fact, if he perceived that you meant him. He said:

"What is a person to do here when he wants a drink of water? drink this slush?"

"Can't you drink it?"

"I could if I had some other water to wash it with."

Here was a thing which had not changed; a score of years had not affected this water's mulatto complexion in the least; a score of centuries would succeed no better, perhaps. It comes out of the turbulent, bank-caving Missouri, and every tumblerful of it holds nearly an acre of land in solution. I got this fact from the bishop of the diocese. If you will let your glass stand half an hour, you can separate the land from the water as easy as Genesis; and then you will find them both good: the one good to eat, the other good to drink. The land is very nourishing, the water is thoroughly wholesome. The one appeases hunger; the other, thirst. But the natives do not take them separately, but together, as nature mixed them. When they find an inch of mud in the bottom of a glass, they stir it up, and then take the draught as they would gruel. It is difficult for a stranger to get used to this batter, but once used to it he will prefer it to water. This is really the case. It is good for steamboating, and good to drink; but it is worthless for all other purposes, except baptizing.

From *Life on the Mississippi*, by Samuel Clemens, Ch. XXII. Copyright, 1874 and 1875, by H. O. Houghton and Company; copyright, 1883, 1899, 1903, by Samuel L. Clemens; 1911, by Clara Gabrilowitsch. New York and London: Harper & Brothers, Publishers.

The Dusty River

The dust blows out of the Missouri River. It is the only river in the world where the dust blows in great columns out of the river bed. The catfish come up to the surface to sneeze. From the great wide-stretching sandbars on the Kansas shore great columns of dust and sand, about two thousand feet high, come whirling and sweeping across the river and hide the town, and sweep through the train and make everything so dry and gritty that a man can light a match on the roof of his mouth. The Missouri River is composed of six parts of sand and mud and four parts of water. When the wind blows very hard it dries the surface of the river and blows it away in clouds of dust. It is just dreadful. The natural color of the river is seal-brown, but when it rains for two or three days at a time, and gets the river pretty wet, it changes to a heavy iron-gray. A long rain will make the river so thin it can easily be poured from one vessel into another, like a cocktail. When it is ordinarily dry, however, it has to be stirred with a stick before you can pour it out of anything. It has a current of about twenty-nine miles an hour, and perhaps the largest acreage of sandbars to the square inch that was ever planted. Steamboats run down the Missouri River. So do newspaper correspondents. But if the river is not fair to look upon, there is some of the grandest country on either side of it the sun ever shone upon. How such a river came to run through such a paradise is more than I can understand.

The Canteen Fish

George [McCarthy] and a partner had been prospecting in the desert till they were far from any road or any other human habitation—or any water. They had built a little shack and were working toward the mouth of a canyon opening out of the mountains, on the theory that the rains and snows of many generations had washed gold down from the mountains. They knew torrents had come out of that canyon mouth at some time, because there was a deep sink in the desert which undoubtedly had been cut by those streams of long ago. But the two prospectors were miles from the nearest water hole, and all the "liquid silver" they had was in a barrel. (In the desert, "liquid silver" means water.) That barrel was their most carefully guarded treasure, for the water hole from which they had brought the water was drying up.

They knew they should turn back, but they had found traces of gold

---

By Robert J. Burdette. From *Gems of Modern Wit and Humor*, with Stories and an Introduction by Robert J. Burdette, Containing All that is Best in the Literature of Laughter of All Nations, pp. 367–368. Copyright, 1903, by L. G. Stahl. [No publisher or place.]

From *It's An Old California Custom*, by Lee Shippey, pp. 195–200. Copyright, 1948, by Lee Shippey. New York: The Vanguard Press, Inc.

and could not till they were down to their last two canteens of water. They were about to give up and return to their shack when they found a little nugget in some gravel. Then they became feverish with excitement. They went on and found some coarse gold in the sand, and then on and on, lured by small but shining pockets of promise.

They had used up all the water in their canteens, and the sun was sinking behind the encircling mountains, before they realized that they were far from their shack and very close to dangerous thirst, and that if darkness caught them they might get lost.

They built a marker of such stones, greasewood, and cactus as they could gather in a hurry and turned back. Then one of the sudden storms which occasionally burst in the mountains blotted out the canyon above them. Realizing that a cloudburst up there might mean a flood in the broad sink in which they had been panning, they hurried. But they were still in the middle of the sink when the flash flood was on them. A wall of water higher than their heads roared down on them and hurled them ahead of it, swimming for their lives. Their situation was desperate, but they were hardy men. Their effort was to keep afloat and let the flood carry them till its force diminished.

They were swimming so when George's outstretched hand closed on something slippery and wriggly. Fearing it might be a rattlesnake, he flung it from him so violently that it landed on the bank, which was dry, as all the rain had fallen in the mountains above them. But as he flung it he saw it was not a snake but a fish. Then both men found themselves in the midst of a veritable school of fish, which apparently were even more helpless in the flood than they were.

The fish swarmed about them, climbing on them. By that time the men had managed to drift toward the side of the sink on which they had made camp and found they were in shallower water. Though the flood was still rushing down the sink, they could touch bottom and could see the way to safety.

Still the fish eddied around them, as purposeful as swarming bees. Thinking a fine fish fry would be good for supper, they began grasping them with both hands and hurling them out on to the bank.

The situation had been so dramatic George hadn't stopped to wonder at the miracle of a school of fish in the desert, but at last, almost exhausted, he called:

"We got more'n we can eat in a week. Let's get out. I've heard of it rainin' fish, but darned if this ain't the first time I ever believed it."

"These didn't come from the sky," said his partner. "These are canteen fish."

"What are canteen fish?"

"You don't find 'em anywhere except in the Mojave," said the other. "They live in the little water holes scattered through the desert, and they're sort of queer shaped. Each one has a hump on its back like a camel, which it can fill with water. That's its canteen, and they always carry a reserve supply. They have some strange way of knowin' when a water hole is goin' to dry up and before it does they all fill their canteens and start off across the desert to some bigger water hole. Guess they can smell water twenty miles away. They march in a regular column, flippin' along on their tails. These poor fish musta been crossin' the sink when the flood hit 'em. They're not used to anything but shallow water, like you'd find around some desert spring, and if it hadn't been for us they'd have all been drowned."

So George and his partner, full of pity, kept on throwing the fish out onto the bank until they had tossed out hundreds. By that time George had noticed that each one did have a queer hump or tank on its back. The fish kept struggling toward the two men instead of striving to elude them, but many were swept away by the turgid waters, and George could not help feeling full of sympathy for them as he saw the despair in their eyes as they were carried out of reach.

When at last the two men climbed out of the sink their sympathy for the creatures whose lives they had saved made it impossible to kill and eat any of them. By that time the water was receding rapidly, and soon the desert, they knew, would swallow it up. So they ran to the sink, filled their canteens, and ran with them to their shack. They emptied them into the barrel and ran back for more water. If they could only get enough water in that barrel to wash out some of the gold, they believed their fortunes would be made. But by that time the water was being blotted up by the sand so rapidly that it was only a forlorn hope.

As they carried back their refilled canteens, and a bucket they had had in the shack, with another load of water, they realized they were leading a procession. All the canteen fish, flipping along on their tails, were following them. The men exchanged ejaculations of surprise but hurried on, having no time to do more than vaguely wonder. But as they emptied their canteens into the barrel the riddle solved itself. The leaders of the fish parade flipped up on top of things piled beside the shack till they reached the level of the barrel-top and emptied their canteens into it. All the other fish followed suit, after which they happily flipped away to the vanishing stream to refill their canteens and bring back more.

"They'd caught on to the fact that we wanted that water mighty bad," George says, "and were so darned grateful to us for savin' their lives they wanted to show their appreciation."

The Friendly Rattlesnake

A Marine I knew was out on the rifle range at San Diego one day, when he heard an ominous rattle close by. He whipped out his .45

From *Tall Tales They Tell in the Services*, edited by Sgt. Bill Davidson, p. 53. Copyright, 1943, by Thomas Y. Crowell Company. New York.

and looked around. There was a coiled young rattlesnake just in front of him. The Marine was about to shoot the reptile, but then he realized that the snake's rattling was not vicious. There was a certain amiable tone to it. The Marine came closer. Sure enough, the snake wanted to make friends.

This Marine took the snake back to the barracks with him. After the objections of the other fellows were overcome, the two became inseparable. The Marine named the snake Jack. He taught Jack to do tricks, and Jack stood guard beside his bed at night to prevent other Marines from absent-mindedly going through his barracks bag while walking in their sleep.

But then the Marine was transferred, and Jack was left behind.

A few months later, this same Marine was leading a patrol along a jungle path. He turned a bend and almost stepped on a huge rattler, which immediately coiled into a striking position. The Marine grabbed his pistol and aimed it at the snake's head. But something made him stop.

"Are you crazy?" yelled the man just behind him. "Shoot!"

"No," said the Marine with a faraway look in his eyes. "Listen!"

They listened.

The snake was rattling in Morse Code.

He was saying, "Don't shoot! It's your old pal Jack!"

The Leaky Stage-Coach Driver

. . . We had breakfasted at Horse-Shoe Station, six hundred and seventy-six miles out from St. Joseph. We had not reached a hostile Indian country, and during the afternoon we passed Laparelle Station, and enjoyed great discomfort all the time we were in the neighborhood, being aware that many of the trees we dashed by at arm's-length concealed a lurking Indian or two. During the preceding night an ambushed savage had sent a bullet through the pony-rider's jacket, but he had ridden on, just the same, because pony-riders were not allowed to stop and inquire into such things except when killed. As long as they had life enough left in them they had to stick to the horse and ride, even if the Indians had been waiting for them a week, and were entirely out of patience. About two hours and a half before we arrived at Laparelle Station, the keeper in charge of it had fired four times at an Indian, but he said with an injured air that the Indian had "skipped around so's to spile everything—and ammunition's blamed skurse, too." The most natural inference conveyed by his manner of speaking was, that in "skipping around," the Indian had taken an unfair advantage. The coach we were in had a neat hole through its front—a reminiscence of its last trip through this region. The bullet that made it wounded the driver slightly, but he did not mind it much. He said the place to keep a man "huffy" was down on the southern Overland, among the Apaches, before the company moved the stage line up on the northern route. He said the Apaches used to annoy him all the time down there, and that he came as near as anything to starving to death in the midst of abundance, because they kept him so leaky with bullet-holes that he "couldn't hold his vittles." This person's statements were not generally believed.

Ear-Marked

Years ago some cowboys were branding in the old Salero corral. The dust was so damn thick you couldn't tell a calf from a cowboy.

The branding and ear marking was going fast so that they could get into camp by dusk. After they were finished and the dust began to settle down a little, one cowboy lifted his hand to scratch his ear and to his surprise, he didn't have any!

The Gold in His Hair

. . . [This] is about the one time, in his youth that [Crazy Quartz Davis] did strike a good pocket, and made money enough to go to New York—or so he always said.

Davis used to love to tell about that trip.

"Made up our minds all at once, we did," he used to say. "Picked up and went, straight from the mines, just as we stood. Mud on our boots, mud in our hair, mud in our beards.

"But we got to New York all right and we set out to get the best there was. Gold? We had plenty of it. Nuggets all through our clothes, and every man had a good-sized sack of dust, too.

"We went to the best hotel we could find, left our gold with the manager and sat down to eat. Would you believe it? They brought us corned beef and cabbage! I told 'em what we thought of 'em and what we wanted. 'Bring the best in the house,' I said to 'em. 'Chicken and apple pie is none too good for us!' They called the manager. 'Give these boys anything they want,' he said. 'They're as rich as anybody in New York!' "

From *Folk Tales from the Patagonia Area, Santa Cruz County, Arizona*, p. 37. University of Arizona Bulletin, General Bulletin No. 13, Vol. XIX (October 1948), No. 4. Copyright, 1949, by the University of Arizona Press. Tucson.

From *Anybody's Gold*, The Story of California's Mining Towns, by Joseph Henry Jackson, pp. 354–356. Copyright, 1941, by D. Appleton-Century Company, Inc. New York and London.

But old Crazy Quartz always saved the best of his yarn to the last.

"After that," he used to go on, "we had to get shaved. Full beards like ours were no style in New York then.

"When we went into the barber shop I told the feller, 'Look here,' I said, 'I'll make a deal with you. Will you shave me for what you can get out of my beard?' He looked at me as though I was crazy. 'Certainly not!' he says. 'Very well,' says I, 'bring me a basin!' When he brought it I told him to see that every hair of my beard when he shaved it, and every hair he clipped off my head, fell into that basin. He didn't know what was up, but he was careful. It all got in. Then I says, 'All right, now get me some water and watch me!'

"He got me the water, and I sloshed all that mess of hair up and down, up and down in the water until every speck of dirt was out of it. Then I scooped it out and settled down to pan out the gravel that was left. Boys, I got five dollars and twenty cents in gold out of my beard, and that barber was the sorriest critter you ever did see!"

Crazy Quartz Davis died years ago, but that story of his lives on in Calaveras County, along with many another one of the old days. . . .

Bemis's Buffalo Hunt

Next morning just before dawn, when about five hundred and fifty miles from St. Joseph, our mud-wagon broke down. We were to be delayed five or six hours, and therefore we took horses, by invitation, and joined a party who were just starting on a buffalo hunt. It was noble sport galloping over the plain in the dewy freshness of the morning, but our part of the hunt ended in disaster and disgrace, for a wounded buffalo bull chased the passenger Bemis nearly two miles, and then he forsook his horse and took to a lone tree. He was very sullen about the matter for some twenty-four hours, but at last he began to soften little by little, and finally he said:

"Well, it was not funny, and there was no sense in those gawks making themselves so facetious over it. I tell you I was angry in earnest for awhile. I should have shot that long gangly lubber they called Hank, if I could have done it without crippling six or seven other people—but of course I couldn't, the old 'Allen's' so confounded comprehensive. I wish those loafers had been up in the tree; they wouldn't have wanted to laugh so. If I had had a horse worth a cent—but no, the minute he saw that buffalo bull wheel on him and give a bellow, he raised straight up in the air and stood on his heels. The saddle began to slip, and I took him round the neck and laid close to him, and began to pray. Then he came down and stood up on the other

From *Roughing It*, by Samuel L. Clemens, Vol. I, Ch. VII. Entered . . . 1871, by The American Publishing Company, copyright, 1899, by Samuel L. Clemens. New York and London: Harper & Brothers, Publishers.

end awhile, and the bull actually stopped pawing sand and bellowing to contemplate the inhuman spectacle. Then the bull made a pass at him and uttered a bellow that sounded perfectly frightful, it was so close to me, and that seemed to literally prostrate my horse's reason, and make a raving distracted maniac of him, and I wish I may die if he didn't stand on his head for a quarter of a minute and shed tears. He was absolutely out of his mind—he was, as sure as truth itself, and he really didn't know what he was doing. Then the bull came charging at us, and my horse dropped down on all fours and took a fresh start—and then for the next ten minutes he would actually throw one handspring after another so fast that the bull began to get unsettled, too, and didn't know where to start in—and so he stood there sneezing, and shovelling dust over his back, and bellowing every now and then, and thinking he had got a fifteen-hundred dollar circus horse for breakfast, certain. Well, I was first out on his neck—the horse's, not the bull's—and then underneath, and next on his rump, and sometimes head up, and sometimes heels—but I tell you it seemed solemn and awful to be ripping and tearing and carrying on so in the presence of death, as you might say. Pretty soon the bull made a snatch for us and brought away some of my horse's tail (I suppose, but do not know, being pretty busy at the time), but *something* made him hungry for solitude and suggested to him to get up and hunt for it. And then you ought to have seen that spider-legged old skeleton go! and you ought to have seen the bull cut out after him, too—head down, tongue out, tail up, bellowing like everything, and actually mowing down the weeds, and tearing up the earth, and boosting up the sand like a whirlwind! By George, it was a hot race! I and the saddle were back on the rump, and I had the bridle in my teeth and holding on to the pommel with both hands. First we left the dogs behind; then we passed a jackass rabbit; then we overtook a coyote, and were gaining on an antelope when the rotten girths let go and threw me about thirty yards off to the left, and as the saddle went down over the horse's rump he gave it a lift with his heels that sent it more than four hundred yards up in the air, I wish I may die in a minute if he didn't. I fell at the foot of the only solitary tree there was in nine counties adjacent (as any creature could see with the naked eye), and the next second I had hold of the bark with four sets of nails and my teeth, and the next second after that I was astraddle of the main limb and blaspheming my luck in a way that made my breath smell of brimstone. I *had* the bull, now, if he did not think of *one* thing. But that one thing I dreaded. I dreaded it very seriously. There was a possibility that the bull might not think of it, but there were greater chances that he would. I made up my mind what I would do in case he did. It was a little over forty feet to the ground from where I sat. I cautiously unwound the lariat from the pommel of my saddle—"

"Your *saddle?* Did you take your saddle up in the tree with you?"

"Take it up in the tree with me? Why how you talk. Of course I didn't. No man could do that. It *fell* in the tree when it came down."

"Oh—exactly."

"Certainly. I unwound the lariat, and fastened one end of it to the limb. It was the very best green raw-hide, and capable of sustaining tons. I made a slip-noose in the other end, and then hung it down to see the length. It reached down twenty-two feet—half way to the ground. I then loaded every barrel of the Allen with a double charge. I felt satisfied. I said to myself, if he never thinks of that one thing that I dread, all right—but if he does, all right anyhow—I am fixed for him. But don't you know that the very thing a man dreads is the thing that always happens? Indeed it is so. I watched the bull, now with anxiety—anxiety which no one can conceive of who has not been in such a situation and felt that at any moment death might come. Presently a thought came into the bull's eye. I knew it! said I—if my nerve fails now, I am lost. Sure enough, it was just as I had dreaded, he started in to climb the tree—"

"What, the bull?"

"Of course—who else?"

"But a bull can't climb a tree."

"He can't, can't he? Since you know so much about it, did you ever see a bull try?"

"No! I never dreamt of such a thing."

"Well, then, what is the use of your talking that way, then? Because you never saw a thing done, is that any reason why it can't be done?"

"Well, all right—go on. What did you do?"

"The bull started up, and got along well for about ten feet, then slipped and slid back. I breathed easier. He tried it again—got up a little higher—slipped again. But he came at it once more, and this time he was careful. He got gradually higher and higher, and my spirits went down more and more. Up he came—an inch at a time—with his eyes hot, and his tongue hanging out. Higher and higher—hitched his foot over the stump of a limb, and looked up, as much as to say, 'You are my meat, friend.' Up again—higher and higher, and getting more excited the closer he got. He was within ten feet of me! I took a long breath,—and then said I, 'It is now or never.' I had the coil of the lariat all ready; I paid it out slowly, till it hung right over his head; all of a sudden I let go of the slack, and the slipnoose fell fairly round his neck! Quicker than lightning I out with the Allen and let him have it in the face. It was an awful roar, and must have scared the bull out of his senses. When the smoke cleared away, there he was, dangling in the air, twenty foot from the ground, and going out of one convulsion into another faster than you could count! I didn't stop to count, anyhow—I shinned down the tree and shot for home."

"Bemis, is all that true, just as you have stated it?"

"I wish I may rot in my tracks and die the death of a dog if it isn't."

"Well, we can't refuse to believe it, and we don't. But if there were some proofs—"

"Proofs! Did I bring back my lariat?"

"No."

"Did I bring back my horse?"

"No."

"Did you ever see the bull again?"

"No."

"Well, then, what more do you want? I never saw anybody as particular as you are about a little thing like that."

I made up my mind that if this man was not a liar he only missed it by the skin of his teeth.

Educating an Englishman

The butler proved to be a genuine blackamoor, a Mr. Waterman, he informed me, his wife, also a black, being the cook. An elderly creature of the utmost gravity of bearing, he brought to his professional duties a finish, a dignity, a manner in short that I have scarce known excelled among our own serving people. And a creature he was of the most eventful past, as he informed me at our first encounter. As a slave he had commanded an immensely high price, some twenty thousand dollars, as the American money is called, and two prominent slaveholders had once fought a duel to the death over his possession. Not many, he assured me, had been so eagerly sought after, they being for the most part held cheaper—"common black trash," he put it.

Early tiring of the life of slavery, he had fled to the wilds and for some years led a desperate band of outlaws whose crimes soon put a price upon his head. He spoke frankly and with considerable regret of these lawless years. At the outbreak of the American war, however, with a reward of fifty thousand dollars offered for his body, he had boldly surrendered to their Secretary of State for War, receiving a full pardon for his crimes on condition that he assist in directing the military operations against the slaveholding aristocracy. Invaluable he had been in this service, I gathered, two generals, named respectively Grant and Sherman, having repeatedly assured him that but for his aid they would more than once in sheer despair have laid down their swords.

I could readily imagine that after these years of strife he had been glad to embrace the peaceful calling in which I found him engaged. He was, as I have intimated, a person of lofty demeanour, with a vein of high seriousness. Yet he would unbend at moments as frankly as a

From *Ruggles of Red Gap*, by Harry Leon Wilson, pp. 101–104. New York: Grosset & Dunlap. Copyright, 1915, by Doubleday, Page & Company.

child and play at a simple game of chance with a pair of dice. This he was good enough to teach to myself and gained from me quite a number of shillings that I chanced to have. For his consort, a person of tremendous bulk named Clarice, he showed a most chivalric consideration, and even what I might have mistaken for timidity in one not a confessed desperado. In truth, he rather flinched when she interrupted our chat from the kitchen doorway by roundly calling him "an old black liar." I saw that his must indeed be a complex nature.

From this encounter I chanced upon two lads who seemed to present the marks of the backwoods life as I had conceived it. Strolling up a woodland path, I discovered a tent pitched among the trees, before it a smouldering campfire, over which a cooking-pot hung. The two lads, of ten years or so, rushed from the tent to regard me, both attired in shirts and leggings of deerskin profusely fringed after the manner in which the red Indians decorate their outing or lounge-suits. They were armed with sheath knives and revolvers, and the taller bore a rifle.

"Howdy, stranger?" exclaimed this one, and the other repeated the simple American phrase of greeting. Responding in kind, I was bade to seat myself on a fallen log, which I did. For some moments they appeared to ignore me, excitedly discussing an adventure of the night before, and addressing each other as Dead Shot and Hawk Eye. From their quaint backwoods speech I gathered that Dead Shot, the taller lad, had the day before been captured by a band of hostile redskins who would have burned him at the stake but for the happy chance that the chieftain's daughter had become enamoured of him and cut his bonds.

They now planned to return to the encampment at nightfall to fetch away the daughter, whose name was White Fawn, and cleaned and oiled their weapons for the enterprise. Dead Shot was vindictive in the extreme, swearing to engage the chieftain in mortal combat and to cut his heart out, the same chieftain in former years having led his savage band against the forest home of Dead Shot while he was yet too young to defend it, and scalped both of his parents. "I was a mere stripling then, but now the coward will feel my steel!" he coldly declared.

It had become absurdly evident as I listened that the whole thing was but spoofing of a silly sort that lads of this age will indulge in, for I had seen the younger one take his seat at the luncheon table. But now they spoke of a raid on the settlement to procure "grub," as the American slang for food has it. Bidding me stop on there and to utter the cry of the great horned owl if danger threatened, they stealthily crept toward the buildings of the camp. Presently came a scream, followed by a hoarse shout of rage. A second later the two dashed by me into the dense woods, Hawk Eye bearing a plucked fowl. Soon Mr. Waterman panted up the path brandishing a barge pole and demanding to know the whereabouts of the marauders. As he had apparently for the moment reverted to his primal African savagery, I deliberately misled him by indicating a false direction, upon which he went off, muttering the most frightful threats.

The two culprits returned, put their fowl in the pot to boil, and swore me eternal fidelity for having saved them. They declared I should thereafter be known as Keen Knife, and that, needing a service, I might call upon them freely.

"Dead Shot never forgets a friend," affirmed the taller lad, whereupon I formally shook hands with the pair and left them to their childish devices.

A Wolfville Thanksgiving

"It's by this time that the drinkin' becomes frequent an' common. The talk gets general, an' the lies them people evolves an' saws off on each other would stampede stock.

"Any day but Thanksgivin' sech tales would shore lead to reecriminations an' blood; but as it is, every gent seems relaxed an' onbuckled that a-way in honor of the hour, an' it looks like lyin' is expected.

"How mendacious be them people? If I recalls them scenes c'rrectly, it's Texas Thompson begins the campaign ag'in trooth.

"This yere Texas Thompson tells, all careless-like, how 'way back in the forties, when he's a boy, he puts in a Thanksgivin' in the Great Salt Lake valley with Old Jim Bridger. This is before the Mormons opens their little game thar.

" 'An' the snow falls to that extent, mebby it's six foot deep,' says Texas. 'Bridger an' me makes snowshoes an' goes slidin' an' pesterin' 'round all fine enough. But the pore animals in the valley gets a rough time.

" 'It's a fact; Bridger an' me finds a drove of buffalos bogged down in the snow,—I reckons now thar's twenty thousand of 'em,—and never a buffalo can move a wheel or turn a kyard. Thar they be planted in the snow, an' only can jest wag their y'ears an' bat their eyes.

" 'Well, to cut it brief, Bridger an' me goes projectin' 'round an' cuts the throats of them twenty thousand buffalo; which we-alls is out for them robes a whole lot. Of course we don't skin 'em none while they's stuck in the snow; but when the snow melts in the spring, we capers forth an' peels off the hides like shuckin' peas. They's froze stiff at the time, for the sun ain't got 'round to thaw the beef none yet; an' so the meat's as good as the day we downs 'em.

" 'An' that brings us to the cur'ous part. As fast as we-alls peels a buffalo, we rolls his carcass down hill into Salt Lake, an' what do you-

From *Wolfville*, by Alfred Henry Lewis, pp. 259–267. Copyright, 1897, by Frederick A. Stokes Company. New York: A. L. Burt Company, Publishers.

alls reckons takes place? The water's that briny, it pickles said buffalo-meat through, an' every year after, when Bridger an' me is back thar, —we're trappin' an' huntin' them times,—all we has to do is haul one of them twenty thousand pickled buffalos ashore an' eat him.

" 'When the Mormons comes wanderin' along, bein' short on grub that a-way, they nacherally jumps in an' consooms up the whole outfit in one season, which is why you-alls don't find pickled buffalo in Salt Lake no more.

" 'Bridger an' me starts in, when we learns about it, to fuss with them polygamists that a-way for gettin' away with our salt buffalos. But they's too noomerous for us, an' we done quits 'em at last an' lets it go.'

"Nobody says much when Texas Thompson is through. We merely sets 'round an' drinks. But I sees the Red Dog folks feels mortified. After a minute they calls on their leadin' prevaricator for a yarn. His name's Lyin' Jim Riley, which the people who baptizes him shorely tumbles to his talents.

"This yere Lyin' Jim fills a tin cup with nose-paint, an' leans back listless-like an' looks at Enright.

" 'I never tells you-alls,' he says, 'about how the Ratons gets afire mighty pecooliar, an' comes near a-roastin' of me up some, do I? It's this a-way: I'm pervadin' 'round one afternoon tryin' to compass a wild turkey, which thar's bands of 'em that Fall in the Ratons a-eatin' of the pinyon-nuts. I've got a Sharp's with me, which the same, as you-alls knows, is a single-shot, but I don't see no turks, none whatever. Now an' then I hears some little old gobbler, 'cross a canyon, a-makin' of sland'rous remarks about other gobblers to some hen he's deloodin', but I never manages a shot. As I'm comin' back to camp—I'm strollin' down a draw at the time where thar's no trees nor nothin'—thar emanates a black-tail buck from over among the bushes on the hill, an' starts to headin' my way a whole lot. His horns is jest gettin' over bein' velvet, an' he's feelin' plenty good an' sassy. I sees that buck—his horns eetches is what makes him—jump eighteen feet into the air an' comb them antlers of his'n through the hangin' pine limbs. Does it to stop the eetchin' an' rub the velvet off. Of course I cuts down on him with the Sharp's. It's a new gun that a-way, an' the sights is too coarse—you drags a dog through the hind sights easy—an' I holds high. The bullet goes plumb through the base of his horn, close into the ha'r, an' all nacheral fetches him sprawlin'. I ain't waitin' to load my gun none, which not waitin' to load, I'm yere to mention, is erroneous. I'm yere to say thar oughter be an act of Congress ag'in not loadin' your gun. They oughter teach it to the yearlin's in the schools, an' likewise in the class on the Sabbath. Allers load your gun. Who is that sharp, Mister Peets, who says, "Be shore you're right, then go ahead"? He once ranches some'ers down on the Glorieta. But what he oughter say is: "Be shore your gun's loaded, then go ahead." '

" 'That's whatever!' says Dan Boggs, he'pin' himse'f an' startin' the bottle; 'an' if he has a lick of sense, that's what he would say.'

" 'Which I lays down my empty gun,' goes on this Lyin' Jim, 'an' starts for my buck to bootcher his neck a lot. When I gets within ten feet he springs to his hoofs an' stands glarin'. You can gamble, I ain't tamperin' 'round no wounded buck. I'd sooner go pesterin' 'round a widow woman.'

" 'I gets mingled up with a wounded buck once,' says Dave Tutt, takin' a dab of paint, 'an' I nacherally wrastles him down an' lops one of his front laigs over his antlers, an' thar I has him; no more harm left in him than a chamber-maid. Mine's a white-tailed deer over on the Careese.'

" 'This yere's a black-tail, which is different,' says Lyin' Jim; 'it's exactly them front laigs you talks of so lightly I'm 'fraid of.

" 'The buck he stands thar sorter dazed an' battin' of his eyes. I ain't no time to go back for my Sharp's, an' my six-shooter is left in camp. Right near is a high rock with a steep face about fifteen feet straight up an' down. I scrambles on to this an' breathes ag'in, 'cause I knows no deer is ever compiled yet who makes the trip. The buck's come to complete by now, an' when he observes me on the rock, his rage is as boundless as the glory of Texas.'

" 'Gents, we-alls takes another cow-swaller, right yere,' shouts Texas Thompson. 'It's a rool with me to drink every time I hears the sacred name of Texas.'

"When we-alls conceals our forty drops in the usual place, Lyin' Jim proceeds:

" 'When this buck notes me, he's that frenzied he backs off an' jumps ag'in the face of the rock stiff-laiged, an' strikes it with them hoofs of his'n. Which he does this noomerous times, an' every hoof cuts like a cold-chisel. It makes the sparks go spittin' an' flyin' like it's a blacksmith-shop.

" 'I'm takin' it ca'm enough, only I'm wonderin' how I'm goin' to fetch loose, when I notices them sparks from his hoofs sets the pine twigs an' needles a-blazin' down by the base of the rock.

" 'That's what comes to my relief. In two minutes this yere spreads to a general conflagration, and the last I sees of my deer he's flyin' over the Divide into the next canyon with his tail a-blazin' an' utterin' shrieks. I has only time to make camp, saddle up, an' line out of thar, to keep from bein' burned before my time.

" 'This yere fire rages for two months, an' burns up a billion dollars' worth of mountains. I'm a coyote if some folks don't talk of lawin' me about it.'

" 'That's a yarn which has the y'ear-marks of trooth, but all the same it's deer as saves my life once,' says Doc Peets, sorter trailin' in innocent-like when this Lyin' Jim gets through; 'leastwise their meat saves it. I'm out huntin' same as you is, this time to which I alloods.

" 'I'm camped on upper Red River; up where the river is only about twelve feet wide. It ain't deep none, only a few inches, but it's dug its banks down about your feet. The river runs along the center of a mile-wide valley, which they ain't no trees in it, but all cl'are an' open.

" 'It's snowin' powerful hard one evenin' about 3 o'clock when I comes back along the ridge towards my camp onder the pines. While I'm ridin' along I crosses the trail of nineteen deer. I takes it too quick, 'cause I needs deer in my business, an' I knows these is close or their tracks would be covered, the way it snows.

" 'I runs the trail out into the open, headin' for the other ridge. The snow is plenty deep out from onder the pines, but I keeps on. Final, jest in the mouth of a canyon, over the other side where the pines begins ag'in, up jumps a black-tail from behind a yaller-pine log, and I drops him.

" 'My pony's plumb broke down by now, so I makes up my mind to camp. It's a 'way good site. Thar's water comin' down the canyon; thar's a big, flat floor of rocks—big as the dance-hall floor—an' all protected by a high rock-faced bluff, so no snow don't get thar none; an' out in front, some twelve feet, is a big pitch-pine log. Which I couldn't a-fixed things better if I works a year.

" 'I sets fire to the log, cuts up my deer, an' sorter camps over between the log an' bluff, an' takes things as ba'my as summer. I has my saddle-blanket an' a slicker, an' that's all I needs.

" 'Thar ain't no grass none for the little hoss, but I peels him about a bushel of quakin'-ash bark, an' he's doin' well 'nough. Lord! how it snows outside! When I peers out in the mornin' it scares me. I saddles up, 'cause my proper camp is in the pines t'other side of this yere open stretch, an' I've got to make it.

" 'My pony is weak, an' can only push through the snow, which is five feet deep. I'm walkin' along all comfortable, a-holdin' of his tail, when "swish" he goes plumb outen sight. I peers into the orifice which ketches him, an' finds he's done slumped off that four-foot bank into Red River, ker-slop! Which he's at once swept from view; the river runnin' in onder the snow like a tunnel.

" 'That settles it; I goes pirootin' back. I lives in that canyon two months. It snows a heap after I gets back, an' makes things deeper'n ever. I has my deer to eat, not loadin' my pony with it when I starts, an' I peels some sugar-pines, like I sees Injuns, an' scrapes off the white skin next the trees, an' makes a pasty kind of bread of it, an' I'm all right.

" 'One mornin', jest before I gets out of meat, I sees trouble out in the snow. Them eighteen deer—thar's nineteen, but I c'llects one, as I says—comes sa'nterin' down my canyon while I'm asleep, an' goes out an' gets stuck in the snow. I allows mebby they dresses about sixty pounds each, an' wallers after 'em with my knife an' kills six.

" 'This yere gives me meat for seventy-two days—five pounds a day, which with the pine bark is shore enough. The other twelve I turns 'round an' he'ps out into the canyon ag'in, an' do you know, them deer's that grateful they won't leave none? It's a fact, they simply hangs 'round all the time I'm snowed in.

" 'In two months the snow melts down, an' I says *adios* to my twelve deer an' starts for camp. Which you-alls mebby imagines my s'prise when I beholds my pony a-grazin' out in the open, saddle on an' right. Yere's how it is: He's been paradin' up an' down the bed of Red River onder that snow tunnel for two months. Oh! he feeds easy enough. Jest bites the yerbage along the banks. This snow tunnel is four feet high, an' he's got plenty of room.

" 'I'm some glad to meet up with my pony that a-way, you bet! an' ketches him up an' rides over to my camp. An' I'm followed by my twelve deer, which comes cavortin' along all genial an' cordial an' never leaves me. No, my hoss is sound, only his feet is a little water-soaked an' tender; an' his eyes, bein' so long in that half-dark place onder the snow, is some weak an' sore.'

"As no one seems desirous to lie no more after Doc Peets gets through, we-alls eats an' drinks all we can, an' then goes over to the dance-hall an' whoops her up in honor of Red Dog. Nothin' could go smoother.

"When it comes time to quit, we has a little trouble gettin' sep'rate from 'em, but not much. We-alls starts out to 'scort 'em to Red Dog as a gyard of honor, an' then they, bustin' with p'liteness, 'scorts us back to Wolfville. Then we-alls, not to be raised out, sees 'em to Red Dog ag'in, an' not to have the odd hoss onto 'em in the matter, back they comes with us.

"I don't know how often we makes this yere round trip from one camp to t'other, 'cause my mem'ry is some dark on the later events of that Thanksgivin'. My pony gets tired of it about the third time back, an' humps himse'f an' bucks me off a whole lot, whereupon I don't go with them Red Dog folks no further, but nacherally camps down back of the mesquite I lights into, an' sleeps till mornin'. You bet! it's a great Thanksgivin'."

Cooking a Horse

In a late letter from the "seat of war" in Mexico, Kendall furnishes some capital sketches of the jokers in the army, from which we quote the following:—

Rare wags may be found among the Texas Volunteers, yet the funniest fellow of all is a happy-go-lucky chap named Bill Dean, one of

"Bill Dean, the Texan Ranger," by Geo. W. Kendall, Esq., of the N. O. *Picayune*, from *A Quarter Race in Kentucky and Other Sketches*, edited by William T. Porter, pp. 122–124. Philadelphia: T. B. Peterson & Brothers. 1858.

Chevallier's spy company, and said to be one of the best "seven-up" players in all Texas. While at Corpus Christi, a lot of us were sitting out on the stoop of the Kinney House, early one morning, when along came Bill Dean. He did not know a single soul in the crowd, although he knew we were all bound for the Rio Grande; yet the fact that the regular formalities of an introduction had not been gone through with, did not prevent his stopping short in his walk and accosting us. His speech, or harangue, or whatever it may be termed, will lose much in the telling, yet I will endeavour to put it upon paper in as good shape as possible.

"Oh, yes," said he, with a knowing leer of the eye: "oh, yes; all going down among the robbers on the Rio Grande, are you? Fine times *you'll* have, over the left. I've been there myself, and done what a great many of you won't do—I come back: but if I didn't see nateral h--ll,—in August at that,—I *am* a teapot. Lived eight days on one poor hawk and three blackberries—couldn't kill a prairie rat on the whole route to save us from starvation. The ninth day come, and we struck a small streak of good luck—a horse give out and broke down, plumb out in the centre of an open prairie—not a stick big enough to tickle a rattlesnake with, let alone killing him. Just had time to save the critter by shootin' him, and that was all, for in three minutes longer he'd have died a nateral death. It didn't take us long to butcher him, nor to cut off some chunks of meat and stick 'em on our ramrods; but the cookin' was another matter. I piled up a heap of prairie grass, for it was high and dry, and sot it on fire; but it flashed up like powder, and went out as quick. But—"

"But," put in one of his hearers, "but how did you cook your horse-meat after that?"

"How?"

"Yes, how?"

"Why, the fire caught the high grass close by, and the wind carried the flames streakin' across the prairie. I followed up the fire, holding my chunk of meat directly over the blaze, and the way we went it was a caution to any thing short of locomotive doin's. Once in a while a little flurry of wind would come along, and the fire would get a few yards the start; but I'd brush upon her, lap her with my chunk, and then we'd have it again, nip and chuck. You never seed such a tight race—it was beautiful."

"Very, we've no doubt," ejaculated one of the listeners, interrupting the mad wag just in season to give him a little breath: "but did you cook your meat in the end?"

"Not bad I didn't. I chased that d——d fire a mile and a half, the almightiest hardest race you ever heer'd tell on, and never give it up until I run her right plump into a wet marsh: there the fire and chunk of horse-meat came out even—a dead heat, especially the meat."

"But wasn't it cooked?" put in another one of the listeners.

"Cooked!—no!—just crusted over a little. You don't cook broken-down horse-flesh very easy, no how; but when it comes to chasing up a prairie fire with a chunk of it, I don't know which is the toughest, the meat or the job. You'd have laughed to split yourself to have seen me in that race—to see the fire leave me at times and then to see me brushin' up on her agin, humpin' and movin' myself as though I was runnin' agin' some of those big ten mile an hour Gildersleeves in the old States. But I'm a goin' over to Jack Haynes's to get a cocktail and some breakfast—I'll see you all down among the robbers on the Rio Grande."

III. SALMAGUNDI AND SLUMGULLION

(Rhymes and Wordplay)

Introduction

One of the main sources of folk laughter is wordplay, which may be simple punning on a word, punning within a joke formula, or playing with the meaning of a trite phrase. The pun is often damned as the lowest form of humor; whether or not it is the lowest, it is at least the commonest. Just as the little child is amused by words which have more than one meaning, so the adult who has retained the wide-eyed exuberance of childhood will probably enjoy the pun, albeit with more selectivity.

Puns are not always meant to be funny, of course, but most modern American puns are so intended, although many of them miss the mark. The reputation of puns has been seriously damaged by forced puns such as this: "As one Arab said to the other, 'Here comes the Caliph on your (California) camel.'" And the pun's good name has not been helped by the continued repetition of such puns as "Charge it to the dust and let the rain settle it" and "He's all right in his way, but he doesn't weigh enough." But puns can be amusing, as these two old ones should prove:

All Mormon women marry Young.

He built a commodious jail and put up a gallows, and to his dying day he claimed with satisfaction that he had had a more restraining and elevating influence on the Indians than any other reformer that ever labored among them.

Often puns are made more palatable by being concealed in some formula framework:

Why is a goose like an icicle? They both grow down.

She was only a postman's daughter, but you ought to have seen her handle the mails.

Run for the roundhouse, Nellie; they'll never corner you there.

Why did the little moron tiptoe past the medicine chest? He didn't want to wake up the sleeping pills.

I should worry like a river and be dammed.

You tell 'em, coffee; you've got the grounds.

Little Audrey saw her father drive off the cliff, but she just laughed and laughed, because she knew her father's car had floating power.

Knock, Knock. Who's there? Agatha. Agatha who? Agatha feeling you're fooling.

Two observations might be made about these formula jokes. One is that they are sometimes used to promulgate bad puns. The Knock-Knock series, for example, usualy incorporates a pun stretched out of all reason. The other observation is that when the formula joke involving a question is used very frequently, a type develops which plays tricks with the formula:

Why did the chicken cross the road? To get on the other side.

Knock, Knock. Who's there? Boo Hoo. Boo Hoo Who? What are you crying about?

Even the simple "Have you heard the one" opening may be made tricky by having the point in the question rather than in a later story:

Have you heard the one about the frustrated young mountain goat who wanted a peak for himself?

The serious writer or speaker avoids clichés, but the humorist turns them to good account. He makes them amusing by stacking them one upon another, as Ring Lardner did, or he leads the reader to expect the usual cliché and then surprises him by making some change in it: "Time and tide wait for no mannikin." A classic in varying a cliché by transposing sounds is that of the news correspondent in the Spanish Civil War who reported that the general had made the mistake of putting all of his Basques in one exit. The Wellerism is a formula joke which plays with clichés, for it begins with a phrase or sentence which we think we know the meaning of, such as "I may be down, but I'm not out." But then the speaker of the words is identified and we realize that our legs have been pulled: ". . . exclaimed the baseball player, as he successfully slid into second."

The poetic devices of rhythm and rhyme are enjoyable in themselves, but they become humorous when they are used with such unpoetic ideas as "Last look, you dirty crook." The use of rhythm, rhyme, and other poetic devices is not restricted to little children, for teen-agers talk of a "zoot-suit with a reat pleat" and dice players of all ages plead for "Little Joe from Kokomo" or "Ada from Decatur."

Comic Rhymes of Childhood

Amen,
Brother Ben,
Shot at a rooster,
Killed a hen.

* * *

Apple core,
Bite no more,
Point him out,
Hit him in the snout.

* * *

Aunt Jemima ate cake,
Aunt Jemima ate jelly,
Aunt Jemima went home
With a pain in her ——

Now don't get excited,
And don't be misled,
For Aunt Jemima went home
With a pain in her head.

* * *

Christmas is coming,
Turkeys are fat,
Please put a nickel
In grandpa's hat.

If you haven't a nickel,
A penny will do.
If you haven't that,
God bless you!

Do you carrot all for me?
My heart beets for you,
With your turnip nose,
And your radish nose;

You are a peach.
If we cantaloupe,
Lettuce marry;
Weed make a swell pear

* * *

Do you like beer?
A sock in the ear.

Do you like butter?
I'll punch you in the gutter.

Do you like jelly?
I'll punch you in the belly.

Do you like pie?
I'll punch you in the eye.

Do you want a nickel?
Suck a pickle.

* * *

Father may I go to war?
Yes you may my son;
Wear your woolen comforter,
But don't let off your gun.

* * *

From *Folk-lore from Adams County, Illinois,* by Harry Middleton Hyatt, pp. 643–656. Copyright, 1935, by the Alma Egan Hyatt Foundation. New York: Memoirs of the Alma Egan Hyatt Foundation. 1935.

Fatty on a steamboat,
Stinks like a nannygoat.

* * *

I had a little dog
And his name was Jack,
I put him in a box,
And he jumped through a crack.

* * *

I should worry, I should care,
I should marry a millionaire.

I should worry, I should cry,
I should marry another guy.

I should worry, I should fret,
I should marry a suffragette.

* * *

I told Ma,
Ma told Pa;
Harry got a licking,
Ha! Ha! Ha!

* * *

The wheel wouldn't run,
Sold it for a gun;
The gun wouldn't shoot,
Sold it for a boot;
The boot wouldn't fit,
So I threw it in the pit.

* * *

Harry, Harry, ain't no good,
We'll chop him up for kindling wood.

* * *

Here I stand all ragged and dirty,
Kiss me quick and I'll run like a turkey.

Here I stand on two little chips,
Come and kiss my sweet little lips.

* * *

I asked my mother for fifty cents,
To see the elephant jump the fence;
He jumped so high, he touched the sky,
And didn't get back till the fourth of July.

* * *

I beg your pardon, I grant your grace,
And hope the cat will scratch your face.

I beg your pardon, I'll grant your grace;
If that won't do, I'll spit in your face.

* * *

I had a little monkey,
I sent him to the country;
They fed him on gingerbread.
Biffo, baffo, they hit him on the head;
Now my poor little monkey is dead.

* * *

A generation ago children used to write rhymes such as the following in their textbooks:

I'm a little curly head,
My father is a preacher.
I love to go to Sunday school,
And listen to my teacher.

* * *

I'm a little Hindoo,
I do all I kindoo;
If my pants and shirt don't meet,
I'll make my little skindoo.

* * *

It is a sin,
To steal a pin;

It is greater,
To steal a potater (*potato*).

* * *

It's raining, it's pouring,
The old man is snoring.

* * *

I've got a rocket,
In my pocket,
I cannot stop to play.
Away she goes,
I've burnt my toes,
'Tis Independence Day.

* * *

If my name you wish to fine (*find*),
Look on page twenty-nine.
If you wish my name to see,
Look on page twenty-three.
If my name you wish to discover,
Turn back ten pages from the cover.
If my name you lack,
Turn four pages from the back.
If my name you want to know,
Look on page 1-2-0.

* * *

When two children separate and each tries to get the last look at the other, one will say:

Last look,
You dirty crook.

Little head, little wit,
Big head, not a bit.

When one child mocked another, the child mocked would say:

Mocking is catching,
Hanging is stretching.

* * *

Raccoon up a persimmon tree,
The possum on the ground;
He said you son of a gun,
Shake those simmons down.

* * *

Raccoon tail is ringed around,
Opossum tail is long and bare;

Rabbit has no tail.
Just a little bunch of hair.

* * *

Ring the bell to go to hell,
Climb the rod to go to God.

* * *

Tit for tat,
You kill my dog,
And I'll skin your cat.

* * *

Opossum up a gum stump
Raccoon in the holler (*hollow*):
Shake him down boy,
And I'll give you a quarter of a dollar.

* * *

Snow is white and coal is black,
If your pants are loose, pull in the slack.

* * *

A Tongue Twister

Peter, reater, eater;
Fish, alligators catch eels.
Eels catch alligators;
Fish eat raw potaters.

* * *

Tom was a bad boy,
Beat a poor cat.
Tom put a stone,
In the blind man's hat.

* * *

Tom was a bad boy,
Wouldn't say his prayers.
Along came the devil,
And kicked him downstairs.

What's your name?
John Brown.
Ask me again,
And I'll knock you down.

* * *

What's your name?
Pudding and tame.
Ask me again and
I'll tell you the same.

* * *

Where do you live?
Down the lane.
What's your number?
Cucumber.

Katydid, katydid, come from your tree,
And tell, little tattler, what did she?

*　*　*

Watchman, watchman, don't catch me,
Catch that —— behind the tree;
He stole gold,
And I stole brass;
Watchman, watchman, go to grass.

*　*　*

Ten little Indians standing in a line,
One went home and that left nine;
Nine little Indians swinging on a gate,
One fell off and that left eight;
Eight little Indians never heard of heaven,
One kicked the bucket and that left seven;
Seven little Indians cutting up tricks,
One broke his neck and that left six;
Six little Indians kicking all alive,
One went to bed and that left five;
Five little Indians on the cellar door,
One tumbled in and that left four;
Four little Indians out on a spree,
One dead drunk, and that left three;
Three little Indians in a canoe,
One tumbled overboard and that left two;
Two little Indians fooled with a gun,
One shot the other and that left one;
One little Indian with his little wife,
Lived in a wigwam the rest of his life;
One daddy Indian one mammy squaw,
Soon raised a family of ten Indians all.

*　*　*

The Irish and Dutch (*Germans*),
They don't amount to much.

*　*　*

Where was Moses when the light went out?
Down in the cellar eating sauerkraut.

Sassy Schooldays

Little bits of nerve,
Little grains of sand,
Make the biggest blockhead
Pass a hard exam.

* * *

Roses are red,
Violets are blue,
You like Miss Jackson,
So phooey to you.

* * *

Tattle tale, teacher's pet!
Tell it quick or you'll forget.

* * *

Monkey see, monkey do,
Copy cat number two.

* * *

Ashes to ashes,
Dust to dust,
Oil those brains
Before they rust.

* * *

Red, white, and blue,
I don't speak to you.

* * *

Flypaper, flypaper,
Gooey, gooey, gooey,
Flypaper, flypaper,
Hope it sticks on Louie.

* * *

Cross my heart and hope to die,
Eat a banana and holler Hi!

Teacher, Teacher,
I declare,
I see Mary's underwear.

* * *

Now you are graduating,
Isn't that fine!
You've been in the eighth grade
Since 1909.

* * *

Cheating shows,
Never goes.
The devil's right behind you.

* * *

Pins and needles,
Needles and pins,
Sass me again
And I'll kick your shins.

* * *

Liar, liar,
Your pants are on fire;
Your nose is as long
As a telephone wire.

* * *

Fatty, fatty,
Two by four,
Swinging on the kitchen door.
When the door began to shake
Fatty had a bellyache.

From *A Dillar A Dollar*, Rhymes and Sayings for the Ten O'Clock Scholar, Compiled by Lillian Morrison, pp. 122–131; 134–144. Copyright, 1955, by Lillian Morrison. New York: Thomas Y. Crowell Company.

Hickory leaves and calico trees,
All schoolteachers are hard to please.

* * *

All the curse words on the earth
All those I have learned from birth
Couldn't express what I feel for you,
Liking Miss Hayward the way you do.

* * *

Teacher, teacher made a mistake,
She sat down on a chocolate cake!
The cake was soft,
Teacher fell off.
Teacher, teacher made a mistake.

* * *

The more we study, the more we know,
The more we know, the more we forget
The more we forget, the less we know.
The less we know, the less we forget.
The less we forget, the more we know.
Why study?

* * *

Hot roasted peanuts
Tell the teacher she's nuts.
If she asks you what's your name
Tell the teacher she's a pain.

* * *

If dumbness were an occupation,
You would be a great sensation.

* * *

Smarty, smarty, smarty,
Thought you'd have a party.
Don't forget what the teacher taught,
You'll be sorry if you get caught.

I'm going to tell your mother,
Now see if you don't care,
You're nothing but a smarty cat
so there, there, there.

* * *

Birds of a feather flock together
And so will pigs and swine;
'Rats and mice will have their choice,
And so will I have mine.

* * *

"Where do you live?"
"On Tough Street. The farther you go, the tougher they get; I live
in the last house."

* * *

"What time is it?"
"Time all fools were dead. Ain't you sick?"

When someone says, "Hey!"

Hay is for horses,
Straw is for cows,
Milk is for babies
For crying out loud

or

Hey!
Straw.
What you can't eat,
You may gnaw.

The Sassy Speller

Spell Tennessee:
One-sy
Two-sy
Three-sy
Four-sy
Five-sy

Six-sy
Seven-sy
Eight-sy
Nine-sy
Ten-a-sy!

* * *

From *A Dillar A Dollar*, Rhymes and Sayings for the Ten O'Clock Scholar, Complied by Lillian Morrison, pp. 19–21. Copyright, 1955, by Lillian Morrison. New
York: Thomas Y. Crowell Company.

On a hill there is a mill,
From the mill, there is a walk,
Under the walk, there is a key.
Can you spell this name for me?

(*Milwaukee*)

* * *

Chicken in the car
And the car won't go.
That's the way to spell
Chicago.

A knife and a fork,
A bottle and a cork.
That's the way to spell
New York.

* * *

P with a little o,
S with a t,
O double f,
And i-c-e.
(*Post Office*)

* * *

A cin and a natty,
A skinny and a fatty,
That's the way to spell Cincinnati.

* * *

Bill had a billboard and also a board bill,
but the board bill bored Bill so that he
sold the billboard to pay the board bill.

A Parody of "Hiawatha"

He had mittens, Minjekahwun,
Buckskin mittens made of deerskin;
Mittens with the fur-side outside,
Mittens with the skin-side inside.
When he turned them inside outside,
When he turned them outside inside,
Then the warm side, fur-side, in was,
And the cold side, skin-side, out was;
When he turned them outside inside,
When he turned them inside outside.

They Have Riddles

In the farm house passing another crock of apples,
On the street car riding to the roller coasters,

Newspaper parody quoted in *The Feminine Fifties*, by Fred Lewis Pattee, p. 171.
Copyright, 1940, by D. Appleton-Century Company. New York.

From *The People, Yes*, by Carl Sandburg, pp. 95–96. Copyright, 1936, by Harcourt, Brace and Company. New York.

American soldiers who compiled them for the amusement of their friends . . . H.H.

1. Two morons joined the cavalry and got horses exactly the same and couldn't tell them apart; so one said he would cut the mane off his. That was O.K. till it grew back in. So then the other said he would cut the tail off his, and that was O.K. till it grew back in. They decided to measure them by hands then, and the black one was two hands higher than the white one.

2. Three little morons were sleeping in a bed. It was kind of crowded so one little moron put his pillow on the floor and slept there. The other one leaned over and said, "You might as well come back in; it's not crowded now."

3. The little moron's feet were hanging out of the end of the bed. The moon went by his window and asked him why he didn't cover them up. He said, "What, put those cold things in bed with me?"

4. The little moron wrote himself a letter and when asked what it said, replied, "I don't know; I won't get it until tomorrow."

5. The little moron told his mother he was glad she had named him Willy 'cause all the kids at school called him that.

6. The little moron was waiting for a 'phone call and couldn't wait any longer, so he took the receiver off the hook and left a note.

7. The little moron lost his watch on a hill, but wouldn't go back for it. He knew it would run down.

8. He wrapped his watch in cellophane to keep the ticks out of his pocket.

9. The little moron wrote letters to his girl very slowly. He said she couldn't read very fast.

10. He went to a show and was asked whether he wanted to sit up in the balcony or on the main floor. He said, "What's playing upstairs?"

11. And one killed his parents so he could go to the Orphan's Picnic.

The Adventures of Little Audrey

Little Audrey is a folk-lore character about whom thousands of nonsensical short tales—during the past five or six years—have been

By Cornelia Chambers. From *Straight Texas*, Publications of the Texas Folk-Lore Society, Number XIII, 1937, edited by J. Frank Dobie and Mody C. Boatright, pp. 106–110. Copyright, 1937, by the Texas Folk-Lore Society. Austin.

told. Sometimes Little Audrey parades as Little Emma or Little Gertrude, but she usually is recognizable by a catch phrase—"she just laughed and laughed." The amusing incident is typically a catastrophe. Little Audrey sees the humor in any situation.

A nice thing about Little Audrey is her integrity. She is no hypocrite; she does what she wants to do, says what she wants to say, and makes no bones about it. Little Audrey will never have inhibitions. Further, she is a very modern girl. She is having new adventures constantly, as indicated by the puns on floating power automobiles and the carioca dance steps. To her, irony predominates over sentiment. She has few illusions.

Little Audrey is nation-wide in distribution. In Texas she is well-known, particularly in universities and high schools. Approximately one out of ten students is a Little Audrey fan with a number of her adventures tucked away in his mind. The following are some of the stories known and collected by the author.

Little Audrey and her papa were out riding one day in their new streamlined car. Papa was proud of the car, and he was giving it the gas; he wanted to see how much it would make. All of a sudden the road turned, but papa did not; he went straight on and into the lake. Little Audrey saw what was going to happen, and she just laughed and laughed. She knew all of the time that their car had floating power.

Once upon a time all the children in Little Audrey's neighborhood were taking lessons. It was the proper thing to do; if you did not take lessons, you simply were not in the social swim. So Little Audrey cried and cried, 'cause she was not taking lessons.

After a while her mama said, "Little Audrey, if you will just stop that bawling, I'll let you take lessons." That made Little Audrey awful happy; so she sat down to think about what kind of lessons she would take. Well, after a long time she decided to take parachute lessons. So Little Audrey practiced and practiced, and after a while it was time to give her recital; you know if you take lessons you just have to give recitals.

Well, people came from far and near to see Little Audrey parachute jump. She went way up high in the airplane and got ready to jump. She looked down and saw all those people watching her, and then she jumped out. On her way down she just laughed and laughed, 'cause she knew she was going to fool those people; she didn't have on her parachute.

Once upon a time Little Audrey got lost on a desert island. Along came a big bunch of black cannibals and kidnapped her. They tied her up to a tree and started their pot to boiling. Little Audrey knew they were going to make stew out of her; so she looked around at those lean, hungry cannibals and counted them. There were nineteen.

Little Audrey just laughed and laughed, 'cause she knew she was not big enough to make enough stew to go around.

One day Little Audrey and her mother went for a walk in the forest where some lumbermen were felling trees. Just as they came along, the men cut down a big oak, and it fell right on mother! Little Audrey just laughed and laughed, 'cause she knew all the time that Mother couldn't carioca.

That night Little Audrey and her mama and papa and her little brunette sister were sitting at the dinner table. Papa said, "Little Audrey, pass the cream, please." So Little Audrey passed the cream to her papa, and he poured some into his coffee. Then he put the pitcher down, and Little Audrey noticed that right on the tip end of the spout there was a little drop of cream all ready to fall. Little Audrey just laughed and laughed, 'cause she knew all the time that the little cream pitcher couldn't go *sniff, sniff*.

One day Little Audrey was standing on the corner just a-crying and a-crying, when along comes a cop, who said, "Little Audrey, why are you crying?" And Little Audrey said, "Oh, I've lost my papa!" The cop said, "Why, Little Audrey, I wouldn't cry about that. There's your papa right across the street leaning against that bank building." Little Audrey was overjoyed; without even looking at the traffic she started across the street. Along came a big two-ton truck that ran over Little Audrey and killed her dead. The cop just laughed and laughed. He knew all the time that that was not Little Audrey's papa leaning against the bank building.

One time Little Audrey and her little brother were inspecting a ship. They went over it from top to bottom, and then little brother decided he wanted to go way up high to the crow's nest. Little Audrey told him he better not go, but he was awful hard-headed; so up he went. When he got up there he waved to Little Audrey, lost his balance, and came tumbling down. Little Audrey looked at the remains and just laughed and laughed, 'cause she knew all the time that her brother just could not stand hard ships.

One time Little Audrey took her grandpa out walking. Little Audrey got awful hot; so she said, "Grandpa, let's go down to the old swimming hole and take a swim." But grandpa didn't much want to, 'cause he was blind. But Little Audrey begged and begged, and finally grandpa agreed to go. So they went down to the old swimming hole and put on their bathing suits. There was a big tree, growing out over the water, that the kids used as a diving board. Little Audrey told her grandpa to climb up the tree and dive off. But he didn't want to; so Little Audrey had to make him. When he jumped off, Little Audrey just laughed and laughed. She knew all the time that the swimming hole had dried up.

Little Audrey's brother was a jailbird. One time when he was up for three years he broke out of jail. The sheriff looked and looked for him, but he couldn't find him anywhere. After about a month the sheriff decided to put the bloodhounds on the trail. And that made Little Audrey just laugh and laugh, 'cause she knew all the time that her brother was anemic.

One day Little Audrey and her mother were driving along when all of a sudden the car door flew open and Little Audrey's mother fell out. Little Audrey just laughed and laughed, 'cause she knew all the time that her mother had on her light fall suit.

The nurse was going to take Little Audrey out for a walk; but the nurse was absent-minded, and she forgot until she was outside to take Little Audrey with her. So she called up to the cook and said, "Cook, throw Little Audrey out the window, and I'll catch her on the second bounce." The cook threw Little Audrey out the window and then she just laughed and laughed. She knew all the time that Little Audrey was not a rubber ball.

One day Little Audrey's mama went to town, and while she was gone Little Audrey decided to bake a cake, 'cause she wanted to show her mama how smart she was. She got down the recipe book and mixed the cake according to directions. She sifted the flour, creamed the butter and sugar, beat the eggs, and stirred the ingredients together. Then she was ready to cook the cake; so she looked at the recipe book and it said: "Now set in the oven for thirty minutes." So Little Audrey crawled into the oven and closed the door.

By and by Little Audrey's mama came home. She looked everywhere for Little Audrey, but she couldn't find her. All of a sudden she smelled something burning. She opened the oven door, and there was Little Audrey, burned to a crisp. Her mother just laughed and laughed. She didn't know that Little Audrey could read.

The next day Little Audrey and her grandma were standing on their front porch watching the men pave their street. There was a cement mixer, a steam roller, and all kinds of things to watch. All of a sudden grandma saw a quarter out there right in the middle of the street. She dashed right out to get it, but just as she picked it up along came that old steam roller and rolled her out flatter than a sheet of theme paper. Little Audrey just laughed and laughed, 'cause she knew all the time it was only a dime.

One day Little Audrey was playing with matches. Mama said, "Ummm, you better not do that." But Little Audrey was awful hardheaded; she kept right on playing with matches, and after a while she set the house on fire, and it burned right down to the ground. Mama and Little Audrey were looking at the ashes, and mama said, "Uh huh, I told you so! Now, young lady, just wait until your papa comes home. You certainly will catch it!" Little Audrey just laughed and laughed. She knew all the time that papa had come home an hour early and had gone to bed to take a nap.

The next night Little Audrey and her date were sitting on the sofa when all of a sudden the lights went out. "Oh," said Little Audrey's boy friend, "it sure is dark in here. I can't even see my hand in front of me." Little Audrey just laughed and laughed, 'cause she knew all the time that his hand wasn't in front of him.

Conundrums

Which of the reptiles is a mathematician? An *adder.*
When is a boat like a heap of snow? When it is *adrift.*
When does a cabbage beat a beet in growing. When it gets *ahead.*
When is a young lady like a music-box? When she is full of *airs.* . . .
Why is the word yes like a mountain? Because it is an *assent.*
When is a dog like a tan-vat? When he's full of *bark.* . . .
Why is hunting for honey in the woods like a legacy? Because it is a *bee-quest.*
What does a drunken husband's thirst end in? Why, in *bier.* . . .
What is the best audience for an auctioneer? Why, *buy standers,* of course.
Why do old maids wear mittens? To keep off the *chaps.* . . .
Why is a cow's tail like a swan's bosom? Because it grows *down.*
When does a farmer act with great rudeness toward his corn? When he pulls its *ears.*
If a woman was to change her sex, what religion would she be? *He-then.* . . .
Why are old maids the most charming of people? Because they are *matchless.*
What fruit does a newly wedded couple most resemble? A green *pair.* . . .
Why is an attorney like a minister? Because he studies the law and the *profits.*

*   *   *   *   *

Why do hens always lay in the daytime? Because at night they become *roosters.*
At what time of life may a man be said to belong to the vegetable kingdom? When long experience has made him *sage.* . . .
Why is a hen immortal? Because her *son* never sets. . . .
Why should a thirsty man always carry a watch? Because there's a *spring* inside it.

*   *   *   *   *

Why is a photographic album like the drainer on a bar counter? Because it is often a receptacle for empty *mugs.*

From "Traditional American Wordplay: The Conundrum," by C. Grant Loomis, in *Western Folklore,* Vol. VIII (1949), pp. 236–241. Examples taken from the San Francisco *Golden Era.*

Why were the Egyptians good sons? Because they paid great respect to their *mummies.*

Why are a good many young men in this city like babies? Because they live on *pap.*

Why is it impossible for a man to boil his father thoroughly? Because he can only be *"par-boiled."*

When is butter like Irish children? When it is made into little *pats.*

If you wish to fatten a thin baby, what should you do with it? Throw it out the window and it will come down *plump.*

*   *   *   *   *

Why are suicides the most successful people in the world? Because they always *accomplish their own ends.* . . .

What is the key-note to good breeding? *B natural.*

What liquor would a lover be? *Beside her.*

Why is a widower like a potato plant? Because his *better half's* underground. . . .

Chain Conundrums

. . . Why is a dying man like a cobbler? Because he gives up his *awl,* looks to his *end,* and prepares his *soul* for the *last.*

Why is a beehive like a rotten potato? A beehive is a *bee-holder,* and a beholder is a spectator, and a *specked tater* is a rotten potato.

Why are ladies like watches? Because they have beautiful *faces,* delicate *hands,* are most admired when *full jeweled,* and need *regulating* very often. . . .

Why are the ladies the biggest thieves in existence? Because they *steel* their petticoats, *bone* their stays, and *crib* the babies. Yes, and *hook* their eyes.

Why is a beautiful young lady like a locomotive? She draws a *train,* scatters the *sparks,* and transports the *mails.*

*   *   *   *   *

What Is the Difference Between

I

What is the difference between stabbing a man and killing a hog? One is *assaulting with intent to kill;* the other is a *killing with intent to salt.*

Ibid., pp. 244–245.

Ibid., p. 245.

What is the difference between a legal document and a cat? One has *pauses at the end of its clauses,* and the other has *claws-es at the end of its paws-es.*

What is the difference between a photographer and the whooping cough? The one makes *facsimiles,* and the other makes *sick families.* ...

What is the difference between a wealthy toper and a skilful miner? One turns his *gold into quarts,* and the other turns his *quartz into gold.*

What is the difference between a schoolmaster and a railroad conductor? One *trains the mind,* and the other *minds the train.* It might be added that the conductor *looks before* when the switch is used, and the schoolmaster *looks behind.*

What is the difference between a piece of honeycomb and a black eye? One is produced by the *laboring bee,* and the other by a *be-laboring.*

What is the difference between a pretty girl and a night-cap? One is *born to wed,* and the other is *worn to bed.*

What is the difference between accepted and rejected lovers? The accepted *kisses the misses,* and the rejected *misses the kisses.* ...

What is the difference between a gambler and a theatrical critic? One is a *player at poker,* and the other is a *poker at players.*

II

... What is the difference between:

a D.D. and a M.D.? One *preaches and does not practice,* and the other *practices and does not preach.* (*Arthur's Home Magazine,* XXVII, 152, 1866)

a young lady and a looking-glass? The former *speaks without reflecting,* and the latter *reflects without speaking.* (*Ibid.,* XXVII, 299, 1866)

a school-boy and a postage stamp? One you *lick with a stick,* and the other you *stick with a lick.* (*Ibid.,* XXXI, 367, 1868)

a postage stamp and a lady? One is a *mail fee,* and the other is a *female.* (*Ibid.,* XXXI, 367, 1868)

* * * * *

an old dame at the spinning wheel and a young urchin chewing tobacco? One *sits and spins,* and the other *spits and sins.* (*Wasp,* III, 458, 1879)

a hungry man and a glutton? One *longs to eat,* and the other *eats too long.* (*Argonaut,* X, 14, 1882) ...

From "What is the Difference Between," by C. Grant Loomis, in *Western Folklore,* Vol. XV, No. 1 (January, 1956), pp. 62–63.

Literally Speaking

. . . Wanted: Some down from the bosom of a lake. . . .

An unfortunate young man is searching everywhere for his sweetheart who was recently carried away by her feelings. . . .

Wanted—The pockets of a coat of paint. . . .

A gentleman who was courting inquiry was found to be wedded to his own views. . . .

Wanted: A rocker for the cradle of the deep. . . .

There is a man in Totres so witty that his wife manufactures all the butter that the family uses from the cream of his jokes. . . .

Wanted—Coffins for the dead of night. . . .

The young woman who was driven to distraction now fears she will have to walk back. . . .

The public lecturer who dwelt upon a topic has changed his residence. . . .

A machine has been invented which is to be driven by the force of circumstances.

The man who ate his dinner with the fork of a river has been endeavoring to spin a mountain top. . . .

The small gentleman who has indulged so freely in biting sarcasm has taken to swallowing affronts. . . .

The man who kept his word gave serious offence to Webster, who wanted it for his dictionary. . . .

The Yankee who was lying on the point of death, whittled it off with his jack-knife and is now recovering.

*   *   *   *   *

The man who was lost in slumber has found his way out on a nightmare. . . .

Wanted: Some of the beer produced when mischief is brewing. . . .

Wanted: A collar for a neck of land. . . .

A thoughtless old gentleman the other day sat down on the spur of the moment. His screams were horrible. . . .

The latest curiosity: The original brush used in painting the signs of the times. . . .

The sieve through which the man strained every nerve is for sale. . . .

The lady who took everybody's eye must have a lot of them. . . .

From "Traditional American Wordplay," by C. Grant Loomis, in *Western Folklore*, Vol. IX (1950), pp. 148–150. Reprinted from *Harper's Weekly* and the San Francisco *Golden Era*.

Appropriate Naming

... Her name was *Ambrosia,* so he nectar. ...

They call her *Checkers.* She jumps when you make a bad move. ...

They call my twin brother *"Encore"* 'cause he wasn't on the program. ...

They call an Indiana judge *"Old Necessity"* because he knows no law.

A boy named his dog *Paste,* because "I want him to stick to me."

She calls him *Pilgrim.* Every time he calls he makes a little progress.

A Connecticut farmer has named a prize rooster *Robinson,* because Robinson Crusoe.

A man in a neighboring city calls his wife *Roe,* because she's a little dear.

A certain young man calls his sweetheart *"Silence,"* because when he wants to kiss she gives consent. ...

She Was Only a . . .

She was only a creditor's daughter, but she allowed no *advances.*

She is only a taxi driver's daughter, but you *auto meter.* ...

She was only a grave-digger's daughter, but you ought to see her lower the *beer.*

She was the village *belle,* so I gave her a *ring.*

She was only a fireman's daughter, but she sure did go to *blazes.* ...

She was only a plumber's daughter, but she had good *connections.*

She was only a milkman's daughter, but she was the *cream* of the crop.

She was only a film censor's daughter, but she knew when to *cut it out.*

She was only a surgeon's daughter, but oh what a *cut-up.*

She was only a photographer's daughter, but she was well *developed.* ...

She was only a hash-slinger's daughter, but how she could *dish it out.* ...

She was only a plumber's daughter, but oh, those *fixtures.* ...

She was only a blacksmith's daughter, but she knew how to *forge ahead.*

She was only a golfer's daughter, but her *form* was perfect. ...

He was only a garage man, but he had the *jack.*

Ibid., pp. 150–151. Examples taken from *The Pelican, Harper's Weekly,* and *The Golden Era.*

Ibid., pp. 151–152. Quoted from *The Pelican,* University of California humor magazine.

She was only a professor's daughter, but she *learned her lesson*.

She was only the daughter of a *mayor,* but she knew her oats.

She was only a lumberman's daughter, but she had been through the *mill*.

She was only a barber's daughter, but what a *mug* she had.

She was only a bar-tender's daughter, but she was a good *mixer*.

She was only a carpenter's daughter, but she *nailed* her man. . . .

She was only a baker's daughter in search of a little '*ovin*'.

She was only a teacher's daughter, but she was the college *pet*.

She was only the stage manager's daughter, but she had the loveliest *props*. . . .

She was only a cowpuncher's daughter, but she knew the *ropes*. . . .

She was only an optician's daughter. Two glasses and she made a *spectacle* of herself.

She was only a bottle-maker's daughter, but nothing could *stopper*. . . .

She was only a taxidermist's daughter, and, boy, she knew her *stuff*. . . .

She was only a watch-maker's daughter, but she gave me a wonderful *time*.

She was only a printer's daughter, but I sure liked her *type*. . . .

Jonathanisms

I

PERSONAL CHARACTERISTICS

. . . *Tallness.* A man who went to Virginia to get his growth, has become so tall that hot soup freezes before it goes down his stomach. When he eats meat, he is obliged to get that which is just killed, or it will spoil before it reaches his gizzard.

There is a boy out west, who is growing so fast that his shadow can't keep up with him. . . .

There is a chap in Albany so tall that he has to stand on a chair to button his shirt collar. This man is a relative to the one mentioned in the San Francisco *Golden Era* in 1869: They are going to have at Wood's Museum a man so tall that he has to go down upon his knees to put his hands into his trouser pockets. . . .

A man "out west" is so remarkably tall that he has to go up a ladder to shave himself. . . .

It is said of the chaps in Vermont who fear to grow tall, that they are about to eat aplenty of lard to make themselves short.

From "Jonathanisms: American Epigrammatic Hyperbole," by C. Grant Loomis, in *Western Folklore*, Vol. VI, No. 3 (April, 1947), pp. 211–227.

. . . This contribution aims to show the variety and range of the subject matter as it appeared chiefly in the three decades prior to the Civil War. . . . C.G.L.

It is reported that there is a boy in Vermont who grows so fast that his clothes are too short for him before the tailor can get them made, and that lately he grew so fast in one day that his head was seen protruding three inches through the crown of his hat. . . .

They have a man out west so tall that he lets himself out at camp meetings for a steeple.

Shortness. There is a man so short in Quebec, that he is obliged to stand on his own head to kiss his wife. . . .

Fatness. . . . The "fat girl" on exhibition at the Museum is so large that the cab is obliged to go twice to transport her from her lodgings to the exhibition room, it being impossible to carry her at one load.

When the fat girl at the Museum is invited out to take tea, her entertainer is obliged to darken the parlor windows, otherwise her shadow would make a huge grease spot on the carpet.

There is a man in Camberwell so fat that they grease the omnibus wheels with his shadow. . . .

They have a man in Mississippi so lean, that he makes no shadow at all. A rattlesnake struck at his leg six times in vain and retired in disgust. . . .

There is a man in Indiana so thin, that when the Sheriff is after him, he crawls into his rifle and watches his adversary through the touch-hole. . . .

Greediness. A man in William Street ate beef till he had horns grow out of his forehead; and he afterwards ate sausages till he barked like a dog. The *Golden Era,* twenty-five years later, presents the big drinker: There is a man out West who drinks so much whisky that mosquitoes that bite him die of delirium tremans (*sic*). . . .

Bigness. Everybody has heard of the man whose mouth was so large that he was afraid to laugh lest his head should fall off. There is a man in Boston whose eyes are so large that when he winks, the wind of his eye-lids will blow out a candle.

There is a man in Boston who was so large when a babe, that it was impossible to name him all at once. He was laid on his left side, when they called him Sam, and as soon as they could turn him over, he was named Snobble. A middle name was intended for him, but his body was so round, that it wouldn't stay.

A man in Kentucky was so enormously big, that when he died it took two clergymen and a boy to preach his sermon. As a contrast may be mentioned the runt who was so small it took two men and a boy to see him. The *Golden Era* in 1867, continues the tradition of Paul Bunyan with a reference: There is a man in Illinois so big that he fishes with a railroad "line" and smokes a stove-pipe.

The Sacramento *Age* tells us of a man in a political procession whose mouth was so large that an Irishman threatened to go and live in it if he didn't shut it. . . .

Deafness. There is a man in this town so deaf that his neighbors can't hear him when he screams. . . .

Age. In Vermont are two men so old they have forgotten who they are, and there are no neighbors living who can remember. . . .

Hair and Features. . . . There is a chap out West with hair so red that when he goes out before day he is taken for sunrise, and the cocks begin to crow. . . .

There was a man who had a nose so large that he couldn't blow it without the use of gunpowder.

There is a man in Farmington, Maine, whose nose is so long that it takes three cents' worth of gunpowder to blow it. He makes money during the cherry season, as he is able to hook his nose over a limb and pick cherries with both hands. . . .

Long Arms. There is a person who never allowed his servant to sit up for him, as he could put his arm down the chimney and unbolt the street door.

Strength. We once heard of a Kentuckian whose amazing strength was attended with fatal consequences. He was cutting a slice of bread and butter when the knife slipped, cut himself in half and two men behind him. The *Golden Era* in 1869, mentions a man so strong that he could lift himself three feet clear of the ground by his overcoat collar. . . .

Laziness. A southern editor declares, upon his honor, that he recently saw a loafer fall over the shadow of a lamp post in trying to catch a lightning bug to light his cigar with. . . .

The people of Peru are said to be so indolent that they open peapods with an oyster knife.

There is a family in Ohio so lazy that it takes two of them to sneeze —one to throw the head back, and the other to make the noise.

This family is obviously related to the one in Vermont mentioned in the *Golden Era* in 1863: There is a family in Vermont so lazy that it takes two of them to chop a stick of wood. Siah chops while Jim grunts, and then for a change, Jim chops and Siah grunts. This idea was expressed on the "Fibber McGee and Molly" program, November 27, 1945. . . .

Speed. There is a man in Oxford who lives so fast that he is now absolutely older than his father.

Uncleanliness and *Cleanliness.* . . . A citizen of Wisconsin, while bathing in the river discovered after an industrious scrub of five minutes a pair of drawers he had lost two years before.

An old maid, who was over-nice in regard to cleanliness about her house, once scrubbed her sitting-room floor until she fell through into the cellar. . . .

Sweetness. A man in Florida, who swallowed an orange seed last fall, has a breath so fragrant, that he says the ladies are constantly teasing him for kisses.

Absentmindedness. . . . A man intending to turn round quickly and look at a pretty girl, forgot to turn his body at the same time, and as he only turned his head, he wrung his own neck off.

* * * * *

A man lately put his dog to bed and kicked himself downstairs. He did not discover his mistake until the next morning. Another paper adds: He didn't discover his mistake until the next morning when he chased a cow and couldn't bark.

A gentleman while in church, intending to scratch his head, in a mental absence reached over into another pew and scratched the head of an old maid. He discovered his mistake when she sued him for a breach of promise of marriage.

An absent-minded Indianian who started out after his cow, found the cow-bell in the road, and pocketing it, followed its tinkling for over twenty miles before he remembered it was not on the cow's neck.

Long Memory. We know a man in this city who has a memory so long that he is obliged to tie a knot in it to enable him to carry it about with him.

Warm, Fond, and Tender Hearts. . . . The most tender-hearted man we ever saw was a shoemaker, who always shut his eyes and whistled when he ran his awl into a shoe.

Ignorance. There is a lady in New York so ignorant of all domestic work that she cannot even knit her brows.

There is a man living at St. Louis who is so wooden-headed that he has to shave himself with a jack-plane.

Modesty. There is a young lady in Maine so very modest that she cannot speak the naked truth.

There is a lady in Boston so modest that she lately discharged her cook for serving up a half-dressed leg of mutton.

There is a young lady in Lafayette, Indiana, so excessively modest, that every night before retiring she closes the window curtains to prevent the man in the moon from looking in. . . .

There is a maiden lady in Connecticut so modest that she turned off her washerwoman because she put her clothes in the same tub with those of a young man. . . .

Temper. There is a man who has such a good temper that he hires himself out in summer to keep people cool.

Meekness. . . . There is a man down East who is such an advocate of peace that he will not have a clock in his house, because it strikes.

Uprightness. There is a Quaker in Philadelphia so upright that he won't sit down to his meals.

Extravagance and *Parsimony.* . . . There is a local editor out West so poor, that he never stands upon more than one foot at a time, for fear that he may wear out his boots too quickly. . . .

There is a grocer who is said to be so mean, that he was seen to catch a flea off his counter, hold him up by his legs, and look into the cracks of his feet to see if he hadn't been stealing sugar. . . .

There was once a man in town so intensely polite that, as he passed a hen on her nest, he said, "Don't rise, ma'am." . . .

II

SKILLS

Artist. . . . A house painter in New York, grained a door so exactly in imitation of oak, that last year it put forth a quantity of leaves, and grew an excellent crop of acorns.

A daguerreotypist in this city lately took the portrait of a lady in such an admirable manner, that her husband preferred it to the original.

An artist of our acquaintance drew a horse and cart so naturally the other day, that when he put on the traces, the horse commenced drawing him. When last seen, the artist was pulling one way and the quadruped the other.

A man said of a painter he knew, that "he painted a shingle so exactly like marble that when it fell into the river it sank."

An artist painted a cannon so naturally the other day, that when he finished the touch-hole it went off. . . .

Shoemaker and Mason. A man down in Lynn, Mass., it is said, made so many pairs of shoes in a day, that it took two days to count them. He was a smart one, but not equal to a mason in New Hampshire who built so many miles of stone wall that it took him all that and the next day to get home again.

Watchmaker. A mechanic up town makes watches that go so fast they get fourteen days into a week.

Pie-Maker. A landlady in Philadelphia, it is said, makes her pies so light that her lodgers can see to go to bed without a candle, after eating a moderate-sized piece.

Boat-maker. A club boat has just been built, which is so nicely balanced, that the rowers are obliged to be particular in parting their hair down the middle to keep their balance.

Carpenter. A carpenter in our vicinity is already in the habit of using moon-beams instead of wooden ones in the erection of houses.

Barber. A barber in Vermont is reported to have three razors of extraordinary powers. The first is so sharp that it goes alone; the second has to be held back, and the third cuts about a quarter of an inch before the edge.

* * * * *

Fisherman. A man in Weston, Missouri, is so successful as a fisherman that he can tie a hook and line to each foot and dive in the river, and bring up a fish on each foot.

III

ANIMALS

Dogs. . . . A boy caught a hungry dog the other day, tied him by his tail, and coaxed him out of his skin with a piece of liver.

Horses. . . . A jockey at the Maze races, England, asked a Yankee if they had any such swift horses in America. "Swift?" said Jonathan, "I've seen a horse at Baltimore beat his own shadow a quarter of a mile at the first heat."

Pigs. They have got a pig in Ohio so thoroughly educated that he has taken to music. They regulate his tune by twisting his tail; the greater the twist, the higher the notes.

The farmer whose pigs were so lean that it took two of them to make a shadow has been beaten by another who had several so thin that they would crawl through the cracks of their pens. He finally stopped that fun by tying knots in their tails. . . .

Duck. A duck hearing the mistress tell the cook to kill and roast it for dinner, went into the garden and stuffed itself with sage and onions. . . .

Firefly. A Californian writes that they have fireflies so large in that interesting State, that they use them to cook by. They hang their kettle on the hinder legs of the fly, which are bent for the purpose like pot-hooks.

IV

WEATHER

Cold. . . . Last winter, it is said, a cow floated down the Mississippi on a piece of ice and caught such a cold that she has yielded nothing but ice cream ever since.

A down east editor has got such a cold in his head that the water freezes on his face when he undertakes to wash.

An exchange says that one of the frozen roosters found hanging by his claws to the limb of a tree at New Albany, Indiana, had his last crow sticking eleven inches out of his mouth and frozen stiff.

Snow. Snow flakes fall so large in Oregon that the ladies put handles to them and use them for parasols. . . .

Fog. They have fogs so thick in the vicinity of Newfoundland that a Yankee is about turning it to account. He intends to dry and use it for stuffing cushions instead of wool. See *Hoosier Folklore Bulletin,* I, 96–97: Fog was so thick that ink was poured on it, and it was sold for coal.

A sailor who has recently returned from Newfoundland says that the fog is so thick there that he used to drive a nail in it to hang his hat on.

Rain. It rained so hard in Arkansas lately that people had to jump into the river to keep from drowning.

Dryness. It is so dry up in Iowa that the steamboat people have to sprinkle the rivers to keep the dust from choking the water wheel.

Wind. Leggett, in one of his naval stories, speaks of a breeze, when "it blew the sheet anchor into the foretop, and took three men to hold the captain's hair on his head."

Healthful Climate. It is so healthy on the prairies that people never really die on them. They keep living until they gradually dry up and then blow away. Sometimes, when they want to die, as they do in the East, they move out of town and go down the river.

It is said that in some of the villages of the West it is so healthy that the folks have to shoot a man to start a burying-ground.

V

NATURE

Land. There is a place in Maine so rocky, that when down-easters plant corn they look for crevices in the rocks and shoot grain in with a musket.

A man who has traveled through New Jersey says that he saw some land there so poor that you couldn't raise a disturbance on it.

Some farms in Vermont are so steep that they require ploughmen with one short leg. . . .

An Illinois paper publishes an account of a queer hole on the side hill out there. The bank caved in, like so many other Illinois banks, and left a hole sticking out about ten feet.

Clear Water. A strange genius, in describing a lake in Minnesota says it is so clear, that by looking into it you can see them making tea in China.

Trees. There are trees so tall in Wisconsin that it takes two men and a boy to look to the top of them. One looks until he gets tired, and another commences where he left off.

The *Picayune* tells of a tree in his neighborhood which has grown so rapidly of late that it has actually pulled itself up by the roots.

VI

NATURAL AND MANUFACTURED OBJECTS

Watches. Some of the Chinese in California have silver watches so large that they use the outside to fry potatoes in. . . .

Steamboats. They are building a steamboat in Ohio so long that it takes two captains to command her, one at each end.

Yankee steamers are so light on the western rivers that they can jump over a sand-bar, float easily on wet grass, and are obliged to lie at anchor when there is a heavy dew.

The Lucy Long, a crack boat made for running in very shallow water, can run anywhere that the ground is a little damp.

When a steamboat gets aground on any of the western rivers, she waits till she gets the fever and ague and then shakes herself off. . . .

Crooked Fence. There is a piece of fence in Indiana made of pine rails so crooked that every time a pig attempts to crawl through it, he comes out on the same side from which he starts.

Dark Room. In a hotel in Washington, they have a room which is lighted only by the key-hole of another room.

Scarce Hay. Hay is so scarce in Texas that a friend informs us that it is served upon the table instead of salad.

Scarce Eggs. Winchell says the people in Alabama are so hard up for eggs that they have to set their turkeys on Carolina potatoes.

Tight Straps. There has been seen recently in Washington Street a young man whose pantaloon straps were so tight that he could not put his feet to the ground. It puts us in mind of a remarkable little dog whose tail curled so tight that it lifted him off his hind legs. . . .

Miscellany. . . . A Yankee in Vermont has such a remarkably hard name that he spoils a gross of steel pens in signing one check.

At a late railway explosion, the fireman was the only one who escaped. He was blown so far from the place that he was completely out of danger. . . .

Wellerisms

Not bigger; darn me, if 'tis, than the leetle eend—o' nothin'—sharpened; as the Irishman said [John Neal], *Brother Jonathan* [Edinburgh, 1825], I, 145).

That's sufficient, as Tom Haynes said when he saw the elephant (A. B. Longstreet, "Georgia Theatrics" [1835], in F. J. Meine, *Tall Tales of the Southwest* [New York, 1930], p. 339; *Colonel Crockett's Exploits and Adventures in Texas* [Philadelphia, 1836], p. 35).

One glance satisfied me that there was no time to be lost, as Pat thought when falling from a church steeple, and exclaimed, "This would be mighty pleasant, now, if it would only last" (*Colonel Crockett's Exploits and Adventures in Texas* [Philadelphia, 1836], p. 153).

I guess he'll re-wive, as the gentleman said when his friend fainted away at his wife's funeral (*ST*, X [1840], 231).

Hard times! and we must make the most of what little we have, as the grocer said when he watered the vinegar (*YN*, I [1852], 9).

Short visits are best, as the fly said when he lit on the hot stove (*YN*, I [1852], 29).

Hard times, and we must make the most of what little we have—

From "American Wellerisms of the Golden Age," by B. J. Whiting, *American Speech*, Vol. XX (Feb., 1945), No. 1, pp. 3–11.

The following abbreviations for sources are used: *ST—The Spirit of the Times, YN—Yankee Notions, NV—The New Varieties, WW—Wit and Wisdom.*

as the grocer said when he sanded the sugar and watered the rum (*YN,* I [1852], 75).

If you bite me, I'll bite you, as the pepper-pod said to the boy (*YN,* I [1852], 78).

Go it, porkey—root, hog, or d-i-e! as Shakepeel said when Caesar stabbed him in the House of Representatives (*YN,* I [1852], 272).

It isn't the size of the present that gives it its value, as the gentleman said when his wife gave him four boys at birth (*YN,* I [1853], 249).

How hot you are, as the roast beef said to the horse radish (*NV,* May 22, 1871, p. 11).

This is brief and to the point, as the man remarked when he got up off a tack (*Keokuk Gate City* [*WW,* June 2, 1881, p. 16]).

Let's shake, as ague said to the earthquake (Erratic Enrique [*WW,* June 2, 1881, p. 16]).

It beats all, as the Yankee shoemaker said when he saw the pegging machine at work (*Cambridge Tribune* [*WW,* June 16, 1881, p. 15]).

I am dressed to kill, as the recruit said when he donned his uniform (*Cambridge Tribune* [*WW,* Nov. 10, 1881, p. 16]).

Everybody to their notion, 's the ol' woman said when she kissed her kyow (Rowland E. Robinson, *Uncle Lisha's Shop* [New York, 1887], p. 139).

Phrenological Wellerisms

Philoprogenitiveness.—What blessings children are! as the clerk said when he took the fees for christening them.

Destructiveness.—It's a to-e-tal loss, as the sailor said when the shark bit his leg off.

Alimentiveness.—We're both matters of taste, as the gingerbread said to the fine picture.

Firmness.—The more you drive me, the firmer I am fixed, as the nail said to the hammer.

Marvellousness.—Shouldn't wonder if that made my head ache! as the sailor said when the cannon-ball smashed his skull.

Veneration.—All the world looks up to me, as the thief said when he stood in the pillory.

Mirthfulness.—I'll die laughing, as the ticklish man said when the sheriff was fixing the rope round his neck to hang him.

From *Yankee Notions,* Vol. III, p. 142. Reprinted in "American Wellerisms of the Golden Age," by B. J. Whiting, *American Speech,* Vol. XX, No. 1 (Feb., 1945), pp. 3–11.

California Wellerisms

1856

"Capital punishment," as the boy said when the mistress seated him with the girls. (*CD*, p. 9)

1857

... "You're just in time," as the watch-spring said to the flea which crept in at the key-hole. (*FJ*, 4.1)

1871

"What is home without a mother?" as the young lady said when she sent her old lady to chop wood. (*CST*, 33.1) ...

1879

... "You are beneath my notice," as the balloonist said to the receding crowd of gaping citizens. (*W*, 3.148.698) ...

"There is music in that sole," said the cook as she threw a fish upon the frying pan and it commenced fizzling. (*W*, 3.146.661) ...

"You be hanged," said the artist to his painting when he sent it in to the exhibition. (*W*, 3.141.581) ...

"Get thee behind me, satin," as the actress said when she kicked the train of her dress out of the way. (*W*, 3.131.426) ...

1881

"I haven't tasted a drop in the last ten years," as the tramp said when the serving-maid tendered him a glass of water. (*W*, 6.254.371)

"It's easy enough after you get your hand in," was the reply of the criminal with the fetters on his wrist. (*W*, 6.250.318) ...

"This suspense will kill me," as the murderer said upon the gallows. (*W*, 7.269.202)

1882

"Down with whisky!" screamed the temperance orator; and then he downed about three fingers of it. (*W*, 9.311.445) ...

1885

... "Come along with me and have a fine time," remarked the policeman to a man he arrested. (*W*, 16.5.10) ...

From "Wellerisms in California Sources," by C. Grant Loomis, in *Western Folklore*, Vol. XIV (October, 1955), No. 4, pp. 229–245.

Abbreviations are as follows: *FJ*—*Fireman's Journal*; *CD*—*Carrie and Damon's California Almanac*; *CST*—*California Spirit of the Times*; *A*—*The Argonaut*; *W*—*The Wasp*; *DE*—*The Daily Examiner*; and *P*—*The Pelican* (Berkeley). All but the latter journal originated in San Francisco. Volume, running number, and page are indicated by Arabic numerals, thus: 1.2.4 means volume one, running number two, page four. When only two numbers are given, volume and page are indicated. C.G.L.

1886

. . . "There are a great many ways of catching flies, but I still adhere to fly paper," as the man said when he sat down on a sheet of it. (*DE*, 42.171.1) . . .

1892

. . . "That was a pretty hard story to swallow," said the cellar when the upper part of the house fell into it. (*A*, 31.18.15) . . .

1893

. . . "Who says two heads are better than one?" exclaimed Jaggs, as he woke up the next morning and took a dose of bromo-soda. (*A*, 33.4.15) . . .

"I beg your pardon!" sang out the convict, as the governor passed by his cell. (*A*, 32.7.12)

1894

"How I pity the poor fellows whose business requires them to be out on a night like this," said the policeman, looking out from the side door. (*A*, 34.11.16)

1895

"One or the other of us is going to be turned down tonight," muttered the young man at the flickering gaslight, as he awaited his beloved in the front parlor. (*A*, 37.21.16) . . .

1898

"Talking about neckties, here's something that is perfectly killing," gayly remarked the Western sheriff, as he deftly arranged the noose. (*A*, 43.1116.16) . . .

1899

"I hope I made myself clear," as the water said when it passed through the filter. (*A*, 44.1153.16)

1903

. . . "One drop too much," mumured the repentant murderer, as he shot through the deadly trap. (*P*, 1.2.7) . . .

"After you," said the chaser to the whisky. (*P*, 1.1.13)

1904

. . . "My life has been a blank," groaned the cartridge, as he lay on the field after the sham battle. (*P*, 2.4.20) . . .

"I have a feeling for you," said the lobster to the bait. "I catch on," said the hook. And the lobster, who had a poor appreciation of humor, didn't see the point. (*P*, 2.1.18) . . .

1905

"I love you, my black darling," breathed the furnace warmly. "Hot air," retorted the Coal. Her thoughts were with a former flame. (*P*, 3.1.16) . . .

1907

... "Home was never like this," said Mr. Henpeck, as he was shown about the deaf and dumb asylum. (*A*, 61.1586.80)

1909

"This is easy picking," remarked the banjo player, as he started in with a new tune. (*P*, 7.4.n.p.) ...

1912

"I'm at my wit's end," said the king, as he trod on the jester's toe. (*P*, 12.1.n.p.) ...

"Blood will tell," quoth Macbeth, as he tried to scrub it off. (*P*, 13.1.n.p.) ...

1913

"Out of sight, out of mind," said the warden, as the escaped lunatic disappeared over the hill. (*P*, 15.1.n.p.) ...

1914

... "That's where I shine," said the young man, as he showed his blue suit to the tailor. (*P*, 16.1.n.p.)

"I'm all in," said the burglar, as he wiggled through the window. "There's something in that," he cried, as he spied the safe. "It's a hard blow," he remarked, as he reached for his nitroglycerine. "I feel blue," he exclaimed, as a policeman caught him in his arms. "I could stay here in a pinch," he said, as they took him to a cell. "That lets me out," he said, when he found a file in his mince pie. (*P*, 16.2.n.p.) ...

"I have a few more points to touch upon," said the after-dinner tramp, as he scaled the barbed wire fence. (*P*, 17.2.12)

"A little will go a long way," said the man, as he spit off the Woolworth building. (*P*, 17.1.27) ...

1918

"It's all up," he cried, as she crossed the floor ventilator. (*P*, 22.5.22) ...

1919

... "Yes, I guess I'll have to hang around here," murmured the convicted murderer, as he entered the prison. (*P*, 25.3.45)

1921

... "This lets me out," said the pickpocket, as he lifted the jailer's pass key. (*P*, 26.5.45) ...

1922

... "This settles you. Your name is mud," said the raindrop to the particle of dust. (*P*, 27.8.47)

"I'm cutting quite a figure," said the chorus girl, as she sat on the broken bottle. (*P*, 27.8.54) ...

1923

"We sure do rate," said Mr. Dun to Mr. Bradstreet. (P, 28.5.43) . . .

"These are the little things that count," cried the salesman, as he demonstrated the adding machine. (P, 29.4.51) . . .

"Now I've got you in my grip," hissed the villain, shoving his toothpaste into his valise. (P, 29.5.37)

1925

. . . "I may be down, but I'm not out," exclaimed the second baseman, as he successfully slid into second. (P, 30.8.42) . . .

"Here's where I shine," said the bootblack, as a customer hove into sight. (P, 31.2.13)

"Shucks!" cried the motorist, as he skidded into the corn field. (P, 31.4.67) . . .

1926

. . . "That's an old gag," said the cashier, as the bandit stopped up his mouth. (P, 31.5.36) . . .

"I'll take charge here," said the murderer, as he seated himself in the electric chair. (P, 32.4.88)

1927

. . . "So long, old top," said the man as his hat rolled into the sewer. (P, 32.7.36) . . .

1929

. . . "Well, I think I'll put the motion before the house," said the chorus girl, as she danced out on the stage. (P, 35.3.46)

"For goodness sake," sighed the young modern, as she wearily trudged home from an auto ride. (P, 35.3.46)

1930

"Man the winches," cried the captain, as he dismissed the crew for shore leave. (P, 35.7.18)

"I'll see you," said our hero, as he laid down four aces in a game of strip poker. (P, 36.1.31)

"This'll be on the house," said the sea gull, as he headed toward shore. (P, 36.1.35) . . .

1931

"Just an udder day," said the cow, as she rolled over for the night. (P, 36.5.2)

"Ah, well," said the painter, preparing a fresh canvas, "while there's still life there's hope." (P, 36.7.22)

"I take my fun where I find it," said the editor, as he looked over the contributions. (P, 37.3.13) . . .

1940

"Spit is such a horrid word," said the pig, as he was about to be barbecued. (P, 47.2.32) . . .

Wellerisms of the Eighteen Thirties

. . . "Come in"—as the spider said to the fly.

"Come on"—as the man said to the tight boot. . . .

"Every evil is followed by some good," as the man said when his wife died the day after he became bankrupt. . . .

"The day we celebrate," as the fat pig said to the cock turkey last Christmas. . . .

"Stick no *bills* here," as the loafer said to the musquitoes. . . .

"Take, oh take those lips away," as the gudgeon said to the shark.

"That's vat I call addin' insult to injury," as the rabbit said, ven they sewed his mouth up, and then told him to vistle.

"Thereby hangs a tail," as the monkey said ven he placed his hand on his rump. . . .

"Werry good, but rather too pointed," as the fish said ven he swallowed the bait.

"I'm up to *snuff*," as the wick said to the snuffers.

"It's of the first *water*," as the milk-man said ven his customers asked him if his milk was good. . . .

"Vot a scrape I'm in now," as the fish said to the voman who vas rubbing down his back vith a knife. . .

"You give me great *relief*," as the marble said to the sculptor.

"I'm winding up my business," as the silkworm said to Mr. Cleveland. . . .

"I'll cut your acquaintance," as the sword said to the gentleman ven he vos a goin' to fight his friend. . . .

"That's a thumper," as the mortar said to the pestle. . . .

"I saw you," as the wood sawyer said to the log of wood.

"I *paws* for a reply," as the cat said to the owl.

"I am clear grit," as the grindstone said to the razor. . . .

Old Saws

Concerning those who came West to the frontier:

"The cowards never started, and all the weak died on the road."

"Texas was fine for men and dogs, but hell on women and horses."

"When a bad man dies he goes either to hell or to the Pecos."

Axiom of the cow country: "A man on foot is no man at all."

Cattleman Bob Beverley, of the great virgin cattle country: "It

From "Wellerisms in *Alexander's Weekly Messenger*, 1837–1839," by James N. Tidwell, in *Western Folklore*, IX (1950), 257–262.

From *Texas Tradition*, by Ross Phares, pp. 190–192. Copyright, 1954, by Ross Phares. New York: Henry Holt and Company, Publishers.

and man, instead of the Federal Land Bank and the

speech to Texas Old-Time Trail Drivers Association:
have lived my whole life and drank out of a gourd
of a paper envelope."

Said of a cowboy pitting his luck against the professional gambler:

"He didn't have no more show than a stump-tailed bull in fly time."

"Never speak of ropes in the house of a man whose father was hanged."

Range-saying about what a man needed in the early West to get a start:

"A rope, a running iron, and the nerve to use it."

Many gems of wisdom are found among the mottoes and slogans of noted Texans:

Colonel Barnard E. Bee's observation on Santa Anna's attitude and consequent rout at San Jacinto:

"It's a dangerous thing to despise your enemy."

Old frontier saying, used by the Reverend Z. M Morrell in a speech:

"Never try to influence a man against his inclination when he is hungry."

Ranch motto:

"Thankful for a rain or a calf any time."

Governor Joseph D. Sayers:

"A Texas governor has only two happy days: the day he is inaugurated and the day he retires."

A rugged individualist, whose name is not known:

"Let's keep this country where every man is entitled to scratch his own itch."

IV. JOE MILLER RIDES AGAIN

(Anecdotes and Such)

Introduction

The anecdote is a short joke with a clear point. Anecdotes may be told either for their own humor or used to illustrate points in serious discourse. Whereas the yarn-spinner concerns himself largely with the manner of telling his tale, the teller of an anecdote is mainly concerned with making his point clearly and quickly. The teller of an anecdote or some speaker within it is figuratively playing a game of "pop-the-whip" with the hearers. In "pop-the-whip" the leader first

gets the line of boys with joined hands moving steadily and rapi‹
in one direction; he then reverses his direction suddenly, thus applyin‿
the "snapper." In a similar manner the teller of anecdotes gives only
enough description of character and narration of events to get the
mind of the listener moving in one direction; then he or some speaker
in the anecdote makes a quick and unexpected change in direction.
In playing "pop-the-whip" and in telling an anecdote it is necessary
to make the change fast and without warning. The point of the anecdote should always be unmistakable even if it is not clear to every
listener. Some people, you see, may be as insensitive to points as the
fellow who challenged a famous swordsman to a duel. During the
fight the swordsman had a good opening and made a fast, deft stroke
at the neck of the challenger, who laughed and said, "You missed."
To which the swordsman replied, "Let's see you shake your head."

Many anecdotes are about character, traits or people who have those
traits—stinginess or generosity, meanness or goodness, slowness or
swiftness, talkativeness or taciturnity, and the like. These stories are
likely to be attached to the name of some famous person with a reputation for that trait: laconic answers to Calvin Coolidge, homely
philosophy to Abraham Lincoln, caustic remarks to Dorothy Parker,
and "boners" in the language to Sam Goldwyn. As Alva Johnston has
pointed out, though, some of the so-called "Goldwynisms" can be
traced to sources other than Sam Goldwyn. The same can probably
be said about many of the jokes attributed to other famous people.

Many anecdotes are told about someone's repartee, the witty retort
which reverses the meaning of a previous remark. One of the best
examples of American repartee is John Randolph's remark to a man
who said, "I had the pleasure of passing your home this morning."
Randolph merely responded, "Thank you." Even more caustic is an
example attributed to Dorothy Parker. When a woman was described
as rude to her inferiors, Miss Parker asked, "Where does she find
them?"

Hacking at the Cherry Tree

In the South Mark Twain once met an exceedingly old servant
who claimed to have crossed the Delaware with Washington.

"Were you with Washington," asked Mark Twain mischievously,
"when he took that hack at the cherry tree?"

This was a poser for the old man; his pride was appealed to, his
character was at stake. After an awkward hesitation . . . "Lord, boss,
I was dar. In cose I was. I was with Marse George at dat very time.
In fac—I done druv dat hack myself!"

From *Mark Twain*, by Archibald Henderson, pp. 187–188. New York: Frederick A.
Stokes Company. 1911.

...ington was once at a dinner party, where his host had ...ı with his back to a fiery red-hot stove. Finding it quite too hot for comfort, after some squirming, he beat a retreat for a more comfortable position, at the same time explaining the reason. "Why," said the hostess, jocularly, "I thought an old general like you could stand fire better than that." "I never could stand a fire in my rear," replied the general.

Headwork

A clergyman in New Jersey owned a slave by the name of *Quash*, who was by no means fond of working, and one day told his master he conceived it a hardship, "dat he poor negar man mus worke so hard and massa do noting." "You are mistaken, *Quash*, my labor is more fatiguing than your's; I do head work, and yours is merely bodily exercise."

This hint was sufficient for *Quash*. The next day he was ordered into the woods to procure fuel; but *Quash* staying longer than usual, the parson repaired to the woods to see what detained him; when behold! the first object that presented itself to his view was *Quash* astride on a large maple log in a pensive attitude. When he enquired the cause, *Quash* starting up, and rubbing his *midnight brow*, "Oh! massa me-me have been doing head work."

"Well let me hear what your head has done."

"Suppose massa, dere be five pigeons on dis tree, and you take a gun and shoot two of dem, how many dere be left?"

"Why three, you old sinner."

"No, massa, dem toder tree fly away."

Goldwynisms

. . . [Goldwyn] can often put things more forcefully in his own medium of expression than they could possibly be said in the king's English. An ordinary man . . . might have turned to his fellow pro-

---

From *The American Jest Book, containing a curious variety of Jests, Anecdotes, Bon Mots, Stories* . . . , p. 184, Philadelphia: Printed for M. Carey & W. Spotswood. 1789.

From *The American Jest Book, containing a curious variety of Jests, Anecdotes, Bon Mots, Stories* . . . Philadelphia: Printed for M. Carey & W. Spotswood. 1789.

From *The Great Goldwyn, by Alva Johnston* . . . , pp. 16–17, 24–25, 27–29, 65–66. Copyright, 1937, by Random House, Inc. New York.

ducers and said, "Gentlemen . . . I have decided to go my own way
Sam said, "Gentlemen, include me out." It would be impossible to
make a more pointed remark than Goldwyn's, "A verbal contract isn't
worth the paper it's written on." One day, after slicing five or six
golf balls, he made a beautiful drive; he turned to the caddy and
asked, "What did I do right?" The true Goldwyn line is seldom a
boner or a howler. It is usually a plain statement with a slight twist;
as, for example, his exclamation at the beach one lovely Sunday morning, "What a wonderful day to spend Sunday!"

* * *

[Sam Goldwyn] stated his philosophy when he had an argument
with another company over the services of William Anthony McGuire,
who wrote *The Great Ziegfeld*. Sam wanted McGuire badly. So did
the other producer. Both sides claimed to have him under contract.
The only solution was arbitration. "All right," said Sam. "I'm a fair
man. I'll submit anything to arbitration. But remember, no matter
what is decided, McGuire goes to work for me."

* * *

Chico Marx said, "Sam [Goldwyn] is the only man in the world who
can throw a seven with one die." Charles MacArthur once slapped
Sam's hand and said, "That's cheating." "What's that between us?"
said Sam.

* * *

Sam [Goldwyn] scolded his partner, Constance Bennett, once for
overbidding her hand.
"How did I know you had nothing?" she asked.
"Didn't you hear me keeping still?" asked Sam.

* * *

Before Sam [Goldwyn] arrived in Hollywood, the official unconscious humorists were two brothers who made short comic pictures.
The brothers became obscure; Sam became famous. The old anecdotes
deserted the brothers and attached themselves to Goldwyn. "Our com-
edies are not to be laughed at" is one of the lines that abandoned the
original author and joined the Goldwyn legend. Another was a telegram sent by one of the brothers after their studio had burned: "If
there is nothing left to watch, fire the watchman." When a director
asked the brothers to send him to the Rockies to shoot cliffs and
forests, the reply was, "A rock's a rock and a tree's a tree; shoot it in
Griffith Park. . . ."
"I can answer you in two words, 'Im possible,' " is almost the cor-
nerstone of the Goldwyn legend, but Sam did not say it. It was printed
late in 1925 in a humorous magazine and credited to an anonymous
Potash or Perlmutter. An executive in the Chaplin studio pointed it

Chaplin, saying, "It sounds like Sam Goldwyn." Chaplin on Sam," and he repeated it until it became a
dwynism. "I read part of it all the way through,"
in. . . .

* * *

. . . The sun-dial story, which is having a vogue now [1937] runs:
"What's that?" asks Sam.
"A sun-dial."
"What's it for?" asks Sam.
"It tells time by the sun."
"My, my, what won't they do next?"

* * *

. . . Probably the most actively circulated Goldwyn story today is
that someone said, "What beautiful hands your wife has," and that
Sam replied, "Yes, I'm going to have a bust made of them."

* * *

. . . There are reliable witnesses who are sure they heard Sam [Gold-
wyn] say, "It rolls off my back like a duck," when Sam's publicity
man showed him a bunch of newspaper reviews damning one of his
pictures. Charles MacArthur, a Goldwyn expert, challenged its au-
thenticity. . . . The duck's-back line was alleged to lack the Goldwyn
rhythm. Later it came to light that it had been invented at the Goldwyn studio restaurant. Members of the staff had amused themselves at
lunch every day for a week by trying to say things as Sam might have
said them. . . .

* * *

. . . One of the standard Goldwyn lines was plagiarized from George
M. Cohan. "Never let that —— in this office again," shouted Cohan;
then, feeling a little ridiculous and turning the joke against himself,
he added, "unless we need him." The conscious humor is omitted
from the line as transplanted to Goldwyn, who is supposed to have
said, "Never let that —— on this lot again unless we need him." . . .

* * *

. . . [Goldwyn] was astonished at the enormous size of a volume
which was brought forth at a Hollywood party to be consulted at the
game of Guggenheim.
"What a big book!" said Sam. "Who wrote it?"
"Webster," was the reply.
"It must have taken him a long time."
"About a century."
"My, my!" said Sam. "Fifty years!"

* * *

Ask a Nasty Question, Get a Nasty Answer

WADE HAMPTON'S STORY

According to a Washington letter, Senator Wade Hampton is a good story teller. As far as is known he is up to this time the only man who has had the temerity to tell the President an impious tale, and General Harrison was actually very much pleased with the narrative. "I always did like army stories," he says, "and you can't expect army stories to be good enough to tell a Sunday-school class. I forgave the profanity of Senator Hampton's story out of consideration for its wit."

"One day during the war," said the Senator, "the Colonel of a South Carolina regiment was making a round of inspection. Sitting lazily on a rail fence whittling at a piece of shingle he found a man whose face was not familiar to him. The Colonel was indignant. Approaching the loafer he called out to him with all proper severity. 'Who the —— are you, sitting here in this fashion?' 'I sir,' responded the man on the fence, continuing his whittling, 'am the chaplain of the ——st regiment. Now, who in —— are you?' "

Pretty Good for an Indian

One day, an Indian in Colorado walked into a country store, with his gun on his shoulder, and told the proprietor he had killed a deer, which he would give him in exchange for a gallon of whiskey.

"Where is your deer?"

"Go down that lane till you come to a field-gate, open it and cross the field, climb over the fence, there is a large oak tree. The deer hangs on that tree."

The gallon of whiskey was delivered. The next day the Indian came into the store.

"You lying Indian," exclaimed the proprietor in a rage, "there was no deer on that oak tree! You shall be punished for lying and cheating."

"Did you find the lane?"

"Yes."

"Did you find the field-gate?"

"Yes."

"Did you find the oak tree?"

"Yes; but I did not find the deer."

"Well, I told you three truths to one lie, and that's pretty good for an Indian."

From *New Yarns and Funny Jokes Comprising Original and Selected American Humor . . .* , p. 57. New York: Excelsior Publishing House. 1890.

From *Funny Stories* told by Phineas T. Barnum, pp. 283–284. Copyright, 1890, by Phineas T. Barnum. New York and London: George Routledge and Sons, Limited.

58

Liquor

...skey and several barrels of wine ranged along the
...e back room beyond the prescription case. It was my father's
...mplaint at home that his clerk, whoever it happened to be, was
selling too much whiskey; and the town made fun of him. The town's
two or three good saloons should have supplied its liquor demand,
but possibly the wine-bibbers and those who desired to be knocked
about by strong drinks thought his liquor was better than saloon
liquor. For it was an everlasting fight between him and his clerks to
keep down the sale of liquor.

One day a town drunk lay in the gutter before his store, and the
town wags, one after another, poked their heads into the store with
raucous taunting and ribald remarks to rile up the proprietor. My
father got two buckets of water at the town pump on the corner, returned with them, sweating, for it was a hot summer day. He stood
over the drunk in the gutter and lifted up a bucket, while the whole
town up and down the street cried, "My God Almighty, Doc, what
are you doing?" *et cetera,* and with variations.

As he soused one of the buckets in the drunk's face, and lifted up
the other, the crowd protested. He roared to the multitude:

"Is freedom dead in this country, that a man has no right to water
his own liquor?" So he soused down the other bucket. Whereupon the
drunk sat up, rubbed his eyes, and walked fairly sober down the street.

The store was so profitable that within a few years my father was
able to trade it for a good farm, and have enough capital to run this
at a loss for a year or two.

A Footless Traveler

The trip was signalized but by one little incident, and that occurred
just as we were about to start. A very seedy-looking vagabond passenger got out of the stage a moment to wait till the usual ballast of
silver bricks was thrown in. He was standing on the pavement, when
an awkward express employee, carrying a brick weighing a hundred
pounds, stumbled and let it fall on the bummer's foot. He instantly
dropped on the ground and began to howl in the most heartbreaking
way. A sympathizing crowd gathered around and were going to pull
his boot off; but he screamed louder than ever and they desisted; then

From *The Autobiography of William Allen White,* p. 33. Copyright, 1946, by
The Macmillan Company. New York.

From *Roughing It,* by Samuel L. Clemens, Vol. II, pp. 118–119. Entered . . .
1871, by The American Publishing Company, in the Office of the Librarian of
Congress, at Washington, 1899, by The American Publishing Company; 1899, by
Samuel L. Clemens. New York and London: Harper & Brothers, Publishers.

he fell to gasping, and between the gasps ejaculated "Brandy! for Heaven's sake, brandy!" They poured half a pint down him, and it wonderfully restored and comforted him. Then he begged the people to assist him to the stage, which was done. The express people urged him to have a doctor at their expense, but he declined, and said that if he only had a little brandy to take along with him, to soothe his paroxysms of pain when they came on, he would be grateful and content. He was quickly supplied with two bottles, and we drove off. He was so smiling and happy after that, that I could not refrain from asking him how he could possibly be so comfortable with a crushed foot.

"Well," said he, "I hadn't had a drink for twelve hours, and hadn't a cent to my name. I was most perishing—and so, when that duffer dropped that hundred-pounder on my foot, I see my chance. Got a cork leg, you know!" and he pulled up his pantaloons and proved it.

Stingy Folks

. . . The central figure was always the husband and father, Mr. Mac (he was not a Mac, actually, but his surname was as Scottish as if he had been), a prosperous farmer; the other members were merely subsidiaries or, perhaps rather, victims.

The most conventional of the tales concerns the father's order that his sons, on the infrequent occasions when they were wearing new shoes, should take especially long steps. The mother, it was sometimes added, finally obtained a withdrawal of this injunction by pointing out that it involved a serious danger of splitting their trousers. . . .

My favorite deals with the father settling his monthly bill at the general store. "Right!" the storekeeper exclaimed. "Thank you very much! And now, if you'll wait just a minute, I'll put up a sack of candy for the children"—as was the genial custom in those days at a settlement of accounts. Mr. Mac put up a restraining hand. "If it's all the same to you," he said, "I think I'll just have the worth of it in assorted nails."

Mr. Mac here appears as a distant relative of the man who, on Christmas Eve, went out into the backyard, fired off a pistol, and rushed into the house to inform his children that Santa Claus had just committed suicide.

So Tight

A Scotchman in order to teach his small son thrifty habits gave him a penny each day and saw to it that he deposited them in a white pig-

From "Thrift and Abstinence Stories," by Kenneth Wiggins Porter, *The Journal of American Folklore*, Vol. LXIII (Oct.-Dec., 1950), No. 250, pp. 467–469.

From *Tall Tales*, compiled by Jim Blakely, p. 54. Copyright, 1936, by Eldridge Entertainment House, Inc. Franklin, Ohio, and Denver, Colorado.

bank. As soon as the boy had five pennies thus saved, the father re-moved the coins and gave the lad a nickel in exchange and had him place it in a larger blue china bank. And when five nickels had been accumulated again the father took the smaller coins and gave him a quarter for them which the boy was taught to place in a large red receptacle. BUT—the LARGE RED RECEPTACLE was a quarter-in-the-slot gas meter.

The Living American Skeleton

. . . Some years ago I engaged a celebrated Living American Skele-ton for a tour through Australia. He was the thinnest man I ever saw. He was a splendid skeleton. He didn't weigh anything scarcely—and I said to myself—the people of Australia will flock to see this tre-mendous curiosity. It is a long voyage—as you know—from New York to Melbourne—and to my utter surprise the skeleton had no sooner got out to sea than he commenced eating in the most horrible man-ner. He had never been on the ocean before—and he said it agreed with him.—I thought so!—I never saw a man eat so much in my life. Beef—mutton—pork—he swallowed them all like a shark—and between meals he was often discovered behind barrels eating hard-boiled eggs. The result was that when we reached Melbourne this infamous skele-ton weighed 64 pounds more than I did!

I thought I was ruined—but I wasn't. I took him on to California—another very long sea voyage—and when I got him to San Francisco I exhibited him as a Fat Man.

* * * * *

I met a man in Oregon who hadn't any teeth—not a tooth in his head—yet that man could play on the bass drum better than any man I ever met.—He kept a hotel. They have queer hotels in Oregon. I remember one where they gave me a bag of oats for a pillow—I had night mares of course. In the morning the landlord said—How do you feel—old hoss—hay?—I told him I felt my oats.

Alexander Stephens' Gastronomical Humor

Wholly fictitious is the anecdote which represents some burly Geor-gian, first Mr. Toombs and then Judge Cone, as saying to Mr. Stephens

From "The Lecture," by Artemus Ward (Charles Farrar Browne), in *Artemus Ward's Panorama*, edited by T. W. Robertson and E. P. Hingston, pp. 66–68, 70. Copyright, 1869, by G. W. Carleton. New York. This lecture, delivered at the Egyp-tian Hall, London, was illustrated with a panorama The footnotes of the previous editors have been omitted.

From "Anecdotes Concerning Noted Men," *Library of Southern Literature*, Edwin Anderson Alderman, Joel Chandler Harris, Editors in Chief, Vol. XIV, compiled by C. Alphonso Smith, pp. 6354–6355. Copyright, 1907, 1910, by The Martin and Hoyt Company. Atlanta.

that if his ears were pinned back and his head was greased he could swallow him whole, and which represents Mr. Stephens as retorting that if the swallower could actually do this he would have more brains in his stomach than he ever had in his head. Perhaps the anecdote has been told around nearly every stove in Georgia. But neither General Toombs nor Judge Cone could have been so stupid as to make the boorish remark, which is supposed to have called forth the famous retort; and General Toombs and Mr. Stephens, it must be remembered, though sometimes at variance upon political issues, were devoted lifelong friends. Some of the graybeards have actually gone so far as to say that they heard Mr. Stephens make the reply in question; but Uncle Ephraim could also swear that "he seed Marse Henry's ghost." . . .

Within the limits of authentic tradition the nearest approach to this specimen of gastronomical humor dates back to the presidential contest of 1860, when Mr. Stephens, who supported the Douglas ticket, engaged in joint debate with Colonel Ranse Wright, afterward General A. R. Wright, who supported the American or Know-Nothing candidates.

Colonel Wright was one of the ablest campaigners in the State, and on this particular occasion he made one of his best efforts. But the effect of the speech was broken by the skillful manner in which Mr. Stephens was reported to have said that, metaphorically speaking, he could eat Ben Hill for breakfast, Ranse Wright for dinner, and Bob Trippe for supper; and of course this ridiculous yarn brought down the house. The laugh was long and continuous as the audience gazed upon the diminutive storage room of the invalid statesman and thought of the little man with the big appetite.

But it came Mr. Stephens' turn to speak; and, after denying that he had made such a statement, he added that if he had contemplated a feast of the character described, he would certainly have changed the order; he would have taken Ben Hill for breakfast, Bob Trippe for dinner, and remembering the advice of his mother, always to eat light suppers, he would have tipped off with his friend Colonel Wright. The building fairly shook with the mirth which followed this sally. Colonel Wright realized that he was worsted in the tilt, but he joined heartily in the laugh at his expense.

A Kentucky Breakfast

This potation, to be thoroughly enjoyed, should be prepared in the following manner:

By Senator Millard Tydings. From *Eat, Drink & Be Merry in Maryland*, An Anthology from a Great Tradition, compiled by Frederick Philip Stieff, pp. 299–300. Copyright, 1932, by Frederick Philip Stieff. New York: G. P. Putnam's Sons.

Supply each guest with a glass containing about one-half inch of water and one-quarter teaspoonful of sugar, and a spoon.

All should sit comfortably and stir the sugar until it is thoroughly dissolved. The host should tell the following story in a low voice while the sugar is being stirred:

"Have you gentlemen ever participated at a Kentucky breakfast?"

The answer is likely to be in the negative. Then some guest will probably ask:

"What is a Kentucky breakfast?"

At this point the sugar is completely dissolved. The host passes around a bottle of Bourbon and each person pours into his glass, containing the dissolved sugar, such amount as suits his inclination. This is stirred for a while, during which time the host replies:

"A Kentucky breakfast is a big beefsteak, a quart of Bourbon and a houn' dawg."

One of the guests will then ask:

"What is the dog for?"

The host then replies:

"He eats the beefsteak."

Ice water is then passed around in a silver pitcher to dilute the drink to meet the requirements of the discriminating taste of each. A part of the Kentucky breakfast is then consumed.

(In order to extract the nth power of enjoyment from this receipt, when stirring the sugar and water, each should sit on the very edge of his chair or sofa, rest his arms on his knees with a slightly forward posture. Unless this is done the drink will taste just a little less good.)

Home-Made Jokes

In Milwaukee last month a man died laughing over one of his own jokes. That's what makes it so tough for us outsiders. We have to fight home competition.

Just get a calm, unpartisan angle on the joke that the man died laughing over. A friend of his, at dinner, said,

"I once shot a rabbit weighing thirty-five pounds."

And the victim-to-be came back with "And I once shot a one three pounds heavier." At which crack he laughed so hard that he slipped off his chair to the floor, dead.

Now, what can you do about that, if your job is supposedly to make people laugh? Of course, there is *nothing* to do about the originator of the joke now. That has all been taken care of. But how is one to get a line on what will knock people off their chairs with laughter and what won't?

From *The Benchley Roundup* [by Robert Benchley], A Selection by Nathaniel Benchley, pp. 283–284. Copyright, 1954, by Nathaniel Benchley. New York: Harper & Brothers.

We might as well face the fact that the whole conversation was pretty comical at that, and that the poor man's return shot was a gem. A rabbit weighing thirty-five pounds has a Gargantuan touch to it, but to have it topped by one weighing thirty-eight pounds (only thirty-eight, mind you! Rabelais would have had it weigh two tons), this is a bit of understatement in exaggeration that marks the deceased as a genius.

But how can one start a conversation in which the other fellow says that he shot a thirty-five-pound rabbit? Things like this can happen only around a dinner table and probably only in Milwaukee.

The only flaw in the make-up of the man who came through with the thirty-eight pound rabbit was that he laughed at his own joke. If he had given it with a dead pan he would be alive today and would have been visiting me in New York at my expense.

Of course, he would have had to bring his thirty-five-pound rabbit man along as a stooge, but I'll bet that, between the two of them, I could have got three more subjects for this department.

Give Him Time

It was about thirty-odd years ago, and there was a Mexican come up from Mexico and got to drinking whiskey. Now he knew all about this mescal they got down in Mexico, but he didn't know nothing about whiskey, so he got to drinking with a man he met and when it was late that night they got a room and went to bed. In the morning the Mexican got up first and accidentally put on the other fella's vest, which had his watch in it. When the other guy woke up later and saw that the Mexican was gone with the vest and the watch in it, he called the cops.

When a cop finally spotted the Mexican with the vest on, he walked up and tapped him on the shoulder and said, "Come along."

Well, the Mexican thought the cop said, "Camalion!" which means "cut-throat" in Mexican, and will make some of them fight. This Mexican started in fighting like hell, but he got dragged in finally.

"Guilty or not guilty?" the judge asked him.

The Mexican said that he was guilty, but he said this rotten whiskey wasn't like the mescal they got down in Mexico.

And he says, "I dreenk thees wheeskey, and I poot on thees vest, and thees watch ees in eet, and so I am here. All because of thees wheeskey, weech I not know."

"Well," says the judge, "you people ought to get familiar with American ways before you come up here."

"Si, senor," says this Mexican. "Send me to San Quentin."

By Thelma Wagner. From Manuscripts of the Federal Writers' Project of the Works Progress Administration for the State of California.

"You ever been in San Quentin?" the judge asks him.

"No, senor."

"Any relatives in San Quentin?"

"No, senor."

"Then why do you want to go there?"

"I hear, senor, San Quentin ees only place to learn all thees American ways."

Everybody in court begun to laugh, and the judge pounds on his desk.

"Well," the judge says, "your sentence'll be light. Let it be ordered and decreed by this court that you be sent to San Quentin for one year—and on good behavior, that means ten months. Now try and reclaim yourself and learn something."

The Mexican shrugs his shoulders and says, "Caramba! What you theenk I learn in ten months?"

Well, sir, you couldn't of kept that court-house from laughing!

Running a Railroad

Some years ago an investigation was under way relative to a most destructive train wreck that had occurred out in the Southwest range country. Two trains had crashed together in a frightful head-on collision at a blind curve where the railway swept around the point of a long, high ridge. Most of the members of both train crews had been killed or injured, but the investigators at last found an old ranchman who had witnessed the disaster.

"Tell us exactly what you saw," demanded the chairman of the investigating committee. "Well, I was ridin' along the backbone of that ridge lookin' for mavericks when I saw off down to the south a train comin' north about fifty miles an hour. Then I looked north an' saw another 'un comin' south at about the same speed and I saw they uz goin' to smash into one another right at that curve."

"What did you do?" asked the chairman.

"Do? I didn't do nothin'."

"Didn't you ride down there and try to stop 'em?"

"No."

"Didn't you even *think* anything?"

"Yes, I thought a little."

"What did you think?"

"Well, I thought to myself that's a helluva way to run a railroad."

From *Cow Country*, by Edward Everett Dale, pp. 145–146. Copyright, 1942, by the University of Oklahoma Press. Norman.

What's His Name?

... In one of the Confederate states ... I came upon a lean Negro, cast in the mold of Stepin Fetchit, standing beside a mule that was hitched to an old wagon. I stopped to talk.

"That your mule?" I asked him.

"Yassuh."

"How old is he?"

"He about sebm years old."

"How long you had him?"

"I had 'im a long time."

"What's his name?"

"Well, suh," he replied uncertainly, "I don't know his name, but I calls him Bill."

No View

"I don't think much of the scenery in this part of the country," said a western man on a Central Hudson train bound north. "Give me a prairie every time." "What's the matter with the scenery in this part of the country?" asked a fellow-passenger. "You can't see any. Them hills and mountains are in the way."

Cussing the Cuspidor

On one of Baker's visits to Denver, while seated in one of the hotels chewing tobacco, he spat on the carpet. A Negro porter who happened to see him moved the cuspidor to the spot where he had expectorated, whereupon Jim turned his head and spat in the opposite direction. The porter again moved the cuspidor to that side. Jim, not heeding this, spat again on the carpet.

Finally the porter made several attempts to place it within the range of his amber spray, and having been unsuccessful, he placed the brass receptacle directly in front of him. Old Jim looked down and replied ..., "You know, by G—, if you keep movin' that thing around I'm li'ble to spit in it."

From *The World, the Flesh, and H. Allen Smith*, edited and with an Introduction by Bergan Evans, p. 255. Copyright, 1954, by H. Allen Smith. Garden City, New York: Hanover House.

From *American Wit and Humor*, Vol. II, p. 73. Philadelphia: George W. Jacobs & Co. 1900.

From *The Life of Jim Baker, 1818–1898, Trapper, Scout, Guide, and Indian Fighter*, by Nolie Mumey, pp. 172–173. Copyright, 1931, by Nolie Mumey. Denver, Colorado: The World Press, Inc.

Don't Monkey with the Buzz Saw

. . . The volume of lumber grew steadily down the Mississippi. Every river led to rich tracts of pine and the stream itself was the road to market. By 1850 developments were growing in all the great Wisconsin pineries, and sawmill towns were springing up on the six great lumber rivers—the Wisconsin, Black, Red Cedar, St. Croix, Chippewa, and Wolf.

In the sawmills changes came quickly to meet the growing trade in finished lumber. The rotary saw replaced the crude "muley" saw and cut twenty times as much lumber in a day's shift. Promptly millmen learned how ruthless that whirling blade could be, and in time the familiar warning passed into common speech: "Don't monkey with the buzz saw."

With the rotary saw spitting its spray of sawdust and the multiple blades snarling through great logs, a mill crew was never far from danger. Every mill town had its men with mutilated hands. Over and over they told the story of big Olaf's explaining to the foreman how he had just lost a finger. The foreman thought the saws were guarded, but Olaf demonstrated how it had happened: "Vell, Ae tak da boord dis vay wit' dis hand an' dis vay wit' da oder. Ae move de boord op to da machine lak dat, an da first ting Ae know—*YUMPIN YIMINY, DAR GOES ANODER VON!*"

Patrick Henry's Reply

Govenor Giles, of Virginia, once addressed a note to Patrick Henry, demanding satisfaction:

Sir, I understand that you have called me a "bob-tail" politician. I wish to know if it be true; and if true, your meaning.

WM. B. GILES

To which Mr. Henry replied in this wise:

Sir, I do not recollect having called you a bob-tail politician at any time, but think it probable I have. Not recollecting the time or occasion, I can't say what I did mean, but if you will tell me what you think I meant, I will say whether you are correct or not. Very respectfully,

PATRICK HENRY

From *Upper Mississippi*, A Wilderness Saga, by Walter Havighurst, p. 157. Copyright, 1937, by Walter Havighurst. *The Rivers of America*, editor, Constance Lindsay Skinner; assistant editor, Elizabeth L. Gilman. New York & Toronto: Farrar & Rinehart, Inc.

From *Bench and Bar:* A Complete Digest of the Wit, Humor, Asperities, and Amenities of the Law, by L. J. Bigelow, p. 155. New York: Harper & Brothers, Publishers. 1871.

About Face

On a cold dreary day an Indian and a white man were making a journey together. The Indian had on no clothing except a blanket, while the white man was bundled up in all the clothes he possessed. The white man continued to complain about the cold and to wonder why the Indian was not freezing. He said to the Indian, "I don't understand it. With all my clothes I am about to freeze, and you, with only a thin blanket, do not seem to be cold at all."

"Is your face cold?" asked the Indian.

"No, my face is not cold, but I'm just about to freeze everywhere else."

"Me all face," said the Indian.

And Then What?

A story is told of a young Indian boy whose dignity and wholesomeness delighted a vacation visitor to the north country. The white man, being childless, but having an abstract taste for paternity, decided in a night of inspiration to make the great gesture and adopt the boy. Agleam with benignity, he announced to the young guide the next day: "I'm going to take you back with me to Chicago. You're to be my son."

The Indian considered the suggestion coolly. What would he do in Chicago, he wanted to know. Well, he would go to school until he was old enough to enter the business. And after that what? Well, he would work his way up through the various departments of the factory. He would be a foreman, then a department head, then general manager. The boy was beginning to look puzzled, and the man who wished to be a foster-father felt his whole scheme of life to be under critical examination. He wanted deeply to justify it. "Finally," he went on in a great burst of generosity, "when I die, you will inherit all that I have, my business, my house, everything." The boy still looked aloof and unpersuaded. "And then what?" he asked once more. "Why, then you'll be a rich man. You can do what you like, you can retire and come up here and spend all your time fishing." The boy's eyes widened in complete despair at being asked to follow such whimsical nonsense. "But I can do that now," he said.

From "Anecdotes from the Brazos Bottoms," by A. W. Eddins, *Straight Texas*, pp. 88–89. Publications of the Texas Folklore Society (1937), No. XIII, ed. by J. Frank Dobie and Mody C. Boatright.

From *Pine Stream & Prairie*, Wisconsin and Minnesota in Profile, by James Gray, pp. 37–38. Copyright, 1945, by James Gray. New York: Alfred A. Knopf, Inc.

Slow Trains

I. Egg Local

"I want to go to bed, so give me a room as soon as you can. I ought to have reached the city early this afternoon, and here it is 11 o'clock."

"What made you so late?" asked a Girard House clerk, as he threw down a key to which was attached a rough-edged brass tag about the size of a buckwheat cake.

"Oh, slow trains! Slow trains! They seem to stop everywhere and at all the little crossroads."

"That's queer."

"I should say it was. Why, at one place they stopped about seven minutes, while half a dozen people came out of the only house to be seen in the neighborhood and boarded the train. Did you ever hear of anything like it?"

"Never."

"I have," said a little old man with long, shaggy hair, who had overheard the conversation while searching the Philadelphia directory for the name of a Boston firm.

"You have?"

"Yes; you may not believe it, but it's a fact. Some years ago I used to travel on the Old Colony Railroad, up in Massachusetts. There was a place called Wheat Sheaf Lane, where the train stopped nearly every day for an old woman, who was always there to send some eggs into town. Now, would you believe it? One day the train stopped as usual for Aunt Betsey, who was there with her eggs, but she only had eleven. She said an old hen was still on the nest, and she wanted the train to wait until she could make up the dozen."

"Yes?"

"Well, I'll be darned if that train didn't wait while the hen laid the extra egg."

The late arrival said he guessed he would go to bed, the bediamoned hotel clerk swooned and the little old man walked down into the corridor and dropped wearily into a chair.

II. Snail Special

Talk about your slow trains through Arkansaw and your snail specials over the Rockies, but I struck a train in Indiana that was sure enough slow. I got on it to go up the state about seventy-five miles. The thing ran so slow that I went to the conductor and said, "Look

From *New Yarns & Funny Jokes comprising Original and Selected American Humor* . . . , p. 38. New York: Excelsior Publishing House. 1890.

From *I Blew in from Arkansaw*, A Trip of Fun through Hoosierdom, by Geo. D. Beason, pp. 48–49. Copyright, 1908, by Geo. D. Beason. Chicago: Geo. D. Beason, Publisher.

here, if you don't ginger the gait of this thing up a little, I'll get out and walk." He flared up and said, "Who's the boss of this train?" I said, "I suppose you are." He said, "Then dry up." I said, "Whose dead body have you on board?" He said, "Nobody's; why?" I said, "Because you're running so slow I thought maybe you were bossing a funeral procession." That made him still madder, and we hooked up. We jumped out on the right-o'-way, and the train running at full speed, and had a fight, and I knocked the breath out of him and ran down to a pond and got my hat full of water and poured it in his face and brought him to, and we both caught the hind end of the train as it came by—and it wasn't a long train either.

But the walloping I gave the conductor didn't make the thing go any faster. A fellow standing on the side of the track held up a knife and hollered, "Got a frog-sticker yer want to swap?" I lit out and looked his knife over, swapped with him and skinned him too bad to talk about, and caught the hind end of the train again as it came by. I went to the conductor next day and apologized for banging him up. He said, "Oh, that's all right. The only thing I regret is, I lost my cap back where we had the fight." I said, "I'll go back and get it." He said, "Don't put yourself to any trouble." I said, "It won't be any trouble." I went back and got his cap and caught up with the train at the next station.

I was on the slow outfit so long that I wore out one of the cushion seats, and had train sores. You may think I'm overdrawing it, but I'm not, when I tell you that a fellow took down with typhoid fever on the thing just after I got on, and when I got off at the end of my journey, he was sound and well, and he had a long siege of it, too.

The Conductor's Lesson

The sturdiest specimen of the hero in Newport history was the late George H. Norman, family-founding forebear of the resort's distinguished Norman dynasty. A dignified gentleman with a long full beard, Norman had no middle name. He thought he ought to have one and so chose the "H," even though the initial never stood for anything. Norman's occupation was that of a hydraulic engineer and, born in Newport, he was a rugged individualist to the end of his days. When a neighbor refused to repaint a barn, which Norman thought was a disagreeable color, Norman, in the owner's absence, had it painted for him. Riding in the train one day in 1900, Norman wrote his will on the back of a paper bag; to this day no one has ever been able to break the trust he thus established.

On another occasion Norman, who never took a parlor car, was reading his paper after the train had started when the conductor,

From *The Last Resorts,* by Cleveland Amory, pp. 246–247. Copyright, 1952, by Cleveland Amory. New York: Harper & Brothers.

coming through the car, noticed a suitcase in the aisle beside him. The train was crowded and the conductor told Norman sharply that he would have to get the suitcase out of the aisle. "No," said Norman, reading his paper, "I don't." The conductor told Norman that a person who tripped over the suitcase might sue the railroad and it would then be Norman's fault. "I mean it," he said, "move it." Norman paid no attention and the conductor became exasperated. "You may be the largest stockholder of this railroad," he said, "but I'll show you who's the captain of this train. If you don't move that suitcase I'll throw it off." Norman still continued to read. The conductor was furious. "I'll count three," he shouted. "I'll throw it off the train!" As the conductor, red in the face and raging, sounded the counts, Norman still read on. At the third count the conductor seized the suitcase, strode down to the end of the car and hurled it out the door. Coming back, he rubbed his hands. "Well," he said, "you Newporters think you own the earth. I guess that will teach you a lesson." For the first time Norman looked up. "Not me, it won't," he said. "It wasn't my suitcase."

Pipe and Poodle

Representative Mercer, of Omaha, contributes the following, which he charges to Joe Teahon, traveling passenger agent of the Wabash.

Teahon had just returned from a trip over the line, and brought this story back with him:

"As we were approaching Talmage the other day a lady with a poodle dog came into the smoker. A traveling man called her attention to the character of the car and told her she had better go into one of the others. She declared that she was going to remain right there, and she told him he must not light and smoke the pipe he was filling with tobacco. He opened the window and calmly lit his pipe, and was puffing away, when she again demanded that he desist. He again told her that she could go into one of the rear cars. It went on for a few minutes, when she leaned over and snatched the pipe from his mouth and threw it out the window. That traveling man was at a white heat with rage, and turning around grabbed the poodle and chucked it out the window. Then she went on the war path. She declared that she would have him arrested at Talmage, where, she said, she knew everybody, and he said if she did he would have her arrested for stealing his pipe. The argument was hot and heavy, and when they got off the train they rustled around for the town marshal, and finally found him, and were telling him their troubles, when the poodle came running up the track with the pipe in his mouth."

From *Waifs of the Press*. Collected and Edited by Harry L. Work, p. 55. Washington: Walter Neale, Publisher. 1898.

The Sit-Down Dance

A young lady . . . had strayed away from the ball-room. Her mother subsequently discovered her in a remote nook, with a gentleman who had his arm around her waist, while she rested the tips of her pretty little fingers upon his manly shoulder. "Daughter, what's all this?" exclaimed the irate mamma. Saucy-cheeks looked up calmly and replied: "Mamma, allow me to introduce Captain X. to you. I had promised him a dance, but I was so tired that I couldn't keep my word, and I'm just giving him a sitting-still waltz instead."

The Going Rate

Jim Smith was fur sartin the coolest feller in the country. He had a little one-room cabin on the banks of the Mississip', an' one night as he sot cleanin' his rifle, one side o' the fire, an' Matty, his wife, on the other, knittin', the' cum a terrible explosion out on the river, an' the next minute somethin' cum plum through the roof an' dropped at their feet, right between 'em, without disturbin' either. Jim went on a-cleanin' his gun an' Matty, she kep' knittin'. The stranger—fur it was a man—was a little dazed at fust, but gittin' up, he squinted at the hole in the roof an', says he, "Well, my man, what's the damage?" Jim put down his rifle, took a careful look at the hole, figured a while an', says he, "Ten dollars." "You be hanged," said the traveler. "Last week I was blown up in another steamboat, opposite St. Louis, and fell through three floors of a new house, and they only charged me five dollars. No, no, my man, I know what the usual figure is in such cases. Here's two dollars; if that won't do, sue me as quick as you please!"

If I Could Swear

. . . What swearing there is among Mormons in general is likely to be fairly tame, and this in spite of the fact that both Brother Brigham and Heber C. Kimball, his right-hand man, were notable swearers and threateners from the pulpit. They were always offering to send their enemies to hell across lots, or give them a dose that would puke

From *Gus Williams' World of Humor.* New York: De Witt, Publishers, 1880.

From *The Lance, Cross and Canoe;* The Flatboat, Rifle and Plough in the Valley of the Mississippi; The Backwoods Hunter and Settler, The Flatboatman, The Saddle-Bags Parson, The Stump Orator and Lawyer, as the Pioneers of Its Civilization; Its Great Leaders, Wit and Humor, Remarkable Extent and Wealth of Resource, Its Past Achievements and Glorious Future, by W. H. Milburn, p. 474. Entered . . . 1892, by William Henry Milburn. . . . New York and St. Louis: N. D. Thompson Publishing Company.

From *Mormon Country,* by Wallace Stegner, pp. 143–144. American Folkways Series, edited by Erskine Caldwell. Copyright, 1942, by Wallace Stegner. New York: Duell, Sloan & Pearce.

them worse than lobelia. A little of that fresh and vigorous tradition remains, though in the staider communities it is likely to be buried under a layer of piety like sausages put up in lard, and to emerge only on great occasions. The story is told of a pious brother in one of the rural settlements who forgot for some reason to milk his cow before he got dressed for Sunday meeting. Rather than change to overalls, he tucked up his coat tails, folded back the lapels of his Prince Albert, and sat down gingerly on the stool. The cow was "ringy." She kept looking around suspiciously and switching her matted tail across the elder's Sunday shirt. He compressed his lips and tied the tail to her leg. For a while he milked steadily, and then in one disastrous motion the cow kicked the bucket into his lap and upset him on the dirty stable floor. The elder, legend says, rose slowly to his feet. His stature grew from second to second, until he stood on tiptoe with the pressure of wrath in him. His hands made futile clawing motions down the stained lapels of his coat. Finally he found words. "If I wasn't a man of God . . . If I wasn't the Bishop of this Ward . . . If I wasn't a member of the Quorum of the Priesthood in this State . . . If I didn't have duties and obligations to live up to . . . If I wasn't called upon to put away wrath and bind the evil passions . . ., *I'd break your God-damned neck!*"

Bringing 'em Back Alive

A party of emigrants were camped in the woods. They had seen bear sign, and as they made their camp they speculated considerably about whether or not they were in any danger.

One man ridiculed their fears, saying that he was not afraid of any bear that ever ate a huckleberry or robbed a bee tree.

The next morning before breakfast he took his rifle and went out by himself for a stroll in the woods. He had not gone far before he stumbled upon a bear. He fired and wounded the animal only slightly, and before he could reload, the bear charged. He dropped his gun and ran for camp, the bear not more than two jumps behind him.

He reached camp shouting, "Shoot him! Shoot him!"

After the bear was killed his companions twitted him about his footrace.

Said one, "I thought you weren't afraid of any bear that ever ate a huckleberry."

"I wasn't scared of that bear."

"Then why were you running away from him?"

"I wasn't running away from him. I was just bringing him back to camp for you."

From *Folk Laughter on the American Frontier,* by Mody C. Boatright, pp. 101–102. New York: The Macmillan Company, 1949.

The Little Frenchman

[Lincoln] had little patience with men who obscured, or tried to obscure, their own trail. It reminded him, he said, of a little Frenchman out west during the "winter of the deep snow" whose "legs were so short that the seat of his trousers rubbed out his footprints as he walked."

The Unreconstructed Rebel

At the time General Banks was in command of New Orleans there resided in that city a young Confederate, who had yet to learn the wisdom of silence. The General sent for him, when the following conversation took place: "Who are you?" said General B. "I am cousin to General ———, of the Confederate army," replied the young man. "You have been using your tongue rather freely, young man. "I have, sir, and don't back down," was the reply. "Then you must either take the oath of allegiance or go to prison," said the General to him in a severe tone. "I don't feel much inclined for either," replied the youth. "Well, I'll give you three days to reflect on the matter." At the end of the three days young secesh returned and said to the General, "I believe I'll take the oath." After the obligation had been complied with, he turned to the General and said, "Well, I suppose we are now good Union friends?" "Yes," replied General B., "there is no reason why we should not be." "Well, General," said the young scamp, with a grin on his countenance, as he rose to depart, "didn't Stonewall Jackson lick *us* most confoundedly?"

Method in His Madness

One day a man riding down the road came to an overturned load of hay. A boy was working frantically, tossing hay in all directions.

The kind traveler stopped and said: "'My young friend, don't you realize that haste makes waste? Instead of scattering the hay all over the road, why don't you load it carefully back on the wagon so that you won't have to handle it again?"

The boy, without pausing, pointed to the pile of hay and said: "Dad's under there."

From *Personal Traits of Abraham Lincoln,* by Helen Nicolay, p. 88. Copyright, 1912, by The Century Company. New York.

From *Flashes and Sparks of Wit and Humor by Our American Humorists . . . ,* p. 18. New York: M. J. Ivers & Co. 1880.

From *Folk Laughter on the American Frontier,* by Mody C. Boatright, p. 105. Copyright, 1949, by The Macmillan Company. New York.

Recipe for Hash

Cooking on the lumber rafts was done under some difficulties. The cook-stove was mounted in a sand-box placed on one of the cribs near the middle of the raft. On windy days a rough screen shelter was erected to protect the cook and his cooking. The raft crew ate their meals from a rough board table, near by. The cooking utensils were a frying pan, coffee pot, and a few pots and kettles. The tableware consisted of tin cups, plates, knives, and forks.

Big John Marshall was the cook on one of Whisky Jack's rafts. He was a good enough lumberjack cook, but one day the crew complained about the meals. They were all pretty much the same, day after day. Whisky Jack thought that the meals could be better, so he talked with Big John and asked him whether he had ever had or seen a cook book. And the cook said, "I got one of them cookery books once but I never could do anything with it. It was just of no use to me." "Was it too fancy for you?" asked Jack. "That was it," said Big John, "every one of the recipes began the same way, 'Take a Clean Dish.' And that settled me."

Big John dished up a lot of hash. It was good, and one of the crew asked him if he had a regular recipe for making it. "No," said the cook, "it just accumulates."

Weather Vanity

I

After a particularly violent rainstorm [in Los Angeles], which was described in the papers as having originated in the Northwest, a Seattle paper retaliated beautifully. It told of the arrest of an itinerant who had fled there to escape the Los Angeles rains and who had a strange type of thermometer in his pocket. Police were baffled by the instrument. Put on a radiator, the mercury went up only a few degrees. Dipped into a pitcher of ice water, it fell only two or three degrees. Finally, the itinerant confessed. It was a Los Angeles Chamber of Commerce thermometer. The temperature was fixed to register a low of seventy-six, a high of eighty.

From *Whisky Jack Yarns*, Short Tales of the Old Time Lumber Raftsmen of the Wisconsin River and Their Mythical Hero, Raft and River Bank Tales, [compiled by Charles E. Brown], p. 8. Madison, Wisconsin: Charles E. Brown, Wisconsin Folklore Society. 1940.

From *My L. A.*, by Matt Weinstock, pp. 35–36. Copyright, 1947, by Matt Weinstock. New York: Current Books, Inc. A. A. Wyn, Publisher.

II

Another apocryphal story deals with an old timer's explanation of a siege of surplus dew.

"Those rain clouds," he said, "were heading for Florida and got off the track."

A newcomer, pointing skyward, said: "Is that so? Then what are those up there?"

"Oh," countered the defender, "those are just the empties coming back."

The Uses of Hadacol

I

" 'Have you heard about the old lady who could neither read nor write? She took a bottle of Hadacol—and went to teachin' school.'

II

" 'There was an old man—real old—was taking Hadacol. He went to bed one night. His wife got up next morning and went to call him. Told him it was getting late. He says, "I'll get up, but I'll not go to school." '

III

"Girl came in and told me (very seriously): 'Have you heard about the ninety-five-year-old lady dying at the hospital?'

"I asked, 'Who was she?'

" 'She was taking Hadacol, too. Too bad; and the Hadacol didn't save her. But they *did* save the baby.' "

V. A FEW FOR THE ROAD
(Yarns)

Introduction

Yarns are rambling tales which are better heard than read. They may have little point, for, as Mark Twain pointed out in "How to Tell a Story," the enjoyment comes from the manner of the telling rather than the matter which is told. When a yarn is written, many devices are used to give it an oral quality, to make it sound as if

From *"Hadacol Stories,"* by Herbert Halpert, in *Kentucky Folklore Record,* Vol. II (1956), pp. 13–14.

someone is talking. At first glance the digressiveness and repetition in a yarn seem to be useless, but they are important in giving the tale the sound of the human voice. A writer of short stories corrects and changes until the story is told with the greatest possible economy, but the writer of yarns allows himself to make all the mistakes you or I would if someone asked us during dinner to tell about our last fishing trip. He repeats parts of the tale, corrects himself, and slips into relations of events and identifications of characters which contribute nothing to the advancement of the story. Jim Blaine carried such digressiveness to an extreme, of course, for he rambled so often and so far that he was unable to finish "The Story of the Old Ram."

Another frequently used device to make a written tale have oral quality is to enclose it in a frame. Thus the writer begins by describing the scene and the characters in standard English prose, but he then lets one of the characters tell the main story in his own language. The writer may then return to make a few remarks at the end. The internal narrator in a story such as this usually speaks some non-standard dialect of English, and his grammar, usage, and pronunciation are thus placed in contrast to the standard English of the frame. The use of dialect by the internal narrator is important. For one thing, the unfamiliar words and locutions are enjoyable, as are the fresh figures of speech like "eyes as big as soap kettles." But a more important reason for the use of dialect is that we are more likely to suspend disbelief of the exaggeration in the yarn when the narrator is a grizzled old mountain man giving us some reminiscences or a hayseedy farmer telling of life in the Ozarks, for such men have obviously experienced a kind of life with which we are unfamiliar. Of course a yarn-spinner makes us further suspend disbelief by using the devices of the tall-tale teller: speaking gravely, exercising care with details, offering proofs, and stopping short of "going the whole hog." Hawley, for example, readily admitted that his story of people who never died seemed incredible, but he went right ahead, told his listeners the number of the sack which contained his Uncle Samuel, and asked them to call on his uncle.

They Have Yarns

> They have yarns
> Of a skyscraper so tall they had to put hinges
> On the two top stories so to let the moon go by,
> Of one corn crop in Missouri when the roots
> Went so deep and drew off so much water

From *The People, Yes,* by Carl Sandburg, pp. 88–93. Harcourt, Brace & Company. New York.

The Mississippi riverbed that year was dry,

Of pancakes so thin they had only one side,

Of "a fog so thick we shingled the barn and six feet out on the fog,"

Of Pecos Pete straddling a cyclone in Texas and riding it to the west coast where "it rained out under him,"

Of the man who drove a swarm of bees across the Rocky Mountains and the Desert "and didn't lose a bee,"

Of a mountain railroad curve where the engineer in his cab can touch the caboose and spit in the conductor's eye,

Of the boy who climbed a cornstalk growing so fast he would have starved to death if they hadn't shot biscuits up to him,

Of the old man's whiskers: "When the wind was with him his whiskers arrived a day before he did,"

Of the hen laying a square egg and cackling, "Ouch!" and of hens laying eggs with the dates printed on them,

Of the ship captain's shadow: it froze to the deck one cold winter night,

Of mutineers on that same ship put to chipping rust with rubber hammers,

Of the sheep counter who was fast and accurate: "I just count their feet and divide by four,"

Of the man so tall he must climb a ladder to shave himself,

Of the runt so teeny-weeny it takes two men and a boy to see him,

Of mosquitoes: one can kill a dog, two of them a man,

Of a cyclone that sucked cookstoves out of the kitchen, up the chimney flue, and on to the next town,

Of the same cyclone picking up wagon-tracks in Nebraska and dropping them over in the Dakotas,

Of the hook-and-eye snake unlocking itself into forty pieces, each piece two inches long, then in nine seconds flat snapping itself together again,

Of the watch swallowed by the cow—when they butchered her a year later the watch was running and had the correct time,

Of horned snakes, hoop snakes that roll themselves where they want to go, and rattlesnakes carrying bells instead of rattles on their tails,

Of the herd of cattle in California getting lost in a giant redwood tree that had hollowed out,

Of the man who killed a snake by putting its tail in its mouth so it swallowed itself,

Of railroad trains whizzing along so fast they reach the station before the whistle,

Of pigs so thin the farmer had to tie knots in their tails to keep them from crawling through the cracks in their pens,

Of Paul Bunyan's big blue ox, Babe, measuring between the eyes forty-two ax-handles and a plug of Star tobacco exactly,

Of John Henry's hammer and the curve of its swing and his singing
of it as "a rainbow round my shoulder."
    "Do tell!"
    "I want to know!"

    "You don't say so!"
    "For the land's sake!"
    "Gosh all fish-hooks!"
    "Tell me some more.
    I don't believe a word you say
    but I love to listen
    to your sweet harmonica
    to your chin-music.
    Your fish stories hang together
    when they're just a pack of lies:
    you ought to have a leather medal:
    you ought to have a statue
    carved of butter: you deserve
    a large bouquet of turnips."

    "Yessir," the traveler drawled,
"Away out there in the petrified forest
everything goes on the same as usual.
The petrified birds sit in their petrified nests
and hatch their petrified young from petrified eggs."

A high pressure salesman jumped off the Brooklyn Bridge and was
saved by a policeman. But it didn't take him long to sell the idea
to the policeman. So together they jumped off the bridge.

One of the oil men in heaven started a rumor of a gusher down in
hell. All the other oil men left in a hurry for hell. As he gets to
thinking about the rumor he had started he says to himself there
might be something in it after all. So he leaves for hell in a hurry.

"The number 42 will win this raffle, that's my number." And when he
won they asked him whether he guessed the number or had a system. He said he had a system, "I took up the old family album
and there on page 7 was my grandfather and grandmother both
on page 7. I said to myself this is easy for 7 times 7 is the number
that will win and 7 times 7 is 42."

Once a shipwrecked sailor caught hold of a stateroom door and floated
for hours till friendly hands from out of the darkness threw him a
rope. And he called across the night, "What country is this?" and
hearing voices answer, "New Jersey," he took a fresh hold on the

floating stateroom door and called back half-wearily, "I guess I'll float a little farther."

An Ohio man bundled up the tin roof of a summer kitchen and sent it to a motor car maker with a complaint of his car not giving service. In three weeks a new car arrived for him and a letter: "We regret a delay in shipment but your car was received in a very bad order."

A Dakota cousin of this Ohio man sent six years of tin can accumulations to the same works, asking them to overhaul his car. Two weeks later came a rebuilt car, five old tin cans, and a letter: "We are also forwarding you five parts not necessary in our new model."

Thus fantasies heard at filling stations in the midwest. Another relates to a Missouri mule who took aim with his heels at an automobile rattling by. The car turned a somersault, lit next a fence, ran right along through a cornfield till it came to a gate, moved onto the road and went on its way as though nothing had happened. The mule heehawed with desolation, "What's the use?"

Another tells of a farmer and his family stalled on a railroad crossing, how they jumped out in time to see a limited express knock it into flinders, the farmer calling, "Well, I always did say that car was no shucks in a real pinch."

When the Masonic Temple in Chicago was the tallest building in the United States west of New York, two men who would cheat the eyes out of you if you gave 'em a chance, took an Iowa farmer to the top of the building and asked him, "How is this for high?" They told him that for $25 they would go down in the basement and turn the building around on its turn-table for him while he stood on the roof and saw how this seventh wonder of the world worked. He handed them $25. They went. He waited. They never came back.

This is told in Chicago as a folk tale, the same as the legend of Mrs. O'Leary's cow kicking over the barn lamp that started the Chicago fire, when the Georgia visitor, Robert Toombs, telegraphed an Atlanta crony, "Chicago is on fire, the whole city burning down, God be praised!"

Nor is the prize sleeper Rip Van Winkle and his scolding wife forgotten, nor the headless horseman scooting through Sleepy Hollow

Nor the sunken treasure-ships in coves and harbors, the hideouts of gold and silver sought by Coronado, nor the Flying Dutchman rounding the Cape doomed to nevermore pound his ear nor ever again take a snooze for himself

Nor the sailor's caretaker Mother Carey seeing to it that every seafaring man in the afterworld has a seabird to bring him news of ships and women, an albatross for the admiral, a gull for the deckhand

Nor the sailor with a sweetheart in every port of the world, nor the ships that set out with flying colors and all the promises you could ask, the ships never heard of again,

Nor Jim Liverpool, the riverman who could jump across any river and back without touching land he was that quick on his feet,

Nor Mike Fink along the Ohio and the Mississippi, half wild horse and half cock-eyed alligator, the rest of him snags and snapping turtle. "I can out-run, out-jump, out-shoot, out-brag, out-drink, and out-fight, rough and tumble, no holts barred, any man on both sides of the river from Pittsburgh to New Orleans and back again to St. Louis. My trigger finger itches and I want to go red-hot. War, famine and bloodshed puts flesh on my bones, and hardship's my daily bread."

Nor the man so lean he threw no shadow: six rattlesnakes struck at him at one time and every one missed him.

The Ram Story

Every now and then, . . . the boys used to tell me I ought to get one Jim Blaine to tell me the stirring story of his granfather's old ram—but they always added that I must not mention the matter unless Jim was drunk at the time—just comfortably and sociably drunk. They kept this up until my curiosity was on the rack to hear the story. I got to haunting Blaine; but it was of no use, the boys always found fault with his condition; he was often moderately but never satisfactorily drunk. I never watched a man's condition with such absorbing interest, such anxious solicitude; I never so pined to see a man uncompromisingly drunk—before. At last, one evening, I hurried to his cabin, for I learned that this time . . . he was tranquilly, serenely, symmetrically drunk—not a hiccup to mar his voice, not a cloud upon his brain thick enough to obscure his memory. As I entered, he was sitting upon an empty powder-keg, with a clay pipe in one hand and the other raised to command silence. His face was round, red, and very serious; his throat was bare and his hair tumbled; in general appearance and costume he was a stalwart miner of the period. On the pine table stood a candle, and its dim light revealed "the boys" sitting

From *Roughing It*, by Samuel L. Clemens, Vol. II, pp. 98–104. Entered . . . 1871, by The American Publishing Company; copyright, 1899, by Samuel L. Clemens. New York and London: Harper & Brothers, Publishers.

here and there on bunks, candle-boxes, powder kegs, etc. They said: "Sh—! Don't speak—he's going to commence."

THE STORY OF THE OLD RAM

I found a seat at once, and Blaine said:

"I don't reckon them times will ever come again. There never was a more bullier old ram than what he was. Grandfather fetched him from Illinois—got him of a man by the name of Yates—Bill Yates— maybe you might have heard of him; his father was a deacon—Baptist —and he was a rustler, too; a man had to get up ruther early to get the start of old Thankful Yates; it was him that put the Greens up to j'ining teams with my grandfather when he moved west. Seth Green was prob'ly the pick of the flock; he married a Wilkerson— Sarah Wilkerson—good cretur, she was—one of the likeliest heifers that was ever raised in old Stoddard, everybody said that knowed her. She could heft a bar'l of flour as easy as I can flirt a flapjack. And spin? Don't mention it! Independent? Humph! When Sile Hawkin come a-browsing around her, she let him know that for all his tin he couldn't trot in harness alongside of *her*. You see, Sile Hawkins was—no, it warn't Sile Hawkins, after all—it was a galoot by the name of Filkins—I disremember his first name but he *was* a stump—come into pra'r-meeting drunk, one night, hooraying for Nixon, becuz he thought it was a primary; and old Deacon Ferguson up and scooted him through the window and he lit on old Miss Jefferson's head, poor old filly. She was a good soul—had a glass eye and used to lend it to old Miss Wagner, that hadn't any, to receive company in; it warn't big enough, and when Miss Wagner warn't noticing, it would get twisted around in the socket, and look up, maybe, or out to one side, and every which way, while t'other one was looking as straight ahead as a spy glass. Grown people didn't mind it, but it 'most always made the children cry, it was so sort of scary. She tried packing it in raw cotton, but it wouldn't work, somehow—the cotton would get loose and stick out and look so kind of awful that the children couldn't stand it no way. She was always dropping it out, and turning up her old deadlight on the company empty, and making them oncomfortable, becuz *she* never could tell when it hopped out, being blind on that side, you see. So somebody would have to hunch her and say, 'Your game eye has fetched loose, Miss Wagner, dear'— and then all of them would have to sit and wait till she jammed it in again—wrong side before, as a general thing, and green as a bird's egg, being a bashful cretur and easy sot back before company. But being wrong side before warn't much different, anyway, becuz her own eye was sky-blue and the glass one was yaller on the front side, so which-ever way she turned it it didn't match nowhow. Old Miss Wagner was considerable on the borrow, she was. When she had a quilting, or Dorcas S'ciety at her house she gen'ally borrowed Miss Higgin's

wooden leg to stump around on; it was considerable shorter than her
other pin, but much *she* minded that. She said she couldn't abide
crutches when she had company, becuz they were so slow; said when
she had company and things had to be done, she wanted to get up and
hump herself. She was as bald as a jug, and so she used to borrow Miss
Jacops's wig—Miss Jacops was the coffin-peddler's wife—a ratty old
buzzard, he was, that used to go roosting around where people was
sick, waiting for 'em; and there that old rip would sit all day, in the
shade, on a coffin that he judged would fit the can'idate; and if it
was a slow customer and kind of uncertain, he' fetch his rations and a
blanket along and sleep in the coffin nights. He was anchored out
that way, in frosty weather, for about three weeks, once, before old
Robbins's place, waiting for him; and after that, for as much as two
years, Jacops was not on speaking terms with the old man, on account
of his disapp'inting him. He got one of his feet froze, and lost money,
too, becuz old Robbins took a favorable turn and got well. The next
time Robbins got sick, Jacops tried to make up with him, and var-
nished up the same old coffin and fetched it along; but old Robbins
was too many for him; he had him in, and 'peared to be powerful
weak; be bought the coffin for ten dollars and Jacops was to pay it
back and twenty-five more besides if Robbins didn't like the coffin
after he'd tried it. And then Robbins died, and at the funeral he
bursted off the lid and riz up in his shroud and told the parson to
let up on the performances, becuz he could *not* stand such a coffin as
that. You see he had been in a trance once before, when he was
young, and he took the chances on another, cal-lating that if he made
the trip it was money in his pocket, and if he missed fire he couldn't
lose a cent. And, by George, he sued Jacops for the rhino and got
judgment; and he set up the coffin in his back parlor and said he
'lowed to take his time, now. It was always an aggravation to Jacops,
the way that miserable old thing acted. He moved back to Indiany
pretty soon—went to Wellsville—Wellsville was the place the Hoga-
dorns was from. Might fine family. Old Maryland stock. Old Squire
Hogadorn could carry around more mixed licker, and cuss better
than 'most any man I ever see. His second wife was the Widder Billings
—she that was Becky Martin; her dam was Deacon Dunlap's first wife.
Her oldest child, Maria, married a missionary and died in grace—
et up by the savages. They et *him,* too, poor feller—biled him. It
warn't the custom, so they say, but they explained to friends of his'n
that went down there to bring away his things, that they'd tried mis-
sionaries every other way and never could get any good out of 'em—
and so it annoyed all his relations to find out that that man's life was
fooled away just out of a dern'd experiment, so to speak. But mind
you, there ain't anything ever reely lost; everything that people can't
understand and don't see the reason of does good if you only hold
on and give it a fair shake; Prov'dence don't fire no blank ca'tridges,

boys. That there missionary's substance, unbeknowns to himself, actu'ly converted every last one of them heathens that took a chance at the barbecue. Nothing ever fetched them but that. Don't tell *me* it was an accident that he was biled. There ain't no such a thing as an accident. When my Uncle Lem was leaning up again a scaffolding once, sick, or drunk, or suthin, an Irishman with a hod full of bricks fell on him out of the third story and broke the old man's back in two places. People said it was an accident. Much accident there was about that. He didn't know what he was there for, but he was there for a good object. If he hadn't been there the Irishman would have been killed. Nobody can ever make me believe anything different from that. Uncle Lem's dog was there. Why didn't the Irishman fall on the dog? Becuz the dog would' a' seen him a-coming and stood from under. That's the reason the dog warn't app'inted. A dog can't be depended on to carry out a special prov'dence. Mark my words, it was a put-up thing. Accidents don't happen, boys. Uncle Lem's dog—I wish you could 'a' seen that dog. He was a reg'lar shepherd—or ruther he was part bull and part shepherd—splendid animal; belonged to Parson Hagar before Uncle Lem got him. Parson Hagar belonged to the Western Reserve Hagars; prime family; his mother was a Watson; one of his sisters married a Wheeler; they settled in Morgan County, and he got nipped by the machinery in a carpet factory and went through in less than a quarter of a minute; his widder bought the piece of carpet that had his remains wove in, and people come a hundred mile to 'tend the funeral. There was fourteen yards in the piece. She wouldn't let them roll him up, but planted him just so—full length. The church was middling small where they preached the funeral, and they had to let one end of the coffin stick out of the window. They didn't bury him—they planted one end, and let him stand up, same as a monument. And they nailed a sign on it and put —put on—put on it—sacred to—the m-em-o-r-y—of fourteen y-a-r-d-s —of three-ply—car—pet—containing all that was—m-o-r-t-a-l—of— of—W-il-l-i-a-m—W-h-e—"

Jim Blaine had been growing gradually drowsy and drowsier—his head nodded, once, twice, three times—dropped peacefully upon his breast, and he fell tranquilly asleep. The tears were running down the boys' cheeks—they were suffocating with suppressed laughter— and had been from the start, though I had never noticed it. I perceived that I was "sold." I learned then that Jim Blaine's peculiarity was that whenever he reached a certain stage of intoxication, no human power could keep him from setting out, with impressive unction, to tell about a wonderful adventure which he had once had with his grandfather's old ram—and the mention of the ram in the first sentence was as far as any man had ever heard him get, concerning it. He always maundered off, interminably, from one thing to another, till his whisky got the best of him, and he fell asleep. What the thing was that happened to him and his grandfather's old ram is a dark mystery to this day, for nobody has ever yet found out.

A Night at the Ugly Man's

. . . My friend, Dick M'Coy, and myself were brought to a sudden halt, on our "voyable" to the Horse Shoe, by the capsizing of our boat . . . We determined, as it was late, to attempt no further progress that day, but to stop until next morning at the house of Old Bill Wallis, the Ugly Man. In accordance with this plan, we bailed the boat and made her fast to a tree on the "Turpingtine" side of the river, and commenced our walk.

Adown the rugged, pine-bearing slope of the hill, on the top of which the Ugly Man's residence was situated, trickled a slender streamlet, pure and sparkling, like a single tear coursing down the rough cheek of manhood. Merrily it leaped along between its tiny moss margins—mere strips of green velvet—tumbling over miniature ledges, and humming forth a tender, complaining sound—the faint, delicate echo, of a fairy chime! Stout poplars and white oaks, at intervals just sufficient to give good sport to the far-jumping gray-squirrels, attested the fertilizing power of the little rill, which the dark intertwining roots seemed striving to grasp—but the streamlet glided through like a silver eel, and kept its downward way, chanting, scarce audibly, its jocund melody. A snowy sheen of dogwood blooms marked its course; and winding beneath these, ran a path leading to the humble cabin we were about to visit.

"This here's Old Bill's spring branch; he lives up there a leetle to the left;" said my companion. A few more strides brought us to the premises of *The Ill-Favoured!*

The cabin was perched on the hill, within twenty yards of a beautiful spring—welling up through the whitest sand and bursting through rock and moss—that supplies the little stream I have described. It was a rough log building. Around it was a low rail fence, enclosing a white and well-swept yard. A dozen clumps of purple altheas and common roses are growing and blooming in front of the house; while a luxuriant cypress vine, with its mimosa-like foliage and brilliant red flowers, clambered around the door, and emulously strove to overspread the roof. On the fence, a huge gobbler, with his meek-looking mate, had gone to their early roost. A dozen fowls clustered on the top of the *ash-gum*, and the projecting corners of the *smoke-house*. These, at the first glance, were all the signs that indicated inhabited premises. Huge, melancholy pines reared themselves gloomily on all

From *The Widow Rugby's Husband, A Night at the Ugly Man's, and Other Tales of Alabama*, by Johnson J. Hooper, pp. 40–51. Philadelphia: T. B. Peterson & Brothers, 1851.

sides, except in front—there, the little spring was in view, with the *oasis* its waters had made—the green line of oak and poplar, with its under-fringe of creamy flowers, winding down the hill—and still further down, the river whirling and frothing along the south-west.

As we stepped over the low fence, I heard the hum of a spinning-wheel, and in another moment one of the sweetest, rosiest faces I ever beheld, looked out at the door. It was Lucy Wallis, the pretty daughter of the Ugly Man! Saluting us modestly, she asked us in—and to be seated—and resumed her work. There be few more lovely girls than Lucy. In her moist blue eye, was a blended expression of mirthfulness and something more tender, that went into your heart without ever asking leave. Clad in a homespun frock, coarse, but tasteful in its colours and adjustment—and oh! how brilliantly spotless—her fingers tipped with the blue of the indigo tub—her little feet in buckskin moccasins—he plied her task industriously; now, with an arch toss, shaking into place her rich auburn hair, and now, with a bound forward, gracefully catching the thread that had slipped from her fingers. Sweet-voiced, too, was Lucy Wallis, as she stood at her wheel, spinning *two* threads, one of cotton on her spindle, and the other of gossip, with my excellent and loquacious friend Dick M'Coy.

Plague take the girl! She has made me forget her ugly father! Mr. Wallis and his "old woman" were from home when we got there—having been on a visit to a sick neighbour—but in half an hour they returned.

"Thar they come," said Dick, as he heard voices outside the cabin; "seat yourself, and don't be scared!" Then Dick looked at Lucy.

"You've never seen daddy, 'squire—have you?" she asked, slightly colouring and pouting.

"Never have—always had a curiosity"—but the wounded expression of the girl stopped me, and in another moment, the Ugly Man was before me.

Truly had McCoy said, "nothing on the breathin' yearth can match him!" His face, generally, had the appearance of a recently healed blister spot. His prominent eyes seemed ready to drop from off his face, and were almost guiltless of lids. Red, red, red, was the all-prevailing colour of his countenance—even his eyes partook of it. His mouth—*ruby-red*—looked as if it had been very lately kicked by a roughly-shod mule, after having been originally made by gouging a hole in his face with a nail-grab! The *tout ensemble* was horribly, unspeakably *ugly!* And yet, in the expression of the whole was legible proof of the paternity of his lovely daughter!

"So you've come to see old Ugly Mug—have you, 'squire? I've hearn of you before. You're the man as took the *sensers* of this country, last time. I was in Georgy then. Well, you're might welcome! Old 'oman, fly around, git somethin' for the 'squire and Dick to eat! Lucy, ain't you got no fresh *aiggs*?"

Lucy went out at this suggestion, and her father went on:

"They call me ugly, 'squire; *and I am;* my father was before me the ugliest man that ever lived in Hancock county. But I'll give you my ixperance after supper. Belikes you've hearn that I've been through the ruffs. No? Well, when we git something down our bellies, I'll tell you all about it. Old 'oman, for God's sake, *do* fly around thar!"

The old lady *did* "fly around," and Lucy got the "aiggs," and between them, they got a most excellent supper. The purity of the table-cloth, the excellence of the coffee, and the freshness of the eggs, not to mention Lucy's good looks, were more than a set-off against the ugliness of old Billy; so that Dick and I continued to eat quite heartily, to the evident gratification of our hospitable, though ugly entertainer.

Supper over, old Bill drew out his large soap-stone pipe, and filling and lighting it, placed it in his mouth. After a whiff or two, he began:

"It's no use argyfyin' the matter—I *am* the ugliest man, now on top of dirt. Thar's narry nuther like me! I'm a crowd by myself. *I allers was.* The fust I know'd of it, tho', was when I was 'bout ten years old. I went down to the spring branch one mornin', to wash my face, and I looked in the water, I seen the shadder of my face. Great God! how I run back, hollerin' for mammy, every jump! That's the last time I seen my face—I darsen't but shet my eyes when I go 'bout water!"

"Don't you use a glass, when you shave?" I inquired.

"Glass! Zounds! What glass could stand it?—'twould bust it, if it was an inch thick. Glass!—pish!"

Lucy told her father he was "too bad," and that "he knew it was no sich a thing;" and the old man told her she was a "sassy wench," and to "hold her tongue."

"Yes," he continued; "it's so; I haven't seen my face in forty years, but I know how it looks. Well, when I growed up, I thort it would be the devil to find a woman that'd be willing to take me, ugly as I was"—

"Oh, you was not so *oncommon* hard-favoured when you was a young man," said old Mrs. Wallis.

"ONCOMMON! I tell you when I was ten years old, *a fly wouldn't light on my face*—and it can't be much wuss now! Shet up, and let me tell the 'squire my ixperance."

"It's no use," put in Lucy, "to be runnin' one's own self down, that way, daddy! It ain't right."

"Runnin' down! Thunder and lightnin', Luce! you'll have me as good-lookin' directly as John Bozeman, your sweetheart."

As he said this, old Bill looked at me, and succeeded in half covering the ball of his left eye, by way of a wink. Lucy said no more.

The old man continued:

"Well, hard as I thort it 'ud be to get a wife, fust thing I knowed, I had Sally here; and she is, or was, as pretty as any of them."

Old Mrs. Wallis knitted convulsively, and coughed slightly.

"However, she never kissed me afore we was married, and it was a long time arter afore she did. The way of it was this: we had an old one-horned cow, mighty onnery (ordinary) lookin', old as the North Star, and poor as a black snake. One day I went out to the lot"—

"Daddy, I *wouldn't* tell *that*," exclaimed Lucy, in the most persuasive tones.

"Drot ef I don't, tho—it's the truth, and ef you don't keep still, I'll send for Bozeman to hold you quiet in the corner."

Lucy pouted a little, and was silent.

"Yes, I went out to the lot, and thar, sure as life, was my old 'oman, swung to the cow, and the old thing flyin' round, and cuttin' up all sorts o' shines! Ses I, 'what the h-ll are you up to, old 'oman?' And with that she let go, and told me she was tryin' to prac*tize* kissin' an old 'Cherry,' and she thort *arter that* she could make up her mind to *kiss me!*"

"Old man, you *made* that! I've hearn you tell it afore—but you *made* it," said the old lady.

"Well, well! I told her, 'squire, ses I, 'come down to it now!—hang the cow—shet your eyes!—hold your breath!'—and upon that she bussed so's you might a heard it a quarter, *and since,* nobody's had better kissin' than me! Now, that was my first ixperance about bein' ugly, arter I was grown, and 'twan't so bad neither!

"The next time my ugly feeturs came into play, was in Mobile; was you ever thar! Worst place on the green yearth; steamboats, oysters, river rats, furrinners, brick houses—hell! *that's* the place! I went down on a flat-boat from Wetumpky, with old John Todd. We had a fust-rate time of it, 'twell we got most to Mobile, and then the d—d steamboats would run so close to us, that the *sloshin'* would pretty nigh capsize us. They done it for devilment. My, how old John cussed! but it done no good. At last, ses I, 'I'll try 'em; ef thar's enny strength in cussin', I'll make 'em ashamed!' So the next one come along cavortin' and snortin' like it was gwine right into us, and did pass in twenty foot! I riz right up on a cotton bag, and ses I to the crowd— which there was a most almighty one on the guards of the boat—ses I, 'you great infernal, racket-makin', smokin', snortin', hell totin' sons of thunder—'

"Afore I could git any furder in my cussin', the crowd gin the most tremenjus, yearth-shakin' howl that ever was hearn—and one fellar, as they was broad-side with us, hollored out, 'It's the old HE UGLY HIMSELF! Great G—d, WHAT A MOUTH!' With that, thar was somethin' rained and rattled in our boat like hail, only hevier, and directly me and old John picked up *a level peck of buck-horn-handled knives!* I'll be darn'd this minit if we didn't!"

Old Mrs. Wallis looked to Heaven, as if appealing there for the forgiveness of some great sin her ugly consort had committed; but she said nothing.

"So I lost nothin' by bein' ugly *that* time! Arter I got into Mobile, howsever, I was bothered and pestered by the people stoppin' in the street to look at me—all dirty and lightwood-smoked as I was, from bein' on the boat."—

"I think I'd a cleaned up a little," interposed tidy Lucy.

"Old 'oman! *ain't* you got nary cold 'tater to choke that gal with! Well they'd look at me the hardest you ever seen. But I got ahead o' my story: A few days afore, thar had been a boat busted, and a heap o' people scalded and killed, one way and another. So at last, as I went into a grocery, a squad of people followed me in, and one 'lowed, ses he, 'it's one of the unfortunate sufferers by the bustin' of the Franklin,' and upon that he axed me to drink with him, and as I had my tumbler half way to my mouth, he stopped me of a sudden—

" 'Beg your pardon, stranger—but'—ses he.

" 'But—what?' ses I.

" 'Jist *fix your mouth that way again!*' ses he.

"I done it, just like I was gwine to drink, and I'll be cussed if I didn't think the whole on 'em would go into fits!—they yelled and whooped like a gang of wolves. Finally, one of 'em ses, 'don't make fun of the unfortunate; he's hardly got over bein' blowed up yet. Less make up a puss for him.' Then they all throwed in, and made up five dollars; as the spokesman handed me the change, he axed me, 'Whar did you find yourself after the 'splosion?"

" 'In a flat-boat,' ses I.

" 'How far from Franklin?' ses he.

" 'Why,' ses I, 'I never seen *her,* but as nigh as I can guess, it must have been, from what they tell me, nigh on to *three hundred and seventy-five miles!'* You oughter 'a seen that gang scatter. As they left, ses one, 'IT'S HIM. *It's the Ugly Man of all!'*

"Knockin' round the place, I came upon one o' these fellers grinds music out'n a mahogany box. He had a little monkey along—the d—dest peartest, least bit of a critter, you ever seed! Well, bein' fond of music and varmints, I gits pretty close to the masheen, and d—d ef 'twan't hard to tell which got the most praise, me or the monkey. Howsever, at last, I got close up, and the darn thing ketch a sight of me and *squalled!* It jumped off'n the box in a fright, and hang'd itself by its chain. The grinder histed it up agin, but it squalled more'n ever, and jerked and twisted and run over the keeper, and jumped off'n his back, and heng'd itself agin. *The sight o' me had run it distracted!* At last the grinder hilt it to his bosom, and ses he,

" 'Go ways, oagley man—maungkee fraid much oagly!' Ses I, 'Go to h-ll, you old heathen'—(you see he was some sort of a Dutch chap or another)—'if you compar me to your dirty monkey agin, I'll throw it hell'ards, and split your old box over your head! And ses he right off agin,

" 'Maungkee ish petter ash dat oagley mans!'

"Ses I, 'Gentle*men*, you heer this crittur compar me, a free Amerakin, to his d—d heathen dumb brute of Afriky;' and with that, I fetched the monkey sailing that sent him a whirlin' about sixty-five yards, over a brick wall, and the next minit the Dutchman and his box was the wost mixed up pile of *rags and splinters* you ever seen in *one* mud-hole! About that time, too, thar was a pretty *up-country* runnin' on top o'them cussed bricks as you'll commonly see. I lay up two or three days, and at last made my passage up to Wetumpky, *in the cabin!*"

"How was that?" I asked.

"An old lady, that was along, 'lowed that it was dangersome for me to stay on the deck, *as I might scare the masheenery* OUT O' JINT. So they tuck me in the cabin afore we started, and I reckon I was treated nigh on to a hundred times, afore we got to Wetumpky."

"That's not the way you told it the last time," remarked Mrs. Wallis.

"Thunder! 'squire, did you ever hear sich wimmen folks—I've hardly had a chance to edge in a word, tonight. Well, my last ixperance was about a year ago. I got ketcht in a hurricane; it was blowin' like the devil, and the thunder and lightnin' was tremenjus—so I gits under a big red-oak, and thar I sot 'twell the lightnin' struck it! I was leanin' agin the tree when the bolt come down, shiverin' and splinterin' all before it. It hit me right here"—"and then"—

"Good Heavens! did *lightning* disfigure your face so?"

"Disfigure h—ll! No! The lightnin' struck right here, as I was sayin', and then—IT GLANCED!"

"Good Lord look down!" ejaculated Mrs. Wallis.

"You'd better go to bed now, 'squire," said old Bill; "and in the mornin' I'll go with you and Dick to the Horse Shoe. *That* was the main feetur' of old Hickory. He was ugly some, hisself. God bless him, I've seed him—but he didn't have the gift like me. Good night."

They Never Died—They Just Sacked Away

. . . EMBOLDENED by his success, Hawley proceeded to relate that there was, in that same section, an area of twenty miles where the air was so pure that people never died, unless by accident.

"Never died!" exclaimed several of his hearers in astonishment.

"No, gentlemen, it was quite possible. The rare purity of the atmosphere prevented it. When persons got too old to be useful, they would sometimes be blown away, and, once outside of the charmed circle, they were lost."

From *Struggles and Triumphs: or The Life of P. T. Barnum*, Written by Himself, edited with an introduction, by George S. Bryan, Volume I, pp. 168–169. Copyright, 1927, by Alfred A. Knopf, Inc. New York and London.

"Is that really possible?" asked one of his hearers, in some doubt.

"A fact, upon my honor," rejoined old Hawley. "Indeed, some years ago several philanthropic gentlemen erected a museum at that place, where persons who became too old for usefulness were put into sacks, labelled, registered at the office, and hung up. If at any subsequent period their friends wished to converse with them, for a fee of fifty cents the old friend would be taken down, placed in a kettle of tepid water, and would soon be enabled to hold a conversation of half an hour, when he would be taken out, wiped off, and hung up again."

"That *seems* incredible!" remarked one of the listeners.

"Of course it does," replied Hawley. "It is nevertheless true. Why, gentlemen," he continued, "on one occasion I went to the museum, and asked if they had a subject there named Samuel Hawley. I had an uncle by that name who went to the Rocky Mountains thirty years before, and we had not heard from him in a long time. The clerk, having examined the register, replied that Samuel Hawley was in Sack No. 367, and had been there nineteen years. I paid the fee and called for an interview. The contents of that particular sack were placed in the warm water, and in a short time I proceeded to inform my old uncle who I was. He seemed pleased to see me, although I was a child when he left our part of the country. He inquired about my father and other friends. His voice was very weak, and after a conversation of twenty minutes, he said his breath was failing him, and if I had nothing more to say he would like to be hung up again. I remarked that I believed he formerly owned a large gun, and asked him where it was. He informed me that it was lying on the cross-beam in my father's garret, and that I was welcome to it. I thanked him, and bidding him good-bye, the keeper of the museum took him in hand, and soon placed him in his proper locality. If any of you should ever go that way, gentlemen, I hope you will call on my uncle and present him my compliments. Remember his number is 367."

The Yankee and the Mermaids

. . . Did *you* ever see a marmaid? Waell, then, I reckon you'd best shut up, cos *I* have—and many on 'em; and marmen too, and marmisses and marmasters, of all sizes from babbies not bigger nor mackrels to regular six-footers, with starns like a full grow'd porpus. I've been at a marmaids' tea-party, and after larnin' the poor ignorant scaly critters how to splice the main brace, I left the hull bilin' on 'em blazin' drunk.

From *The Yankee Amongst the Mermaids, and Other Waggeries and Vagaries*, by William E. Burton, Comedian, pp. 10–11, 17–26. Philadelphia, T. B. Peterson & Brothers. 1843.

You see when our craft was cruisin' up the Arches, we cast anchor one mornin' in pretty deep water just abrest of a small green island as wasn't down in the chart, and hadn't got no name, nyther. But our capting know'd what he was arter, abeout as right as nine-pence, cos a small skewner came along-side pretty sune, freighted with brandy and wine for the officers, what they'd ordered for their own private stores. Waell, the slings was run up to the end o' the main-yard, and the waisters were busy hoistin' up the barrils, when a cask o' brandy slipped from the slings as it was being canted round, and dropped right splash into the sea, sinkin' right away. Upon 'zamination-tioning the manifest, it proved to be the best cask o' brandy in the skewner, imported from Boardo direct for the capting himself. He raised a gretty muss, I guess, right off the reel. "You d—— etarnal lazy suckers," said he, "look here! take all the boats' anchors, lash 'em together in tews so as to form grapnels o'four pints each, and drag all about here for that ar' brandy—and mind you find it, or I'll put every mother's son of you on short allowance o' rye for the next month."

Waell, the boats was ordered out, and a gropin' we went. I was placed in the jolly, with Sy Davis and Pete Slinks, and a middy to direct. The middy was a pretty considerable smart fellow, and jest as we was puttin' off, he nodded up to the chaplin as was leanin' over the side, and says, "What say you to an hour's float upon this here glassy sea?" The parson was down by the man ropes in a minnit, and off we sot a fishin' for the brandy tub.

* * * * *

The barrel of brandy had not been found, and I wish I may be sniggered if the capting did not fly into the biggest kind o' quarter-deck passion I ever did see. He stormed great guns and fired hull broadsides at the boat's crews, swearin' that they should keep on dredgin' till the tub was found, if it was the day arter eternity. So, you see, the hands was piped to dinner, but I was ordered tew keep in the boats and take keare they didn't stave each other.

Waell, I laid down in the capting's gig, and what with the parson's licker, and the talk abeout marmaids and syringes and water galls, and one thing and t'other, a very pretty muss began mixin' in my brain pan. So, as I was layin' comfortably moored in the starn sheets, with my head a leetle over the boats' quarter, I thought it highly unwrong that the brandy's tub hadn't been fotched up, and that the men usin' the grapnels must have shirked as we did, cos, if they'd sarched as they oughter, they must have seed the barrel, for the water was so petickler clear that you could dissarn the crabs crawlin' over the korril rocks at the bottom o' twenty fathom.

Waell, while I was lookin' into the ocean to see if I could light upon the barrel, a leetle o' the largest fish I ever did see, come and swum right close to the bottom of the sea, jest under the boats. Then it kept risin' and risin' till I seed its long fins were shaped like men's arms; and when it come near the sarfis, it turned on its back and then I seed a human face! I know'd at once that it was a marmaid, or a marman—or one o' them amfibberus critters called fabbelus syringes as the chaplain had been spinning' his yarns abeout. So, the critter popt its head up jest above the water, which was smooth as glass, and a little smoother tew by a darned sight, and jest as clear and jest as shiny, and says he to me, "Look here, strannger, you and your ship-mates ain't doin' the genteel thing to me no how you can fit it, for they're playin' old hub with my garding grounds and oyster beds by scratchin' and rakin' 'em all over with them ar' darned anchors and grapnel fixins, in a manner that's harrowin' to my feelins. If the capting wants his thundernation licker tub, let him jest send eeny decent Christian down with me, and I'll gin it him."

Waell, I'm not goin' to say that I didn't feel kinder skeered, but the chaplain's yarns had rubbed the rough edge off, and the notion o' findin' the capting's cask pleased me mightily, cos I knowed it would tickle the old man like all creation, and sartingly get me three or four liberty days for shore goin' when we returned to Port Mahon. So, as I hadn't on nothin' petikler as would spile, only a blue cotting shirt and sail-cloth pantys, and the weather bein' most uncommon warm, I jest told the marman I was ready, and tortled quietly over the boat's side into the blue transparent sea.

The marman grappled me by the fist, and we soon touched bottom, now I tell ye. I found as I could walk easy enough, only the water swayed me abeout jest as if I war a leetle tight, but I didn't seem to suffer nothin' for want o' breath, nyther.

We soon reached whar' the brandy cask was lyin' right under the ship's keel, which accounts for its not bein' seen nor nothin' by the boats' crews. I felt so ever-lastingly comical abeout findin' the tub, that I told the half-bred dolphing feller as pinted it out, that if I knowed how to tap it, I wish I might die if I wouldn't give him a gallon o' the stuff as a salvage fee.

"What's in it?" says the marman.

"Why, licker," says I.

"Waell," says the marman, "so I heerd them scrapin' fellers in the boats say; but I guess I've licker enough to last my time, tho' I recking your licker is something stronger than salt water, seein its hooped up in that almighty way."

"Why, you lubber," says I, "its brandy—the raal ginnewine coney-hack."

"And what's that?" says the marman.

"Why, dew tell—want to know?" says I, "have you lived to your time o' life without tastin' spirretus licker? Waell, I swow, you oughter be the commodore of all them cold water clubs, and perpetual president of all temp'rance teetotallers. Go ahead, matey; pilot the way to your shanty, and I'll roll the barrel arter you. I'll sune give you a drink o' licker that will jest take the shirt tail off eeny thing you ever did taste, now I tell you."

Waell, the critter flopped ahead, for you see its the natur' o' the marmen, seein' as they've no legs, only a fish's tail what's bent under them, jest like the lower part o' the letter J, to make way by floppin' their starns up and down, and paddlin' with their hands—somethin' between a swim and a swagger—but the way they get through the water is a caution. I rolled the tub along over the smooth white shiny sand, and the crabs and lobsters skeeted off right and left sides out o' my way regular skeered, and big fishes of all shapes and makes, with bristlin' fins, swum close alongside me, and looked at me quite awful with their small gooseberry eyes, as much as to say "What the nation *are* you at?"

Bymeby, the marman brought up in front of rayther a largeish cave or grotto of rock and shell work, kivered with korril and sea weed. So, you see, the tub was put right on eend in one corner; I made an enquirry o' the marman if he had a gimblet, and he said he b'leved there was sitch a thing in the hold or cellar; he'd found a carpenter's tool-chest in a wreck a few miles to the easterd, and he fotched away six or seving of the leetle fixins, thinkin' they might be useful to hum —so, he opened the back door and hailed a young marman to bring him the gimblet.

Seein' as there was no benches nor nothin' to sit down on, which marmen and marmaids don't desire, cos they've no sittin' parts to their bodies, which is all fish from their waistbands, I jest sot on the top o' the brandy tub, and took an observation of the critter before me. His face was reglar human, only it looked rayther tawney and flabby like a biled flounder, with fishy eyes, and a mouth like a huge tom cod. His hair hung stret down his shoulders, and was coarse and thick like untwisted rattlin'; his hands were somethin' like a goose's paw, only the fingers were longer and thicker—and his body was not exactly like an Injin's nor an African's, nor a white man's—nor was it yaller, nor blue, nor green—but a sorter altogether kinder mixed up colour, lookin' as if it were warranted to stand the weather. Jest abeout midships, his body was tucked into a fish's belly, with huge green scales right down to the tail.

Whilst I was surveyin' the marman fore and aft, the back door opened and a she critter flopped in, with a young marman at the breast. The leetle sucker was not bigger than a pickerel, with a tail of a delicate sammon colour, and a head and body jest like one o' them small tan monkeys, with a face as large as a dollar. The marman introduced the she critter as his wife, and we soon got into a coil of talk right slick, all abeout the weather, and the keare and trouble o' a young family—and I wished I may be swamped if the marmaid warn't a dreadful nice critter to chatter. Like all wimming folk, she was plaguey kewrous as to whar' I was raised and rigged—and when I said I guess I hailed from Cape Cod, and all along shore thar', she looked at the marman, and said to me, "Waell, I never—Cape Cod! why, strannger, I guess there must be some finnity in our breeds."

Waell, you see, I grew rayther kewrous tew, and wanted to log the petiklers o' the nateral history o' the race o' marmen—so I made a few enquerries respectin' their ways o' life. "I guess," says I, "you've a tarnal good fish market in these here parts, and keep your table well supplied with hallibut and sea-bass, and black-fish, eh?"

"Why, strannger," says the marman, rayther wrathy, "seein' its you I won't be offended, or, by hevving, if that speech ain't enough to make a marman feel scaly, why then it ain't no matter. We claim to be half fish in our natur', and I reckon you don't kalkilate we gobbles our relations? there's sea varmint enough in all conscience, sitch as oysters, and clams, and quahogs, and muscles, and crabs, and lobsters. We go the hull shoat with them; and then we cultivates kail and other sea truck in our gardings, and sometimes we swims under the wild fowl as they're floatin', and jerks down a fine duck or a gull, or gathers their eggs off the rocks, or the barnacles off drift wood."

Jest then, the marman's eldest son-fish fotched in the gimblet, and brought up the marman's jawin' tacks with a round turn. The young un was about the size of an Injin boy jest afore he runs alone—half papoose, half porpus. He got a leetle skeered when he clapt eyes on me, but I guv' him a stale quid o' backer to amuse himself, and the sugar plum made the marmaster roll his eyes above a bit, now I tell you.

Waell, I bored a hole in the brandy tub, and pickin' up an empty clam shell, handed a drink to the lady, and told her to tote it down. She swaller'd it pretty slick, and the way she gulped arterwards, and stared, and twisted her fishy mouth, was a sin to Davy Crockett. The marman looked rayther wolfy at me, as if I'd gin her pison; so I drawed a shell-full and swallered it myself. This kinder cooled him down, and when the marmaid got her tongue tackle in runnin' order agin, she said she guessed the licker was the juice of hevving, and she'd be darned if she wouldn't have another drink right off the reel.

Seein' this, the marman swallered his dose, and no sooner got it down than he squealed right out, and clapped his webby hands together, and wagged his tail like all creation. He swore it was elegant stuff, and he felt it tickle powerful from the top of his head to the eend of his starn-fin. Arter takin' two or three horns together, the sonny cried for a drink, and I gin him one that sent him wrigglin' on the sand like an eel in an uneasiness. So, the marman said as the licker was raal first rate, and first rater than that tew, he guessed he'd ask in his next door neighbour and his lady, jest to taste the godsend. Waell, in a minnit, in comes a huge marman of the most almighty size.

looking jest like Black Hawk when he was bilious; he fotched up his lady with him, and his eldest son, a scraggy hobbadehoy marman, and his darters, two young marmaids or marmisses, jest goin' out o' their teens, who flapped their yaller-skinned paws over their punking-coloured chops, pretendin' to be almighty skeered at comin' afore a strannge man in a state o' natur'—but they forgot all abeout that thar' when the licker was handed to them.

Arter takin' a few smallers, the fresh marman said he guessed the clam shell was altogether tew leetle to get a proper amount of licker whereby a feller could judge correctly of the raal taste o' the stuff—so he went to his berth in the next cave, and fotched a large blue and silver shell that held abeout a pint.

The news o' the brandy tub spred pretty slick, for in half an hour, I'd the hull grist o' the marmen belongin' to that settlement cooped up in the cavern. Sitch a noisy swillin' set o' wet souls I never did see; the drunk com' on em almighty strong, for they kept me sarvin' out the licker jest as quick as it would run. I thought if the capting could have seen me astridin' his brandy cask, in an underground grocery at the bottom o' the sea, surrounded by sitch a skeul of odd fish, how many dozen at the gangway would he have ordered the bosen's mate to have sarved me out?

The way the drunk affected the different critters was right kewrous, now I tell you. One great scaly feller stiffened his tail all up, and stood poppindickler erect on the peaked pints of the eend fin, like a jury-mast, and jawed away raal dignified at all the rest, wantin' them to appoint him a sort o' admiral over all the hull crew. Another yeller feller with a green tail, was so dreadful blue, that he doubled himself into a figgery 5, and sung scraps and bits o' all sort of sea songs, till he got tew drunk to speak at all. Some o' the marmen wanted to kiss all the marmaids, and tew o' the ladies begun scratchin' and fightin' like two pusseys, cos one trod on t'other's tail. Some went floppin' and dancin' on the sand like mad, raisin' sitch a dust that I could not see to draw the licker—but the party round the tub soon druv' them to the right abeout, as interferin' with the interest o' the settlement. Every minnit some fresh marman dropped on the ground with the biggest kind of load on; I never seed a set o' critters so almighty tight, yellin', swearin,' huggin', and fightin,' till they growed so darned savagerous that I kinder feared for my own safety amongst them drunken moffradite sea aborgoines. So, you see, I up and told them that I'd clapt my veto on the licker, and that they should not have any more.

Waell, if ever you did hear a most etarnal row, or see a hull raft o' drunken fellers cut didoes, then *was* the time. It was voted that I were a public enemy, and every half drunken marman suddenly became very 'fishus to have me Lynched, and it were settled at last that I were to be rode on a rail, and then tarred and feathered. But, while some o' the varmint went arter the rail and the tar, the rest o' the critters begun quarrelin' who was to sarve out the licker; and as each marman, drunk or sober, wanted to have the keare o' the precious stuff, they soon raised a pretty muss, and kept on tearin' at each other like a pack o' wolves. Seein' this, I jest kinder sneaked quietly away from the cave grocery till I com' in sight o' the ship, when I struck upperd for the sarfis, and swum for dear life. I soon seed that the boats' crews were musterin' for another bout o' draggin' for the brandy cask; so, fearin' least the capting should miss me, I jest laid hold o' the edge o' the gig, and crawled in pretty quickly, and laid myself down in the starn sheets, as if I'd never been out o' the boat.

I hadn't laid thar' half a second, when I heerd a noise jest for all the world as if somebody was squeezin' a small thunder cloud right over my head. I ruz up, and thar' were the capting and the hull crew lookin' over the ship's side at me—the officers in a tarnal rage, and the men grinnin' like so many hyenas.

"Rouse up, you long-sided lazy swab, and bring the boats in from the boom. Are you goin' to sleep all day?"

"Ay, ay, sir," said I, jumpin' up in the boat, when all the water run off me like forty thousand mill streams—I'd been so outrageous soaked while down with the marmen. I felt kinder skeered lest the capting should see it, but when I stood up he laughed right out, and so did the hull crew tew.

"Why, he's not awake yet," said the capting. "Bosen, give him another bucket."

You see they wanted to persuade me that I'd fell asleep in the gig, as fast as a meetin' house, and slept thar' the hull while the crew were at dinner, and that no shoutin' nor nothin' couldn't waken me up—so, the bosen run along the boom and jest give me a couple o' buckets o' sea-water right over me. When I told 'em my yarn abeout the marman poppin' up his head, and invitin' me down, and all abeout findin' the brandy tub and the rest, they swore that I'd got drunk on the parson's licker, and dreamt it all in the boat. But I guess I know what I did see, jest abeout as slick as anybody; and the chaplain b'lieved the hull story; and said that as I'd learnt the marmen the valley o'licker, they'd get huntin' up all the tubs and barrels out of the different wrecks in all the various seas; and that intemperance would spile the race, and thin 'em off till they became one o' the things that was—jest like the Injins what's wastin' away by the power o' rum and whiskey given 'em by the white men.

I recking the parson warn't far out of his kalkilashing. The love o' licker has had its effect upon the marmen and the marmaids; they must have thinned off surprisin'ly, for I aint seed none since, nor I don't know nobody that has, nyther.

Big-Foot Wallace Describes Texas Varmints

A few weeks after my arrival I went to a "fandango" that was given for my especial benefit. There was a great crowd there, and everybody was anxious to see the "Wild Texan," as they called me. I was the "lion" of the evening, particularly with the young ladies, who never tired of asking me questions about Mexico, Texas, the Indians, prairies, etc. I at first answered truly all the questions they asked me; but when I found they evidently doubted some of the stories I told them which were facts, I branched out and gave them some "whoppers," which they swallowed down without "gagging." For instance, one young woman wanted to know how many wild horses I had ever seen in a drove. I told her perhaps thirty or forty thousand.

"Oh! now! Mr. Wallace," said she, "don't try to make game of me in that way. Forty thousand horses in one drove! well, I declare you are a second 'Munchausen'!"

"Well, then," said I, "maybe you won't believe me when I tell you there is a sort of spider in Texas as big as a peck measure, the bite of which can only be cured by music."

"Oh, yes," she answered, "I believe that's all so, for I have read about them in a book."

Among other "whoppers," I told her there was a "varmint" in Texas called the "Santa Fé," that was still worse than the tarantula, for the best brass band in the country couldn't cure their sting; that the creature had a hundred legs and a sting on every one of them, besides two large stings in its forked tail, and fangs as big as a rattlesnake's. When they sting you with their legs alone, you might possibly live an hour; when with all their stings, perhaps fifteen or twenty minutes; but when they sting and bite you at the same time, you first turn blue, then yellow, and then a beautiful bottle-green, when your hair all fell out and your finger nails dropped off, and you were as dead as a doornail in five minutes, in spite of all the doctors in America.

"Oh! my! Mr. Wallace," said she, "how have you managed to live so long in that horrible country?"

"Why, you see," said I, "with my tarantula boots made of alligator-skin, and my centipede hunting-shirt made of tanned rattlesnake's hides, I have escaped pretty well; but these don't protect you against the stinging scorpions, 'cow-killers,' and scaly-back chinches, that crawl about at night when you are asleep! The only way to keep them at a distance is to 'chaw' tobacco and drink whisky, and that is the reason the Temperance Society never flourished much in Texas."

From *The Adventures of Big-Foot Wallace*, by John C. Duval, pp. 293–294. Entered . . . 1870, by J. W. Burke & Co.

"Oh!" said she, "what a horrible country that must be, where the people have to be stung to death, or 'chaw' tobacco and drink whisky! I don't know which is the worst."

"Well," said I, "the people out there don't seem to mind it much; they get used to it after a while; in fact, they seem rather to like it, for they chaw tobacco and drink whisky even in the winter-time, when the 'cow-killers' and stinging-lizards are all frozen up!"

The Meanest Man Contest

I was talking with Senator Blaine in Saratoga one day about mean men when Sam Cox stepped up and said he knew a very mean man— the meanest man on earth.

"'How mean is that?" I asked.

"Why, Eli," he said, "he is so mean that he keeps a five-cent piece with a string tied to it to give to beggars; and when their backs are turned he jerks it out of their pockets!

"Why, this man is so confounded mean," continued Mr. Cox, "that he gave his children ten cents apiece every night for going to bed without their supper, but during the night, when they were asleep, he went upstairs, took the money out of their clothes, and then whipped them in the morning for losing it."

"Does he do anything else?"

"Yes, the other day I dined with him, and I noticed the poor little servant girl whistled all the way upstairs with the dessert; and when I asked the mean old scamp what made her whistle so happily, he said: 'I keep her whistling so she can't eat the raisins out of the cake.'"

I was down in Uncle Hank Allen's grocery today, telling about Sam Cox's mean man, when Oliver Wilcoxen remarked:

"That was a pretty mean man, but I could tell you about meaner men than that right in this town. Now there is old Backus Long. You remember about the sausage skins?"

"No, what was it?" asked several voices at once.

"Well, I don't speak of this as a case of meanness, but I put it forward as an instance of careful thrift when I say that when I ran the butcher's shop Backus Long always used to send back his sausage skins and have them refilled."

"That was simply business shrewdness," said John Whitney. "Now I always do those kind of things myself. For instance, it is always my cutom to stop the clock nights."

From *Library of Wit and Humor by Mark Twain and Others, with the Philosophy of Wit and Humor,* by Melville D. Landon, A. M. (Eli Perkins), pp. 203–205. Copyright, 1883, by L. W. Yaggy and, 1898, by Star Publishing Co. Chicago: Thompson and Thomas.

"What for?" asked Stanley Westfall.

"I do it to keep it from wearing out the cogs."

"I call that rather close," said Deacon Monson. "I call that mean, but we've got a man over in Lebanon who beats that. Old Calkins over there is so mean that he skims his milk on top, and then, when no one is looking, he turns it over and skims it on the bottom."

Uncle Hank now uncrossed his legs, took a quid of fine cut, and remarked:

"Gentlemen, you don't appear to be aware of the many mean things done every day in this community. I tell you there is an all-killin' sight of meanness in this town."

"Who's meaner than old Calkins?" asked Calvin Morse.

"Why, the meanest man in this town, and none of you seems to have heard of him," said Uncle Hank. "I say the meanest man in this town, if my memory does not fail me, is old Deacon Crawford, and—"

"What was the meanest thing he ever did?" asked a dozen voices.

"Well, gentlemen, you may call me a liar, but it's the solemn truth. One day Deakin Crawford found a stray bung hole over around Stanley Westfall's cooper shop, and—"

"What did he do with a stray bung hole?" asked Jonas White.

"Why, gentlemen, you may call it a lie, but if he didn't take it up to Morse's cooper shop, and, handing it out, ask Gardner Morse to please give him a barrel to fit that ere bung hole. He did, by gosh!"

Col. Hawkins and the Court

Some years ago, I knew an individual whose *sobriquet* was "Col. Hawkins," and who was the most perfect specimen of the dare-devil frontier-man, that I ever saw, at least in Alabama. His real name was Jim Fielder—to which his neighbours frequently added the expressive prefix "Devil." And he *was* a devil, fearing neither God, man, nor beast, and if not invulnerable, possessing at least a tenacity of life that was most astonishing. He had been once struck down with a broadaxe, and his brain absolutely cloven to a considerable depth, and for several inches in length; yet he made no particular difficulty of surviving, and that, too, with all his faculties uninjured.

The "Colonel" being what, in his region and times, was called a cow-driver, had cultivated the art of equitation, until he and his favourite bay, whom he named "*Hell*," had become a perfect centaur. No feat was too difficult for them. I have seen them myself do things which would make the gallant Col. May's blood run cold. Hell was

From *The Widow Rugby's Husband . . . and Other Tales of Alabama,* by Johnson J. Hooper, pp. 102–108. Entered . . . 1851, by A. Hart. Philadelphia: T. B. Peterson & Brothers. Published in The New York *Spirit of the Times,* December 1, 1849, with credit to the New Orleans *Delta.*

the most perfectly trained animal that I ever saw; followed his master like a dog, and when the Colonel got drunk and lay in the road, would stand by him and guard him for hours.

"Col. Hawkins" used to be very fond of attending the circuit courts of his county, at which, after a time, he became an insufferable nuisance. The sheriffs were always afraid of him; the tavern-keepers dreaded him; and the judge never could get hold of him. In one of his mad freaks, I have seen him, while court was in session, mounted on "Hell," charge up to the steps, and into one door of the court-house, dash furiously along the aisle, and, with a tremendous leap, clear the steps out of the other.

I remember well the first session at which I ever saw him. Court was held, temporarily, in a two-story wooden building; one end of which rested on the ground; the other (the front) being on brick-work, or blocks, two or three feet high. A judge was presiding, whose distinguishing trait was a tyrannical petulance—a judicial wasp, whose sting was ever protruding. His Honour, however, met his match in "Col Hawkins," and, no doubt, thinks of him to this day with emotions of horror.

For the first day or two of the court, our hero, being rather sober, behaved remarkably well; but about the middle of the week he got on a regular frolic, and immediately turned his attention to the disturbance of the court. For this purpose, he had prepared a number of loaves of bread, and collecting all the scraps of the kitchen of his tavern, he proceeded to "fort" himself *under* the court-house. His citadel was impregnable on one side, by reason of the house having one end on the ground; and all the other approaches the Colonel industriously fortified by building walls of large rocks leaving only a single entrance, and a few port-holes through which he might cast his missiles at any adventurous besieger.

Here it must be remarked, that the town was particularly populous *in the dog way*—if that be not a solecism—and Jim being aware of the fact, had provided himself with a hunting horn, an instrument on which he was a most capital performer. There were in the village, at the time, I think, three full packs of hounds; and as to the curs, though I never took *their* census, I can certify that they were multitudinous.

Prepared now, at all points, the Colonel took his place within his "fort," and waited until a sound of bustling from above indicated that the court was transacting business. Then, *toot, toot, to-too, to-too—toot, toot, toot!* went his horn.

Three "several and distinct" simultaneous howls from different quarters of the town, responded to the blast!

Toot! toot! to-too! to-too! toot! toot! toot!

Again three dire howls responded; but this time they seemed converging to a common centre—Jim's *subcurian* fortification.

"My God, Mr. Sheriff," said the little tiger on the bench, "what is all that blowing and howling about?"

"I s'pose," replied the Sheriff, with a wild look, for he knew the Tartar he had to deal with, " I s'pose it's a comp'ny of hunters going out after deer."

"Wal"—the Judge invariably sounded the *e* in *well*, *a* short—"Wal, my God! do the hunters in this country *hunt on the public square?*"

Toot! toot! toot! to-to-to-to-to-to-hoot! went Jim's horn again; and the hounds, with a multitude of their half-brethren "of low degree," having by this time assembled under the house, sent up a long, a loud, and a most deafening response. Jim then gave them all some bread and meat-scraps, in token of their approval. He then blew "another blast," and again fifty or sixty canine throats belched forth the hideous sounds!

"My God! Mr. Sheriff, I fine you ten dollars," said the irritated Judge—"Go and stop that noise."

The Sheriff went down, and having ascertained the strength of the Colonel's position, endeavoured to coax him out.

"Come out, Jim, old fellow, and I'll stand a treat; I will, by George!"

"Toot! toot!" was the reply; and then the howl from the dogs, who began "to let themselves out."

The Judge fined the first deputy, up stairs, five dollars, for the new attack upon his nerves.

Several adventurous special deputies at length went under, to take our hero "by storm"; but they very soon returned with bruised heads and defiled clothing. Jim, with inimitable *sang froid,* held the horn to his mouth with one hand, while with the other he sent his rocks with terrible effect at his assailants. His allies, too, the dogs, gave him occasional sly assistance, by nibbling at the more exposed parts of the persons of the invaders; and these being obliged to go "upon all-fours," under the house, these "attacks in the rear" were in the highest degree vexatious and unpunishable

Toot! toot! toot!
Howl! howl! howl!

The contagion spread to the crowd assembled on the public square.

"And each—for madness ruled the hour—
Would try his own expressive pow'r."

Yell after yell went up from the crowd! All was confusion; and as peal after peal of the odd and mingled discord floated up, roar after roar of unsuppressed laughter shook the court-room!

The Judge was pale with rage. Every fibre of his frame trembled with excitement; but he could only fine—so he fined the Sheriff an hundred dollars for reporting the Colonel's fort impregnable, himself invincible, and his forces determined to stand to him, *to a dog!* He then adjourned court, "until the nuisance could be abated."

As soon as the Colonel perceived that he had stopped all legal proceedings, he suspended his blasts, and dealt out double rations to his forces. From one of the port-holes in front, observing that the Judge was strolling about on the square, and that the Sheriff was consulting with a dozen or so of friends, he watched his opportunity, horn in hand, he slipped out, unperceived except by friends, and reached his steed, which was tied in the bushes near by. Mounting "Hell," he "blew a blast so loud and long," that every hound responded at once, and in a moment more, dashed in upon the square, with his followers in full cry! Here he went, "like mad," now clearing an old woman and her cake-stand at a jump, and now bounding lightly over a group of a half dozen on a fallen log. Ye gods! how the crowd scattered! Espying the Judge, he dashed up to him—circled round him, in Cumanchee style, and blowing his horn the while, evoked the most hideous howls from his troop! Round and round he dashed—the judge petrified in the centre, pawed, mouthed, and smelt of by the hounds, and stunned—overpowered by their hideous din! Never before (I speak metaphorically) was the ermine so villanously defiled!

Having accomplished his purpose of "bedeviling" a Judge, who had the reputation of being a martinet, Jim retreated, in good order, from the square to the thicket at the back of the court-house. He knew what would follow, and fully prepared for it. He had procured him a whiskey-barrel, *minus* one head, and, a foot or so above the bung-hole, had cut an opening about six inches in diameter. By small cords he had attached to the outside of the barrel two large bundles of fodder, a fragment of old stove-pipe, and three super-annuated coffee-pots.

As soon as Jim had left the square, the Judge ordered the Sheriff to summon a *posse,* and take him, at all risks—and the Sheriff instantly summoned twenty or thirty of the hundreds who had horses hitched on the square, and ordered them into line to receive his directions. The Judge borrowed a pony, to go along and see his mandate executed.

Jim, who had been watching their operations slily, as soon as they seemed nearly complete, blew a blast, mounted "Hell," and drawing the barrel up after him, placed it over himself; and taking the reins through the hole, rode leisurely on, till in view of the Sheriff's squad, when, with a loud toot, a howl from his dogs, the rustling of his fodder, the clangour of his coffee-pots, and the sonorous *gong*-notes of his stove-pipe, he charged at full speed upon the Sheriff and his *posse comitatus!*

Talk of *May!* Talk of *Murat!* There was never a charge so reckless or effective as Jim Fielder's charge upon the sheriff and his squad.

Toot! toot! toot! bang! clang! bang! howl! howl! howl! and he was in their midst! The horses of the squad, maddened with fright, reared and plunged, and either threw their riders, or dashed off with them precipitately from the field. The horses hitched about at racks and trees, participated in the panic, and in five seconds there was a universal *stampede.*

The Judge's pony dashed off with a speed that was highly creditable to his short legs and Indian origin; and after *him* the Colonel dashed, with all his dreadful din, in full blast! On, on, on! at a killing lick! Down, down the hill to the old tan-yard!—where suddenly Judge and pony find a "tight fit" in an ancient, but not inodorous vat!

Satisfied—almost—with his victory, our hero charged back to town —putting to flight everything equine, of which he came in view, and leaping his horse into the piazza of a grocery, pitched his barrel through the window upon the head, and other frangible property of the proprietor—like lightning passed in at one door and out at another —and whooping at the top of his voice, rode furiously out of town.

Why Bowleg Bill Let the Biggest One Get Away

The boys of the trap fleet are setting on the wharf as usual between trips, betting on the gulls as to which will be the next to decorate the spiles, when Bowleg Bill the sea-going cowboy shows up.

We have been hearing yarns for years of this wild Wyoming bronco-buster, and the uncommon happen-quences which are told of him since he took to seafaring, and now all of a sudden on our own water-front here he is personal. But for all his rare seamanship, not even Bowleg Bill himself—personal as a spinster's dream—is going to take up much slack among the boys that goes out for swordfish or hoss-mackerel.

"Hoss-mackerel" is the name we give in Cape Cod waters to what off-Cape furriners calls "tuna." For a few days each summer they strike here and git caught in the weirs and float-traps which we set in the harbor for smaller fish. This summer the run of hoss-mackerel is heavy in the traps, and while the boys are talking of the elegant stocks it is rolling up for them, Bowleg Bill paces for'ard and aft on that wharf like a tomcat on one side of the fence which figures he is missing something on tother.

Finally the talk is more than he can put up with, and he walks over to Yank Daggett, who skippers the *Tossup,* and who is high-line fisherman of the harbor fleet.

"This here hoss-mackerel," Bowleg inquires, "he's a sassy varmint, is he, stranger?"

Yank nods. "The strike is running uncommon heavy this season, with a long streak of hell in each of 'em."

"Mmm. Real cornfed he-man's work, is it, ridin' herd on 'em?"

From *Bowleg Bill, The Sea-Going Cowboy* . . . , by Jeremiah Digges, pp. 21–28. Copyright, 1938, by Josef Berger. New York: The Viking Press.

"Well, you got to know how to gaff 'em in. Hoss-mackereling is no business for a green hand."

Bowleg Bill paces the wharf a couple more times, and comes back.

"What do you reckon the critters will weigh on the hoof?"

"Up to rising a thousand pounds. Most of 'em come a hundred to eight-nine hundred."

"Now, hain't that a shame!" says Bowleg. "Not enough to kick dust in yore eye! I was figgering I might admire to rope in a few, but where I come from, we don't bother with a rope on nawthing under a couple ton—that is, if it's extry good, smoke-snortin' bull with half a ton of devilment throwed in."

Yank bends a long grin between his ears.

"You jest throw back the small fry, eh?"

"Wa-al, them little fellers we pick up barehanded by the belly-slack, and toss 'em into the pens."

Yank nods. "Makes it handy, don't it? But with us, we got to watch out for the tail. A hoss-mackerel's tail ain't no slack hawser abaft, ending in a bunch of loose rope-yarns. When you git hoss-mackerel, you want to make sartin-sure you don't git slapped over the gunnels with his tail."

"Huh!" says Bowleg. "I have yet to meet up with the critter—two-legged or four, stranger—which I couldn't take keer of in that section. Where's yore foreman? I see I'll have to show you fellers how to haze yore herd, the way it's done back in old Wyoming!"

"I'm skipper here," Yank says, "but we ain't taking on no greenies while the run of hoss-mackerel keeps up."

"Mister," says Bowleg, "if you are a betting man, I'll jest hit the trail with you to them corral-things out yonder. And if I don't cut me out one of yore full-growed hoss-mackerel and bring him in bare-handed, without using none of them long-handled prod-sticks, I'll pay you twenty silver dollars and marry yore meanest of kin!"

Well, Yank figures this big cowboy has missed stays in the August heat, but he has heard so many yarns about him that finally he takes the bet. The boys at the wharf hurry upstreet to spread the news, and before dark the whole town is talking of the off-Cape lunatic who is going after hoss-mackerel barehanded. Big odds is offered against Bowleg, but these people knows fish, and there is no takers amongst 'em.

Next morning the whole harbor is cluttered up with dories, pungoes, and anything down to harness-casks, which the citizens can climb aboard to watch the *Tossup* draw the traps. As a fishing port, the town has took Bowleg's bet to heart as an insult, and he gets hootcalls aplenty on the way out. Even poor old Cap'n Dyer, who's been shore-bound twenty years with the backsliding vertigo, is out there in one of the boats.

"Better go back inland, young feller!" he hollers. "Ye don't know what's waiting for ye in that net!"

"Don't you fret over me, grandpaw!" Bowleg calls back. "That's a mighty shaky caboose yo're driving there. You get for cover pronto if I start a stampede!"

At the first trap, there is thrashing and white water, a commotion like a hurricane stoppered up under them net-buoys, and in the middle of it, the biggest hoss-mackerel Yank Daggett has ever seen. And the minute Yank does see him, he forgets all about Bowleg Bill, he forgets everything but that great blue-silver body and six foot of slapping, thrashing tail. And he stands ready with his gaff while the boys haul on the net.

Bowleg gets the measure of this big feller, and he climbs over, alongside Yank.

"That one over yonder!" he says. "Will he weigh up to our bet?"

"Will he weigh up to it! He's two thousand pounds if he's a Scotch ounce, you lubber!"

"All right, boys," Bowleg sings out, "give me a clear field!" And he pushes Yank and a couple of others aside and yells to the hoss-mackerel. "Come along, leetle dogie!"

"Hey, git aft, you blasted pig-farmer!" Yank hollers. "That fish is big money, and I ain't leaving it to no gawd-damned greeny to lose him!"

"Now, jest keep yore britches dry, boss," says Bowleg, "and lift that daggone spear out o' my road. I've picked my animal and I'm a-going after him for all creation and a barbwire fence! *Hy-up!* Come along, leetle dogie, come along!"

He reaches out, he gets hold of the fish in the small, and he heaves —though how in etarnity he figures to swing aboard two thousand pounds of game fish that way, only an inland furriner might know! The tail slips clear of his hands, and the moss-mackerel slips clear of the backbone of the net.

"Look out!" Yank hollers. "He's clear! He's clear and away!"

"Oh, no, he hain't," Bowleg answers. Over the side he goes, boots and all, and before the fish has got under way, there is this shatter-witted cowpuncher, setting astride, whipping astern with his hat, and hollering like the yoho-bird of every dead sailor come home from hell!

"*Whoop-ee-ee! Hy-ee-ee—up!* Show some buck, now, you white-livered snubbin'-beetle, before I sell you off to a livery stable. Come on here, Slickbritches, *hy-up!*" And away goes that silver divil, and up he jumps, breaching clean out of the water like a porpoise. But when he comes down again, there is Bowleg Bill, still astraddle, still fanning his tail with the wide out-rigger hat.

Yank gives a groan. "There goes the biggest catch—and the gawd-damnedest fool—that was ever set loose in these waters!"

But somebody aboard one of the craft hard by sets up a cheer: "Ride him, cowboy!" And other folks takes it up, till all over the harbor there is a wide sing-out of cheers for Bowleg Bill and the hoss-mackerel which he has named Slickbritches.

But the worst yells is from Bowleg himself, who is whooping like a wild Injun with the galloping chin-cough.

"*Yip, yip, yip-ee-ee!* Come on, you two-dollar fly-roost, hain't you going to throw no sand in their eyes?"

I don't know where he larned it, but somehow that cowboy has took a grip on the foretops'l fin, and no matter how bad Slickbritches broaches to, he can't shake him loose. They go scudding a wide circle of the harbor, with the big hoss-mackerel getting madder every minute. He dives to starboard, he lashes to larboard, he all but pitchpoles head-over. But somehow—and may the divil spit me over hell's hottest hearth if I can explain it!—Bowleg hangs on, with his knees bearing in close amidships, riding easy as grandmar in the Sunday-parlor rocker. Then Slickbritches makes one last big leap, like the flurry of an ironed whale—up in the air and clean over the bow of the *Tossup!*

"Buck away, you overgrown sardine!" yells Bowleg. "I'll peel you if it takes to Kansas City!"

But after that last jump, it is plain that Slickbritches is losing wind. He stops pitching, and jogs along easy among the harbor craft. And Bowleg, setting there and showing out of water from the knees up, starts stroking the fish abaft the gills, and talking to him, and—so help me Gawd!—little by little larning him to answer the helm! He hauls taut on that fin, and Slickbritches takes one tack; and he hauls again, and Slickbritches takes another tack; and when he has rode all the crank notions out of him, Bowleg veers about and heads in for the beach.

They make inshore till the hoss-mackerel is chafing his chin on the tideflats. Then—just when the whole town is fixing to send up a cheer for the landing of the biggest fish in history—this big beef-farmer gives a performance which none of us human folks will ever understand, and which I respectfully leave to some gawd-damned inlander to explain.

Instead of beaching that fish, he all of a sudden warps him around and jumps off!

Slickbritches heads for the open water, and Bowleg speeds him on his course, splashing after him and flogging him over the tail.

A crowd is gathered on the beach, and they are mad as a school of bees in a tar-barrel; for any man which lets a big fish get away has got some explaining to do before the law-abiding citizens of this town. When Bowleg wades out of the water, they all want to know why he done it, and is he gone clean whacky, and hadn't they better get him arrested and locked up as a dangerous character.

But Bowleg Bill just shakes his head at the crowd, and there is a sad, long-frayed look in his eyes, and he knuckles a tear off his cheek, and he says:

"That pore old windbroke waterbug! I tell you, folks, there ain't

nawthing that'll break a cowhand's heart so quick as to find a critter—
two-legged or four—with the rough all rode off at first mount!"

The Bear That Was

"Talkin' about Christmas," said Bedrock, as we smoked in his cabin
after supper, an' the wind howled as it sometimes can on a blizzardy
December night, "puts me in mind of one I spent in the '60s. Me an'
a feller named Jake Mason, but better knowed as Beaver, is trappin'
an' prospectin' on the head of the Porcupine. We've struck some
placer, but she's too cold to work her. The snow's drove all the game
out of the country, an' barrin' a few beans and some flour, we're plum
out of grub, so we decide we'd better pull our freight before we're
snowed in.

"The winter's been pretty open till then, but the day we start there's
a storm breaks loose that skins everything I ever seed. It looks like the
snow-maker's been holdin' back, an' turned the whole winter supply
loose at once. Cold? Well, it would make a polar bear hunt cover.

"About noon it lets up enough so we can see our pack-hosses. We're
joggin' along at a good gait, when old Baldy, our lead pack-hoss, stops
an' swings 'round in the trail, bringin' the other three to a stand. His
whinner causes me to raise my head, an' lookin' under my hat brim,
I'm plenty surprised to see an old log shack not ten feet to the side
of the trail.

" 'I guess we'd better take that cayuse's advice,' says Beaver, pintin'
to Baldy, who's got his ears straightened, lookin' at us as much as to
say: 'What, am I packin' fer Pilgrims; or don't you know enough to
get in out of the weather? It looks like you'd loosen these packs.' So,
takin' Baldy's hunch, we unsaddle.

"This cabin's mighty ancient. It's been two rooms, but the ridge-
pole on the rear one's rotted an' let the roof down. The door's wide
open an' hangs on a wooden hinge. The animal smell I get on the
inside tells me there ain't no humans lived here for many's the winter.
The floor's strewn with pine cones an' a few scattered bones, showin'
it's been the home of mountain-rats an' squirrels. Takin' it all 'n all,
it ain't no palace, but, in this storm, it looks mighty snug, an' when
we get a blaze started in the fireplace an' the beans goin' it's comfortable.

"The door to the back's open, an' by the light of the fire I can see
the roof hangin' down V-shaped, leavin' quite a little space agin the
wall. Once I had a notion of walkin' in an' prospectin' the place, but
there's somethin' ghostly about it an' I change my mind.

From *Trails Plowed Under*, by Charles M. Russell, pp. 9–14. Copyright, 1927, by
Doubleday, Page & Company. Garden City, N. Y.

"When we're rollin' in that night, Beaver asks me what day of the month it is.

" 'If I'm right on my dates,' says I, 'this is the evenin' the kids hang up their socks.'

" 'The hell it is,' says he. 'Well, here's one camp Santy'll probably overlook. We ain't got no socks nor no place to hang 'em, an' I don't think the old boy'd savvy our foot-rags.' That's the last I remember till I'm waked up along in the night by somethin' monkeyin' with the kettle.

"If it wasn't for a snufflin' noise I could hear, I'd a-tuk it fer a trade-rat, but with this noise it's no guess with me, an' I call the turn all right, 'cause when I take a peek, there, humped between me an' the fire, is the most robust silvertip I ever see. In size, he resembles a load of hay. The fire's down low, but there's enough light to give me his outline. He's humped over, busy with the beans, snifflin' an' whinin' pleasant, like he enjoys 'em. I nudged Beaver easy, an' whispers: 'Santy Claus is here.'

"He don't need but one look. 'Yes,' says he, reachin' for his Henry, 'but he ain't brought nothin' but trouble, an' more'n a sock full of that. You couldn't crowd it into a wagon-box.'

"This whisperin' disturbs Mr. Bear, an' he straightens up till he near touches the ridge-pole. He looks eight feet tall. Am I scared? Well, I'd tell a man. By the feelin' runnin' up and down my back, if I had bristles I'd resemble a wild hog. The cold sweat's drippin' off my nose, an' I ain't got nothin' on me but sluice-ice.

"The bark of Beaver's Henry brings me out of this scare. The bear goes over, upsettin' a kettle of water, puttin' the fire out. If it wasn't for a stream of fire runnin' from Beaver's weapon, we'd be in plumb darkness. The bear's up agin, bellerin' an' bawling', and comin' at us mighty warlike, and by the time I get my Sharp's workin', I'm near choked with smoke, the barkin' of the guns an' the bellerin' of the bear, it's like hell on a holiday.

"I'm gropin' for another ca'tridge when I hear the lock on Beaver's gun click, an' I know his magazine's dry. Lowerin' my hot gun, I listen. Everythin's quiet now. In the sudden stillness I can hear the drippin' of blood. It's the bear's life runnin' out.

" 'I guess it's all over,' says Beaver, kind of shaky. 'It was a short fight, but a fast one, an' hell was poppin' while she lasted.'

"When we get the fire lit, we take a look at the battle ground. There lays Mr. Bear in a ring of blood, with a hide so full of holes he wouldn't hold hay. I don't think there's a bullet went 'round him.

"This excitement wakens us so we don't sleep no more that night. We breakfast on bear meat. He's an old bear an' it's pretty stout, but a feller livin' on beans and bannocks straight for a couple of weeks don't kick much on flavor, an' we're at a stage where meat's meat.

"When it comes day, me an' Beaver goes lookin' over the bear's bedroom. You know, daylight drives away ha'nts, an' this room don't look near so ghostly as it did last night. After winnin' this fight, we're both mighty brave. The roof caved in with four or five feet of snow on, makes the rear room still dark, so, lightin' a pitch-pine glow, we start explorin'.

"The first thing we bump into is the bear's bunk. There's a rusty pick layin' up against the wall, an' a gold-pan on the floor, showin' us that the human that lived there was a miner. On the other side of the shack we ran onto a pole bunk, with a weather-wrinkled buffalo robe an' some rotten blankets. The way the roof slants, we can't see into the bed, but by usin' an axe an' choppin' the legs off, we lower it to view. When Beaver raises the light, there's the frame-work of a man. He's layin' on his left-side, like he's sleepin', an' looks like he cashed in easy. Across the bunk, under his head, is an old-fashioned cap-'n-ball rifle. On the bedpost hangs a powder horn an' pouch, with a belt an' skinnin' knife. These things tell us that this man's a pretty old-timer.

"Findin' the pick an' gold-pan causes us to look more careful for what he'd been diggin'. We explore the bunk from top to bottom, but nary a find. All day long we prospects. That evenin', when we're fillin' up on bear meat, beans and bannocks, Beaver says he's goin' to go through the bear's bunk; so, after we smoke, relightin' our torches, we start our search again.

"Sizin' up the bear's nest, we see he'd laid there quite a while. It looks like Mr. Silvertip, when the weather gets cold, starts huntin' a winter location for his long snooze. Runnin' onto this cabin, vacant, and lookin' like it's for rent, he jumps the claim an' would have been snoozin' there yet, but our fire warmin' up the place fools him. He thinks it's spring an' steps out to look at the weather. On the way he strikes this breakfast of beans, an' they hold him till we object.

"We're lookin' over this nest when somethin' catches my eye on the edge of the waller. It's a hole, roofed over with willers.

" 'Well, I'll be damned. There's his cache,' says Beaver, whose eyes has follered mine. It don't take a minute to kick these willers loose, an' there lays a buckskin sack with five hundred dollars in dust in it.

" 'Old Santy Claus, out there,' says Beaver, pointin' to the bear through the door, 'didn't load our socks, but he brought plenty of meat an' showed us the cache, for we'd never a-found it if he hadn't raised the lid.'

"The day after Christmas we buried the bones, wrapped in one of our blankets, where we'd found the cache. It was the best we could do.

" 'I guess the dust's ours,' says Beaver. 'There's no papers to show who's his kin-folks.' So we splits the pile an' leaves him sleepin' in the tomb he built for himself."

Index